USA West

"West of the Mississippi it's a little more look,
see, act. A little less rationalize, comment, talk."

F. Scott Fitzgerald, 1934

"Go West, young man, and grow up with the country."

Horace Greeley, 1850

D0300689

Travel Publications

Michelin North America
One Parkway South, Greenville SC 29615, U.S.A.
Tel. 1-800-423-0485
www.michelin-travel.com
TheGreenGuide-us@us.michelin.com

Manufacture Française des Pneumatiques Michelin
Société en commandite par actions au capital de 2 000 000 000 de francs
Place des Carmes-Déchaux – 63000 Clermont-Ferrand (France)
R.C.S. Clermont-Fd B 855 200 507

© Michelin et Cie, Propriétaires-éditeurs, 2000
Dépôt légal mai 2000 – ISBN 2-06-155901-8 – ISSN 0763-1383

Printed in the EU 07-00/1

Compogravure, impression et brochage : I.M.E.–P.P.C., Baume-les-Dames
Maquette de couverture extérieure : Agence Carré Noir à Paris 17e

THE GREEN GUIDE:
The Spirit of Discovery

*The exhilaration of new horizons, the
fun of seeing the world, the
excitement of discovery: this is what
we seek to share with you. To help
you make the most of your travel
experience, we offer first-hand
knowledge and turn a discerning eye
on places to visit.*

*This wealth of information gives you
the expertise to plan your own
enriching adventure. With THE GREEN
GUIDE showing you the way, you can
explore new destinations with
confidence or rediscover old ones.
Leisure time spent with THE GREEN
GUIDE is also a time for refreshing
your spirit, enjoying yourself, and
taking advantage of our selection of
fine restaurants, hotels and other
places for relaxing.*

*So turn the page and open a window
on the world. Join THE GREEN GUIDE
in the spirit of discovery.*

Contents

Gaslamp Quarter,
San Diego, California

© Jeff Greenberg/FOLIO, Inc.

Navajo Jewelry,
Northeastern Arizona

Practical Information 396

Old Route 66 Stagecoach, Gallup, New Mexico

Totem Bight State Historical Park, Ketchikan, Alaska

Maps and Plans

COMPANION PUBLICATIONS

Map 493 Western USA and Canada

Large-format map providing detailed road systems; includes driving distances, interstate rest stops, border crossings and interchanges.
– Comprehensive city and town index
– Scale 1:2,400,000 (1 inch = approx. 38 miles)

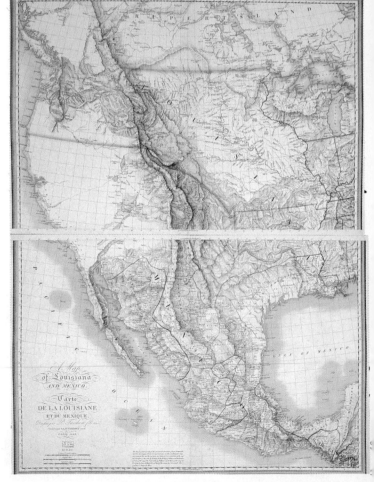

Western United States (1820), by Tardien

Map 491 Northeastern USA/ Eastern Canada and Map 492 Southeastern USA

Large-format maps providing detailed road systems; include driving distances, interstate rest stops, border crossings and interchanges
— Comprehensive city and town index
— Scale 1:2,400,000 (1 inch = approx. 38 miles

Map 930 USA Road Map

Covers principal US road network while also presenting shaded relief detail of overall physiography of the land.
— State flags with statistical data and state tourism office telephone numbers
Scale: 1:3,450,000

Map 933 USA Recreational

Descriptive section, with color photos and profiles of 51 national parks, complements a fold-out US map designating 500 parks, monuments, historic sites, scenic rivers and other points of interest.

LIST OF MAPS AND PLANS

Using this guide

- The guide is organized by geographic region, each with its own introduction. Within each chapter, the text is broken down by **Entry Heading**, each followed by a map reference, the time zone, population figure (where applicable), tourist information phone number and Web site when available.
- Within the text, information such as sight location, directions, telephone numbers and Web addresses appears in *italics*. Additional information is indicated by the following symbols: ♿ handicapped access, ✗ on-site eating facilities, ⚠ camping facilities, 🅿 on-site parking, Kids sights of interest to children, and ⅡⅡ long lines. The presence of a swimming pool is indicated in **Address Book** sections by the symbol 🏊.
- Sections with a blue background offer practical information—such as transportation, how to contact visitors bureaus, and recreational activities—for a city or region. Blue sections edged in a marbleized band also provide hotel and restaurant suggestions.
- We welcome corrections and suggestions that may assist us in preparing the next edition. Please send comments to Michelin Travel Publications, Editorial Department, P. O. Box 19001, Greenville, SC 29602-9001 or to TheGreenGuide-us@us.michelin.com.

© Claire Curran

Joshua Tree National Park, California

Legend

★★★ **Worth the trip**
★★ **Worth a detour**
★ **Interesting**

Sight Symbols

▬▬●▬▬▬▬▬▬▬▬▬▬ Recommended itineraries with departure point

⛪ ✝ ✡	Church, chapel – Synagogue	▰ Building described
○	Town described	▱ Other building
AZ B	Map co-ordinates locating sights	▪ Small building, statue
▪ ▲	Other points of interest	◎ ∴ Fountain – Ruins
⚒ ∩	Mine – Cave	🛈 Visitor information
🛆 ⌁	Windmill – Lighthouse	⬭ ✺ Ship – Shipwreck
☆ ⛪	Fort – Mission	⁂ ψ Panorama – View

Other Symbols

🛡 Interstate highway (USA)   🛡 US highway   (180) Other route

🍁 Trans-Canada highway   🛡 Canadian highway   🛡 Mexican federal highway

══	Highway, bridge	═══ Major city thoroughfare
══	Toll highway, interchange	═══ City street with median
══	Divided highway	◄═══ One-way street
──	Major, minor route	═══ Pedestrian Street
15 (21)	Distance in miles (kilometers)	✢∶✣ Tunnel
2140/666	Pass, elevation *(feet/meters)*	▦▦▦▦ Steps – Gate
△6288(1917)	Mtn. peak, elevation *(feet/meters)*	◮ 🗼 Drawbridge - Water tower
✈ ✛	Airport – Airfield	🅿 ✉ Parking – Main post office
⛴	Ferry: Cars and passengers	🖼 ✚ University – Hospital
⛴	Ferry: Passengers only	🚆 🚌 Train station – Bus station
⟨⟨ ▷	Waterfall – Lock – Dam	● Ⓜ Subway station
·—··—··	International boundary	● ⚲ Digressions – Observatory
------	State boundary	⊞ ⟁ Cemetery – Swamp

Recreation

▪-○-○-○-○-○-▪	Gondola, chairlift	⟨᠆᠆⟩ ⚑ Stadium – Golf course
🚂	Tourist or steam railway	❄ ▦ ▩ Park, garden – Wooded area
⚓ ⚑	Harbor, lake cruise – Marina	Ⓢ Wildlife reserve
🏄 ☑	Surfing – Windsurfing	◉ ψ Wildlife/Safari park, zoo
🤿 🚣	Diving – Kayaking	------ Walking path, trail
⛷ 🎿	Ski area – Cross-country skiing	🚶 Hiking trail

Kids Sight of special interest for children

Abbreviations and special symbols

NP	National Park	NMem	National Memorial	SP	State Park
NM	National Monument	NHS	National Historic Site	SF	State Forest
NWR	National Wildlife Refuge	NHP	National Historical Park	SR	State Reserve
NF	National Forest	NVM	National Volcanic Monument	SAP	State Archeological Park

🛡 National Park   🛡 State Park   🛡 National Forest   🛡 State Forest

All maps are oriented north, unless otherwise indicated by a directional arrow.

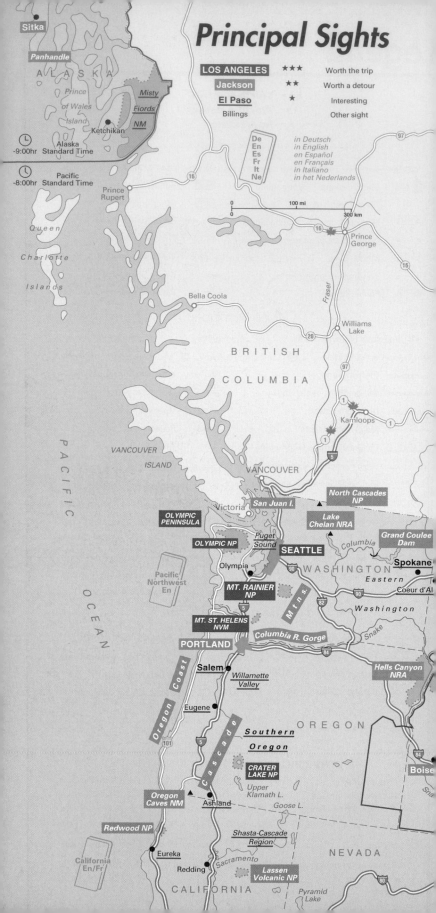

Principal Sights

LOS ANGELES   ★★★   Worth the trip

Jackson   ★★   Worth a detour

El Paso   ★   Interesting

Billings   Other sight

De   in Deutsch
En   in English
Es   en Español
Fr   en Français
It   in Italiano
Ne   in het Nederlands

0   100 mi
0   300 km

Sitka

Panhandle

ALASKA

Prince
of Wales
Island

Misty
Fiords
NM

Ketchikan

🕐 -9:00hr   Alaska
Standard Time

🕐 -8:00hr   Pacific
Standard Time

Prince
Rupert

Queen

Charlotte

Islands

PACIFIC

OCEAN

Bella Coola

BRITISH

COLUMBIA

Fraser

Williams
Lake

Prince
George

Kamloops

VANCOUVER
ISLAND

VANCOUVER

Victoria

San Juan I.

North Cascades
NP

**OLYMPIC
PENINSULA**

OLYMPIC NP

Puget
Sound

Lake
Chelan NRA

Grand Coulee
Dam

Spokane

SEATTLE

Columbia

Olympia

WASHINGTON

Eastern

Pacific
Northwest
En

**MT. RAINIER
NP**

Coeur d'Al

Washington

C a s c a d e   M t n s.

**MT. ST. HELENS
NVM**

Snake

PORTLAND

Columbia R. Gorge

Hells Canyon
NRA

Salem

Willamette
Valley

Oregon
Coast

Eugene

OREGON

Southern

Oregon

Boise

**CRATER
LAKE NP**

Upper
Klamath L.

Oregon
Caves NM

Ashland

Goose L.

Redwood NP

Shasta-Cascade
Region

NEVADA

California
En/Fr

Eureka

Redding

Sacramento

Lassen
Volcanic NP

Pyramid
Lake

CALIFORNIA

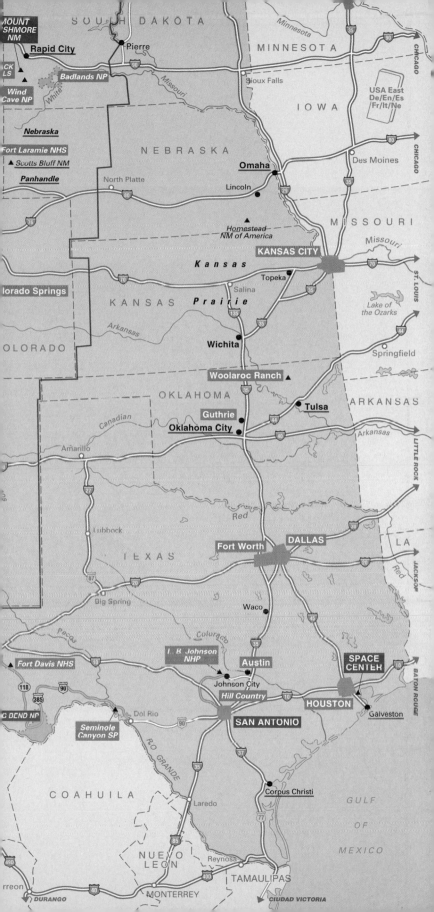

Historic Moulton Barn, Grand Teton National Park, Wyoming

Introduction
USA West

Western US Landscapes

It would be simple to divide the United States into "East" and "West" at the Mississippi River, but the entire Mississippi Valley belongs to the East: The Mississippi is a distinctly Midwestern river north of its confluence with the Ohio River, an indisputably Southern river south of there. By this reckoning, the West starts with the tier of Great Plains states west of the Mississippi—Texas, Oklahoma, Kansas, Nebraska and the Dakotas—and includes all of the continent beyond to the Pacific Ocean, as well as the isolated states of Alaska and Hawaii.

The simplest account of western US topography describes its eastern third as plains that rise gradually from the Gulf of Mexico and Mississippi Valley; the western two-thirds constitute a vast, corrugated expanse of hills, mountains and plateaus interposed with canyons, valleys and basins of varying size. Although landforms have been more than 2 billion years in the making, the current uplift began 130 million years ago, after the Pacific Plate subducted the North American Plate. The tectonic collision brought island masses crashing into the continent and slowly raised vast areas of what previously had been a shallow sea, forming new uplands in a process known as orogenesis. Magma intruded through weakened parts of the earth's crust, welling over as volcanoes and volcanic plateaus. Faults (most aligned north-south) thrust mountain ranges sharply upward, creating abrupt escarpments; or dropped blocks of land to form grabens, typical of the Great Basin region. Streams, rushing from the rising highlands, cut deep canyons. Sediments flowing to lowlands deposited valley soils and built the Great Plains on the eastern side of the Rocky Mountains.

The subduction zone where the Pacific and North American Plates meet is part of the Ring of Fire, the geologically unstable zone that circles the Pacific Ocean. In the American West, its most volatile indicators are the San Andreas Fault, the volcanic Cascade Range and Alaska's Aleutian volcanoes; Yellowstone National Park is the world's largest geothermal area. The San Andreas Fault buffers a strip of California coastline; other major fault lines underlie the Rockies, the Pacific Northwest and Alaska, creating earthquake hazards with potential to disrupt the lives of millions of people.

Before about 5000 BC, cool, wet conditions prevailed in what is now the American West. A drier, hotter climate subsequently began to dominate. During the early Pleistocene Epoch some 2 million years ago, when ice age glaciers pushed down over Canada and much of the midwestern and northeastern US, the West remained largely free of ice. Alpine glaciers, however, covered high-mountain expanses of the Rockies, Cascades, Sierra Nevada and Alaskan coastal ranges, sculpting glacial troughs, hanging valleys, cirques and other features, including Alaska's deep Pacific fjords. Enormous pluvial lakes covered thousands of square miles in the Great Basin. Cataclysmic floods periodically washed over the Pacific Northwest when glacial dams melted and broke. The continental ice sheets diminished the water level of the oceans, exposing a land bridge across the Bering Strait and promoting the migration of animals and humans between Asia and North America.

Despite areas of high rainfall in the Pacific Northwest and the Gulf Coast of Texas, much of the West today is characterized by aridity, especially in comparison with the eastern half of North America. The 100th meridian, which runs through the heart of the Great Plains, marks the approximate division between traditional farming and ranching economies. East of the meridian, annual precipitation averages more than 20in per year; west, rainfall rapidly diminishes, making agriculture impractical without irrigation. Travelers heading west across the Great Plains can observe cultivated corn rows and wheat fields giving way to short grass, and know that they are passing from the Midwest into the West.

Regional Landscapes and Climates

Coastal Pacific Northwest – The **Coast Ranges** of Oregon and Washington fall steeply to a rugged shoreline. Mild summers and wet, cool winters encourage the prolific growth of Douglas fir, spruce, hemlock and other evergreens. Broken only by the **Columbia River** and **Strait of Juan de Fuca** between California and Canada, the ranges are drained by short, swift streams. The western slope of the **Olympic Peninsula** receives more than 150in of annual rainfall, creating rain forests in the canyons beneath 7,965ft **Mt. Olympus.** Rainfall decreases steadily as one travels south down the coast, to about 60in per year on the California border. East of the Olympics, the Strait of Juan de Fuca opens into the many-isled harbor of **Puget Sound.** On its eastern shore is **Seattle,** largest city of the region. The fertile and populous lowland that extends south between the Coast Ranges and Cascades encompasses the city of Portland and, below it, the lush **Willamette River Valley**.

The Cascades – This barrier of volcanic peaks, stretching over 600mi from Canada to California's **Lassen Peak,** is breached only by the Columbia—largest river in the West and a natural highway between the dry Columbia Plateau and the farmland to the west. Two dozen peaks rise in relative isolation, presenting a line of majestic domes, many capped by brilliant glaciers. Highest are Washington's **Mt. Rainier** (14,410ft) and California's **Mt. Shasta** (14,162ft). Snowy winters and mild summers, often doused with showers, keep slopes lush with evergreen forests, a boon to timber and recreation industries. The volcanoes are dormant, but scientists monitor signs of life that may escalate to explosive eruptions, as at Lassen in 1914 and **Mt. St. Helens** in 1980. Fewer than 8,000 years ago, the mere blink of an eye in geologic time, massive Mt. Mazama exploded, leaving a gaping crater that filled with snowmelt and rain to form Oregon's **Crater Lake**.

The Lava Plateaus – Extensive lava plateaus spread eastward in the rain shadow of the Cascades at 2,000-3,000ft elevation. The **Columbia Plateau** covers most of eastern Washington and parts of Oregon and Idaho. The **Modoc Lava Plateau** covers the northeastern corner of California and part of Oregon. Between them rise several small ranges, including the Wallowas, which form the western wall of enormous, 8,000ft-deep Hells Canyon of the Snake River. Upstream, the **Snake River Plain** of Idaho and northern Nevada form yet a third extensive lava plateau, tracing its origins not to the Cascades but to clusters of spatter cones and volcanoes south of the Idaho Rockies. The Columbia Plateau and Snake River Plain have proven very fertile under irrigation from the Columbia and Snake Rivers. Washington's southeastern corner, known as the Palouse, is rich in wheat.

Coastal Northern California – The 600mi shoreline of northern and central California embraces a climate that varies from moist and mild (near Oregon) to semiarid Mediterranean. Washed by the Alaska Current, the rough, cold Pacific waters are rich in sea life but dangerous for shipping and swimming. The rugged **Coast Ranges** are breached only at the **Golden Gate**, entrance to **San Francisco Bay**. At several points, mountains push inland to yield narrow strips of fertile lowlands—the verge of **Monterey Bay** and the agriculturally rich **Napa, Sonoma and Salinas Valleys**. Redwood forests grow profusely in the north and intermittently as far south as **Big Sur**. Drier chaparral, grasses and live oak predominate inland and to the south.

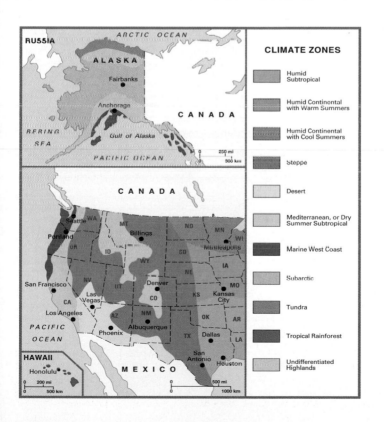

After Glenn T. Trewartha, Elements of Physical Geography, 1957

19

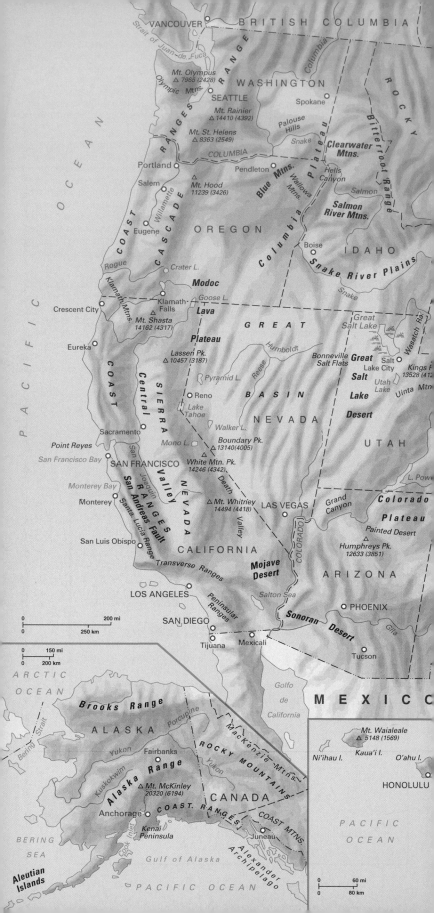

ALBERTA

SASKATCHEWAN

CANADA

MANITOBA

Lake Manitoba

Lake Winnipeg

WINNIPEG

Great Falls

MONTANA

Fort Peck L.

Missouri

L. Sakakawea

Mouse

Souris

Red

Red L.

Helena

Crazy Mtns.

Yellowstone

Billings

Bighorn

NORTH DAKOTA

Badlands

Bismarck

James

Fargo

MINNESOTA

△ Granite Pk. 12799 (3901)

Absaroka Range

Powder

Lake Oahe

GREAT

SOUTH DAKOTA

Gannett Pk. △ 13804 (4207)

Big Horn Mtns.

Black Hills

Harney Pk. 7242 (2207) △

Rapid City

Pierre

Minnesota

Des Moines

WYOMING

Wind River Range

Great Divide Basin

Laramie Mtns.

North Platte

Cheyenne

BADLANDS

Niobrara

Sioux Falls

MISSOURI

Cheyenne

NEBRASKA

IOWA

MOUNTAINS

Park Range

Front Range

Cheyenne

South Platte

Sand Hills

Platte

Omaha

Des Moines

Colorado

DENVER

Lincoln

Mt. Elbert 14433 (4399) △

Pikes Pk. 14110 (4301)

P L A I N S

Gunnison

COLORADO

Arkansas

Kansas

KANSAS

Kansas City

MISSOURI

San Juan Mtns.

n San Juan

Rio Grande

Sangre de Cristo Mtns.

△ Wheeler Pk. 13161 (4014)

Wichita

Springfield

MISSOURI

Jefferson City

Ozark Plateau

Santa Fe

Canadian

Tulsa

Albuquerque

Oklahoma City

Boston Mtns.

Little Rock

NEW MEXICO

Estacado

OKLAHOMA

Ouachita Mtns.

ARKANSAS

ihuahuan Desert

Llano

Lubbock

Red

Abilene

Fort Worth

DALLAS

Sabine

LOUISIANA

udad uarez

El Paso

RIO GRANDE

Pecos

Odessa

Colorado

Brazos

Trinity

MISSISSIPPI

T E X A S

Austin

HOUSTON

Baton Rouge

NEW ORLEANS

Hill Country

SAN ANTONIO

G U L F   C O A S T

Galveston I.

Moloka'i I.

Shelf

na'i I.

Maui I.

Kaho'olawe I.

Corpus Christi

Matagorda I.

Gulf of

Padro I.

HAWAI'I

Hawai'i I.

Mauna Loa 13677 (4169) △

△ Kilauea 4091 (1247)

Continental

Mexico

The **San Andreas Fault** parallels the coastline from Point Reyes (north of San Francisco) to Point Concepcion (northwest of Los Angeles), where it cuts inland.

Coastal Southern California – Shielded from the cold waters of the Alaska Current, the southern California coast is relatively warm and hospitable. Rainfall seldom exceeds 15in per year, giving Santa Barbara, Los Angeles and San Diego an enviable Mediterranean climate, free of winter snows except in the highest mountains. The **Los Angeles Basin**, California's largest and most heavily populated coastal plain, is hemmed on the north by the **San Gabriel Mountains**. These are a part of the **Transverse Ranges** that follow the San Andreas Fault eastward from the coast, rendering southern California one of the most seismically active regions of the US. East of the basin are the lower **Santa Ana Mountains**, part of the **Peninsular Ranges** that run south through Mexico's Baja Peninsula. The Los Angeles Basin has grown to become the West's largest and most culturally influential metropolitan area.

The Sierra Nevada – Running southeasterly almost 400mi from the Cascades, 50-80mi wide, the fault-block Sierra Nevada rises in an abrupt escarpment on the east to heights of more than 2mi above the **Owens Valley** at **Mt. Whitney** (14,494ft)—highest peak in the contiguous US. The lofty crest hinders weather systems from passing, creating a rain shadow to its east. Westward slopes descend gradually through alpine high country, evergreen forests and rugged foothills. Streams and rivers run through great canyons to feed the Central Valley, a fecund plain with the richest agricultural land in the US. Remarkable **Yosemite Valley** is the best place to see the Sierra's sculpted peaks and U-shaped glacial valleys. Although its winter snowfall is the greatest in the US, providing excellent skiing, the Sierra also enjoys plenty of summer sun. **Lake Tahoe** is a year-round recreation center.

Great Basin – Lying east of the Sierra Nevada and west of the Rocky Mountains, the sagebrush-cloaked Great Basin embraces a high desert of hot, dry summer days, cool nights and cold winters. It is corrugated with parallel fault-block mountain ranges, some above 13,000ft, divided by valleys known as grabens. Escarpments of 5,000-6,000ft are common; below the 11,200ft Panamint Range, **Death Valley** falls to 282ft below sea level, lowest point in the Western Hemisphere. No streams that flow into the Great Basin drain to the sea; they evaporate or disappear into lakes or marshy sinks. Utah's **Great Salt Lake** is a remnant of prehistoric Lake Bonneville, which once covered some 20,000sq mi. Other salt lakes also are vestiges of pluvial seas. For 150 years, mining towns have boomed and busted in this resource-rich, water-poor region. Except for cities at the foot of well-watered mountains—**Reno** in the west, **Salt Lake City** in the east—population density is the lowest of any region of comparable size in the contiguous US.

Colorado Plateau – The nation's highest plateau region covers 130,000sq mi of Utah, Colorado, New Mexico and Arizona at a mile above sea level. Scattered mountain ranges punch up as high as 11,000ft, but the most remarkable features are the myriad canyons carved by the **Colorado River** and its tributaries—thousands of feet deep, through aeons-old rock strata. More than 25 national parks and monuments—including **Grand Canyon, Zion, Bryce Canyon** and **Canyonlands**—preserve arches, eroded pinnacles, natural bridges and immense gorges in rainbow hues, all carved by wind and water. With a semiarid climate and a dearth of fruitful soil, the area is home to such hardy plant species as sagebrush, juniper and piñon pine. The ruins of ancient Anasazi Indian cliff villages may still be seen at **Mesa Verde** in Colorado, **Chaco Canyon** in New Mexico, and at the Betatakin and **Canyon de Chelly** ruins on the Navajo Indian Reservation. Rugged terrain discouraged American exploration until the late 19C; today tourism and recreation ensure that marvelous scenery remains the region's principal commercial asset.

The Desert Southwest – North America's largest arid region spreads east from California to Texas, containing at least three distinct deserts with vague transition zones. The mountainous **Mojave Desert**, which ranges into Death Valley, is home to the Joshua tree, a yucca that may grow 50ft tall. The Mojave fades into the Great Basin north of **Las Vegas** and meshes with the lower-elevation Sonoran Desert through the **Colorado Desert**, west of the Colorado River. The **Sonoran Desert**, which extends through southern Arizona and northwestern Mexico, boasts a profusion of cacti—including the giant saguaro—dependent on intense cloudbursts that bring temporary relief from summer heat. Winters are mild and sunny, luring thousands of seasonal residents to Arizona. The large **Chihuahuan Desert** of southern New Mexico, west Texas and northeastern Mexico is a high-elevation desert of parched mountain ranges, extensive grasslands, cold winters and torrid summers. The **Rio Grande** flows through its heart, scribing the huge hook of **Big Bend National Park.**

Rocky Mountains – Reaching from New Mexico to Canada, this sprawling mountain system comprises scores of subranges interposed with high basins, plateaus and plains. Modern resort villages, founded as mining towns, nestle in broad valleys. A key resource for timber, mining, grazing and recreation, the Rockies are vitally important as a source of water. Most major rivers of the western US, including the Snake, Columbia, Yellowstone, Missouri, Colorado, Rio Grande, Arkansas and Platte, originate here, flowing to the Pacific or Atlantic Ocean (or the Gulf of Mexico) from either side of the **Continental Divide**. The Northern Rockies are typified by the highly stratified, precipitous mountains of **Glacier National Park** in Montana, southern bulwark of the Canadian Rockies. Ranges like the Tetons rise above open plains or forested plateaus in the Middle Rockies of southern Montana and Wyoming. In the Southern (Colorado) Rockies are dozens of peaks above 14,000ft in elevation. The Rockies diminish in stature in New Mexico, growing generally more rounded and drier.

Great Plains – Built of sediment washed eastward from the Rocky Mountain slopes, the plains extend 1,000mi to the Mississippi. Semiarid high plains (the western third) naturally support short grass, ideal for bison and cattle; the tapping of aquifers permits more varied farming. East of the 100th meridian, better soil and higher rainfall nourish taller grasses, and agriculture thrives. Some areas are so flat that one can discern the curvature of the earth's horizon, but rolling landscapes are more typical. South Dakota's **Black Hills** and **Badlands**, and the Texas **Hill Country**, enhance an otherwise monotonous landscape. Fierce thunderstorms and tornadoes are frequent in summer; frigid blizzards mark the winters.

Tornado near Wichita, Kansas
© E. R. Degginger/DPA

Gulf Coast – Deep, rich soils extend along the Gulf of Mexico coast of Texas to Louisiana. High humidity and rainfall, and temperatures over 90°F, make summers muggy; winters are mild and snow-free. Numerous rivers—chief among them the **Rio Grande** on the US-Mexico border—water this naturally forested swath. Protecting most of the coast is a string of sandy barrier islands and peninsulas, including **Padre, Matagorda and Galveston Islands**, whose inland lagoons serve as tranquil intracoastal waterways. These islands support rich bird colonies, provide extensive recreational opportunities and help shield the mainland from hurricanes.

Alaska The largest US state contains more than 570,000sq mi of forests, mountains, glaciers and tundra. Bounded by the Pacific Ocean (south), Arctic Ocean (north) and Bering Strait (west), Alaska is a massive peninsula. The **Brooks Range** spans its northern tier, dividing oil-rich tundra from interior plains. The **Yukon River** flows through the center, bounded by the Alaska Range and North America's highest summit, 20,320ft **Mt. McKinley**. Southern coastal ranges straggle west as the volcanic **Aleutian Islands** and arc east through the **Panhandle**, a fjord-riddled archipelago that shelters the Inside Passage from the heavy seas of the Gulf of Alaska. Although the interior is very cold and dry in winter, summer can bring high temperatures and clouds of insects that attract enormous bird migrations. The Panhandle is cool and wet year-round.

Hawaii – The world's most remote archipelago with a substantial population, Hawaii comprises 132 volcanic islands, of which the eight most southeasterly—seven of them inhabited—are largest. The earliest islands surfaced as volcanoes about 5 million years ago; the most recent (the "Big Island" of Hawai'i) is still growing from eruptions at Kilauea Volcano. The **Big Island** embraces the world's largest volcano, 13,677ft Mauna Loa, while the huge dormant volcano of Haleakala dominates the eastern half of nearby **Maui**. Its tropical climate moderated by trade winds, Hawaii is diverse in weather, foliage and topography, with dramatic differences in rainfall between the wetter windward and drier leeward sides of each island. Mount Waialeale on **Kaua'i** receives as much as 500in of rain a year, while the Big Island's Ka'u Desert is exceedingly arid. Fine beaches and lush foliage contribute to the islands' tourism fame. The main city of **Honolulu** is on the island of **O'ahu**.

History

The Early Migrations

Archaeological sites throughout the Americas yield many clues about the origins of Native Americans, but not enough to support a definitive theory as to when or by what route they arrived in the New World. Most scientists believe that ancestral Native Americans walked from northeastern Asia across the Bering land bridge during the Pleistocene Epoch, when continental ice sheets locked up enough water to reduce sea levels. Finding the coast blocked by maritime glaciers, they would have moved south via an ice-free corridor that opened through Canada during a warming period. An intriguing newer theory postulates that some may have arrived from Siberia in skin boats—some settling in Alaska, most coasting around the maritime glaciers and quickly moving south to settle the most promising temperate coastal spots, then moving out from there to inhabit inland regions over succeeding generations.

Prehistoric emigrants apparently arrived in four distinct migratory cycles, the first as many as 30,000 years ago. These **Paleo-Indians** found a land rich in mammoths, camels, large bison, mastodons, prehistoric horses and other big game. Whether the Paleo-Indians died out or were absorbed into later populations is unknown, but judging from the scant remains they left, they were racially distinct from contemporary Native Americans. The oldest complete human corpse discovered in North America, the **Spirit Cave mummy** from central Nevada, was radiocarbon-dated to about 9,400 years ago and apparently has no direct descendants. The skeleton of 9,300-year-old **Kennewick Man,** found in a burial site near the Columbia River in Washington, indicates racial links nearer to southern Asian or Polynesian people than to modern Native Americans. Traces of Paleo-Indian flint projectile points have been found at Folsom and Clovis, New Mexico, and elsewhere.

The ancestors of most modern Native Americans arrived during the second migration, beginning about 15,000 years ago. Descended from northeastern Asian peoples, they also hunted big game, although larger mammals began to disappear as the climate warmed about 10,000 years ago. Succeeding generations of these **Archaic hunters and gatherers** fanned out across the Americas, adapting to specific territorial homelands. As populations grew, so did interaction between tribes, as well as conflict over resources. Even up to historic times, migrations within the continent forced entire nations to readapt cultures to new homes and conditions.

A third migration about 9,500 years ago brought the **Athabascan** ancestors of the Navajo, Apache and peoples of the Alaskan and Canadian interior. Ancestors of the **Inuit and Aleut** people arrived in a fourth migration from Siberia about 4,500 years ago, occupying lands hitherto deemed less hospitable for settlement, specifically the frigid Arctic and stormy Aleutian Islands.

Hawaiians trace their ancestry to two distinct waves of Polynesian settlers who sailed northward in double-hulled canoes. The first wave arrived between AD 400 and 750, probably from the Marquesas Islands. The second migration, likely from Tahiti, arrived around 1100. These newcomers vanquished the earlier inhabitants and developed a society in which chiefs and hereditary priests held social ascendancy over large classes of commoners, mostly farmers and fishermen.

Indian Nations of the US West

When Europeans arrived in the Western Hemisphere at the end of the 15C, scores of nations occupied America's West. Some were migratory hunters and gatherers; others lived in fixed villages. In Mexico, large cities with trade routes influenced cultures far to their north. (The first Europeans called these tribes "Indians," erroneously assuming that they had landed in the East Indies; although scholars may refer to Native Americans or Amerindians, still the most popular general term used today, even among most tribal leaders, is "American Indian.")

Of the 54 million people who some anthropologists estimate were living in the Americas at the time of Columbus' "discovery" in 1492, 4 million may have dwelled north of Mexico. At least 300 distinct languages were spoken. West of the Mississippi River, anthropologists count 56 language families, although six predominated (with more than half of the native population communicating in one of that halfdozen). **Uto-Aztecan** prevailed from central Mexico into Texas; it was spoken by the Comanche, Shoshone, Paiute, and the Pueblo cultures of New Mexico. **Siouan** was the dominant language of the Great Plains and Missouri River Valley. **Algonquian** was spoken by the Blackfoot, Cheyenne and Arapaho peoples who had migrated to the northern plains from northeastern woodlands. **Salish** was dominant in the Northwest coastal region. **Athabascan** was spoken in western (but not coastal) Canada and central Alaska, and by Navajo and Apache in the Southwest. **Eskimo-Aleut** was the tongue of the Inuit and Aleut people of Alaska. In California alone, there was a veritable Babel of 120 dialects (of seven separate language families).

Although Europeans had scant contact with western Indians until the late 17C and 18C, numerous migrations predated their arrival. Among the most important was

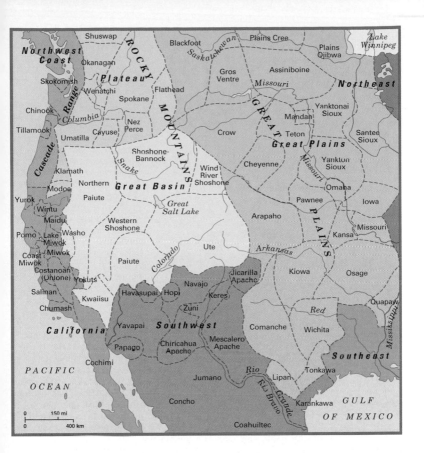

the movement of woodland farmers, including the **Mandan, Omaha, Osage, Pawnee** and **Wichita**, from the East to the western prairies between 100 BC and AD 900. Later European settlement along the eastern seaboard spurred the **Lakota** and other nations to the Great Plains. Many tribes, like the Mandan, remained in permanent farming villages after their migration, while others abandoned villages after Spanish horses were introduced in the 17C, choosing a nomadic lifestyle following bison herds. Horses also brought greater leisure and a cultural renaissance to the Lakota, **Crow, Assiniboine, Cheyenne, Comanche, Blackfoot, Arapaho** and other tribes, all of whom developed elaborate religious rites and highly codified warrior rituals. Plains tribes entered the Rocky Mountains in summer to hunt or to trade with tribes farther west. Some of the broader Rockies basins provided winter homes.

The desert Southwest experienced even more profound cultural upheaval in the millennia before the Spanish conquests. Archaic people in Mexico began cultivating corn, gourds, chilies and avocados about 5000 BC, beans and squash by 3500 BC. Farming culture spread by 300 BC into southern Arizona, where the **Hohokam** irrigated corn. Farming influenced the peoples of the southern Rockies and Colorado Plateau to settle in villages, precursors of the agricultural **Mogollon, Anasazi** and **Fremont** cultures. The Anasazi in particular built cliff dwellings and sophisticated towns that maintained elaborate trade links as far distant as the Aztec cities. The Anasazi cities were abandoned by AD 1200, perhaps because of drought; archaeologists surmise they transformed into the modern **Hopi** and **Pueblo** cultures. Their lands were occupied first by nomadic Shoshonean tribes, later by ancestors of the **Navajo** and **Apache** in the 14C.

The arid and mountainous reaches of the Great Basin supported smaller nomadic populations. When Shoshonean tribes (including **Paiute** and **Ute**) replaced the Fremont culture after the 10C, they developed a wandering lifestyle better suited to the prevailing desert climate. The nutritious piñon nut served as a dietary staple, supplemented with deer, small game, lizards, insects and seeds.

An abundance of food in Pacific Coast micro-environments encouraged the greatest diversity of Native American cultures, languages and societies. The population of California on the eve of the Spanish conquests is estimated to have been over 300,000. With shellfish, game, roots, seeds and acorns readily available, there was never a need for farming, except among **Yuman**-speaking desert tribes of the lower Colorado River. Coastal tribes, including **Ohlone, Chumash, Yurok** and **Pomo**, traded with inland

Cayuse Indian in Ceremonial Dress, Northeastern Oregon

Howdyshell Photo/Tamastslikt Cultural Institute

tribes such as **Miwok, Maidu** and **Yokut** on the west side of the Sierra Nevada, who in turn traded eastward with Shoshonean tribes of the Great Basin.

The populous tribes of the Northwest coast, from northern California to Alaska—including **Chinook, Tillamook, Skokomish** and **Tlingit**—were likewise rich in resources, particularly fish and shellfish. Early on, they developed technologies for preserving and storing seasonal foods. They built sturdy homes, canoes and furniture of hemlock, spruce, bone and other resources, and cultivated highly refined notions of the relative values of material goods and social status. The acquisition of material wealth—and especially its redistribution at a ceremony known as the potlatch—was a prime determiner of social status among individuals.

The tribes along the upper Columbia River and its tributaries, including the Snake River, migrated from the Pacific coast. Although culturally adapted to a drier, more severe climate, they depended upon the salmon run for a major part of their diet, supplementing fish with game and plants, including the nutritious camas bulb. The arrival of the horse to this region in the 18C increased the tribes' mobility and trading contacts. Among the larger tribes were the **Nez Percé, Cayuse** and **Flathead**.

Despite the ubiquity of the American Indian tribes, new diseases—which swept the Americas ahead of European migration—thinned their populations by as much as 90 percent. The depopulation of vast areas was perhaps the most lethal pandemic ever visited upon human beings.

Early European Inroads

The conquest of the Aztec empire in 1521 by **Hernán Cortés** (1485-1547) enormously enriched the Spanish treasury and plunged the Spanish government into the colonization of their vast new territories in the New World. From the Europeans' perspective, the terrain north of central Mexico was peripheral, a sere and underpopulated wasteland, definitely of less significance than the civilizations (and gold reserves) of Central and South America.

Spanish exploration of North America trailed upon rumors of gold carried by the remnants of a Florida expedition shipwrecked on the barrier islands of Texas in 1528. **Alvar Núñez Cabeza de Vaca** (c.1490-1557) straggled back to Mexico in 1536 with tales of treasures hoarded in the fabulous Seven Cities of Cibola. A succession of explorers penetrated the unknown land—most prominently the expeditions of **Hernando de Soto** (1496-1542), who entered Oklahoma from the east in 1541, and **Francisco Vásquez de Coronado** (1510-54). Coronado marched north from Mexico in 1540, wreaking mayhem among the Pueblos, pushing as far north as the Grand Canyon and possibly as far east as Kansas, but failing to find another Aztec or Inca empire. Sailing in 1542, **Juan Rodríguez Cabrillo** (d.1543) explored the coast of California for Spain and put San Diego Bay on European maps.

Disappointed by a lack of conspicuous gold, Spain allowed its colonization of New Mexico and California to languish until **Sir Francis Drake** (c.1540-96) landed on California's north coast and claimed it for England in 1579. That sparked a northward expansion of Spanish frontiers. Although early missionary attempts failed, successful trade expeditions encouraged **Juan de Oñate** (c.1549-1630), with a party of missionaries, soldiers, black slaves and Indians, to establish a tenuous colony at San Juan Pueblo, north of what now is Santa Fe, in 1598.

Throughout the 17C, expansion of Spanish settlements—and with them, the forced conversion of Indians to Catholicism—progressed with checkered success throughout the Rio Grande Valley. The colonies survived despite periodic setbacks including the devastating **Pueblo Revolt of 1680,** when Indians drove the Spanish from New Mexico for more than a decade. Spanish policy thereafter was reformed to permit native religious practices to continue, and the majority culture of New Mexico developed into a blend of Spanish and Pueblo, with its political, social, cultural and commercial capital at **Santa Fe**.

The French, meanwhile, were scouring the USA West for a different treasure: pelts. **French fur trappers and traders** first arrived by way of the Great Lakes and inland rivers, developing such favorable relations with native tribes that many Frenchmen married into Indian families and adopted the lifestyle. The full story of French exploration was never written down, although "naturalized" French must have penetrated far into the West in the 17C and 18C. Their biracial children also became effective guides, translators and trappers.

The French seized the key to the Great Plains in the 17C by building trading posts along the Mississippi River at St. Louis and other strategic points. They called the region Louisiana after King Louis XIV. By 1682, when **René-Robert Cavelier de la Salle** (1643-87) navigated the river to its mouth and claimed the Mississippi and its tributaries for France, the vast territory stretched from Canada to the Gulf of Mexico. Separating Florida from Mexico, it prompted a Spanish frenzy to colonize Texas. French New Orleans, however, was not founded until 1718.

Over the next half century, French traders explored every western tributary to the Rockies, even mounting an expedition to Santa Fe in 1739. The French did not pursue a vigorous colonization of Louisiana, however, so the tribes of the Great Plains lived unaffected by their paper affiliation with the French empire. Territorial settlements developed a Creole character born of French, African slave and Native American populations. Greater numbers of American adventurers arrived after 1763, when the **Treaty of Paris**—ending the French and Indian War—extended the borders of British colonies from the Atlantic Ocean to the Mississippi River. France had ceded the Louisiana Territory west of the Mississippi to Spain one year earlier in an effort to prevent it from falling into British hands, but Spain's energies were more focused on settling California.

Neglected for more than a century, Spain's claims to Alta (Upper) California were revived by fears of foreign incursions. Under **Aleksei Chirikov** (1703-48) and Dane **Vitus Bering** (1681-1741), Russians began probing Alaskan waters in 1728, sparking an influx of pelt hunters and fortified colonies along that coast. English ships also investigated the Pacific: **James Cook** (1728-79) claimed British Columbia for England in 1768. Cook subsequently visited the Pacific Northwest and Hawaii in 1778, and **George Vancouver** (1757-98) mapped the Canadian coast in 1792-94.

Goaded into action, a Spanish expedition organized by Padre **Junípero Serra** (1713-84) and **Gaspar de Portolá** (c.1723-86) pushed, by land and sea, to San Diego harbor, where Serra dedicated the first of California's 21 missions on July 16, 1769. Over the next decade, a string of missions, pueblos and presidios was erected along a coastal strip that stretched from San Diego to San Francisco Bay, with a provincial capital at **Monterey**.

Acting from the most righteous of intentions, though beset with a catastrophic disregard for native cultures, the Spanish set about converting California Indians to Catholicism. Their goal was to create an agrarian civilization by pressing the natives into service on the mission lands, consolidating them without regard to language or clan, and segregating them by sexes. Thousands died of foreign diseases and mistreatment during this calamitous cultural uprooting.

The Louisiana Purchase

Despite the long and arduous attempts of European countries to settle portions of the West, all (except the British in western Canada) were eclipsed during the 19C by the rapid growth of the United States. The westward expansion of the US in the late 17C and 18C—both as a collection of British colonies and as an independent republic after 1776—had inexorably progressed despite warfare with Native Americans and complex political and military maneuvering among European powers in North America. The westerly movement enabled Americans to obtain new resources, farmlands and trade relations, while satisfying a taste among many for adventure and freedom from social, religious or political constraints. The rallying cry that justified and even glorified this expansion was **"Manifest Destiny."** Born in colonial times, the idea that the US was destined to push its borders to the Pacific reached its apex in the 19C, when politicians, editors and missionaries presented Manifest Destiny as America's divine right, its sacred duty.

Following the 1763 Treaty of Paris, Americans quickly immigrated to Kentucky, Tennessee and the "northwest" territories. Conflicts with Indians were legion. Americans were alarmed when they learned that **Napoléon**, leading an ascendant France, had persuaded Spain to cede Louisiana back to France in 1800. But after a disastrous campaign in Haiti, a shortage of funds convinced Napoléon to sell Louisiana to the US in 1803 to support his war against Great Britain. Negotiators for President **Thomas Jefferson** settled with Napoléon for about $15 million.

Lewis & Clark at Three Forks - (1912) by Edgar S. Paxson

The exact boundaries of the Louisiana Territory were undefined. Pressed as much by personal curiosity as national interest, Jefferson enlisted congressional approval for a military expedition to explore the area. He selected his personal secretary, **Meriwether Lewis** (1774-1809), to spearhead the expedition, and Lewis invited his boyhood friend, career soldier **William Clark** (1770-1838), as co-leader. Instructed to promote trade with the Indians, observe flora and fauna, map major rivers and their sources, and make records of soils, minerals and climate, the Corps of Discovery set course up the Missouri River on May 14, 1804, with a trained party of stalwart frontiersmen.

Wintering at a Mandan village in what is now North Dakota, they enlisted a French Canadian trapper, Toussaint Charbonneau, as an interpreter for their journey. Charbonneau's Shoshone wife, **Sacagawea** (c.1786-1812), unexpectedly proved a far greater asset. The presence of a native woman signaled to western tribes that this was not a war party. Sacagawea was instrumental in obtaining horses when the expedition dramatically encountered a Shoshone tribe, led by her own brother, near the Continental Divide. After a strenuous descent of the Rockies, Lewis and Clark arrived at the Pacific Ocean on November 7, 1805. They wintered at Fort Clatsop at the mouth of the Columbia River and returned to St. Louis in September 1806, having lost only one man to appendicitis.

The extraordinary success of the Lewis and Clark Expedition overshadowed other government-funded forays into the West. After leading an expedition to the upper Mississippi in 1805-06, **Zebulon Pike** (1779-1813) investigated the Colorado Front Range headwaters of the Arkansas and Red Rivers; arrested by Spanish soldiers, he was held in Mexico for several months. Another party, led by Major **Stephen H. Long** (1784-1864), ascended the Platte River and looped back through the high plains; Long branded the region "the Great American Desert."

Pelts, Hides and Blubber

Others headed west without government support, seeking adventure and profit from the burgeoning fur trade. These "mountain men" sought buffalo robes, bear and deer hides, the pelts of otter and fox, and especially beaver furs, which earned high prices in Chinese and European markets. Among them was **John Colter** (c.1774-1813), who left the eastbound Lewis and Clark party and became the first person to describe the Yellowstone country. **Jedediah Smith** (1799-1831) was a Bible-toting teetotaler who blazed trails across the Great Basin to California and north to the Columbia River. Others included **Kit Carson** (1809-68), **Jim Bridger** (1804-81), **Jim Beckwourth** (c.1800-66), **Joe Walker** (1798-1876) and the Sublette brothers, William and Milton. Although they worked in extreme isolation and independence, most of these men were nominally employed by trading companies such as the Rocky Mountain Fur Company and the Canada-based North West and Hudson's Bay Companies. They became thoroughly acquainted with the West, blazing the first transcontinental trails or bringing long-established Indian trails to the attention of travelers. Their lonely lives were enlivened by annual rendezvous, a tradition started in 1825 to facilitate the collection of furs, but also serving as a good excuse for festivities, contests and debauchery.

After Mexico overthrew Spanish rule in 1821, Santa Fe began welcoming American traders. **William Becknell** (c.1790-1865) became the first American to push wagons through the plains to the New Mexico outpost, opening the **Santa Fe Trail** and earning large profits by exchanging hardware and dry goods for livestock. Indian raids forced later traders to gather for safety in wagon trains, while clustering in defensive camping positions at night.

The fur trade heated up on the Pacific slope, too, especially after New Englander **Robert Gray** (1755-1806) made a fortune on a round-the-world voyage, gathering pelts along the Northwest coast in 1789 and selling them in China for vast profits. The name of his ship, *Columbia*, was bestowed upon the Northwest's great river. British Canadian trading posts were already established on the Columbia in 1811 when a subsidiary of John Jacob Astor's American Fur Company founded the post of **Astoria** near the river mouth. Although Fort Astoria fell peacefully to the British in the War of 1812, the Treaty of Ghent soon returned it to US interests. Another treaty in 1818 established joint occupation of the Oregon Country by both nations and set a northern boundary (along the 49th parallel) to the Louisiana Territory.

As New England merchants pushed deeply into the China trade, clipper ships took on the trans-Pacific shipment of Russian pelts from Alaska. (This encouraged a short-lived Russian expansion to northern California.) Clipper ships also called at San Diego, Santa Barbara, Monterey and San Francisco Bay, resupplying and trading for tallow and cowhides. California's enviable climate and excellent harbors became common knowledge along the Eastern seaboard after **Richard Henry Dana** published his best-seller, *Two Years Before the Mast* (1840).

Yankees also reaped great profits in the Pacific from hunting whales, the primary source of lamp oil in the mid-19C. A particularly rich hunting ground was the Hawaiian Islands. Soon after Captain Cook had introduced the remote archipelago (dubbed the "Sandwich Isles") to the world, **King Kamehameha I** (c.1758-1819) unified the islands in 1795. The new dynasty dismantled the ruling tradition in which an aristocratic class of warriors and priests dominated the majority through a system of *kapus* (taboos). Whaling rapidly became the economic mainstay, increasing the kingdom's reliance on foreign advisers while enabling hundreds of sturdy Hawaiian sailors to ship out. The whalers' most insidious contributions to local culture were smallpox, syphilis and other epidemics that ravaged the indigenous population, hewing their numbers from 300,000 at the time of Cook's visit to 54,000 a century later. Far-reaching also were the social effects sparked by the journey to New England of a Hawaiian, Opukahaia, whose conversion to Christianity encouraged the first Protestant missionaries to move to Hawaii in 1820—engendering enormous changes in local culture, religion and politics.

Reports circulating in the East about the Great Plains and Rockies signaled that those regions were useless for agriculture or civilization, but would serve well as buffer zones against hostile attacks from foreign nations. As bloody warfare between Indians and settlers continued to rage through the Midwest and South, some Americans proposed to remove all Indians to the remote lands west of the Mississippi, then home primarily to nomadic tribes. The **Indian Removal Act of 1830** saw the Cherokee, Chickasaw, Chocktaw, Creek and Seminole nations uprooted from their homelands in the South and forced to march to the **Indian Territory**, now Oklahoma. Ironically known as the Five Civilized Tribes for their adoption of American clothing and agricultural methods, the populations were decimated by the internment and grueling march, since referred to by the Cherokee tribe as the "Trail of Tears."

In the 19C, Easterners were increasingly in favor of conciliatory measures to assimilate Indians by religious conversion or schooling, while Westerners favored policies that wavered between enforced banishment on guarded reservations and outright extermination. The dichotomy between the attitudes played dynamically through the US government's 19C Indian policy.

Eastern sensibilities were moved by a delegation of Flathead Indians that arrived in St. Louis in 1831 seeking information on Christianity. Methodist and Presbyterian missionaries set out for the isolated Oregon Country. A mission near modern Walla Walla, Washington, was built by **Marcus Whitman** (1804-47); in 1836, his wife, **Narcissa Whitman**, and her companion, **Eliza Spaulding**, became the first American women to cross the continent. Jesuit priest **Pierre Jean de Smet** (1801-73), a Belgian who founded a string of missions across Idaho and Montana, won the respect and affection of the Teton, Sioux and Blackfoot peoples by his great strength and integrity. The Church of Jesus Christ of Latter-day Saints, founded in 1830, also undertook extensive proselytizing work among the Indians of the Mississippi Valley.

The Pioneer Movement

The three Western destinations that most appealed to early pioneers were each claimed by a foreign nation. The promised land in the 1830s was Texas, then governed by Mexico. In the 1840s, new streams of pioneers set out for the Oregon Country, jointly (though sparsely) occupied by Britain and the US. Other pioneers had their sights on California, a neglected Mexican outpost.

Anglo-American traders and squatters had been unwelcome residents of Texas since the late 18C. When Mexico broke from Spain in 1821, it opened the borders of Texas to immigration, assuming that Texas would assimilate newcomers by requiring them to adopt Mexican citizenship and Catholicism. But most Americans flooding into Texas had no intention whatsoever of respecting Mexican law or culture. Anglo Texans proved so assertive of their independence that before the end of a decade, Mexico attempted to close its borders again.

By then, political tensions had degenerated to skirmishes, and Mexico resolved to put down the rebellion by force. In 1836, Mexican General **Antonio López de Santa Anna** (1794-1876) took 4,000 troops to San Antonio and slaughtered a party of insurrectionists sequestered at a former mission, the Alamo. Santa Anna then marched east to San Jacinto, near modern Houston, to dispatch another small Texas army, this one led by **Sam Houston** (1793-1863). Rallying under the battle cry "Remember the Alamo!" the Texans captured Santa Anna, defeating his troops and winning their independence. The new **Republic of Texas** elected Sam Houston as its president.

Beset by debt, Indian hostilities and conflict with a Mexico unwilling to recognize its independence, Texas was steered by Houston toward statehood. In the growing crisis that soon would lead to the American Civil War, however, Congress was politically reluctant to admit another "slave state," so Texas remained a republic until 1845. By that time, its burgeoning population of 142,000, bolstered by thousands of immigrants from the US South and Europe, could no longer be denied statehood, slavery or no—even though most Americans recognized that this annexation would antagonize Mexico and lead to war with that nation.

Oregon proved a less contentious acquisition. Praised for its salubrious climate and soil, the Oregon Country's graces were well advertised in the East. Many Americans were doubly motivated by the patriotic goal of securing the country from Britain by the simple act of occupying the land. Convoys of Conestoga wagons pushed west from Independence, Missouri, guided by scouts familiar with a route soon known as the **Oregon Trail.** Stretching some 2,000mi, the Oregon Trail followed the Platte River across Nebraska; surmounted the Rockies at broad South Pass, between Fort Laramie and Fort Bridger; then crossed the Snake River Plain and Blue Mountains to Whitman's Walla Walla mission. A final stretch down the Columbia River brought tired travelers to the lush Willamette River Valley. Hardships wracked the six-month journey, but thousands completed the crossing between 1842 and 1869, when the trail was rendered obsolete by the completion of the transcontinental railway.

In 1843, the Oregon Country petitioned Congress for protection from British claims and marauding Indians. Two years later, US President **James Polk** (1795-1849) called for a renegotiation of the joint occupation agreement with Great Britain; in 1846, they compromised on the 49th parallel as their boundary. The slaughter of Whitman and his fellow missionaries by Indians in 1847 provoked another demand for federal protection, and in 1848 the Oregon Territory was formally established. Five years later, the Washington Territory was divided off. North of the Columbia and centered around Puget Sound, this region lacked the economic diversity of Oregon's rich farms; its population survived mainly by supplying timber to San Francisco and the California mines. Greater economic strength followed the completion of the Great Northern Railroad in the 1870s.

Smaller parties of transcontinental migrants left the Oregon Trail near Fort Bridger for California. The Mexican residents of California, known as **Californios,** were a self-sufficient lot; they received scant attention from Mexico's government, which was content to let the landholders rule themselves. Rancho owners prospered by selling hides to Yankee trading ships. A growing population of Yankees and other foreigners were living in Monterey and other settlements, having jumped ship, adopted the Catholic religion and become naturalized Mexican citizens. Many married local girls and became prominent in Californio society.

Poster Promoting Western Migration

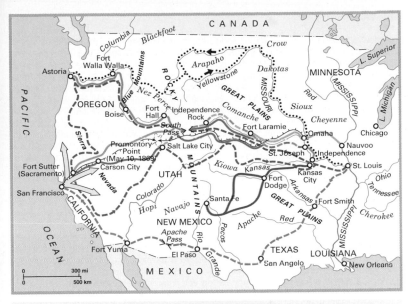

Among the foreign residents was **John Augustus Sutter** (1803-80), a Swiss adventurer with vast land grants along the American River in the Sacramento Valley. Sutter entertained many travelers and immigrants at his walled fort, including US Army surveyor **John C. Frémont** (1813-90) after his exhausting 1844 winter crossing of the Sierra Nevada. Frémont's published report of his California journey became the standard guidebook for westbound travelers.

The Mexican War

James Polk gained election in 1845 on a platform of expansion through the annexation of Texas and Oregon. In the inevitable war with Mexico, Polk was anxious to obtain the provinces of New Mexico (including Arizona) and Alta California, a block of land that stretched from the Rockies to the Pacific Ocean and north to Oregon. He successfully achieved these objectives within two extraordinary years of his administration.

Although Polk was motivated by territorial gain as championed by the policy of Manifest Destiny, his official reason for going to war was a border dispute. Mexico viewed US annexation of Texas as an illegal transgression and, as expected, promptly severed relations. Polk ordered troops under General **Zachary Taylor** (1784-1850) to the Rio Grande, where they were attacked by Mexican forces. US troops marched down the Santa Fe Trail under General **Stephen Kearny** (1794-1848), capturing Santa Fe in June 1846 and continuing into Mexico. Kearny then marched west with a detachment to California, which he helped to secure in a small but decisive battle near Los Angeles, concluding a coup that had begun several weeks earlier.

California's capitulation had been orchestrated to coincide with the start of the Mexican War. When the US annexed Texas in 1845, Mexico banned Americans from emigrating to California. After armed foreigners, including Frémont and scout Kit Carson, were ordered out of California in March 1846, Frémont defiantly raised the US flag on Gabilan Peak, a prominent height northeast of Monterey, before retreating into Oregon. When he returned three months later, a band of American settlers hoisted their Bear Flag above the Mexican barracks in Sonoma, north of San Francisco, and declared California an independent republic. Less than a month later, American naval officer **John D. Sloat** (1781-1867) seized the California capital at Monterey and made the territory an American possession. Skirmishes continued in southern California until Kearny's arrival ended the fighting in January 1847.

Polk, meanwhile, sent General **Winfield Scott** (1786-1866) and his army to the Mexican port of Veracruz, from where they marched on Mexico City, capturing their foes' capital in February 1848 and bringing the war to an end. Provisions of peace were hammered out in the **Treaty of Guadalupe Hidalgo**, formalizing the American seizure of the vast territory stretching from Texas to the Pacific and north to Oregon.

The Mormons

The new territories acquired from Mexico embraced a vast, high, mountainous desert between the Rockies and the Sierra Nevada: the Great Basin. Even before it was relinquished by Mexico, the Great Basin already had been proclaimed the State of Deseret by a sect of pioneers who called themselves Latter-day Saints, or Mormons. The Church of Jesus Christ of Latter-day Saints was founded in 1830 in New York by **Joseph Smith** (1805-44). His zealous missionary work reaped new members, but he antagonized many others with his determined espousal of Old Testament views on polygamy and by his adherence to the unorthodox *Book of Mormon;* attributed to divine revelation, it propounded that Jesus had taught in North America after his biblical resurrection. Mormon community clannishness—especially their enthusiasm for hard work, their consequent prosperity and their disinclination to patronize non-Mormon establishments—further aroused ire and intolerance. When the sect moved West to facilitate its missionary work, the Mormons were violently driven from Ohio to Missouri to Illinois, where Smith was murdered by an armed mob. **Brigham Young** (1801-77) assumed the role of prophet and leader.

Young led his people to the Far West, where they could practice their religion without hindrance. Their migration culminated in their settlement of the Great Salt Lake Valley in 1847. Young directed the construction of **Salt Lake City** ; he returned East to bring more Mormon immigrants, encouraged others from Europe, and exhorted all to bring the tools, seeds and zeal they would need to establish a self-sufficient nation in a hard land. Thousands made the trek across the Plains and Rockies in ensuing decades, swelling the closely knit population and making the desert bloom with cooperative effort and irrigation from the Wasatch Mountains. The Mormons also established forts and built agricultural communities throughout Utah and parts of many other states.

The Utah Territory was established in 1850, but friction soon developed over questions of loyalty. Federally appointed territorial leaders felt unwelcome and even imperiled by Young's anti-government rhetoric. The institution of polygamy, and rumors of Mormon-inspired Indian uprisings, raised alarm in the East. Convinced of impending rebellion, the US government in 1857 ordered 2,500 troops to march to Utah to install a new governor to replace Young, and to instill a sense of respect for federal authority. Overreacting in kind, Young portrayed the invasion as a tool of Mormon persecution. He declared martial law, mobilized a militia, recalled the distant Mormon outposts, burned down Fort Bridger, fortified the western boundary of the Utah Territory, and even ordered Mormons to be ready to torch their own settlements. Tensions peaked when zealots slaughtered a party of non-Mormon pioneers at the Mountain Meadow Massacre in southern Utah. But with both sides perched on the brink of disaster, common sense prevailed, and diplomats negotiated a peaceful resolution.

The Gold and Silver Rushes

A few weeks before the formal peace with Mexico in 1848, flecks of gold were discovered in the sand at John Sutter's lumber mill on California's American River. The news spread like wildfire. The next year, **Forty-Niners** began pouring by land and sea into California from the eastern US, Europe, Australia, Asia, Mexico and South America. Though not the first gold rush in American history (Georgia had seen one in 1828), this one was unlike anything seen before. In just weeks, the port city of **San Francisco** grew from a sleepy village of 800 to a cosmopolitan hive of 90,000. In January 1849 alone, 61 vessels arrived at San Francisco Bay from the Eastern seaboard after sailing around stormy Cape Horn. As passengers and crews set off for the gold mines, abandoned ships rotted or were dragged ashore to serve as hotels, warehouses and offices. Meanwhile, thousands of prospectors—as well as tradesmen, money lenders, innkeepers, teamsters, preachers, gamblers, gunslingers and prostitutes—set out overland along the Oregon, California and Santa Fe Trails.

Mining camps with names like Rough and Ready, Hangtown, Poker Flat and Murderers Bar sprang up in the canyons and foothills, and California's Caucasian population mushroomed from 15,000 in 1848 to almost 100,000 in 1850, when California joined the Union as the 31st state. The frenetic activity died down toward the end of the 1850s with the decline of surface gold; individual gold miners gave way to mining corporations, companies with stockholders and the capital to build and operate hard-rock, dredging and hydraulic mining operations. Thousands of fortune hunters returned home or settled into new opportunities in California, where ranching, farming, construction, manufacturing and other jobs were becoming increasingly available. The California gold rush was the archetype of a series of mining rushes that marked the West for the next 60 years, instantly peopling remote corners with camps and makeshift towns. Ore-hungry miners established local governments that protected their claims and property rights, occasionally resorting to vigilante justice against more violent trespassers. Strikes in Colorado and Nevada started new stampedes just as the California rush was settling down.

California Gold Diggers, Ballou's Pictorial (1856)

The Pikes Peak gold rush hit pay dirt in 1858; the adjacent city of **Denver** was platted by speculators over that winter, and by spring 1859 a real rush was on. New lodes were discovered higher in the Rockies; Denver's first newspaper, *The Rocky Mountain News*, began publication in April, and a US mint opened the following year. Hostile confrontations with Indians increased; reservations were established deeper into the plains, and Indians were rounded up in campaigns that degenerated into the full-blown **Indian Wars**. As in California, corporate mining interests eventually prevailed in Colorado, especially after silver was discovered. Lone prospectors set out for other strikes—Idaho in 1860, Montana in 1862.

The 1859 discovery of Nevada's vast **Comstock Lode** of silver and gold produced a very different kind of mining rush. Initially some 10,000 hopeful prospectors poured into the desert to excavate the dry mountainside. Of the many claims along the buried vein, 12 proved bonanzas; but the difficulties of mining ore required capital investment and sophisticated engineering. Speculators from California bought up stock in the richest mines, while San Francisco merchants, farmers and transport companies earned good profits shipping supplies, food and people to the town that grew atop the mines. **Virginia City**. As newly minted millionaires built elegant mansions atop Nob Hill in San Francisco, Virginia City emerged as the first truly industrialized city west of the Mississippi. The glittering city on the side of Mount Davidson boasted an opera house, churches, saloons, schools and newspapers, while far beneath its streets, miners worked for wages in shifts by candlelight, in the most debilitating conditions of extreme heat and moisture.

The Civil War in the West

Westerners generally avoided the bloodshed of the Civil War, at least on their own territory. The issue of slavery had little effect on economies and did not arouse the strong passions it did in the cotton states of the South, nor among Northern abolitionists. Aside from a handful of skirmishes, although every state had to take sides, only Kansas and Texas were deeply affected by the war—Texas by its alignment to the Confederacy out of sympathy for its Southern immigrants, Kansas through the disastrous political machinations of the US Congress.

Problems began affecting the West in the 1820s, when the number of free and slave states was equal. This political reality forced Congress over the next four decades to postpone the entrance of new Western states to the Union until the balance of parity could be ensured, by admitting one slave state for every free state. This issue delayed Texas' entry into the Union for nine years. When the war started, Governor Houston was voted out of office after advocating a policy of non-involvement, and Texas voted overwhelmingly to join the Southern cause.

Federal politics played a dirty hand when Congress voted to allow Kansas to determine its standing on the slave-versus-free issue by popular sovereignty. Partisans from both sides converged on Kansas to sway the issue, and when violence flared in 1855, the territory slipped into national notoriety as "Bleeding Kansas." Finally admitted to the Union as a free state in 1861, Kansas continued to smolder. In one of the most brutal actions of the Civil War, raiders burned the free-state stronghold of Lawrence in 1863, killing at least 150 civilians.

None of the skirmishes in the Far West affected the outcome of the Civil War. Texans themselves fought prominently in many Eastern battles, although the state itself was successfully embargoed and never invaded. Confederates briefly occupied Arizona, whose provisional government joined the Southern cause in 1861. A force of 1,750 Confederates marched up the Rio Grande Valley in 1862 in an attempt to force Union troops from New Mexico, seize matériel and gain control of gold and silver supplies from Colorado, Nevada and California. They were stopped at the **Battle of Glorieta Pass**, just east of Santa Fe, and retreated back into Texas, leaving the West in Union hands. Union authorities in New Mexico then decided to end Navajo raids on pueblos and settlements. Colonel Kit Carson was chosen to lead a punitive expedition. Although he had a natural sympathy for the Indians' plight, he followed orders, surprising the Navajo at Canyon de Chelly, destroying their fields, butchering their sheep and leading some 7,000 survivors in **The Long Walk** to a fortified reservation in New Mexico. They were allowed to return to their homeland in 1868.

Linking East and West

The first overland transcontinental mail and passenger-coach service was contracted in 1857 to **John Butterfield, William G. Fargo & Associates,** who selected a year-round route from St. Louis and Memphis to El Paso, Tucson and Los Angeles. This low-elevation corridor avoided the snows of the Rockies, passing through lands acquired in 1853 as the **Gadsden Purchase** (named for the diplomat who negotiated that treaty with Mexico). New routes quickly followed.

Faster service came with the **Pony Express,** which transported express mail by relays from St. Joseph, Missouri, to Sacramento, California, and by ship to San Francisco. Riding in 75mi increments, day and night, changing ponies at stations spaced every 10-15mi, a team of riders could transport the mail pouch in 10 days. The route grew shorter as telegraph lines edged across America; they joined in 1861. Yet the legend of the Pony Express has long outlasted its 18 months of service.

Eastern railroads reached the Mississippi as early as 1854. The first rail lines on the river's west bank went to St. Joseph in 1859 and to Kansas City in 1865. The US government, eager to ensure a steady flow of California gold and Comstock silver during the Civil War, pushed for a transcontinental railroad that would link California and Nevada with the East Coast. As incentive, Congress offered land grants and subsidies to rail companies for every mile of track laid. Two companies formed to build lines from opposite ends: the **Central Pacific** eastward from California and the **Union Pacific** westward from Missouri.

In 1857, construction engineer **Theodore Judah** (1826-63) had developed and published a plan for building a railroad through Donner Pass in the Sierra Nevada, the most difficult stretch of terrain on the transcontinental route. Financiers **Collis P. Huntington** (1821-1900), **Mark Hopkins** (1814-78), **Charles Crocker** (1822-88) and **Leland Stanford**

The Last Rails of the Union Pacific and Central Pacific Railroad,
May 10, 1869, Promontory Point, Utah

(1824-93)—who became known as "The Big Four"—signed on to Judah's plan and established the Central Pacific in 1861. Construction over the most difficult sections of the Sierra depended heavily upon 15,000 laborers from China, who laid the track. The Union Pacific, employing large numbers of Irish, set out across the Great Plains under chief engineer **Grenville Dodge** (1831-1916). Despite Indian resistance, the rolling terrain permitted faster progress than in the Far West. The project was known as "Hell on Wheels," both for its rambunctious crews and for the army of rascally camp followers, saloons, gambling dens and brothels that flourished in their wake. The two crews joined east and west with the **Golden Spike** at Promontory Point, Utah, on May 10, 1869.

Though the railroad was undeniably a great national asset, it proved disastrous for the short-term economy of California. The ready import of cheaply made goods from the East Coast undercut factories, throwing thousands out of work. As many factory owners rehired Chinese, willing to work for lower wages than Americans, anti-Asian resentment rose to fever pitch. Riots and murder ensued in some areas.

The railroads, however, prospered, and their boards and presidents acquired great political and economic clout. By deftly wielding their vast real-estate grants, these corporations could determine where cities and towns would be built, and which counties could prosper. Profitable spur lines and new overland routes connected mining and farming areas, opening vast sections of the nation to settlement. The **Northern Pacific** opened the Dakota Territory and Montana to easier settlement by linking Minnesota with Portland, Oregon, in 1883, and with Seattle in 1887. The **Southern Pacific** extended a line from New Orleans to Los Angeles and San Francisco.

The Cattle Industry

The Great Plains obviously were ideal for livestock. Herds of **bison** numbered at least 15 million, and perhaps 50 million, prior to the arrival of Europeans. Between the 1850s and 1880s, however, the beasts were nearly wiped out in an orgy of slaughter that climaxed in the 1870s, when buffalo were wantonly killed from trains or massacred en masse for their hides. Their extermination crushed the independence of the Indians, but it also opened the ranges for cattle.

The **longhorn range cattle** of the Texas plains were descended from breeds brought north from Mexico in the late 17C. Most of the techniques of livestock husbandry used in 19C Texas likewise were developed from methods used in Spanish New Mexico: Cattle were grazed on open ranges, gathered by roping from horseback in annual roundups, branded and driven to market in herds. Even the clothing, saddle and lingo of the Anglo cattle industry were largely adapted from the *vaqueros.*

After the Civil War, with beef in Northern markets earning 10 times as much as on the Southern plains, enterprising Texans contrived a scheme to round up wild cattle. They were driven to railheads and shipped to stockyards and meat-packing plants in Chicago, Omaha and Kansas City, thence to the Northeast. Crews of cowboys branded and drove the cattle along what soon became well-established routes, including the **Chisholm, Goodnight-Loving, Sedalia and Western trails.** The drives were fraught with danger and discomfort. Rivers had to be forded; bandits, hostile Indians, wildfires, disease and extreme weather conditions took their toll.

After weeks in the saddle, cowboys were ecstatic to return to some semblance of civilization. The arrival of a cattle drive in a terminal town among them Fort Worth, Texas; Cheyenne, Wyoming; Wichita, Abilene and Dodge City, Kansas—was marked by days and nights of frantic celebration and wild roughhousing by the pleasure-starved wranglers. The excitement and ready money in cow towns attracted saloon keepers, prostitutes, gamblers and various riffraff to service or fleece the cowboys. Gunplay was common, giving rise to a tough breed of lawmen who sometimes were hard to distinguish from hired gunslingers. Some names have become part of Western legend: **Wyatt Earp** (1848-1929), **William Barclay "Bat" Masterson** (1853-1921), **James Butler "Wild Bill" Hickok** (1837-76).

Many early Texas cattlemen—including **Jesse Chisholm** (1805-68), **John Chisum** (1824-84) and **Charles Goodnight** (1836-1929)—grew wealthy from the cattle drives and staked out huge ranches on the plains. Soon the introduction of barbed wire in the 1870s offered a practical method of fencing large, treeless areas. Some cattlemen continued to pursue open range by driving herds to the northern plains of Wyoming, Montana and the Dakotas, but even there, fences were cutting the land into individual ranches by 1885.

Consolidation of the cattle industry on large ranches encouraged the formation of cooperative organizations to fight rustlers, look after business interests and make rules governing roundups, quarantines, branding and mavericks (unbranded stray cattle). As the industry became more regulated, it attracted well-moneyed Eastern and European investors. Powerful organizations and cattlemen sometimes tried to hinder "nesters" (homesteaders) and small ranchers from gaining footholds, and to intimidate them with vigilantism. Dangerous and widespread range wars, such as New Mexico's 1878 Lincoln County War, brought notoriety to gunmen like **William "Billy the Kid" Bonney** (c.1859-81).

Other conflicts pitted cattlemen versus sheepherders. Cattle and sheep competed for similar resources yet were incompatible, as sheep destroyed turf and cattle wouldn't drink from holes where sheep had watered. Pitched battles between gregarious cowboys and lonely sheepherders were seldom fairly matched. Ironically, a more potent challenge to the economic dominance of the cattle barons was the late-19C discovery on the Great Plains of petroleum. This industry eventually would revolutionize the economies of Texas and Oklahoma.

The Indian Wars

As hordes of miners, cattlemen, railroad builders, soldiers and pioneers pushed across the Great Plains and Rockies, overrunning what had been designated "Indian land," the federal government sought to redraw the boundaries of native homelands. Reservations for the Cheyenne, Arapaho, Blackfoot, Sioux, Crow and other tribes were reduced in size and placed as far as possible from railways and settlements. The Army set about enforcing the tribes' removal to the reservations.

Although the resettlement of eastern tribes to Indian Territory had been hard, the lands of eastern Oklahoma were fertile and well-watered, and the Five Civilized Tribes could make a go of farming. It was far more difficult for the nomadic tribes of the plains to adapt to new homes. Even if the new reservation lands had not been unsuited for farming by conventional methods, the relocated Indians lacked tools and skills to cultivate them. As buffalo herds dwindled, and with federal troops fighting the Civil War in the East, some tribes stepped up depredations against settlements and travelers in the high plains.

When one renegade band of Cheyenne sued for peace in 1864, a Colorado militia force led by Methodist minister John Chivington ambushed their camp, killing more than 300 men, women and children in what became known as the **Sand Creek Massacre.** The news struck foreboding in many whites, for it predictably enraged thousands of Indians from Texas to Montana and kindled the bloodiest sessions of the Indian Wars. Already angered by the decimation of bison herds, by countless trespasses on their hunting grounds and by broken treaties, the massacre further convinced the Native Americans that they must fight to survive. The 1870s saw repeated insurrections. Among the bloodiest were the 1874-75 Red River War, staged by Comanche and Kiowa led by **Quanah Parker** (c.1845-1911); and the four-month, 1,200mi odyssey of the Nez Percé under **Chief Joseph** (c.1840-1904), who was determined not to be confined to a reservation.

The Sioux offered the most dogged resistance on the Great Plains. After the Bozeman Trail to Montana mines was cut through Sioux hunting grounds east of the Big Horn Mountains, **Red Cloud** (1822-1909) led the tribe in an 1866 campaign that forced the US Army to surrender and abandon Fort Phil Kearny. Red Cloud also secured guarantees for South Dakota's sacred Black Hills in exchange for his promise to never again go to war against the US. But when prospectors discovered gold in the Black Hills in 1874 and a full-blown gold rush ensued, the Sioux returned to war under **Crazy Horse** (c.1842-77) and **Sitting Bull** (1831-90).

Peace negotiations failed dismally. As the Sioux and their Cheyenne allies rode west toward the Big Horns, pursued by the Army, they established camp on the Little Bighorn River of Montana. When Lt. Col. **George Armstrong Custer** (1839-76) and his 7th Cavalry attacked without ascertaining the Indians' full force, he and all 225 of his troops, plus another 47 under command of other officers, were massacred. A single horse survived what became known as "Custer's Last Stand." The nation was shocked. The Indians could not exploit their resounding victory, however. With winter they were forced to return to the reservation.

Another resilient people were the Apaches, who for centuries raided their Indian neighbors and played havoc with Spanish and Mexican settlers. Attacks continued against Americans in the 1850s and 1860s, growing more severe during the Civil War. Aided by familiar terrain and climate, the Apaches—under such leaders as **Cochise** (c.1812-1874) and **Geronimo** (c.1829-1909)—for decades were able to evade Army campaigns by retreating into mountain strongholds.

In the 1880s, the messianic **Ghost Dance** religious movement swept from California to the Dakotas. Originating among the Paiutes, the cult exhorted followers to dance trance-like in a circle to commune with dead ancestors. The cult promised the resurrection of ancestors and old ways, a resurgence of the buffalo and the disappearance of the whites. In 1890, when they became alarmed by dances on the Pine Ridge Reservation in South Dakota, soldiers tried to disarm the Sioux, who fled into the nearby Badlands. In an ensuing melée, soldiers opened fire and killed about 250 men, women and children. The **Wounded Knee Massacre** was the last major conflict of the Indian Wars.

The **Dawes Act of 1887** attempted to redress the failure of the reservation system by redistributing parcels to individual Indians. Though well intended, it proved a failure in many cases, as Indians sold their lands for pittances to outsiders. White settlers also pressured the government to open for settlement some former reservation lands of Oklahoma, seized from the Indians as Civil War reparation for their support of the Confederacy. In several government-organized land runs, the first in 1889, contenders for homesteads were assembled on the edge of each new tract and released en masse at an appointed hour. Numbering as many as 100,000 when the 6-million-acre **Cherokee Outlet** was opened in 1893, the emigrants fanned out at full speed in wagons and buggies. They overran each new territory within hours, seizing farmsteads and city lots in Oklahoma City, Norman, Guthrie and other paper settlements that vaulted to life overnight.

Acquisition of Alaska and Hawaii

Overburdened by the settlement of Siberia, fearing Alaska's imminent seizure by the British Navy, and with the sea-otter population in rapid decline from over-hunting, Russia sold its vast North American territories to the US government for $7.2 million in 1867. Secretary of State **William Seward** (1801-72) negotiated the purchase, for which he was ridiculed by a handful of politicians and newspapermen. When the Army took control of "Seward's Icebox" later that year, expeditions began to map the interior and churchmen established missions.

Few settlers, however, ventured to Alaska until 1897-98, after gold was discovered on a tributary of the Klondike River in Canada's Yukon Territory. Because it lay on the primary route to the gold fields, the Alaskan port of Skagway boomed. Some 100,000 stampeding prospectors poured off steamships from Seattle and San Francisco, setting off on a long slog over White Pass via the Chilkoot Trail. Many were unprepared for the exertion, isolation or severe climate; fewer than half arrived at the gold fields. The hardy survivors—known thereafter as Sourdoughs for the starter they used to leaven camp bread—went on to strike gold in the Yukon and Tanana River Valleys, and in far-western Alaska at Nome.

Half an ocean away, Hawaii by the mid-19C boasted one of the world's highest English literacy rates, the fruit of New England missionaries. Yankee advisers to the Kamehameha Dynasty also engendered a land-reform plan that promoted private property but disenfranchised small farmers. Enormous blocks of land were bought up by Americans and other foreigners, consolidated and developed as sugar plantations. Thousands of contract laborers from China, and later from Japan, Korea, the Philippines and Portugal, met labor demands. When Hawaiian sugar was granted duty-free access to the US market in 1874, American business interests in Honolulu began to clamor for more power in the government.

In 1887, businessmen induced King **David Kalakaua** (1836-91) to adopt a constitution that reduced him to a figurehead. An attempted palace coup to replace the weakened king with his sister, **Liliuokalani** (1838-1917), was suppressed by US Marines. When Liliuokalani became queen by succession in 1891, her efforts to regain monarchical power prompted a prominent newspaperman, Lorin Thurston, to lead the bloodless Revolution of 1893, establishing the **Republic of Hawaii**. Calls for US annexation were parried by Congress until the Spanish-American War, when the invasion of the Philippines demonstrated Hawaii's usefulness as a mid-Pacific supply station. Annexed in 1898, Hawaii achieved territorial status in 1900.

The Preservation Movement

The closing of the frontier brought some hard recognition that the resources of the West, once seemingly boundless, were not inexhaustible. Water produced the longest and most intractable dispute. Everyone acknowledged the relative aridity of Western lands; but the Mormons had shown that irrigation could accommodate a deficiency in rainfall and make the desert bloom. Unlike rainfall, however, streams and rivers could be privately owned and, to a large measure, controlled.

Dangers and inequities were pointed out early by **John Wesley Powell** (1834-1902). A naturalist who had lost his arm as an artillery battery commander in the Civil War, Powell achieved near-legendary status by twice leading wooden-boat expeditions through the rugged drainage of the Colorado River, including the Grand Canyon, the last major unexplored region of the continental US. Sponsored by the Smithsonian Institution, Powell's first expedition descended the Green and Colorado Rivers on dories in 1869. The small party provided a geological survey of the Colorado Plateau in which Powell illuminated the role of erosion on landforms. Powell was instrumental in creating the US Geological Survey, an agency he later headed. His respect for the miracles wrought by irrigation was tempered by warnings that the public lands of the West be rationally managed to conserve water and other resources—an opinion fervently attacked by mining, cattle and timber interests, among whom any talk of government regulation was repellent.

© Matthew McVay/FOLIO, Inc.

Environmental Protester,
Portland, Oregon

The federal government followed Powell's visionary lead in the 20C by sponsoring massive reclamation projects, constructing dams, reservoirs, canals and irrigation systems that turned California's Central Valley into the richest agricultural region in the world. Large dams built on the Columbia, Snake, Colorado, Missouri, Arkansas and other Western rivers supply electricity and preserve water for public consumption, agriculture and recreation. On the Great Plains, aquifers were tapped for irrigation; coupled with the development of dry-farming techniques in the late 19C, the plains states became major producers of wheat and other grains.

Reclamation projects, however, also undercut Powell's forewarning, enabling the sprawl of vast urban tracts on arid lands. The explosive growth of Los Angeles after the capture of Owens River water in the early 20C was later followed by the runaway expansions of Las Vegas and Phoenix, beginning in the 1970s.

Since the late 19C, meanwhile, large natural areas had come under the protective umbrella of the National Park Service. The paintings and photographs of **Thomas Moran** and **William Henry Jackson** (p 379), which accompanied the first detailed descriptions of the wondrous Yellowstone Country, provoked public interest and motivated Congress to create the world's first national park in 1872. Protection for California's giant sequoias and peerless Yosemite Valley followed in 1890, inspired by the writings of **John Muir** (1838-1914). The Preservation Movement found a friend in President **Theodore Roosevelt** (1858-1919), whose own experiences on a North Dakota ranch had brought him joy and robust health. Though a Division of Forestry had been established in the 1870s, Roosevelt quadrupled the amount of national forest land and gave a boost to the creation of national parks and monuments in the 20C.

The National Park Service today manages 82.5 million acres (129,000sq mi) of parklands, while another 91 million acres (142,000sq mi) are protected by the US Fish and Wildlife Service as wildlife refuges. Managed for commerce, recreation and environmental purposes are 191 million acres (298,000sq mi) of national forest and 270 million acres (421,000sq mi) of public domain under the Bureau of Land Management (BLM). These lands lie, overwhelmingly, in western states.

The West Grows Up

The unsettled West provided ample space for criminals and unsociable elements to hide from the law. Known for robbing coaches, trains and banks, **Jesse James** (1847-82), the four **Dalton Brothers** (b.1861-71) and the Hole-in-the-Wall Gang of **Robert "Butch Cassidy" Parker** (1866-1909?) and **Harry "Sundance Kid" Longabaugh** (1870-1909?) were among the nefarious felons. As settlements grew, however, so did demand for law and order. The frontier sheriff or marshal enforced laws against carrying firearms in towns, an unglamorous and sometimes-risky task that contributed enormously to social order. Judges often relied more upon common sense than legal basis, but their decisions carried weight and reinforced stability.

As the percentage of women in the Western population increased, so did family life and the stability it represented. Drinking and gambling had been conspicuous features of the overwhelmingly male societies of mining settlements, lumber camps and cow towns. A scarcity of females has been cited as a reason why the **women's suffrage movement** achieved its earliest successes in the Rocky Mountains, where male voters conceivably hoped enfranchisement might attract more women settlers. Wyoming Territory was the first US entity to grant women the vote, in 1869; it was followed by Utah in 1870, Colorado in 1893 and Idaho in 1896.

Government regulation, anathema throughout the 19C West, became a salvation in the 20C. The Great Depression of 1929 and the 1930s coincided with one of the historically worst droughts on the Great Plains. As crops failed, winds blew away the parched topsoil and the region became known as the **Dust Bowl**. Thousands of farmers and ranchers became debtors. Foreclosures sent up to 400,000 migrant farmers, many from Oklahoma, in search of work to California (where they were labeled Okies). President **Franklin Roosevelt** (1882-1945) took revolutionary action with his New Deal, introducing bold programs to control erosion, regulate farm production to raise agricultural prices, provide drought relief, and fund huge reclamation and irrigation projects. The **Civilian Conservation Corps** (CCC) employed thousands in public construction projects. Federal and state governments spent millions upgrading roads, a program that culminated with the interstate highway system in the 1970s, and facilitated the growth of tourism throughout the West.

World War II heralded an era of unprecedented growth and change. Burgeoning shipyards and war industries brought thousands of workers to Pacific Coast cities from other parts of the US. The Army and Navy established huge training bases and missile-testing ranges in the wide-open desert and plateau lands, while Alaska and Hawaii boomed with an influx of military personnel. The **aerospace industry** took root in southern California, Seattle and Houston, bringing lucrative defense contracts, demands for labor, government jobs and subsidies for universities.

The booming post-war economy brought huge growth, especially in California, which overtook New York as the most populous state in the 1960s. Fueled by Asian and Latin American immigration, the demographic makeup of Western cities changed dramatically; Los Angeles and San Francisco became the most ethnically diverse regions of the US. Growth also brought many problems long associated with Eastern cities—

Japanese Attack on Pearl Harbor, Hawaii, December 7, 1941

scarce housing, urban blight, crime, poverty, traffic jams and pollution. Politically, the Pacific coastal cities became among the most liberal in the nation, now having more in common with the Eastern seaboard than with the Western hinterland, which has remained more politically conservative. Specifically Western political interests often are motivated by concern over environment.

The **high-technology** revolution brought great wealth to California, major Northwest cities and other areas. It also created a trend that worries preservation-minded Westerners: Telecommuters now may live wherever they wish, instead of being concentrated where jobs dictate. Many scenic areas, especially near national parks, have become highly desirable real estate. Ranchers find that subdividing their lands may be more profitable than agriculture. As new housing developments encroach upon diminishing wildlife habitats, they also crowd the sensibility of wide-open spaces that has always set the West apart from the Eastern US.

■ Presidents of the United States

George Washington (1789-97)
John Adams (1797-1801)
Thomas Jefferson (1801-09)
James Madison (1809-17)
James Monroe (1817-25)
John Quincy Adams (1825-29)
Andrew Jackson (1829-37)
Martin Van Buren (1837-41)
William Henry Harrison (1841)
John Tyler (1841-45)
James Polk (1845-49)
Zachary Taylor (1849-50)
Millard Fillmore (1850-53)
Franklin Pierce (1853-57)
James Buchanan (1857-61)
Abraham Lincoln (1861-65)
Andrew Johnson (1865-69)
Ulysses S. Grant (1869-77)
Rutherford B. Hayes (1877-81)
James A. Garfield (1881)
Chester A. Arthur (1881-85)

Grover Cleveland (1885-89)
Benjamin Harrison (1889-93)
Grover Cleveland (1893-97)
William McKinley (1897-1901)
Theodore Roosevelt (1901-09)
William Howard Taft (1909-13)
Woodrow Wilson (1913-21)
Warren Harding (1921-23)
Calvin Coolidge (1923-29)
Herbert Hoover (1929-33)
Franklin D. Roosevelt (1933-45)
Harry S Truman (1945-53)
Dwight D. Eisenhower (1953-61)
John F. Kennedy (1961-63)
Lyndon B. Johnson (1963-69)
Richard M. Nixon (1969-74)
Gerald Ford (1974-77)
Jimmy Carter (1977-81)
Ronald Reagan (1981-89)
George Bush (1989-93)
William J. Clinton (1993-2001)

Time Line

c.30,000 BC	Paleo-Indians begin arriving in North America, probably across the Bering Land Bridge.
c.300 BC	Irrigated farming enters Arizona from Mexico.
c.AD 1200	Anasazi cliff dwellings abandoned.
1492	Columbus lands in the Western Hemisphere.
1521	Cortés defeats the Aztecs and claims Mexico for Spain.
1540-42	Coronado marches through the Southwest in search of the Seven Cities of Cibola.
1542	Cabrillo explores the California coast.
1579	Drake lands in California, claiming it for England.
1609	Santa Fe is founded.
1680	Spanish colonists flee northern New Mexico after more than 400 are slaughtered in Pueblo Revolt; they return in 1692.
1682	La Salle sails down the Mississippi, claiming the river and its western drainage for France.
1728	Bering explores the coast of Alaska for Russia.
1762	France cedes Louisiana Territory to Spain to avoid losing it to England.
1763	Treaty of Paris extends British (American colonial) frontier west to the Mississippi River.
1768	Cook claims coastal Canada for Great Britain.
1769	Serra establishes first of 21 missions along California coast.
1776	The future San Francisco is founded at Mission Dolores.
1778	Cook makes first landing in Hawaii.
1781	Los Angeles is founded.
1784	Russia establishes settlements at Kodiak and Sitka, Alaska.
1792-94	Vancouver charts Pacific coast from San Diego to Alaska, giving rise to competing British and US claims to Oregon Country.
1800	Napoleonic France regains Louisiana Territory from Spain.
1803	US buys Louisiana Territory from France for $15 million.
1804-06	**Lewis and Clark** journey up Missouri River, across Rocky Mountains and down Columbia River to Pacific Ocean.
1811	Fur traders found Fort Astoria at mouth of Columbia River.
1812	Russians establish Fort Ross on northern California coast.
1818	Treaty with Great Britain establishes northern US territorial border.
1821	Mexico declares independence from Spain. Santa Fe Trail opens.
1824	US War Department creates Bureau of Indian Affairs.
1830	Indian Removal Act mandates relocation of Five Civilized Tribes from southeastern US to Indian Territory (now Oklahoma).
1834	Mexico secularizes California missions.
1835	Dana voyages up the California coast, a trip he describes in *Two Years Before the Mast* (1840).
1836	Texas wins independence from Mexico six weeks after slaughter at The Alamo. Whitmans establish Walla Walla mission.
1842	First settlers leave Missouri on Oregon Trail.
1845	Republic of Texas becomes US state.
1846	US acquires Oregon Territory south of 49th parallel in negotiations with Great Britain.
1847	Brigham Young leads Mormons into Great Salt Lake Valley. Whitman missionaries slain by Cayuse Indians.
1848	US wins New Mexico and California in treaty ending **Mexican War**. Gold discovered in California, igniting gold rush of 1849.
1850	California enters Union.

1858-59	Gold discovered in Colorado; Comstock Lode (silver) revealed in Nevada.
1858-61	Butterfield stagecoaches run from St. Louis to Los Angeles.
1860-61	Pony Express.
1861-65	Civil War.
1861	First transcontinental telegraph line completed.
1866	Led by Red Cloud, Sioux eject Army from Wyoming's Fort Phil Kearny. First cattle drive on Goodnight-Loving Trail.
1867	US buys Alaska from Russia for $7.2 million.
1869	Transcontinental railroad completed in Utah. Wyoming grants suffrage to women. Powell charts Grand Canyon by boat.
1872	Yellowstone is established as first national park.
1876	Custer and his troops annihilated by Sioux and Cheyenne at **Battle of the Little Bighorn**.
1877	Chief Joseph and his band of Nez Percé are captured after a 1,200mi flight.
1878	Billy the Kid begins a short but notorious outlaw career by killing a sheriff during the Lincoln County War.
1883	"Buffalo Bill" Cody launches his renowned Wild West Show.
1887	Dawes Act redistributes reservation land to individual Indians.
1889-93	Land rushes bring 150,000 homesteaders to Oklahoma.
1890	Wounded Knee Massacre.
1892	Sierra Club founded with John Muir as president.
1893	US planters depose Hawaii's Queen Liliuokalani, establishing republic accepted in 1898 as US territory.
1896	Utah becomes state after Mormons de-sanction polygamy.
1897	Klondike gold rush begins, drawing prospectors to Alaska; oil gusher at Bartlesville, Oklahoma, signals start of industry.
1900	More than 6,000 people die in Galveston hurricane.
1902	Reclamation Act diverts funds from sale of public lands to construct dams and other irrigation projects in West.
1906	Great earthquake and fire devastate San Francisco.
1913	Los Angeles Aqueduct brings water from Owens Valley to L.A. Hollywood's first feature film, *The Squaw Man*, is released.
1916	William Boeing founds aircraft company in Seattle. National Park Service established in Washington DC.
1919	Grand Canyon National Park created.
1927-41	Mount Rushmore chiseled by sculptor Gutzon Borglum.
1936	Hoover Dam completed. Sun Valley resort opens.
1937	Golden Gate Bridge spans entrance to San Francisco Bay.
1941	Japanese attack **Pearl Harbor**, Hawaii; US enters World War II.
1953	War hero Gen. Dwight Eisenhower, a Texas-born Kansan, succeeds Harry S Truman as US president.
1959	Alaska and Hawaii become 49th and 50th states.
1962	Cesar Chavez organizes United Farm Workers in California.
1963	President John Kennedy is assassinated in Dallas and succeeded by Lyndon Johnson, a native Texan.
1971	Alaska Native Land Claims Settlement Act distributes $1 billion and 44 million acres of land to indigenous tribes.
1975	Bill Gates and Paul Allen establish Microsoft in Albuquerque, New Mexico; four years later, they move it to a Seattle suburb.
1980	Washington's Mount St. Helens erupts, killing 57. California governor Ronald Reagan, a former actor, elected US president.
1989	Tanker *Exxon Valdez* spills 11 million gallons of oil into Alaska's Prince William Sound.
1995	Terrorist bombing of Oklahoma City federal building kills 168.

Government and Politics

When delegates gathered in Philadelphia in 1787 to set up the government of the infant United States, they had varying ideas as to how it should be organized. Influenced by 18C philosophers, they believed government should exist to protect the rights of the people, and that the will of the citizenry, rather than a monarch, should prevail. But certain delegates also worried that placing too much power in popular hands could lead to mob rule. They saw a need for a strong leader, but not one so powerful as to become a tyrant. The federal structure devised by the delegates divided power, providing a system of checks and balances whereby no one branch of government could wield total control.

Federal Government

The US Constitution divides the government into three separate branches. Although the Constitution leaves all powers not specifically delegated to the federal government to the states and municipalities, there is overlap in certain areas.

Executive Branch – This branch is headed by the president and vice president, elected together to four-year terms of office. Both must be 35 years old, native citizens, and have lived in the US for at least 14 years prior to taking office.

Although the president's candidacy is submitted to popular vote, the country's leader is elected by an elaborate system called the **electoral college.** Citizens' votes are actually cast for a slate of electors committed to a specific candidate. The electors cast their pro forma votes several weeks after the popular election.

The constitution designates the president as head of state, chief treaty maker and commander-in-chief of the armed forces. He appoints ambassadors, Supreme Court justices and lower-court judges, federal department heads, and other office holders. His appointments require Senate approval. The president has the power to veto legislation, though both houses of Congress can override his veto by a two-thirds vote. The president's responsibilities have expanded over the years to include drafting domestic legislation and devising and implementing foreign policy.

The vice president has no specific duties except to step into the breach if the president dies or becomes so disabled as to be unable to perform his duties.

Also within the Executive Branch are 14 cabinet departments: State, Treasury, Defense, Justice, Interior, Agriculture, Commerce, Labor, Health and Human Services, Education, Transportation, Housing and Urban Development, Energy, and Veterans Affairs. The secretary (head) of each department advises the president on national policy, along with other designated officials. Another 80 agencies help carry out executive branch functions, including the Central Intelligence Agency, National Security Agency and National Aeronautics and Space Administration.

Most administrative work of the executive departments and agencies is performed by civilian employees. Numbering approximately 2.5 million, this cadre works in Washington DC and other major US cities. Most (70 percent) are employed by the departments of Treasury, Defense, Justice and Veterans Affairs.

© FOLIO, Inc.

President Bill Clinton Addressing Congress, January 19, 1999

Legislative Branch – The US Congress is the bicameral legislative, or lawmaking, branch of government. It comprises the 435-member **House of Representatives**, with states represented according to population; and the 100-member **Senate**, which contains two members from each of the 50 states, no matter how large or small.

Senate candidates run for six-year terms in staggered years; that is, about one-third of the Senate faces re-election every two years. Senators must be 30 years old. Representatives, all of whom run in biennial elections, must be 25 years old. Legislators are not required to have been born in the US, but senators must have lived in this country for nine years, representatives for seven.

Powers granted to Congress include declaring war, levying taxes, regulating interstate commerce and impeaching or otherwise trying government officials, including judges and presidents. The Senate confirms all presidential appointees and ratifies all treaties made with other governments. The responsibility for originating tax and appropriations bills rests with the House of Representatives.

Most congressional business today is taken up with domestic legislation. Although many of today's legislative subjects were never envisioned by the founding fathers, most scholars agree that Congress' power to consider and pass laws on these matters comes from certain "implied powers" inherent in the Constitution.

Judicial Branch – The judicial branch consists of the US Supreme Court (the country's highest tribunal), some 94 district courts of original federal jurisdiction, and 13 appellate courts. There are also a number of special courts, among them US Claims Court, Tax Court and the Court of Military Appeals.

The Supreme Court considers constitutional questions arising from both the lower federal courts and the state court systems. This power gives it a check on Congress by allowing review of laws passed by that body. Beginning its term the first Monday in October, and lasting through June, the court usually hears about 150 cases per year. Its nine justices—one chief justice and eight associates—are appointed by the president and confirmed by the Senate. Lifetime tenure gives judges a large measure of independence, helping to ensure that political pressures do not unduly influence judicial opinions. District and appeals-court judges likewise are appointed to lifetime terms.

Revenue – About $1 trillion, the lion's share from personal income taxes, is collected each year to operate the US government. Other revenue sources include corporate income taxes; excise taxes on such items as gas, cigarettes and liquor; energy and timber sales; Social Security taxes; customs duties, and estate taxes.

Armed Forces – The US maintains some 1.4 million military forces in the form of a full-time army, navy, marine corps and air force. Additional forces are available from reserves, which may be called upon in times of war. Military service has been voluntary since 1973, when conscription ended.

State Governments

The structure of most state governments is closely akin to that of the federal government, with a governor as chief executive; a two-house legislature (except in Nebraska, which is unicameral); and a system of trial and appellate courts. As provided in the US Constitution, each state operates under its own constitution.

As in the federal system, the chief executive and legislators are elected. While most state judges once were also elected, this practice has begun to change, with many now appointed by the governor.

State government responsibilities, beyond passing and enforcing laws, include the regulation of businesses and professions; the maintenance of state roads and facilities; the regulation of driver and motor-vehicle licensing; the setting of standards for schools; and the regulation of liquor and tobacco sales.

Laws and regulations can vary widely among states. Most Western states require vehicles to be tested for exhaust emission levels before a license tag can be issued; others do not. Some states allow civilians to carry concealed firearms as long as they have a valid permit; in other states, this practice is strictly forbidden. Liquor laws and motor-vehicle speed limits may vary considerably from state to state.

Political Parties

Since the presidency of Abraham Lincoln (1861-65), two major political parties—the more liberal **Democrats** and more conservative **Republicans**—have dominated US politics. While third parties, such as the Reform and Libertarian parties, often field candidates, it is difficult for them to gain enough followers to win an election. Most voters choose to remain within the mainstream rather than vote for a candidate who has little chance of winning. Although most Americans over the age of 18 are eligible to vote, only about half participate in national elections.

Economy

The United States economy thrives on its unique historical system of free enter-prise—a laissez-faire capitalism whereby individuals can create, own and control the production of virtually any marketable good or commodity they can conceive, without undue government interference except in consumer protection. As might be expected, such unfettered freedom can inspire both the sublime (replacement valves for the human heart, for instance) and the ridiculous (the marketing of "pet rocks").

A federal income tax on earnings helps support government activities, including national defense, space exploration, public schools and major public-works projects, such as airports and interstate highways. In addition, most Americans are required to contribute a small percentage of their annual income to the federal Social Secu-rity system, which provides retirement benefits and medical care for older citizens. Like other industrialized nations, the US has undergone a profound transformation over the last few generations, from an agriculturally based economy to one based on service industries and manufacturing. Its 21C economy is complex and varied, and its $8 trillion gross national product (GNP)—the combined value of all goods and services—is the largest in the world.

Natural Resources – Americans were first lured westward by an abundance of free natural resources: pelts, minerals, fossil fuels, grazing lands, fertile soil, fish-eries and timber. Except for pelts, these resources still constitute a substantial portion of the Western economy. Private companies engaged in timber harvesting, mining and grazing benefit from favorable contracts for the lease of public lands managed by the US Forest Service or Bureau of Land Management. Altogether, mining accounts for some $56.6 billion of the US GNP; Nevada is at the forefront of non-fuel production with $3 billion annual earnings, mostly from gold, silver and copper. Crude oil is concentrated in pockets along the Gulf of Mexico and in Texas, Oklahoma, California, Alaska and Wyoming, while a vast reserve of oil shale underlies the central Rocky Mountains and Col-orado Plateau.

Irrigation has allowed agri-culture to thrive despite arid or semiarid conditions over much of the West. With nearly $25 billion in annual sales, California leads the nation in overall agricultural production, fol-lowed by Texas with more than $13 billion; Nebraska ranks fourth, after Iowa.

The most diverse Western farmlands are valleys near the Pacific coast. These include Oregon's Willamette Valley, which lured pioneers after being acclaimed by Lewis and Clark. With more sunshine but greater need for irrigation, Califor-nia's fertile valleys—partic-ularly the Central and Sali-nas—yield some of the richest harvests in the world. Its Napa and Sonoma Valleys are famed for wine grapes, while elsewhere in the state, farmers produce arti-chokes, tomatoes, citrus,

© David Barnes/Tony Stone Images

Offshore Oil Derrick, Santa Barbara, California

nuts and other vegetables and fruits. Washington is noted for apples, Idaho for potatoes, the Great Plains for wheat and grains. Livestock, especially sheep and cattle, are vital to the economies of several Western states, especially in the Rocky Mountains and Great Plains.

Once supreme for pineapples and sugar, Hawaii has had to downsize and diversify under foreign competition. A broader threat to agriculture is urban growth and com-petition for water. The supplanting of family farms by more efficient corporations is a blow to the social fabric of small towns across the Great Plains.

Diversified Economies – The growing Pacific coastal cities were the first to diversify from resource- and agricultural-based economies. During the 20C, manufacturing and service industries inexorably moved to other Western cities. Regional banking centers like Denver and Reno grew from mining and railroad-supply settlements in the 19C, though San Francisco remained the West's preeminent financial hub from the 1850s to the mid-20C.

By then, Los Angeles had grown into the West's largest, wealthiest, most culturally influential metropolitan area. With an artificial harbor, proficient railroad connections and ambitious engineering projects that delivered freshwater from the Sierra Nevada, Colorado River and northern California, L.A. set the example for other sprawling, prosperous and economically diversified Western cities of the later 20C, such as Houston, Phoenix and Seattle.

Ready access to large testing facilities brought the aerospace industry to southern California, Arizona and Washington. The high-technology electronics revolution of the final quarter of the 20C spread from enormously successful beginnings in Silicon Valley (near San Jose), California, to Seattle and other regional centers in Oregon, Texas, Colorado and Idaho.

Service industries are the fastest growing employers in the West. Government is responsible for much of this growth, especially in California, with 153,000 federal civilian employees, and Texas, with 108,000. Large military bases in Hawaii, California's Mojave Desert and San Diego area, Nevada, Texas and Washington's Puget Sound introduced thousands of military personnel.

Tourism and travel-related services (lodging, restaurants, entertainment, transportation) account for an increasing proportion of US employment, goods, services and tax revenues—as much as $515 billion per year. Tourism earns $62 billion annually in California, followed by Texas ($27 billion), Nevada ($18 billion) and Hawaii ($14 billion).

■ Economies of the Western United States

	*GSP (mil.$)	Principal Industries
California	$1,033,016	manufacturing, tourism, crops, oil, film
Texas	601,643	oil, livestock, cotton, manufacturing
Washington	172,253	fishing, timber, manufacturing, wheat
Colorado	126,084	tourism, manufacturing, mining, oil, corn
Arizona	121,239	manufacturing, mining, tourism
Oregon	98,367	timber, fishing, fruit, manufacturing
Oklahoma	76,642	natural gas, oil, wheat, livestock
Kansas	71,737	wheat, corn, livestock, oil, manufacturing
Nevada	57,407	gambling, tourism, mining, hydroelectric
Utah	55,417	mining, oil, livestock, manufacturing
Nebraska	48,812	corn, wheat, livestock, manufacturing
New Mexico	45,242	mining, manufacturing, livestock
Hawaii	38,024	tourism, sugar, pineapple, military
Idaho	29,141	potatoes, wheat, timber, mining
Alaska	24,494	fishing, oil, natural gas, mining, timber
South Dakota	20,186	corn, wheat, mining, manufacturing
Montana	19,160	mining, wheat, forage crops, livestock
Wyoming	17,561	mining, oil, sheep, forage crops
North Dakota	15,768	wheat, potatoes, oil

*Gross State Product (1997), from US Bureau of Economic Analysis

People of the USA West

The American West has always been perceived as a land of hope, a place to wipe clean the slate and to start anew. Its population is largely composed of immigrants and their recent descendants, people who set out in quest of quick fortunes or the American dream.

The West remains the fastest growing region of the US. The demographic trend is playing out dramatically in booming communities like Las Vegas, Tucson, Fresno, Santa Fe and Boise, as the largest cities—Los Angeles, San Diego, Houston, Dallas, Denver, Phoenix, San Antonio, Kansas City, and the San Francisco Bay and Puget Sound metropolitan areas—continue to drive the West's economic engines.

Most population growth has occurred in the Sun Belt of New Mexico, Arizona and California's Mojave Desert, where winters are milder. Retirees account for large numbers of new residents here, although many of them are "sunbirds" who depart for cooler climates when summer temperatures begin to rise.

Population growth is balanced by another demographic shift away from the smaller towns of the Great Plains, in effect leaving broad swaths with fewer people than they had 50 years ago. Other parts of the West, particularly the Great Basin, the Chihuahuan Desert of west Texas and southern New Mexico, the northern Rockies and Alaska, still contain thousands of square miles that are very sparsely inhabited.

The steady influx of migrants to the West has brought with it a heady mix of cultural traditions. Their influences and customs are scattered in pockets across the West. Recent foreign immigration has revolutionized demographics in the coastal metropolitan areas. San Francisco, Oakland, Los Angeles and Seattle are among the most ethnically diverse cities in the world, with significant Chinese, Japanese, Filipino, Hispanic, Italian, Greek, Portuguese and African-American populations. Despite the cultural domination of Anglo-Saxon language and custom throughout the hinterland, ethnic festivals remain strong and vigorous in many isolated communities. Mining towns of the Rockies and Southwest annually recall the contributions of miners of all European nationalities. The Texas Hill Country has strong ties to Germany. Alaska celebrates Russian heritage in Sitka and Kodiak, although Scandinavians and others now outnumber the Russians. Basque sheepherders exert their influence on the hearty restaurants and small hotels of the Great Basin, Idaho and Wyoming. The ubiquitous Irish, who supplied so much of the labor force and soldiery of the early West, have rendered St. Patrick's Day a nearly universal and all-inclusive celebration.

Cowboys and Indians – The popular depiction of the West in literature and film favors the notion that settlement was primarily a contest between Indians and Americans of European heritage. Historians since the 1960s have made strong efforts to correct the picture, pointing out the contributions of African-American regiments—called Buffalo Soldiers by the Plains Indians—in the Indian Wars and in the early protection of national parks. Although statistics are debated, a high percentage of cowboys in the late 19C, and rodeo circuit riders of the early 20C, were black. Many others were Hispanic and Indian.

Chinese workers represented up to 60 percent of the miners in California and in the Northwest during the late 19C. They also represented a majority of fishermen, railroad workers, road builders and construction workers. Hispanic farmworkers continue to dominate the ranks of migratory field laborers throughout the West.

Most Indians have adopted popular American dress and customs, and many have intermarried with other races and moved to urban areas. But a highly visible segment still dwells on reservations throughout the West, especially in Arizona, New Mexico, South Dakota and Montana. The most tradition-bound are the Hopi, who still live in pueblos on high desert mesas, completely surrounded by the Navajo Reservation. Other Pueblo tribes and the Navajo maintain a balance between the old ways and the new, operating lively tourist industries noted for their blankets, pottery and jewelry. The reservations of the Great Plains and the Pacific slope are decidedly less tied to the nomadic ways of the past, but likewise are less inclined to welcome tourism. A recent trend is for reservations to open public gambling casinos; these have revitalized the economies of many tribes despite social concerns by more traditional tribal members.

Independent Thinkers – Regardless of where they live, Americans are known as ardent defenders of the individual rights and freedoms defined in the Constitution to exercise free speech, to assemble, to keep and bear arms, and to enjoy the freedoms of religion and privacy, among others. Such liberties come at a price, however, as recent and ongoing debates over abortion and gun control attest.

The people of the United States, a country still in the process of defining itself, defy most attempts at classification. Social scientists, demographers and the media are quick to tag segments of society with labels such as "baby boomers" (the generation born immediately after World War II) and "Generation Xers" (persons born in the late 1960s and 1970s). Yet exceptions contradict every rule, keeping alive the challenge to create a definitive description of mainstream America.

Cultural Arts

Architecture

Native Americans built homes to suit their environment and culture with available materials. Nomadic Plains tribes adopted buffalo skins spread over lean-to timber frames to build highly mobile **tepees**. Farming tribes of the lower Great Plains, like the Mandans and Pawnees, built permanent **earthen lodges**. Northwestern tribes erected sturdy **plank houses**, while the people of the Great Basin and California lowlands preferred light summer lean-tos of thatch and brush, using more substantial materials in winter.

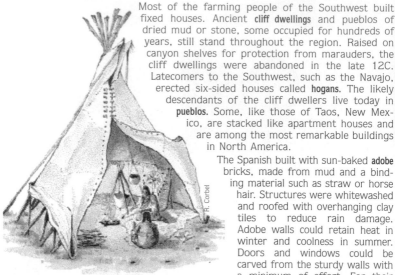

Most of the farming people of the Southwest built fixed houses. Ancient **cliff dwellings** and pueblos of dried mud or stone, some occupied for hundreds of years, still stand throughout the region. Raised on canyon shelves for protection from marauders, the cliff dwellings were abandoned in the late 12C. Latecomers to the Southwest, such as the Navajo, erected six-sided houses called **hogans**. The likely descendants of the cliff dwellers live today in **pueblos**. Some, like those of Taos, New Mexico, are stacked like apartment houses and are among the most remarkable buildings in North America.

The Spanish built with sun-baked **adobe** bricks, made from mud and a binding material such as straw or horse hair. Structures were whitewashed and roofed with overhanging clay tiles to reduce rain damage. Adobe walls could retain heat in winter and coolness in summer. Doors and windows could be carved from the sturdy walls with a minimum of effort. For their ecclesiastical buildings, Spanish architects tried to copy structures they knew from Spain or Mexico. Though painted with Christian themes, the interiors often retained details reflective of local culture, particularly in pattern and color scheme.

Sioux Tepee, Upper Great Plains

Most Western settlements in the American era were initially built of wood, the cheapest and most readily available material. A prominent exception was the **sod house** of the Great Plains which, though warm, was dark and readily abandoned when wood became available. Rudimentary **log cabins** were usually superseded by **frame houses**, while commercial establishments achieved a tone of respectability by sporting facades of brick (often imported from the Midwest or East) or dressed stone, locally quarried. A characteristic feature of many towns was the **false front**, which served to make one-story shanties look larger and more reputable.

Large cities looked East for architectural inspiration in the 19C, often drawing upon the Greek Revival style for banks, or a hodgepodge of styles for the mansions and row houses of residential districts. Romanticized throwbacks to the Old West have

Salish Village, Northwest Coast

Traditional Mandan Lodges, Missouri River

remained popular through the 20C, especially at dude ranches, resorts and national parks—a singularly spectacular example being the **Old Faithful Inn** (1904, Robert Reamer) at Yellowstone National Park.

Widespread prosperity in the 20C enabled Westerners to experiment more with architectural style. In California, some builders put form before practicability, so that wealthier residential districts in some cities were imbued with a bewildering array of styles in close juxtaposition. In Los Angeles, one residential block might boast Tudor, Norman and Mission-style houses between a Japanese garden and Swiss chalet. The 1920s and 1930s popularized whimsical structures built to resemble extraneous objects (giant oranges, derby hats, even cartoon animals) to attract clientele. A paucity of materials and workers during World War II left a spate of flat-roofed houses in places not burdened by snowfall, such as California.

More thoughtful architectural fashions of the 20C included the **Mission Style**, which resurrected the arched doorways and windows, red-tile roofs and white earthen walls of Spanish missions; **Art Moderne**, with streamlined contours and Art Deco detailing; and the **Prairie School**, emphasizing strong, horizontal lines and a lack of superfluous decoration. The latter, a creation of architect **Frank Lloyd Wright** (1867-1959), stressed organic architecture harmonizing with specific landscapes. Of hundreds of buildings designed by Wright in the West, the most important is **Taliesin West** (1937) in Scottsdale, Arizona. With its low-profile buildings of indigenous materials, uneven rooflines and deeply shaded entrances, Taliesin West remains a strong influence on design.

Low-density sprawl—an outgrowth of abundant land, cheap gasoline and relaxed zoning laws—has long characterized Western towns and cities. Post-World War II prosperity heralded a boom in **suburban residential tracts** on the edge cities. Typified by single-story, ranch-style houses on rectangular plots, landscaped with front and back lawns that served the purpose of private parks, these suburbs were linked to cities by freeways, and thus were dependent upon automobiles. Suburbs were perceived as safe, healthy, comfortable and democratic. As land prices rose and population increased toward the end of the 20C, building trends in more populous metropolitan areas switched to favor two-story houses covering as much of their lots as could be allowed by local codes.

Anasazi Cliff Dwelling, Four Corners Region

49

Visual Arts

No word for art existed in any Native American language—not because the Indians didn't create works of art, but because everything had a utilitarian or religious purpose. Some of the finest baskets ever created were the work of Washoe artisans, of whom **Datsolalee**, of the late 19C, is the best known. Coastal California tribes also wove baskets in a variety of shapes and designs exceptional for their beauty and utility, and woven so tightly they could hold water. Peoples of the Northwest coast and Alaska excelled in the art of carving soapstone and walrus tusk, cedar masks and totem poles that portrayed clan lineage. Hawaiians created coral jewelry and finely decorated robes and helmets adorned with bird feathers. All the tribes of the Southwest fashioned decorated pottery, although the art had slipped into a utilitarian mold by the early 20C. Potter **María Montoya Martínez** (c.1881-1980) of New Mexico's San Ildefonso Pueblo is credited with inspiring the revival of the potter's art in the 1930s when she produced exquisite black-on-black ware. Southwest Indian artists also made names for themselves as painters, among them **Pablita Velarde** (b.1918) and **Harrison Begay** (b.1917). Although they originally learned the skill from the Pueblo Indians, Navajo women today are the only Southwest Indians who still weave rugs, crafted in distinctive regional styles. Aficionados of detailed craftsmanship, the Spanish decorated their missions with silver work and wood carvings, much of it made in Mexico and carried north by mule train. The Spanish probably also taught lapidary skills to the Pueblo Indians, who today produce some of the finest stone and silver jewelry in the US.

Georgia O'Keeffe at the exhibition *Life and Death* (1931)

UPI/CORBIS-BETTMANN

The American West provided an exceedingly rich canvas for artists and other chroniclers of frontier life and scenery. Early explorers often were accompanied by sketch artists, some of whom went on to become noted artists. **Karl Bodmer** (1809-93) and **George Catlin** (1796-1872) both recorded Indians and mountain men in the 1830s, while **John James Audubon** (1785-1851) made his own journey west to sketch birds and wildlife. Artist-photographer **Solomon Nuñes Carvalho** (1815-94) accompanied Frémont during a survey of the Far West. The paintings of **Thomas Moran** (1837-1926) and photographs of **William Henry Jackson** (1843-1942), part of the Hayden Expedition to Yellowstone in 1871, were crucial evidence in swaying the public and Congress to create the first national park. **Alfred Jacob Miller** (1810-74), a Baltimore artist, made a trip west in the company of fur traders in 1837 and capitalized upon it in creating a series of paintings of great documentary value. German-born **Albert Bierstadt** (1830-1902) painted Western landscapes in a particularly Romantic style. Grittier and more lifelike are the sketches, paintings and sculptures of cowboys, Indians and other Western characters by **Frederic Remington** (1861-1909) and **Charles M. Russell** (1864-1926).

New Mexico, with its pueblos and unusual scenery, became a popular magnet for artists in the late 19C. Santa Fe, long the cultural center of the Southwest, today is the third-largest art market in the US after New York and Los Angeles. Taos boasted an artist colony in the very early 20C. **Georgia O'Keeffe** (1887-1986), an annual Taos visitor who later moved to the New Mexico desert, painted austere landscapes and decorated more than one famous painting with a parched cow skull against a bright Southwestern sky.

The stop-action photography of **Eadweard Muybridge** (1830-1904) preceded the invention of his zoopraxiscope, a landmark in pioneering the moving-picture industry. The haunting black-and-white shots of Western landscapes by **Ansel Adams** (1902-84) inspired generations of photographers and conservationists. Through her poignant portraits of farm migrants and photos of vast public-works projects rising amid arid landscapes, **Dorothea Lange** (1895-1965) dramatized the tragedies and triumphs of the Depression-era West. Photographers **Edward Weston** (1886-1958) and **Imogen Cunningham** (1883-1976) were among the more influential members of a West Coast coterie known as Group f.64.

The west coast of California also exerted a strong influence on 20C painting and sculpture. Artist colonies at Carmel, La Jolla and Laguna Beach spawned the California Impressionism and Plein-Air movements, including **Franz Bischoff** (1864-1929), creating landscapes inspired by the unique light and natural features of the area. During the 1930s, abstraction, surrealism and social realism came into play. In San Francisco, **Mark Rothko** (1903-70) and **Clyfford Still** (1904-80) inspired an explosion of abstract painting by their students, who included **Robert Motherwell** (1915-91). Painters such as **Richard Diebenkorn** (1922-93) and **David Park** (1911-60) responded with a representational movement known as Bay Area Figurative. The impact of the culture of the 1960s inspired pop artists and photorealists, followed by conceptualists. An influential art scene that has developed in southern California since the 1950s includes **David Hockney** (b.1937).

Literature

Tall tales and colorful humor were popular on the frontier. Westerners were notorious for finding amusement in telling tall tales—which is why John Colter's earliest descriptions of Yellowstone's geysers, petrified trees and astringent streams were thought to be lies. Humorists like **Mark Twain** (né Samuel Clemens, 1835-1910), **Dan DeQuille** (1829-98) and **Edgar "Bill" Nye** (1850-96) carried on the tradition of exaggeration in print, writing satire that turned on common sense and droll humor. Twain made a name for himself with his stories filled with pungent Western color. His first break in the East came with "The Celebrated Jumping Frog of Calaveras County" (1867). *Roughing It* (1872) is considered by most critics to be his richest and funniest description of a dude's life in Virginia City, San Francisco, Hawaii and other parts of the Wild West.

More serious Western observations also were widely read in the East. Francis Parkman's exciting account of *The Oregon Trail* (1849) remains in print today. John C. Frémont's reports of his forays to the West, scribed with governmental precision, were rewritten with dramatic flair by his wife, **Jesse Benton Frémont** (1824-1902); they were best-sellers in their day and made John Frémont's guide, Kit Carson *(p 340)*, into a great Western hero. The laconic Carson himself told his own story with less flamboyance in an autobiography not published until 1926. Other accounts of Western experiences embraced a wide range of views, including those of Indians (*Black Elk Speaks*, 1932) and homesteaders (the works of **Laura Ingalls Wilder**, 1867-1957). Historians like **Frederick Jackson Turner** (1861-1932), **Bernard De Voto** (1897-1955) and **Wallace Stegner** (1909-93) added heft and drama.

Sentimental stories, exemplified by the California gold-rush tales of **Bret Harte** (1836-1902), were popular throughout the 19C, but it was adventure and derring-do that gave the real impetus to a new brand of fiction, the Western. The first mass market adventure fiction set in the Wild West appeared in the 1860s. The prototype of the modern Western is generally considered to be Owen Wister's *The Virginian* (1902), which combined a love interest with all the elements of frontier lore: chivalrous cowboys, treacherous Indians and a brooding bad man. Among the most enduring work is that of **Zane Grey** (1875-1939); his *Riders of the Purple Sage* appeared in 1912. The Western occasionally rose to high levels of literary complexity, as in the psychological narrative of a lynching in Walter Van Tilburg Clark's *The Ox-Bow Incident* (1940), Willa Cather's *Death Comes for the Archbishop* (1927) and Wallace Stegner's *Angle of Repose* (1971). Jack London's novel of man and dog in the Klondike gold rush, *The Call of the Wild* (1903), probably has been translated into more languages than any other novel set in the West. Few books have sparked so large a following as Jack Kerouac's awakening call to the Beat Generation, *On the Road* (1957), a fictionalized account of aimless journeys through the contemporary West.

Other writers alerted public opinion to regional problems. Helen Hunt Jackson's *Century of Dishonor* (1881) helped awaken sentiment to the mistreatment of Indians, a forerunner to Dee Brown's *Bury My Heart at Wounded Knee* (1971). **Frank Norris** (1870-1902) attacked the problem of greedy railroad barons in *The Octopus* (1901). **John Steinbeck** (1902-68) won the Pulitzer Prize for *The Grapes of Wrath* (1939), a depiction of impoverished farmers migrating from the Oklahoma Dust Bowl to California. John Muir's books and articles helped arouse Eastern support for greater protection of Western lands and resources. Among the defenders of the deserts' fragile beauties were **Mary Austin** (1868-1934), whose *The Land of Little Rain* exalted the Owens Valley and Mojave Desert; and the irascible **Edward Abbey** (1927-89), author of *Desert Solitaire* (1968).

Another stalwart of Western fiction is the hard-boiled detective. **Dashiell Hammett** (1894-1961) created the tone with Sam Spade in *The Maltese Falcon* (1930), set in San Francisco. **Raymond Chandler** (1888-1959) followed suit in *The Big Sleep* (1939) by introducing Philip Marlowe, a cynical, self-sufficient but honorable detective who guarded the mean streets of Los Angeles. **Tony Hillerman** (b.1925) blends Western and detective fiction in his books, which recount the adventures of Navajo policemen Joe Leaphorn and Jim Chee in the Indian lands of the Southwest.

Audience at Rock Concert, Seattle, Washington

© Tim Thompson

Music

Native Americans employed music and dance in all their ceremonies, both religious and social. The Spanish, who introduced the guitar to the West, also used music for sacred and social purposes, and took pains to instruct their mission neophytes in playing instruments. The bulk of popular music today, carried West in the folk music of pioneers and the hymns of missionaries, has roots in the British Isles. Fiddle, harmonica and banjo were the instruments of choice on wagon trains, where popular Oregon Trail tunes included "The Arkansas Traveler" and "Sweet Betsy from Pike." Accompanied by stomping feet, clapping hands and instructional dance calls, the fiddle gave life to capers, jigs and square dances at rural festivals, and entertained cowboys on cattle drives and soldiers in lonely barracks. After railroads pushed west, many saloons imported pianos.

The archetype of contemporary Western music is a highly commercialized hybrid of cowboy songs, themselves descended from Scottish, English and Irish ballads by way of the rural South. After collections were published in the early 20C, the genre achieved wider interest when it was popularized on radio and in film by cowboy singers like **Roy Rogers** (1912-98) and **Gene Autry** (1907-98). Influenced by well-traveled rural singers like **Buck Owens** (b.1929), cowboy music absorbed elements of swing in the 1940s, picking up the tempo, heavier rhythms and twanging guitar that characterizes popular country-and-western music today. National radio has eroded regional distinctions.

The West has made conspicuous contributions in the realm of rock music. In the early 1960s, as the Beatles emerged in England, southern California originated its own brand of lighthearted "surf" music; its best-known ambassadors, **The Beach Boys**, sang in great harmony of waves, hot rods and "girls on the beach." Later in the decade, the social upheaval in San Francisco, culminating in 1967's "Summer of Love," drew numerous prominent singers and performers—including Texan **Janis Joplin** (1943-70) and Seattleite **Jimi Hendrix** (1942-70)—to a local scene already celebrated for its "San Francisco Sound." The music of Jerry Garcia's **Grateful Dead**, Grace Slick's **Jefferson Airplane**, John Fogarty's **Credence Clearwater Revival** and other top groups was characterized by driving guitar riffs and influenced by more traditional blues. In the early 1990s, Seattle became the center of a style termed "grunge rock," with bands like Kurt Cobain's **Nirvana** and Eddie Vedder's **Pearl Jam** noted as much for their appearance as for their music.

Theater and Film

Nineteenth Century miners were noted for their love of opera. They were so generous in supporting fine opera houses in remote towns that Eastern and European companies routinely toured San Francisco, Virginia City (Nevada), Central City (Colorado) and other thriving mining frontiers. Stage plays, running the gamut from Shakespearean excerpts to melodramas, were also popular. Among the famous actors who toured the Western mining camps were **Edwin Booth** (1833-93), **Helena Modjeska** (1840-1909) and the unconventional **Sarah Bernhardt** (1844-1923). Less exalted entertainment was offered by the scandalous exotic dancer **Lola Montez** (1818-61) and her comedic successor, **Lotta Crabtree** (1847-1924).

Today, San Francisco remains among the preeminent opera cities of the West, staging lavish productions with renowned casts. The Dallas Opera and Houston Grand Opera also are highly regarded, the latter known for its modern world premieres of *Nixon in China* (1987) and *The Death of Klinghoffer* (1991). Since 1957, one of the brightest lights in the American opera scene has been the Santa Fe Opera Company, which offers outdoor summer performances. Live stage plays continue to attract tourists and local audiences in Los Angeles, San Francisco, Seattle and smaller cities like Ashland, Oregon, and Cedar City, Utah, both of which mount internationally recognized annual Shakespeare festivals.

Of all the Western-themed entertainment, nothing was more popular during the late-19C and early-20C than Buffalo Bill's Wild West Show, a commercial extravaganza. Theater on an epic scale, the show thrilled East Coast and European audiences with dramatized excepts from **William F. "Buffalo Bill" Cody** (1846-1917) himself. Drawing on Cody's remarkable life as a Pony Express rider, bison hunter, Army scout and soldier, the show re-created famous Western battles and presented feats of sharpshooting, an Indian attack on a stagecoach, trick riding and roping, bucking broncos, bull-riding, steer wrestling and other rodeo events. Among the most famous cast members were Sitting Bull *(p 36)*, **Gordon "Pawnee Bill" Lillie** (1860-1942), sharpshooter **Annie Oakley** (1860-1926) and Cody himself.

Spectacular live shows continue to be a hallmark of the Western stage, particularly in resort centers like Lake Tahoe, Reno and especially Las Vegas. The prototypes of Las Vegas-style performers were stand-up comedians, torch singers and chorus-line Parisian showgirls like the Folies Bergères. Shows now embrace a mind-boggling array of magician acts, circuses, water choreography, and spectacles of electronic and pyrotechnic wizardry, as well as concerts by famous singers.

No other medium has propounded the myth of the Old West more successfully than the **Western movie**. Like Medieval morality plays, Westerns depict history selectively but irresistibly, winning audiences who root for heroes and boo villains without complicating conflicts with ambiguities. Larger than life, Westerns helped to establish Hollywood as the world capital of film-making.

From the first silent Westerns in the early 20C through the 1950s, Westerns' cowboy heroes were chivalrous characters; Indians were usually villains, and other ethnic minorities were rarely depicted despite the prominent roles played by Chinese, black and Hispanic people throughout the American West. That some of these Westerns were also dramatically powerful is undeniable. Among the most emotionally satisfying, if conventional, Westerns were *Red River* (1948), starring **John Wayne**; *High Noon* (1952), starring **Gary Cooper**; *Shane* (1953), starring **Alan Ladd**; *The Searchers* (1956), starring Wayne; and many visually exciting works by director **John Ford**, beginning with *Stagecoach* (1939), also starring Wayne. Television Westerns of the 1950s and 1960s tended to reinforce the Western myth in shows like *The Lone Ranger*, *Gunsmoke* and *Bonanza*.

Since the 1960s, Hollywood has produced ever-greater numbers of offbeat, thoughtful, brooding Westerns that run against the grain of earlier productions. Protagonists are anti-heroes in *Lonely Are the Brave* (1962), starring **Kirk Douglas**; *Hud* (1963), starring **Paul Newman**; *The Wild Bunch* (1969), directed by **Sam Peckinpah**; and a series of "spaghetti westerns" (including *The Good, the Bad and the Ugly*, 1967) directed by **Sergio Leone** and starring **Clint Eastwood**. Another recent trend reverses old roles by placing Indians as heroes and soldiers as villains, as in *Little Big Man* (1970), starring **Dustin Hoffman**, and *Dances with Wolves* (1989), starring **Kevin Costner**. Film festivals throughout the West continue to influence the world and disseminate the medium. Among the most famous is Utah's Sundance Film Festival, the creation of actor-director **Robert Redford**.

John Ford Directs *My Darling Clementine* (1946), Monument Valley, Arizona

Cuisine

Although the West offers an extraordinary range of cuisines, the most distinguished dining experiences are concentrated in a few large cities and along the coast—especially Los Angeles, northern California and Seattle. The small towns of the vast rural expanses of the Western hinterland are better known for large portions of decent, hearty meals—a cuisine best described, even when borrowed from other cultures, as American. This includes the ubiquitous hamburger, french fries and milkshake, of course, but also steaks, spaghetti, pizza, tacos, fried chicken, meat loaf, apple pie with ice cream, and "bottomless" cups of coffee.

Regional differences in Western cooking styles are determined less by geography than they are in Europe or the Eastern US, ethnicity and settlement patterns being far more scattered here. Modified immigrant cuisines such as Mexican, Italian and Chinese are readily available in nearly every large town of the inland West.

The most important regional distinction arises from the concentration of Hispanic settlement along the Mexican border states—Texas, New Mexico, Arizona and California—where the supremacy of wheat and potatoes as staples is rivaled by maize (corn). At its root lies the native cuisine of the Pueblo Indians, whose corn comes in many colors, including blue, white and yellow. Dried kernels are ground and made into breads, baked in ovens or on hot stones. This cuisine is famed for its tacos, tamales and fry bread. In Texas, such foods are popularized as Tejano or Tex-Mex; most celebrated is chili, a spicy meat dish served with or without beans.

Historical Fare – The most important contributions of indigenous American cultures are tomatoes, beans, squash, chilies and corn—all originally cultivated in Mexico, but widely distributed throughout the Southwest and southern Great Plains when the first Europeans arrived. The dried meats of Plains Indian hunters and the *carne seco* of Southwestern farmers were forerunners of today's popular "jerky" snack. Foods like prickly pears, sunflower seeds, wild berries, mushrooms, piñon nuts, wild game and fish were readily adapted.

The stampede of American settlers during gold and silver rushes depended initially upon game for food, but their taste for tinned foods and bread gave strong impetus to the growth of a transport system. While desperate invention produced oddities like the Hangtown Fry (an omelet made from eggs, bacon rind and preserved oysters), immigrants brought such simple recipes as Cornish pasties, French ragouts, Irish stews and the Chinese hash known as chop suey.

A scarcity of yeast prompted a method of leavening bread with a starter, or large pinch of the latest dough, left to ferment in a warm spot until it grew as a result of its own healthy bacterial culture. The resultant sourdough bread, descended from the California gold rush, is still being baked in San Francisco.

The era of the cowboy has associated beef with the West, although wranglers themselves were more likely to enjoy beans, stews and organ meats than the tough, stringy steaks served on a cattle drive. Well-fattened and far tastier beef emerged after a session in the stockyards at the end of the trail drives, to this day giving Kansas City and Omaha an excellent reputation for tender steaks and exceptional barbecue. Barbecue has become a hallmark of Western dining, a staple of every ranch and resort, and a popular excuse for weekend gatherings at countless homes. Though grilling over coals or mesquite remains the most popular method of barbecuing meat, the traditional method in Texas is to bury a prepared carcass with the coals, allowing it to cook underground.

All-American Cuisine: Hamburger and Coca-Cola

© Ian O'Leary/Tony Stone Images

Nature's Bounty – Though over-fishing threatens wild stock, commercial fisheries along the Gulf Coast are famed for shrimp catches, San Francisco for its Dungeness crabs, northern California for abalone, the Pacific Northwest for shellfish and salmon, Alaska for salmon and king crab. Western farms, particularly in the fine soils and climate of California's inland valleys, are world leaders in developing new crop strains. The world's most productive wheat fields, vegetable farms and livestock ranches are in the West. Washington is celebrated for apples, Idaho for potatoes, California for citrus crops and truck gardens.

Westerners have long been known for their penchant for red meat and fried potatoes. Some interesting culinary reactions developed in the 1960s. Chief among these was the evolution of California cuisine, credited to Alice Waters and her Berkeley restaurant, Chez Panisse, which emphasized using fine local seasonal ingredients, lightly prepared and presented artistically. Asian cooking also helped popularize the light cooking of vegetables. Fusion cuisine blending Asian, French and other culinary styles and ingredients to produce new flavors has become very popular in coastal cities. Organic farming, which eschews any artificial fertilizers, hormones or toxic sprays, has become a minor industry in its own right.

Refined tastes for wine have encouraged the expansion of acreage planted with grapes, especially in California. Commercial viticulture has become highly successful in the Pacific Northwest as well, and has expanded to a lesser degree into the Rockies, the desert Southwest, Texas and even Hawaii. Demand for exceptional beer also has fueled the growth of small breweries across the West.

■ Cooking Schools

Following is a selection of well-regarded culinary academies across the American West for non-professional cooks and gourmets.

Arizona - Les Gourmettes Cooking School, 6610 N. Central Ave., Phoenix AZ 85012; ☎ 602-240-6767; http://cookforfun.shawguides.com.

California - Eat Your Way Through L.A., 267 S. El Molino Ave., Pasadena CA 91101; ☎ 626-744-3174 or 323-666-9061; http://cookforfun. shawguides.com.

Epicurean School of Culinary Arts, 8759 Melrose Ave., Los Angeles CA 90069; ☎ 310-659-5990; http://cookforfun.shawguides.com.

Tante Marie's Cooking School, 271 Francisco St., San Francisco CA 94133; ☎ 415-788-6699; www.tantemarie.com.

Colorado - Cooking School of Aspen, 414 E. Hyman Ave., Aspen CO 81611; ☎ 970-920-1879; www.aspen.com/cookingschool.

Cook Street School of Fine Cooking, 1937 Market St., Denver CO 80202; ☎ 303-308-9300; www.cookstreet.com.

Hawaii - Grand Chefs On Tour, Kea Lani Hotel, 4100 Wailea Alanui Dr., Wailea, Maui HI 96753; ☎ 808-875-4100; www.kealani.com.

Kansas - Baron's School of Pitmasters, 3625 W. 50th Terr., Shawnee Mission KS 66205; ☎ 913-262-6029; www.bbqcookoff.com/school.htm.

Nevada - Nothing To It! Culinary Center, 225 Crummer Ln., Reno NV 89502; ☎ 775-826-2628; www.nothingtoit.com.

New Mexico - Santa Fe School of Cooking, 116 W. San Francisco St., Santa Fe NM 87501; ☎ 505-983-4511; www.santafeschoolofcooking.com.

Oklahoma - Bama Cooking School of Tulsa, 8264 S. Lewis St., Tulsa OK 74137; ☎ 918-732-2110; www.bama.com.

Oregon - Cooks, Pots & Tabletops, 2807 Oak St., Eugene OR 97405; ☎ 541-338-4339; http://cookforfun.shawguides.com.

Canterbury Farms, 16185 SW 108th Ave., Tigard OR 97224; ☎ 503-968-8269; www.canfarms.com.

Texas - Central Market Cooking School, 4001 N. Lamar Blvd., Austin TX 78756; ☎ 512-458-3068; www.centralmarket.com.

Culinary Academy of Austin, 2823 Hancock Dr., Austin TX 78731; ☎ 512-451-5743; http://chefs.home.texas.net.

Star Canyon, 3102 Oak Lawn Ave., Dallas TX 75219; ☎ 214-520-8111; www.guidelive.com.

Washington - Cook's World, 2900 NE Blakely St., Seattle WA 98105; ☎ 206-528-8192; http://cookforfun.shawguides.com.

Sports and Recreation

For exercise, entertainment, drama and fellowship, Americans love to play and watch sports. No event may inspire more patriotic fervor than the quadrennial Olympic Games, but a year-round slate of professional ("pro"), collegiate and amateur competition keeps the fever pitch high. College sports, especially football and basketball, attract the excited attention of fans and alumni nationwide, especially during the annual football "bowl game" series over the Christmas-New Year holidays, and the "March Madness" championship basketball tournament.

Take Me Out to the Ball Games – Sometimes called the national pastime, **baseball** inspires legions of devoted fans who follow teams with religious intensity. Played on a diamond-shaped field with bases in each corner, the game tests the individual skills of batters, who try to strike a thrown ball, against pitchers and fielders. The game may appear slow-paced but can be fraught with suspense, the outcome often resting on a final confrontation between pitcher and batter. In March, when pro teams engage in their annual spring training in Arizona and Florida, seats at practice games are the hottest tickets in town. The Major League Baseball season runs from April to October, culminating in the World Series, a best-of-seven-games matchup between the American League and National League champions.

Fast-paced **basketball** draws participants and spectators from every walk of life. In part because it requires a smaller playing area than most sports, the game is often played outdoors in crowded urban areas. Players score by throwing a ball through a suspended hoop. The 29 teams of the National Basketball Association (NBA) begin play in November, competing for a berth in the NBA Finals held in June. The 12-team Women's National Basketball Association (WNBA), founded in 1997, has inspired a new host of professional female players around the country.

With its unique combination of brute force and finely tuned skill, **American football** demands strength, speed and agility from players in their quest to pass, kick and run with the football down a 100-yard field to the goal. The National Football League (NFL) oversees 32 teams in two conferences, the champions of which meet in late January in the annual Super Bowl, a game that draws more television viewers than any other event. Football season begins about September 1.

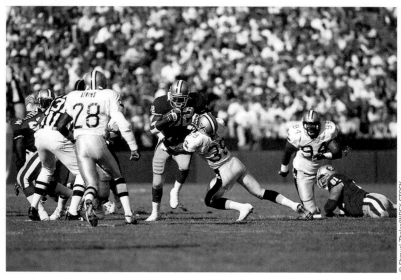

American Football: San Francisco 49ers vs. New Orleans Saints

© Shmuel Thaler/INDEX STOCK

Other Professional Sports – Although **ice hockey** was born in Canada, the US has adopted the game in a big way. In this breakneck sport, skated players use sticks to maneuver a hard rubber puck into a goal at either end of an ice arena. The 29-team National Hockey League (NHL) pits professional Canadian and American teams in annual competition for the coveted Stanley Cup, with finals held in June.

The US may be the world's preeminent **golf** nation, attracting golfers from around the globe to its challenging, well-manicured courses. Public and private links abound throughout much of the West, especially California, Arizona, Las Vegas and Hawaii, where the climate permits year-round play. Audiences flock to such important annual tournaments as the US Open in mid-June and the National Pro-Am Tournament in early February, both at Pebble Beach on California's Monterey Peninsula, and to the ladies' tour championship in Las Vegas in November.

Descended from frontier horsemanship contests, **rodeo** (p 132) celebrates the skills developed by generations of cowboys. Members of the Professional Rodeo Cowboys Association (PRCA) compete for millions of dollars in bronc-riding, calf roping, steer wrestling and other events. Most dangerous is bull-riding, in which a cowboy tries to remain on the back of a rampaging bull for all of eight seconds; rodeo clowns distract the bull from goring the rider after he has been thrown. Hugely popular pro rodeos are held in Cheyenne (Wyoming), Pendleton (Oregon), Las Vegas, Oklahoma City, Fort Worth, Denver and other cities.

A Recreational Paradise – **Skiing** in the Colorado Rockies; **surfing** the big waves on the north shore of O'ahu. Whitewater **rafting** down Idaho's Salmon River; **backpacking** the 2,550mi Pacific Crest Trail. **Mountain-biking** through Utah's slick-rock canyons; **fly-fishing** isolated lakes in Alaska's vast interior: Seekers of physical fitness and natural beauty take full advantage of the wealth of mountains, forests, lakes, rivers and oceanfront, as well as urban parks and biking/running paths.

In-line skating, snowboarding and mountain biking are recent additions to the panoply of popular recreational sports. **Sky-diving** and **mountain climbing** attract increasing numbers of mainstream participants. Adventure-travel agencies design vacations around bicycling, canoeing, wildlife viewing and other themes.

Hiking, **horseback riding** and river rafting provide the best access to thousands of square miles of Western backcountry and parkland. A vast network of trails probes remote corners of the Rockies, Sierra Nevada and Cascades. Undeveloped Alaska offers plenty of true wilderness for adventurers—even for comfort-loving anglers or hunters who hire bush pilots to find the perfect lake. Throughout the West, guest ranches offer room, board and riding opportunities to "city slickers"; some even sponsor working cattle-drive vacations. The Colorado River of Utah and Arizona might be the most celebrated rafting challenge, but most Western states offer whitewater to match the skill level of any rafter or kayaker.

■ 50 Greatest US Athletes of the 20th Century

At the end of 1999, the ESPN sports television network named these individuals (and one horse) as the most influential sports figures in modern US history.

1. Michael Jordan, basketball	26. Kareem Abdul-Jabbar, basketball
2. Babe Ruth, baseball	27. Jerry Rice, football
3. Muhammad Ali, boxing	28. Red Grange, football
4. Jim Brown, football	29. Arnold Palmer, golf
5. Wayne Gretzky, ice hockey	30. Larry Bird, basketball
6. Jesse Owens, track and field	31. Bobby Orr, ice hockey
7. Jim Thorpe, football, track	32. Johnny Unitas, football
8. Willie Mays, baseball	33. Mark Spitz, swimming
9. Jack Nicklaus, golf	34. Lou Gehrig, baseball
10. Babe Didrikson Zaharias, golf, track	35. Secretariat, horse racing
11. Joe Louis, boxing	36. Oscar Robertson, basketball
12. Carl Lewis, track and field	37. Mickey Mantle, baseball
13. Wilt Chamberlain, basketball	38. Ben Hogan, golf
14. Hank Aaron, baseball	39. Walter Payton, football
15. Jackie Robinson, baseball	40. Lawrence Taylor, football
16. Ted Williams, baseball	41. Wilma Rudolph, track and field
17. Magic Johnson, basketball	42. Sandy Koufax, baseball
18. Bill Russell, basketball	43. Julius Erving, basketball
19. Martina Navratilova, tennis	44. Bobby Jones, golf
20. Ty Cobb, baseball	45. Bill Tilden, tennis
21. Gordie Howe, ice hockey	46. Eric Heiden, speed skating
22. Joe DiMaggio, baseball	47. Edwin Moses, track and field
23. Jackie Joyner-Kersee, track and field	48. Pete Sampras, tennis
24. Sugar Ray Robinson, boxing	49. O. J. Simpson, football
25. Joe Montana, football	50. Chris Evert, tennis

Laguna Beach, California

© Claire Cuneen

Sights

Alaska

Mount McKinley, Denali National Park

A land of superlatives, Alaska covers an area more than twice the size of Texas, the next largest US state, and is bigger than all but 16 of the world's nations. It claims the 16 highest peaks in the US and far more wildlife and national parkland than any other state. A huge knob at the northwestern corner of North America, "The Great Land" spans 2,350mi from the border of Canada to the western tip of the Aleutian Islands in the Pacific Ocean. Although separated from Russian Siberia by a mere 51mi of water, Alaska lies 500mi northwest of the nearest US mainland state, Washington. Only 619,000 people live in this vast (570,000sq mi) state, ranking it third to last in US population and dead last in population density.

Sometime between 15,000 and 30,000 years ago, nomadic bands crossed an exposed land bridge from Asia to America, with Alaska thus functioning as the gateway to this new world. Living along the coast and in the interior, native groups were well established by the time Europeans arrived in the 18C. Driven by fantastic prices on the furs of sea otters, the Russians developed a trade empire that eventually stretched all the way from Siberia to California. But as hunting pressures hastened the decline of the otter population, the Russians withdrew, selling the vast Alaska territory to the US in 1867 for $7.2 million.

Though many in the lower 48 states considered the area a frozen wasteland, others began to grow curious about what might lay within the mysterious northern realm. One thing they found was gold: Its glitter helped to swell settlement in Alaska with rushes to Juneau (1880), Skagway (1897-98), Nome (1899) and the Fairbanks area (1902). A much larger influx arrived during World War II with the buildup of military installations and a communications and transportation network that included the fabled Alaska Highway, linking Canada's Yukon Territory to Fairbanks through 1,500mi of rugged wilderness.

With Alaskan statehood in 1959 came a broader recognition of the state's riches and its strategic importance. Alaska also inherited a responsibility to grapple with the issues of oil development and land rights—a complex web of native claims, developers' interests, and the ideals of conservationists who believe that within Alaska lies the last best hope for true wilderness, undisturbed by man. It is for that latter experience that visitors come. More than one-quarter of Alaska's land is protected as park, refuge and wilderness, varying from spectacular coastal mountains and island-studded fjords to windswept tundra and bear-haunted boreal forests. Outdoor recreational possibilities are almost endless.

THE PANHANDLE★★

Michelin map 930 Inset   Alaska Standard Time
Tourist Information ☎ 907-586-4777 or www.alaskainfo.org

A complicated puzzle of land and water stretching north 540mi from Misty Fiords National Monument to Malaspina Glacier, the Panhandle reaches like an appendage from the body of Alaska toward the lower 48 states, separating Canada from the Gulf of Alaska. Constituting only 6 percent of the state's land area, the Panhandle (often called the Southeast) nevertheless totes up 10,000mi of shoreline with its irregular coast and its 1,000-island Alexander Archipelago.

In addition to islands, the landscape is distinguished by a chain of coastal mountains that crests at more than 15,000ft, making it the highest maritime range in the world. Glaciers slip from the heights to deep fjords where seals bask on ice floes and seabirds nest on granite islands. The region receives some of the heaviest rainfall in the state, which, coupled with a sea-tempered climate, has created a lush covering of spruce-hemlock rain forest. The largest US national forest, the Tongass contains more than 75 percent of the Panhandle's land area.

Historical Notes – For thousand of years, Tlingit *(KLINK-it)* Indians carved cedar canoes and harvested an easy living from the sea. They traded otter furs and dried salmon to Athabaskans of the Interior for copper and caribou skins. When the Russians arrived in the late 18C, they found millions of fur-bearing sea mammals whose pelts went for fabulous prices in Europe and China. The Russian capital in the New World, Sitka, acquired the look of a European enclave—for a time, it was the largest city on North America's west coast—until the near-extinction of sea otters and withdrawal of the Russians in the mid-19C.

Today ferries and cruise ships thread the island-sheltered Inside Passage on their way north from Ketchikan to Skagway. While fishing is still the main industry in most Panhandle areas, tourism and timber production also bolster the economy. Nearly half the old-growth forest of the Tongass had already been clear-cut before restrictions came to its rescue in the 1990s; debate continues over the right proportions of logging, conservation and recreation.

SIGHTS

Ketchikan – *285mi south of Juneau.* ☎ *907-225-6166. www.visit-ketchikan.com.* The southernmost town in Alaska and one of the wettest, Ketchikan bills itself as the salmon capital of the world. Closer to Seattle (650mi) than to Anchorage (900mi), Ketchikan once was known as the town "where fish and fishermen went upstream to spawn." Its **Creek Street Historic District** preserves a boardwalk that until 1954 was Alaska's most notorious red-light district.

Several attractions honor the Tlingit, Haida and Tsimshian cultures. The **Totem Heritage Center★** *(601 Deermount Ave.;* ☎ *907-225-5900)* displays nearly three dozen 19C totem poles salvaged from abandoned villages. With a population of 350 Tlingits, the **Saxman Native Village★** *(S. Stedman St.;* ☎ *907-225-9038)* offers tours that cover the tribal house, schoolhouse, carver's shed and a park punctuated with 28 totem poles. Visitors may watch master carvers and their apprentices at work, and view native dance performances at the clan house.

■ Alaska by Sea Bus

Southeast Alaska, with its chain of islands, was not made for cars. Planes and boats are the rule. Voyaging by water not only makes economic sense for those with time; it can be a memorable part of an Alaskan vacation in itself.

The **Alaska Marine Highway System** *(*☎ *907-465-3941 or 800-642-0066)* is the alternative to roads. Used by commuters and sightseers alike, the ferry system links 14 towns in the Panhandle; there also are networks in south-central Alaska and the Aleutian Islands. A ferry connects Bellingham, Washington *(p 355)*, with major stops along the Inside Passage the 1,000mi waterway from Puget Sound to Skagway—making for a less expensive travel option than luxury cruise lines.

Naturalists often are on board in the summer to interpret marine mammal and bird life. Comfortable overnight cabins are available. Those planning to book a cabin, or to transport a car in summer, should reserve several months ahead. Port stops generally are brief; travelers wishing to get off and explore will pay a somewhat higher total fare for consecutive one-way tickets. Many travelers bring a kayak or bicycle aboard, adding an adventure option for a small fee.

Getting There & Getting Around – Alaska's main airports serving flights from the US mainland are **Anchorage International Airport (ANC)** (☎ 266-2525, www.dot.state.ak.us/external/aias/aia/aiawlcm.htm), **Fairbanks International Airport (FAI)** (☎ 479-8700, www.dot.state.ak.us/external/aias/aias_fairbanks.html) and **Juneau International Airport (JNU)** (☎ 789-7821, www.juneau.lib.ak.us/cbj/airport/airport.htm). **Alaska Airlines** (☎ 800-426-0333) offers the widest range of flights to and within the state. Other regional airlines offering internal con- nections are **ERA Aviation** (☎ 248-4422) and **PenAir** (☎ 243-2323).

Alaska Railroad Corp. (P.O. Box 107500, Anchorage AK 99510; ☎ 265-2494) links Seward, Anchorage, Denali National Park and Fairbanks. There is bus service between Anchorage and Whitehorse, Canada, via **Alaska Direct Bus Lines** (☎ 277-6652). Independent tour companies offer travel throughout Alaska by coach.

Scheduled **ferry** service from Bellingham WA to Juneau and several other ports in Alaska is provided by the **Alaska Marine Highway System** (P.O. Box 25535, Juneau AK 99802; ☎ 465-3941). Reservations are required. For a listing of **cruise** companies, consult the Alaska State Division of Tourism (below).

Accommodations – **Alaska Windsong Lodges** (☎ 907-245-0200, www.alaska- parks.com) are located in and around national parks and in gateway cities. For **bed-and-breakfast reservations**: Alaska Private Lodgings/Stay with A Friend (P.O. Box 200047, Anchorage AK 99520; ☎ 258-1717, www.alaskabandb.com). For a list of public **campgrounds** and maps contact the Alaska State Division of Tourism.

Motels along highways usually have a restaurant, gasoline and repair facilities. Call for availability, especially Oct–mid-May. Sights and services are listed in Alaska Milepost, available in bookstores or by mail (Vernon Publications, 3000 Northup Way, Suite 200, Bellevue WA 98004; ☎ 800-726-4707).

Salmon Catch

Sightseeing – **Adventure Tourism**: Alaska Wildland Adventures (P.O. Box 389, Girdwood AK 99587; ☎ 783-2928, www.alaskawildland.com). MarkAir (P.O. Box 196769, Anchorage AK 99519; ☎ 243-6275). **Biking**: Alaskan Bicycle Adventures (907 E. Dowling Rd., Anchorage AK 99518; ☎ 243-2329, www.alaskabike.com). **Escorted tours**: Gray Line of Alaska (745 W. Fourth Ave., Anchorage AK 99501; ☎ 277-5581). **Multi-sport excursions**: REI Adventures (P.O. Box 1938, Sumner WA 98390; ☎ 253-395-8111, www.rei.com/travel).

For a list of ecotourism outfitters and for further information on adventure travel, contact the **Alaska Wilderness Recreation & Tourism Association** (P.O. Box 22827, Juneau AK 99802; ☎ 463-3038, www.alaska.net/~awrta).

Visitor Information – For further information on points of interest, accom- modations, sightseeing, tour companies and seasonal events, or to request the Alaska State Vacation Planner, contact the **Alaska State Division of Tourism** (P.O. Box 110801, Juneau AK 99811-0801; ☎ 465-2010, www.travelalaska.com).

* Misty Fiords National Monument – *Headquarters, 3031 Tongass Ave., Ketchikan.* ☎ *907-225-2148.* *www.gorp.com/gorp/resource/US_Wilderness_Area/ak_misty.htm.* A 3,580sq mi preserve of lushly forested mountains, glacial fjords flanked by 3,000ft granite cliffs, and mist-enshrouded islands rich in wildlife, this hauntingly beautiful park holds many wonders for visitors who boat its shores and take to its dense forests. Hidden waterfalls, spouting whales, blue tidewater glaciers and spruce-top bald-eagle aeries are a few of its delights.

** Sitka – *136mi southwest of Juneau.* ☎ *907-747-5940. www.sitka.org.* Sheltered by small islands, with a mountain backdrop, this lovely and historically important towns occupies a point on the west side of Baranof Island. Tlingit life was uninterrupted for 6,000 years until the arrival of Russian traders in 1799. Directed by Alexander Baranof, the Russians established a fortress, Redoubt Arkhangelsk Mikhailovsk, and solicited native help in fur trapping. But Indian suspicions erupted in violence in 1802; Tlingits attacked the redoubt and killed nearly all the Russians. The Russians returned two years later, outfought the Tlingits and began displacing Indian clan houses with fort-like dwellings.

Upon the sale of Alaska to the US in 1867, Sitka became the new territorial capital. After Juneau claimed that office in 1906, Sitka accepted a role as a peaceful fishing hamlet. Its Russian heritage is symbolized by **St. Michael's Cathedral** *(Lincoln & American Sts.;* ☎ *907-747-8120)*, which dominates the town center; it was rebuilt in 1976 on the site of the original 19C church, destroyed by fire. Now with a population of 9,000, Sitka holds all the charms of an old seaside village.

* Sitka National Historical Park – *106 Metlakatla St.; Bishop's House at Monastery & Lincoln Sts.* ☎ *907-747-6281. www.nps.gov/sitk.* This 107-acre park has two parcels. Exhibits at the visitor center, at the mouth of the Indian River, examine the cultural clash created by the arrival of Europeans in the New World. The adjacent **Fort Site** recalls the 1804 Battle of Sitka. A 1mi loop trail through a spruce forest passes the clearing where a Tlingit fort stood. After withstanding six days of bombardment from Russian ships, the Indians slipped quietly away. When the Russians entered the fort, all they heard was the maniacal cackling of ravens.

The long, ocher **Russian Bishop's House**** (1843), near downtown, was sturdily built by Finnish shipwrights. First-floor exhibits cover Russian history; guided tours of the upstairs bishop's quarters interpret the ecclesiastical lifestyle.

* Sheldon Jackson Museum – *104 College Dr.* ☎ *907-747-8981. www.educ.state .ak.us/lam/museum.* The oldest museum and best trove of artifacts in Alaska is located on the campus of little Sheldon Jackson College, where author James Michener lived from 1984-86 while researching his novel *Alaska*. The four major native groups—Southeast and Athabaskan Indians, Aleuts and Eskimos—are featured. Bentwood baskets, ivory tools, painted drums and other artfully executed pieces show a remarkable adaptation to a demanding environment.

* Admiralty Island National Monument – *Headquarters, 8461 Old Dairy Rd., Juneau.* ☎ *907-586-8790. www.fs.fed.us/r10/chatham/anm/frmain.htm.* This pristine 1,709sq mi island is famous for its brown bears. Some 1,500 of them inhabit the dense forest, mountains and rocky beaches, feeding on salmon from streams and wild berries in high meadows. The presence of so many well-fed bears led early dwellers to dub the place Kootznoowoo, "fortress of the bears." Visitors with permits may visit **Pack Creek Bear Preserve** on the northeast shore.

* Juneau – *650mi southeast of Anchorage.* ☎ *907-586-2201. www.juneau.com.* Tucked along the narrow strip of land between Gastineau Channel and high mountains, the capital of 30,000 is accessible only by air or sea. Juneau is the most visually appealing of Alaska's cities, having the look and feel of a quaint European city with narrow streets that curve up from the waterfront.

The discovery of gold in 1880 led to the establishment of a town site that became the territorial capital in 1906. Through World War II, miners removed 88 million tons of rock from Mt. Roberts, riddling the mountain with so many passages that there remain more miles of tunnel than road in Juneau. Though the city lies far from Alaska's population center at Anchorage, a move to relocate the capital was rejected by voters in 1982. The presence of state power brokers continues to give the town a solid footing, as do boatloads of summer cruise visitors.

Near the cruise-ship terminal, the **Mt. Roberts Tramway*** *(490 S. Franklin St.;* ☎ *907-463-3412)* ascends 1,880 vertical feet to wonderful views of town and harbor. A short stroll from People's Wharf, through the heart of the historic district on Franklin and Main Streets, brings visitors to the **Alaska State Capitol** *(4th & Main Sts.;* ☎ *907-465-2479)*, ornamented with marble quarried on Prince of Wales Island in the southern Panhandle.

** Alaska State Museum – *395 Whittier St.* ☎ *907-465-2901.* The state's finest museum of history and culture holds more than 23,000 artifacts and works of art. The Alaska Native Gallery defines the four main native groups and features such splendid examples of their craftsmanship as ceremonial masks and sealskin kayaks. A life-size diorama of a treetop eagle's nest highlights the Natural History ramp, while upstairs, the State History Gallery limns important events in the Russian-American period, the gold-mining era and other early chapters.

* **Mendenhall Glacier** – *Mendenhall Loop Rd., 13mi northwest of downtown Juneau via Egan Dr.* ☎ *907-789-0097.* An easily accessible natural wonder, this 1.5mi-wide glacier arcs 12mi from the Juneau Icefield down to Mendenhall Lake, where it calves into the water. A .3mi trail leads to the water's edge, while the 3.5mi **East Glacier Loop** gets hikers close to the glacier's edge. Though sliding forward 2ft per day, the river of ice is actually losing ground, retreating about 25ft per year uphill as a result of a climatic warming trend of 250 years.

ADDRESS BOOK

Staying in Alaska

The accommodations listed below have been chosen for their location, character or value for money. Rates are for a standard room, double occupancy in high season; some hotels offer lower weekend rates.

$$$$	over $250	$$	$100-$175
$$$	$175-$250	$	less than $100

Great Alaska Adventure Lodge – *33881 Sterling Hwy., Sterling AK.* ✗ ☎ *907-262-8797. www.greatalaska.com. 22 rooms.* **$$$$** The front door of this knotty-pine lodge swings open into the Kenai National Wildlife Refuge. Fishing, canoeing, kayaking, hiking and even bear-viewing excursions depart from here. A seaplane delivers guests to wilderness camps where gourmet meals are flown in daily.

Hotel Captain Cook – *939 W. 5th Ave., Anchorage AK.* ✗ ⅙ 🄿 🏊 ☎ *907-276-6000. www.captaincook.com. 557 rooms.* **$$$** With spectacular vistas on Cook Inlet and the Chugach Mountains, this high-rise was Alaska's first luxury inn, built to rejuvenate Anchorage after the 1964 quake. **The Crow's Nest** on the 20th floor serves fresh seafood with views of Mt. McKinley.

Denali National Park Hotel – *Denali National Park AK.* ✗ ⅙ 🄿
www.denalinationalpark.com. 100 rooms. **$$** Built in the 1920s, this hub of activity is the only hotel within Denali Park. The lone telephone is in the lobby, which resembles an old railroad depot. Shuttles whisk visitors to gold-panning, river rafting, flightseeing and dinner theater; in-house programs are presented in a 300-seat auditorium.

Glacier Bay Country Inn – *Gustavus AK.* ✗ ☎ *907-697-2288.*
www.glacierbayalaska.com. 6 rooms, 5 cabins. **$$** Visitors who arrive by air or ferry are rewarded by the solitude of this rambling inn, isolated in meadows of wild-flowers. Guests spend days fly-fishing, whale-watching or cruising the bay, and evenings dining on halibut with plum sauce or grilled salmon with Mongolian glaze.

Dining in Alaska

The list below represents a sample of some popular establishments. Prices indicate the average cost of an entrée, an appetizer or dessert, and a beverage for one person (not including tax and tip, or alcoholic beverages). Reservations are highly recommended for $$$ and $$$$ restaurants.

$$$$	over $100	$$	$30-$65
$$$	$65-$100	$	less than $30

The Marx Brothers Café – *627 W. 3rd Ave., Anchorage AK.* ☎ *907-278-2133. www.marxcafe.com.* **$$$ Creative American.** This quaint, wood-frame café changes its menu daily, always featuring local seafood: king salmon, sautéed Kodiak scallops, or broiled marlin with blood-orange vinaigrette.

Red Dog Saloon and Cookhouse – *278 S. Franklin St., Juneau AK.* ☎ *907-463-3777.* **$$ American.** Photos of the old mining days—tough faces and hard work—surround diners. The Red Dog specializes in hearty seafood and steak dishes. Read the writing on the wall: "The cooking has never killed anyone but the miners have hung more than one cook." Watch for the noose that drops from the ceiling.

*** Glacier Bay National Park and Preserve – *Gustavus, 65mi west of Juneau.* ☎ *907-697-2230. www.nps.gov/glba.* Encompassing 4,297sq mi at the northern end of the Panhandle, Glacier Bay showcases the best that Alaska's wild lands have to offer: stunning views of ice-clad mountains, a rich variety of marine and land animals, and seemingly limitless miles of wilderness. No roads traverse this watery sanctuary. Visitors have a distinct sense of being privileged to enter this natural kingdom by the sea, ruled by whales and bears and the dramatic forces of nature. Recognizing the unique value of this glacial landscape, UNESCO declared it an International Biosphere Reserve in 1986 and a World Heritage Site in 1992.

© Art Wolfe/Tony Stone Images

Kayaker, Glacier Bay

When explorer George Vancouver sailed past in 1794, he saw only an icy shoreline, with barely an indentation to suggest a retreating glacier. The first person to seriously study the area and bring it to the attention of the outside world, naturalist John Muir *(p 320)*, traveled here in 1879 and inspired potential visitors with bold descriptions of "the intensely white, far-spreading fields of ice." But visits to these remote haunts remained sparse until Inside Passage cruise ships added the bay to their itineraries in the 1970s. Today, frigid inlets reach back 65mi to where numerous tidewater glaciers continue to reshape the land, scooping out fjords and carving mountain valleys and peaks.

Unforgettable day-long cruises depart Bartlett Cove aboard the park's **Spirit of Adventure★★★**. The boat maneuvers close to glaciers while offering waterborne comfort, view windows and outdoor decks. In the lower bay, naturalists point out sea otters at play; humpback whales breaching, their tails fanning as they dive; and pods of orcas (killer whales) rolling in unison like black and white waves. Tours pause at **Marble Island★★** where thousands of kittiwakes, puffins, cormorants, murres and other birds noisily commune on the rocks, and sea lions growl, snort and nose each other for better places in the sun. At the head of the bay, spectacular glaciers rear up 200ft; tours venture close enough to witness tremendous splashes as building-size chunks of ice calve into the water.

★ Skagway – *80mi north of Juneau.* ☎ *907-983-1898. www.skagway.org.* Northern terminus of the Inside Passage, historic Skagway was the rollicking frontier town through which tens of thousands of gold seekers passed on their arduous way up the 33mi **Chilkoot Trail** to the goldfields of the Yukon in 1897-98. To prevent their perishing in the wilderness, prospectors were required by law to carry one ton of supplies over the pass, which meant 40 back-breaking ascents. Many fell prey to the dance halls and streetwalkers of Skagway, where outlaws like nefarious gang leader Jefferson "Soapy" Smith lay in wait for green young men.

Klondike Gold Rush National Historical Park *(2nd Ave. & Broadway;* ☎ *907-983-2921; www.nps.gov/klgo)* preserves the Chilkoot Trail (now a recreational byway) and much of the historic district, with its false-fronted buildings and wooden sidewalks. *(Also see p 347).* Brothels and gambling dens have been converted to gift shops and eateries. The 41mi **White Pass & Yukon Route★** *(2nd Ave. & Spring St.;* ☎ *907-983-2217)* is a narrow-gauge railway that takes tourists through the same breathtaking mountain scenery witnessed by the prospectors—but in much less time and with much greater ease.

ANCHORAGE★

Michelin map 930 Inset   Alaska Standard Time
Population 254,982
Tourist Information ☎ 907-276-4118 or www.anchorage.net

Sprawled over the one piece of flat ground between the arms of Cook Inlet and the sharp peaks of the Chugach Range, Alaska's largest city holds nearly half the state's population. Its maritime proximity gives Anchorage a more moderate climate than most of Alaska. As the state's center of commerce and culture, the city welcomes business travelers and summer visitors heading out into the wild.

Historical Notes – Starting as a tent city of pioneers and rail workers in 1914, Anchorage grew into a frontier town. Fort Richardson and Elmendorf Air Force Base helped push population over 30,000 by 1950. Cold War defense-system headquarters added to the city's size and problems: inadequate housing, vice crimes and heavy traffic. The Good Friday earthquake of 1964 rocked Anchorage to its foundations. Rebuilding in its aftermath proved an economic slingshot, invigorating the skyline with new life. The rich 1968 oil strike in Prudhoe Bay, in the Arctic, provided another boost. Anchorage today offers fine restaurants, upscale galleries, beautifully landscaped parks and numerous cultural events.

The modern Iditarod, beginning the first Saturday of March, spans wind-raked tundra, frozen rivers and icy mountain ranges, with winners typically covering the ground to Nome, on the Bering Sea, in just over nine days. Improved equipment, trail conditions, breeding and training have whittled the course time from 20 days in 1973. First-place finishers win a purse of $52,500, a four-wheel-drive truck and the accolades of the international dogsled-racing world.

SIGHTS

★**Anchorage Museum of History and Art** – *121 W. 7th St.* ☎ *907-343-4326. www.ci.anchorage.ak.us.* Covering most of a city block, this repository of history, ethnography and art presents an in-depth look at Alaskan culture. The first-floor art collection highlights people and landscapes; included are striking **canvases**★ by Sydney Laurence (1865-1940), Alaska's most famous painter. Upstairs, the Alaska Gallery holds more than 1,000 historical objects in exhibits of Indian, Aleut and Eskimo lifestyles, proceeding into the era of European contact. A highlight is the life-size diorama of an 18C Aleut house of whalebone, grass and sod.

★**Alaska Aviation Heritage Museum** – 🅺🅸🅳🆂 *4721 Aircraft Dr., Lake Hood Air Harbor.* ☎ *907-248-5325.* The din of seaplanes on the lake outside—85,000 takeoffs and landings a year, the most of any air harbor on earth—adds realism to a compendium of history in a state that relies on aircraft to access "the bush." Displays include two dozen vintage bush planes, a restoration room, photos and a theater. Exhibits chronicle the World War II Battle of Attu, the heroics of aviation pioneer Carl Ben Eielson (1897-1929) and the tragic 1935 flight that killed aviator Wiley Post and humorist Will Rogers near Barrow.

EXCURSION

★**Girdwood Area** – *37mi southeast of Anchorage via Seward Hwy. (Rte. 1).* A national scenic byway, the Seward Highway takes motorists from Anchorage along lovely **Turnagain Arm,** whose 38ft bore tide in spring is the second-greatest in North America. Beluga whales sometimes spout and breach here. The road continues through Chugach National Forest to the Kenai Peninsula *(opposite).*

Less than an hour from the city, the **Alyeska Resort Tramway**★ *(Alyeska Hwy., 3mi east of Girdwood;* ☎ *907-754-1111)* whisks visitors 2,300ft above the valley to the top of Alaska's premier ski mountain for stunning **views**★★ of Turnagain Arm and ice-bitten peaks. Nearby **Crow Creek Mine** 🅺🅸🅳🆂 *(Crow Creek Rd., 2mi east of Girdwood;* ☎ *907-278-8060)* harbors a clutch of weathered buildings from the turn-of-the-20C gold-rush era. The **Portage Glacier Recreation Area**★ *(5.5mi east of Seward Hwy., Milepost 79;* ☎ *907-783-3242)* offers a short course on glacial geology and a chance to reach out and grab chunks of ice in a glacial lake. On 1hr boat tours, visitors see and hear Portage Glacier calve. Interpretive trails explore a moraine and provide a close look at Byron Glacier.

■ Dogsled Racing

A team of huskies mushing across frozen tundra is a quintessential image of Alaska. As the starting point for the arduous 1,049mi **Iditarod**, "the last great race on earth," Anchorage shares mightily in this vision. Sled dogs are a reminder that this modern city is not far removed from primitive wilderness.

For millennia, working sled dogs provided travel and communication in the far north. More than 4,000 years ago, nomadic Eskimos and Indians enlisted native malamutes to help pull loads and take them to hunting and fishing grounds. Their stamina and sense of direction made them invaluable to later explorers. In his 1903 classic, *The Call of the Wild*, Jack London wrote of gold seekers using dogs to haul equipment and provisions. With the arrival of air transport in the 1920s, dogsledding nearly died out; backcountry mushers kept the practice alive. In 1967, during Alaska's centennial celebration, a race was held to commemorate the Iditarod Trail, a gold-rush route blazed in 1910 to deliver mail from Seward to Nome, and renewed in 1925 to relay diptheria serum.

© Kevir Horan/Tony Stone Images

Start of the Iditarod

SOUTH CENTRAL ALASKA★★

Michelin map 930 Inset   Alaska Standard Time
Tourist Information ☎ 907-283-3850 or www.kenaipeninsula.org

South of the Alaska Range, the land gentles into fertile valleys and rolling forests, then suddenly buckles into another cordillera of glacier-capped peaks along the Gulf of Alaska. Land, sea and sky meet in grand proportion in this diverse region where goats clamber on steep cliffs in sight of spouting whales, and fishing villages reap the bounty of tens of millions of spawning salmon.

The ice-free ports of Valdez, Cordova, Seward, Homer and Kenai were early staging points for exploitation of copper, coal and gold. In the 1910s the railroad linked Seward with Anchorage and the Interior, but not until the 1950s did a highway traverse the 225mi from Anchorage to Homer.

South of Anchorage lies the **Kenai Peninsula**, a place where knife-ridged mountains seem to rise directly from the sea. Clouds accumulate often in the moist sea air, saturating the coastline in summer with light but frequent rains.

The region continues to recover from the massive *Exxon Valdez* oil spill of 1989, which affected more than 1,500mi of shoreline from Prince William Sound to Kodiak Island. Lingering effects are not evident to visitors, however.

SIGHTS

★ **Seward** – *Seward Hwy. (Rte. 9), 130mi south of Anchorage.* ☎ *907-224-8051. www.seward.net/chamber/.* A spirited town of bright stucco-and-clapboard bungalows, Seward rests at the head of mountain-rimmed **Resurrection Bay**. Starting in 1902 as the southern terminus of the Alaska Railroad, Seward became known as the "Gateway to Alaska"; it remains a rail center and a port for cruise ships. Visitors shop and eat at the picturesque **Small Boat Harbor**, watch fishermen returning with their catches, and take wildlife cruises into the bay.

★ **Alaska SeaLife Center** – 🅚🅘🅓🅢 *301 Railway Ave.* ☎ *907-224-6300.* This modern research, rehabilitation and education facility was funded by a legal settlement from the *Exxon Valdez* spill. The center offers two floors of exhibits on marine animals and ongoing projects to protect local ecosystems. Viewing platforms allow visitors to gaze into pools for sea lions, seals and sea otters; marine birds have a rock pool and cliffs.

★★ **Kenai Fjords National Park** – *Visitor center at Small Boat Harbor on 4th Ave., Seward.* ☎ *907-224-3175. www.nps.gov/kefj.* Covering 1,045sq mi of coastal fjords and glacier-clad mountains on the southeastern side of the Kenai Peninsula, this park preserves a wilderness where thousands of marine mammals and seabirds find sanctuary. More than 30ft of snow a year replenish the 300sq mi Harding Icefield, which feeds 30 glaciers; eight descend all the way to tidewater, where they calve icebergs with such force that explosions may be heard up to 20mi away.
Boat tours★ vary from 2hr 30min cruises around Resurrection Bay to 9hr voyages down the coastline to Harris Bay and Northwestern Glacier. Passengers have plenty of opportunities to spot diverse wildlife, from murres and horned puffins to sea otters and humpback whales.
On the north side of the park, the **Exit Glacier**★ area *(Exit Glacier Rd., 9mi west of Seward Hwy.; first 4mi paved)* has a network of trails to bring visitors close to the 3mi-long, .5mi-wide river of ice. The **Glacier Access Trail** *(.5mi)* is an easy stroll to a glacial viewpoint. The more strenuous **Harding Icefield Trail**★ *(3.5mi one-way)* ascends 3,000ft to spectacular views of the vast icefield. From this frozen sea jut jagged nunataks, an Eskimo word meaning "lonely peaks."

Steller Sea Lions

© Buddy Mays/TRAVEL STOCK

★ **Homer** – *Sterling Hwy. (Rte. 1), 225mi southwest of Anchorage.* ☎ *907-235-7740. www.xyz.net/~homer.* Guarding the entrance to Kachemak Bay in the lower Kenai Peninsula, the individualistic town of Homer is framed by lovely Cook Inlet and the jagged graph of the Kenai Mountains. The town has a gentler setting than Seward; for decades it has attracted artists, retirees, fishermen and, more recently, tourists. The 4.5mi **Homer Spit** acts as nerve center of an extensive commercial and recreational fishing industry, with halibut the leading catch.

★ **Pratt Museum** – *3779 Bartlett St.* ☎ *907-235-8635. www.prattmuseum.org.* A first-rate collection of art and natural history, the Pratt offers a gut-wrenching exhibit on the Valdez spill, an interesting display about the ongoing spruce-beetle epidemic, and a hands-on video monitor for viewing nesting birds on nearby Gull Island via remote-control camera.

** Halibut Cove – *Access by Danny J ferry (4hr 30min tours) from the Homer Spit Marina.* ☎ *907-235-7847 or 800-478-7847. www.central-charter.com.* A 32-person ferry takes locals and tourists to this tranquil curve of beach backed by a lagoon dotted with houses on stilts. Stroll the boardwalks, visit the handful of galleries, and absorb the beauty of a watery paradise.

* Prince William Sound – ☎ *907-835-2984.* Basking in the protective embrace of the Chugach Mountains on the north and the Kenai Peninsula on the west, Prince William Sound offers a quiet 15,000sq mi seascape for kayaking, cruising and studying marine wildlife. Only one road links the Sound with the Interior—the scenic Richardson Highway to **Valdez** *(val-DEEZ)*, a port town sitting at the end of the Trans-Alaska Pipeline and servicing the giant tankers that haul oil away. Free tours of the **Alyeska Pipeline Terminal** *(Dayville Rd., 13mi east of Valdez;* ☎ *907-835-2686)* are offered daily. Valdez was destroyed by a tidal wave from the 1964 earthquake and was subsequently relocated.

* Wrangell-St. Elias National Park – *Headquarters at Mile 105.5 Old Richardson Hwy. (Rte. 4), Copper Center, 10mi south of Glenallen.* ☎ *907-822-5234. www.nps.gov/wrst.* A magnificent wilderness of glaciers, streams and towering snow-crowned peaks, the park's 20,600sq mi make it the largest national park in the US. Encompassing an area larger than Switzerland, it tops out at 18,008ft **Mt. St. Elias**, second-highest summit in the US, and contains nine of the 16 highest mountains in the country.

EXCURSIONS

Lake Clark National Park and Preserve – *Headquarters, 4230 University Dr., Suite 311, Anchorage.* ☎ *907-271-3751. Field headquarters, Port Alsworth; 150mi southwest of Anchorage.* ☎ *907-781-2218. www.nps.gov/lacl.* This realm of active volcanoes, glacial highlands and cobalt-blue lakes may be the perfect Alaskan retreat. A stunning range of landscapes varies from coastal wetlands rich in marine mammals, to alpine tundra thick with bears, to 50mi-long **Lake Clark**, host to an immense run of sockeye salmon.

* Katmai National Park and Preserve – *Headquarters, 1 King Salmon Mall, King Salmon; 290mi southwest of Anchorage.* ☎ *907-246-3305. www.nps.gov/katm.* Rich in wildlife and geological history, Katmai embraces 6,250sq mi at the head of the Alaska Peninsula. The 1912 eruption of 2,700ft Novarupta shook the Northern Hemisphere for five days and spread ash as far as Texas. Adjacent Mt. Katmai collapsed into a chasm. As molten earth poured into a once-green valley, steam and gases emitted from thousands of vents. Four years later, a National Geographic Society team saw these fumaroles spewing smoke and steam up 1,000ft. They named the area the **Valley of Ten Thousand Smokes***. After 20 years, the smokes trailed off, although wisps are still sometimes visible.

Katmai is well-known for its large population of Alaskan brown bears. Viewing platforms at Brooks Camp and at the **McNeil River State Game Sanctuary*** allow visitors a chance to observe bears up close. McNeil draws the most brown bears of anywhere in the world—up to 60 at a time may be fishing on the falls—and human visitation is controlled by lottery.

Aniakchak National Monument – *Headquarters, 1 King Salmon Mall, King Salmon.* ☎ *907-246-3305. www.nps.gov/ania.* This isolated, otherworldly tract of volcanic land south of Katmai boasts an active volcano with one of the world's largest calderas, 6mi wide and 2,000ft deep. Reached by plane from Anchorage in three stages, the park is often raked by high winds and foul weather; visitors must wait for a break in the weather, then land on the lake or in the caldera. Visitor facilities are nonexistent but adventurous kayakers and river rafters can navigate a 32mi river from Surprise Lake in the caldera to saltwater Aniakchak Bay.

INTERIOR AND ARCTIC*

Michelin map 930 Inset   Alaska Standard Time
Tourist Information ☎ 907-465-2012 or http://apr.travelalaska.com

A great rolling plain sandwiched between the Alaska and Brooks Ranges, the Interior has long been a haven for wildlife. Much in the landscape has remained the same for millennia. The taiga—a forest of spruce, alder and willow—supports a chain of mammalian life from bear and moose down to snowshoe hare and lynx. Birds in the millions migrate through as they have for tens of thousands of years, wings drumming, responding to the call of the north.

The Interior surged in population during the 1890s gold rush as thousands of prospectors made their ways to the Klondike River in Canada using the Yukon River as a western corridor. The grittiest stayed, turning log-cabin settlements into a few sparse towns. One of them, Fairbanks, grew into a small city that is now home to the University of Alaska. Elsewhere, the region remains largely undeveloped and inaccessible by road. A paved highway does, however, lead to that mecca of Alaskan wilderness seekers, Denali National Park.

North of the Interior sprawls the vast and forbidding Arctic, an alien region that occupies nearly a third of Alaska and claims very few human residents. In this unforgiving land of extremes, the sun never sets in the summer, never rises in the winter. A major mountain range, largely unexplored, arcs across its midriff; frozen deserts dot the hinterlands; shimmering streams etch sinuous patterns across the tundra. Life bursts forth in the brief summer: Wildflowers bloom bravely in chill winds and herds of caribou thunder north to calving grounds.

SIGHTS

* **Fairbanks** – *Alaska Hwy. (Rte. 2) & George Parks Hwy. (Rte. 3), 358mi north of Anchorage.* ☎ *907-456-5774. www.explorefairbanks.com.* Spread among rolling hills along the Chena River, Alaska's second-largest city (34,000 people) serves as the business, military and transportation hub for the Interior. Beginning as a trading post for gold miners in 1901, the town prospered with the building of military installations in World War II and the construction of the Trans-Alaska Pipeline in the 1970s. A resourceful and often eccentric citizenry copes with brutal winters, tempered somewhat by the spectacle of the northern lights, and open their arms to the nightless days of summer and the curious visitors who stop by.

* **Alaskaland** – **Kids** *Airport Way & Peger Rd.* ☎ *907-459-1087.* Among the state treasures in this 44-acre history theme park is the National Historic Landmark S.S. *Nenana,* a restored sternwheeler that plied the Yukon River from 1933 to 1952. There's also a plush railcar that carried President Warren Harding to the Interior in the 1920s, and a street of turn-of-the-20C wooden buildings moved from downtown Fairbanks, now operating as gift shops and snack stands.

* **Riverboat Discovery** – **Kids** *Steamboat Landing, Discovery Rd.* ☎ *907-479-6673. www.riverboatdiscovery.com.* A 20mi cruise down the Chena and Tenana Rivers is enlivened by bush-plane and sled-dog demonstrations, an Indian fishing camp display and a visit to a re-created Athabaskan Indian village.

University of Alaska Museum – *907 Yukon Dr., west end of campus.* ☎ *907-474-7505. www.uaf.edu/museum.* Mounted animals, dioramas, hands-on objects and video programs outline the history and culture of the state, while daily shows highlight native lifeways and the *aurora borealis,* or northern lights.

*** **Denali National Park and Preserve** – *George Parks Hwy. (Rte. 3), Denali Park; 125mi south of Fairbanks & 240mi north of Anchorage.* ☎ *907-683-2294. www.nps.gov/dena.* At 9,375sq mi, Denali offers an incomparable cross section of the untamed Alaska Range, including the highest peak in North America, 20,320ft **Mt. McKinley.** A primeval world of grand design and dimension, the park's geography varies from spruce forest to grassy tundra to austere granite pinnacles mantled with snow and ice. Glaciers have scoured cirques, and chiseled ridges and steep valleys, to create a remote Olympian landscape that often appears to float in a world of its own above the clouds.

Set aside as a refuge in 1917, the park harbors a remarkable wildlife community. Thirty-seven mammals and 157 bird species reside in Denali. Moose favor the boggy, moist forest-tundra transition zone, while wolves and grizzly bears roam throughout. Small herds of caribou graze the tundra; Dall sheep dot the highlands.

Since the first successful climb in 1913, more than 10,000 people have reached the summit of "The High One," as it was called by Athabaskans. At least 88 climbers have died trying. With its tremendous girth, McKinley is the single largest mountain and highest exposed mountain in the world. Rising 18,000ft above the lowlands of **Wonder Lake,** it is 7,000ft higher than Everest from base to summit.

Most visitors will be lucky to obtain a view of the often cloud-covered peak; early mornings provide the best chance. Popular shuttle-bus tours carry visitors deep into the park, crossing forested taiga and open tundra, offering myriad opportunities for wildlife sightings. Few trails cross this wilderness park; hikers head out on river bars or ridgetops, finding their own square miles of solitude.

* **The Arctic** – Spreading from Canada 700mi to the Chukchi Sea, the Arctic claims as its northern border the frigid Beaufort Sea, while to the south runs the Yukon River. The dominating feature of the landscape rises just north of the Arctic Circle—the ancient Brooks Range, with its 9,000ft peaks running east to west in endless, sharp spires. Access is mainly by air.

Gates of the Arctic National Park – *Headquarters, 201 First Ave., Fairbanks.* ☎ *907-456-0281. Field office, Bettles; 180mi northwest of Fairbanks.* ☎ *907-692-5494.* Bush pilots fly visitors to this sprawling (12,816sq mi) national park. With no formal trails or facilities, hikers and canoeists are on their own in the Brooks Range. Guided adventures, booked well in advance, begin either in the Inupiat Eskimo village of **Anaktuvuk Pass** or in the century-old trading village of **Bettles.**

Prudhoe Bay – *380mi north of Fairbanks.* ☎ *907-659-2368*. Half-day tours of the oil and gas production facilities here on the Arctic Ocean take in wells, drill pads, housing facilities, Pump Station One at the beginning of the 800mi Trans-Alaska Pipeline, and a wide variety of Arctic tundra flora and fauna.

Barrow – *500mi north-northwest of Fairbanks.* ☎ *907-852-5211*. Northernmost town in the Western Hemisphere, this Inupiat community clings to a treeless tundra on the edge of the Arctic icepack. It has modernized in recent decades, but whaling and dogsledding remain from earlier times. The Inupiat have lived in these climes for 1,500 years; archaeologists are excavating an ancient village on a bluff near downtown. Tourists may visit the **Wiley Post-Will Rogers Memorial** *(15mi southwest)*, where the pilot and humorist died in the 1935 crash of a small plane.

★ **Kotzebue** – *450mi west-northwest of Fairbanks.* ☎ *907-442-3301*. Alaska's most populous native community with nearly 4,000 residents, Kotzebue is a living cultural museum. Visitors can learn how Eskimos have lived in this unrelenting environment for millennia. The **NANA Museum of the Arctic** *(2nd Ave.)* features a 90min presentation on culture, crafts and livelihood that concludes with a traditional blanket toss, once used to help hunters scout prey on a flat landscape. Alaska's only jade factory is next door to the museum.

Kotzebue's **Public Lands Information Center** *(☎ 907-442-3890)* is headquarters for three vast National Park Service expanses. **Noatak National Preserve** harbors the largest virgin river basin in the US; UNESCO has designated the 425mi Noatak River an International Biosphere Reserve. **Kobuk Valley National Park**, at the remote west end of the Brooks Range, has 100ft-high dunes (the largest active Arctic dune field in the world), limpid streams and relict flora. **Cape Krusenstern National Monument**, across Hotham Inlet from Kotzebue, has coastal landscapes of harsh beauty, its lateral ridges rife with 6,000 years of Eskimo artifacts.

Nome – *520mi west of Fairbanks.* ☎ *907-443-5535*. With the discovery of gold here in late 1898, Nome's population soared to 20,000. Those rambunctious frontier days long gone, the town of 3,500 now serves as the commercial hub of northwestern Alaska and its constellation of Eskimo villages. It is best known as the finish line for the annual Iditarod Trail dogsled race *(p 67)* in March.

Bering Land Bridge National Preserve – *Visitor center, 240 Front St., Nome.* ☎ *907-443-2522. www.nps.gov/bela.* Hot springs, extinct volcanoes, stunningly clear lakes and prehistoric camping sites dot the peninsula where Siberian nomads first crossed into Alaska, discovering abundant game and not a living human soul.

■ Arctic Wildlife

Though the woolly mammoth and saber-tooth cat have long since vanished, the vast roadless expanse of the Arctic remains to a large extent an unaltered ecosystem of animals that have been here since the end of the Ice Age.

Among large mammals, the semi-aquatic **polar bear** is one of the most elusive. Living on ice floes in the far north, this rare and fierce predator hunts walruses, seals and whales, sometimes waiting four hours for prey to surface at a breathing hole, then pouncing like a swift cat.

Polar Bear

Unlike polar bears, **grizzly bears** will eat food other than meat, often grazing on blueberries near Antigun Pass off the Dalton Highway. Though not quite as large as their cousins, the brown bears that inhabit Alaska's south coast, Arctic grizzlies can top 900 pounds and live up to 30 years. The heaviest polar bears weigh about 1,200 pounds; Alaskan brown bears may exceed 1,400 pounds.

Musk Ox

Re-introduced to the Arctic, **musk oxen** are exceptionally adapted to extreme cold. A layer of fat topped by thick skin, a heavy undercoat and silky hair 15-20in long keeps them comfortable at -80°F. Their wool, or *qiviut*, is prized for its softness and warmth. Chief among their enemies, **wolves** hunt in packs on the dry alpine tundra. When under attack, the musk oxen herd will circle up like a wagon train, shaggy heads facing defiantly outward.

Magnificent **caribou** migrate to the tundra in summer across cold rivers and through mountain passes, their herds sometimes numbering in the thousands.

Black Hills Region

Mount Rushmore National Memorial

Rolling hills seem to go on forever in the northern Great Plains, punctuated only by an occasional ranch house or pumping oil well. Here and there, a rancher may ride over the crest of a hill, sheepdogs in the lead, to corral 100 head of cattle in a draw. Multiple thunderstorms move through the expanse of sky like ships adrift in a deceptively placid sea. In places, these wide-open spaces are impaled with high buttes that once were landmarks for westbound pioneers.

The dominant landforms in the region are the Black Hills and Badlands of western South Dakota. Sixty million years ago, the Black Hills were becoming a major mountain range, forced by the earth's internal heat to heights of 14,000ft. Ravaged for millions of years by inland seas and thundering upheavals, the domed range today stands 3,000ft-4,000ft above the surrounding plains. From a distance, the heavily wooded hills appear dark, even black: thus their name. East of the hills, across the Cheyenne River, the rapid erosion of sedimentary shale in the past 500,000 years has created the Badlands.

The area's human history goes back 11,000 years. Ancient mammoth hunters were followed by nomadic tribes. The Lakota Sioux, having domesticated horses, prevailed by the 18C and ruled the northern plains until Northwest and Hudson's Bay Company fur-trading posts, on the Red and Missouri Rivers, put the Europeans in control. Beginning in the 1850s, soldiers, miners and homesteaders moved in; European immigrants, who came with the railroad, soon followed them.

In the 1870s, gold was discovered in the Black Hills, the Lakotas' sacred hunting ground. The treaty that had granted them this territory in perpetuity was rendered obsolete, as prospectors rushed in to separate the earth from its treasure. This inevitably led to conflict. The Sioux and Cheyenne prevailed at the Battle of the Little Bighorn in adjacent Montana in 1876, but that was their final hurrah. The massacre at Wounded Knee in 1890 completed the subjugation of the native tribes.

The 20C has seen the growth of tourism, triggered by the sculpting of Mt. Rushmore and establishment of numerous national parks throughout the region. Today, everyone from backpackers to cave explorers, motorcyclists to gamblers, is drawn to the greater Black Hills region.

BLACK HILLS★★

Map p 76   Mountain Standard Time
Tourist Information ☎ 605-355-3700 or www.travelsd.com

The elliptical uplift of the Black Hills, 125mi long and 65mi wide, has a rugged core of granite spires, knobs and mountains. It is flanked in the west by a limestone plateau, framed by the Cheyenne and Belle Fourche Rivers, encircled by steep Hogback Ridge and the appropriately named Red Valley.

Black Hills National Forest cloaks the central hills and covers much of western South Dakota and parts of northeastern Wyoming. It surrounds or abuts Custer State Park, Jewel Cave National Monument, Wind Cave National Park and eight communities, including Deadwood, and approaches the gateway town, Rapid City.

The Black Hills are renowned for their caves. The same geological forces that caused them to uplift, 60 million years ago, cracked the limestone layers deposited by a previous inland ocean. Water seeped in, slowly wearing away the rock into a maze of passages. The "racetrack" of limestone that circles the hills is strewn with hundreds of miles of ancient caverns, constituting the second-longest cave system in the world. Eight caves—two of them administered by the National Park Service—are developed for public viewing.

Historical Notes – For centuries Native Americans came to worship amid these dark, ponderosa-laden hills—as they called them, Paha Sapa, "hills that are black." After a member of Lt. Col. George Custer's expedition discovered gold here in 1874, South Dakota's gold rush began. It wasn't until almost a quarter-century later, in 1897, that President Grover Cleveland established the Black Hills Forest Reserve, later renamed Black Hills National Forest. The Homestake Gold Mine in Lead is the world's oldest continuously operated gold mine.

SIGHTS

★★★ **Mt. Rushmore National Memorial** – Kids IIII *Rte. 244, 3mi west of Keystone.* ✗ ♿ 🅿 ☎ *605-574-2523. www.nps.gov/moru.* Carved from the face of a granite cliff over a period of 14 years (1927-41) by Gutzon Borglum, Mt. Rushmore was intended as a "shrine to democracy," recognizing the country's greatest leaders. Borglum chose to depict four US presidents who brought the nation from colonial times into the 20C—George Washington, first president and commander of the Revolutionary Army; Thomas Jefferson, author of the Declaration of Independence; Abraham Lincoln, whose Civil War leadership restored the Union and ended slavery in the US; and Theodore Roosevelt, whose progressive stance led to key reforms in conservation, business and world trade.

An injection of $56 million since 1993 has vastly upgraded visitor facilities. The **Avenue of Flags**, representing all US states and territories, leads to the **Grand View Terrace**, outdoor amphitheater and **Lincoln Borglum Visitor Center**, which includes a museum, bookstore and theaters. Ten foot historical photos, jackhammers and comparative storyboards tell the story of the making of Mt. Rushmore. Six TV monitors flicker with historical clips; on one of them, visitors can touch an image, depress a plunger and watch a dynamite blast on the screen.

The **Presidential Trail** *(.5mi)* takes walkers to the talus slope of the mountain and around to the Sculptor's Studio. A wooded trail offers a tranquil diversion. In summer, ranger programs include a 30min evening lighting ceremony.

★ **Crazy Horse Memorial** – *US-16/385, 4mi north of Custer.* ✗ *(summer only)* ♿ 🅿 ☎ *605-673-4681. www.crazyhorse.org.* The world's largest sculptural undertaking features the slowly emerging 563ft-high image of Sioux Chief Crazy Horse (c.1842-77) mounted upon his steed. The warrior's face, higher than the Sphinx, was completed in 1998. The colossal carving-in-progress began in 1948 after sculptor Korczak Ziolkowski (1908-82) was invited by Sioux chiefs to create a work to complement Mt. Rushmore; the Sioux wanted "the white man to know the red man has great heroes, too." Ziolkowski's family carries on the project.

Native artisans from many tribes demonstrate their skills in the **Native American Educational and Cultural Center** Kids at the foot of the mountain. The adjacent **Indian Museum of North America** presents traditional crafts and early-20C sepia-tone photos of native life. Sculpture and antiques are on display in Ziolkowski's log studio home. From a verandah, the profile of Crazy Horse's nine-story head is visible in the distance, behind a full-scale model.

★★ **Jewel Cave National Monument** – *US-16, 13mi west of Custer.* ♿ 🅿 ☎ *605-673-2288. www.nps.gov/jeca.* Jewel Cave was declared a national monument in 1908, eight years after it was discovered by prospectors. Since then, spelunkers have mapped more than 120mi of passages, a mere 2 percent of what is estimated to exist. In the world, only the Mammoth Cave system in Kentucky (with more than 350mi mapped) is known to be longer.

The 80min **Scenic Tour**★ starts with a 234ft elevator descent. Visitors then follow a concrete path and aluminum stairways to 370ft below the surface, where it is a constant, cool 49°F. Massive chambers glitter with the calcite formations—elon-

ADDRESS BOOK

Please see explanation on p 64.

Staying and Dining in the Black Hills

Hotel Alex Johnson – *523 6th St., Rapid City.* ✗ ⅇ 🄿 ⤒ ☎ *605-342-1210. www.alexjohnson.com. 143 rooms.* **$$** When Alex Johnson built his seven-story hotel in 1928, he foresaw a showplace for Sioux Indian culture, with hand-painted buffalo tiles and a chandelier made of spears. Each floor honors a tribe, from "Black Spirit Horse" to "White Calf Buffalo." Sample regional cuisine (rainbow trout or buffalo) at the hotel's **Landmark Restaurant**.

Franklin Hotel – *700 Main St., Deadwood.* ✗ 🄿 ☎ *605-578-2241. www.deadwood.net/franklin. 81 rooms.* **$** The historic Franklin has hosted stars since 1903. Rooms are dedicated to movie stars (John Wayne), motorcycle men (Harley Davidson), presidents (William Howard Taft) and rodeo riders (Casey Tibbs). In the antiques-laden lobby, rife with slot machines, is a hand-operated elevator.

Powderhouse Lodge and Restaurant – *US-16A, Keystone.* ✗ ⅇ 🄿 ⤒ ☎ *605-666-4646. www.powderhouselodge.com. 37 rooms.* **$** Once a cache for blasting powder used on Mount Rushmore, the log-cabin Powderhouse also hid bootleg liquor under its tin roof in the 1930s. Today, spirits are served in the tree-branch legs of big oak tables, along with breaded mushrooms, prime rib, and buffalo stew in a homemade bread bowl.

Spearfish Canyon Resort – *US-14A, Spearfish.* ✗ ⅇ 🄿 ☎ *605-584-3435. www.spfcanyon.com. 54 rooms.* **$** This rustic resort is more than a hotel: it has a pioneer-style cultural center with artifacts and antique furniture. One log building houses The **Latchstring Restaurant**, offering Black Hills trout pan-seared, deep-fried or almandine.

gated crystals of dogtooth spar and nailhead spor—for which the cave is named. On the 1hr 45min **Candlelight Tour**, visitors carry candle lanterns while following a half-mile of early explorers' paths. Before going on the very strenuous 4hr **Spelunking Tour**, visitors must first show they can squeeze through an 8.5in-high, 24in-wide block on the patio.

★★Custer State Park – *US-16A & Rte. 87. Park headquarters are about 23mi south of Mt. Rushmore.* ⚠ ✗ ⅇ 🄿 ☎ *605-255-4515. www.state.sd.us/sdparks.* One of the largest state parks in the US, Custer includes 114sq mi of swelling blond grasslands, prairie swales, lush forest and granite peaks. Elk, deer, pronghorn, bighorn sheep and songbirds—and a publicly owned bison herd of 1,400—are at home among wildflowers, cacti, pine and spruce.

Three scenic driving routes wind through the park, two of them segments of the 66mi **Peter Norbeck Scenic Byway** *(US-16A, Rtes. 87, 89 & 244)*. As governor in 1919, Norbeck spurred the creation of park. The 18mi **Wildlife Loop Road★★** runs south and west from the State Game Lodge to Blue Bell Resort, with wide vistas of grasslands and forested slopes, plus bison, pronghorn, prairie dogs and the park's resident "begging" burros. The 17mi **Iron Mountain Road★★** *(US-16A)*, which extends to Mt. Rushmore, features several pigtail bridges designed in the 1930s to span steep climbs in short distances. Three narrow tunnels frame Rushmore as drivers pass through them. Slender granite peaks—including 7,242ft Harney Peak, highest point in South Dakota—flank the spectacular 14mi **Needles Highway★★** *(Rte. 87)*, which traverses the northwestern panhandle of the park. The road threads around hairpin curves and past pinnacle-like rock formations, one of which resembles the eye of a needle. Just off this highway is the long-established **Black Hills Playhouse** *(Rte. 753;* ☎ *605-255-4141)*, whose summer offerings range from drama to comedy to musicals, from Shakespeare to Andrew Lloyd Webber.

★★Wind Cave National Park – *US-385, 10mi north of Hot Springs & 22mi south of Custer.* ⚠ ⅇ 🄿 ☎ *605-745-4600. www.nps.gov/wica.* Beneath a single square mile of surface land is an underground wilderness considered one of the 10 longest caves in the world. Wind Cave's 85 surveyed miles of passages may represent just 5 percent of its entire subterranean system.

Although Indian legends addressed holes that "blew wind," the cave's recorded discovery came in 1881, when a man named Tom Bingham, curious about a whistling sound, found a hole that expelled a wind so strong it blew his hat off. In 1903, Wind Cave was the first cave included in the national park system.

Ranger-led tours range from the 1hr, 150-stair **Garden of Eden Tour** to the 4hr, lots-of-crawling **Caving Tour**. Close walls, narrow passageways and low ceilings make the Wind Cave experience more intimate than that of Jewel Cave.

Unique, honeycomb-like boxwork is the trademark of Wind Cave. Created by calcite left by dissolved limestone, boxwork was named for its resemblance to old postal sorters—a diagonal crisscross of fragile-looking lines of calcite protruding from walls. A 44sq-mi wilderness spreads above Wind Cave—two-thirds of it mixed-grass prairie, the remainder ponderosa-pine forest.

★★ **Deadwood** – *US-14A, 13mi west of Sturgis.* An adage of the Old West is that "dead men tell no tales," but Deadwood tells a great many of them. Nestled in the northern Black Hills, the town—once the wildest gold camp in the West—has undergone the largest historic restoration effort in the US.

By the spring of 1876, within a year and a half of the discovery of gold, 25,000 people had swarmed down the hillsides of Deadwood Gulch. Fortune seekers, cavalrymen, Chinese laborers, trollops and gun-slinging gamblers established a main street of tents, stores, banks, 53 saloons and 33 brothels. Fifty-two trains came and left each week.

Gambling was banned in 1905, but was legalized again in 1989. With it came a resurgence of money to revitalize the town. Today visitors can be entertained 24 hours a day with nightclubs, dinner theaters, museums and other attractions. Buildings that were once banks, brothels and gaming halls are now shops, restaurants and, well, gaming halls—80 in all. Extensive Victorian architecture lines a dozen downtown blocks, especially **Main Street★★**. At the **Deadwood History and Information Center** *(US-14A; ☎ 605-578-1102),* visitors can pick up a "Historic Deadwood Walking Tour" map. The **Adams Historical Museum★** *(54 Sherman St.; ☎ 605-578-1714)* exhibits a 7.75oz gold nugget found by "Potato Creek Johnny" Perrett in 1929. The **Old Style Saloon No. 10** *(657 Main St.; ☎ 605-578-3346),* where "Wild Bill" Hickok *(see sidebar)* met his demise, is now filled with antique paraphernalia; the floor is cloaked in sawdust, once a ploy to recover gold dust. The **Broken Boot Gold Mine** Kids *(Upper Main St. & US-14A; ☎ 605-578-9997)* offers underground tours and gold panning.

★★ **Homestake Gold Mine** – *160 W. Main St., Lead, 3mi southwest of Deadwood.* ℗ ☎ 605-584-3110. www.homestaketours.com. The world's oldest continuously operated gold mine is just uphill from Deadwood in the town of **Lead★** *(LEED),* whose old miners' homes crawl up steep hillsides. The Homestake extracts gold from one of the richest veins of gold ever discovered—by three prospectors, in 1876. They sold the mine to a San Francisco syndicate, which incorporated Homestake Mining Co. with $10 million capital. By 1945, 40 million tons of ore had been taken from the once-solid mountain. Mining continues 1.5mi beneath the surface. The heart of the Homestake is the **Open Cut★★**, an enormous pit 1,800ft wide, 4,500ft long and 968ft deep.

■ **Wild Bill Hickok**

One hot August night in 1876, US marshal and army scout James Butler Hickok was invited to join a poker game in Deadwood's Saloon No. 10. The only empty chair faced away from the door. "Wild Bill," as Hickok was known, wasn't happy about this, but he sat down amid the chiding of his fellow players and ordered a gin. After losing heavily, Hickok borrowed $15 from the bartender and studied his next hand. A drifter named Jack McCall strolled into the bar, drew a rusty revolver and fired. Hickok, 39, died instantly. He dropped a pair of black aces and eights, since known among poker players as "the dead man's hand."

Wild Bill confessed to having killed between 15 and 100 men before he was 27—"but never unless in absolute self-defense, or in the performance of an official duty," he claimed. "I never, in my life, took any mean advantage of an enemy... But I may die yet with my boots on."

Sharp-shooting Wild Bill was in Deadwood for only 67 days, but his legacy colors the city and, indeed, the Black Hills to this day. In the **Adams Museum** *(above)* is an original pencil sketch of Hickok by artist Nathaniel Wyeth. Hickok's murder is reenacted in a mini drama at **Old Style Saloon No. 10** *(above)* and in a diorama, complete with honky-tonk music and gunshots, at the **Journey Museum** *(below)* in Rapid City. On Lee Street in Deadwood stands a bust of Wild Bill, a gift of Crazy Horse sculptor Korczak Ziolkowski.

Wild Bill Hickok is buried in **Mt. Moriah Cemetery★**, Deadwood's "Boot Hill," next to Martha "Calamity Jane" Canary, America's most famous bullwhip-toting dame. One-hour trolley tours depart Main Street for the cemetery, which holds thousands of tombstones engraved with epigraphs such as "Died of Softening of the Brain."

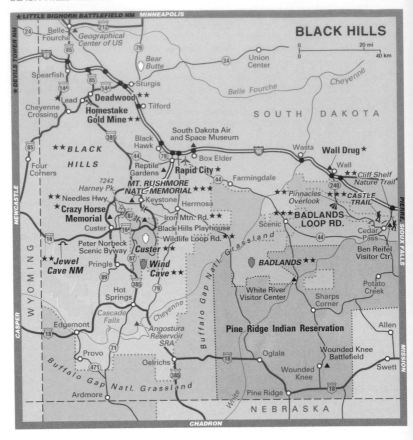

★ Rapid City – *US-16 & Rte. 79 at I-90.* ☎ *605-343-1744. www.rapidcityvb.com.*
The principal Black Hills gateway community was established on a foundation of
mining, lumber and ranching, but trade and tourism now support its 58,000 people. Besides sights of the hills, there are numerous attractions. One of the best is
the **Black Hills Reptile Gardens** Kids *(US-16, 6mi south of downtown;* ☎ *605-342-*
5873), where exotic snakes and lizards share a tropical garden. The **South Dakota**
Air and Space Museum *(Ellsworth Air Force Base, I-90 Exit 66;* ☎ *605-385-5188)* displays stealth bombers and other aircraft.

★★ The Journey Museum – Kids *222 New York St.* ♿ 🅿 ☎ *605-394-6923. www.journey-*
museum.org. State-of-the-art multimedia techniques relate the 2.5-million-year
history of the Black Hills region. This expansive building incorporates the collections of five separate museums—the **Museum of Geology★** of the South Dakota
School of Mines and Technology; the **Archaeological Research Center** of the State Historical Society; the **Sioux Indian Museum★★** of the US Department of the Interior; the
Duhamel Plains Indian Collection; and the **Minnilusa Pioneer Museum★★**.
Visitors watch a 14min orientation film in a 150-seat theater, then continue
through the exhibit area on self-guided audio tours with Lakota or American nar-
rators. Provocative displays offer insight into the minds of Indian warriors and
the secrets of the Sioux's sacred Black Hills. A resident archaeologist answers
questions about prehistoric digs. A hologramic Lakota storyteller, illuminated story
walls and ambient sounds enhance exhibits.

EXCURSIONS

★ Devils Tower National Monument – *Wyoming Rte. 110 off Rte. 24; 10mi*
south of Hulett WY & 52mi southwest of Belle Fourche SD via Rte. 34. △ ♿ 🅿
☎ *307-467-5501. www.nps.gov/deto.* Sacred to Native Americans, Devils
Tower was designated a national monument by President Theodore Roosevelt
in 1906. The fluted monolith rises 867ft from its base; the top covers 1.5
acres. A scored butte with a talus slope, Devils Tower is the core of an

igneous intrusion that became exposed as surrounding sedimentary rock eroded. Today it is most readily identified as the landmark for interplanetary spacecraft in the 1977 Steven Spielberg movie *Close Encounters of the Third Kind*. The first ascent of the peak was made on July 4, 1893, as more than 1,000 spectators watched; today 5,000 climbers a year challenge themselves on its vertical rock walls.

Although the parking lot gets crowded, the butte is worth the bother, especially for those who hike the paved, interpretive 1.3mi **Tower Trail★** around its base. The more rugged 3mi **Red Beds Trail**, from which the Bighorn Mountains can be seen 150mi to the west, also has a trailhead in front of the Visitor Center.

★**Little Bighorn Battlefield National Monument** – *US-212, Crow Agency MT; 15mi south of Hardin MT & 201mi northwest of Belle Fourche SD.* ♿ 🅿 ☎ *406-638-2621. www.nps.gov/libi.* Here on June 25-26, 1876, in one of the last armed efforts to preserve their way of life, Lakota Sioux and Cheyenne warriors killed 272 US cavalrymen, including Lt. Col. George A. Custer. Natives know the conflict as the Battle of Greasy Grass; Americans often refer to it as Custer's Last Stand.

In fact, it was the last major victory for Native Americans in the western US. Visitors can peruse the maps, photos and dioramas in the **visitor center and museum**, and roam outside among memorials and a national cemetery. In late June each year, the battle is reenacted at Hardin, 15mi north of the battlefield, and at Garryowen, 5mi south.

■ Sturgis Rally and Races

Bikers from all over North America know South Dakota as the home of a motorcycle rally that is among the largest in the world. Every year during the second week of August, an estimated 350,000 riders roll across the US and Canada to the little town of Sturgis (population 6,700), 27mi northwest of Rapid City.

The event originated in 1938, when motorcycle-shop owner J.C. "Pappy" Hoel held the first rally with 19 racers. Today poker runs, drag races, hill climbs, road tours and riding exhibitions are among events on a full seven-day schedule. Even nonbikers attend to see what's new in the motorcycle world and to view more than 100 antique bikes—including the oldest unrestored running 1907 Harley-Davidson and actor Steve McQueen's 1915 Cyclone—at the **National Motorcycle Museum & Hall of Fame** *(2438 Junction Ave.;* ☎ *605-347-4875).* For more information: www.rally.sturgis.sd.us.

Ready for the Sturgis Rally

BADLANDS★★

Map p 76   Mountain Standard Time
Tourist Information ☎ 605-355-3600

The play of dawn's light tints the rock faces a gentle bluish-pink that warms to red, gradually covering existing layers of purple shale, chestnut sand, orange iron oxide and white volcanic ash. Dark shadows lie sharp off the wind-honed edges of the buttressed hills. While the Badlands boast a remarkable geological history, it is the rare and not-so-subtle beauty of a landscape that changes seasonally, and even hourly, that visitors are compelled to see again and again.

Although the Badlands are eroding at a pace of an inch per year, modern tourists needn't worry: Another half-million years will pass before the fantastic shapes and colors disappear. The range of spires and sawtooth ridges—a sculpted mudstone wall roughly 1,000ft at its highest—runs 90mi from South Dakota into Nebraska, and is bounded on both sides by prairies.

Historical Notes – The term "Badlands" was bestowed by the Lakota Sioux, who called the area *mako sica*. French trappers referred to the country as *les mauvaises terres à traverser*—"bad lands to cross." Fossils as old as 77 million years have been unearthed here; of particular note are those of early mammals, such as the rhinoceros-like *brontotheres* from the Eocene era.

SIGHTS

★★ **Badlands National Park** – *Rte. 240 (Badlands Loop Rd.), 8mi south of I-90 Exit 110 at Wall, 51mi east of Rapid City.* △ ✕ *(summer only)* ⚹ ◨ ☎ *605-433-5361. www.nps.gov/badl.* Most visitors see only one strip of this 375sq-mi park, but it is the most dramatic. The 39mi **Badlands Loop Road**★★★ traverses the northern rim of the Badlands, where prairie grasslands give way to buttes and hoodoos. The road passes long blond grasses that shimmer in the wind like a shaken sheet, then straddles and dips down into the gullies. Wildflowers speckle narrow stream canyons, steep and barren or intricately carved slopes, high-ridged and tiny sodded buttes. **Pinnacles Overlook**★★ is a sweeping viewpoint to the south. Formations are bleached white on top, then bleed pinkish to a tawny yellow. Tiny white flowers—Hood's phlox—bloom in the broad expanse of gray. The **Castle Trail**★★★ *(4.5mi)* is spectacular in early morning when the moonscape valley and pointed spires get their first dose of light. The **Cliff Shelf Nature Trail**★★ *(.5mi)* is popular for its shady juniper trees. The boardwalk winds through a "slump," a wet place in dry country, where water retention has created an oasis of green.

Four units comprise Badlands National Park. Park headquarters are located at the **Ben Reifel Visitor Center** *(Cedar Pass, 8mi south of I-90 Exit 131),* at the east end of the park road. The North Unit, through which Badlands Loop Road runs, and the adjoining wilderness Sage Creek Unit are surrounded by **Buffalo Gap National Grassland**. The undeveloped Stronghold and Palmer Creek Units are within the Pine Ridge Indian Reservation, to the south; they are served by the **White River Visitor Center** *(☎ 605-455-2878, 25mi north of Wounded Knee, open Jun-Aug).*

Badlands National Park

Pine Ridge Indian Reservation – *US-18 & connecting routes south of Badlands National Park.* ☎ *605-867-5301.* The home of the Oglala Sioux tribe covers nearly 3,000sq mi of western South Dakota, south of I-90 and southeast of the Black Hills. About 20,000 Oglala live on the reservation, established in 1878. The chief attraction is the **Wounded Knee battlefield** *(Rte. 27 just east of Rte. 28),* a landmark in American Indian history.

By 1890, the Sioux had embraced the teachings of Paiute medicine man Wovoka, who had a vision that the white man would vanish and bison would return as the Indians' ancestors rose from the dead. But, Wovoka said, Native Americans must perform the ritual Ghost Dance to show their faith. A skeptical US government assigned troops to subdue the Ghost Dancers. In late 1890, two weeks after Chief Sitting Bull was killed during a "precautionary" arrest further north, Chief Big Foot and his band left Pine Ridge to hide in the Badlands. The cavalry intercepted them. On December 29, as troops searched the band for weapons, a rifle was fired, setting off a barrage that didn't stop until Big Foot and some 250 Oglala men, women and children were dead. Thirty soldiers also died, many from their own crossfire. A gray stone monument and wooden sign today mark the massacre site. There are plans for a national memorial park.

★**Wall Drug** – **Kids** *510 Main St., Wall; 51mi east of Rapid City off I-90 Exit 109 or 110.* ✕ ♿ 🅿 ☎ *605-279-2175. www.walldrug.com.* Wall Drug is the world's most famous "drug store," with visitors lured by signs as far away as Easter Island. Don't expect just a pharmacy. Behind a Western storefront and block-long awning is a 76,000sq-ft space with over more than 20 shops, filled with 1,400 historical photos, 6,000 pairs of cowboy boots, wildlife exhibits and more. An expansive Western art collection is displayed in five dining rooms. In the backyard is a children's play area with ice-water wells and a roaring, steaming 80ft **Tyrannosaurus** that sends toddlers running every 12min.

Since the 1930s, when Ted and Dorothy Hustead began offering free ice water to travelers, three generations of Husteads have turned a faltering pharmacy into a tourist oasis. Wall Drug greets more than 15,000 visitors a day during the busy summer season and generates more than $11 million in annual sales.

EXCURSION

Pierre – *US-14, US-83 & Rte. 34. 188mi east of Rapid City. Central Time Zone.* ⚠ ✕ ♿ 🅿 ☎ *605-773-3301. www.pierrechamber.com.* Seven other towns in South Dakota are larger than the quaint state capital, located near the geographical center of the state. Some 13,000 people live in Pierre *(pronounced "peer").* The town sits on the banks of the Missouri River just below meandering **Lake Oahe**, which extends 231mi upstream into North Dakota.

The four-story **South Dakota State Capitol** *(500 E. Capitol Ave.;* ☎ *605-773-3765)* is a modified Greek structure with Ionic columns. Built in 1910 of native fieldstone, Indiana limestone and Italian marble, it was restored in 1989. Unique to the building is its terrazzo flooring: The 66 contributing Italian artisans were told to place a blue signature tile wherever they liked.

NORTH DAKOTA★

Michelin map 491 I, J, K, 4, 5   Central and Mountain Standard Times
Tourist Information ☎ 701-328-2874 or www.ndtourism.com

North Dakota typifies the Great Plains—from the small lakes and forested hills of the glaciated north, where every mile has a pair of mallards in a bulrush-buttressed pothole, to the rugged badlands of the Little Missouri and the rolling hills that cross into South Dakota. This is a land where ranchers are more likely to herd their cattle on all-terrain vehicles (ATVs) than on horseback, of small towns that boast Western-façade storefronts and bear-trap door handles. It is a land of climate extremes, of frigid winter blizzards and violent summer thunderstorms. But the wide open spaces also boast a stark beauty. Outdoor recreation, prolific wildlife and vast fields of grain attract visitors from near and far.

Historical Notes – Inhabited by Native Americans for at least 15,000 years, the state's high plains were visited by European fur traders in the mid-18C. After the Louisiana Purchase in 1803, explorers Meriwether Lewis and William Clark wintered with the Mandan tribe on the Missouri River, where they were joined by Sacagawea, the Shoshone woman who helped guide them to the Pacific. The region developed slowly until the 1870s, when the advent of the railroad brought many wheat-farming homesteaders to the area. Statehood came in 1889. Since the late 1950s, multitudes of oil derricks have dotted the landscape.

SIGHTS

★★Theodore Roosevelt National Park – *Off I-94 & US-85 between Medora & Watford City (3 units).* ⚠ ♿ 🅿 ☎ *701-623-4466. www.nps.gov/thro.* Theodore Roosevelt once said that, had it not been for his experiences in North Dakota, he never would have become US president. Such is the power of this park's savage beauty. The 110sq mi park is backdropped by badlands, run through with river-bottom cottonwoods, and flanked by brush and prairie. The Little Missouri River links its South, Elkhorn Ranch and North Units.

Bands of lignite coal, petrified trees and fossil-rich bentonite clay began piling one atop another 58 million years ago. Lightning can ignite underground fires that turn clay, silt and sand to hard rock in this massive geological torte. Erosion—by wind, water and ice—is the lazy artist, paring down softer rock, leaving behind the razor-sharp ridges, scoria-red hillsides and rugged buttes now called badlands.

★★South Unit – *Rte. 10 Bypass off I-94, Medora, 16mi west of Belfield.* ☎ *701-623-4466. Mountain Standard Time.* By far the most visited unit, if only for its proximity to the interstate, this area is best seen on a paved 36mi scenic loop drive. **Scoria Point Overlook** and **Boicourt Overlook** offer panoramas of yellow, gray and burnt-red buttes. **Wind Canyon Trail** *(.2mi)* leads along the very steep edge of a ridge to views of sculpted canyon walls. Wild horses grazing upland plateaus may be a vision to behold, but prairie dogs are the darlings of the park. The small rodents live in colonies that number in the thousands, entertaining visitors with their high-pitched squeaks and plump scurrying bodies.

Behind the **Medora Visitor Center** is Theodore Roosevelt's original Maltese Cross Cabin, restored and relocated here. Inquire about access to the undeveloped site of **Elkhorn Ranch** *(35mi north of Medora)*, where foundation blocks are all that remain of Roosevelt's 1885 ranch. Part of the backcountry route may require fording the Little Missouri, depending upon the road taken.

★★North Unit – *US-85, 16mi south of Watford City.* ☎ *701-842-2333. Central Standard Time.* Dramatically overlooking the broad plains of the Little Missouri, a 14mi scenic drive climbs to Oxbow Overlook, 500ft above the river. Several turnouts offer viewpoints along the road. Five trails, ranging from the **Little Mo Nature Trail** *(1mi)* to the **Achenbach Trail** *(16mi)*, lead through river woodlands, grassy hills and badlands. A 1.5mi segment of the Achenbach from Oxbow Overlook approaches **Sperati Point★**, the narrowest gateway in the badlands.

★Fort Union Trading Post National Historical Site – *Rte. 1804 (Lewis & Clark Trail) 25mi southwest of Williston. Central Standard Time.* ♿ 🅿 ☎ *701-572-9083. www.nps.gov/fous.* The 18ft palisades of Fort Union gleam white in the middle of a high embankment near the confluence of the Yellowstone and Missouri Rivers. Inside the reconstructed fort, the setting is dominated by the manager's **Bourgeois House**, a lavish reminder of the thriving trade sustained here by John Jacob Astor's American Fur Company. From 1828 to 1867, Native Americans exchanged beaver pelts and other furs for cloth, Sheffield knives and Venetian beads. Exhibits in the Bourgeois House, now the fort visitor center, trace the history of the fur trade at Fort Union and in North America. Living-history demonstrations are frequently offered in summer.

United Tribes Powwow Celebrants, Bismarck

Bismarck – *I-94 & US-83.* ☎ *701-222-4308. Central Standard Time.* Established as a rail camp in 1872, Bismarck boomed as a Missouri riverboat port. It was named for German Chancellor Otto von Bismarck. Now a city of 54,000, it is an agricultural center and nexus for water sports on Lakes Oahe and Sakakawea, to its south and north. Its highlight is the stark **North Dakota State Capitol** *(600 E. Boulevard Ave.;* ☎ *701-328-2471),* a 19-story limestone structure built in 1933. Its Art Deco centerpiece is the high-ceilinged Memorial Hall, with Belgian black-marble walls and 12ft lights resembling wheat shafts.

★ **North Dakota Heritage Center** – 🄺🄸🄳🅂 *612 E. Boulevard Ave.* ♿ 🄿 ☎ *701-328-2666. www.state.nd.us/hist.* Exhibits at this museum of history and natural history, on the south side of the capitol grounds, explore Northern Plains life—beginning with the State Fossil Collection and continuing to the present day. Displays in the Main Gallery include a superb exhibit on North Dakota birds and their eggs, a mastodon skeleton and examples of Native American culture.

★ **Fort Abraham Lincoln State Park** – 🄺🄸🄳🅂 *Rte. 1806, 7mi south of Mandan.* ⚠ 🄿 ☎ *701-663-4758.* Spread across 1,000 acres at the confluence of the Heart and Missouri Rivers opposite Bismarck, this park combines history and recreation. There are three primary sites. **Cavalry Square** includes the Custer House, from which Lt. Col. George Custer set out in 1876 for his "last stand" at the Little Bighorn. Costumed guides offer tours of the home and other structures in Fort Abraham Lincoln, abandoned in 1891 and later restored. Portions of **On-A-Slant Indian Village**, including four Mandan earth lodges used from the mid-16C to mid-18C, have been reconstructed. High on a hill are the blockhouses of an old **Infantry Post**, with an interpretive center nearby.

■ The Lewis and Clark Expedition

The 1803 Louisiana Purchase from Napoleonic France gave US President Thomas Jefferson cause to commission a geographic and scientific expedition to explore the new land. The two men who led the expedition—Meriwether Lewis, Jefferson's personal secretary, and William Clark, a career soldier—have forever since been inextricably linked in American minds.

The Corps of Discovery set off from St. Louis on May 14, 1804. It returned 28 months later, on September 23, 1806, after traveling more than 8,000ml up the Missouri River, across the Rocky Mountains, down the Snake and Columbia Rivers, and back again. Though not the first to reach the Pacific Ocean overland from the east—Canadian explorer Alexander McKenzie had done that a decade earlier—Lewis and Clark succeeded in making the unknown known to a growing nation and opening the gates to further exploration and settlement.

As the 200th anniversary of the expedition approaches, facilities along the **Lewis and Clark National Historic Trail** *(☎ 608-264-5610; www.nps.gov/lecl)* are being improved in all 11 states along the explorers' route. In the Dakotas, visitors can follow the Missouri River by car, boat or foot, stopping at interpretive signs, museums and visitor centers. In many places, the trail is geographically as well as historically spectacular.

The explorers negotiated passage upriver with Sioux warriors near the site of modern Pierre, at the mouth of the Bad River, in September 1804. They camped near On-A-Slant Village in October and spent that winter beside the Missouri across from its confluence with the Knife River. Exhibits at the **North Dakota Lewis and Clark Interpretive Center** *(US-83 & Rte. 200-A, Washburn;* ☎ *701-462-8535, www.fortmandan.org)* include a 55ft cottonwood being carved into a canoe, and artifacts of every tribe the party encountered between the Plains and Pacific. An art gallery contains a full set of Karl Bodmer's prints, realistic images of upper Midwest Indian cultures and lifestyles. **Fort Mandan Historic Site** *(2mi west)* replicates the triangular fort where the party wintered.

At **Knife River Indian Villages National Historic Site** *(Rte. 37, .5mi north of Stanton;* ☎ *701-745-3309),* 3mi farther upriver, a 15min film describes the Hidatsa Mandan tribe that helped Lewis and Clark through that harsh winter. Eleven miles of trails weave past three buried villages and a re-created earth lodge. One village was the home of French interpreter Toussaint Charbonneau, who signed on with the expedition here, and his Shoshone wife, Sacagawea, who guided the Corps west and smoothed relations with Sioux and other tribes.

NEBRASKA PANHANDLE★

Michelin map 491 I 7, 8   Mountain Standard Time
Tourist Information ☎ 308-632-2133 or www.westnebraska.com.

Three easterly flowing rivers help define the Nebraska Panhandle, which extends 135mi from the Black Hills to the Colorado border. In the north, above the White River, the white cliffs and buttes of rugged Pine Ridge extend in a 100mi arc to South Dakota's badlands. Farther south, the Niobrara River slices past 19-million-year-old fossils and through the expansive ranch and dune country of the Sand Hills. Overlooking the North Platte River, the geological formations of Chimney Rock and Scotts Bluff were significant milestones for westbound travelers.

Historical Notes – Western Nebraska was an important 19C transition area from the Great Plains to the Rocky Mountains. The Oregon Trail followed the North Platte to Fort Laramie, Wyoming; fur merchants plied their trade farther north, on the White River. After the 1874 gold strike in the Black Hills, Fort Robinson was constructed to defend settlers and travelers from Indian attacks.

SIGHTS

The Museum of the Fur Trade – *US-20, 3mi east of Chadron.* ♿ �🅿 ☎ *308-432-3843. www.furtrade.org.* An important collection of 6,000 pieces represents every type of object exchanged by Indians and European-Americans in the 18-19C fur trade. Displays include 234 trade guns, the largest collection of those made for the Indian trade between 1750 and 1900. Behind the museum is a small earthbound trading post, built in 1833 and operated independently by James Bordeaux for the Sioux trade until 1872.

★**Fort Robinson State Park** – *US-20, 3mi west of Crawford.* △ ✗ ♿ �🅿 ☎ *308-665-2900.* Nebraska's largest and most historic state park, Fort Robinson covers 34sq mi in the heart of the Pine Ridge region. Established in 1874, the fort was in active use until 1948. Many pivotal events of the late-19C Indian Wars occurred here, including the 1877 killing of Chief Crazy Horse and the 1879 Cheyenne Outbreak, an abortive escape attempt by 149 imprisoned and starving Cheyenne men, women and children. In the late 19C and early 20C, this was home to the African-American garrison known as the Buffalo Soldiers.
The **Fort Robinson State Park Inn & Lodge**, in the 1909 enlisted men's barracks, serves as a visitor center. Tour trains and walking tours depart from this point. Opposite, in the 1905 post headquarters facing the parade grounds, the **Fort Robinson Museum** has exhibits on military history, including an unusual account of the war dogs trained to sniff out mines, carry messages and pull sleds.

★**Agate Fossil Beds National Monument** – *River Rd. off Rte. 29, 44mi north of Scottsbluff.* ♿ �🅿 ☎ *308-668-2211. www.nps.gov/agfo.* Some 3,000 acres of grassy plains surround a striking visitor center nestled beside the Niobrara River. Preserved are the 19-million-year-old fossil remains of rhinoceroses and other animals that roamed these plains more than 40 million years after dinosaurs disappeared. A life-size diorama describes an ancient waterhole, the remains of which are accessible via the **Fossil Hills Trail** *(2mi),* just outside. Another highlight is the **James H. Cook Collection★**, an impressive display of over 100 Oglala Sioux artifacts. The pieces include a whetstone that once belonged to Crazy Horse. The **Daemonelix Trail** *(1mi),* off Route 29 near the west entrance to the monument, features preserved corkscrew-like burrows of a palaeocastor or prehistoric beaver.

★**Scotts Bluff National Monument** – *Rte. 92, 5mi southwest of Scottsbluff.* ☎ *308-436-4340. www.nps.gov/scbl.* Immense sandstone and clay bluffs stand some 800ft higher than the North Platte River. A section of the Oregon Trail runs past the visitor center at their foot. Beginning in 1838, following a corridor of tracks long used by Indians and, later, European trappers, waves of wagon convoys followed the 2,170mi Oregon Trail across the plains. Along with Chimney Rock, 25mi east, these 20-million-year-old bluffs marked the start of the last two-thirds of the journey for more than 350,000 emigrants.
The **Oregon Trail Museum** offers interpretive exhibits along with work by noted pioneer photographer-artist William Henry Jackson. A 1.6mi paved road leads to a parking area atop the summit. The **Saddle Rock Trail,** also 1.6mi, takes hikers to the same place for sweeping **views★★** over the North Platte Valley.

Chimney Rock National Historical Site – *Rte. 92, 23mi east of Scottsbluff.* ♿ �🅿 ☎ *308-586-2581. www.nps.gov/chro.* Westbound pioneers scrawled descriptions in their journals of this unique spire visible along both sides of the North Platte. Designated a national site in 1956, the grounds include a visitor center and museum, whose windows frame the 350ft spire of Chimney Rock about .75mi away.

Canyonlands

Delicate Arch, Arches National Park

The dimension of vast and distorted space is the first thing that strikes visitors to southern Utah's Canyonlands region. As far as the eye can see, for hundreds of miles in all directions, undeveloped land extends in undulating contours and sharp angles, its vivid colors bent in whimsical and tortured shapes. Earth, water and sky hold sway here. Visitors come for the experience of nature, not of man, and southern Utah delivers on an epic scale.

Most of this land is owned by the federal government, and much is protected for public recreational use. Enormous Canyonlands National Park is split into three distinct areas by the confluence of the Colorado and Green Rivers, its colorful rock strata witness to billions of years of geologic history. Arches National Park is a fantastic landscape of wind and water-sculpted rocks, formed into improbable swirls, graceful freestanding arches and impressive natural bridges spanning hundreds of feet. Capitol Reef National Park, whose central feature is a 100mi-long rock form known as Waterpocket Fold, is an isolated moonscape of buttes, mesas and other monoliths that stand 500ft or higher above a level desert floor.

Bryce Canyon National Park features an astonishing concentration of dizzying, multicolored rock spires and evocatively shaped rocks called hoodoos. Cedar Breaks National Monument is a mini-Bryce Canyon, but without the crowds. The canyons of Zion National Park are surrounded by cliffs as high as 3,000ft. Water only now seeping through the porous sandstone to the canyon floor fell as rainfall atop these cliffs 1,500 years ago.

At Natural Bridges National Monument, three mammoth stone spans are set in a convoluted network of narrow canyons. The Navajo tribe considers Rainbow Bridge National Monument a sacred place; it is now most easily reached via boat on Lake Powell, centerpiece of Glen Canyon National Recreation Area. The serenely beautiful reservoir was created in the 1960s when the controversial Glen Canyon Dam was constructed on the Colorado River at Page, Arizona, just below the Utah border. Grand Staircase-Escalante National Monument, dedicated in 1996, adjoins Glen Canyon and provides many more thousands of square miles of natural lands.

Cities are few and far between. St. George is historically important as the earliest Mormon colony in southern Utah, as directed by church leader Brigham Young. Cedar City hosts a renowned annual Shakespearean festival. Across the state, Moab, despite its biblical name, might more appropriately be called Mecca, considering its importance to river rafters and mountain bikers as an outdoor-recreation center.

ADDRESS BOOK

Please see explanation on p 64.

Staying in the Canyonlands

Bryce Canyon National Park Lodge – *Bryce Canyon National Park UT.* 🍴 ♿ 🅿 ☎ *435-834-5361. www.amfac.com. 114 rooms.* **$$** A shingled roof, stone piers and green shutters reflect the restoration of this 1930s National Historic Landmark to its former rustic elegance. Its porch overlooks the brilliant colors of Bryce's famed hoodoos—tall, red-rock pinnacles. Exhibits on park history are integrated right into the design.

Boulder Mountain Lodge – *Junction of Burr Trail and Rte. 12, Boulder UT.* 🍴 🅿 ☎ *435-335-7460. 20 rooms. www.boulder-utah.com.* **$** Boulder was the final community in America to have postal trucks replace mule trains for mail delivery. This complex of detached buildings, surrounding a lake and bird sanctuary, still seems undiscovered. Rooms have wooden furniture, quilts and exposed beams and an eclectic architectural amalgam of sandstone and timber.

Grist Mill Inn – *64 S. 300 East, Monticello UT.* 🅿 ☎ *435-587-2597. www.gristmillinn.com. 11 rooms.* **$** Built in 1933 as a flour mill, this wooden building has been restored as a B&B. Both the main house and neighboring Granary are outfitted with claw-footed tubs, floral patterns and iron beds. There is a quaint book- and crafts store (The Flour Shoppe) next door.

Sunflower Hill B&B Inn – *185 N. 300 East, Moab UT.* 🅿 ☎ *435-259-2974. www.sunflowerhill.com. 11 rooms.* **$** The wooded pathways and flower gardens of this charming house provide a quiet retreat from the bustle of downtown Moab, three blocks away. Guests relax on wicker chairs on the covered porch, savor the stone fireplace in the living room, or just collapse into antique iron beds.

Valley of the Gods B&B – *East of Rte. 261, north of Mexican Hat UT.* 🅿 ☎ *970-749-1164. www.hkhinc.com/vog.html. 4 rooms.* **$** This solar- and wind-powered stone ranch house is located in a mini-Monument Valley just north of the San Juan River. Visitors take in the sights of Red Rock country from the long front porch, or relax in rooms with exposed-rock walls and wood stoves.

Dining in the Canyonlands

Cafe Diablo – *599 W. Main St., Torrey UT.* ☎ *435-425-3070.* **$$$ Southwestern.** Local trout gets a pumpkin-seed crust, poblano peppers are buried beneath hominy, rattlesnake cakes are topped with rosemary aioli: At Cafe Diablo, everything has a desert twist. Chef Gary Pankow's "painted chicken" is coated with honey, lime and tomatillo salsa, and the chipotle-fired ribs heat up diners' tongues.

Adriana's – *164 S. 100 West, Cedar City UT.* ☎ *435-865-1234.* **$$ Continental.** Located in a 1916 Victorian mansion, this Olde English-style eatery offers steaks, chicken and chops served by waitresses in Renaissance costume. Strains of Medieval English music accompany dishes like tenderloin of pork with apricot-ginger sauce and grilled Rocky Mountain trout with roasted almonds. The restaurant is especially popular during the summer Shakespearean festival.

Slick Rock Cafe – *5 N. Main St., Moab UT.* ☎ *435-259-8004.* **$$ Southwestern.** This hip spot, with murals and petroglyph replicas on walls, is a hangout for mountain bikers and river rafters. Diners may munch a platter of "Macho Nachos" at a table overlooking Main Street activity, or dine inside on Utah red trout with herbed cornmeal or a chili verde burrito stuffed with pork, black beans and rice.

BRYCE-ZION AREA★★★

Considered by some to be the most appealing area in all of Utah, this region contains three national parks (Zion, Bryce Canyon and Capitol Reef), two national monuments (Grand Staircase-Escalante and Cedar Breaks), stunning state parks and national forests, accented by an annual dose of Shakespeare in Cedar City.

Considerably more developed than the Colorado River canyonlands to the east and south, this area actually has a small metropolitan center. St. George is the largest city in southern Utah; nearby, once-small towns like Hurricane are rapidly transforming into booming desert retirement communities.

Still, the dominant features for most visitors are the unique and spectacular natural lands. It's often hard to tell where parks begin and end: The beauty of the region is nearly equal outside their boundaries.

SIGHTS

★ **St. George** – *I-15 Exit 8.* ✗♿🅿 ☎ *435-628-1658*. Mormons sent south from Salt Lake City settled St. George during the Civil War. Unable to procure cotton from the American South for textiles during the war, the pioneers grew their own in this hot, dry climate. Since that time, the region has been known as "Utah's Dixie." The city of 46,000—two hours' drive from Las Vegas but five hours from Salt Lake City—is one of Utah's fastest growing communities, its numbers swelled by throngs of snowbirds and retirees.

The **St. George Mormon Temple** *(440 S. 300 East; ☎ 435-673-5181)*, constructed between 1869 and 1877, was the first Mormon temple in Utah. Admission to the temple is restricted to baptized Mormons, but nearby, the red sandstone **Mormon Tabernacle** *(Main & Tabernacle Sts.; ☎ 435-628-4072)*, built between 1863 and 1876, is open to visitors. Guided tours explain Mormon beliefs and describe the function of the temple as a religious and civic center.

Brigham Young's Winter Home *(67 W. 200 North; ☎ 435-673-2517)* was built in 1873 by the Mormon leader. The restored property holds period furnishings.

The **Jacob Hamblin Home** *(US-91, 3mi west of St. George; ☎ 435-673-2161)* was the original homestead of the first Mormon missionary in 1863. Most furnishings are from the 1880s. Hamblin, who gained a reputation for social skills with previously hostile Indians, converted many of them to Mormonism.

★★★ **Zion National Park** – *Rte. 9, Springdale, 42mi east of St. George & 23mi west of US-89.* ⛺✗♿🅿 ☎ *435-772-3256. www.nps.gov/zion.* Surrounding a scenic, 2,500ft-deep sandstone canyon decorated with waterfalls and damp hanging gardens, Zion is one of the oldest (1919) national parks in the US. More than 65mi of hiking trails, some of them steep and strenuous, lead into its backcountry wilderness. Non-hikers can go on horseback or join shuttle-bus tours of the valley *(Apr-Oct)*.

The massive sandstone features began forming 225 million years ago, when the park was an ancient sea floor. Later, it was a river delta and a lake bottom, and was covered in ash by volcanic eruptions. Shellfish flourished here; dinosaurs walked here. Around 170 million years ago, huge deposits of wind-blown sand left the region covered in dunes. Over time, the sand hardened into the 2,000ft-thick compacted sandstone that is now Zion's major geologic feature.

Over the last 15 million years, a short span of geological time, the forces of the Virgin River began carving **Zion Canyon**. Older features flatten out over

The Narrows

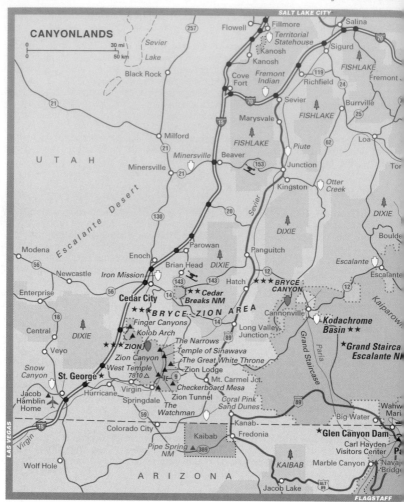

time, so the steep vertical walls of Zion Canyon are evidence of its relative youth. Even today, the river continues its carving: A million tons of rocky sediment are washed out of Zion Canyon yearly, flowing with the Virgin River into the Colorado River at Lake Mead, west of the Grand Canyon.

Zion Canyon—8mi long, .5mi wide and .5 mi deep—begins at the park's south entrance off Route 9. **Zion Scenic Canyon Drive** runs 8mi to the **Temple of Sinawava**, a natural sandstone amphitheater. (From April to November the road is closed to private vehicles beyond historic **Zion Lodge**, 1mi from Route 9.) From the Temple, a paved 1mi trail follows the Virgin River to **The Narrows**, barely 20ft wide in the river bottom, squeezed between rock walls rising 2,000ft above it. In good weather, wading is permitted; but flash-flood danger is always present. Hikers are advised to check river conditions, posted daily at the visitor center.

Other sandstone monoliths include **The Watchman**, rising 2,555ft above the canyon floor; and the massive 7,810ft **West Temple**, standing more than 4,100ft above the river road. **The Great White Throne** is a prominent monolith that rises majestically 2,400ft behind a red-rock saddle. Over aeons, iron minerals leached from the upper reaches of the formation have settled at its base, leaving the top white and the bottom red. An attraction of a different sort is **Weeping Rock**, a cool rock niche carved over millennia by seeping water. Fertile hanging gardens thrive in the damp confines of its cave-like grotto.

The **Kolob** area of Zion Park—accessible only by road from I-15 Exit 40, 20mi south of Cedar City—features a 5mi scenic drive along the Hurricane Fault, where twisted layers of exposed rock may be seen. Kolob's **Finger Canyons** extend southeast toward the main park area and are favored by backcountry hikers. A strenuous 7mi hike from Lee Pass, on La Verkin Creek, leads to **Kolob Arch**, one of the world's largest stone spans at 310ft across.

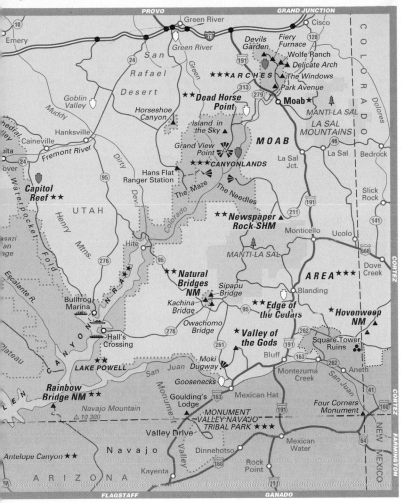

The Route 9 roadway east from Springdale to US-89, through **Zion Tunnel**, is considered an engineering marvel. The road features six switchbacks; the 5,607ft-long tunnel was blasted from solid sandstone between 1927 and 1930. Built for that era's smaller cars, the road now requires oversize vehicles to pay a fee to be escorted through the low-clearance tunnel as all other traffic waits. At the east end of the tunnel is **Checkerboard Mesa:** A pattern of horizontal and vertical lines etched into the sandstone were produced by geological fractures eroded by rain and snow.

Cedar City – *Rtes. 14 & 56 at I-15 Exit 59, 51 miles northeast of St. George & 252mi southwest of Salt Lake City.* △ ※ & P ☎ *435-586-5124. www.utahsplayground.org.* A onetime mining and livestock-raising community, this town of 19,000 was the site of the first US iron foundry west of the Mississippi River. At **Iron Mission State Park** *(Rte. 91; ☎ 435-586-9290),* the old foundry (1851-58) has been converted into a museum of farm and industrial machinery and horse-drawn vehicles.

Cedar City is best known for its annual **Utah Shakespearean Festival★** *(☎ 435-586-7880),* held from late June through early October. The primary venue is a replica of the Bard's own open-air Globe Theatre, built on the campus of Southern Utah University. Evening performances include an Elizabethan "Greenshow" with mimes, jugglers, falconers and storytellers in period costumes. Performers mingle with crowds before showtime, remaining in character. Other events include literary and production seminars, backstage tours and a Renaissance Feast sans cutlery.

★★ Cedar Breaks National Monument – *Rte. 14, 23mi east of Cedar City & 3mi south of Brian Head.* △ & P ☎ *435-586-9451. www.nps.gov/cebr. Facilities open late May-mid-Oct.* A 3mi-wide sandstone amphitheater is rimmed by bristlecone pines, some of the oldest living plants on earth. Cedar Breaks' heavily eroded features are sculpted to a depth of 2,500ft below the 10,000ft rim in a series of rugged, narrow walls, fins, pinnacles, spires and arches that resemble Bryce Canyon in shape, structure and color. Mormon settlers misnamed the site for trees they saw growing in the canyon bottom—they were junipers, not cedars.

In winter *(mid-Nov-mid-May)*, due to the 10,000ft elevation, snow makes the Cedar Breaks road impassable. But that makes it more appealing to cross-country skiers, who easily ascend the unplowed road from **Brian Head Resort** *(Rte. 143; ☎ 435-677-2035)*, just 3mi north. Brian Head is southern Utah's largest ski area, with six lifts and 53 runs; its base elevation of 9,600ft is the state's highest.

© Ric Ergenbright

Silent City Formation, Bryce Canyon National Park

***Bryce Canyon National Park** – *Bryce Canyon, 24mi southeast of Panguitch & 77mi east of Cedar City.* △ ✕ ♿ 🅿 ☎ *435-834-5322. www.nps.gov/brca.* This 56sq mi park contains an enchanting array of rock spires, pinnacles, arches and hoodoos tinted in a palette of rich shades, considered by some to be the most brightly colored rocks on earth. Red, yellow and brown shades derive from the iron content in the rocks. Purple and lavender rocks contain more manganese.

The odd rocks rise from the floor of a series of vast horseshoe-shaped natural amphitheaters. They reflect an astonishing 60 million years of the effects of wind and water on the layers of limestone.

The sculpted rock forms began forming during the Cretaceous Period, around the time that dinosaurs disappeared and flowering plants appeared. Deposits of sand and minerals, uplifts forced out of the earth, and erosional effects of rain and running water combined with snowfall, freezing and thawing to gradually remove billions of tons of rocks from the amphitheater rim. Eventually this debris was washed away by the Paria River, a tributary of the Colorado. Fins, spires, arches and balanced rock pillars are the colorful remnants.

Southern Paiute Indians lived around Bryce Canyon for several hundred years prior to white settlement in the late 1800s. Native Americans called this place "red rocks standing like men in a bowl-shaped canyon." Americans shortened it to Bryce Canyon after rancher Ebenezer Bryce, who first grazed livestock in the canyon bottoms in 1875 and called it "one hell of a place to lose a cow." President Warren Harding declared the area a national monument in 1923, and it became a national park five years later.

An 18mi (one-way) scenic drive leads along the pine-clad rim top to popular views and trailheads leading down into the maze-like amphitheaters. Hiking into Bryce Canyon, as opposed to looking at it from the rim, provides a very different perspective of the rock forms. Rim spots such as Sunrise, Sunset, Rainbow and Inspiration Points, all around 8,000ft elevation, afford differing views of the crenellated and sculpted rocks. They are especially magnificent, revealing unexpected subleties of shading and form, in the glow cast by early-morning or late-afternoon sunlight.

The park has more than 50mi of trails for hiking and horseback riding. Winter visitors, for whom the park may be virtually empty, cross-country ski on park roads or borrow snowshoes (gratis) from the Bryce Canyon Visitor Center.

★ **Grand Staircase-Escalante National Monument** – *Access from Rte. 12 between Cannonville & Boulder or US-89 west of Page.* ⚠ ♿ 🅿 🕿 *435-826-5499 (Escalante visitor center) or 435-644-4300 (Kanab headquarters). www.ut.blm.gov/monument.* This new (1997) national monument occupies 1.9 million acres of southern Utah wilderness west of the Waterpocket Fold and north of Lake Powell. This was one of the last regions in the continental US to be mapped. High, rugged and remote, it rises as many as 4,500ft above the Colorado River and Lake Powell, and is considered a geological sampler, containing a huge variety of sedimentary rock formations. It is also a world-class paleontology site; remnants of Anasazi Indian settlements may be found throughout the monument.
The **Grand Staircase**, a series of mammoth cliffs and miles-long ledges formed into natural steps of different-colored rock strata, dominates its western third. Stretching across the distant horizon for a distance of more than 100mi is layer upon layer of rock comprising the Pink, Gray, White, Vermilion and Chocolate Cliffs. In clear weather, the layers are clearly defined.
The area is partly named for the **Escalante River**, which flows from Boulder Mountain to Lake Powell in Glen Canyon National Recreation Area *(p 90)*. The Escalante has carved deep canyons and gorges into an immense puzzle of sandstone mazes and slot canyons that offer extensive opportunities for self-sufficient and well-prepared backpackers and hikers.
There are no services whatsoever within the large and remote backcountry that comprises this park. Services are available only in the adjacent communities of Boulder, Escalante, Cannonville and Kanab, or at Kodachrome Basin State Park, adjacent to the monument.

★★ **Kodachrome Basin State Park** – *9mi south of Cannonville off Rte. 12.* 🕿 *435-679-8562.* The primary distinguishing characteristic of the unique desert terrain in this park is the concentration of numerous tall sandstone chimneys—sand pipes—that rise from the desert floor. The spires appear white or gray in midday light. In low-angle sun of early morning or late afternoon, they begin to glow in unexpected shades of crimson, mauve and burnished orange. Hiking and horseback trails lead to peaceful desert vistas across Grand Staircase-Escalante National Monument, which surrounds the park.

★★ **Capitol Reef National Park** – *Rte. 24, 11mi east of Torrey.* ⚠ ♿ 🅿 🕿 *435-425-3791. www.nps.gov/care.* This park displays an amalgam of rocks of numerous varieties and colors—great slabs of white, pink, gold, purple, orange and red rocks combined into immense, vividly colored 1,000ft-tall cliffs, stone arches and natural bridges. Primarily a backcountry park, it features hundreds of miles of unpaved driving roads as well as hiking, biking and Jeep trails leading toward remote wilderness. A visitor center is located in the heart of the park, 9mi east of the junction of Routes 12 and 24.
The park was named by 19C Mormon pioneers, whose travels across Utah were impeded by a huge, convoluted, eroded rock uplift known as the **Waterpocket Fold.** Stretching 100mi to Lake Powell, it impeded their progress as a coral reef would a ship. This "reef" is crowned by prominent white domed rock that reminded pioneers of the US Capitol building in Washington DC. Waterpocket Fold itself is named for its eroded rock basins, also called pockets or tanks, that can hold thousands of gallons of water after a rainfall. In the desert, this helps to sustain various life forms, including humans.
The fold is a classic monocline, thrusting the earth's crust upward, with one extremely steep side, in an area otherwise characterized by flat layers of horizontal rocks. The fold is thought to be 50 million to 70 million years old and the result of movement along an ancient fault line. Geological layers reveal evidence of more than 200 million years of the earth's history—periods when this area contained rivers, swamps, huge deserts and shallow oceans.
Around AD 700, the Fremont culture established farming communities in the area. They were drawn by the water reserves of the rock pockets, and by the **Fremont River,** which also attracted abundant game and nourished wild foods. Their residency lasted 600 years. Fremont cultural history is told in petroglyphs (rock carvings) and painted pictograph panels throughout the park.
In the 1880s, Mormon pioneers established farms and orchards along the Fremont River at **Fruita,** in the vicinity of today's park visitor center. Their descendants raised cattle and fruit here until 1969, two years before Congress declared Capitol Reef a national park. The orchards are still maintained, and visitors may pick fruit in season. Surviving remnants of the pioneer community include a one-room schoolhouse, the Gifford Farmhouse and the Behunin Cabin.
A 10mi (one-way) scenic drive from the visitor center leads to overlooks of remote canyon country, slick-rock terrain, arches and spires. Turnouts offer views of such geological features as Capitol Dome, Chimney Rock, Egyptian

Temple and The Goosenecks. A short, moderately strenuous hike leads to Hickman Bridge, a natural stone bridge. A short, steep hike climbs to the Golden Throne and Capitol Gorge. Numerous other trails lead to a variety of overlooks and points of interest.

Unpaved roads, such as the one north from Route 24 into **Cathedral Valley**, an area of stunning sandstone buttes and 500ft-tall, freestanding monoliths, are suitable for high-clearance or four-wheel-drive vehicles only.

GLEN CANYON AREA**

Map pp 86-87   Mountain Standard Time
Tourist Information ☎ 520-608-6404 or www.nps.gov/glca

Environmentalists still lament the damming of the Colorado River to form Lake Powell in 1963. Glen Canyon, they say, was even more beautiful than its southerly neighbor, the Grand Canyon, though not as deep. They are a minority: Most visitors acclaim the 186mi-long lake, whose 1,960mi shoreline are longer than California's Pacific coast. Lake Powell is the centerpiece of an area characterized by a relative lack of human intrusion throughout history. In places such as the remote Valley of the Gods or Natural Bridges National Monument, it's clear that nature holds sway, not people. Even Rainbow Bridge National Monument—revered by the Navajo Indians, whose reservation lands surround it, and visited by hundreds of tourists traveling by Lake Powell tour boats daily—retains its natural grandeur, arcing in a great curve over lake-lapped desert beaches.

In other places, however, man has produced obvious changes. The town of Page, Arizona, the primary gateway to Lake Powell (most of which lies within Utah's borders), didn't exist before the Glen Canyon Dam was built. The dam, considered an engineering marvel, was constructed between 1956 and 1963 to store water for development of the desert Southwest. Nearby, the Four Corners Power Generating Station spews smoke from tall stacks into an otherwise clear-blue sky.

SIGHTS

** **Glen Canyon National Recreation Area** – *US-89 at Page AZ; Rte. 276 at Bullfrog Marina & Hall's Crossing, 158mi southwest of Moab UT; Rte. 95 at Hite UT, 155mi southwest of Moab.* △ ✕ ㅅ 🅿 ☎ *520-608-6404. www.nps.gov/glca.* This vast, federally protected area extends from Canyonlands National Park southwest to Grand Canyon National Park, covering more than 1,900sq mi around Lake Powell and the Colorado River. Its centerpiece is **Lake Powell****, a vast recreational playground whose watery fingers reach into sandy coves, inlets and slot canyons, coursing between towering red-rock cliffs to depths of 500ft. The waters, which took 17 years—until 1980—to fill to a surface elevation of 3,700ft above sea level, provide opportunities for houseboating and power boating, fishing and water skiing. On the lake are five marinas and several campgrounds. A visitor center at Bullfrog Marina, midway up the lake, features a life-size model of a slot canyon.

Lake Powell occupies only one-eighth of the parkland's acreage. The surrounding lands, with their myriad inlets and coves, are fascinating as well. Side canyons protect Indian ruins and a full array of natural stone features, including arches and bridges, pinnacles, fins, towers and stone chimneys known as sand pipes. Extensive backcountry hiking, biking and Jeep trails may be found throughout. Food, water and gasoline services, however, are generally available only in small communities on the periphery of the national recreation area. It is not a region to be explored without serious advance planning.

Page – *US-89, 157mi east of St. George UT & 135mi northeast of Grand Canyon Village AZ.* ✕ ㅅ 🅿 ☎ *520-645-4095. www.page-lakepowell.com.* Established during the construction of the Glen Canyon Dam in 1956 to house workers, this Arizona town, at the northwest corner of the huge Navajo Indian Reservation, grew as the enormous lake behind the dam began filling with water in 1963. The national recreation area has its headquarters here.

The **John Wesley Powell Museum & Visitor Information Center*** *(6 N. Lake Powell Blvd.; ☎ 520-645-9496)* features a fascinating collection of artifacts from the earliest recorded exploration of the region, about 130 years ago. The museum describes the exploits of Major Powell, a one-armed Civil War veteran who first charted the waters of the Colorado River in a wooden boat in 1869. Additional displays describe slot canyons and other local geology. Century-old black-and-white photographs of Glen Canyon are shown side-by-side with recent photos made from the same locations. The terrain appears remarkably unchanged.

Tours of **Antelope Canyon**** *(5mi east of Page off Rte. 98)* may be booked through the Powell Museum. Here on the Navajo Reservation is one of the colorful, swirling, narrow slot canyons so often seen in photographs of the Southwest. A millennium

Wahweap Marina, Lake Powell

of rain and wind has sculpted the porous sandstone into a slender crevice, 130ft deep and only 3ft wide in places. Undulations in the rock reveal colorful layers of stone that take on a photogenic glow at midday, the only time sunlight can penetrate the narrow canyon. Tours are permitted only with a licensed guide.

★ Glen Canyon Dam – *US-89, 2mi northwest of Page.* The Glen Canyon Dam produces more than 1.3 kilowatts of electricity daily, serving 1.5 million users in five states: Utah, Colorado, Wyoming, Arizona and New Mexico. With all eight of its generators operating, 15 million gallons of water pass through the dam each minute. (Radical environmentalists propose removing the 710ft-tall dam to return Glen Canyon to its original undammed state. But engineers believe it should last 300 to 500 years.) The **Carl Hayden Visitors Center** *(US-89; ☎ 520-608-6404)* provides photos and displays pertaining to the construction of the dam and the adjacent Navajo Bridge, as well as free tours of the dam.

★★ Rainbow Bridge National Monument   *☎ 520-608-6404. www.nps.gov/ rabr.* The world's largest known natural bridge, Rainbow Bridge stands 290ft above the waters of Lake Powell, beside an inlet just inside the Utah border with Arizona. Higher than the US Capitol, it spans 275ft, nearly the length of a football field, and is considered one of the seven natural wonders of the world. Called Nonnezoshi—"rainbow turned to stone"—by the Navajo, it's easy to see how the graceful curves earned that name. Navajo believe that passing beneath Rainbow Bridge without offering special prayers will bring misfortune. In an effort to respect these beliefs, the National Park Service asks visitors to refrain from walking under the bridge.
Boat tours depart several times daily from **Wahweap Marina**, north of the Glen Canyon Dam, and cover the 50mi to Rainbow Bridge. Tours also depart from **Bullfrog Marina** and **Hall's Crossing** at mid-lake.
Hikers may reach the bridge by a 14mi trail around Navajo Mountain from Tribal Road 16, about 85mi east of Page. Permission must first be obtained from the Navajo Tribe *(Parks and Recreation Dept., PO Box 308, Window Rock AZ 86515; ☎ 520-871-6647).*

★★ Natural Bridges National Monument – *Rte. 275 off Rte. 95, 42mi west of Bland ing UT.* △ ♿ 🅿 *☎ 435-692-1234. www.nps.gov/nabr.* One of the most remote areas in a state noted for its remote places, this parkland contains the eroded stone networks of Armstrong and White Canyons. Over hundreds of centuries, seeping water and seasonal runoff have worn away vast sections of rock walls to create three stunning and impressive natural stone bridges that are among the largest in the world. The three bridges may be seen from overlooks along a 9mi paved park road. Short hiking trails lead to each site, and an 8.5mi trail links all three bridges. The bridges were given Hopi Indian names. **Sipapu Bridge** is the longest (268ft) and highest (220ft); it is thought to be the second-largest natural bridge in the world. **Kachina Bridge** is 204ft long, 210ft high and 93ft thick. **Owachomo Bridge** is the oldest and smallest of the park's natural bridges; it spans 180ft in length, but is only 9ft thick in spots and barely 27ft wide. Owachomo is considered a late-stage natural bridge. Someday relatively soon, although no one knows exactly when, it will collapse to the canyon floor.

★Valley of the Gods – *Rte. 261, 10mi north of Mexican Hat UT & 35mi south of Natural Bridges National Monument.* 🅿 ☎ *435-587-1500.* Characterized by protruding rock monoliths rising from a level desert floor, Valley of the Gods is similar, though smaller in scale, to its southerly neighbor, Monument Valley *(p 169).* Valley of the Gods is far less visited, far less crowded.

A rough 17mi dirt road passes through the valley. A four-wheel-drive vehicle is recommended, with plenty of gas for the car and water for its passengers. Hardy bike riders particularly enjoy the Valley of the Gods loop for its isolation and lack of motor traffic. There are no services whatsoever.

Perhaps the best view of Valley of the Gods is from the **Moki Dugway** *(Rte. 261),* where it descends in 1,000ft of steep switchbacks from Cedar Mesa to the valley floor. Just past Valley of the Gods, a side road leads 3mi to **Goosenecks State Park** *(Rte. 316;* ☎ *435-678-2238),* a clifftop aerie offering an eagle's-eye view of the loop-like bends of the meandering San Juan, 500-1,000ft below.

MOAB AREA★★★

Map pp 86-87   Mountain Standard Time
Tourist Information ☎ 435-259-8825 or http://canyonlands-utah.com

A town of 5,000 that serves as gateway to the Arches and Canyonlands National Park areas, Moab is surrounded by breathtaking scenery of carved rock and powerful flowing water. It is the stage for a wide range of outdoor activities, particularly Colorado River rafting and "slick-rock" mountain biking.

A large number of expedition outfitters and guided-tour operators make their headquarters in Moab, which offers far more lodging and dining options than any other southeastern Utah community. Limited services may be found in the smaller towns of Monticello, Blanding and Bluff.

SIGHTS

★Moab – *US-191, 244mi southeast of Salt Lake City.* ⬘ ✗ 🅿 ☎ *435-259-8825.* A 1950s uranium boomtown, Moab is the center of an adventure travel industry built around the spectacular rugged terrain of two national parks, Arches and Canyonlands; a handful of state parks; and adjacent public lands straddling the Colorado and Green Rivers.

Named for a region in the Book of Mormon, Moab was first settled near the banks of the Colorado River in 1855 by Mormon colonists dispatched from Salt Lake City by Brigham Young. But white farmers didn't make lasting peace with local Indians until 1876. In subsequent decades, the eroded deserts around Moab have been a hideout for such outlaws as Butch Cassidy, a dock for a Colorado River boat company, and a setting for novels by Zane Grey and numerous Hollywood movies. Uranium mining sustained the community until the 1980s, when adventure travel took hold.

■ **Edward Abbey**

Author Edward Abbey (1927-89) gained fame in the late 20C as a champion of the pristine desert environment. A park ranger at the Arches in the 1950s, he immortalized his experiences in a book called *Desert Solitaire* (1968), now considered a classic of the ecology movement. Abbey, who called himself "a man with the bark still on," wrote of the seasonal changes in the then-largely deserted park. Living alone in a small, isolated trailer, he found time to note and describe subtleties in the rock formations as well as the interplay of weather conditions, plant and animal life and humans' place in it all.

The cynical Abbey considered humans to be insignificant but vicious and short-sighted creatures. He felt man lacked the good sense to preserve the wilderness areas where primitive human urges could be expressed harmlessly.

Other books by the gruff philosopher include the nonfiction *The Journey Home* (1977), *Abbey's Road* (1979) and *Down the River* (1982). His best-known novels are *The Monkey Wrench Gang* (1975), a humorous but insightful look at environmental terrorism, and *The Brave Cowboy* (1956), made into a 1962 movie (starring Kirk Douglas) called *Lonely Are the Brave.* Other novels include *Good News* (1980), *The Fool's Progress* (1988) and *Hayduke Lives!* (1990).

Today mountain biking, golf, river rafting and kayaking, hiking and Jeep driving appear to be the primary pursuits of residents and visitors alike. Winter attracts cross-country skiers to the La Sal Mountains, which rise east of Moab to more than 13,000ft.

The town's **Dan O'Laurie Canyon Country Museum** *(118 E. Center St.; ☎ 435-259-7985)* displays artifacts of ancient Indians and exhibits on Moab's role in the uranium boom. The Nature Conservancy's **Scott M. Matheson Wetlands Preserve** *(Kane Creek Blvd.; ☎ 435-259-4629)* protects a riparian slough rich in bird and plant life.

★★★ **Arches National Park** – *Off US-191, 5mi northwest of Moab.* △ ⚹ ▣ ☎ *435-719-2299. www.nps.gov/arch.* The greatest concentration of natural stone arches in the US are found in this rugged 120sq mi park. An arch is a vertical sandstone slab with an opening of at least 3ft, created over aeons by wind and water. More than 2,000 arches are within this park's serpentine network of multicolored canyons, distinguished by enormous, narrow rock fins, slender spires and improbably balanced rocks hundreds of feet high.

Arches' unique terrain represents the effects of 150 million years of erosion on 5,000 vertical feet of rock, revealing a porous layer of 300ft-thick Entrada Sandstone, out of which today's arches were formed. The thick sandstone is composed of fused grains of sand held together by minerals, through which water may slowly seep. Over 10 million years, this seepage—and the accumulated effects of wind—created cracks in the areas of weakest mineral concentration. The park's dramatic rock towers, spires and fins broke along these vertical cracks. Additional aeons of seepage, freezing and thawing caused pieces of the fins to fall out, creating apertures that in freestanding fins became arches.

Created as a national monument in 1929, Arches was upgraded to a national park in 1971. Previously, only Native Americans had lingered long in this arid and daunting landscape. One rare settlement was established in the late 19C by Civil War veteran John Wesley Wolfe and his son Fred. They raised cattle for 20 years at **Wolfe Ranch**; the ruins of their log cabin and corrals remain today.

Many geological attractions may be seen from the park's 18mi (one-way) main road. Short hikes from the roadway offer more intimate perspectives on some of the most dramatic and impressive features.

Two miles from the visitor center, **Park Avenue** is the name given to a tapering redrock canyon resembling a city skyline. Seven miles farther, a paved spur road leads 3mi to a clustered group of geological features, including numerous large and small arches, in **The Windows** section of the park. Short trails lead to the major features, which include the North and South Windows, Double Arch and Turret Arch.

Returning to the main road, another spur road *(2.5mi farther)* leads to Wolfe Ranch and the **Delicate Arch** viewpoint. Delicate Arch is perhaps the park's most recognizable feature. A steep hike *(1.5mi)* from Wolfe Ranch leads to the base of the 46ft-high, 35ft-wide arch, which frames the La Sal Mountains in the eastern distance. A paved road accesses a viewpoint.

At the end of the main road, the **Devils Garden** area contains numerous arches, including Skyline Arch and Landscape Arch—one of the world's longest, spanning 306ft although it is only 10ft thick in one spot. A mostly level trail *(2mi one-way)* reaches many of the Garden's highlights.

The **Fiery Furnace** area contains a jumble of rock fins, towers, pinnacles and twisting canyons. Although the strenuous round-trip hike covers only 2mi, it takes 3hrs to accomplish. It is considered so confusing to navigate that visitors are encouraged to walk only with a park ranger as a guide *(Mar-Oct only)*.

★★★ **Canyonlands National Park** – *Island in the Sky District, Rte. 313, 35mi southwest of Moab via US-191. The Needles District, Rte. 211, 87mi south of Moab via US-191. The Maze District, Rec. Rd. 633, 136mi southwest of Moab via US-191, I-70, Rte. 24 & Lower San Rafael Rd.* △ ▣ ☎ *435-719-2313. www.nps.gov/cany.* Trisected by the deep canyons of the Colorado and Green Rivers, Canyonlands' three main sections are reached via different routes, each one far from the other. Utah's largest national park was so designated in 1964.

It contains 527sq mi of deep, eroded canyons, characterized by sheer cliffs, outstanding mesas and all other varieties of bizarrely shaped hoodoos, balanced rocks, spires, pinnacles, fins and arches that characterize southeastern Utah. None of the rugged and largely barren park areas have seen much human settlement, save for an odd cattle-ranching operation or law-evading outlaw.

The Green River flows into the Colorado below Moab, proceeds through the strong rapids of Cataract Canyon, and empties into Lake Powell before continuing through the Grand Canyon. The rivers are separated by the **Island in the Sky** District, a gigantic level mesa reached via a spur road that turns south off US-191 about 9mi north of Moab. At its tip, 3,000ft above the confluence, is **Grand View Point**, with panoramic views of 100mi of tiered canyons in all directions, changing colors in dramatic red, orange and pink layer-cake slices in the low-angle light of the late-afternoon or early-morning sun. About 1,000ft below Grand View Point lies the pale White Rim, a rocky sandstone bench that traces the mesa's sinuous,

Mountain Biking, Canyonlands National Park

Mountain Biking

The diverse terrain and moderate desert climate of the Canyonlands make this region irresistible to mountain bikers. Two-wheel adventurers can be found from the river-carved red-rock canyons to the heights of 13,000ft mountains, in between tackling Moab's challenging, world-famous slick-rock hills.

The **Slickrock Bike Trail** is probably the best-known trail of its type any-where. It stretches over 11 technically demanding miles on undulating slickrock, a form of eroded sandstone that takes on graceful curved shapes and swirls, becoming dangerously slippery when wet. Riders fol-low a track, indicated by dotted white lines painted on red rocks, that hugs cliff faces and potentially lethal drop-offs.

Other biking trails with international reputations include the 100mi **White Rim Trail** (also suitable for Jeeps) through Canyonlands National Park, and the shorter, off-road Hurrah Pass Trail and Poison Spider Trail. The paved roads through Arches National Park are likewise popular with bik-ers, although off-road biking is prohibited in Arches.

One of the most demanding bike trails anywhere, the **Kokopelli Trail**, begins at the Slickrock Trail and covers 128mi from Moab to Grand Junction, Colorado. Along the way, the multi-day route traces the route of the Col-orado River, passing from the desert canyon country of Utah into the pine-and-aspen forests of neighboring Colorado.

Each year, Moab is host to several of the biggest mountain-biking events anywhere, luring riders from around the world. Numerous bicycle shops in Moab provide full retail and rental services, and link riders with special-ized tour operators for group biking adventures.

erosion-made curves. Farther below, curving through on their meandering journey south, are the Colorado River (to the east) and Green River (to the west).

The Needles District, reached from a westbound turnoff 39mi south of Moab, is separated from Island in the Sky by more than 100 road miles, although their respective paved roads end just 10mi apart, the Colorado flowing between. Incredible rock forms protrude from the vast canyons, spires and arches. The Needles are a massive city-size formation of vertical standing rocks huddled con-spiratorially. In early morning and late afternoon, glowing shades of red, pink, orange and rust deepen and fade with dramatic impact.

The road entrance to **The Maze** District is hours from the rest of the park. From Route 24, 90mi west of Moab via I-70 at the town of Green River, drivers must navigate the dirt Lower San Rafael Road, maintained by the Bureau of Land Man-agement, another 46mi southeast to **Hans Flat Ranger Station**. Although most high-clearance vehicles can travel it with ease, the road may nonetheless be impassable in wet weather. Considered one of the most remote locations in the continental US, the 30sq mi Maze District contains a severely convoluted canyon network. Rock fins, towers and mesas are found in great concentrations and given names like the Doll House and the Land of Standing Rocks.

Ancient Indian pictograph panels, depicting ghostly characters twice human size, are seen in the Great Gallery at **Horseshoe Canyon** *(Lower San Rafael Rd., 30mi north of Hans Flat)*. These primitive paintings may be as old as 2,000 years. Relatively few visitors have passed since that time; hence the panels have remained intact. Even today, the dark grotto may be reached only after a steep 2mi hike down hidden Barrier Creek Canyon, protected by rock overhangs.

★★ **Dead Horse Point State Park** – *Rte. 313, 32mi southwest of Moab via US-191.* ⛺ ♿ 🅿 ☎ *435-259-2614. www.nr.state.ut.us/parks/utahstpk.htm.* This park, en route to the Island in the Sky, was named for a herd of wild horses once corralled and forgotten on this isolated point 2,000ft above the Colorado River. All of the equines died of thirst within view of the river. Some consider the sunset views from this point, light tracing across the multi-hued sandstone canyons, cliffs and mesas, to be among the most dramatically beautiful in all the Canyonlands.

★★ **Newspaper Rock State Historical Monument** – *Rte. 211, 51mi south of Moab via US-191.* This small roadside park, 12mi west of US-191 on the route to The Needles District, contains a rock wall virtually covered in hundreds of Indian pictographs and etched petroglyph carvings. Portrayed in or on the stone wall is nearly every figure found in ancient Indian art throughout the Southwest: the hunchbacked flute player Kokopelli, hunters with bows and arrows, horses and wild animals. Archaeologists believe the site was actually a message board for ancient people, a way for far-flung regional residents to keep in touch over long periods of time.

Petroglyphs on Newspaper Rock

★★ **Edge of the Cedars State Park** – *660 W. 400 North, Blanding, 74mi south of Moab.* ♿ 🅿 ☎ *435-678-2238.* This small and very well done museum contains the remains of a pre-Columbian Anasazi Indian village, occupied from AD 700-1200. The ruins include six partially excavated dwellings. There is also a modern museum, which contains a fine collection of artifacts, including pottery and weavings. This important facility serves as the main archaeological repository for all of southeastern Utah.

★ **Hovenweep National Monument** – *Square Tower Ruins, Hovenweep Rd. (County Rd. G), 46mi west of Cortez CO & 31mi east of US-191 south of Moab UT.* ⛺ 🅿 ☎ *435-459-4344. www.nps.gov/hove.* Founded in 1923 to preserve six Anasazi Indian villages on both sides of the Utah-Colorado border, Hovenweep includes the unusual **Square Tower Ruins**, where a small visitor center offers exhibits. The unique square, oval, circular and D-shaped towers provided residents, as recently as 800 years ago, with extensive views of their surroundings. A fairly level 8mi trail system, beginning at the Square Tower Ruins, passes the remains of an irrigation system along with pit dwellings, ceremonial places and burial sites. Roads to other sites are unpaved and dusty, but the main route to the Square Tower Ruins is now paved.

Colorado Rockies

Maroon Bells Near Aspen

Nowhere else in the continental United States are the mountains as high, nor the terrain as challenging, as in the Colorado Rockies. Climaxed by no fewer than 53 peaks of 14,000ft elevation or higher, the Rocky Mountains—actually a series of north-south-running ranges—dominate the western two-thirds of the state of Colorado. Many of North America's most famous ski resorts are found here, along with fascinating pieces of mining and railroad heritage.

The Continental Divide winds through this mountainous domain, headspring of three of North America's six longest rivers. The Colorado, which begins as a trickle in Rocky Mountain National Park, flows southwesterly 1,450mi through Arizona's Grand Canyon to the Sea of Cortez. The Arkansas, whose modest source is beneath 14,433ft Mount Elbert, Colorado's highest summit, runs east 1,459mi and joins the Mississippi River. The Rio Grande, which rises in the San Juans, courses south through New Mexico and sculpts an international border before reaching the Gulf of Mexico, 1,900mi from its font.

Originally inhabited mainly by Ute tribes, Colorado's mountains were divided between Spain and France as the 19C opened. The US acquired the eastern flank of the Rockies in the Louisiana Purchase of 1803, the balance in 1848 by treaty from Mexico, which had assumed Spain's colonial mantle. But this elevated land was rarely visited; westbound pioneers followed the Oregon Trail through lower mountains to the north, or took the Santa Fe Trail to the south. Not until the discovery of gold in 1858, soon followed by an even larger silver boom, was there stimulation to settle here. Even when mining was at its acme, and narrow-gauge rail lines threaded over, around and through the highest ranges, the mountains were considered so formidable that the transcontinental railroad was routed through neighboring Wyoming in 1869.

Today, the Colorado Rockies combine modern resorts, authentic Western towns and easy highway travel with natural beauty. Bicycle paths parallel roads and rivers between many towns; hiking, golf and whitewater rafting are other popular summer activities. In winter, skiing turns the Rockies into America's leading recreational playground. Most mountains are national forest land owned by the US government, which limits resort growth and restricts overt development of valleys that are private land. Thus both historic mining towns and new resorts are tightly built and densely settled, yet often are surrounded by protected wilderness areas.

Colorado Rockies
CO

HIGH ROCKIES★★★

Map pp 100-101   Mountain Standard Time
Tourist information 303-837-0793, www.colorado.com

There's no "best" way to tour Colorado's High Rockies. Spread across more than 20,000sq mi, yet crossed by only a handful of major highways, this lofty zone teases travelers with the promise of views that are always "just around the next bend." But it rewards the intrepid with a rich flora and fauna, evocative mining heritage, and some of the most spectacular mountain scenery in the country.

Historical Notes – The Utes were dominant from the 17C to mid-19C; Arapaho and Cheyenne also hunted in these mountains. After the US acquired the territory, Zebulon Pike explored rivers and valleys in 1806-07, Major Stephen Long ventured up the South Platte and Arkansas valleys in 1820, and John C. Frémont visited northern Colorado in 1842. Still, the mountains seemed impenetrable to anyone but fur trappers and mountain men. It wasn't until the Civil War era that the promise of mineral wealth attracted permanent residents.

The war had a sobering effect on the gold rush that began in 1859, but silver created another flurry of prospecting. Narrow-gauge railroads began serving mining camps in the 1870s. When resources were exhausted, some settlements faded into ghost towns; others persisted. Central City, Georgetown, Breckenridge, Leadville, Aspen, Crested Butte and Telluride are among the survivors.

★★★ROCKY MOUNTAIN NATIONAL PARK DRIVING TOUR

2-3 days, 205mi round-trip

Denver is closer to high mountains than any other major American city. Yet these very heights keep the city's growth spreading across the plains to its south, east and north. The peaks rise literally from the western suburbs, making state and national parks and forests easy getaways for city dwellers.

From Golden (p 128), west of Denver, drive 13mi west on US-6 through Clear Creek Canyon to Rte. 119, then 5mi south.

★ **Black Hawk and Central City** – *Rtes. 119 & 279.* ☎ *303-582-5077.* ✗ ㄴ ▣
Spawned by 1859 gold strikes that claimed "the richest square mile on earth," these once-forlorn foothills towns, a mile apart, are booming again. Limited-stakes gambling ($5 maximum), legalized in 1991, features blackjack, poker and acres of slot machines in 31 casinos.

The original excavation at Gregory Gulch marks the entrance to Central City, a few steep streets with narrow sidewalks. Brick masonry in the wake of a devastating 1874 fire resulted in sturdy Victorian buildings that still stand. Among them is the 1878 **Central City Opera**★ *(120 Eureka St.,* ☎ *303-297-8306),* whose six week summer season *(*☎ *303-202-6500; performances late Jun-early Aug)* was launched by silent-screen star Lillian Gish in 1932. Next door is the 1872 **Teller House** *(110 Eureka St.;* ☎ *303-582-3200),* an elegant hotel famed for a legendary painting dubbed "The Face on the Barroom Floor."

Return to Rte. 119 & continue north 65mi on the Peak to Peak Highway.

★★ **Peak to Peak Highway** – *Rtes. 119, 72 & 7.* △ ✗ This scenic route winds through pine woods that periodically open to offer tantalizing mountain views. In **Nederland**★, a small, lively, former mining-supply town, Route 119 branches east toward Boulder *(p 128).* Proceed north on Route 72. After 14mi, look for a left turn to **Brainard Lake**★, surrounded by the soaring snow-cloaked summits of the Indian Peaks Wilderness on the Continental Divide.

Return to Route 72, continue north 9mi and turn left on Route 7 to Estes Park.

★★ **Estes Park** – *US-34, US-36 & Rte. 7.* △ ✗ ㄴ ▣ ☎ *970-586-4431.*
www.estesparkresort.com. A tourist town of shops, inns and restaurants, Estes Park nestles at the east edge of Rocky Mountain National Park. An **aerial tramway**★ *(420 E. Riverside Dr.;* ☎ *970-586-3675)* climbs 8,900ft Prospect Mountain in summer, with fine views of adjacent summits. Winter offers snowshoeing and cross-country skiing in the park, and chances to see deer and elk right in town.

Take US-36 west from the south side of Estes Park to the main national park entrance station and the Beaver Meadows Visitor Center.

★★★ **Rocky Mountain National Park** – *US-34 & US-36.* △ ㄴ ▣ ☎ *970-586-1206.*
www.nps.gov/romo. This magnificent landscape boasts craggy mountains, glaciated valleys, perpetual snowfields, small lakes and vast alpine tundra that covers one-third of its 415sq mi. It features more than 100 mountains of 11,000ft or higher, reaching its apex at 14,255ft **Longs Peak**, whose distinctive flat-topped summit dominates the park's southeast corner. The **Beaver Meadows Visitor Center** has park maps and information on ranger-led tours and lectures. From here, 10mi **Bear Lake Road**★ runs south, providing access to trailheads.

Rocky Mountain Aspen Forest

★★★ **Trail Ridge Road** – *US-34, 50mi from Estes Park to Grand Lake.* △ ⚫ ▣ *Open late May-Oct, depending upon weather conditions.* Constructed in 1932, this is the highest continuous paved highway in North America, ascending rapidly from coniferous and aspen forests to treeless tundra at 12,183ft, and offering outstanding mountain panoramas. Viewing areas include **Many Parks Curve**★★ and **Forest Canyon Overlook**★★. The **Tundra Trail at Rock Cut**★★ *(.5mi),* an interpretive path with signs describing the geology, botany and wildlife of this harsh environment, is short and gentle, but at this elevation it may be exhausting for flatlanders. After passing its high point, the road curves downhill past the **Gore Range Overlook**★ and the **Alpine Visitor Center** *(closed in winter),* crossing the Continental Divide at 10,758ft Milner Pass. Roadside picnic areas are steps from the uppermost Colorado River, only a modest stream here.

★ **Grand Lake** – *Rte. 278 off US-34.* △ ✗ ⚫ ▣ ☎ *970-627-3402. www.grandlakechamber.com.* A small town at the west entrance to the park, Grand Lake boasts Old West-style log buildings and boardwalks. It is named for its large glacial lake (1.2mi long, 1mi wide, 400ft deep), fed by the Colorado River. Below Grand Lake, the river is dammed twice to form **Shadow Mountain Lake** and large **Lake Granby,** popular with water-sports enthusiasts. Water is pumped via pipeline from here to quench the thirsts of Front Range residents.

Continue south 15mi on US-34 from Grand Lake to Granby. Turn left (southeasterly) on US-40 and proceed 46mi to I-70 at Empire.

Middle Park – *Fraser River Valley, US-40 south of Granby.* △ ✗ ⚫ ▣ ☎ *800-903-7275. www.winterpark-info.com.* Cattle graze in this broad, flat valley whose mountain-sheathed location renders it one of the coldest places in the continental US. **Cozens Ranch**★ *(US-40 south of Fraser;* ☎ *970-726-6514)* displays pioneer and Ute artifacts in an 1870s ranch house, stagecoach stop and post office. The resort community of **Winter Park**★ *(US-40;* ☎ *970-726-4221)* is known for mountain biking and winter skiing on two mountains. The route crosses the Continental Divide at 11,315ft **Berthoud Pass** and swings through Empire, a 19C mining town.

Return 29mi via I-70 & US-6 to Golden.

★★ DENVER-VAIL-ASPEN DRIVING TOUR *3 days, 276mi one-way*

Interstate 70 is Colorado's principal east-west thoroughfare. Between Denver and Glenwood Springs it is one of America's most scenic highways and the gateway to some of the West's leading mountain resorts. For early settlers here, wealth came from the earth as gold, silver and other minerals. Today's gold is white at ski areas, green at golf courses. Both proliferate on either side of this busy ribbon.

From Denver, drive west 32mi on I-70.

Idaho Springs – *I-70 Exit 241.* △ ✗ ⚫ ▣ ☎ *303-567-4382.* Nineteenth-century commercial buildings line the main street of this old mining town. The 1913 **Argo Gold Mill & Mine** *(2350 Riverside Dr.;* ☎ *303-567-2421)* is an ore-processing mill open for self-guided tours, with a small mining museum and a chance to pan for gold. At the **Phoenix Mine**★ *(right on Stanley Rd., left on Trail Creek Rd.;* ☎ *303-567-0422),* a retired miner leads an underground tour.

© Ric Ergenbright

★★ Mount Evans – *Mt. Evans Rd. (Rte. 5), off I-70 Exit 240 via Rte. 103 to Echo Lake.* ▣ ☎ *303-567-2901; summers only.* This is one of only two 14,000ft mountains with a road to the top; the other is Pikes Peak *(p 131).* En route to its 14,264ft summit, the 14mi road passes a grove of ancient **bristlecone pines★**. At Summit Lake, which is not in fact at the summit, bold Rocky Mountain goats often approach cars. From the mountaintop parking lot, a short trail leads to the true summit and a 360-degree panorama. This drive is best done early in the day, as lightning is common on summer afternoons.

Return to I-70 & continue 14mi west.

★ Georgetown – *I-70 Exit 228.* △ ✕ ⚹ ▣ ☎ *303-569-2840.* When the new state of Colorado was determining a site for its capital in 1876, Georgetown was a contender. The old town center is immaculately preserved. The **Hotel de Paris★** *(Taos & 6th Sts.; ☎ 303-569-2840),* built in 1875 by French immigrant Louis Dupuy as one of the most elegant hotels in the West, is now a museum. The 1879 **Hamill House★** *(305 Argentine St.; ☎ 303-569-2840)* demonstrates the luxury in which the family of silver baron and civic leader William Hamill lived.
Tickets for a 1hr summer round-trip outing on the **Georgetown Loop Railroad★★** *(1100 Rose St.; ☎ 303-569-2403)* are available at the historic train depot. The 4.5mi of track between Georgetown and Silver Plume, another 19C mining town, feature a 360-degree loop on a bridge high over Clear Creek.

Continue 23mi west on I-70.

The highway climbs steadily to the **Eisenhower Tunnel,** bored under the Continental Divide at 10,700ft. North America's highest road tunnel enables vehicles to avoid 11,992ft **Loveland Pass★**—a scenic but time-consuming 20mi detour. Take Exit 216 and follow US-6 for dramatic views of mountains, valleys, lingering snowfields and (at 13,050ft) the **Arapahoe Basin Ski Area** *(☎ 970-496-7030),* which stays open later than any other Rocky Mountain resort—until July 4. The highway passes modern **Keystone Resort★** *(☎ 970-496-4242),* famed for its night skiing, en route back to its junction with I-70 at **Silverthorne,** noted for its factory outlet stores.

Continue 5mi west on I-70 to Exit 203. Turn south and take Rte. 9 for 9mi.

On the left is **Dillon Reservoir,** cradled by mountains. Route 9 passes quaint **Frisco** and follows the Blue River. The Tenmile Range—mountains numbered (north to south) "Peak 1" through "Peak 10"—forms the western backdrop.

★★ Breckenridge – *87mi west of Denver.* △ ✕ ⚹ ▣ ☎ *970-453-5579. www. gobreck.com.* Now a resort town, Breckenridge was founded in 1859 by gold miners. In 1887, prospectors in French Gulch found a gold nugget weighing more than eight pounds and nicknamed it Tom's Baby; the rock is now displayed at the Denver Museum of Nature and Science *(p 126).* The **Country Boy Mine★** **Kids** *(452 French Gulch Rd.; ☎ 970-453-4405)* offers tours and gold panning in French Creek.
Main Street is lined with restaurants and shops, most housed in colorfully painted Old West-style buildings. The **Summit Historical Society** *(☎ 970-453-9022)* offers walking tours and mining-district tours. Historic buildings include the **Barney Ford**

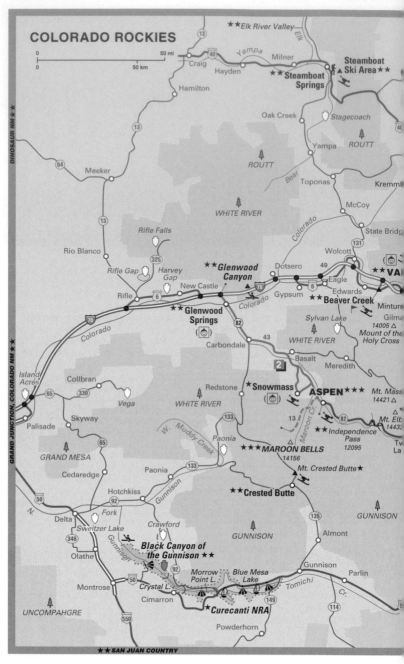

COLORADO ROCKIES

0 ——————— 50 mi
0 ——————— 50 km

★★Elk River Valley

★★Steamboat Springs

Steamboat Ski Area ★★

Craig   Milner
Hayden
Hamilton

Oak Creek   Stagecoach

Yampa   ROUTT

ROUTT

Meeker

Bear

Toponas   Kremml

WHITE RIVER

McCoy

State Brid

Rifle Falls   Wolcott   131

Rio Blanco

Rifle Gap   Harvey Gap   ★★Glenwood Canyon   Dotsero   49   ★★VA

New Castle   Eagle

Rifle   Gypsum   6   Edwards

Colorado   ★★Beaver Creek   Mintur

★★Glenwood Springs   Sylvan Lake   Gilma

14005 △
Mount of the Holy Cross

Carbondale   WHITE RIVER

43

Basalt   Meredith

Island Acres   Collbran   Redstone   ★Snowmass   ASPEN★★★   Mt. Mass
14421 △

WHITE RIVER   △
Mt. Elb
14433

Vega   13   △

Skyway   ★★Independence Pass   Tv
12095   La

Palisade   Paonia

GRAND MESA   ★★★MAROON BELLS
14156

Cedaredge   Paonia   133   Mt. Crested Butte★

Hotchkiss

Sweitzer Lake   ★★Crested Butte

Delta   Crawford   135

GUNNISON

Olathe   GUNNISON   Almont

Black Canyon of the Gunnison ★★   Gunnison   Parlin

Montrose   Morrow Point L.   Blue Mesa Lake   Tomichi   Cr.

Crystal L.   149

Cimarron   ★Curecanti NRA

UNCOMPAHGRE   Powderhorn

★★SAN JUAN COUNTRY

House *(Washington & Main Sts.)*, owned by a freed slave who became a 19C business and civic leader. The small **Father Dyer United Methodist Church** *(Wellington & Briar Rose Sts.)* is dedicated to a roving preacher who carried mail and the word of God to remote mining camps.

A bike path along the Blue River becomes a cross-country skiing thoroughfare in winter. Ski lifts serve downhill terrain that spreads across three mountains—Peaks 8, 9 and 10—with off-piste skiing available on Peak 7.

Return to I-70 and continue west 6mi to Exit 195. Take Rte. 91 south 24mi to Leadville.

Exiting the interstate at **Copper Mountain Resort** *(Rte. 91 at I-70 Exit 195; ☎ 970-968-2882)*, Route 91 cuts across 11,318ft **Fremont Pass**. It passes the open pit of the defunct American Climax Molybdenum Mine before descending into Leadville.

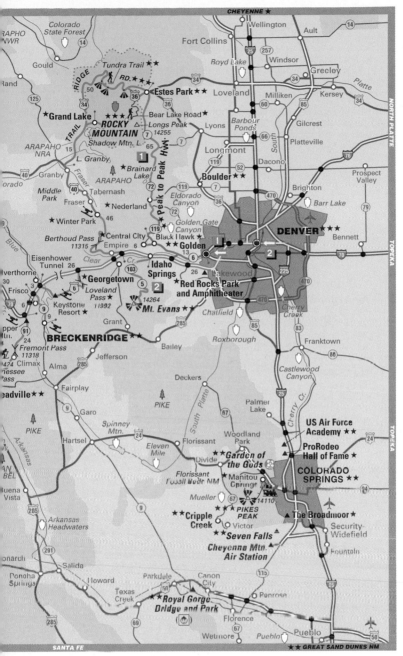

★★ Leadville – *US-24 & Rte. 91, 103mi west of Denver.* △ ╳ & 🅿 ☎ *719-486-3900. www.leadvilleusa.com.* Situated at 10,152ft, Leadville was once Colorado's silver capital. Mines also yielded gold, lead, molybdenum, manganese and turquoise; in 1880, population soared to 24,000. The wide main street is flanked by fine Victorian commercial architecture, and the side streets are lined with brightly painted dwellings, from mansions to modest miners' cottages.

Tickets for *The Earth Runs Silver,* a multimedia show about the town's history, are available at the **Leadville Visitor Center** *(809 Harrison Ave.; ☎ 719-486-3900).* The nearby **National Mining Hall of Fame and Museum★★** *(120 W. 9th St.; ☎ 719-486-1229)* has exhibits on historic and contemporary mining, including a full-size, walk-through replica of a hard-rock mine. The elaborate **Tabor Opera House★**

(315 Harrison Ave.) was built in 1879 and was reputedly the finest theater west of the Mississippi River. The remnants of millionaire Horace Tabor's **Matchless Mine** *(E. 7th St., 1mi east of downtown)* can also be visited.

About 5mi west of town is **Leadville National Fish Hatchery★** *(Rte. 300)*, built in 1889; tanks hold millions of trout for release into Colorado's streams. Behind the hatchery, a network of hiking trails begins from the foot of 14,421ft **Mount Massive**, the state's second-highest peak. Immediately south of that summit, also in the Sawatch Range, is the state's highest crest, 14,433ft **Mount Elbert**.

Beginning 13mi south of Leadville, the Independence Pass Highway *(Rte. 82)*, linking US-24 with I-70 at Glenwood Springs, crosses 12,095ft **Independence Pass★★** and offers incredible views from its numerous hairpin turns. The 38mi stretch from **Twin Lakes** *(6mi west of US-24)* to Aspen, however, is normally closed by snow from mid-October to Memorial Day.

From Leadville, take US-24 north 33mi to I-70.

ADDRESS BOOK

Please see explanation on p 64.

Staying in the Colorado Rockies

The Home Ranch – *Rte. 129, Clark CO, 19mi north of Steamboat Springs.* ✗⌖ 🄿 ⌁ ☎ *970-879-1780. 6 rooms, 8 cabins.* **$$$$** To stay here is to experience the best in "Western hospitality": 80 horses, gourmet family-style meals, private cabins with wood-burning stoves and lofts. The minimum summer stay (with fly-fishing and fireside sing-alongs) is one week. Nightly rates are available in winter.

The Lodge at Vail – *174 E. Gore Creek Dr., Vail CO.* ✗⌖ 🄿 ⌁ ☎ *970-476-5011. www.lodgeatvail.com. 123 rooms.* **$$$$** Tyrol meets the Rockies in an opulent mix just 30 yards from Vail's chairlifts. A wide staircase leads to rooms of polished woods, high-backed leather chairs and private balconies. Dining on Colorado lamb at the luxurious **Wildflower Restaurant** continues the splurge.

Hotel Jerome – *330 E. Main St., Aspen CO.* ✗⌖ 🄿 ⌁ ☎ *970-920-1000. www.hoteljerome.com. 92 rooms.* **$$$** Over a century ago, the rich mining crowd bellied up to the cherry-wood bar to celebrate silver strikes. Today, Aspen's elite still frequent the same terra-cotta brick landmark. Glass-cut doorknobs open to mining-camp Victorian rooms decorated in raspberry and hunter green. Old mining maps and silver-etched lamps line the hallways.

The Stanley Hotel – *333 Wonderview Ave., Estes Park CO.* ✗⌖ 🄿 ⌁ ☎ *970-586-3371. www.grandheritage.com/Hotels/Namerican/Stanley. 135 rooms.* **$$** Ailing F.O. Stanley went to Estes Valley for mountain air in 1903 on his doctor's orders, and he never left. Instead, he built a white-pillared Georgian hotel high in the Rockies. While the rooms are modern, double fireplaces and double staircases still grace the lobby, and Palladian windows provide spectacular views.

Strater Hotel – *699 Main Ave., Durango CO.* ✗⌖ 🄿 ☎ *970-247-4431. www.strater.com. 93 rooms.* **$$** The Strater is a palace of red brick and white trim with a hint of the Wild West, furnished with one of the world's largest collections of Victorian walnut antiques, and embellished with glistening brass rails and brocaded settees. The diary in each room contains affectionate accolades to mighty four-posters and ornate wallpapers.

Dining in the Colorado Rockies

Piñon's – *105 S. Mill St., Aspen CO.* ☎ *970-920-2021. www.pinons.com.* **$$$ Creative regional.** Sautéed elk loin, sesame-crusted ahi and coriander-grilled caribou hardly seem fare for ski bums, but this cuisine fits right into the calm earth tones and high ceilings of the casual-elegant town favorite.

Sweet Basil – *193 E. Gore Creek Dr., Vail CO.* ☎ *970-476-0125.* **$$$ Mediterranean and Asian fusion.** The menu changes seasonally, but this contemporary bistro always remains packed from wall to mustard-colored wall. Unique dishes include crispy quail with mango chutney and saffron pasta with lobster.

The Powderhouse – *226 W. Colorado Ave., Telluride CO.* ☎ *970-728-3622.* **$$ Creative regional.** The atmosphere here harks back to old mining days. Specialties focus on Rocky Mountain cuisine: elk tenderloin, rainbow trout and stuffed quail bathed in red wine, mushrooms and pearl onions.

The site of **Camp Hale**, a World War II army training base for the 10th Mountain Division, the US ski and mountaineering contingent, is atop 10,424ft **Tennessee Pass**—where a monument to "The Tenth" stands, appropriately, 10mi from Leadville. Descending the pass, US-24 follows the upper Eagle River through a little-developed valley below 14,005ft **Mount of the Holy Cross**, so-named for its distinctive, intersecting, perpetually snow-packed gullies in the shape of a cross. US-24 meets I-70 near **Minturn**, a former rail town now becoming a Vail suburb.

Backtrack east 5mi on I-70 to Vail.

★★ **Vail** – *98mi west of Denver.* △ ✗ � 🄿 ☏ *970-476-1000. www.visitvailvalley.com.* One of North America's premier mountain resorts, Vail was founded in 1963 by veterans of the World War II 10th Mountain Division. Vail Village boasts winding, pedestrian-only streets and chalet-style buildings with fashionable shops and restaurants. The **Colorado Ski Museum★** *(231 S. Frontage Rd.;* ☏ *970-476-1876)* documents the state's skiing and snowboarding heritage and commemorates the skiing soldiers, who trained at Camp Hale *(above).* The **Vail Nature Center★** 𝖪𝗂𝖽𝗌 *(831 Vail Valley Dr.;* ☏ *970-479-2291)* offers naturalist tours and guided hikes year-round. The tranquil and lush **Betty Ford Alpine Garden★★** *(173 Gore Creek Dr.;* ☏ *970-476-0103),* established by the former First Lady, boasts 1,500 varieties of annuals and perennials, with a special focus on high-elevation plants.

The town is tightly packed into the Gore Creek valley, resulting in satellite developments that extend from East Vail to West Vail, including Lionshead and Cascade Villages. All sit at the foot of mammoth **Vail Mountain★★★**, the continent's largest single-mountain ski area with 31 lifts, more than 4,600 acres of terrain, and a 3,330ft vertical drop. **Adventure Ridge★** 𝖪𝗂𝖽𝗌 is the site of outdoor ice-skating, snow tubing, night ski-biking and high-mountain snowmobile and snowshoe tours. In summer, the domed VistaBahn chairlift and the 12-passenger Lionshead Gondola ascend for mountain biking, hiking and outstanding views.

Drive 10mi west from Vail on I-70.

★★ **Beaver Creek** – *From I-70 Exit 167 at Avon, take Village Rd. 3mi south.* ✗ � 🄿 ☏ *970-845-2500. www.visitbeavercreek.com.* This elegant and exclusive ski-and-golf resort community was created by the operators of the Vail resort in 1980. The ski terrain, which twice has hosted men's world-championship downhill races, connects two developments, Arrowhead and Bachelor Gulch. **Vilar Center for the Arts★** *(*☏ *970-834-8397),* an acoustically precise and attractive theater, hosts classical and popular performances.

Continue 50mi west on I-70.

★★ **Glenwood Canyon** – *I-70 between Exits 133 & 116.* Colorado's geological history is written on the sedimentary walls of this spectacular 18mi gorge. The oldest rock was formed 570 million years ago in the Precambrian era. The youngest rock, up to 1,500ft above the river, is iron rich sandstone. This portion of I-70, completed in 1992, is an engineering marvel: The divided highway was cantilevered from granite walls and routed through short tunnels to minimize damage to rock and vegetation. A paved biking and jogging trail runs the entire length of Glenwood Canyon. Exits access raft-launch areas and the **Hanging Lake Trail★★**, which ascends 1,000ft in 1mi to an exquisite lake in a small basin.

★★ **Glenwood Springs** – *Rte. 82 at I-70 Exit 116, 158mi west of Denver.* △ ✗ � 🄿 ☏ *888-445-3696. www.glenwoodchamber.com.* This lively town is situated where the Roaring Fork meets the Colorado River below Glenwood Canyon. The **Hot Springs Pool★★** 𝖪𝗂𝖽𝗌 *(401 N. River St.;* ☏ *970-945-7131)* is claimed to be the world's largest naturally spring-fed hot pool. Areas of different temperatures invite swimming, playing or simply relaxing in therapeutic waters.

Hourly tours visit lighted portions of the **Historic Fairy Caves and Glenwood Caverns★★** 𝖪𝗂𝖽𝗌 *(509 Pine St.;* ☏ *970-945-4228),* high above Glenwood Canyon. Closed in World War I, it was not reopened until 1999. Exquisitely decorated chambers, discovered in the intervening 82 years, display untouched and brilliant formations.

Take Rte. 82 southeast 42mi to Aspen and conclusion of driving tour.

★★★ **Aspen** – *200mi southwest of Denver.* △ ✗ � 🄿 ☏ *970-925-1940. www.aspenchamber.com.* Aspen is synonymous with glamour. Its ski terrain ranks among the finest in North America, as four separate resort mountains rise within 12mi of one another. High-season guests and part-time residents include many celebrities. It also is a notable art and intellectual center.

The Aspen Skiing Company and Aspen Institute for Humanistic Studies, both founded in the late 1940s, revived a rundown silver-mining town. Aspen's development into a world-class resort became a model for other Rocky Mountain communities, although no other has achieved the same status.

Downtown Aspen in Winter

Downtown Aspen – Known for chic boutiques and fashionable restaurants, historic downtown focuses around a three-block pedestrian mall. Jerome B. Wheeler, president of Macy's department store in New York, came to Aspen during its boom years and in 1888 and 1889 built three enduring landmarks. The elaborate **Wheeler Opera House**★★ *(320 E. Hyman Ave.;* ☎ *970-920-5770)* hosts films and live entertainment. The **Hotel Jerome**★ *(330 Main St.;* ☎ *970-920-1000)* has been luxuriously restored. The **Wheeler-Stallard House**★ *(620 W. Bleeker St.;* ☎ *970-925-3721),* a Victorian showplace, is a museum of the Aspen Historical Society.
The **Aspen Art Museum**★ *(590 N. Mill St.;* ☎ *970-925-8050)* offers exhibits of various works, many by local artists. The **Aspen Center for Environmental Studies** *(100 Puppy Smith St.;* ☎ *970-925-5756)* is set on Hallam Lake, maintained as an in-town nature preserve and wildlife sanctuary. The **Aspen Music Festival and School**★★★ *(5th & Gillespie Sts.;* ☎ *970-925-3254)* presents summer concerts that often feature world-renowned musicians.

★★ **Aspen Mountain** – ✕ 🅿 ☎ *970-925-1220. www.skiaspen.com.* Aspen's original ski mountain rises directly behind town, its slopes luring some of the world's best skiers—but no snowboarders. The **Silver Queen Gondola**★★ operates in summer for sightseeing; views from its 11,212ft summit take in four surrounding wilderness areas. Immediately northwest of town are two more resorts, **Aspen Highlands** *(Maroon Creek Rd. via Rte. 82)* and novice-oriented **Buttermilk Mountain** *(Rte. 82).*

★ **Snowmass** – *Brush Creek Rd. via Rte. 82, 12mi northwest of Aspen.* ✕ ♿ 🅿 ☎ *970-925-1220; www.skiaspen.com.* Created in 1967 as a modern alternative to historic Aspen, Snowmass has the most expansive and varied terrain of the four mountains. **Krabloonik Kennels**★★ 🄺🄸🄳🅂 *(Divide Rd. off Brush Creek Rd.;* ☎ *970-923-3953)* operates dog-sled rides in winter. The **Anderson Ranch Art Center**★ *(5263 Owl Creek Rd.;* ☎ *970-923-3181)* offers exhibits and highly regarded workshops.

★★★ **Maroon Bells** – *13mi southwest of Aspen in the Maroon Bells-Snowmass Wilderness.* ⛺♿🅿 The view of Colorado's most oft-photographed mountains is particularly inspiring across **Maroon Lake**★★, whose still waters reflect their elegant summits—topping out at 14,156ft—and distinctive rock bands. Summers and weekends, private vehicles are prohibited from 10mi Maroon Creek Road, so shuttle buses make the trip from Rubey Park Transit Center *(Durant Ave. between S. Galena & S. Mill Sts.).* In winter, the **T-Lazy-7 Ranch** 🄺🄸🄳🅂 *(Maroon Creek Rd.;* ☎ *970-925-4614)* operates snowmobile tours and sleigh rides.

ADDITIONAL SIGHTS

★★ **Steamboat Springs** – *US-40, 74mi north of I-70 Exit 157, 19mi west of Vail.* ⛺✕♿🅿 ☎ *970-879-0880. www.steamboat-chamber.com.* A relaxed, true Western town in the broad Yampa River Valley, Steamboat has preserved its ranch heritage to maintain an authenticity lacking in many other mountain resort communities. Lincoln Avenue, the main street, has a refreshing mix of utilitarian stores with its chic boutiques and galleries; **F.M. Light & Sons**★ *(830 Lincoln Ave.;* ☎ *970-879-1822)* has

sold Western clothing from the same location since 1905. The **Eleanor Bliss Center for the Arts** *(13th & Stockbridge Sts.;* ☎ *970-879-9008)*, in a renovated 1908 rail depot, offers exhibits and performances. The **Tread of the Pioneers Museum** *(800 Oak St.;* ☎ *970-879-2214)* exhibits historical artifacts in a 1908 Queen Anne-style home. The paved 3mi **Yampa River Trail★**, core of a large recreational trail system, invites walkers and cyclists just south of downtown.
Steamboat Ski Area★★ *(US-40, 3mi south of downtown;* ☎ *970-879-6111; www.steamboat-ski.com)* has 20 lifts, 3,000 skiable acres and a 3,668ft vertical. It is fabled for its abundant, ultra-light snowfall dubbed "champagne powder." The **Silver Bullet Gondola★** runs in summer for sightseeing, hiking and mountain biking. **Howelsen Hill★** *(River Rd.;* ☎ *970-879-4300)*, Steamboat's original hometown ski hill, has a historic ski-jumping facility. A large spring near its foot was deemed by early visitors to sound like a steamboat—thus the town's name.
North of Steamboat, numerous working and guest ranches are located 20mi and farther up the **Elk River Valley★★** *(County Rd. 129 off US-40)*.

★★ Crested Butte – *Rte. 135, 28mi north of US-50 at Gunnison, 66mi west of Salida.* △ ✕ ㄴ 🅿 ☎ *970-349-6438. www.crestedbuttechamber.com.* This entire former mining town is a National Historic District, its false-front Victorian buildings conveying an Old West flavor. Adjacent **Mt. Crested Butte★** *(Rte. 135, 2mi north of Crested Butte;* ☎ *800-544-4505)* has off-piste terrain that is challenging enough to host extreme skiing competitions; in summer, these wildflower-cloaked slopes offer some of Colorado's best mountain-biking trails.

★★ Royal Gorge Bridge and Park – [Kids] *Off US-50, 8mi west of Cañon City.* ✕ ㄴ 🅿 ☎ *719-275-7507. www.royalgorgebridge.com.* The Denver & Rio Grande Railroad laid a route through this spectacular Arkansas River chasm in 1877. A suspension bridge claimed as the world's highest, 1,053ft above the river and more than a quarter-mile long, opened in 1929. A funicular railway (1931) plunges precipitously from the rim; an aerial tramway (1969) spans the gorge. Rafting companies have run its whitewater for decades. In 1999, the **Royal Gorge Route★★** again began operating passenger trains through the gorge. Trains depart from Cañon City's Santa Fe Depot *(401 Water St.;* ☎ *888-724-5748)*. On the rim, a 160-acre park features a theater and miniature railway.

★★ Great Sand Dunes National Monument – [Kids] *Rte. 150, 90mi south of Salida via US-50, US-285, Rte. 17 & 6N Ln.* △ ㄴ 🅿 ☎ *719-378-2312. www.nps.gov/grsa.* North America's tallest sand dunes, nearly 750ft high, spread across 39sq mi on the flank of the Sangre de Cristo Mountains. Formed by winds over thousands of years, the dunes seems totally out of place here, far from any ocean or major desert. Changing light and deceptive shadows color the sand gold, pink and tan.

WESTERN SLOPE★

Michelin map 493 G 8, 9 and map pp 100-101   Mountain Standard Time
Tourist Information ☎ 970 242-3214 or http://colorado.com/info.html

Rivers rushing west from the Rockies give life to this vast semi-desert land. Population centers are few and far between; the only major town is Grand Junction, whose 42,000 people huddle near the confluence of the Gunnison and Colorado Rivers. These two streams—and, to a lesser extent, the Yampa and White Rivers farther north—provide lifeblood for ranching and an agriculture industry that has expanded from soybeans to peaches, pears and wine grapes.
The Western Slope's unique geology has made it a treasure trove of natural resources, especially oil, coal and uranium, all of which have inspired exploitation. But the rivers' influence is much more apparent in the stunning canyons they have gouged over tens of thousands of years—canyons now preserved in three separate national monuments and parks.

SIGHTS

Grand Junction – *US-50, 3mi south of I-70 Exit 31.* △ ✕ ㄴ 🅿 ☎ *970-244-1480. www.grand-junction.net.* Founded in 1882 as a rail town, Grand Junction became the principal trade and distribution center between Denver and Salt Lake City. Irrigated soil and a mild climate enabled it to grow as an agricultural area. Early heritage is recalled at the **Cross Orchards Living History Farm★** [Kids] *(3079 F Rd.;* ☎ *970-434-9814)*, where a fruit-packing shed, blacksmith's shop and laborers' bunkhouse share space with displays of vintage farming and railway equipment. The original 243-acre farm nurtured 22,000 apple trees between 1896 and 1923. Today it is a division of the **Museum of Western Colorado** *(248 S. 4th St.;* ☎ *970-242-0971)*, whose displays focus on regional geology, history and native culture.

** **Colorado National Monument** – *Off Rte. 340, via I-70 Exit 19 at Fruita, 12mi west of Grand Junction.* △ ▣ ☏ *970-858-3617. www.nps.gov/colm.* Memorable for its sandstone monoliths and sheer-walled canyons, this 32sq mi wilderness rises more than 2,000ft above the Colorado River along the northern rim of the Upcompahgre Plateau. **Rim Rock Drive**★★★ *(23mi)* weaves past such red-rock formations as the Kissing Couple, whose respective "lips" lightly graze; Devils Kitchen, strewn with boulders; and aptly named Window Rock. Trails access these and other features, including petroglyphs and fossils.
Bighorn sheep, mule deer, golden eagles and a few mountain lions prowl the rugged landscape, created by upward lifts, volcanic eruptions and wind and water erosion. Exhibits on geology and nature are presented at a **visitor center** near the Saddlehorn Campground.

** **Dinosaur National Monument** – *31mi north of US-40 at Dinosaur, 108mi north of Grand Junction.* △ ▣ ☏ *970-374-3000. www.nps.gov/dino.* Although this 325sq mi parkland extends into Utah, its headquarters and **visitor center** are 2mi east of tiny Dinosaur, Colorado. A scenic drive to **Harpers Corner** climaxes with a 1.5mi hike to a viewpoint over the confluence of the Yampa and Green Rivers at **Echo Park**. Side roads to other overlooks are fit for four-wheel-drive vehicles only.
To see dinosaur skeletons, visitors must travel west 20mi on US-40 to Jensen, Utah, then north 7mi on Rte. 149 to the **Dinosaur Quarry**. About 150 million years ago, such creatures as the herbivorous apatosaurus and stegosaurus, and the carnivorous allosaurus, lived and died here. The Quarry was once a sandbar where carcasses accumulated, covered with sediment and preserved.

** **Black Canyon of the Gunnison National Park** – *Rte. 347, 5mi north of US-50, 8mi east of Montrose & 58mi west of Gunnison.* △ ▣ ☏ *970-641-2337. www.nps.gov/blca.* Neither the deepest nor the narrowest canyon in Colorado, this chasm combines both aspects for its dramatic appearance. The westward-flowing Gunnison River has scoured a virtually impenetrable 53mi-long, 2,700ft-deep, 1,000ft-wide path through Precambrian gneiss and schist. A 7mi road along the south rim offers 12 scenic overlooks. Adventurous rock climbers test canyon walls in summer as expert kayakers ride the rapids below.

* **Curecanti National Recreation Area** – *US-50 between Montrose & Gunnison.* △ ▣ ☏ *970-641-2337. www.nps.gov/cure.* Three consecutive reservoirs on the Gunnison River, within and above the Black Canyon, are the heart of this recreational heaven for water-sports lovers. Farthest upstream is **Blue Mesa Lake**, Colorado's biggest lake and the largest kokanee salmon fishery in the US. Below Blue Mesa are **Morrow Point Lake**, locked into the upper Black Canyon, and **Crystal Lake**. Three visitor centers provide information on activities; one (Elk Creek on Blue Mesa Lake) is open year-round.

SAN JUAN COUNTRY★★

Michelin map 493 F, G 9, 10   Mountain Standard Time
Tourist Information ☏ 970-247-9621 or www.swcolotravel.org

Colorado's southwestern corner is a largely mountainous area dominated by the sharply angled slopes and precipices of the San Juan Mountains. The Rockies' youngest range includes more than 2 million acres of national forests, parks and designated wilderness areas laced with scenic rivers and lakes. Fourteen lofty peaks surpass 14,000ft; at lower elevations, agriculture still holds sway.
Historic 19C mining towns characterize human settlement in the high San Juans. But long before white settlement, the Anasazi were present. Between AD 600 and 1300, they built primitive cities amid the piñon-and-sage mesas feathering off the San Juans. Abandoned seven centuries ago, these communities are now some of the best preserved archaeological sites in the Southwest. The foremost cliff-dwelling sites in the world are contained within Mesa Verde National Park.
Much later, pioneers seeking gold and silver discovered the San Juans. In 1880, a railroad—a portion of which survives today as the Durango & Silverton Narrow Gauge Railroad—was built to haul ore and supplies. The Million Dollar Highway was blasted through the mountains to link far-flung sites with service towns like Durango and Cortez; wealth from the mines built their Victorian main streets. Many mines failed by the early 20C, but the towns' architecture was preserved in national historic districts. Most of the old sites are now ghost towns frequented by hikers, horseback riders, cross-country skiers and off-road vehicle enthusiasts.

DRIVING TOUR 2-3 days, 290mi

★**Durango** – US-160 & US-550. ☎ 970-247-0312. www.durango.org. This Animas River town of 14,000 is by far the largest in the region. It was founded in 1880 when the Denver and Rio Grande Railroad built a rail line to alpine mines near remote Silverton. The **Durango & Silverton Narrow Gauge Railroad**★★★ **Kids** *(479 Main Ave.; ☎ 970-259-2733, www.durangotrain.com)* still employs coal-fired steam locomotive engines to pull impeccably restored narrow-gauge cars, hauling 200,000 tourists a year 45 slow miles through the heart of San Juan National Forest. The route skirts a wilderness of spruce and aspen trees, plunging canyons, powerful waterfalls and snow-covered peaks.

The train depot anchors the **Main Avenue National Historic District**★ *(Main Ave., 5th-12th Sts.)*. While virtually every building has historic appeal, the star attraction is the **Strater Hotel**★ *(699 Main Ave.; ☎ 970-247-4431)*, a four-story brick Victorian that first let rooms in 1887. It contains a hiss-the-villain summer theater and the Diamond Belle Saloon, a bar with a honky-tonk pianist and garter-clad waitresses like those of the old *Gunsmoke* television series.

Drive north 50mi from Durango on US-550.

★**Silverton** – US-550 & Rte. 110. △ ✗ & 🄿 ☎ 800-752-4494. www.silverton .org. A boom town in the 1880s when miners were moving "silver by the ton," Silverton now relies largely upon rail tourists for its survival. Train passengers have a two-hour layover here, ample time to explore the 50-or-so distinctive Victorian buildings of the historic district *(between 10th, 15th, Mineral & Snowden Sts.)*. Though a shadow of its former self, Silverton has a fascinating history, expressed at the **San Juan Historical Society Museum** in the old country jail.

North of town, US-550 cores through country pocked by abandoned mines along the **Million Dollar Highway**★. Sheer drops plunge from the shoulders of this roadway to jagged rocks hundreds of feet below. Some say its name came from the high cost of construction; others cite gold chips embedded in the original roadway by mining operators with money to spare for such extravagances.

Continue north 25mi from Silverton on US-550.

★**Ouray** – 73mi north of Durango. △ ✗ & 🄿 ☎ 970-325-4746. www.ouraycolorado. com. The seven-block **Main Street Historic District** of this "Switzerland of America,"
founded by miners in 1876, lies in a dramatic, narrow canyon. Ute Indian Chief Ouray is said to have enjoyed soaking in the natural hot springs here. Especially in winter, visitors can see steam rising from the **Ouray Hot Springs Pool** *(US-550, north end of Ouray; ☎ 970 325-4638)*, its million gallons of thermal water as hot as 104°F. South of town in a slender gorge are the impressive **Box Canyon Falls**, a county park devoted to the winter sport of ice climbing. In summer, Ouray is a center for Jeep excursions.

Drive north 10mi from Ouray on US-550; at Ridgway, turn west (left) on Rte. 162; after 23mi, turn east (left) on Rte. 145 and continue 17mi to Telluride.

★★**Telluride** – 125mi north of Durango. △ ✗ 🄿 ☎ 970-728-3041. www.tvs.org. This beautiful mountain resort town is actually two separate communities. The

© John Gottberg

Telluride Ski Resort

1878 **National Historic District**, nestled in a steep-sided glacial box canyon, is linked with ultra-modern **Mountain Village** by a state-of-the-art gondola, installed in 1996. Rich veins of silver and gold made Telluride a boisterous, Wild West town in the late 19C. Its affluence was not lost on Butch Cassidy, who in 1889 launched his prolific career as an outlaw by robbing the Bank of Telluride. Nine years later, American politician William Jennings Bryan delivered his famous "Cross of Gold" speech (defending the falling gold standard) from the steps of **The New Sheridan Hotel** *(231 W. Colorado Ave.;* ☎ *970-728-4351)*. Today the Victorian downtown —three blocks on either side of Colorado Avenue—is the heart of local commerce.

At the east end of Telluride's box canyon is Colorado's longest free-flowing waterfall, 365ft **Bridal Veil Falls★**. A track leads to remnants of the world's first hydroelectric power plant, built beside the cataract in 1905.

Mountain Village is 6mi by road from downtown. The European-style complex has massive stone-and-wood structures, including a luxury spa, around a golf course. Adjacent private homes look like 21C castles. The high-speed gondola linking town and village has greatly reduced dependence on motor vehicles.

Telluride Ski Resort★★ *(*☎ *970-728-6900)* is one of the Rockies' most acclaimed and challenging. Its 3,522ft vertical drop (climaxing at 12,266ft) is accessible from downtown or Mountain Village. In summer, Telluride is noted for its diverse festivals—bluegrass, jazz and chamber music, film and hang-gliding.

Drive south 77mi from Telluride on Rte. 145.

Dolores – *Rtes. 145 & 184, 45mi west of Durango.* △ ✗ ♿ 🅿 ☎ *970-882-4018. www.doloreschamber.com.* Travelers transiting this small town may visit its historic train station and rare **Galloping Goose** *(Rte. 145;* ☎ *970-565-8227)*, a hybrid train/bus contraption that once simultaneously carried passengers and removed snow from the railroad tracks. Three miles west is the **Anasazi Heritage and Cultural Center★** *(Rte. 184;* ☎ *970-565-8227)*, a museum with displays of native artifacts removed from a valley before it was flooded by a reservoir.

Continue south 12mi from Dolores on Rte. 145.

Cortez – *US-160, US-666 & Rte. 145, 46mi west of Durango.* △ ✗ 🅿 ☎ *970-565-3414. www.swcolo.org.* An agricultural town separating the San Juan Mountains from desert lands to the south and west, Cortez features a small historic district that stretches eight blocks along Main Street.

Cliff Palace, Mesa Verde National Park

The **Ute Mountain Tribal Park**★★ *(12mi southwest via US-160; visit by guided tour only)* contains a cluster of excavated cliff dwellings, many unexcavated sites, petroglyphs and thousands of pottery shards. It's one of the most evocative ancient sites in North America, although it requires a difficult drive of 82mi on unpaved backroads and several miles of hiking and climbing.

Another hour's drive is the **Four Corners Monument** *(US-160, 76mi southwest of Cortez)*, the only place where four US states intersect. Flags surround a cement marker where Colorado, New Mexico, Arizona and Utah meet.

The **Lowry Ruins** *(County Rd. GG, 12mi northwest of Cortez)* include examples of two different ancient cultural traditions. Farther west, the various parcels of **Hovenweep National Monument**★ *(McElmo Canyon Rd., 100mi west of Cortez)* preserve the ruins of six Anasazi villages *(p 95)*.

Take US-160 east 10mi from Cortez; turn south into Mesa Verde National Park.

★★★**Mesa Verde National Park** – US-160, Mancos. △ ✗ 㐁 🅿 ☎ *970-529-4465*. *www.nps.gov/meve*. The first US national park to preserve the works of man (as opposed to nature), Mesa Verde was created by Congress on September 29, 1906. Today it attracts 650,000 annual visitors, most of them in summer, when they can walk through five major cliff dwellings and additional mesa-top structures displaying primitive construction methods used by ancestral Puebloans between AD 750 and 1300.

The 21mi drive from the park entrance to the **Chapin Mesa Archaeological Museum**★ winds around the mesa, offering spectacular views of four states. Adjacent is **Spruce Tree House**★★★, a major cliff dwelling and the only one open year-round. Nearby, the 6mi **Mesa Top Loop Road** is also open year-round. Overlooks provide views of **Square Tower House**★★, the **Twin Trees**★ site and **Sun Temple**★. In warmer weather, guided tours are offered to spectacular sites built into overhanging cliffs at **Cliff Palace**★★ and **Balcony House**★★.

Continue east 36mi on US-160 to return to Durango.

■ **UNESCO World Heritage Sites**

The following locations in the western United States have been designated by the United Nations Educational, Scientific and Cultural Organization as "World Heritage Sites" for their outstanding natural or cultural significance:

Carlsbad Caverns National Park, New Mexico
Chaco Culture National Historic Park, New Mexico
Glacier Bay National Park, Alaska
Grand Canyon National Park, Arizona
Hawaii Volcanoes National Park, Hawaii
Mesa Verde National Park, Colorado
Olympic National Park, Washington
Pueblo de Taos, New Mexico
Redwood National Park, California
Waterton-Glacier International Peace Park, Montana and Alberta (Canada)
Wrangell-St. Elias National Park and Preserve, Alaska
Yellowstone National Park, Wyoming-Montana-Idaho
Yosemite National Park, California

Dallas-Fort Worth Area

Dallas Skyline

The twin cities of Dallas and Fort Worth, together with their patchwork of suburbs, constitute the sprawling expanse of prairie termed the Metroplex. It is the single largest urbanized area in Texas, with a combined population of 4.5 million. Landlocked and lacking navigable waterways, Dallas and Fort Worth have nonetheless flowered. Though united by their physical proximity, the cities vary widely in history and character.

The gleaming towers of downtown Dallas are firmly anchored in trade and commerce. Although the city is deservedly famous for its roots in the oil business, petroleum is by no means the only industry in its portfolio. Dallas is a major center for banking, transportation and retailing, and is home to a host of US and international companies. Along with its corporate image, Dallas also enjoys cultural prestige. Institutions such as the Dallas Museum of Art and the Morton H. Meyerson Symphony Center have made the Dallas Arts District one of the largest and most significant in the US.

One of Dallas' darkest moments occurred in 1963 when US President John F. Kennedy was assassinated while touring the city in a motorcade. The tragic episode is remembered at Dealey Plaza, where a memorial commemorates the location, and in The Sixth Floor Museum, situated in the former Texas School Book Depository building from which the alleged assassin's shots were fired.

Fort Worth trades heavily on its "Cowtown" image, bringing its Old West heritage to life in the Stockyards National Historic District and the restored downtown, known as Sundance Square. Smaller and less hurried than its neighbor to the east, Fort Worth offers a surprisingly diverse array of attractions beyond its Wild West flavor, including a first-rate zoo and a cluster of renowned museums in the Cultural District.

DALLAS★★

Map pp 114-115   Central Standard Time
Population 1,075,894
Tourist information ☎ 214-571-1301 or www.dallascvb.com

Dallas has a certain familiarity for visitors—even those who haven't previously been to "The Big D." It's the city where President Kennedy was assassinated, venue of the Dallas television series, home of the Dallas Cowboys football team. Shoppers know the **Dallas Market Center** *(2100 Stemmons Fwy.; ☎ 214-670-1700)*, largest wholesale merchandise market in the world, and the original **Neiman-Marcus department store** *(1618 Main St.; ☎ 214-741-6911)*, a symbol of Texas wealth.

Many attractions are concentrated in three areas. Museums are clustered at Fair Park, site of the largest state fair in the US each October. The Dallas Arts District is the nation's largest urban arts district. The West End Historic District, occupying renovated warehouses, holds some of the city's best shopping and nightlife.

Historical Notes – Dallas began in 1841 as a trading post near a crossing on the Trinity River. By the time the US annexed Texas in 1845, the town's population had grown to 430, mostly farmers, traders and shopkeepers. It prospered as a supply station for settlers in the great westward expansion and as an agricultural center, particularly for the export of cotton. After suffering severe economic and social problems in the wake of the Civil War, during which it supported the Confederacy, Dallas rebounded as a trade center and a shipping point for the buffalo market. In the 1870s railway and telegraph lines further enhanced its position as a hub of commerce. The Federal Reserve Bank selected Dallas as the site for a regional bank in 1911 and established the city as a financial center.

Dallas' strong ties with the aviation industry began with World War I, when Love Field was founded as an air-training facility. Today, although Love still operates as a commercial airport, it is overshadowed in suburban Grapevine by the enormous Dallas-Fort Worth International Airport, world headquarters of American Airlines.

★★DOWNTOWN DALLAS

Downtown Dallas combines commerce and culture with shopping, dining and entertainment. The four-story **West End Marketplace** *(Lamar St. north of Pacific Ave.; ☎ 214-748-4801; www.dallaswestend.org)* is a renovated warehouse home to more than 50 shops, restaurants, nightclubs and a cinema complex. **Deep Ellum** *(Elm St. east of Good-Latimer Expwy.; ☎ 214-747-3337)*, a former industrial neighborhood east of downtown, now boasts a thriving bohemian night scene ranging from jazz and blues to alternative music. In recent years, the scope of the avant-garde has spread beyond Elm Street (where speakeasies flourished during Prohibition) to nearby Main and Commerce streets.

★★ **Dallas Museum of Art** – *1717 N. Harwood St.* ✕ ⅋ 🄿 ☎ *214-922-1344. www.dm-art.org*. A collection of global scope is presented in this vast, stair-stepped building (1984, Edward L. Barnes). Its highlight is **Arts of the Americas★★★**, a unique survey of human cultural evolution in the Western Hemisphere. Beginning with amulets and jewelry of prehistoric civilizations, it follows creative man through the Spanish and British colonial periods, right up to 20C Texas. Highlights include paintings by Albert Bierstadt, Andrew Wyeth and Georgia O'Keeffe, as well as Frederic Church's *The Icebergs* (1861), Thomas Hart Benton's *The Prodigal Son* (c.1939-41) and sculptor James Earl Frasier's *End of the Trail* (c.1918).

The **European Painting & Sculpture★★** galleries offer classical antiquities; 19C canvases by Manet, Degas, Monet, Renoir, Van Gogh and Gauguin; and 20C works by Mondrian, Picasso, Braque and Modigliani. There are sculptures by Rodin, Moore and Oldenburg. The **Contemporary Gallery★**, one of the largest collections of post-1945 art in the Southwest, presents works by Rothko, Pollock, Motherwell, Warhol, Diebenkorn and other mid- to late 20C artists.

The **Wendy & Emery Reves Collection★** features 19-20C European painting and diverse decorative arts. Its setting recalls a French Riviera villa, and it has a full room devoted to paintings and memorabilia of Sir Winston Churchill. The **Arts of Africa** and **Arts of Asia and the Pacific** exhibits show a wide range of world cultures.

Nearby is the **Morton H. Meyerson Symphony Center★** *(2301 Flora St.; ☎ 214-670-3600)*, home of the Dallas Symphony Orchestra. The only such building designed by I.M. Pei (1989) incorporates the Eugene McDermott Concert Hall, whose unique tuning features were the creation of acoustician Russell Johnson.

★★★ **The Sixth Floor Museum at Dealey Plaza** – ▐▌▐▌ *411 Elm St. at Houston St.* ⅋ 🄿 ☎ *214-747-6660. www.jfk.org*. On November 22, 1963, alleged assassin Lee Harvey Oswald fired shots at President Kennedy from this level of the former Texas School Book Depository building. Today the entire 9,000sq-ft floor holds an impressive and moving tribute to Kennedy's life and career. Although the mood is hushed and reverential, exhibits do not canonize JFK. Audio programs *(included with admission)*, descriptive text, archival photographs and film footage (including 45min of video) treat the 35th president as a historical figure.

After a look at JFK's family history, marriage and early career, exhibits focus on the 1960 election campaign and the 1,000 days of the Kennedy presidency, especially the events leading to the assassination. The southeast corner window—from

ADDRESS BOOK

Please see explanation on p 64.

Staying in the Dallas-Fort Worth Area

The Mansion on Turtle Creek – *2821 Turtle Creek Blvd., Dallas.* ✕ ♿ 🅿 ⚓ ☏ *214-559-2100. www.rosewood-hotels.com. 141 rooms.* $$$$ Consistently ranked among the finest US hotels, the Mansion has soaring marble rotundas, elaborate floral arrangements and impeccable service. The wood-paneled dining room is famous for its haute Southwestern cuisine.

Hotel Adolphus – *1321 Commerce St., Dallas.* ✕ ♿ 🅿 ☏ *214-742-8200. www.adolphus.com. 433 rooms.* $$$ This 80-year-old creation of unabashed Baroque flamboyance and period furniture, with lacquered chinoiserie, tapestries, and chandeliers, was built by a beer baron. The crown jewel is **The French Room**, serving creative cuisine under vaulted ceilings and gilded rococo arches.

The Worthington – *200 Main St., Fort Worth.* ✕ ♿ 🅿 ⚓ ☏ *817-870-1000. www.worthingtonhotel.com. 504 rooms.* $$$ Spanning two city blocks and joined together by a glassed-in bridge, the Worthington stands on Sundance Square as Fort Worth's ultra-modern luxury hotel. Its restaurant is award-winning, and the interior design creates a plush escape.

The Melrose Hotel – *3015 Oak Lawn Ave., Dallas.* ✕ ♿ 🅿 ☏ *214-521-5151. 184 rooms.* $$ What once was a luxury, U-shaped apartment building is now a small hotel and historic landmark. The understated exterior is simple brick with a carved frieze; the handsome porte-cochere leads to marble floors, tall columns and newly renovated rooms. **The Landmark** serves fine regional cuisine.

Stockyards Hotel – *109 E. Exchange Ave., Fort Worth.* 🅿 ☏ *817-625-6427. www.stockyardshotel.com. 52 rooms.* $$ Located in the historic cowtown district, this Old West hostelry recalls early Texas history: Some rooms are decorated with rawhide lamps and steer skulls. The Davy Crockett Suite even boasts a coonskin cap from the days when cattle barons and rustlers sat in the saddles at the bar.

Dining in the Dallas-Fort Worth Area

Star Canyon – *3102 Oak Lawn, The Centrum, Dallas.* ☏ *214-520-7827.* $$$ **New Texas.** An open kitchen is the centerpiece of a room adorned with cowgirl murals and barbed-wire motifs. Offering salmon with black-bean banana mash, a foie-gras and corn-pudding tamale and rock-shrimp taquitos, it's top end for creativity.

Riscky's Steakhouse – *120 E. Exchange Ave., Fort Worth.* ☏ *817-624-4800.* $$ **American.** The interior of this local favorite resembles a street of old downtown Fort Worth, with a typical menu. Come for Texas T-bone or chicken-fried steaks; ask about batter-dipped "calf fries," cooked to a crispy golden brown.

Sonny Bryan's BBQ – *2202 Inwood Rd.* ☏ *214-357-7120. www. sonnybryansbbq.com.* $$ **Barbecue.** Sonny's opened in 1958 as a drive-in. The recipes for slow-smoked brisket have been passed through the family for a century; today, Texans slather Sonny's secret BBQ sauce onto spareribs, chicken and pulled pork. The double-dipped onion rings are delectable.

Joe T Garcia's – *2122 N. Commerce St., Fort Worth.* ☏ *817-626-4356.* $ **Mexican.** Joe T's is the epitome of Tex and Mex, where the Mexican beer is freely consumed by cowboy-clad customers on a patio that regularly fills to its capacity of 300. Visiting celebrities gobble up renowned menudos and enchiladas, or buy a round of potent margaritas to enjoy in the mini-park.

where Oswald allegedly shot the president—has been re-created to look as it did when investigators discovered it, with cardboard boxes stacked to create a hiding place. Newscaster Walter Cronkite's poignant announcement of the president's death is rebroadcast in a TV clip. Nearby is a photo of Lyndon Johnson taking the presidential oath with Jacqueline Kennedy by his side.

A final area considers a variety of conspiracy theories—including shots reputed to have come from an adjacent "grassy knoll"—and possible motives for Kennedy's murder. Display cases showcase international tributes; visitors also are encouraged to share their personal reflections in "memory books."

The Sixth Floor Museum is within **Dealey Plaza National Historic Landmark** district, six square blocks that encompass sites important to the Kennedy assassination and its aftermath. East of Dealey Plaza, **John F. Kennedy Memorial Plaza** centers on a cenotaph, or open tomb, designed by Philip Johnson and dedicated in 1970.

President John F. Kennedy, Texas Governor John Connally
and Mrs. Jacqueline Kennedy Moments Before the Assassination, November 22, 1963

★★ Pioneer Plaza – **Kids** *Young & Griffin Sts.* The world's largest bronze monument occupies this 4.2-acre park area north of the Dallas Convention Center *Cattle Drive* (1994, Robert Summers) features 40 longhorn steers being herded by a trio of mounted cowboys down a limestone ledge, past native plants and through a flowing stream.

★FAIR PARK

Built to host the 1936 Texas Centennial Exhibition, these 277-acre grounds, a short distance east of downtown, host the largest state fair in the US. Running for 24 days of September and October, the fair attracts the lion's share of 7 million annual visitors to Fair Park *(1300 Robert E. Cullum Blvd.; ☎ 214 670-8400).* Even during its "off-season," it bustles as a cultural center with its **Cotton Bowl** stadium *(☎ 214-939-2222);* the **Music Hall at Fair Park** *(909 First Ave.; ☎ 214-565-1116),* home of the Dallas Opera, the **Starplex Amphitheater** *(1818 First Ave.; ☎ 214-421-1111)* for open-air concerts; and 115 annual events. Also here are numerous museums, many of them—including the Hall of State, aquarium and natural-history museum—built in 1930s Art Deco style.

Scheduled to open in October 2000 is **The Women's Museum,** a $25 million interactive facility highlighting women's achievements in culture, commerce, politics, art, music and the sciences from the 19C into the 21C.

Hall of State – *3939 Grand Ave.* ♿ 🅿 ☎ *214-421-4500. www.hallofstate.com.* An exposition hall that showcases Texas history, the Hall of State is built of limestone in the shape of an inverted T. Larger-than-life bronze statues by Pompeo Coppini commemorate six of Texas' founding fathers, including

Stephen Austin, Sam Houston and Alamo defender William Travis. Ornate murals in the Great Hall depict historical events; side halls illustrate various regions of Texas.

★**African American Museum** – *3536 Grand Ave.* ♿ 🅿 ♨ *214-565-9026.* The only major facility in the Southwest devoted to African-American history, art and culture occupies a unique two-story building (1993, Arthur Rogers). Made of ivory stone with a 60ft dome in the shape of a 12C Ethiopian Orthodox cross, its design motifs symbolize pre-industrialized African cultures. Exhibits, centering around a rotunda, include selections from the **Billy R. Allen Folk Art Collection**, considered among the best contemporary collections in the US.

Dallas Museum of Natural History – **Kids** *3535 Grand Ave.* ♿ 🅿 ♨ *214-421-3466. www.dallasdino.org.* Move past the traditional exhibits on the ground floor—four dozen dated dioramas of Texas wildlife and habitats—and climb the stairs to see the first dinosaur discovered in this state (it's mounted) and interactive ecology exhibits. The entrance is marked by a bronze sculpture by Tom Tischler, based on a mammoth skeleton excavated in Dallas.

The Science Place – **Kids** *1318 Second Ave.* ♿ 🅿 ♨ *214-428-5555. www.scienceplace.org.* More than 300 interactive displays explore scientific principles. In Hands-On Physics, children learn to lift a 1,000-pound steel ball; in a medical gallery, visitors use microscopes to study bacteria and viruses. *Dallas: A Unique Place in Time* is shown before every feature in the IMAX theater. Less than a block away is **The Science Place Planetarium** *(First Ave. & Martin Luther King Blvd.).*

★**The Dallas Aquarium at Fair Park** – **Kids** *1462 First Ave. & Martin Luther King Blvd.* ♿ 🅿 ♨ *214-670-8443. www.dallas-zoo.org.* Operated by the Dallas Zoo, the aquarium is home to about 5,000 aquatic animals of 400 species, many of them anomalous fresh- or saltwater creatures—like fish with four eyes, fish that walk on land, and fish that are virtually invisible. Highlights include an Amazon River exhibit and tanks of native Texas species, including the rare Texas blind salamander, a 135-pound alligator snapping turtle and a 5ft electric eel. Visitors may attend public feedings of piranhas and sharks, and peer through windows to a breeding lab for endangered species.

Dallas Horticulture Center – *3601 Martin Luther King Blvd.* ♿ 🅿 ♨ *214-428-7476.* A resource for urban horticulture, this facility spans 7.5 acres of both decorative and native Texas plants. Its most notable feature is the **William Douglas Blanchly Conservatory**, a 6,800sq-ft glass facility that houses more than 250 species of African plants. Outside is a series of smaller specialty gardens.

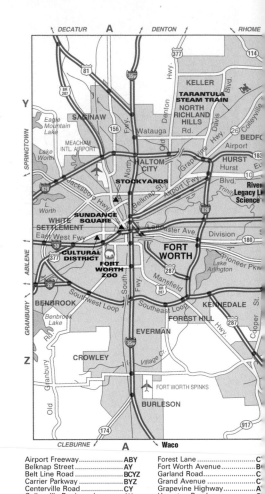

Airport Freeway	ABY	Forest Lane	C
Belknap Street	AY	Fort Worth Avenue	B
Belt Line Road	BCYZ	Garland Road	C
Carrier Parkway	BYZ	Grand Avenue	C
Centerville Road	CY	Grapevine Highway	A
Colleyville Boulevard	AY	Hampton Road	C
Collins Street	BY	Hawn Freeway	B
Cooper Street	AZ	Hurst Boulevard	A
Davis Boulevard	AY	Industrial Drive	B
Davis Street	BCZ	International Parkway	B
Denton Tap Road	BY	Jacksboro Highway	A
Division Street	AZ	Kiest Boulevard	B
East West Freeway	AZ	Lake Ridge Parkway	A
Euless Boulevard	AY	Lancaster Avenue	A
Ferguson Road	CY	Lancaster Road	C

ADDITIONAL SIGHTS

⋆**Old City Park** – 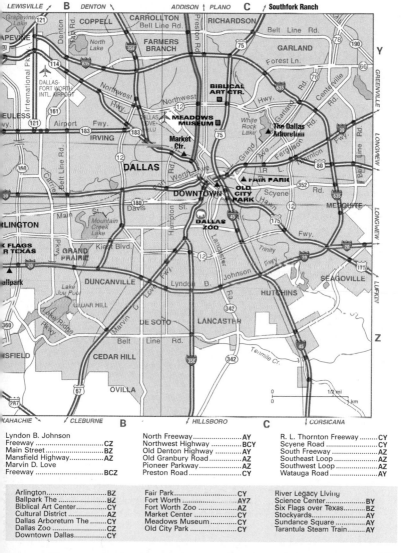 **Kids** *1717 Gano St.* ✕ & 🅿 ☎ *214-421-5141. www.oldcitypark .org.* This 13-acre museum village, south of downtown, contains 37 restored buildings dated 1840-1910, moved here and maintained by the Dallas County Heritage Society. Structures include a rail depot, hotel, bank, doctor's office and school, plus several private homes. Costumed docents carry on chores in the garden, curing shed and livestock lot of the Living Farmstead; a blacksmith, potter and printer may be on hand as well. McCall's 1907 general store offers shopping and the little Pilot Grove Church hosts weddings.

⋆**Dallas Zoo** – **Kids** *650 S. R.L. Thornton Fwy., 3mi south of downtown at Marsalis Exit, I-35.* ✕ & 🅿 ☎ *214-670-5656. www.dallas-zoo.org.* Founded in 1888, the zoo keeps 2,000 animals in two sections of 85 developed acres. The larger **ZooNorth** is in transition, its containments being replaced by new habitat areas such as a tiger exhibit. In the Bird & Reptile Building is a rare tuatara; the New Zealand lizard is considered the only surviving direct descendant of dinosaurs.

The more modern **Wilds of Africa**⋆⋆, south of Cedar Creek, boasts six expansive habitats of forest, mountain, woodland, river, desert and bush landscapes. From the Iliff Environmental Gallery, visitors take a .25mi nature trail to the Hamon Gorilla Conservation Research Center, where gorillas forage on two lush acres, and an African aviary. A 1mi **Monorail Safari** takes in 25 acres of habitats, featuring a prolific okapi population (26 have been born here) and other antelope and birds.

The Dallas Arboretum and Botanical Garden – *8525 Garland Rd.* ♿ 🅿 ☎ *214-327-8263.* Located on the southeast shore of White Rock Lake, this 66-acre expanse is highlighted by the **Jonsson Color Garden★**, the largest publicly maintained azalea garden in the US, with 20,000 bushes of more than 2,000 varieties. Other features are the 1940 Spanish Colonial-style **DeGolyer House** *(tours daily)* and a half-dozen children's **storybook playhouses** Kids.

★**Biblical Art Center** – *7500 Park Ln. at Boedeker St.* ♿ 🅿 ☎ *214-691-4661. www.biblicalarts.org.* Heavy wooden doors and a limestone gate—modeled after Paul's Gate in Damascus—greet visitors. Several galleries filled with Bible-themed artwork focus around a life-size replica of Christ's Garden Tomb in Jerusalem. The collection, ranging from Old Masters to contemporary art, is modest but diverse. It includes oils, pen-and-ink, woodblock, sculpture, stained glass and decorative furniture. The highlight is *The Miracle at Pentecost*, a 124ft-long mural by Torger Thompson depicting more than 200 biblical personalities. The mural is housed in its own theater and unveiled with a 30min sound-and-light presentation.

★★**Meadows Museum** – *Bishop Blvd. at Binkley Ave., Southern Methodist University.* ☎ *214-768-2516. www.smu.edu/meadows/museum.* Its interior fashioned after Madrid's famed Prado, this small university museum houses an outstanding collection of Spanish art. Oils, sculptures and works on paper span 1,000 years. Beginning with 10C Medieval and Renaissance paintings, it moves through Baroque Castillian (Velázquez) and Andalusian (Murillo) art to 18C dry-point etchings by Goya. There are 20C works by Miró and early Cubist still-lifes by Picasso. The museum is part of a larger arts complex that also features the Bob Hope Theatre.

EXCURSIONS

Southfork Ranch – *3700 Hogge Dr., Parker; 16mi north of downtown Dallas off US-75, Exit 30 East.* 🍴♿ 🅿 ☎ *972-442-7800. www.southforkranch.com.* J.R. Ewing may be gone and his *Dallas* soap opera relegated to syndicated television reruns, but the Ewing presence lives on at Southfork Ranch. Originally built as a residence and quarter-horse training ranch, the sprawling mansion was used in exterior shots for the long-running TV series. Visitors may board a tram to reach the Ewing Mansion for a guided tour. The "Dallas Legends" exhibit recalls famous moments with TV clips, star interviews and "the gun that shot J.R." Evening guests may take a haywagon to a chuckwagon dinner event.

Arlington – *I-30, 16mi west of Dallas & 15mi east of Fort Worth.* ☎ *817-461-3888.* A city of just over 300,000, Arlington is best known for its theme parks and as the home of major league baseball's Texas Rangers.

The Ballpark in Arlington – IIIII *1000 Ballpark Way.* 🍴♿ 🅿 ☎ *817-273-5222.* Built in 1994 (David M. Schwarz) in the style of early-20C ballparks, this $190 million stadium offers year-round tours of its dugouts, clubhouse, press box and owner's suite. The **Legends of the Game Museum and Learning Center★** Kids *(☎ 817-273-5098)* displays the largest collection of memorabilia from the Baseball Hall of Fame outside of Cooperstown, New York; third-floor exhibits present baseball as a medium for teaching principles of physics, history, geography and mathematics.

River Legacy Living Science Center – Kids *703 NW Green Oaks Blvd.* ♿ 🅿 ☎ *817-860-6752.* This nature-education facility, set on 1,000 acres of forest and floodplain beside the Trinity River, explores North Texas flora and fauna. There are quiet viewing rooms for bird- and river-watching and interactive videos.

★**Six Flags Over Texas** – Kids   IIIII *I-30 & Rte. 360.* 🍴♿ 🅿 ☎ *817-640-8900. www.sixflags.com.* The state's tallest and fastest roller coaster, "Mr. Freeze," is in this 221-acre theme park, as is the Texas Giant, rated the world's No. 1 wooden roller coaster. A $14 million expansion has resulted in new shows and thrill rides. The seasonal **Six Flags Hurricane Harbor** *(1800 E. Lamar Blvd.; ☎ 817-265-3356)* boasts water rides, slides and more than 3 million gallons of water.

FORT WORTH★★

Map p 114   Central Standard Time
Population 491,801
Tourist information ☎ 817-336-8791 or www.fortworth.com

The city that calls itself "the place where the West begins" wears its heritage like a Medal of Honor. Established in 1849 as a US Army outpost on the Trinity River, Fort Worth was named for Mexican War hero William Jenkins Worth. In the 1860s the town became a shipping point for buffalo hunters on the Great Plains. No city nickname has endured like "Cowtown," a moniker adopted in the 1870s when beef cattle were driven up the Chisholm Trail from South Texas. Fort Worth was first a supply station and later, with the arrival of the railway, a major terminus itself.

With the founding of the Stockyards in 1887, the town assumed a Wild West reputation. Saloons and brothels proliferated. The infamous Hell's Half Acre district served for a time as headquarters for Butch Cassidy and his Wild Bunch. By 1904, more than 1 million head of cattle had passed through the Stockyards; Fort Worth was the second largest beef, hog and sheep market in the US. Cattle pens extended for nearly a mile. So influential was the exchange, it became known as the Wall Street of the West.

During the early 20C, Fort Worth expanded and diversified, especially in the aviation and oil industries. But its "aw, shucks" image has remained, despite the enviable collection of world-class museums in its Cultural District.

At the heart of downtown Fort Worth is historic Sundance Square, a revitalized 20-block neighborhood named for notorious Western bandit Harry Longabaugh, "The Sundance Kid." The Stockyards National Historic District is 2mi north.

★★STOCKYARDS NATIONAL HISTORIC DISTRICT

An Old West flair persists in old Cowtown *(www.fortworthstockyards.org)*. A steam train, year-round rodeos and top country-and-western nightlife couple with historic hotels, steak houses and Western wear shops to give it a frontier flavor. The small **Stockyards Museum** *(131 E. Exchange Ave.; ☎ 817-625-5087)*, in the 1902 Livestock Exchange Building, chronicles history with a clutter of antiques and photos. At the century-old **White Elephant Saloon** *(106 E. Exchange Ave.; ☎ 817-624-1887)*, hundreds of patrons have left their Stetson hats nailed to the ceiling.

Cowtown Coliseum – **Kids** *121 E. Exchange Ave.* ♿ ☎ *817-625-1025. www.cowtowncoliseum.com.* Built in 1908, the coliseum presented the world's first indoor rodeo in 1918. Weekend evenings today, the Stockyards Championship Rodeo features bull riding, calf roping and barrel racing. Also presented is Pawnee Bill's Wild West Show, a revival of a traveling Western show—with rope tricks, cowboy songs and trick riding—that first played here in 1909.

Cattle Pens, Fort Worth Stockyards

© Tim Thompson

★**Billy Bob's Texas** – IIIII *2520 Rodeo Plaza.* ✗♿️📶 ☎ *817-624-7117. www.billybobstexas.com.* Billed as "the world's largest honky-tonk," this huge nightclub seats 6,000 and boasts 40 bar stations, line-dancing lessons, two separate music stages and an indoor professional bull-riding arena. Many of the top names in the country-music industry have performed here; autographed cement impressions of their hands are exhibited in a hallway gallery.

★**Tarantula Steam Train** – Kids *140 E. Exchange Ave.* ☎ *817-625-7145. www.tarantulatrain.com.* With the oldest "puffer-belly" locomotive in the US (c.1896), the fully restored Tarantula pulls a chain of Victorian coaches and open-air cars on a 75min, 21mi ride between the Stockyards and suburban Grapevine. Passengers may visit craftspeople at the Grapevine Heritage Center or attend tastings offered by award-winning wineries on Grapevine's historic Main Street. The trip is especially popular in spring and fall.

★SUNDANCE SQUARE

Sundance Square is not a square in the traditional sense. It is the heart of downtown Fort Worth, a revitalized district of brick streets lined with shops and restaurants, hotels and museums. Anchoring the district is the 1895 **Tarrant County Courthouse**★ *(100 W. Weatherford St.;* ☎ *817-884-1111)*, patterned after the Texas State Capitol. Often featured in the *Walker: Texas Ranger* TV series, it boasts an unusual *trompe l'oeil* paint job that gives a building extension the same appearance as the original stone structure.

The $65 million **Nancy Lee and Perry R. Bass Performance Hall**★ *(555 Commerce St.;* ☎ *817-212-4200)*, designed by David M. Schwarz (1998), occupies a full city block. It is identified by its twin 48ft limestone sculptures—trumpet-heralding angels by Marton Varo. The Bass is home to the Fort Worth symphony, ballet and opera, and the Van Cliburn International Piano Competition.

★**Sid Richardson Collection of Western Art** – *309 Main St.* ♿️📶 ☎ *817-332-6554. www.sidrmuseum.org.* Five dozen paintings by Charles M. Russell and Frederic Remington (the latter known best for his bronze sculptures) are showcased in this Sundance Square museum. Pieces include Remington's *Self-Portrait on a Horse* (1890) and *The Puncher* (1895), and Russell's *Returning to Camp* (1901) and *The Tenderfoot* (1900), the latter a comic piece that portrayed the urban East meeting the rugged West. The paintings were the personal collection of billionaire oilman Sid W. Richardson (1891-1959).

★**Cattle Raisers Museum** – *1301 W. 7th St.* ♿️📶 ☎ *817-332-8551. www. cattleraisersmuseum.org.* The evolution of the Texas ranching industry is portrayed in this museum, west of Sundance Square. A 14min multimedia show introduces ranch life; interactive exhibits allow "interviews" of 19C sheriffs and rustlers, ranch hands and ranch wives. Collections of saddles, spurs and branding irons represent cattlemen from Stephen F. Austin and Lyndon Johnson to actor John Wayne and baseball star Nolan Ryan. Plans call for the museum to relocate to the Cultural District by 2004, with a location adjacent to the proposed **National Cowgirl Museum and Hall of Fame** *(111 W. 4th St., Suite 300;* ☎ *817-336-4475)*.

★★CULTURAL DISTRICT

Trinity Park is the focus of this district, which includes four major museums as well as Fort Worth's zoo and botanical garden.

★★★**Kimbell Art Museum** – IIIII *3333 Camp Bowie Blvd.* ✗♿️📶 ☎ *817-332-8451. www.kimbellart.org.* A modern showcase building and a remarkable survey collection have made the Kimbell one of the finest small public art museums in the world. The building (1972, Louis Kahn) makes innovative use of natural light and enables curators to subtly rearrange its generous space for special exhibitions.

Although space limits the museum from displaying more than a fraction of its permanent collection at any one time, visitors might see such masterworks as Rubens' *The Duke of Buckingham* (1625); Rembrandt's *Portrait of a Young Jew* (1663); Cézanne's *Glass and Apples* (c.1879-82); Van Gogh's *Daubigny's Garden* (1890); Gauguin's *Two Women* (1902); and Matisse's *L'Asie* (1946). Works by Titian, El Greco, Goya, Pissarro, Degas, Monet, Picasso and Miró are also in the collection. There are changing exhibits of pre-Columbian, African and Asian art, from ancient Assyrian sculpture to Ming bronzes.

** Amon Carter Museum – *3501 Camp Bowie Blvd.* ☎ *817-738-1933.* *www.cartermuseum.org. Closed for renovation and expansion; scheduled reopening autumn 2001.* Oilman-publisher Amon G. Carter's private collection of 391 Charles Russell paintings and Frederic Remington sculptures provided the foundation for this museum. Two full galleries remain devoted to these documentalists of the old American West. After this International-style building (1961, Philip Johnson) opened, the collection expanded to encompass a wider range of Western art. The collection of more than 100,000 photographs is considered among the most historically important in the US.

* Fort Worth Museum of Science and History – **Kids** *1501 Montgomery St.* ✗ ♿ 🅿 ☎ *817-255-9300. www.fwmuseum.org.* Nine exhibit galleries, covering subjects from computers to anthropology, are featured at this family-oriented museum. It is renowned for its interactive exhibits, including an outdoor "dinosaur dig" and a preschoolers' science-discovery area. The museum is also home to an OMNI theater and a planetarium.

* Modern Art Museum of Fort Worth – *1309 Montgomery St.* ♿ 🅿 ☎ *817-738-9215. www.mamfw.org.* Ironically the oldest (1892) art museum in Texas, the Modern houses a modest collection of works iby the likes of Picasso, Rothko, Pollock, Motherwell, Warhol, Basquiat and Lichtenstein. Outdoor sculptures include George Segal's *Chance Meeting* (1974)—three bronze figures at a street sign—and Anthony Gormley's double-sized *Sculpture for Derry Walls* (1987). A satellite model, **The Modern at Sundance Square** *(410 Houston St.; ☎ 817-335-9215),* is in downtown Fort Worth.

** Fort Worth Zoo – **Kids** *1989 Colonial Pkwy.* ✗ ♿ 🅿 ☎ *817-871-7050. www.fortworthzoo.com.* Acclaimed both for its visitor accessibility and its animal-friendly habitats, this growing zoo is home to more than 6,000 animals of Texas and exotic species. In **Asian Falls,** waterfalls tumble through hillside precincts for tigers and sun bears, overlooking rhinoceroses and elephants. Viewing windows in **World of Primates** permit visitors to virtually enter the gorilla habitat. **Thundering Plains** showcases bison and other animals of the Great Plains. Wooded walkways connect the areas. Among indoor facilities are one of the largest freshwater aquariums in the US, a good-sized herpetarium and an enlightening **Insect City**.

* Fort Worth Botanic Garden – *3220 Botanic Garden Blvd. (off University Dr.).* ♿ 🅿 ☎ *817-871-7689.* Texas' oldest botanic garden began as a Depression-era relief program in 1933. The 109-acre gardens include more than 2,500 native and exotic species. The rose garden is abloom in late April and October. A Japanese garden features waterfalls and colorful koi. An impressive begonia collection is in the Exhibition Greenhouse; tropical plants fill the lush, 10,000sq-ft Conservatory.

EXCURSION

Waco – *On I-35, 87mi south of Fort Worth (via I 35W) and 90mi south of Dallas (via I-35E).* ☎ *254-750-8696.* A cattle and cotton-farming center of 108,000 on the Brazos River, Waco is home to Baylor University. It came to world attention during the March April 1993 standoff between Branch Davidian cultists and agents for the Federal Bureau of Investigation; an exhibit at the **Taylor Museum of Waco History** *(701 Jefferson St.; ☎ 254-752-4774)* interprets the tragic incident.

* The Texas Ranger Hall of Fame and Museum – *Fort Fisher Park off University Parks Dr. (I-35 Exit 335B).* ⚠ ♿ 🅿 ☎ *254-750-8631. www.texasranger.org.* The lawmen responsible for the taming of Texas are remembered in this museum. Displays include Billy the Kid's Winchester carbine, weapons packed by Bonnie and Clyde, and a gem-encrusted saddle from the 101 Ranch Wild West Show. Dioramas recount the early days of the Rangers, beginning in the 1840s.

Dr Pepper Museum and Free Enterprise Institute – **Kids** *300 S. 5th St.* ♿ 🅿 ☎ *254-757-1025. www.drpeppermuseum.com.* The Dr Pepper soft drink was invented in 1885 by pharmacist Charles Alderton at Waco's Old Corner Drug Store. Today, in the original 1906 Dr Pepper bottling plant, a lifelike model of Alderton describes his concoction. Exhibits and films look at manufacturing and marketing, including an amusing series of old TV commercials. The third-floor Free Enterprise Institute lauds the soft-drink industry as a success story of American capitalism.

** Armstrong Browning Library – *700 Speight Ave., Baylor University.* ♿ 🅿 ☎ *254-710-3566. www.baylor.edu/Library/LibDepts/ABL/ABL.html. Obtain parking permit at Wiethorn Visitors Center, University Parks Dr. at Baylor St.* ☎ *254-710-1921.*

Central Texas seems an unlikely place to find the world's largest collection of the works and belongings of British poets Robert Browning (1812-89) and Elizabeth Barrett Browning (1806-61). Dr. A.J. Armstrong, chairman of Baylor's English department for 40 years until his death in 1954, donated his personal Browning collection to the university in 1918; it grew in one room of the campus library until this two-story Italian Renaissance-style building was erected in 1951. Bronze doors, modeled after 15C Florentine baptistry doors by Ghiberti, were engraved by Robert Weinman; 56 stained-glass windows, the world's largest secular collection, illustrate works of both writers, including Robert Browning's *The Pied Piper of Hamelin* and his wife's *Sonnets from the Portuguese*. Also displayed are original manuscripts of Charles Dickens, Ralph Waldo Emerson and other authors.

■ Cattle Drives

By the end of the Civil War, severe meat shortages in the East led Texas ranchers to employ new strategies to get beef to market. Most dramatic was the cattle drive: Cowboys in South Texas collected enormous herds of wild and range cattle ("mavericks") and drove them north to railroads in Kansas. Although the heyday of the cattle drive lasted only a dozen years, its influence persists in popular myth.

Descendants of Andalusian and Castilian breeds brought to the New World by Spaniards, Texas Longhorns roamed freely over the grasslands of Texas and Mexico, numbering in the millions by the time of the first cattle drives in the late 1860s. Cowboys roamed the unfenced plains, gathering herds for the long trip to the markets. Along the way lay many hazards—hostile Apache and Comanche Indians, thieves and rustlers, treacherous rivers and inclement weather, not to mention the normal hardships of life on the range.

The Chisholm Trail was the most famous of the cattle-drive routes. In 1870 alone, 300,000 cattle were driven through San Antonio, Austin and north to Fort Worth, the last "civilized" stop before Indian Territory. In Cowtown, cowboys girded themselves for the rigors of the trail in saloons and brothels. As their herds thundered down Commerce Street, townsfolk knew to stay off the streets.

By the late 1870s, the railroad was pushing south and west, eventually making the cattle drive obsolete.

© Walter Frerck/Odyssey

Longhorn Cattle Roundup

Denver Area

Larimer Square

Nicknamed the "Mile High City" because its elevation is exactly 5,280ft above sea level, Denver is a rapidly growing metropolis of more than 2.3 million people. As the largest urban center within a 550mi radius—between Phoenix and Chicago, Dallas and Seattle—it is the focus of commerce, government, sports and the arts for the greater Rocky Mountain region.

Denver is nestled near the foothills of the Rockies on a high plain that originally was Arapaho and Cheyenne Indian land. The alpine panorama to its west has become North America's greatest mountain playground, with many famous ski resorts (such as Vail and Aspen) and a remarkable concentration of peaks higher than 4,000m (13,124ft). To the east are a few topographic rolls, then flat land stretching across the prairie states to the Mississippi River.

Neither the mountains nor the prairie is heavily populated. The main towns north and south of Denver cling to the Front Range, as the eastern fringe of the Rockies is called. Little more than an hour's drive south is Colorado Springs, sprawling at the foot of immense Pikes Peak, its 14,110ft summit a landmark to westbound travelers since it was first sighted by Lieutenant Zebulon Pike in 1806. The burgeoning city is home to the US Air Force Academy, the high-altitude US Olympic Training Center and numerous unique geological and architectural attractions. Two hours north by interstate freeway is Cheyenne, the small Wyoming state capital that clings to its Wild West heritage. Cheyenne is quiet except during 10 days in late July and early August when it hosts Cheyenne Frontier Days, the world's largest outdoor rodeo.

Denver owes its origin to mining. Although fur trader Luis Vásquez had a trading post here as early as 1832, pioneers showed no inclination to settle until gold was discovered nearby in late 1858. Denver grew as a miners' supply center near the confluence of Cherry Creek and the South Platte River. When the gold supply dwindled, silver became king. The city continued to thrive through many subsequent boom-and-bust cycles. Colorado Springs, by contrast, thrived as a spa and tourism center—the first genuine resort community west of Chicago—and Cheyenne began as a transcontinental railroad construction camp.

DENVER★★★

Maps p 101 and 127   Mountain Standard Time
Population 499,055
Tourist Information ☎ 303-892-1112 or www.denver.org

Denver today has replaced mining with manufacturing as its economic base. Telecommunications and computer industries contribute to the economy. With thousands of state, local and federal employees, Denver has the country's second-highest percentage of government workers after Washington DC.

The city is an important cultural and entertainment center with museums, theaters and concert venues, and is one of only eight US cities with franchises in all four major-league sports: football, baseball, basketball and ice hockey. The annual National Western Stock Show & Rodeo ties Western tradition to modern times.

Historical Notes

Denver City was formed in 1860 by the merger of two gold-rush settlements. The community at first rode an economic roller coaster with a stream of prospectors, some of whom came from the East, others from the California gold rush a

ADDRESS BOOK

Please see explanation on p 64.

Staying in the Denver Area

The Brown Palace Hotel – *321 17th St., Denver.* ✗ ♿ 🅿 ☎ *303-297-3111. www.brownpalace.com. 230 rooms.* **$$$$** When entrepreneurs seeking silver and gold flocked west in 1892, they stayed at the distinguished Brown Palace. Presidents still shake hands in the grand atrium, with seven tiers of balconies lined in Mexican white onyx and topped with a stained-glass dome. Celebrities dine at the formal **Palace Arms** among European battle flags.

The Broadmoor – *1 Lake Ave., Colorado Springs.* ✗ ♿ 🅿 🏊 ☎ *719-634-7711. www.broadmoor.com. 700 rooms.* **$$$** At first a casino, by 1918 it was a grand resort nestled against the Rocky Mountain foothills. Today it displays the same pink-stucco facade and curved marble staircase. Nine restaurants, a world-class spa, three golf courses and four swimming pools add to its charms.

The Oxford Hotel – *1600 17th St., Denver.* ✗ ♿ 🅿 ☎ *303-628-5400. www.theoxfordhotel .com. 80 rooms.* **$$$** French and English antiques adorn rooms at Denver's oldest grand hotel. The red-brick exterior is classic; careful restorations have revealed false ceilings and silver chandeliers previously coated in paint. Built in 1891, it is on the National Register of Historic Places.

The Warwick – *1776 Grant St., Denver.* ✗ ♿ 🅿 🏊 ☎ *303-861-2000. www .warwickhotels.com. 215 rooms.* **$$$** This elegant midsize hotel has undergone extensive renovation, with data-ports and tasteful new furnishings. An atrium, fitness center, rooftop pool and restaurant add to the first-class image.

Hotel Boulderado – *2115 13th St., Boulder.* ✗ ♿ 🅿 ☎ *303-442-4344. www.boulderado.com. 160 rooms.* **$$** A bright lobby, with a canopied ceiling of stained glass and mosaic tile, recalls the era of Victorian elegance. It has been intertwined with Boulder history for over 90 years. Furniture is antique, but **Q's Restaurant** serves contemporary award-winning cuisine.

Cheyenne Cañon Inn – *2030 W. Cheyenne Blvd., Colorado Springs.* 🅿 ☎ *719-633-0625. www.cheyennecanoninn.com. 10 rooms.* **$** The Inn has had a turbulent history——bordello, gambling house and orphanage—— but is now an outstanding B&B. The mansion has over 100 windows, providing canyon and mountain views, and an international flair: Lodgings range from Swiss chalet to Oriental teahouse.

Dining in the Denver Area

Bravo! – *1550 Court Pl., Adam's Mark Hotel, Denver.* ☎ *303-626-2581.* **$$$** **Italian.** The staff here are not only servers; they also are professional singers: When they set down big bowls of seafood *capelli di angelo*, they serenade diners with Italian opera or Broadway tunes. An open kitchen lets the chefs perform as well, and a 1,700-bottle wine cellar adds to the conviviality.

decade earlier. Despite Indian skirmishes, fire, flood, spotty communications and a transient population laden with outlaws and tricksters, the frontier town survived the pioneer era as capital of the Colorado Territory.

Denver's ultimate prosperity was pegged to silver. Between the mid-1870s and mid-1890s, strikes in Leadville, Aspen and other camps turned miners into millionaires. Successful silver production required banks to underpin the enterprises, mercantiles to outfit them, smelters to extract precious metals from ore, and trains to connect the mountain towns with Denver and the East.

By 1890 Denver was a fashionable city of 106,000 with fine hotels, stores, the- aters and mansions. Electric lights were installed in 1883; the first streetcars began running five years later. Although many mining towns were devastated in the financial panic of the 1890s and in the switch from gold to silver as the US currency standard, Denver weathered the economic storm.

Today the railroads are all but gone. But Interstates 70 and 25 cross in Denver, and the 1995 opening of Denver International Airport, one of the busiest in the world, assured the city's importance as a locus of transportation systems.

Buckhorn Exchange – *1000 Osage St., Denver.* ☎ *303-534-9505. www.buckhorn.com.* **$$$ Regional.** Like Theodore Roosevelt and his contempo- raries, diners at Denver's oldest restaurant can try elk, pheasant and rat- tlesnake in the company of more than 500 animal trophies and 125 guns. The eatery uses such indigenous Old West ingredients as chilies and juniper berries.

John's Restaurant – *2328 Pearl St., Boulder.* ☎ *303-444-5232.* **$$$ Conti- nental.** Dining here is like dining in a quaint private home: Only 30-40 peo- ple a night are served, but these few are rewarded with chef-owner John Bizzarro's weekly choices, from Basque seafood stew to turkey breast with mole sauce. His caramel cheesecake has been a house favorite for 22 years.

Craftwood Inn – *404 El Paso Blvd., Manitou Springs.* ☎ *719-685-9000. www.craftwood.com.* **$$ Regional.** This Tudor style restaurant of beamed ceil- ings and stained- glass windows, once a coppersmith shop, began serving food in 1940. Views of Pikes Peak are spec- tacular. The cuisine is hearty and robust Colorado: noisettes of caribou, loin of wild boar, grilled pheasant sausage and piñon trout.

Wynkoop Brewing Company – *1634 18th St., Denver.* ☎ *303-297-2700.* **$$ American.** As the biggest brewpub in the US, the Wynkoop tallies over 5,000 barrels a year on its Barrel-O-Meter. The LoDo warehouse has many whimsical annual "competi- tions," but normal days see the con- sumption of pub fare: hot artichoke dip, beer-braised pot roast and plenty of signature RailYard Ale.

© David Falconer/FOLIO, Inc.

Lunch at the Buckhorn Exchange

Practical Information .... Area code: 303

Getting There – Denver International Airport (DEN) (☎ 342-2200, www .diaweb.com) is 24mi northeast of downtown. Rental car and shuttle service counters are in the main terminal. Ground transportation is on baggage-claim level. RTD SkyRide and SuperShuttle (☎ 370-1300, www.supershuttle.com) run buses and vans to downtown and surrounding areas.

Amtrak train: Union Station (1701 Wynkoop St.; ☎ 800-872-7245, www.amtrak.com). Greyhound and regional buses: Main terminal (20th & Curtis Sts.; ☎ 293-6555 or 800-231-2222, www.greyhound.com).

Getting Around – The Regional Transportation District (RTD) operates local and regional buses and a light rail line that runs through downtown (☎ 299-6000, www.rtd-denver.com). Local fares $1.50 during rush hours, 75¢ all other times. Transfers free; exact change required. Coupons and tokens at Market Street and Civic Center stations and some grocery stores. The Cultural Connection Trolley (daily $3) operates summers between major museums, hotels and shopping areas . The 16th Street Mall Shuttle (free) runs between Market Street and Civic Center. Taxi: American Cab (☎ 321-5555), Metro Taxi (☎ 333-3333), Yellow Cab (☎ 777-7777), Zone Cab (☎ 444-8888).

Accommodations – Contact the Denver Metro Convention & Visitors Bureau (below) for area lodging and reservations. Hotel Reservations Network (☎ 214-361-7311, www.hoteldiscount.com) provides free reservations service.

Entertainment – Consult the Friday and Sunday editions of the Denver Post and Rocky Mountain News, or the weekly Westword, published Thursdays, for listings of current events, theaters and concert halls. Favorite venues: Denver Center for the Performing Arts (☎ 893-4100), Historic Paramount Theatre (☎ 220-7000), Fiddler's Green Amphitheater (☎ 220-7000), Red Rocks Amphitheater (☎ 640-7334).

Visitor Information – The Denver Metro Convention & Visitors Bureau (DMCVB) (1555 California St., Suite 200, Denver CO 80202; ☎ 892-1505, www.denver.org) operates three visitor information centers: Denver International Airport main terminal, Tabor Center (entrance facing Larimer Square.) and Cherry Creek Shopping Center. The free Official Visitors Guide of the Denver Metro Chamber of Commerce (1445 Market St., Denver CO 80202; ☎ 620-8075, www .denverchamber.org) contains detailed information on accommodations, area events and attractions, and dining (available in visitor centers and hotels).

★DOWNTOWN DENVER

The revitalization of downtown Denver began in the Lower Downtown Historic District, best known as "LoDo." The neighborhood has been gradually reborn since the 1965, when historic preservationists reinvented Larimer Square, the city's oldest commercial block. LoDo is linked to Civic Center Park by mile-long 16th Street Mall, a promenade that continues to attract slick new construction.

★★ **LoDo** – Between Larimer & Wynkoop Sts., 20th St. & Speer Blvd. ✕ ▣ ☎ 303-628-5428. Ardent preservationists fought for the renovation of 17 neglected c.1870-90 buildings. Their efforts culminated in 1973 in **Larimer Square**★★ (1400 block of Larimer St.; ☎ 303-534-2367), a lively, pedestrian-friendly thoroughfare. The restoration movement boomed in the 1990s as LoDo became Denver's most energetic neighborhood. A multitude of 19C commercial buildings and warehouses were revitalized into 60 restaurants and clubs, 40 galleries and shops, and upper-story apartments. The 1995 opening of **Coors Field** 🄺🄸🄳🄳 ⅢⅢ (2001 Blake St.; ☎ 303-292-0200), a baseball stadium, climaxed the transformation.
Larimer Square anchors the southern end of the 26-block historic district. The 1895 **Union Station** (1701 Wynkoop St.) remains a Beaux-Arts landmark on its northern fringe. Across the street from the depot is the **Wynkoop Brewing Company** (1634 18th St.; ☎ 303-297-2700), Denver's original microbrewery and one of America's first when it opened in 1988.

★ **16th Street Mall** – 16th St. between Market St. & Broadway. ✕ ♿ ▣ Extending southeast from the bus terminal to Civic Center Plaza, the tree-lined Mall was created in 1982. The route is flanked by office towers, street-level cafes and shops, and 11 fountains. Horse-drawn carriages and free shuttle buses are the only vehicles permitted. Highlights include the 1910 **D & F Tower**★ (at Arapahoe

St.), a 325ft replica of the campanile of St. Mark's Basilica in Venice, Italy; and the 1891 **Kittredge Building** *(at Glenarm Pl.),* a handsome Romanesque Revival structure housing restaurants and offices. The **Historic Paramount Theatre** *(1631 Glenarm Pl.;* ☎ *303-825-4904),* built in 1929, has one of two operating dual-console pipe organs in the US (the other is at New York's Radio City Music Hall). The $100 million **Denver Pavilions** *(between Welton St. & Glenarm Pl.;* ✕ ♿ 🄿 ☎ *303-260-6000)* is Denver's newest shopping-dining-entertainment complex.

★ **Brown Palace Hotel** – *321 17th St. at Tremont Pl. & Broadway.* ✕ ♿ 🄿 ☎ *303-297-3111. www.brownpalace.com.* Five US presidents and the Beatles have stayed at "The Brown," Denver's grandest hotel (1892, Frank Edbrooke). The nine-story Italian Renaissance landmark is made of red granite and sandstone. Twenty-six stone medallions depicting Rocky Mountain animals are set between the seventh-story windows. Interior balconies, framed by ornate ironwork, rise eight stories above the atrium beneath a stained-class ceiling. Afternoon tea is served in the lobby, itself trimmed with Mexican white onyx.

★★ CIVIC CENTER

Some of Denver's most important public buildings surround **Civic Center Plaza**★ *(between Broadway & Bannock St., W. Colfax & 14th Aves.),* at the southeast edge of downtown. The grandiose green space, sweeping westward from the capitol steps, was designed in 1904 by landscape architect Frederick Law Olmsted Jr. and Chicago city planner E.H. Bennett. Dominating the west side is the **City & County Building** (1932), Denver's city hall. It continues the park's classical themes with Doric columns on a concave granite facade flanking a large portico with Corinthian columns. The slim central tower houses the **Speer Memorial Chimes.**

★★ **Colorado State Capitol** – *East side of Civic Center Plaza facing Lincoln St.* ♿ ☎ *303-866-2604.* As the seat of state government, the imposing hilltop capitol (1886, Elijah Myers) is home to the General Assembly and offices of the governor and other officials. Constructed over 22 years in the shape of a Greek cross, the granite capitol is a smaller version of the US Capitol. Its gilded gold-leaf dome, a gleaming 272ft-high landmark, once dominated the city scene. From the third-floor rotunda, 93 steps climb into the dome for a commanding **view**★★ of the surrounding city. Senate and House chambers are on the second floor; visitor galleries are open when the legislature is in session *(Jan-Apr).*

★ **Molly Brown House** – *1340 Pennsylvania St., 3 blocks east of the capitol.* ☎ *303-832-4092. www.mollybrown.org.* Made famous by a Broadway musical and an Oscar-nominated 1964 movie, the "unsinkable" Molly Brown experienced new popularity after the 1998 movie *Titanic.* Visits to her home surged as well. Guided tours *(60min)* of the 7,700sq ft sandstone house (1889, William Lang) offer a glimpse into Denver's Gilded Age through the prism of this remarkable woman. In spring 1912, having raised two children and separated from her wealthy miner husband, Molly boarded the ill-fated *Titanic.* First as the liner was sinking and later aboard the rescue ship, Carpathian, she tried to bring order to chaos. She subsequently organized relief efforts for survivors. Molly ran for US Congress three times — twice before women were granted the right to vote.

★ **Colorado History Museum** – 🄺🄸🄳🅂 *1300 Broadway.* ♿ ☎ *303-866-3682. www.coloradohistory.org.* Galleries include an 1800-1949 timeline and exhibits on cowboys, pioneer lifestyle, transportation, and black and Hispanic cultures. Of note are numerous artifacts from Mesa Verde, removed in the late 19C before the establishment of the national park; and a display of heavy mining machinery with interpretive text describing mineral production processes.

★★ **Denver Art Museum** – *100 W. 14th Ave. Pkwy.* ✕ ♿ 🄿 ☎ *303-640-4433. www.denverartmuseum.org.* This thin, twin-towered building, faced with iridescent tile, is a modern fortress looming over Civic Center Plaza, with exhibits on seven vertically stacked, 10,000sq-ft gallery floors.

The Cheyenne (1901),
Bronze by Frederic Remington

Highlights of a renowned 17,000-item **Native American Collection**★★★ *(2nd & 3rd floors)* include an 1840s house panel from a southeast Alaskan Tlingit chief; a Salish spirit figure and an Iroquois war club, both from the mid-1850s; Plains Indian horse trappings from the 19C; and a modern Navajo sand painting.

Maya, Aztec and Inca pieces contrast dramatically with European aesthetic in the **Pre-Columbian and Spanish Colonial**★★ collections (4th floor). **Asian Art**★ (5th floor) includes Hindu sculptures, Islamic textiles and Japanese scrolls. **European and American Art**★ (6th floor) is organized thematically—landscapes in one area, portraits in another. Highlights include Monet's *Waterloo Bridge* (1903) and Warhol's *Liz* (1965). **Western Art**★★ (7th floor) includes a casting of *The Cheyenne* (1901) widely regarded as the best Remington sculpture in existence.

★**The Denver Public Library** – *10 W. 14th Ave. Pkwy.* ☐ ☎ *303-640-6200. www.denver.lib.co.us.* A striking Postmodern structure (1995, Michael Graves & Brian Klipp), this library—largest in the US between Chicago and Los Angeles—boasts six public floors and 47 miles of shelves. Seventy panels by artist Edward Ruscha adorn its main hall and atriums. The acclaimed **Western History Collection** includes important early maps, documents and photographs; a $20 million art collection features work by Remington, Bierstadt and Moran.

★★**US Mint** – Kids ‖‖‖ *W. Colfax Ave. & Cherokee St. (east of Civic Center Park). Visit by guided tour only.* ☐ ☎ *303-405-4761. www.usmint.treas.gov.* This mint, one of four in the country, produces half the coins circulated in the US. It strikes 10 billion coins a year, producing an average of $3.5 million each day, and tends one-fourth of America's gold reserves—shipped from San Francisco in 1934 because Denver is not as vulnerable to earthquakes or wartime attacks.

The elegant, five-story, granite-and-marble building (1906, James Knox Taylor) was modeled after the Medici Riccardi Palace in Florence, Italy. Displays of coins and currency, mint equipment and historic photos line visitors' galleries. Free weekday tours *(20min)* offer views of the stamping and counting rooms as a guide describes the process of striking, counting and bagging coinage.

WEST OF DOWNTOWN

For decades, the area along the South Platte River, just west of downtown, was neglected. Today Denver is reclaiming its riverfront. New attractions include the **Pepsi Center** (Speer Blvd. & Auraria Pkwy.) basketball and ice-hockey arena.

Six Flags Elitch Gardens – Kids ‖‖‖ *2000 Elitch Cir. off Speer Blvd. (I-25 Exit 212A). Open May-Sept.* ✗☐ ☐ ☎ *303-595-4386.* Established in 1890 in northwest Denver, Elitch Gardens moved in 1995 to this site and became part of the Six Flags chain. Thrill rides and a cartoon town are among its draws.

★★**Colorado's Ocean Journey** – Kids ‖‖‖ *700 Water St. at 23rd Ave. (I-25 Exit 211).* ✗☐ ☐ ☎ *303-561-4450. www.oceanjourney.org.* Opened in 1999, this modern aquarium incorporates the sights, sounds and climate of simulated American and Asian river habitats, from their headwaters to the Pacific Ocean. **Colorado River Journey** begins in the trout-rich streams of the Rockies and depicts a 1,500mi course through the arid Grand Canyon to the subtropical Sea of Cortez. **Indonesian River Journey** follows Sumatra's 300mi Kampar River through similarly dramatic transitions from lush jungle (where two rare Sumatran tigers live near a freshwater pool) to a coral lagoon.

★★CITY PARK

The grand space was established in 1881 and modeled after the urban parks of Boston, New York, London and Paris. From the east end of the park—which occupies 314 acres between Colorado Boulevard and York Street, 17th and 26th Avenues—visitors get a fine **view**★★ of the Denver skyline and mountains beyond. The park has two lakes, a rose garden, a golf course and a playground.

★★**Denver Museum of Nature and Science** – Kids *2001 Colorado Blvd., City Park.* ✗☐ ☐ ☎ *303-322-7009. www.dmnh.org.* From a modest origin in 1900, this three-story museum has grown to become one of the largest in the US, with more than 500,000 specimens and artifacts. Included are 95 natural-history dioramas and exceptional collections of fossils, minerals and cultural artifacts. There are interactive displays for students, a planetarium *(closed for renovation through 2001)* and an IMAX theater.

A section of the alpine Sweet Home Mine is re-created in the heralded gem display of **Coors Mineral Hall**★★★. A central room showcases Tom's Baby, at 135 ounces the largest gold nugget ever found in Colorado. Immensely popular

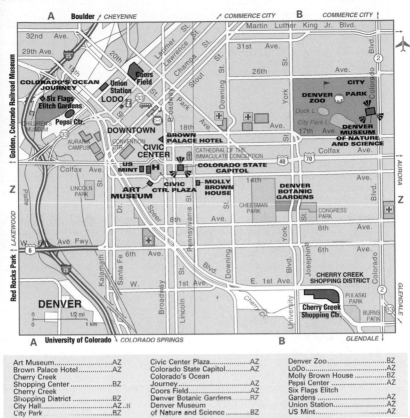

with children is **Prehistoric Journey★★**, a 3.5-billion-year timeline that depicts the history of life on earth, from single-cell organisms through huge dinosaurs to modern man. **Dioramas★** on the second and third floors present flora and fauna of the Rocky Mountains and the wider world, including South America and Africa. Other exhibits examine Native American and ancient Egyptian cultures.

★Denver Zoo – [Kids] *2300 Steele St., City Park.* ✗ ♿ 🅿 ☎ *303-376-4800. www.denverzoo.org.* Nearly 4,000 animals of 700 species are at home in this 80-acre zoo, laid out on an oval around a 1.5mi loop. Summer visitors may tour the grounds aboard the Safari Shuttle, an open-air electric bus, or the Pioneer Train, a scale model of an 1878 train, powered by natural gas.
Tropical Discovery★★, a $10 million rain-forest habitat under a huge glass pyramid, is home to many species, including deep-sea chambered nautiluses. **Primate Panorama★** features nocturnal lemurs, Asian orangutans and endangered African lowland gorillas. Feeding time at **Northern Shores**, an Arctic habitat for harbor seals, sea lions and otters, is among the zoo's most popular spectacles.

ADDITIONAL SIGHTS

★Denver Botanic Gardens – *1005 York St. (4 blocks south of E. Colfax Ave.).* ✗ ♿ 🅿 ☎ *303-331-4000. www.botanicgardens.org.* With 30 themed areas, these gardens are a tranquil oasis amid urban congestion. From early spring to the first hard frost, rose, lilac, peony, iris and daylily gardens attract birds and butterflies. The Rock Alpine Garden mimics high-altitude life zones. The soaring glass dome of **Boettcher Memorial Conservatory★★** shelters tropical plants in a startlingly humid environment. Gentle paths meander through this paradise, best viewed from a platform suspended 40ft in an artificial banyan tree.

Cherry Creek Shopping District – *1st Ave. between Steele St. & University Blvd.* ✗ ♿ 🅿 Denver's single most popular visitor attraction is the **Cherry Creek Shopping Center** *(3000 E. 1st Ave.; ☎ 303-388-3900)*, an elegant indoor mall just north of Cherry Creek Park. The adjacent streets of **Cherry Creek North** *(1st* *to 3rd Aves.;* ☎ *303-394-2903)* are lined with boutiques, restaurants, galleries, salons and day spas. The **Tattered Cover★** 🄺🄸🄳🄸 *(2955 E. Milwaukee St.;* ☎ *303-322-7727)* is one of the country's best bookstores. **The Rink at Cherry Creek** 🄺🄸🄳🄸 *(E. 1st Ave. & Fillmore St.;* ☎ *303-394-9170)* offers winter ice skating and rentals.

EXCURSIONS

★★ **Golden** – *15mi west of downtown Denver via I-70 (to Rte. 58) or US-6 (to 19th St.).* 🅇🅖 🄿 ☎ *303-279-3113. www.goldenchamber.org.* The Colorado territorial capital from 1862 to 1867, Golden lost the state capital to Denver by one vote; population now exceeds 15,000. Walking tours begin at the tourist office *(1010 10th St.)* and take in the **Astor House Museum** *(822 12th St.;* ☎ *303-278-3557),* first brick hotel west of the Mississippi River when built in 1867; the **Golden Pioneer Museum** *(923 10th St.;* ☎ *303-278-7151),* and the **Rocky Mountain Quilt Museum** *(1111 Washington Ave.;* ☎ *303-277-0377).*

★ **Coors Brewing Co.** - 13th & East Sts. Visit by guided tour only. 🅖 🄿 ☎ *303-277-2337 or 303-277-2552 (foreign-language tours).* The world's largest brewing complex, founded in 1873 by immigrant brewer Adolph Coors, stretches for 2mi along Clear Creek. Tours follow the 16-week beer-making process through malting, brewing and packaging. Some 1.5 million gallons of beer are produced daily.

★ **Colorado Railroad Museum** – 🄺🄸🄳🄸 *17144 W. 44th Ave.* 🄿 ☎ *303-279-4591. www.crrm.org.* The largest rail museum in the Rocky Mountains displays more than 70 examples of trains that brought development and settlement to the frontier West.

Buffalo Bill Grave & Museum – *987 1/2 Lookout Mountain Rd. (I-70 Exit 256, 5mi west of Golden).* 🅇🅖 🄿 ☎ *303-526-0747. www.buffalobill.org.* The inimitable "Buffalo Bill" Cody *(p 389)* died while visiting his sister in Denver in 1917 and was buried atop Lookout Mountain. The gravesite, a simple stone plot near the museum and its extensive gift shop, affords a fine **view★** of the Front Range.

★ **Red Rocks Park and Amphitheater** – *Hogback Rd., Morrison (via Rte. 26 off I-70 or Morrison Rd. off Rte. 470).* 🅇🅖 🄿 ☎ *303-697-8935. www.Red-Rocks.com.* The 9,450-seat outdoor amphitheater is cradled by a vast natural bowl sculpted between two 300ft sandstone outcroppings high on a ridge. Major concert events are staged here. The 630-acre park also has trails for hiking and biking.

★★ **Boulder** – 🄺🄸🄳🄸 *29mi northwest of Denver via US-36.* △🅇🅖 🄿 ☎ *303-442-2911. http://visitor.boulder.co.us.* This attractive city of 90,000 people nestles against uplifted red-rock mountains called The Flatirons. Founded in 1859, it boomed after Colorado established its state university here in 1876. Modern Boulder is largely defined by the pioneering limits on residential construction it adopted in 1977, and by the 84sq mi greenbelt that surrounds it—providing 200mi of trails for bicycling, skating, jogging and walking. Some 25,000 University of Colorado students, including more than 1,000 from abroad, contribute a youthful flavor.
Lively **Pearl Street Mall★** *(11th to 15th Sts.)* is a brick-paved pedestrian zone of shops, galleries and sidewalk cafes; landmark buildings are the 1933 **Art Deco Boulder County Courthouse** *(13th & Pearl Sts.)* and the 1909 **Hotel Boulderado★** *(2115 13th St. at Spruce St.;* ☎ *303-442-4344),* a red-brick Italianate structure. The **Boulder Creek Path★** 🄺🄸🄳🄸 *(☎ 303-442-2911)* runs creekside for 16mi through the heart of the city. The dramatic glass architecture of the new **Boulder Public Library★** *(1000 Canyon Blvd.;* ☎ *303-441-3100)* straddles the creek near downtown. Facing a block of farmers' markets is The **Boulder Dushanbe Teahouse★★** *(1770 13th St.;* ☎ *303-442-4993),* an elaborate, polychrome-tile restaurant, handcrafted and assembled by Tajikistani artisans in 1998 as a gift from Boulder's sister city of Dushanbe in their central Asian country. Nearby, the **Boulder Museum of Contemporary Art** *(1750 13th St.;* ☎ *303-443-2122)* offers a rotating series of exhibits.

★ **University of Colorado** – *Broadway to 28th St. & University Ave. to Baseline Rd.* 🅇🅖 🄿 ☎ *303-492-1411. www.colorado.edu.* Two hundred buildings spread over this 786-acre campus. **Old Main** (1877), the university's first structure, is a turreted brick Victorian, but most buildings are pink sandstone with red-tile roofs—the legacy of Charles Klauder's 1917 plan inspired by the hill towns of Tuscany. Visitors are welcome at the **University of Colorado Museum of Natural History** *(Henderson Bldg., 15th St. & Broadway;* ☎ *303-492-6892)* and **Fiske Planetarium & Observatory** *(Regent Dr. at Kittredge Loop Dr.;* ☎ *303-492-5001).*

Chautauqua Park – *Baseline Rd. & 9th St. Vehicle entrance at 6th St.* ✂♿ 🅿 ☎ *303-442-2911.* In the late 19C, when the nationwide Chautauqua movement encouraged retreats to nurture body, mind and spirit. This park opened in 1898 with tent lodgings and two buildings that still stand—the **Auditorium** (site of the Colorado Music Festival) and **Dining Room** (a restaurant). Trails ascend from broad lawns into alpine meadows beneath The Flatirons and the 33,000-acre **Boulder Mountain Parks**★ *(☎ 303-441-3408).* Those who don't hike **Flagstaff Mountain**★ can drive a twisting byway from Baseline Road to numerous scenic overlooks.

★ **National Center for Atmospheric Research** – *1850 Table Mesa Dr.* ✂♿ 🅿 ☎ *303-497-1174. www.ncar.ucar.edu.* The stunning Mesa Laboratory (1966, I.M. Pei) is a fortuitous blend of style and science. Pei's international reputation was secured by this building, dramatically set against the Flatirons and inspired by Anasazi cliff dwellings (and featured in Woody Allen's 1973 movie, *Sleeper*). Guided 1hr tours include hands-on displays illustrating atmospheric phenomena, real-time weather and climate change, robotic meteorological instruments and aviation hazards.

Department of Commerce Laboratories – *325 Broadway at 27th Way.* ✂♿ 🅿 ☎ *303-497-5500. www.nist.gov.* The National Institute of Standards and Technology and National Oceanic and Atmospheric Administration share a large campus. Displays study electromagnetic interference, communications satellites and weather. Guided tours (2hrs) include a cryogenics demonstration and a look at the atomic clock that keeps the most accurate time in the US.

COLORADO SPRINGS★★

Map p 101 Mountain Standard Time
Population 344,987
Tourist Information ☎ 719-635-7506 or www.coloradosprings.travel.com

Nestled at 6,035ft at the foot of soaring Pikes Peak, Colorado Springs enjoys one of the most beautiful settings of any city in North America.

Civil War Gen. William Jackson Palmer, builder of the Denver & Rio Grande Railroad, founded the city in 1871 on a rail link to the mining towns of Cripple Creek and Victor. He called it "Springs" to attract Easterners accustomed to fashionable health resorts. Spencer Penrose, who made a fortune in gold and copper, matched the general in ambition and concept. In the early 20C he built the Pikes Peak Auto Highway, developed The Broadmoor as a world-class resort hotel, and endowed many of Colorado Springs' enduring cultural institutions. During the Cold War, "The Springs" established itself as the hub of US military air defense with its Cheyenne Mountain Operations Center. Many defense contractors also are based in the city, a home for numerous fundamentalist Protestant organizations.

Downtown Colorado Springs reflects the grandiose vision of its founders in broad avenues, an elegant layout and fine old buildings. Early years are documented at the **Colorado Springs Pioneers Museum** *(215 S. Tejon St.; ☎ 719-578-6650)* in the 1903 courthouse. The **Colorado Springs Fine Arts Center**★ *(30 W. Dale St.; ☎ 719-634-5581)* features paintings by O'Keeffe, Russell and Audubon in an Art-Deco landmark (1936, John Gaw Meem) that recalls Pueblo style in limestone and steel.

SIGHTS

★ **US Olympic Complex** – Kids *Boulder St. & Union Blvd.* ♿ 🅿 ☎ *719-632-5551, www.usoc.org.* One of three national training centers for amateur athletes (along with San Diego, California, and Lake Placid, New York), this complex was built in 1978 on the grounds of a former Air Force base. A visitor center houses the US Olympic Hall of Fame. Free tours *(60min)* take visitors down the colorful Olympic Path pedestrian walkway to watch gymnasts and swimmers hone their skills; the International Center for Aquatic Research and a state-of-the art sports-medicine clinic are of particular interest. More than 550 coaches and athletes, in two dozen sports, live here at one time.

★ **Old Colorado City** – *Colorado Ave. & cross streets from S. 24th to S. 27th Sts.* ✂♿ 🅿 *http://history.oldcolo.com.* Before Colorado Springs there was El Dorado, settled in 1859 and soon renamed Colorado City. It became part of Colorado Springs in 1917. The **Old Colorado City History Center** *(S. 24th St. at Pikes Peak Ave.; ☎ 719-636-1225)*, in an 1890 church, exhibits historic photographs, documents and memorabilia. Colorado Avenue is lined with restaurants, artists' studios and Western collectibles galleries in charmingly restored commercial buildings. **Van Briggle Art Pottery** *(600 S. 21st St.; ☎ 719-633-7729)* is a century-old facility whose works have been displayed at the Louvre and Metropolitan Museum of Art.

*The Broadmoor – *1 Lake Circle; west end of Lake Ave. via I-25 Exit 138.* ✗ ♿ 🅿
🕿 *719-634-7711. www.broadmoor.com.* Born in 1891 as a small casino at the
foot of Cheyenne Mountain, The Broadmoor was reincarnated when Spencer Penrose bought the 40-acre site (and 400 adjoining acres) in 1916 and turned it into
a world-class resort. European artisans created ornate frescoes and tile work,
marble fixtures and other design elements in the pink-stucco, Italianate hotel.
Today three 18-hole golf courses, 12 tennis courts, four swimming pools, riding
stables, nine restaurants and lounges, a conference center and spa make up the
700-room complex. A 17C pub, the Golden Bee, was imported from England.
Penrose's widow, Julie, built the **Carriage House Museum** in 1947 for antique vehicles.
A 1mi loop circles the original hotel and the resort's private lake.

One block north of The Broadmoor, the **World Figure Skating Hall of Fame** 🄺🄸🄳🅂 *(20 1st
St.; 🕿 719-635-5200),* offers ice-skating memories from the 17C to the present.
Skating and hockey competitions are held at the 8,000-seat **Colorado Springs World
Arena** *(3185 Venetucci Blvd. at Circle Dr.; 🕿 719-477-2100),* opened in 1998.

*Cheyenne Mountain Zoo – 🄺🄸🄳🅂 *4250 Cheyenne Mountain Zoo Rd. From The
Broadmoor, take Lake Circle south to Mirada Rd. & west to Cheyenne Rd.* ✗ ♿ 🅿
🕿 *719-633-9925. www.cmzoo.org.* Built in 1926 by Penrose on a pine-forested
hillside to house exotic animals he had received as gifts from around the world,
America's only mountain zoo was deeded to Colorado Springs in 1938. It is home
to more than 500 animals of 146 species. In 1998, 29 of its 74 animal births
were endangered species, including a spectacled bear and a Sichuan takin. Other
rare species include the snow leopard, black rhinoceros and Sumatran orangutan.
Paved paths wind up the hill; summer guests may ride a tram.

To reach the **Will Rogers Shrine of the Sun*** *(🕿 719-634-5975),* motorists drive cau-
tiously through the zoo grounds and up a 1.5mi winding road to a plateau
2,000ft above Colorado Springs. The 100ft granite tower, resembling a Medieval
castle, was built as a Penrose family tomb but was rededicated to philosopher-
actor Will Rogers when he died in a 1935 plane crash. Tower landings are photo
galleries of Rogers' life: a 94-step climb reveals an outstanding **view**** east.

Cheyenne Mountain Air Station Visitors Center – *1 NORAD Rd.* ♿ 🕿 *719-
474-2238. www.spacecom.af.mil/usspace.* Visitors must book two months ahead to
attend public briefings *(3 times weekly, 75min)* that consist primarily of a multimedia presentation. Security is tight; entrance is not permitted to the Cheyenne
Mountain Operations Center itself. In the early 1960s, 693,000 tons of solid
granite were carved from within the peak to house the North American Aerospace
Defense Command (NORAD) and US Space Command, in a facility insulated
against earthquakes and nuclear explosions. Today, 1,450 employees work underground in 15 independent buildings, each with its own tunnel.

**Seven Falls – 🄺🄸🄳🅂 *West end of Cheyenne Blvd.; off Mesa Dr. via Lake Ave. from
The Broadmoor.* ✗ ♿ 🅿 🕿 *719-632-0765. www.sevenfalls.com.* A road threads
through the Pillars of Hercules, a slot in South Cheyenne Canyon, and terminates
at this impressive 181ft series of waterfalls. Eagle's Nest, accessed by elevator or
185 steep steps, overlooks the falls. Another staircase *(224 steps)* ascends beside
the falls to the start of the **Inspiration Point Trail** *(0.5mi).*

*ProRodeo Hall of Fame and Museum of the American Cowboy – 🄺🄸🄳🅂 *101
ProRodeo Dr.; at Rockrimmon Blvd. off I-25 Exit 147.* ♿ 🅿 🕿 *719-528-4764.
www.prodeo.com.* Two multimedia presentations trace the lifestyle of rodeo,
"America's original sport" *(p 132),* from its 19C origins to the present. The hall of
fame honors the most skillful cowboys, clowns, showmen and behind-the-scenes
personnel with plaques or bronze statues. Further displays highlight cowboy gear
and garb, saddles, ropes and personal souvenirs.

**US Air Force Academy – *Academy Dr. West off I-25 at Exit 156-B (North Gate
Blvd.); 12mi north of downtown.* ⛺ ✗ ♿ 🅿 🕿 *719-333-8723. www.usafa.af .mil.*
On 29sq mi at the foot of the Rampart Range, this is the only US service academy
in the West. A self-guided auto tour includes a B-52 display and scenic overlooks.
The highlight is the **Cadet Chapel***** (1959-63, Skidmore, Owings & Merrill),
designed by Walter Netsch. Topped by 17 aluminum spires, each 150ft high, this
soaring cathedral comprises individual Protestant, Catholic, Jewish and interfaith
chapels. At 11:35am each weekday, the academy's 4,000 cadets march smartly to
lunch across the square beside the chapel. The nearby **Barry Goldwater Visitor Center***
(🕿 719-333-2025) explains cadet life in interactive displays.

**Garden of the Gods - 🄺🄸🄳🅂 *Garden Dr. (north of US-24) or Gateway Rd. (west of
30th St.).* ✗ ♿ 🅿 🕿 *719-634-6666. www.GardenOfGods.com.* Fabulous red-rock
formations within this 1,400-acre city park, a geological showcase, soar up to
300ft. Paved roads offer easy access to the best-known formations—Balanced

Rock, Cathedral Spires, Kissing Camels, Three Graces and Tower of Babel—rising dramatically from a landscape of greenery. Most are better seen via foot, bicycle or horseback on trails of .5mi to 3mi in length.

Guided walks and nature programs begin on the east side of the park at a new **visitor center** Kids *(1805 N. 30th St.)*, which offers an orientational 12min multimedia show. Just south at the **Rock Ledge Ranch Historic Site** *(Gateway Rd. & 30th St.; ☎ 719-578-6777)*, costumed docents portray life on an 1860s homestead, an 1880s ranch and an early-20C estate. The landmark 1901 **Garden of the Gods Trading Post** *(324 Beckers Ln.; ☎ 719-685-9045)*, a sprawling Pueblo-style structure, is on the south side of the park.

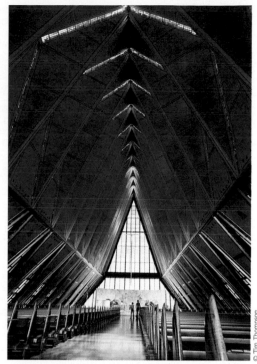

Cadet Chapel, Interior

© Tim Thompson

***Pikes Peak** – ✕ ⬚ ⯈ P ☎ 719-385-7325. *www.pikespeakcolorado.com*. At 14,110ft elevation, Pikes Peak is not the highest mountain in the US nor even Colorado. But it is arguably the most imposing high peak, probably the most famous, definitely the most accessible. Named in 1806 by Army Lieutenant Zebulon Pike, who declared the mountain "unconquerable," it has proven anything but. A railway mounted its flank as early as 1891. Developer Spencer Penrose built a motor road in 1916 and bought the railway in 1925.

Visitors today ascend to the **Summit House** cafe and gift shop via railway, car or foot. The peak is often cold and windy, and snow may fall at any time. But when skies are clear, unrivaled **views***** extend west into the snow-capped Rockies, east across the plains, north to Denver and south to the Sangre de Cristo range.

The **Pikes Peak Cog Railway***** Kids ⅧⅢ *(515 Ruxton Ave., Manitou Springs; ☎ 719-685-5401)* remains a great excursion. Small black coal-fired steam locomotives, tilted to keep the boilers level, originally pushed trains up the mountain's eastern side. Now diesel electric models do so *(late Apr-early Nov; round-trip 3hrs includes 30min at summit)*. From its picturesque depot, the train climbs more than 6,500ft in a series of steep grades with constantly changing views. Marmots and bighorn sheep cavort among the rocks.

At the peak's broad summit, the cog railway meets the **Pikes Peak Highway**** *(☎ 719-385-7325)*, a meandering 19mi toll road. It begins at Cascade *(15mi west of Colorado Springs on US-24)*; after 7mi, at the **Crystal Reservoir and Visitor Center**, pavement is replaced by gravel. Hikers may ascend Pikes Peak via the **Barr Trail** *(☎ 719-578-6640)*. Challenge Unlimited *(☎ 719-633-6399)* offers a downhill alternative in a guided convoy of mountain bikes with good brakes.

Manitou Springs** – *4mi west of Colorado Springs on US-24 bypass.* △ ✕ ⬚ P ☎ 719-685-5089. *www.manitousprings.org*. Long before Gen. Palmer began to promote Manitou Springs as a resort in the early 1870s, Indians and mountain men knew of the restorative waters that bubbled from the ground northeast of Pikes Peak. A spa and hotels were established in the 1890s. Today galleries and bed-and-breakfast inns occupy many charming, if aging, structures, and open-air street trolleys make 1hr summer circuits of the quaint downtown. **Miramont Castle *(9 Capitol Hill Ave.; ☎ 719-685-1011)*, the imposing 1895 sandstone mansion of a wealthy French priest, combines elements of nine design styles in its 28 rooms.

***Cave of the Winds** – Kids ⅧⅢ *US-24 Bypass, 2mi west of Manitou Springs.* ✕ P ☎ 719-685-5444. *www.caveofthewinds.com*. After two boys discovered a cavern entrance in 1880, Manitou resident George Snider began exploring its passages. He broke through to a chamber—200ft long and 50ft high—that now is the centerpiece of a commercial cave still owned by the Snider family. It is reached by a steep, winding 1mi road. Guides on the **Discovery Tour** *(45min)* explain limestone cave formation to visitors walking a well-lit concrete path. Participants in the **Lantern Tour** *(75min)* follow a guide in 1880s garb who emphasizes history and legend.

Manitou Cliff Dwellings Museum – **Kids** *US-24 Bypass, just above Manitou Springs.* ✗ 🅿 ☎ *719-685-5242. www.cliffdwellingsmuseum.com.* The 40 rooms and towers in Phantom Cliff Canyon were dismantled by archaeologists in the Four Corners area at the end of the 19C and reconstructed here as a re-creation of 12-13C Anasazi culture. Native Americans built the adjacent pueblo in 1896 as a residence and lived here until 1984. Their descendants still dance in summer. A large retail shop and two museums display artifacts.

EXCURSIONS

★★ Cripple Creek – *45mi west of Colorado Springs via US-24 to Divide, then Rte. 67 south.* ⚠ ✗ ♿ 🅿 ☎ *719-689-3315.* When gold was discovered on the east flank of Pikes Peak in 1890, this town at 9,396ft elevation became the world's greatest gold camp. Within 10 years its population reached 25,000. It boasted 16 churches, 73 saloons, streetcars, and 18 rail arrivals and departures daily. Neighboring **Victor**, 6mi south, had 18,000 residents. Mining continued until 1961, by which time more than $800 million worth of ore had been taken.

Today a different kind of gold flows: Limited-stakes gambling was legalized in 1991 and Cripple Creek has been revitalized. Visitors who tire of casinos can take a trip on the **Cripple Creek & Victor Narrow Gauge Railroad★** *(east end of Bennett Ave.; ☎ 719-689-2640)*. A 15-ton steam locomotive pulls the train on a 4mi

---

■ Eight Seconds: The World of Rodeo

A quarter-million rodeo fans attend Cheyenne Frontier Days, the world's largest professional outdoor rodeo, in late July each year. Well over 100,000 descend upon Denver in January for the National Western Stock Show and Rodeo, the world's largest livestock show and indoor rodeo. Parades, barbecues and top-end country-and-western music complement the action in the dusty arenas.

Throughout much of the West, rodeo is more popular than baseball, football or golf. Like their late-19C forebears who originated the sport, young ranch hands vie to see who is the best rider, roper or wrestler on the spread. Those who fare well may continue to regional competitions in which silver belt buckles and prize money are awarded to winners. They may earn just enough to reinvest their earnings in another event. Losers often gain nothing but broken bones.

The best athletes, members of the Professional Rodeo Cowboys Association, may earn jackpots of many thousands of dollars. From headquarters adjacent to the ProRodeo Hall of Fame in Colorado Springs, the PRCA oversees a year-round national circuit culminating in the National Finals Rodeo in Las Vegas, Nevada, in December.

A typical rodeo has six events: bull riding, saddle- and bareback-bronc riding, steer wrestling, team and individual roping, plus women's barrel racing. Scoring is based on style and difficulty in the first three events; stronger,

© Robert Holmes

journey past abandoned mines to the ghost town of Anaconda *(late May-early Oct)*. In the depot is the **Cripple Creek District Museum** *(☎ 719-689-2634)*. At the **Mollie Kathleen Gold Mine**★★ *(1mi north on Rte. 67; ☎ 719-689-2465)*, visitors descend 1,000ft into a hard-rock mine, where veteran miners demonstrate the mining process.

Florissant Fossil Beds National Monument – *35mi west of Colorado Springs via US-24.* & ▯ ☎ *719-748-3253. www.nps.gov/flfo.* More than 50,000 fossils— one of the most extensive records of the Oligocene epoch, 35 million years ago— have been removed from the shale bed of ancient Lake Florissant. Among them are an astounding 14,000 species of insects. Fifteen miles of nature trails pass sequoia stumps petrified by volcanic mud flows.

CHEYENNE★

Michelin map 493 H 7, 8   Mountain Standard Time
Population 53,640
Tourist Information ☎ 307-778-3133 or www.cheyenne.org

Cheyenne, today Wyoming's capital and largest city with a population nearing 54,000, was founded in 1867 as a construction camp for rail workers just 10mi north of the Colorado border. With the train came thousands of immigrants—some real-estate speculators and confidence men, but more honest merchants, tradesmen and cowboys, who worked the surrounding grasslands. Local citizens formed vigilante committees to rid the town of outlaws. Cheyenne then settled into frontier comfort with streets of handsome mansions and a thriving social scene. When Wyoming joined the Union in 1890, Cheyenne was chosen capital.

temperamental animals can earn more points. Skill and courage are critical, but the luck of the draw plays a part. In wrestling, roping and racing, speed is paramount.

Bull riding is the most perilous event—"no doubt one of the most dangerous you can do," said seven-time world all-around champion Ty Murray. "If it wasn't, guys probably wouldn't do it, and people certainly wouldn't come watch it." Eight seconds must seem like a lifetime to riders who, in order to score, cling for that long to the back of a one-ton bull, clenching a single thick rope wrapped around the animal's chest. If the bull throws its rider by jumping, kicking and ramming the arena wall, it may then turn and attack with its horns or hooves. Many riders have been seriously injured; some have died. Fallen riders put their faith in daring rodeo clowns who lure bulls away from cowboys while risking their own lives.

Bronco rides, a progression from the traditional cowboy "breaking" of wild horses, also last eight seconds. Mounted horses, released from fenced chutes, buck wildly to eject their riders. Cowboys employ a rhythmic rocking motion to stay on top. Bareback riders cling to nothing but a single-hold rigging; saddle-bronc riders have a thick rope rein and stirrups. When the time has elapsed, cowboys slide to safety on another horse ridden by a "pickup man."

Steer wrestling, or bulldogging, was invented in the early 20C by a famous black cowboy named Bill Pickett. A mounted "hazer" forces the steer to run straight ahead; a "dogger" leaps from his horse onto the back of a 700-pound steer, grabs its horns and wrestles it to the ground with its feet and head facing the same direction, often in less than seven seconds.

Perhaps the best test of a true cowboy is roping, a skill still used for branding young cattle on the open range. Horses must be specially trained. In team roping, a pair of riders lassos a young steer by its horns and hind legs. In individual roping, the cowboy dismounts from his horse to tie three legs of the calf he has roped. The animal, which weighs 250-300 pounds, has six seconds in which to free itself; it is quickly liberated when that time has passed.

Barrel racing, the lone event for women, requires speed and agility. Riders on horseback follow a cloverleaf course around three barrels spaced 100ft apart. Penalty seconds are added to times if any barrels are knocked over.

Cheyenne Frontier Days (☎ 307-778-7222) were first held in 1897; today the world's largest outdoor rodeo, parade and carnival consumes all of southeastern Wyoming in late July and early August. At other times, even in winter when the legislature is in session, Cheyenne remains startlingly serene. Walking tours of the downtown historic district begin at the 1886 **Union Pacific Depot** (121 W. 15th St.; ☎ 307-637-3376), currently being restored as a transportation museum.

SIGHTS

★Wyoming State Capitol – 24th St. & Capitol Ave. ♿ 🅿 ☎ 307-777-7021. As statehouses go, this gray sandstone building (1890) is modest, but with such elegant fittings as a 24-carat gold-leaf dome and interior woodwork of maple and cherry. The stained-glass dome ceiling was imported from England. The third-floor Legislative Conference Room features a half-ton Tiffany chandelier and a 22ft mural by Mike Kopriva that depicts Wyoming history.

Wyoming State Museum – [Kids] 2301 Central Ave. ♿ 🅿 ☎ 307-777-7022. http://spacr.state.wy.us/cr/wsm. Sharing two floors of the Barrett Building just southeast of the capitol, 10 galleries depict Wyoming's human and natural history. Exhibits focus on dinosaurs; Shoshone and Arapaho culture; gold, uranium and coal mining; jade prospecting; cowboy traditions, and more.

Warren ICBM & Heritage Museum – 7405 Marne Loop, Francis. E. Warren Air Force Base. 🅿 ☎ 307-773-2980. Established in 1867 as a cavalry post to protect rail workers from Indians, Warren was the most powerful US missile base in the Cold War and remains the Intercontinental Ballistic Missile (ICBM) command center. Building 210, the former commander's headquarters, houses exhibits on military life. Building 211 has two missile launch setups and ground capsules, one interactive so visitors can "launch" missiles and monitor progress.

★Cheyenne Frontier Days Old West Museum – [Kids] 4610 N. Carey Ave. Frontier Park. ♿ 🅿 ☎ 307-778-7290. Housed in one wing of the Cheyenne Frontier Days headquarters is this year-round tribute to the event's exciting century of history. Dust and Glory, a 55min audiovisual presentation, spotlights this biggest and most important event on the professional rodeo circuit.

EXCURSIONS

Laramie – 46mi west of Cheyenne via I-80 or Rte. 210. Founded like Cheyenne as a railroad town, Laramie took a different path with the founding in 1886 of the University of Wyoming. Today at least half of the town's 25,000 residents are students, faculty or staff. Just off the 780-acre campus is the **Laramie Plains Museum** (603 Ivinson Ave.; ☎ 307-742-4448), an 1892 Victorian mansion.

University of Wyoming – Ivinson Ave. & 9th St. ⚹♿ 🅿 ☎ 307-766-4075. Most buildings surrounding the campus quadrangle are limestone. A standout is the **Geological Museum** (S.H. Knight Bldg.; ☎ 307-766-4218), notable for a full-size copper tyrannosaur outside and a full apatosaur skeleton inside. Exhibits range from jade and uranium to core samples from oil drilling. The **American Heritage Center** (22nd St. & Willett Dr.; ☎ 307-766-4114), housed in Antoine Predock's futuristic Centennial Complex, has sections on industry, environment and Western art, including works by Catlin, Remington and Moran.

★Wyoming Territorial Prison & Old West Park – [Kids] 975 Snowy Range Rd. at I-80. ⚹♿ 🅿 ☎ 307-745-6161. www.wyoprisonpark.org. Commemorating Old West heritage, this theme park includes Wyoming's original Territorial Prison (1872-1901). Tours include cell blocks that held such outlaws as Butch Cassidy, who served 18 months for horse-stealing. In **Frontier Town**, men and women in 19C garb perform crafts and trades in buildings moved from other parts of Wyoming. One structure holds the National US Marshals Museum; another has a dinner theater.

★★Fort Laramie National Historic Site – 113mi north of Cheyenne via I-25, US-26 & Rte. 160. ♿ 🅿 ☎ 307-837-2221. www.nps.gov/fola. Built by fur traders near the North Platte River in 1834, this key Oregon Trail fort was garrisoned by the Army in 1849. Fort Laramie helped pave the way for the Pony Express, transcontinental telegraph and overland stage routes. Major campaigns against hostile Indian tribes were launched from this bastion until it closed in 1890.
Half of its 22 buildings have been restored and furnished to their 19C appearance. The 1884 commissary holds a visitor center and museum with artifact displays, historic photos and other exhibits, including a scale model of the fort in its heyday.

El Paso Area

Prickly Pear Cacti. Big Bend National Park

E l Paso is, seemingly, a world apart from the rest of Texas. Separated from the Lone Star State's other population centers by more than 500mi of high desert, this bilingual city is the largest US-Mexico border city after metropolitan San Diego. Geographically and culturally, it is far nearer to Albuquerque and Tucson—and, indeed, to Ciudad Juárez. Mexico—than to Houston or Dallas. It's even in a different time zone than other Texas cities.

Fully three-quarters of its population are of Spanish heritage. Traditional Native American cultures of the Southwest, particularly the Pueblo tribe known as the Tigua, also had a major impact on the region's development, as did white Americans, including railroad builders and soldiers.

Within a few hours' drive in any direction from El Paso, explorers can look 8,000 years into the past—and perhaps an equal distance into the future.

Geography is dominated by the Rio Grande, the great river that rives the state of New Mexico and sculpts the international boundary between Texas and Mexico. The most dramatic scenery is found 300mi southeast of El Paso in the canyons of isolated Big Bend National Park. Much of this wilderness belongs to wild animals like mountain lions and javelinas, but not far downriver are human habitation sites considered among the oldest in North America.

Other national parks and monuments are within an easy day's drive east or north of El Paso, most of them in southern New Mexico. Best known of the New Mexico parks is Carlsbad Caverns National Park, one of the world's largest and most complex underground labyrinths. Other attractions range from the very ancient to the unfathomably futuristic. Near centuries-old Anasazi cliff dwellings and pueblos, radio telescopes send high-frequency messages into outer space. Not far from the site of Billy the Kid's most famous and brutal jailbreak is the location of the world's best-documented crash of a supposed UFO, an unidentified flying object. A stone's throw from the charred forest home of Smokey Bear is the wasteland that witnessed the world's first atomic bomb test.

ADDRESS BOOK

Please see explanation on p 64.

Staying in the El Paso Area

Camino Real Hotel, El Paso – *101 S. El Paso St., El Paso TX.* ✗♿ 🅿 ⛓ ☎ *915-534-3000. www.caminoreal.com/elpaso. 359 rooms.* **$$** At 17 stories, this historic landmark overlooks three states in two nations. Decked in brass, cherry and marble, the lobby is topped by a Tiffany glass dome of mosaic leaves and blue sky. The ambience of the **Dome Restaurant** takes fine dining back to the turn of the 20C.

Lajitas Resort – *Rte. 170, Terlingua TX.* ✗♿ 🅿 ⛓ ☎ *915-424-3471. www.lajitas.com. 119 rooms.* **$** Remote and historic, this 1915 cavalry post once protected the Big Bend area from Mexican bandits. Now it's a full Old West experience—with modern additions like swimming pools and golf courses. Lodgings include the Badlands Hotel and the Officer's Quarters, with planked facades and covered wooden sidewalks, on the dusty main drag.

The Lodge – *1 Corona Pl., Cloudcroft NM.* ✗♿ 🅿 ⛓ ☎ *505-682-2566. 61 rooms.* **$** At 9,200ft elevation, The Lodge was built in 1899 as a retreat for overheated Texans. Paddle fans and gently clanging radiators remain. Guests perch on the copper-domed observatory for views that stretch for 150mi, and eat creative Southwestern cuisine at award-winning **Rebecca's Restaurant.**

Dining in the El Paso Area

Los Bandidos de Carlos and Mickey – *1310 Magruder St., El Paso TX.* ☎ *915-778-3323.* **$$ Mexican.** With cathedral ceilings and terra-cotta tiles, this hacienda-style tribute to the Revolution is the prettiest Mexican restaurant in El Paso. Walls have photos of everyone from Pancho Villa to Miss Texas to five-star generals. The menu features green chile stew and tacos in adobe sauce.

Flying "J" Ranch – *Rte. 48, Ruidoso NM.* ☎ *505-336-4330.* **$ Barbecue.** Offering a foot-stompin' night of gunfights, pony rides, gold panning and cowboy fixin's, this chuck-wagon supper of beef, beans and biscuits recalls what cowboys once ate on the trail. Guests wander through an Old West village until the dinner bell rings, then are entertained by a world-champion yodeler.

EL PASO★

Michelin map 492 G, H 12   Mountain Standard Time
Population 615,032
Tourist Information ☎ 915-534-0653 or www.visitelpaso.com

Located in Texas' westernmost corner, El Paso is linked to adjacent Ciudad Juárez, Mexico, just across the Rio Grande. International trade keeps the border busy in both directions. El Paso is a manufacturing center, especially active in the production of cotton clothing. The newly renovated El Paso Museum of Art is the vanguard of downtown revitalization in the 14-block **Union Plaza** cultural and entertainment district; it is scheduled for completion in 2003.

Rising behind the city are the Franklin Mountains, southernmost tip of the Rockies. This warm, dry region is part of the Chihuahuan Desert; altitudes range from 3,800ft in the city to 7,200ft in the mountains, so climate may vary.

Historical Notes – El Paso originally was home to Manso Suma Indians. The region was claimed for Spain in 1598 by Juan de Oñate, who named it El Paso del Rio del Norte. Six decades later, priests arrived to establish a series of missions on the Juárez side of the Rio Grande. In 1680, the Pueblo Indians in northern Mexico drove out Spanish settlers, who fled to the El Paso region with Christianized Indians known as Tiguas and Piros. They founded Ysleta and Socorro, and together with Franciscan padres built the first Texas missions.

In the mid-19C, the US Army constructed Fort Bliss for defense of the city and surrounding areas. El Paso was incorporated in 1873; it became a boomtown a decade later with the arrival of the railroad. Throughout the late 19C, the city had a Wild West reputation, with gunfights and a renegade atmosphere.

SIGHTS

** **El Paso Museum of Art** – *1 Arts Festival Plaza at Santa Fe & Main Sts.* ☎ *915-532-1707. www.elpasoartmuseum.org.* With an $8 million renovation completed in 1998, this spacious two-level museum includes a reference library, auditorium and the Arts Festival Plaza, which features a reflecting pool, waterfall and performance areas.

The **Works on Paper Collection** showcases drawings and prints from the 16-20C, including Cézanne, Degas, Picasso, Goya and Rivera. The **American Collection** (late 18C-mid-20C) has works by Frederic Remington and post-Depression Figurative painter Moses Soyer. The **Samuel Kress Collection** highlights 13-18C European paintings and sculpture, including pieces by Canaletto and Van Dyck. The **Spanish Viceroyal Collection** features 17-19C artists and includes Mexican folk retablos. The **Contemporary Collection** emphasizes pieces created in the American Southwest and Mexico since 1945.

* **El Paso Holocaust Museum and Study Center** – *401 Wallenberg Dr.* ♿ 🅿 ☎ *915-833-5656. www.flash.net/~epholo.* Memorializing the Holocaust's 6 million victims and its survivors, this museum's bone-chilling exhibits include a three-quarter-scale model of a railroad used to carry victims to concentration camps, a facsimile of an underground gas chamber and models of Nazi death camps. The Garden of the Righteous, shaded by cypress, commemorates non-Jews who risked their lives to assist Jews during the war.

* **Chamizal National Memorial** – *800 S. San Marcial Dr.* ♿ 🅿 ☎ *915-532-7273. www.nps.gov/cham.* Located near the Bridge of the Americas, this memorial to peaceful US-Mexico relations recalls the 1963 resolution of a century-old border dispute caused by the shifting of the Rio Grande's course. A visitor center presents a 12min video on border history; **Los Paisanos Gallery** exhibits paintings, sculpture and photography from several countries. A 120ft-long mural by Carlos Flores, *Nuestra Herencia* ("Our Heritage"), depicts in four panels the blending of American and Hispanic cultures. Within the 55-acre park is the **Córdova Island Trail** *(1.8mi)*, with views of the El Paso skyline and surrounding mountains. On many evenings, the park's 500-seat indoor theater offers performances by *ballet folklórico* troupes or modern dancers.

* **Mission Trail** – *I-10 Zaragoza Exit, 4mi southeast of downtown.* ♿ 🅿 ☎ *915-534-0677. www.missiontrail.com.* Stretching south of El Paso along the Rio Grande are three 17C missions that once lured settlers as farming and ranching centers. All are listed on the National Register of Historic Places.

Northernmost is **Mission Ysleta** *(Zaragoza Ave. at S. Old Pueblo Dr.;* ☎ *915-859-9848),* built for Spanish and Tigua refugees from the Pueblo Revolt in 1680. Floods destroyed the original mission; this one dates from 1851. Descendants of those Tiguas still use the mission for religious services. Their **Tigua Indian Cultural Center** ★ *(305 Ya Ya Ln.;* ☎ *915-859-5287)* has a museum, restaurant, gallery and weekend dances.

Mission Ysleta

© Tim Thompson

Mission Socorro★ *(Socorro Rd., 2.6mi south of Mission Ysleta;* ☎ *915-859-7718)* also was built for refugees and rebuilt after a 19C flood. An outstanding example of Spanish Mission architecture, with roof beams hand-sculpted by Piro Indians, the mission is the oldest continuously active parish in the US.

Also still in use, the gilded **Presidio Chapel in San Elizario★** *(Socorro Rd., 6mi south of Mission Socorro;* ☎ *915-851-2333)* is noted for its late adobe architectural style. It combines Southwestern attributes with European architectural characteristics such as buttresses.

★Franklin Mountains State Park – *I-10 to Canutillo Exit, Loop 375 east 4mi to entrance.* ⚠ ☎ *915-566-6441. www.tpwd.state.tx.us/franklin/ franklin.htm.* The largest urban wilderness park in the US spans 37sq mi of Chihuahuan Desert, from El Paso to the Texas-New Mexico state line. It is a favorite of hikers, mountain bikers, rock climbers and nature lovers. Along with desert plants such as sotol and ocotillo, the park is home to mule deer, many birds and occasional mountain lions.

Fort Bliss – *Fred Wilson Rd. east of US-54.* ☎ *915-568-4518.* This fort was established in 1848 to protect the region from Indian attack and to enforce US authority over the territory obtained that year from Mexico. During the Civil War, it was headquarters for the Confederate forces of the Southwest, and later was a post for troops charged with capturing Apache chief Geronimo. The **Fort Bliss Museum** *(Bldg. 5051;* ☎ *915-568-4518),* in a replica of a c.1857 adobe fort, recalls this history. Exhibits include uniforms and tools, as well as the riding crop brandished by Gen. John Pershing during his pursuit of the outlaw Pancho Villa.

Today Fort Bliss is a US Army Air Defense Center. The **US Army Air Defense Museum** *(Bldg. 5000;* ☎ *915-568-5412)* is the only one of its kind, with exhibits on the history of air defense including weapons, ammunition, photographs and dioramas. At the Robert E. Lee entrance gate stands the **Buffalo Soldier Monument**, executed in bronze by sculptor Jimmie Bemont. Feared and respected, the African-American Buffalo Soldiers defended the Western frontier during the late 19C.

EXCURSIONS

Ciudad Juárez – *Several international bridges cross the Rio Grande from downtown El Paso. For vehicles: Bridge of the Americas, Córdova Bridge, Zaragosa Bridge. For vehicles & pedestrians: Santa Fe Bridge, Stanton Bridge.* ☎ *915-533-3644.* Steps from El Paso is this city of more than 1 million, named for former Mexican president Benito Juárez. Business and family ties give Juárez a strong bond with El Paso that grew in the 1970s with the development of *maquiladoras,* or sister factories. Raw materials—everything from electronic goods to clothing—are gathered in El Paso and transported into Mexico for assembly by laborers at the plants there; completed goods are shipped back to the US for retailing.

Besides car and foot, visitors may enter Juárez on trolleys of the **El Paso-Juárez Trolley Company** *(*☎ *915-544-0061),* departing from the El Paso Convention and Performing Arts Center on Arts Festival Plaza. Day-trippers cross the border to shop at the two-story **Mercado** *(Avenida 16 de Septiembre),* near downtown. Handicrafts, silver jewelry, glassware and leather goods are sold. At night, Juárez has a lively nightlife that includes cabarets, casinos and bullfights.

★Parque Chamizal – *Directly south of Bridge of the Americas.* This city park opposite Chamizal National Memorial includes an **anthropology museum** with displays on Mexican history. Exhibits include replicas of some of Mexico's most famous Aztec and Mayan sites, including Uxmal, Chichén Itzá and Teotihuacán.

★Misión de Nuestra Señora de Guadalupe – *Avenidas 10 y 16 de Septiembre, south of the Stanton Bridge.* Constructed in 1658-68, this adobe mission is noted for its magnificent carved ceiling and richly decorated log beams made from Spanish palms. Legend says the shadows from the mission point to the Lost Padre Mine in the Franklin Mountains, where Spanish gold allegedly was hidden.

★★Guadalupe Mountains National Park – *US-62/180, 110mi east of El Paso.* ⚠ 🅿 ☎ *915-828-3251. www.nps.gov/gumo.* The only true mountains in Texas rise to 8,749ft at Guadalupe Peak, the state's highest point. Home to part of the most extensive Permian limestone fossil reef in the world, this terrain ranges from lowland desert to a high-country conifer forest. Mescalero Apaches hunted these mountains beginning in the early 16C.

At Pine Springs' **Headquarters Visitor Center**, a slide show and exhibits delineate the ecology and geology of the mountains. There are other exhibits at **Historic Frijole Ranch**. Visitors may hike more than 80mi of trails; most popular are those to El Capitan limestone formation and to **McKittrick Canyon**, where maple, walnut, ash, oak and madrone trees provide some of the best fall color in the Lone Star State.

BIG BEND AREA★★

Michelin map 492 H, I 13, 14   Central Standard Time
Tourist Information ☎ 915-837-3638 or www.visitbigbend.com

Much of this rugged and sparsely populated region is preserved within sprawling Big Bend National Park, located where the Rio Grande takes a sharp turn from southeast to northeast. More than 100mi is edged by the Rio Grande's swirling waters, which have carved the Santa Elena, Mariscal and Boquillas Canyons. Cut deep into the Chisos Mountains, these limestone chasms at first appear barren. But closer inspection reveals them—and the surrounding Chihuahuan Desert—to be rich with animal, bird and plant life.

Historical Notes — Man has lived in the Big Bend area at least 8,000 years. Ancient residents—who relied upon bison, and later agriculture, for sustenance—left pictographs and petroglyphs on canyon walls. By 1535, when the first Spanish arrived, the region was a seasonal home to the nomadic Chisos Indians. They were displaced by Mescalero Apaches and finally by Comanches, who moved through the area, making raids on Mexico, into the mid-19C.

After the Mexican War, US forts, including Fort Davis, gave security to modern settlement. Early 20C mining brought prospectors. In the 1930s, the state of Texas began to acquire and preserve land in the Big Bend area, consolidating it as Texas Canyons State Park. The state deeded the land to the US government in 1944 and the site became Big Bend National Park.

DRIVING TOUR *4 days, 581mi one-way.*

From El Paso, take I-10 east 157mi to Kent, then Rte. 118 south 37mi.

★ **McDonald Observatory** – 〖Kids〗 *Rte. 118, 16mi northwest of Fort Davis.* 🅿 ☎ 915-426-3640. http://www.vc.as.utexas.edu. Located far from city lights, this University of Texas facility is one of the world's best astronomy research centers. Visitors join tours of the 107in Harlan J. Smith Telescope and the Hobby-Eberly Telescope, third largest in the world. Public viewings (by reservation) and family-oriented "star parties" are scheduled year-round.

Continue 16mi southeast on Rte. 118.

★★ **Fort Davis National Historic Site** – *Main St. (Rtes. 17 & 118), Fort Davis.* ⅁ 🅿 ☎ 915-426-3224. www.nps.gov/foda. Fort Davis is one of the best surviving examples of a frontier post. Built in 1854 to protect the El Paso-San Antonio road from Indian attack, it was abandoned during the Civil War; troops found mainly ruins when they returned in 1867. Rock and adobe were used in reconstructing buildings. Fort Davis' role as a bulwark for mail and wagon-train routes continued until 1891. Today costumed docents staff some of the buildings. Historical exhibits are at the fort museum, in a reconstructed barracks. The fort anchors the community of Fort Davis, home to about 1,200.

Follow Rte. 118 south 103mi through Alpine to Study Butte, at west entrance to Big Bend National Park.

★★★ **Big Bend National Park** – *Rte. 118 south of Alpine or US-385 south of Marathon; Panther Junction is 320mi southeast of El Paso.* △ ✕ ⅁ 🅿 ☎ 915-477-2251. www.nps.gov/bibe. Big Bend spans 1,252sq mi of spectacular canyons, lush bottomlands, sprawling desert and mountain woodlands on the north side of the Rio Grande. Ranging over 6,000ft of elevation changes, it boasts a wealth of animal and plant life, a remarkable geological history, and a long and fascinating chronology of human habitation.

The oldest rocks, nearly 300 million years old, were deposited as sediment on an ancient ocean floor. Marine fossils in Persimmon Gap predate dinosaurs, which wandered a swampy Cretaceous landscape 100 million to 65 million years ago. Among them was the largest flying creature ever known, a pterodactyl with a 51ft wingspread. Volcanism and tectonic buckling, taking place between 42 million and 26 million years ago, created the Chisos Mountains, a range that tops out at 7,835ft Emory Peak. The park's canyons were carved only over the past 3 million years during the ice ages.

Ten thousand archaeological sites tell of hunters who ventured into the area 11,000 years ago pursuing giant bison and woolly mammoths. Artifacts found in caves and rock shelters indicate that these paleo-Indians had settled into a nomadic lifestyle by 6000 BC. Ruins of pueblo villages in the Rio Grande floodplain document a culture well established by AD 500. Cabeza de Vaca noted this farming culture in 1535 as he crossed the region. Later, Big Bend was a sanctuary for Apaches driven south by warlike Comanches in the 17C.

Survey parties explored Big Bend by riverboat and camel in the late 1850s. Ranching and mining achieved minor success. A small factory at **Glenn Spring** produced wax from the candelilla, a perennial desert plant, until Mexican bandits destroyed the community in 1916. The US Army then began an aerial border patrol in an attempt to capture the infamous Pancho Villa.

White-Water Rafting, Santa Elena Canyon

Big Bend has more species of migratory and resident birds—over 450—than any other national park. Bats, rodents and other small mammals are nocturnal; javelina and deer are often seen, mountain lions rarely. Reptiles thrive in the extreme climate. Torrential thunderstorms may follow droughts. Temperatures approach 120°F in summer but may drop below 10°F in winter.

Park headquarters and the main visitor center are at **Panther Junction** (*US-385 & Rio Grande Village Rd.*) in the heart of Big Bend. Other visitor centers—at **Persimmon Gap** (*US-385 at north entrance*), **Chisos Basin** (*Basin Rd.*) and **Rio Grande Village** (*Rio Grande Village Rd.*)—also provide information on archaeology and ecotourism activities. Campgrounds and rustic lodges are at various locations. Hikers can choose from 200mi of trails in the park, ranging from easy to strenuous. Naturalists guide walks year-round: several times daily between November and April. Outfitters based outside the park offer Rio Grande float trips through rugged canyons.

From Panther Junction, 25mi east of Study Butte, take US-385 north 69mi to Marathon. Turn east on US-90 for 115 mi to Langtry.

★ **Judge Roy Bean Visitor Center** – *.5mi south of US-90 on Loop 25, Langtry.* ♿ 🅿 ☎ *915-291-3340.* The story of the Wild West's most famous frontier judge is told in dioramas and exhibits. Adjacent stands **The Jersey Lilly,** the restored saloon and courtroom used by Judge Bean in the 1880s. The center includes a cactus garden with desert plants from throughout the Southwest.

Continue east on US-90 for 18mi.

★★ **Seminole Canyon State Park** – *US-90, 133mi east of Marathon.* ⛺♿ 🅿 ☎ *915-292-4464. www.tpwd.state.tx.us/park/seminole/seminole.htm.* On the limestone walls of this park are pictographs drawn by ancient Indians 4,000 years ago. Symbols represent animals, Indians and supernatural shamans, although their meaning is unknown. Archaeologists believe the early residents of Seminole Canyon were hunter-gatherers, living on plants such as sotol, prickly pear and lechugilla. Ranger-led tours *(Wed-Sun)* take visitors to the **Fate Bell Shelter,** an overhang that displays the oldest rock art in North America.

Continue east on US-90 for 27mi.

★ **Amistad National Recreation Area** – 🄺🄸🄳🅂 *US-90 between Langtry and Del Rio, 160mi east of Marathon.* ⛺ 🅿 ☎ *830-775-7491. www.nps.gov/amis.* Surrounding Lake Amistad on the US-Mexico border, this recreation area is popular for water sports. The 85mi-long lake is formed by a dam built in 1969 below the confluence of the Pecos and Devils Rivers with the Rio Grande. Amistad, the Spanish word for "friendship," was a joint US-Mexico project. Much of the lake is lined with limestone canyons, some containing caves with prehistoric pictographs. There are more than 250 sites within 100sq mi.

Driving tour concludes in Del Rio, 41mi farther east.

■ **Judge Roy Bean**

The self-proclaimed "Law West of the Pecos" was one of the most color-ful characters of the 19C US West. From behind the bar of his saloon, The Jersey Lilly, Judge Roy Bean served up frontier justice with beer and whiskey, leaving a mingled legacy of fact and fiction.

A silver spike driven at Dead Man's Gulch, near Langtry, linked the final section of Southern Pacific track between New Orleans and San Francisco in 1882. With the railroad came an influx of rowdy construction crews and their attendant evils— stealing, gambling and prostitution. With no law enforcement office within 100mi, shopkeeper Roy Bean was named Justice of the Peace.

Bean chose his jurors from among saloon customers. He presided over trials with a six-shooter at one hand and his single book of law at the other. He kept a pet bear named Bruno. His favorite punishment was to exile offenders into the desert without food, water, weapons or money.

Bean was obsessed with British actress Lillie Langtry, known as "The Jer-sey Lily." He named his saloon in her honor and wrote many letters beg ging her to visit. After several years—and his implication that the town had been named for her—Lillie agreed to stop on a 1904 tour. Bean died in 1903, a few months too soon.

SOUTHERN NEW MEXICO★

Michelin map 493 G, H 11, 12   Mountain Standard Time
Tourist Information ☎ 505-827-7400 or www.newmexico.org

Southern New Mexico is a crossroads of sorts. Here the Hispanic culture of Mexico meshes almost indecipherably with the Native American culture of the American Southwest, its glaze of "Anglo" society seeming out of place. Extending north of El Paso 150mi, from the Texas and Mexico borders through numerous fertile valleys and basins amid mountainous areas, this expansive region contains a mind-boggling variety of natural and historical attractions.

Historical Notes – Hundreds of millions of years ago, this was the floor of an inland sea. When the waters receded, a rich store of fossils was left. Carlsbad Caverns, today one of the world's most complex cave systems, began forming within this fossil reef 250 million years ago. Relative newcomers, Anasazi and Mogollon Indians established a foothold only 8,000 years ago. Their legacy remains in the ruins of cliff dwellings and pueblo communities.

Ranching, farming and mining have supported the regional economy since the first Spanish missions were built in the 17C. In the late 19C, Las Cruces grew from a mining supply center to become the largest city in the area.

On July 16, 1945, the first atomic bomb (p 336) was exploded at the Trinity Site near White Sands. Two years later, some folks contend, an interplanetary spacecraft crash-landed near Roswell, its alien crew put under lock and key by the US Army. The International UFO Museum heads efforts to substantiate the claim. Meanwhile, the world's most powerful radio telescopes send signals toward unseen civilizations, and The Space Center in Alamogordo is a tribute to aerospace fact.

DRIVING TOUR *5 days, 969mi round-trip*

Tour begins and ends in El Paso. Take I-10 north 42mi to Las Cruces.

Las Cruces – *I-10, I-25 & US-70.* ✕ ♿ 🅿 ☎ *505 541 2444. www.lascrucescvb .org.* Located in the fertile Mesilla Valley between the Rio Grande and the Organ Mountains, this city of 76,000 is one of the fastest growing in the Southwest. Modern history dates from 1598, when Juan de Oñate founded the village of La Mesilla while searching for gold. Las Cruces was founded in 1849 on the east bank of the Rio Grande, US territory after the Mexican War ; it was named for "the crosses" that marked primitive graves of travelers. In 1854, La Mesilla became part of the US when the Gadsden Purchase formalized the sale of another 45,000sq mi of Mexican territory to the US.

Built in 1851 and reconstructed in 1906, San Albino Church towers over **Old Mesilla Plaza★** *(Rte. 28, 4mi southwest of downtown Las Cruces)*. Colorful cafes, galleries and antique shops occupy its 19C buildings. In the Masonic cemetery

is the grave of Sheriff Pat Garrett, who tracked and shot down Billy the Kid *(p 144)* after the outlaw fled La Mesilla jail while awaiting execution.
The Mesilla Valley is a leading producer of chiles, pecans and cotton. Farm and factory tours can be arranged.

Fort Selden State Monument – *Between I-25, exit 19, & Rte. 185, 15mi north of Las Cruces.* ♿ 🅿 ☎ *505-526-8911. www.nmculture.org.* Two historical facts inspire a visit to the ruins of this adobe fort, built in 1865 and abandoned in 1891. It was home to the Buffalo Soldiers, the famed African-American cavalry that shielded settlers from Indians. And it was the boyhood home of Gen. Douglas MacArthur, the World War II hero whose father was stationed here. A visitor center has a series of photo displays.

Take I-10 west 59mi to Deming, then US-180 north 53mi to Silver City.

Silver City – *Rte. 90 & US-180.* 🍴♿ 🅿 ☎ *505-538-3785. www.silvercity.org.* In the foothills of the Piños Altos Range, this town of 12,000 was founded as a mining community in the 1870s. Its downtown historic district features extensive brickwork in mansard-roofed Victorian homes, cast iron in commercial buildings. The 1881 H.B. Ailman House is home to the **Silver City Museum** *(312 W. Broadway;* ☎ *505-538-5921).* Silver City is surrounded by the 3.3-million-acre Gila National Forest, whose Gila Wilderness Area was the first designated by the US Congress.

★**Gila Cliff Dwellings National Monument** – *Rte. 15, 44mi north of Silver City.* ♿ 🅿 ☎ *505-536-9461. www.nps.gov/gicl.* The cliffside stone-and-masonry homes of a late-13C Mogollon agricultural village are preserved within this park, a narrow, winding, 2hr drive from Silver City. In a side canyon above the West Fork of the Gila River, in a half-dozen shallow caves in a sandstone bluff, are 42 mostly intact rooms, believed to have housed as many as 50 Indians. A **loop trail** *(1mi)* climbs 175ft to the dwellings, giving visitors a rare glimpse of a prehistoric culture.
The Mogollon were fine builders. Stones were anchored by clay mortar, roof beams cut with stone adzes and shaped by fire. The people hunted and tended fields of corn, squash and beans in the rich soil of the Gila floodplain.
The dwellings were occupied for only a generation. But relics of thousands of years of settlement can be found nearby. Rangers staffing a **visitor center**, 1.5mi from the cliff dwellings trailhead, can direct the curious to various locations.

Turn northwest on US-180 along the scenic Mogollon Rim for 93mi, then easterly on Rte. 12 for 74mi to Datil, at junction of US-60.

★**Very Large Array** – *VLA Access Rd. west of Rte. 52 & south of US-60, 9mi east of Datil and 50mi west of Socorro.* 🅿 ☎ *505-835-7000. www.nrao.edu.* Operated as the National Radio Astronomy Observatory and completed in 1981, the Very Large Array is the world's most powerful radio telescope. The structure, featured in the 1997 Jodie Foster movie *Contact,* is used by astronomers to research the nature and processes of the universe. Composed of 27 dish-shaped metal mirrors, each 82ft in diameter, extending across the Plains of San Agustin in a trio of 13mi-long arms, the facility gathers radio signals from the Milky Way galaxy and beyond. At the **visitor center**, guests may view a slide show and displays on radio astronomy, then take a self-guided tour of one of the 230-ton antennae.

Continue east 61mi on US-60 to Socorro; then north 26mi on I-25 to Bernardo; then east 39mi on US-60 to Mountainair.

★**Salinas Pueblo Missions National Monument** – *Headquarters on US-60, one block west of Rte. 55, Mountainair.* ♿ 🅿 ☎ *505-847-2585. www.nps.gov/sapu.* Stone ruins are all that remain of the pueblos of the Salinas Valley, inhabited by descendants of Anasazi and Mogollon peoples in the 13-17C. The communities served as trading posts dealing in agriculture, hides and flints. Franciscan missionaries moved in to Christianize the population in the late 16C, built chapels of native adobe in European styles, and ultimately hastened the pueblos' demise. Conflicts with Apaches, as well as a severe drought and famine, led to their final abandonment during the 1670s. The **visitor center** in Mountainair has exhibits.
The **Abó Ruins** *(9mi west on US-60 & .5mi north on Rte. 513)* have an unexcavated pueblo and ruins of Misión de San Gregorio de Abó. The **Quarai Ruins★** *(8mi north on Rte. 55, then 1mi west)* include walls of Misión de Nuestra Señora de la Purisima Concepción de Cuarac, most complete of the Salinas chapels. The **Gran Quivira Ruins★** *(25mi south on Rte. 55)* have a small museum, excavations of the San Isidro Conventio and ruins of the Misión de San Buenaventura.

From Mountainair, drive east 12mi on US-60 to Willard; southeast 38mi on Rte. 42 to Corona; then south 47mi on US-54 to Carrizozo.

Trinity Site – *Range Rd. 7 in the White Sands Missile Range, 21mi south of US-380, 54mi west of Carrizozo.* At this location in the Jordana del Muerto desert, the world's first atomic bomb was exploded on July 16, 1945. It is closed to the public except on rare tour days. *(See p 336)*

Continue south 57mi on US-54 to Alamogordo.

Alamogordo – *US-54 & 70.* ✗ & 🄿 ☎ *505-437-6120. www.alamogordo.com.* The "Rocket City" was a mere desert oasis until World War II. Flanked on the north by lava fields, on the south by white sand dunes and on the east by the 1.1-million-acre Lincoln National Forest, this community has grown into a boomtown of 28,000 people. Holloman Air Force Base, home to the Stealth F-117A aircraft, and the White Sands Missile Range administer hundreds of square miles of uninhabited land to train bombing crews and to undertake rocket research.

★★ **The Space Center** – **Kids** *Rte. 2001 via Indian Wells Rd. & Scenic Dr., off US-54.* & 🄿 ☎ *505-437-2840. www.spacefame.org.* A five-story, gold-colored cube at the foot of the Sacramento Mountains, this complex salutes man's exploration of space through exhibits on history, science and technology. Displays in the **Space Museum**★★ range from examples of Robert Goddard's early experiments in rocketry, to the capsule flown in 1961 by the first astrochimp, to futuristic models of space stations. The **International Space Hall of Fame** pays tribute to 142 space pioneers, including US and Soviet astronauts. **John P. Stapp Air and Space Park**★, named for the man who rode the *Sonic Wind 1* rocket sled at 634mph, exhibits full-size spacecraft. The **Astronaut Memorial Garden**★ honors the seven men and women who lost their lives in the 1986 *Challenger* space-shuttle disaster. The **Clyde W. Tombaugh IMAX Dome Theater and Planetarium** presents a regular schedule of movies and star shows. Tombaugh (1906-97), who discovered the planet Pluto in 1930 *(p 164)*, also originated the astronomy research program at New Mexico State University in Las Cruces.

★★ **White Sands National Monument** – **Kids** *US-70, 15mi southwest of Alamogordo.* & 🄿 ☎ *505-679-2599. www.nps.gov/whsa.* The world's greatest expanse of white gypsum sand dunes, this mountain-ringed northern edge of the Chihuahuan Desert is preserved as a delicate ecological system. Nearly half of the sands are contained within this 240sq mi site on the Tularosa Basin, inhabited only by a few hardy plant species, a few small birds and other animals (some of which have evolved a white camouflage). The visitor center features displays on the ever-moving dunes, driven by a relentless southwesterly wind; they can be seen on an 8mi *(one-way)* drive through the park. The **Alkali Flat Trail** *(4.6mi)* is designed for backcountry hikers; the **Interdune Boardwalk** *(& 0.25mi)* has interpretive exhibits on dune ecology.

From Alamogordo, return 3mi up US-54, then east 16mi on US-82.

Soaptree Yuccas, White Sands National Monument

■ Billy the Kid and Smokey Bear

Tributes to two American legends—one a notorious outlaw, the other an animal rescued from a fire—stand only 12mi apart on US-380 north of Ruidoso. **Lincoln State Monument** *(36mi northeast of Ruidoso; ☎ 505-653-4372)* preserves a historic 19C village that recalls the life of Billy the Kid. **Smokey Bear Historical Park Kids** *(118 Smokey Bear Blvd., Capitan, 24mi north of Ruidoso; ☎ 505-354-2748)* honors a real-life creature that became a national symbol.

Billy the Kid – A few dusty miles outside Fort Sumner, the grave of Billy the Kid lies imprisoned behind iron bars. The site attracts a stream of sightseers drawn by one of the West's most compelling sagas, about a young outlaw who gunned down maybe a dozen men before being killed himself by an officer of the law.

Born of poor Irish immigrants in New York City or Indianapolis, Henry McCarty (1859?-81), alias William Bonney, moved to Silver City, New Mexico, with his widowed mother sometime after the Civil War. He was orphaned when she died of tuberculosis in 1873. Working as a cowboy in Arizona, he was pursued for thefts and one killing as he fled back to New Mexico in 1877.

In Lincoln County, a savage range war raged between two groups of businessmen who sought control of government contracts. It began with cattle rustling but climaxed in 1878 with a five-day gun battle. Billy figured prominently in the carnage, ambushing and killing a sheriff and deputy while evading capture.

Bonney eventually was caught and sentenced to hang in Lincoln. As he awaited execution, he was left alone with only one guard, whom he tricked and overpowered. While making his escape, he shot and killed two more deputies.

For months the Kid hid, making his way to Fort Sumner, where he found refuge in the abandoned fort now preserved as **Fort Sumner State Monument** *(Rte. 272, 7mi southeast of Fort Sumner off US-60/84; ☎ 505-355-2573)*. On the night of July 14, 1881, Sheriff Pat Garrett, who had tracked him from Lincoln, found Bonney and shot him through the heart.

Smokey Bear – The real-life Smokey Bear emerged from the devastation of a huge Lincoln National Forest fire in 1950. Although badly burned, the rescued black-bear cub was nursed back to health and adopted by the US Forest Service. Smokey became a living symbol of a campaign, launched during World War II, to prevent fires caused by careless humans. His cartoon image had already begun to capture American minds and hearts via billboards, print media and radio by the time the real cub was introduced.

Smokey lived out his life in the National Zoo in Washington DC, where he was a popular attraction until his death in 1976. He was returned to New Mexico and buried in Smokey Bear Historical Park. In addition to the gravesite, the park contains exhibits of Smokey memorabilia, a film documentary on the Smokey Bear phenomenon, historical displays on forest-fire prevention and management, and a nature walk through native New Mexico plant species.

Over the years, Smokey's message—"Only you can prevent forest fires"—has become part of American popular culture. In 1984, a US postage stamp was issued honoring Smokey's contributions to national fire awareness. The stamp featured a bear cub clinging to a tree, superimposed over the official Smokey Bear emblem. It was the first US postage stamp to honor an individual animal.

Cloudcroft – *US-82.* ✗ ᕦ 🄿 ☎ *505-682-2733. www.cloudcroft.net.* Located at 8,663ft, about twice the elevation of Alamogordo, this mountain village of 600 offers hiking and mountain biking in summer, skiing in winter. **The Lodge at Cloudcroft** *(1 Corona Pl.; ☎ 505-682-2566)* is a Victorian gem built in 1898 for rail workers. The **National Solar Observatory** *(Rte. 6563, 17mi south of Cloudcroft; ☎ 505-434-7000)* is located atop 9,255ft Sacramento Peak; tours begin at the **Sunspot Astronomy and Visitor Center** *(Sunspot Scenic Byway).*

Take Rte. 244 east and north 29mi to US-70 in the Mescalero Apache Indian Reservation, then east 12mi on US-70 to Ruidoso.

Ruidoso – *US-70 & Rte. 37.* ⚠ ✗ ♿ 🅿 ☎ *505-257-7395. www.ruidoso.net.* A resort town of 8,500 on a Sacramento Mountain stream, Ruidoso *(ree-uh-DOH-so)* is famous for horse racing. On Labor Day, the All-American Futurity—the world's richest quarter-horse race, with $2.5 million at stake—is run at **Ruidoso Downs** racetrack *(US-70, 4mi east of Ruidoso;* ☎ *505-378-4431).* The Futurity is the final event of a 77-day season that begins in mid-May.

Ruidoso is on the northern edge of the 723sq mi Mescalero Apache Indian Reservation, highlighted by the luxurious **Inn of the Mountain Gods** resort *(Carrizo Canyon Rd.;* ☎ *505-257-5141).* The tribe also owns southern New Mexico's largest winter resort, **Ski Apache** *(Forest Rd. 532;* ☎ *505-336-4356),* with a gondola and eight chairlifts on a flank of 12,003ft Sierra Blanca.

⭐⭐ **Hubbard Museum of the American West** – 🔲Kids 841 *US-70 West, Ruidoso Downs.* ♿ 🅿 ☎ *505-378-4142. www.zianet.com/museum.* More than 10,000 historical and cultural items chronicle the relationship between horse and man. Firearms, farm tools, wagons and carriages are on display, along with a fine art collection that includes works by Russell and Remington. At the entrance is one of the world's largest equine monuments, *Free Spirits at Noisy Water,* by Ruidoso sculptor Dave McGary. The bronze is more than 300ft long and stands over three stories high.

⭐ **Spencer Theater for the Performing Arts** – *Airport Rd. 220, Alto, 5mi north of Ruidoso.* ♿ 🅿 ☎ *505-336-4800. www.spencertheater.com.* Designed to echo the surrounding Capitan and Sacramento Mountains with white limestone and steep angles, this $20 million, 514-seat theater (1997, Antoine Predock) also showcases the glass art of Dale Chihuly *(p 355).* Dramatic, musical and dance performances are regularly scheduled.

Continue east 71mi on US-70 to Roswell.

Roswell – *US-70, 285 & 380.* ✗ ♿ 🅿 ☎ *505-623-5695. www.roswellnm .org.* This city of 48,000 once was known merely for its ranching economy and esteemed military school. Then the "Roswell Incident" occurred. In 1947, a "flying saucer" or unidentified flying object (UFO) allegedly crashed in a field 20mi northwest. The incident was reported by local media but quickly hushed up by the US Army. Some locals conjecture that alien bodies were removed from the crash site to a research facility. In recent years, television shows like *The X Files* and movies like *Independence Day* have focused new attention on the controversy.

The **International UFO Museum & Research Center**⭐ 🔲Kids *(114 N. Main St.;* ☎ *505-625-9495)* features exhibits both on the Roswell Incident and cover-up, and on UFO sightings around the world. Documentary films are presented in a video room; a research library provides reading space.

At the **Roswell Museum and Art Center** *(11th & Main Sts.;* ☎ *505-624-6744)* are the Robert H. Goddard Planetarium and the workshop of Goddard, father of

The Big Room, Carlsbad Caverns

modern rocketry. The art collection has works by Peter Hurd, Henriette Wyeth and Georgia O'Keeffe; the Rogers Aston Collection features Western history.

From Roswell, drive south 76mi on US-285 to Carlsbad. Turn southwest on US-62/180 for 16mi to Whites City, at entrance to Carlsbad Caverns National Park.

★★★ **Carlsbad Caverns National Park** – Kids ▐▐▐▐ *Off US-62, 23mi southwest of Carlsbad.* ✕ & ▣ ☎ *505-785-2232. www.nps.gov/cave.* One of the largest cave systems in the world, the labyrinth of Carlsbad Caverns takes in 88 known caves, including Lechuguilla Cave, at 1,567ft the deepest limestone cavern in the US.

The caverns were discovered in the early 1900s. Cowboy Jim White saw a cloud of dark smoke, rising on the horizon near dusk, that turned out to be hundreds of thousands of Mexican free-tailed bats. Bats still cling to the roof of the cave entrance by day before beginning their nightly insect-hunting ritual. White descended on a rope ladder to the cave floor, where he was stunned by the formations: soda straws and ice-cream cones, strings of pearls and miniature castles. By 1923 the caves were part of the national park system.

Perpetually 56 degrees, the damp caves can be entered through their natural entrance or by elevator. Tour highlights include such beautiful formations as the Temple of the Sun, the Frozen Waterfall and the King's Palace. Spelunkers can take "wild cave" tours to see formations few other visitors view.

Continue west on US-180, 35mi to Guadalupe Mountains National Park (p 138) and another 110mi to El Paso.

Glacier Park Region

Swiftcurrent Valley and Grinnell Lake, Glacier National Park

One of the most awe-inspiring destinations in North America is Waterton/Glacier International Peace Park, its jagged peaks, glacial lakes and U-shaped valleys straddling the US-Canada border. Lying 400mi east of Seattle and 270mi north of Yellowstone National Park, relative isolation has enhanced its wilderness charms.

About 100 million years ago, the continental plate moved over the Pacific plate, colliding with a flat plain that bordered an ancient sea. The earth's crust buckled and folded, creating the Rocky Mountains. During the ice ages, glaciers plowed down river valleys, shaving mountains into horns and arêtes and gouging the valleys and lake bottoms of Glacier and Waterton Lakes National Parks.

Some glaciers flowed far enough south to impound the Clark Fork River at the present site of Lake Pend Oreille, creating glacial Lake Missoula. Larger in volume than Lakes Ontario and Erie combined, the inland sea spread from the Flathead region to the Bitterroot Mountains. At least 40 times, whenever an ice dam broke, floods raged down the Columbia River drainage to the Pacific; each time, another glacier plugged the outlet and the lake refilled. Fertile sedimentary deposits are the lake's legacy in the Mission and Bitterroot Valleys.

Lewis' and Clark's 1804-06 odyssey took them across this ruggedly beautiful land: through the Bitterroot Valley, down the Columbia drainage. Even before the Corps of Discovery returned east, mountain men were headed west into these reaches. On their heels were Christian missionaries; behind them, settlers traveling by Missouri River steamboat and, later, railroad. Open-range cattle ranching evolved. Prospectors struck gold and silver, attracting hordes of miners to the rich veins of Montana and Idaho. The pioneer influx led to conflict with Native Americans, whose free-roaming lifestyle disappeared into a new, oppressive reservations.

Mining and logging supported regional economies until plunging markets and decreased resources downsized these industries. To survive, communities reinvented themselves. They turned to cultural and recreational tourism, cashing in on magnificent wide-open spaces, snow-dusted peaks and pristine lakes.

Visitors still can see bison and eagles, grizzly bears and mountain goats here. They still can meet real cowboys and Indians, stride across glaciers or into gold mines. America's Western heritage lives on through national and state parks, wildlife refuges, museums and historic preservation efforts.

147

GLACIER NATIONAL PARK★★★

Shaped by glaciers, the Glacier Park area is characterized by rugged mountains, lakes and valleys. About 75 million years ago, a geological phenomenon known as the Lewis Overthrust tilted and pushed a 3mi- to 4mi-thick slab of the earth's crust 50mi east, leaving older Proterozoic rock atop younger Cretaceous rock. These mountains now rise 3,000-7,000ft above valley floors, partially forming the Continental Divide. A wet coniferous ecosystem on the west side of the Divide is balanced by dry, sparsely vegetated terrain on the east side.

SIGHTS

★★★ **Glacier National Park** – *Going-to-the-Sun Road off US-2, 35mi east of Kalispell.* ⚠ ✕ ᴦ ᴘ ☎ *406-888-7800. www.nps.gov/glac.* Known to native Blackfeet as the "Land of Shining Mountains," Glacier Park was homesteaded in the late 19C. Pressure to establish the park began in 1891 with the arrival of the Great Northern Railway; Congress gave its nod in 1910. The railroad built numerous delightful Swiss-style chalets and hotels, five of which still operate.
Glacier's rugged mountainscape takes its name not from living glaciers, but from ancient rivers of ice that carved the peaks, finger lakes and U-shaped valleys. The remoteness of the park's 1,584sq mi makes it an ideal home for grizzly bears and mountain goats, bighorn sheep and bugling elk.

Western Approaches – Coming from Kalispell, visitors pass through the village of Hungry Horse, named for two lost horses that nearly starved one long-ago winter. **Hungry Horse Dam** *(West Reservoir Rd., 4mi south of US-2; ☎ 406-387-5241),*

ADDRESS BOOK

Please see explanation on p 64.

Staying in Montana and Northern Idaho

The Coeur d'Alene – *115 S. 2nd St., Coeur d'Alene ID.* ✕ ᴦ ᴘ ⌁ ☎ *208-765-4000. www.cdaresort.com. 336 rooms.* **$$** Consistently voted one of America's top resorts, this golf, sailing and tennis complex offers lodgings that range from economy to tower penthouses. Saturated with amenities, it perches beside Lake Coeur d'Alene with a private beach and marina.

Glacier Park Lodge – *US-2, East Glacier Park MT.* ✕ ᴦ ᴘ ☎ *602-207-6000. www.glacierparkinc.com/gpl.htm. 161 rooms.* **$$** The Great Northern Railway created the pitched roofline and rustic rooms in 1913 to attract wealthy travelers to the frontier. The vast lobby is one highlight of this grand building: Huge 48ft timbers, with bark intact, create a rectangular basilica flanked by galleries on either side and illuminated by skylights.

The Copper King Mansion – *219 W. Granite St., Butte MT.* ☎ *406-782-7580. 5 rooms.* **$** Built for a self-made copper millionaire in 1888, this opulent Victorian residence even offers a guided tour. It starts with the main hall's Staircase of Nations and moves to the ballroom, library and billiard room, all rich with stained-glass windows, gold-embossed leather ceilings, and inlaid woodwork.

The Garden Wall Inn – *504 Spokane Ave., Whitefish MT.* ᴘ ☎ *406-862-3440. www.wtp.net/go/gardenwall. 5 rooms.* **$** With clapboard siding and claw-foot tubs, this charming Colonial Revival bed-and-breakfast inn is named for the sheer cliffs that form the Continental Divide. The innkeepers, keen explorers of the Montana outdoors, concoct gourmet breakfasts that might include huckleberry-pear crepes.

Dining in Montana

The Stonehouse – *120 Reeder's Alley, Helena MT.* ☎ *406-449-2552.* **$$** American. In the 1890s, fine dining meant white linen, even if the atmosphere was rustic. This former miners' boardinghouse and four adjacent historic cabins perpetuate that theme. Evening specials include corn-fed steaks, stuffed catfish and wild game, and the Friday-night seafood buffet is always bustling.

which impounds a 34mi-long reservoir, offers grand **views** up the South Fork of the Flathead River, into the Bob Marshall Wilderness. Guided tours from a visitor center lead to the massive turbines and generators of the 564ft-high arched concrete dam.

Charming **West Glacier**, a park gateway town, is an outfitting center. Amtrak trains stop at a renovated depot that now houses the nonprofit Glacier Natural History Association. **Belton Chalet** *(US-2;* ☎ *406-888-5000)*, built by the Great Northern Railroad in 1910, is restored and listed on the National Register of Historic Places.

★★★ **Going-to-the-Sun Road** – *52mi from US-2 at West Glacier to US-89 at St. Mary. Closed mid Oct-late May due to snow.* This National Historic Landmark may be America's most beautiful highway. Deemed an engineering marvel when completed in 1932, the narrow, serpentine roadway climbs 3,500ft to the Continental Divide at Logan Pass, moving from forested valleys to alpine meadows to native grassland as it bisects the park west to east. Passenger vehicles (size restrictions prohibit large RVs) share the route with Glacier's trademark red buses, which have carried sightseers over this road for more than 50 years. *(In summer 1999, the red buses were replaced by a fleet of white vans, considered a temporary move.)*

Two miles from the road's beginning is **Apgar**, an assemblage of lodgings, cafes and shops at the foot of mountain-ringed **Lake McDonald★**. Like most park waters, this lake is fed by snowmelt and glacial runoff, and summer surface temperatures average a cool 55°F. The launch *DeSmet*, a classic wooden boat handcrafted in 1928, cruises from the rustic **Lake McDonald Lodge** *(Mile 11)*, open summers. There's been a hotel here since 1895.

At **Trail of the Cedars★** *(Mile 16.5)*, a wheelchair-accessible boardwalk winds through old-growth cedar-hemlock forest and past a sculpted gorge. Able-bodied hikers can amble uphill another 2mi to Avalanche Lake, fed by waterfalls

Rocky Mountain Goat

© Buddy Mays/TRAVEL S°CCK

spilling from Sperry Glacier. Beyond, the road climbs a castellated arête called the Garden Wall. **Bird Woman Falls** cascades from Mt. Oberlin and the **Weeping Wall★** gushes or trickles—depending on the season—from a roadside rock face.

At 6,680ft **Logan Pass★★★** *(Mile 33)*, visitors enjoy broad alpine meadows of wildflowers and keep their eyes open for mountain goats on the 1.5mi walk to **Hidden Lake Overlook★★**. White-flowered beargrass is beautiful in summer. Ripple-marked rocks more than 1 billion years old lie along the route to the observation post, which looks into a cirque lake surrounded by mountains. A visitor center is atop the pass, but parking is often at a premium.

Descending Logan Pass, travelers may stop at the **Jackson Glacier Overlook** *(Mile 37)* or continue to **Sun Point★** *(Mile 41)*, where there is picnicking beside **St. Mary Lake** and a trailhead to **Baring Falls** *(1mi)*. From **Rising Sun** *(Mile 45)*, scenic 90min **lake cruises★** aboard the 49-passenger *Little Chief*, built in 1925, are launched. The **St. Mary Visitor Center** *(Mile 51)* is a mile west of **St. Mary** village.

★★ **Eastern Valleys** – A 21mi drive northwest from St. Mary leads to **Many Glacier★★★** *(12mi west of Babb off US-89)*. Three small glaciers provide a memorable backdrop to the valley above Grinnell Lake. They may be reached by a 5mi hiking path (part of Glacier Park's stalwart 735mi trail network), or viewed from the landmark 1915 **Many Glacier Hotel★**, once a showcase of the Rockies, or from a boat on sparkling Swiftcurrent and Josephine Lakes.

Two Medicine★ *(13mi northwest of East Glacier Park off Rte. 49)* is tucked into a carved glacial valley 38mi south of St. Mary via US-89. The serene spot has a general store and guided boat tours but no lodgings except a campground.

President Franklin Roosevelt once broadcast a "Fireside Chat" from here, telling America: "The great mountains, the glaciers, the lakes and the trees make me long to stay here for all the rest of the summer."

East Glacier Park – *US-2 & Rte. 49.* This small town on the Blackfeet Indian Reservation is home to the 1913 **Glacier Park Lodge**★, whose lobby is columned with old-growth Douglas fir logs. Besides the usual amenities, the village boasts youth hostels, bicycle rentals, horseback outfitters and an Amtrak train depot.

Southern Boundary – Between East Glacier Park and West Glacier, a 57mi stretch of US-2 divides the park from the Great Bear Wilderness. From 5,220ft **Marias Pass** on the Continental Divide, there are superb views of the Lewis Overthrust. Tiny **Essex** *(25mi east of West Glacier),* on the Middle Fork of the Flathead River, is home to the **Izaak Walton Inn** *(off US-2; ☎ 406-888-5700),* built in 1939 for rail crews. Today the half-timbered inn is a mecca for rail-road fans (who sleep in vintage cabooses and peruse historical memorabilia) and cross-country skiers.

Blackfeet Indian Reservation – *US-2 & US-89.* △ ☒ ▣ Bordered on the north by Canada, the Blackfeet Reservation stretches east from Glacier Park across 50mi of rolling hills and prairies notorious for hot, dry summers and wind-whipped winters. Blackfeet migrated west from the Great Lakes around 1700 and settled in bison country. By the mid-18C they ruled the northwest plains and gained a reputation for aggressiveness. Today three Blackfeet confederacy tribes live in Montana and adjacent Alberta, earning livelihoods mainly in ranching and farming.

Undistinguished **Browning** is the administrative center and largest town (with 1,200 people) on the 2,383sq-mi reserve. It comes to life during North American Indian Days, a colorful four-day July powwow. The **Museum of the Plains Indian**★ *(US-2 & US-89; ☎ 406-338-2230)* presents art and history of the Northern Plains peoples, with artifacts from war bonnets to dolls. The **Scriver Museum of Montana Wildlife and Hall of Bronze** *(US-2 near US-89; ☎ 406-338-5425)* exhibits sculpture and taxidermy by late Western artist Bob Scriver, who lived on the reservation.

Great Bear and Bob Marshall Wilderness Areas – *Access from US-2 south or forest roads south & east of Hungry Horse Reservoir.* △ ☎ *406-329-3511.* Two vast wilderness areas lie south of Glacier Park. The 446sq-mi **Great Bear Wilderness** is a forested corridor that preserves grizzly habitat and watershed for North America's longest "wild and scenic river" system, the Flathead. **Bob Marshall Wilderness**, named for a conservationist forester, is a roadless area of meadows and mountains whose 1,577sq mi attract big-game hunters, rafters, backpackers and horseback riders. The most photographed sight in "The Bob" is the **Chinese Wall**, a towering, 12mi-long limestone escarpment along the Continental Divide.

EXCURSION

★★ **Waterton Lakes National Park** – *Alberta Rte. 5 off Chief Mountain International Hwy.* △ ☒⅘ ▣ ☎ *403-859-2224.* Yoked like oxen since 1932 as an official World Heritage Site, Glacier Park and Canada's adjacent Waterton Lakes National Park share a similar topography and a history of cooperation. Together they form Waterton/Glacier International Peace Park.

The 203sq mi Waterton Lakes Park focuses around the distinctly Canadian townsite of **Waterton Park,** hugging the shoreline of Upper Waterton Lake. The community is a charming place to browse and watch bighorn sheep and mule deer intermingling with pedestrians. Visitors can walk to Cameron Falls *(.5mi),* take a **lake excursion**★ aboard the launch *International, and enjoy high tea at the gabled 1927* **Prince of Wales Hotel**★★, whose stunning hilltop setting and commanding lake views befit its regal namesake. Waterton visitors also enjoy the park's drive-through bison paddock and a scenic 9mi drive to **Red Rock Canyon.**

FLATHEAD REGION★

Michelin map 493 E 3, 4   Mountain Standard Time
Tourist Information ☎ 406-756-9091 or www.fcvb.org

Wherever the eye rests in the Flathead Valley, mountains loom. They follow the traveler like a shadow. Ice Age glaciers left behind these jagged peaks and a fertile river valley that now supports an agricultural economy. The Flathead Indian Reservation and Flathead Lake are both found in this striking land, where outdoor recreation is gradually supplanting logging as the major industry.

SIGHTS

Kalispell – *US-2 & US-93 west of Glacier Park.* ⚠ ✕ ⚫ 🅿 ☎ *406-758-2800. www.fcvb.org.* Flathead County's commercial center, this town of 16,000 melds old and new Montana. The elegant **Conrad Mansion**★ *(313 6th Ave. E.; ☎ 406-755-2166)*, a 26-room Norman-style home built in 1895, is Kalispell's crown jewel. It contains mostly original furnishings and stands near the town's lovely Woodland Park. The **Hockaday Museum of Art** *(302 2nd Ave. E.; ☎ 406-755-5268)*, in a 1903, Classical Revival-style Carnegie Library building, displays rotating exhibits of regional art in five galleries.

★**Whitefish** – *US-93, 14mi north of Kalispell.* ⚠ ✕ ⚫ 🅿 ☎ *406-862-3501. www.whitefishchamber.com.* This small town gracefully balances its dual identity as a Western community and resort center. **Whitefish Lake**★ draws campers, anglers and water skiers in summer; in winter, 7,000ft **Big Mountain**★ *(Big Mountain Rd., 8mi north of Whitefish; ☎ 406-862-2900)* lures ski and snowboard enthusiasts. Summer visitors ride the gondola to the summit for wonderful **views**★★ into Glacier National Park and the Canadian Rockies.

■ Where the Buffalo Roam

Fifty million bison once migrated across North America from central Mexico to Canada. For thousands of years they sustained generations of Plains Indians. Hides provided clothing and lodging; bones became tools and weapons; flesh and organs fed families. The herds flourished until the late 19C, when hunters slaughtered them for tongues and hides, leaving carcasses to rot.

The **National Bison Range**★★ *(Rte. 212, Moiese, 31mi south of Polson;* ⚫ 🅿 ☎ *406-644-2211)* was set aside in 1908 to preserve a small herd of buffalo, by then approaching extinction. About 370 buffalo now roam the range and provide breeding stock for private North American bison ranches, where as many as 200,000 of the great beasts are raised. Visitor center displays examine the behavior and history of these strong, temperamental animals. Drivers on the 19mi Red Sleep Mountain tour may view not only bison but also pronghorn, bighorn sheep, elk and mountain goats on more than 18,500 scenic acres.

© Matthew McVay/FOLIO, Inc.

★★ Flathead Lake – *Between US-93 & Rte. 35, 11 to 38mi south of Kalispell.* ⚠ This 27mi-long lake, largest natural freshwater lake west of the Mississippi River, offers boating, sailing and fishing with gorgeous mountain **views★**. It fills a basin formed after rivers of ice scooped a trench in the valley floor and deposited a terminal moraine where the town of Polson now stands.

With its Western-theme architecture and storybook lakeside setting, **Bigfork★** *(Rte. 35, 17mi southeast of Kalispell;* ⚠ ✗ ♿ ♿ 🅿 ☎ *406-837-5888)* is a center for the arts and fine dining. Galleries and gift shops line its main street, and the Bigfork Summer Playhouse draws sellout crowds. South of Bigfork, cherry orchards and roadside stands stud the lake's eastern shoreline.

Flathead Indian Reservation – *US-93 between Kalispell & Missoula.* ✗ ♿ 🅿 ☎ *406-675-2700.* Montana's Salish, Kootenai and Pend d'Oreille tribes reside on this reservation, established in 1855. Mostly farm and range land, the 1,942sq-mi reserve embraces the southern half of Flathead Lake and the Mission Mountains. Every July, traditional **celebrations★** in the villages of Elmo and Arlee welcome visitors to see Native American dancing, music and games.

The reservation's commercial center is **Polson** *(US-93 & Rte. 35, 49mi south of Kalispell & 65mi north of Missoula;* ☎ *406-883-5969),* a boating and outfitting hub that hugs the foot of Flathead Lake. Nearby **Kerr Dam Overlook** *(Kerr Dam Rd., 6mi west of Polson;* ☎ *406-883-4450)* faces a 204ft-high arched dam (1938) in Buffalo Rapids Canyon downstream from Flathead Lake. At the powerhouse is an English-style village with an adjacent recreation area. Ownership of the dam is in the process of transfer to the Confederated Salish and Kootenai Tribes.

Six miles south of Polson, **The People's Center★** *(US-93, Pablo;* ☎ *406-675-0160)* relates the history of the reservation's tribes; its Native Ed-Ventures offers guided tours from an Indian perspective. Numerous prairie potholes, formed by glaciers 12,000 years ago, attract more than 180 bird species to **Ninepipe National Wildlife Refuge** *(US-93, 15mi south of Polson;* ☎ *406-644-2211),* a 2,000-acre wetland. The 1891 **St. Ignatius Mission★** *(US-93, 29mi south of Polson;* ☎ *406-745-2768)* is graced with handsome frescoes and murals and backdropped by the majestic Mission Mountains.

UPPER MISSOURI RIVER★

Michelin map 493 F 4   Mountain Standard Time
Tourist Information ☎ 406-761-5036 or http://visitmt.com/russell

The Missouri River played a key role in US westward expansion. Besides bringing the Lewis and Clark Expedition, fur traders, gold seekers and pioneer settlers into the region, it was part of a vast water-land route from St. Louis to the Pacific Ocean. Today, 149mi of the Missouri are a "wild and scenic" corridor rich in wildlife and pristine canyon scenes. Coursing through a land of buttes and prairies immortalized by cowboy artist Charles M. Russell, it's the last free-flowing remnant of a historic waterway.

SIGHTS

★★ Great Falls – *US-87 & US-89 at I-15.* ⚠ ✗ ♿ 🅿 ☎ *406-761-5036.* A hub of commerce and culture, Great Falls drew national attention when explorers Lewis and Clark portaged five local waterfalls (now submerged or reduced by dams). Great Falls is Montana's second-largest city, with 56,000 residents.

The **Lewis & Clark Interpretive Center★★** *(4201 Giant Springs Rd.;* ☎ *406-727-8733)* honors the Corps of Discovery and the Plains Indians who assisted them. Following a **film★** by director Ken Burns, visitors may explore interactive displays and exhibits that chronicle the voyageurs' odyssey. Outside, the 10mi **River's Edge Trail** entices bicyclists and walkers. Down the road at **Giant Springs Heritage State Park★** *(4600 Giant Springs Rd.;* ☎ *406-454-5840)* is one of the nation's largest freshwater springs and shortest rivers—the Roe, 201ft long.

Artist Charlie Russell (1864-1926), who portrayed the vanishing American West in oils, watercolors and sculptures, made his home in Great Falls. The **C.M. Russell Museum★★** *(400 13th St. N.;* ☎ *406-727-8787)* features the world's largest collection of Russell masterpieces, plus the artist's home and log-cabin studio. Not far away, Romanesque 1896 **Paris Gibson Square** *(1400 1st Ave. N.;* ☎ *406-727-8255)* has a contemporary art museum and a historical society.

C. M. Russell Museum, Great Falls, Montana

Fireboat (1918) by C. M. Russell

Outside the city, exhibits at **Ulm Pishkun State Park** *(Ulm-Vaughn Rd., 10mi southwest of Great Falls;* ☎ *406-866-2217)* tell the story of the bison's heyday and near-extinction. A visitor center explains how Indians once used *pishkuns* (buffalo jumps) to coax bison over cliffs.

★**Fort Benton** – *Rte. 80 off US-87, 38mi northeast of Great Falls.* △ ✗ ♿ ▣ ☎ *406-622-5316. www.fortbenton.com.* The farthest point to which steamboats could travel up the Missouri, Fort Benton developed as a river port. It was the east end of the 642mi Mullan Road to Walla Walla, Washington, linking the Missouri and Columbia River drainages. The **Bureau of Land Management Visitor Center** *(Front St.;* ☎ *406-538-1916)* is a helpful starting point for exploring. Sights along the **Front Street Levee** encapsulate Fort Benton's past as a frontier town, as told in the compact **Museum of the Upper Missouri** *(Front St. in Old Fort Park).* The **Montana Agricultural Center and Museum of the Northern Great Plains**★ *(20th & Washington Sts.;* ☎ *406-622-5316)* presents a vivid picture of farm life over the past century.

Charles M. Russell National Wildlife Refuge – *Road access via US-191, 174mi east of Great Falls.* △ ☎ *406-404-5101. www.r6.fws.gov/feature/cmr.html.* Surrounding Fort Peck Reservoir, this refuge holds 1,719sq mi of Missouri River wilderness. Home to elk, pronghorn, prehistoric paddlefish and 200 species of birds, the terrain looks much as it did when steamboats plied the waters. A 20mi self-guided **auto tour** begins 67mi northeast of Lewistown.

★★**Helena** – *US 12 at I-15* ✗ ♿ ▣ ☎ *406-442-4120.* Montana's capital, Helena sits atop Last Chance Gulch, one of America's richest gold strikes. A genteel town of 28,000 with a rough-and-tumble heritage, Helena is full of old mansions and mining legends. The **Last Chance Tour Train** *(*☎ *406-442-1023)* introduces the twin-spired **St. Helena's Cathedral**★ *(Lawrence & Warren Sts.;* ☎ *406-442-5825)* and the 1888 Queen Anne-style **Original Governor's Mansion**★ *(304 N. Ewing St.).*
Situated on a hillside facing the Helena Valley, the copper-domed **Montana State Capitol**★★ *(6th Ave. between N. Roberts & Montana Sts.;* ☎ *406-444-4789)* is a grand structure with an elegant French Renaissance rotunda. Charles Russell's monumental *Lewis and Clark Meeting Indians at Ross's Hole* (1912) hangs here. While the capitol undergoes renovation *(scheduled reopening 2001),* the **Montana Historical Society**★ *(225 N. Roberts St.;* ☎ *406-444-2696)* presents a vicarious video trip to the landmark. The society has a fine collection of Russell canvases; its Montana Homeland exhibit depicts the lifestyles of native peoples.
At **Gates of the Mountains**★★ *(I-15 Exit 209, 18mi north of Helena;* ☎ *406-458-5241),* the Missouri River weaves through a spectacular canyon formed from Precambrian sedimentary rock and Mississippian limestone. An optical illusion makes the towering rock walls appear to act as waterway guardians—thus Meriwether Lewis dubbed them "gates." Narrated 13mi cruises from Upper Holter Lake interpret the natural and human history of the area.

GOLD WEST COUNTRY★

Michelin map 493 E, F 4, 5   Mountain Standard Time
Tourist information ☎ 800-879-1159 or http://visitmt.com/goldwest

About 75 million years ago, molten granite surged into the earth's crust to create the mineral-laden Boulder Batholith—the genesis of southwestern Montana's wealth and outlaw lore. Gold, silver and copper drew settlers to the area in the mid- to late 19C. The charm of this historic region remains today.

SIGHTS

Butte – *I-15 & I-90.* ✗ & 🄿 ☎ *406-723-3177. www.butteinfo.org.* An erstwhile mining town of 34,000, Butte calls itself "The Richest Hill on Earth." Tunnels beneath the town, if unfurled, would stretch the length of Montana— more than 500mi. In the 1950s, labor strikes shut down underground hard-rock mining and left behind headframes and handsome fin-de-siècle buildings.

A **trolley tour** through historic Uptown includes the **Berkeley Pit★** *(east end of Mercury St. off Continental Dr.)*, the largest truck-served open-pit copper mine in the US from 1955 to 1982, when it produced more than 290 million tons of copper ore. Over a mile in diameter and 1,600ft deep, the pit harbors a toxic lake 650ft deep. The **Granite Mountain Mine Memorial** *(N. Main St., Walkerville)* honors 168 men who died in 1917 during hard-rock mining's worst disaster. Poignant quotes penned by several of the trapped men tell their tragic story.

Visitors may roam a reconstructed mining camp and hoist house at the **World Museum of Mining★** *(west end of Park St.; ☎ 406-723-7211)*, or tour Butte's last intact mine yard, the **Anselmo Mine★** *(600 block of N. Excelsior St.)*.

With its stained-glass windows and frescoed ceilings, the **Copper King Mansion★** *(219 W. Granite St.; ☎ 406-782-7580)* recalls Butte's glory days.

★**Deer Lodge** – *I-90, 41mi northwest of Butte.* △ ✗ & 🄿 A traditional ranching town, Deer Lodge today has captured the attention of Old West aficionados. At the 1,500-acre **Grant-Kohrs Ranch National Historic Site★★** *(.75mi west of I-90 Exit 184; ☎ 406-846-3388; www.nps.gov/grko)*, costumed Park Service rangers share the story of a working ranch that once was headquarters of a four-state cattle empire. Tours include the sumptuous 1890 ranch house.

Old Montana Prison★ *(1106 Main St.; ☎ 406-846-3111)*, the West's first territorial prison, provides a glimpse of yesteryear's convicts. Adjacent is the **Montana Automobile Museum★** *(☎ 406-846-3114)*, which features antique roadsters and novelty cars. **Frontier Montana** *(☎ 406-846-0026)*, showcasing cowboy collectibles, is across Main Street.

★★**Pintler Scenic Route** – *Rte. 1 between I-90 Exits 208 & 153.* △ ✗ & 🄿 This splendid 63mi road winds past ranches, over a mountain pass and along lakes. At one end is **Anaconda★** *(Rte. 1, 24mi west of Butte via I-90; ☎ 406-563-2400)*, known for its Art Deco theater and a landmark smelter stack. The highlight of quaint **Philipsburg★★** *(Rte. 1, 55mi northwest of Butte; ☎ 406-859-3388)*, a historic mining community, is the **Granite County Museum★** *(155 S. Sansome St.; ☎ 406-859-3020)*, which holds the Montana Ghost Town Hall of Fame. Within 60mi are 21 ghost towns, best preserved of which is the 1890s gold camp of **Garnet★★** *(39mi east of Missoula via Rte. 200 & Garnet Range Rd., or 57mi northwest of Philipsburg via I-90 & rugged Bear Gulch Rd.)*.

★**Missoula** – *US-12 & US-93 at I-90.* ☎ *406-543-6623.* A commercial and cultural center and home to the University of Montana, Missoula is a lively town of 52,000 residents. Built in 1877 for protection against Indians, **Fort Missoula** *(South Ave. west of Reserve St.; ☎ 406-728-3476)* served as a World War II internment center for Italians and Japanese Americans. The **US Forest Service Smokejumpers Training Center★** *(5765 W. Broadway; ☎ 406-329-4934)* prepares an elite corps of men and women to fight wildfires; public tours introduce a uniquely Western profession. The **Rocky Mountain Elk Foundation** *(2291 W. Broadway; ☎ 406-523-4545)* has bird, mammal and trophy-size elk mounts.

EXCURSION

★★**Bannack** – *South of Rte. 278, 26mi southwest of Dillon.* & 🄿 ☎ *406-834-3413.* A booming 1860s mining camp near the Pioneer Mountains, Bannack was Montana's first territorial capital. Its 50-plus buildings stand as abandoned when the gold played out. Self-guided tours lead through a deserted main street that comes to life during July's **Bannack Days**, a full-dress 19C re-creation.

Bannack's most notorious citizen, sheriff Henry Plummer, secretly led a gang of outlaws who killed and robbed more than 100 men. Vigilantes hung Plummer, but the loot he stole was supposedly never found.

CŒUR D'ALENE COUNTRY★

Michelin map p 493 D, E 3, 4   Pacific Standard Time
Tourist information ☎ 800-292-2553

In the early 1800s, fur trappers began trading for pelts with the Indians of Idaho's Panhandle. The natives proved shrewd bargainers, inspiring the trappers to say they had hearts like awls—*les coeurs d'alênes*. When the Mullan Road was completed in 1862, linking the Missouri and Columbia River watersheds, mountainous northern Idaho opened for settlement. Miners came for gold but stayed for other riches in what became one of the world's foremost regions for the production of silver, lead and zinc.

SIGHTS

★**Coeur d'Alene** – *I-90, 32mi east of Spokane, Washington.* △ ⚔ ♿ 🅿 ☎ *208-773-5016.* The former steamship port of 32,000 is now a summer playground for jet-skiers, parasailers, golfers and other recreation lovers. **Coeur d'Alene Lake**★★, once named by *National Geographic* magazine as one of the five most beautiful lakes in the world, extends 23mi south. Visitors may tour the lake by cruise ship, or bicycle the paved 62mi **Centennial Trail** between Coeur d'Alene and Spokane *(p 361).* The **Museum of North Idaho** *(115 Northwest Blvd.; ☎ 208-664-3448)* and **Fort Sherman Museum** *(Empire St. & College Dr., North Idaho College; ☎ 208-664-3448)* provide details of the region's history.

The **Coeur d'Alene** resort *(Front Ave. at 2nd St.; ☎ 208-765-4000)* boasts a marina surrounded by a .75mi boardwalk and an 18-hole golf course with the world's only floating green. Nearby, extending into the lake, is wooded **Tubbs Hill** promontory, a city park with coves, beaches and great lake views.

Hidden Creek Ranch Guest, Coeur d'Alene Lake

★★**Silver Valley** – *I-90, 20 to 60mi east of Coeur d'Alene.* △ ⚔ ♿ 🅿 The Silver Valley was named for the abundant mineral deposits found in the mountains overlooking the Coeur d'Alene River. More than a billion ounces of silver were extracted in the 20C at **Wallace**★★ *(I-90 Exit 62, 49mi east of Coeur d'Alene; ☎ 208-753-7151),* self-proclaimed "Silver Capital of the World." At the **Sierra Silver Mine**★★ *(420 5th St.; ☎ 208-752-5151),* retired miners demonstrate such equipment as muckers and slushers at a mine shaft; tours include a narrated trolley ride through town. A handsomely restored train depot (1901) houses railroad mementos at the château-style **Northern Pacific Railroad Museum**★ *(219 6th St. at Pine St.; ☎ 208-752-0111).* The **Wallace District Mining Museum** *(509 Bank St.; ☎ 208-556-1592)* shows films explaining how Idaho's mining industry evolved, along with displays of mineral samples and antiques.

Kellogg★ *(I-90 Exit 49, 36mi east of Coeur d'Alene;* △ ⚔ ♿ 🅿 ☎ *208-784-0821),* Wallace's larger neighbor, has shifted haltingly from mining to tourism. Its unique **junk-art sculptures**★ whimsically color the landscape. Summer weekends, a gondola and chairlifts at the **Silver Mountain** ski area *(610 Bunker Ave.; ☎ 208-783-1111)* carry visitors to the top of 6,300ft Kellogg Peak, where spectacular 360-degree **views**★★ encompass parts of Canada, Washington and Montana. The **Staff House Museum** *(820 W. McKinley Ave.; ☎ 208-786-4141)* features an extensive mineral collection and a mine model representing 135mi of tunnel.

All that remains of **Murray**★ *(Forest Rd. 9 via Forest Rd. 456, 18mi north of Wallace;* ☏ *208-682-4653),* a gold-rush boomtown, are two vintage saloons, a bank-turned-inn, an old cemetery and memories. This mining camp remnant comes complete with creekside tailings and gold panning.

Old Mission State Park★★ *(I-90 Exit 40, Cataldo, 24mi east of Cœur d'Alene;* ☏ *208-682-3814)* preserves Idaho's oldest structure, the 1850 Cataldo Mission. Modeled on Doric Roman lines, the restored church sits on a grassy knoll overlooking the Coeur d'Alene River valley. The well-interpreted visitor center shows an 18min film about the Indians and "Black Robes."

★**Lake Pend Oreille** – *East of US-95 & south of Rte. 200, about 25-50mi north of Cœur d'Alene.* △ ⟁ ▣ World War II history buffs recall 1,150ft-deep Lake Pend Oreille as the site of Farragut Naval Training Center. Farragut also served as a prisoner-of-war camp for Germans. The museum at **Farragut State Park** *(Rte. 54, 4mi east of Athol off US-95;* ☏ *208-683-2425)* shows how the region, now an outdoor recreation getaway, has evolved.

Sandpoint★ *(US-2 & 95, 46mi north of Cœur d'Alene;* ☏ *208-263-2161),* Lake Pend Oreille's largest town (with 5,200 people), has quaint shops and a small historical museum. Nearby **Schweitzer Mountain** *(Schweitzer Mountain Rd.;* ☏ *208-263-9555),* a popular ski area, offers summer-weekend chairlift rides to its 6,400ft summit and memorable lake-to-mountain **views**★★.

■ **State Capitals of the West**

Juneau,	Alaska
Phoenix,	Arizona
Sacramento,	California
Denver,	Colorado
Honolulu,	Hawaii
Boise,	Kansas
Helena,	Montana
Lincoln,	Nebraska
Carson City,	Nevada
Santa Fe,	New Mexico
Bismarck,	North Dakota
Oklahoma City,	Oklahoma
Salem,	Oregon
Pierre,	South Dakota
Austin,	Texas
Salt Lake City,	Utah
Olympia,	Washington
Cheyenne,	Wyoming

Grand Canyon Region

Bright Angel Trail, Grand Canyon National Park

The Grand Canyon is more than impressive. It is the largest chasm on earth, nearly 2 billion years in the making, 277mi long and averaging 10mi wide and 1mi deep. Hundreds of side canyons, creeks and trails lie within the boundaries of Grand Canyon National Park. No other place has so much of the earth's physical surface and geological history on display.

Most visitor services are centered on the canyon's South Rim. One may also explore the less commercialized North Rim and, beyond that, the largely undeveloped wilderness of the Arizona Strip just south of the Utah border. But the drive from South Rim to North Rim takes a good four hours, and many visitors opt for a shorter hop to Williams (56mi south), terminus for the Grand Canyon Railway, a driving alternative for national-park visitors. Northwest of Williams via old Route 66— the historic pre-interstate highway that linked Chicago with Los Angeles in the 1940s and '50s— lie the Native American reservation lands of the Havasupai and Hualapai tribes. Each offers access to remote areas of the Grand Canyon far from the busy South Rim.

Some 80mi southeast of the South Rim is cool and mountainous Flagstaff, the region's biggest city. Nearby are the world's largest stand of ponderosa pines and Arizona's tallest mountains —the San Francisco Peaks, rising to 12,633ft at Humphreys Peak. The 30mi drive south from Flagstaff to Sedona, descending from 7,000ft to 4,500ft through the diverse forests and famed red-rock scenery of Oak Creek Canyon, is brief but captivating. Sedona has lured artists and other creative types for a century; in recent decades, the influx has included New Age devotees who claim to be drawn by a mystical energy ascribed to the rocks.

Northeast of Sedona, occupying nearly one-sixth of the state of Arizona, are the Navajo and Hopi Indian reservations. The Navajo is the largest US Indian reservation; within its boundaries are some of the Southwest's most revered locales, including Canyon de Chelly and Monument Valley, plus numerous ancient Indian ruins and exhibits. Immediately south of the reservation is Petrified Forest National Park and the westward-stretching Painted Desert, a subtly colorful wilderness marked by jewel-like specimens of wood turned to stone.

157

Map pp 164-165   Mountain Standard Time
Tourist Information ☎ 520-638-7888 or www.nps.gov/grca

If any single geographical feature symbolizes the United States in the minds of world travelers, it is Arizona's Grand Canyon.

This 1,904sq-mi national park, located entirely in northwestern Arizona, extends from Lees Ferry, in Glen Canyon National Recreation Area, west to the Grand Wash Cliffs, in Lake Mead National Recreation Area. Waters from seven western states— Arizona, Utah, New Mexico, Colorado and Wyoming, plus Nevada and California below the Grand Canyon—drain into the mighty Colorado River, 1,450mi long from its source in Colorado's Rocky Mountains to Mexico's Gulf of California.

The Grand Canyon was carved over aeons by the powerful waters of the Colorado River, forcibly aided by wind and water erosion. Today a giant swath of the earth's geological history is visible in the colorfully striated layers of rock that reach down more than a mile below the canyon's rim.

This is not the world's deepest canyon. In North America alone, there are deeper chasms in Mexico (Copper Canyon), California (Kings Canyon) and the Pacific Northwest (Hells Canyon). Older rocks may be found in northern Canada and elsewhere. But the Grand Canyon of the Colorado River is known throughout the world for its immense and labyrinthine rock landscape as well as its special, almost mystical characteristics.

At dawn and dusk, in particular, the low-angle sun highlights the vividly colored canyon walls. Bands of green, blue, purple, pink, red, orange, gold, yellow and white define a succession of exposed ancient rock layers. It is one of the most extreme cases of erosion anywhere, and a site few humans can experience without feeling humbled by the relentless sculpting power of nature.

Flowing water, rainfall and melting snow cause some layers to erode more quickly than others. Some form slender spires, others plunging cliffs. Mineral variation within the rocks gives each stratum a distinctive color. The sequence of layers—so well preserved in the semiarid climate—offers striking examples of Precambrian (up to 2 billion years old) and Paleozoic (250-550 million years old) rock.

Historical Notes

Early Civilization – The Grand Canyon has been inhabited for at least 4,000 years, as evidenced by small hunting fetishes of the Desert Archaic culture, found hidden in niches in the canyon walls. By AD 500, the Anasazi culture was established. About 2,000 sites, including cliff-wall petroglyphs, have been found within park boundaries;

South Rim, Grand

most impressive is Tusayan Pueblo (c.1185) on the South Rim. These Puebloans, ancestors of the modern Hopi, had left the canyon by the late 13C, to be replaced by the Cerbat—forebears of the Hualapai and Havasupai tribes, who today have reservations in the western canyon.

The earliest recorded European visit to the Grand Canyon was by Francisco Vásquez de Coronado's gold-hungry 1540 expedition. But except for brief Spanish exploration in the 18C, the region was neglected for more than three centuries until 1869, when a one-armed Civil War veteran named John Wesley Powell led an expedition of nine men in small wooden boats through the length of the canyon. Six men survived the journey through uncharted whitewater rapids, including Powell, who was at times lashed by ropes to his boat for safety. Two years later, the fearless Powell led a second expedition.

Late-19C mining efforts in the canyon generally failed, but they opened the doors for a Grand Canyon-based tourism industry. The first rim-top hotels were little more than mining camps. Guided mule trips took visitors to the canyon floor.

The Harvey Legacy – The Grand Canyon was earmarked for protection in 1893, but not until 1919 was it set aside as a park. Much credit goes to the Fred Harvey Company, which built railroad hotels and restaurants throughout the Southwest. The Santa Fe Railroad built a line from Williams to the South Rim in 1901; tourism began in earnest with the 1905 completion of the El Tovar Hotel, the most elegant in the West. Designer Mary Colter conceived many of the Harvey buildings, including the Pueblo-style Hopi House (1905), Lookout Studio (1914), Hermits Rest (1914), canyon-floor Phantom Ranch (1922), Desert View Watchtower (1932) and Bright Angel Lodge (1935). Most were staffed by "Harvey Girls," well-dressed and educated young women, usually from the East, who offered a civilized sort of tourism in a rather uncivilized place. The "Girls" are gone, but the lodges continue to serve visitors.

In its first year as a national park, over 44,000 people visited the Grand Canyon. Today, about 5 million tourists enter the park each year. Their impact on the environment has led the National Park Service to take dramatic action to protect the Canyon for future generations, and to establish a model that likely will be adapted at other US national parks.

By 2002, passenger vehicles will park at Tusayan, 6mi south of Grand Canyon Village, and take a light rail system to **Canyon View Information Plaza** on the South Rim. This orientation hub at Mather Point is scheduled to open in fall 2000. It will provide visitors with their first view of the canyon and a menu of activities to plan their visit, including hiking, biking, horseback, mule and rafting trips.

Canyon National Park

SIGHTS

★★★ **South Rim** – **Kids** IIIII Most visitor activities in Grand Canyon National Park are focused along a 35mi strand of paved road that extends from the East Rim Entrance Station (29mi west of US-89 at Cameron) to Hermits Rest.

Grand Canyon Village – △ ✕ ⅙ ▣ Site of park headquarters, the main visitor center and the lion's share of historic hotels, restaurants and tourist facilities within the park, this community links East Rim and West Rim drives with Williams (56mi south via Rte. 64) and Flagstaff (80mi southeast via US-180).

The **Grand Canyon Village Historical District★** comprises nine buildings, including the El Tovar Hotel, Hopi House, Bright Angel Lodge and Lookout Studio. Trains still arrive at the **Santa Fe Railway Station** (1909, Francis Wilson), one of three remaining log depots in the US. The **Buckey O'Neill Cabin** (1890s) was built by a miner-politician who rode with Teddy Roosevelt's Rough Riders in 1898 during the Spanish-American War assault on San Juan Hill.

Perched on the rim west of the Bright Angel Lodge is the **Kolb Brothers Studio** (1904). The two brothers photographed tourists descending by mule into the canyon. They processed the film at Indian Garden, 4.5mi (by trail) and 4,000ft below the rim, where they maintained a lab with readily available water. One of them would run back uphill in time to sell the photos to returning tourists. The building is now operated as a bookstore and art gallery.

A mile east of the visitor center, itself east of the historical district, the **Yavapai Observation Station** acts as a sort of geology museum. Exhibits focus on the Grand Canyon's fossil record; guided geology walks depart several times daily. The **Rim Trail** *(9.4mi)* extends gently west from here to Hermits Rest, its first 2.7mi (to Maricopa Point) paved and highly accessible.

ADDRESS BOOK

Please see explanation on p 64.

Staying and Dining in Northern Arizona

Enchantment Resort – *520 Boynton Canyon Rd., Sedona.* ☎ *520-282-2900. www.enchantmentresort.com. 266 rooms.* **$$$** Low-profile, adobe-style casitas, with beehive fireplaces and private balconies, are nestled in the red rocks of Boynton Canyon. The spa offers restorative Native American earth-clay wraps. Diners enjoy rack of lamb with a pistachio crust at the award-winning **Yavapai Restaurant,** which has a 180-degree panoramic view.

El Tovar Hotel – *Grand Canyon Village.* ✕ ⅙ ▣ ☎ *303-297-2757. www .amfac.com. 78 rooms.* **$$** Native stone and heavy Oregon pine logs create the atmosphere of an old European hunting lodge, and the views are out of this world: El Tovar has offered perspective on the Grand Canyon since 1905. Fresh Atlantic salmon, flown in daily, is a highlight of the **Dining Room.**

L'Auberge de Sedona – *301 L'Auberge Ln., Sedona.* ✕ ⅙ ▣ ﹗ ☎ *520-282-1661. www.lauberge.com. 100 rooms and cottages.* **$$** The main lodge's huge rolling logs and stone columns blend into the chiseled buttes and spires of Sedona's geology. The 33 cottages, on the other hand, have a country-French feel. Eleven acres of botanical gardens are joined to the award-winning creek-side **L'Auberge Restaurant** by paths that wind past fruit trees and lilacs.

Hotel Weatherford – *23 N. Leroux St., Flagstaff.* ✕ ▣ ☎ *520-779-1919. www.weatherfordhotel.com. 8 rooms.* **$** Nearly 100 years ago, the local paper claimed the Weatherford to be "first class in every aspect." Since then, it has been a telephone exchange and theater. After 20 years of restoration to its brick façade and double-tiered balconies, it now offers a handful of basic, economical rooms.

La Posada – *303 E. 2nd St., Winslow.* ▣ ☎ *520-289-4366.* **$** Fred Harvey used his Santa Fe Railroad to civilize the West with silverware and china, and La Posada was his last and most elegant hotel. Designed as a Spanish hacienda, with garden, ballroom and arcade, it was in its heyday a favorite retreat for Hollywood stars and a popular stop on Route 66.

★★ West Rim Drive – Only free shuttle buses may ply this 8mi road west from Grand Canyon Village in summer. (For now, private vehicles are permitted October to April.) The drive passes **viewpoints★★★** at Maricopa Point, the John Wesley Powell Memorial, Hopi Point, Mohave Point and Pima Point before ending at **Hermits Rest★**. Built as a tourist stop with a fireplace and picture windows, Hermits Rest was named for a 19C prospector, loner Louis Boucher.

★★★ East Rim Drive – The 24mi road from Grand Canyon Village to the East Rim Entrance Station passes numerous dizzying viewpoints, including Yaki, Grandview, Moran and Lipan Points. Grandview Point was the site of the Grand Canyon's first tourist hotel, a guest ranch that fell into disuse when the train chose Grand Canyon Village over Grandview for its depot in 1901.

A small pueblo ruin marks the **Tusayan Ruin and Museum★**, 20mi east of the village. Displays trace the primitive Native American culture of pueblo-dwelling Anasazi in the Grand Canyon region prior to the 13C.

The **Desert View Watchtower★**, 22mi from Grand Canyon Village, may be the most photographed structure in the park. Modeled after an ancient Pueblo lookout, the three-story building is dominated by a circular 70ft tower that commands expansive **views★★★** of the convoluted canyon and Colorado River far below. The Painted Desert appears on the far eastern horizon.

★ Canyon Floor Trails – From Grand Canyon Village, the depth of the Grand Canyon—South Rim to canyon floor—is about 5,000ft. The distance on foot, via any of several steep and narrow trails, is 7mi to 10mi. Trailheads for a variety of steep routes may be found at three viewpoints.

Most popular is the **Bright Angel Trail**, originating at Bright Angel Lodge in Grand Canyon Village. The trail descends 4,460ft in 9mi to the Colorado River at Phantom Ranch, which lodges adventurers in cabins or dormitories. The trail is recommended only for exceptionally fit individuals. Signs posted prominently along the canyon rim, and at nearly every trailhead, caution hikers not to try hiking to the river and back to the rim in a single day. Hikes that continue across the river and up to the North Rim typically require three days. An option for descending to the canyon floor is by commercial **trail ride** on the back of a mule: one day down, one day back *(reservations, booked well in advance:* ☎ *435-679-8665)*.

On the banks of the river, 16 different concessionaires offer commercial rafting trips in a range of distances and vessel sizes. Bookings are essential months in advance. Trips can be as short as two days and as long as three weeks. Private rafting permits are available, but the waiting list is 12-15 years long.

★★ North Rim – *Open May 15-Oct 16, weather permitting.* △ ⅄⅁ ₽ As the desert raven flies, the North Rim is only 10mi across the canyon from the South Rim, but hiking the 21mi from rim to rim takes two to three days. The drive from Grand Canyon Village (South Rim) to Grand Canyon Lodge on the North Rim *(Rte. 64 east to Cameron, US-89 north to Marble Canyon, US-89A west to Jacob Lake, then Rte. 67 south)* covers 214 road miles and requires at least 5hrs of travel time.

The North Rim is far less developed than the South Rim. It has the feel of a wilderness outpost cloaked in pine forest, rather than a crowded resort village. At 7,700-8,800ft above sea level, it is about 1,200ft higher than the South Rim; and it is several degrees cooler, with midsummer temperatures averaging in the high-70s (Fahrenheit) rather than mid-80s. To many visitors, the North Rim offers a connoisseur's experience of the Grand Canyon.

The National Park boundary is 30mi south of Jacob Lake on Route 67; it's another 14mi to the North Rim. The visitor center, adjacent to the Grand Canyon Lodge complex, is a good place to get one's bearings. A paved .5mi trail leads from here to Bright Angel Point, with glorious **views★★★** of the canyon. Also visible is the strenuous **North Kaibab Trail** *(14.2mi)*, which descends 5,840ft to Phantom Ranch. Day hikers should not venture beyond Roaring Springs *(4.7mi each way)*, water source for the entire Grand Canyon National Park. Full- and half-day mule trips are available from the North Rim, but do not descend all the way to the river.

The **Cape Royal Road★** extends 23mi from the Grand Canyon Lodge southeast across the Walhalla Plateau to Vista Encantadora and Cape Royal, with a spur route to Point Imperial, the highest point on the canyon rim at 8,803ft.

★ Grand Canyon Railway – *233 N. Grand Canyon Blvd., Williams, 65mi south of Grand Canyon Village.* ⅄⅁ ₽ ☎ *520-635-4253. www.thetrain.com.* The Territorial-style town of **Williams** has long been a starting point for canyon tours. The Atchison Topeka-Santa Fe Railroad operated between here and the canyon from 1901 to 1968; service was re-established in 1989. Today the restored Grand Canyon Railway runs daily trips from the 1908 Williams Depot. The one-way trip takes 2hrs 15min, and is made even quicker by strolling musicians and the antics of Wild West characters on board. It is a worthy alternative to driving and parking at the South Rim, a potential problem any time of year.

Havasupai Indian Reservation – *From I-40 at Seligman, 44mi west of Williams, drive 34mi northwest on Rte. 66, then 65mi north on Tribal Road 18 to Hualapai Hilltop. Supai is another 8mi by foot or mule.* △ ✗ ☎ *520-448-2121.* Together with the adjacent Hualapai reservation, this tribal grant includes lands along the South Rim of the western Grand Canyon. The village of **Supai**, site of the Havasupai tribal center, is at the bottom of the Canyon, where the Havasupai have lived at least since the 16C. Several hundred tribal members continue to farm the fer-

■ How the Grand Canyon Was Formed

In the earth's infancy, the area now defined by the Grand Canyon was covered by shallow coastal waters and accented by active volcanoes. Over millions of years, layers of marine sediment and lava built to depths thousands of feet thick. About 1.7 billion years ago, heat and pressure from within the earth buckled the sedimentary layers into mountains 5-6mi high, changing their composition to a metamorphic rock called Vishnu schist. Molten intrusions in the mountains' core cooled and hardened into pink granite. Then erosion took over, reducing the mountains to mere vestiges over millions of years.

The process repeated itself, another shallow sea covering the land, more layers of sediment—12,000ft thick—being laid down. A new mountain range formed; erosion again assaulted the peaks so thoroughly that only ridges remained and, in many places, the ancient Vishnu schist was laid bare.

The horizontal layers above the schist, to 3,500ft below the modern canyon rim, were formed over 300 million years as oceans advanced across the Southwest, perhaps as many as seven times, and each time regressed. The environment was alternately marsh and desert, subject to rapid erosion. The era coincided with the age of dinosaurs and concluded about 65 million years ago with the end of the Cretaceous period. Then the Colorado River began to cut the canyon, gouging through rock and soil and carrying the debris away to sea. As erosion thinned the layer of rock above the earth's core, lava spewed to the surface. In fact, there have been several periods of recent volcanic activity in the Grand Canyon area, most recently in the 11C at Sunset Crater, southeast of the park.

Today, water and wind continue to chisel the Grand Canyon ever deeper.

GEOLOGIC LAYERS OF THE GRAND CANYON

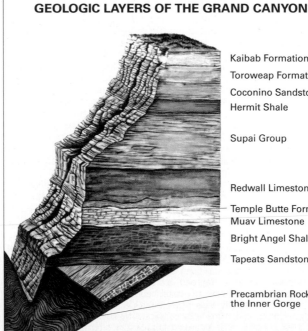

Kaibab Formation

Toroweap Formation

Coconino Sandstone

Hermit Shale

Supai Group

Redwall Limestone

Temple Butte Formation
Muav Limestone

Bright Angel Shale

Tapeats Sandstone

Precambrian Rocks of
the Inner Gorge

Frank Sierra/Courtesy National Park Service

tile bottomlands and provide basic tourism services. Accessible only by foot, mule or helicopter, Supai has a small tourist lodge, a restaurant, several shops and a post office. Visitors can see the farms and livestock areas kept along Havasu Creek by the Havasupai, and hike a mile or two to several beautiful and distinctive turquoise-colored **waterfalls** pouring out of steep cliffs.

Hualapai Indian Reservation – *From I-40 at Seligman (44mi west of Williams), drive 41mi northwest on Rte. 66 to Peach Springs.* △ ✕ ☎ *520-769-2230.* The Hualapai control a 108mi-long portion of the South Rim, beginning about 50mi west of Grand Canyon Village. The tribe operates bus tours and one- or two-day rafting trips on the Colorado River from Diamond Creek to Pearce Ferry. A permit, available in Peach Springs, is required for private car travel off Route 66.

FLAGSTAFF-SEDONA AREA★★

Map pp 164-165   Mountain Standard Time
Flagstaff Tourist Information ☎ 520-774-9541 or www.flagstaff.az.us
Sedona Tourist Information ☎ 520-282-7722 or www.sedonachamber.com

Towering red-rock spires and buttes, and history-rich Native American sites, have long attracted visitors and new residents to these north-central Arizona towns. Flagstaff, established as a logging and livestock-ranching center, grew as a transportation hub—first for the railroad (beginning in 1882), later for auto travelers on historic Route 66. Today it is home to 57,000 people. Sedona, 28mi south, renowned for its wind- and water-sculpted scenery, is a magnet for artists, tourists and (more recently) New Age aficionados who claim the red rocks are imbued with a mystical aura. The cities are linked by spring-fed Oak Creek Canyon, a 1,200ft-deep gorge that descends 2,500ft down the southern escarpment of the vast Colorado Plateau.

Historical Notes

Redwall Limestone, the first stratum of sedimentary rock exposed in the red-rock formations, began to form 330 million years ago when seawater blanketed the area. A series of oceanic advances and retreats deposited layers of sediment visible today. The black basaltic lava that now caps the walls of Oak Creek Canyon was the result of volcanic activity some 7 million years ago.

Hunter-gatherer groups of Paleo Indians probably occupied the Flagstaff-Sedona region as early as 11,000 years ago. Over the centuries, various tribes of Indians, including the Hohokam and Sinagua, thrived here. In modern times, the Yavapai and Tonto Apaches made this area their home.

Flagstaff traces its history to 1876, when New England immigrants attached a US flag to the top of a tall, trimmed pine tree to honor their nation on Independence Day. That original flagstaff became a trail marker for westbound travelers. The opening in 1899 of Northern Arizona Normal School (now University) cemented the town's future. In the 1950s and '60s, Flagstaff was a key stop on historic Route 66, the "Mother Road" that ran 2,000mi from Chicago to Los Angeles in the days before the interstate highway system. A strip of neon motels, mom and pop cafes and "last chance for gas" truck stops recalls that era. Other evocative remnants exist east and west of town just off the Interstate 40 corridor.

Settlers trickled into Oak Creek Canyon after the first homesteader set up house-keeping in 1876, but by 1900 there were only about 20 families in the area. Sedona evolved after World War II into a destination that is part resort town, part artist colony and part New Age center. Today the town accommodates some 9,230 permanent residents and attracts about 2.5 million tourists each year.

SIGHTS

★ **Flagstaff** – *I-40 & US-89.* △ ✕ ♿ 🅿 This city—nestled at the foot of the San Francisco Peaks, crowned by 12,633ft Humphreys Peak—is the commercial hub for a huge and sparsely populated area. Within the boundaries of Coconino County are Sedona, the Grand Canyon *(p 158)*, Glen Canyon Dam *(p 91)*, the western third of the Navajo Indian Reservation *(p 167)* and three national monuments—Wupatki, Sunset Crater and Walnut Canyon *(below)*.

From a visitor center in the 1926 Tudor Revival **railway station** *(1 E. Rte. 66 at Leroux St.;* ☎ *520-774-9541)*, walking tours depart for the downtown **historic district**, whose highlights include the 1889 Hotel Weatherford *(23 N. Leroux St.)*. Seven sandstone structures on the **Northern Arizona University** campus *(Kendrick St. & Ellery Ave., south of Butler Ave.;* ☎ *520-523-5511)*, built between 1894 and 1935, are on the National Register of Historic Places. The 13,000sq ft **Riordan Mansion** *(1300 Riordan Ranch St., east of Milton Rd.; visit by guided tour only, ☎ 520-779-4395),* 1904 home of two timber-baron brothers, features log siding, volcanic stone arches and an array of original Craftsman-style furniture.

★ **Lowell Observatory** – 🄺🄸🄳🄢 *1400 Mars Hill Rd.* ♿ 🅿 ☎ *520-774-3358.* Astronomer Percival Lowell established this facility in 1894, 1mi west of downtown Flagstaff. Here in 1930, Clyde Tombaugh *(p 143)* discovered the tiny outer planet Pluto by photographing sections of the night sky at six-day intervals and looking for movements in the minuscule dots of light. Stars don't change position; the tiny point of light that did was identified as a planet. Lowell's own 24in Clark refracting telescope is on display and in use during frequent nighttime sky-viewing sessions. Interactive exhibits focus on basic astronomy and space travel.

★ **Museum of Northern Arizona** – 🄺🄸🄳🄢 *3101 Fort Valley Rd. (US-180 North).* ♿ 🅿 ☎ *520-774-5213. www.musnaz.org.* Well-considered exhibits provide an overview of southwestern Native American cultures, both ancient and modern, as well as an introduction to the geology, archaeology, anthropology and arts of northern Arizona. It's a helpful first stop before visiting regional sites.

★ **Wupatki National Monument** – *Sunset Crater-Wupatki Rd., east of US-89, 33mi northeast of Flagstaff.* ♿ 🅿 ☎ *520-679-2365. www.nps.gov/wupa.* Hundreds of Pueblo-style masonry ruins are spread across this vast volcanic plain, remains of a Sinagua farming community that lived here 800 years ago. The highlight of the 55sq-mi preserve is the **Wupatki Ruins,** accessible from an overlook or a .5mi trail. The extraordinary site includes a 100-room pueblo, ball court and amphitheater. The **Wukoki Ruins,** reached by a .2mi trail, comprise an isolated square tower and several rooms, surrounded by the pastel shades of the Painted Desert.

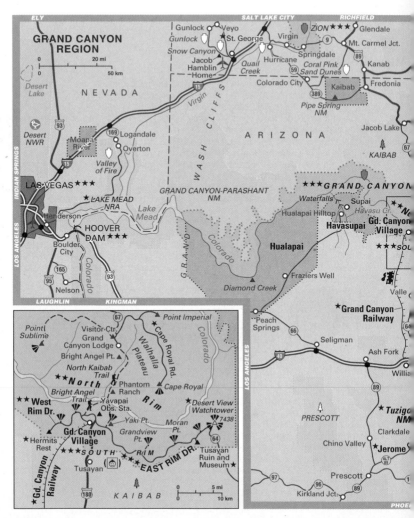

*Sunset Crater Volcano National Monument – *Sunset Crater-Wupatki Rd., east of US-89, 14mi northeast of Flagstaff.* ♿ 🅿 ☎ *520-526-0502. www.nps.gov/sucr.* A 1,000ft-high cinder cone, which erupted in 1064, is surrounded by hundreds of acres of black lava flows and cinders, out of which sprouts an improbable pine forest. A 1mi trail skirts the base of the volcano. You cannot climb Sunset Crater itself, but trails access smaller, nearby cinder cones, including Lenox Crater *(1mi round-trip).*

*Walnut Canyon National Monument – *Walnut Canyon Rd., 3mi south of I-40, 7.5mi east of Flagstaff.* ♿ 🅿 ☎ *520-526-3367. www.nps.gov/waca.* A set of Sinagua cliff dwellings, occupied from the early 12C to mid-13C, are built into the 350ft-high walls of Walnut Creek canyon. Most ruins are well below the canyon rim, nestled in alcoves in the overhanging rock. The **Island Trail** *(.9mi)* requires a degree of high-altitude fitness, but visitors who descend 185 ft (via 240 steps) are rewarded with the chance to crawl through two dozen ancient dwellings. Ruins may be viewed from farther away by those walking the more-level **Rim Trail** *(.7mi).*

*Meteor Crater – *Meteor Crater Rd., 8mi south of I-40, 38mi east of Flagstaff.* 🍴♿ 🅿 ☎ *520-289-2362.* The best-preserved meteor impact site on earth was created 50,000 years ago. A relatively small meteorite, 150ft in diameter, left a hole 570ft deep and nearly 1mi across when it crashed into the earth; a .8mi trail *(by guided tour only)* now follows the crater rim. In the visitor center, the **Museum of Astrogeology** has interactive displays on meteors and the threat of collisions with earth, and an **Astronaut Hall of Fame** cites achievements of US space pioneers who once trained in the crater's virtual moonscape.

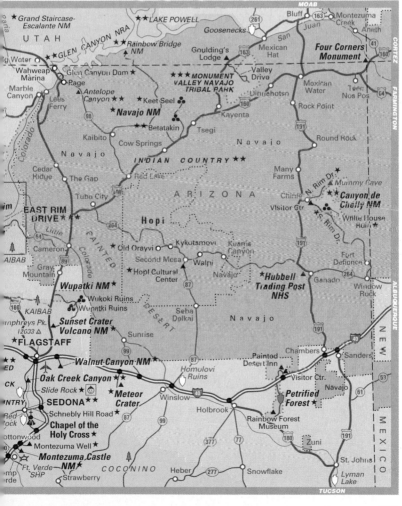

Slide Rock State Park

Oak Creek Canyon – *Take US-89A south 14mi from Flagstaff to Oak Creek Vista to begin scenic drive. Note: The two-lane highway is often crowded with traffic. Drivers are cautioned to be patient; passing other vehicles may be difficult or impossible.* Oak Creek began cutting its gorge into a fault line about 1 million years ago. Today a beautiful 14mi scenic drive plunges more than 2,000ft through a steep-walled, 1,200ft-deep canyon, about a mile wide. The main descent begins at **Oak Creek Vista** (elevation 6,400ft) with a dramatic 2mi series of switch-backs. Stunning views down the gorge encompass forests of ponderosa pine and fir trees crowning the Mogollon Rim. Enormous bright-red rocks jut out above, interspersed with white and gold rocks and spotted with piñon and juniper.

The creek pours over tiers of smooth sandstone at **Slide Rock State Park*** [Kids] *(8mi north of Sedona; ☎ 520-282-3034)*, a popular swimming hole on hot summer days. Just outside Sedona, the road skirts the banks of sparkling Oak Creek (elevation 4,300ft), where ash, cottonwood, sycamore, willow and walnut thrive.

Sedona – *US-89A & Rte. 179.* △ ✕ ❺ ▣ This small city, its economy based upon tourism and the arts, owes its beauty and mystique to the variety of striking red buttes and spires that surround it. It is located in the heart of **Red Rock Country***, bounded by Oak Creek and Sycamore Canyons, the Mogollon Rim and Verde Valley. The region takes its name from rust color exposed in three mid-level strata of the Supai Group, the Hermit Formation and the Schnebly Hill Formation, sculpted of sandstone between 270 million and 300 million years ago.

Maps of the Sedona area identify such landmarks as Cathedral Rock, Bell Rock and Boynton Canyon. In the 1980s, these sites and others were identified as "vortices," where concentrated electromagnetic energy emanates from the earth. Native Americans had long imputed inspirational characteristics to these sites. Sedona's red rocks have now become a beacon for the New Age, attracting hosts of visitors seeking spiritual enlightenment. *(Vortex maps are available at New Age shops and at the Sedona-Oak Creek Chamber of Commerce, US-89A at Forest Rd.; ☎ 520-282-7722.)*

To experience Red Rock Country and the Sedona vortices up close, you'll need sturdy hiking boots or a four-wheel-drive vehicle. Several companies provide off-road **Jeep tours** to vista points, vortices, wildflower meadows, Sinagua ruins and other sites. If you are driving yourself, the most convenient backcountry access is via **Schnebly Hill Road*** *(off Rte. 179, across the Oak Creek bridge from the US-89A "Y" junction).* This 12mi road—pavement gives way to rutted dirt after the first mile—has provided a route from town to the Mogollon Rim, the edge of the Colorado Plateau, since 1904. A drive along its rough switchbacks rewards visitors with stunning **views***** of red-rock formations and a panorama that spans the valley below.

Sedona's original commercial core is called not "downtown" but **Uptown.** Just north of the "Y" intersection on US-89A, a plethora of shops and galleries in Old West-style structures offer everything from Native American crafts to New Age items. Down the hill on Route 179 sits **Tlaquepaque Arts & Crafts Village** *(☎ 520-282-4838)*, a charming shopping complex modeled after the village of San Pedro de Tlaquepaque in Guadalajara, Mexico. Narrow passageways and tiled plazas are planted with profusions of bright flowers and shaded by venerable sycamore trees.

★**Chapel of the Holy Cross** – *End of Chapel Rd. off Rte. 179, 7mi south of uptown Sedona.* ♿ 🅿 ✆ *520-282-4069.* This awe-inspiring contemporary Catholic chapel was completed in 1956 (Anshen & Allen), the brainchild of local artist and rancher Marguerite Brunswig Staude. Characterized by its cruciform shape, the concrete aggregate-and-glass chapel rises 90ft from the base of a red-rock butte. **Views**★★ from the stark interior of the "spiritual fortress," as Staude called it, look south to Courthouse Butte and Bell Rock.

★**Tuzigoot National Monument** – *Tuzigoot Rd. off Rte. 279, Clarkdale; 23mi southwest of Sedona via US-89A to Cottonwood.* ♿ 🅿 ✆ *520-634-5564. www.nps.gov/tuzi.* Occupied from 1000 to 1400, this ancient Sinagua pueblo tops a ridge 120ft above the Verde River. At its height in the late 1300s, Tuzigoot (Apache for "crooked water") was home to about 225 people, who lived in 86 ground-floor rooms and perhaps 15 second-story rooms, and farmed the fertile valley. Rooftop ladders offered entry to most rooms. Limestone and sandstone river boulders, bound together with mud mortar, formed the pueblo's walls.

Modern visitors, following a gently sloping .25mi trail through the ruins, may enter several rooms to glimpse how the Sinaguans lived. Artifacts, excavated on site and displayed in the visitor center, help interpret cultural practices.

★**Jerome** – *US-89A, 29mi southwest of Sedona.* ✕ ♿ 🅿 ✆ *520-634-2900. www.jeromechamber.com.* Clinging precipitously to the slope of Cleopatra Hill, 2,000ft above the adjacent plain, Jerome began as a rough-and-tumble mining camp in 1876. One of the world's richest veins of copper ore—more than $4 billion worth was drawn from this earth—had the community flourishing by the early 20C. In the late 1920s, population stood at 15,000. The Great Depression, however, took its toll; Jerome went into a steady decline until the last mine closed in 1953.

Today the erstwhile copper town has 470 residents, 300 historic structures and a handful of artisans' galleries along its winding streets. Booklets for self-guided tours are available at the visitor information trolley on Hull Avenue.

Exhibits at **Jerome State Historic Park**★ *(Douglas Rd.; ✆ 520-634-5381)*, in a 1916 adobe mansion built for mine owner "Rawhide Jimmy" Douglas, explore town history. Displays include tools and equipment, minerals and photographs, and a model of the network of underground mine shafts that weave beneath the streets.

★**Montezuma Castle National Monument** – *Montezuma Rd., Camp Verde, 1mi east of I-17 Exit 289.* ♿ 🅿 ✆ *520-567-3322, www.nps.gov/moca.* Impossibly tucked into a natural limestone alcove 50-100ft above the floor of Beaver Creek, Montezuma Castle formed part of a larger early-12C Sinaguan community. The five-story, 20-room "castle" was misnamed by Europeans, who presumed it had been constructed for 16C Aztec emperor Montezuma.

Not intended as a fortress, the dwelling's location protected its occupants from the elements and supplied natural insulation against heat and cold. Nor did it take up valuable farmland. Sinaguans created the rooms by hauling chunks of limestone and baskets of mud mortar up crude pole ladders. About 5mi north of Montezuma Castle, the monument's **Montezuma Well**★ unit *(Rte. 119, Rimrock, 4mi east of I-17 Exit 293; ✆ 520-567-3322)* preserves a 55ft-deep limestone sink formed millions of years ago by the collapse of an underground cavern. Sinagua farmers diverted water from this spring-fed "well" to irrigate crops. On the edge of the well are remnants of several additional Sinaguan dwellings and a c.1100 Hohokam pit house.

INDIAN COUNTRY★★

Map pp 164-165   Mountain Standard Time
Tourist Information ✆ 520-871-6659

The largest of all Native American reservations, the **Navajo Indian Reservation** covers more than 27,000sq mi of mountains, forests, buttes, mesas and other wide-open desert spaces whose imagery is so often associated with the Southwest. The reservation mainly cloaks northeastern Arizona, although small portions extend into southeastern Utah and northwestern New Mexico.

Most tribal land is used as open range. The Navajo—descended from nomadic hunter-gatherers, who migrated around 1600 to the Four Corners area after the disappearance of the earlier Anasazi and Sinagua cultures—have raised sheep on isolated homesteads for centuries. The wool produces the distinctive Navajo rug and blanket weavings renowned around the world for color, design and fabric.

After the Mexican War gave the US control of the Southwest, Navajo raids induced the Army to invade tribal lands. In 1863-64, troops razed the earth, destroying homes and crops, killing people and livestock. The 8,500 survivors were marched nearly 300mi to a reserve in eastern New Mexico, a tragic ordeal etched firmly in Navajo memory as the "Long Walk." But the Army's plan to turn nomadic herdsmen into sedentary farmers failed, and in 1868, the Navajo were allowed to return to their own land with enough sheep to start anew.

About 100,000 Navajo live on their reservation today; a similar number have left to seek work in towns and cities. Many of those who remain continue to ranch tribal lands and speak the Navajo language, a complicated tongue used successfully during World War II as an unbreakable code against the Japanese in the Pacific.

It is increasingly common on the reservation to see contemporary homes with satellite dishes and new cars. Typically, alongside these icons of modernity stands at least one hogan, a traditional round ceremonial structure made of logs and mud. The hogan always faces east to greet the sunrise.

Surrounded by the Navajo Reservation is the 2,400sq mi **Hopi Indian Reservation,** home to about 10,000 descendants of the fabled Anasazi. Arizona's only Pueblo tribe (most are in New Mexico), the Hopi live in 12 villages, most on a trio of 6,000ft mesas. Masters of dry-land farming, the Hopi have lived here since the 11C; they remain perhaps the most traditional of any Native American tribe. Their devotion to the spiritual world is reflected in their carvings of colorful *kachinas,* benevolent cloud dwellers supplicated for rain, good crops and a harmonious life. (Hopi means "people of peace.")

Both the Navajo and the Hopi are sovereign entities within Arizona and the United States. Both enforce tribal regulations as well as state and federal laws. Tourists are welcome on reservations; however, alcohol is prohibited. Because there is no private land ownership, and nearly all reservation land is part of someone's traditional use area, cross-country and off-road travel require special permission.

SIGHTS

* **Navajo National Monument** – *Rte. 564, 10mi north of US-160, 21mi west of Kayenta.* ⚠ 🅿 ☎ *520-672-2366. www.nps.gov/nava.* Two of the finest Anasazi ruins are located here at 7,300ft elevation in little-visited Tsegi Canyon. The 135 rooms of **Betatakin★★** ("ledge house"), late-13C home of a community of 100, nestle into a huge, south-facing, vaulted alcove in a sandstone cliff. **Keet**

Navajo Weaver, Monument Valley

Seel★ ("remains of square houses"), occupied about AD 950 to 1300, was larger (160 rooms) and of different design than Betatakin, and probably was home to 150.

From a visitor center and museum, a steep trail *(.5mi)* leads to a spectacular over-look of Betatakin, across a narrow canyon. The only way to visit the ruins up close is on a ranger-led hike *(5mi round-trip)*, offered daily *(May-Sept)* to 20 25 visitors on a first-come, first-served basis. Keet Seel, an overnight trek, is an arduous 8.5mi each way *(60-day advance reservations recommended)*.

★★★ Monument Valley Navajo Tribal Park – *Tribal Rd. 42, 4mi east of US-163, 24mi north of Kayenta.* △ ※ & ▣ ☎ *435-727-3287.* To many visitors, Monument Val-ley represents the essence of the American Southwest as conveyed in movies, commercials and print ads. The distinctive landscape—Tse' Bii' Ndzisgaii to the Navajo—covers 150sq mi on both sides of the Arizona-Utah border. Massive sandstone monoliths rise up to 1,000ft from a relatively flat desert floor. In early morning or late afternoon, the low sun highlights the red color of the rock and the valley takes on an otherworldly glow.

The unpaved, 17mi **Valley Drive**, for high-clearance or four-wheel-drive vehicles only, loops through the park and past many of its most prominent features, including The Mittens, Elephant Butte, Camel Butte, The Thumb and the Totem Pole. Other monoliths like Sentinel Mesa, Castle Butte and The King on His Throne are easily viewed from the visitor center. Guided Jeep tours and horseback tours access parts of Monument Valley that are off-limits to private vehicles, including several Navajo homesteads and isolated petroglyphs.

Hollywood director John Ford set many of his Western movies here, beginning with *Stagecoach* in 1938. Ford cast John Wayne as his star in such movies as *Fort Apache* (1948) and *She Wore a Yellow Ribbon* (1949). Visiting production crews are often seen today. At **Goulding's Lodge** *(Goulding's Rd., 2mi west of US 163 in Utah; 435-727-3225)*, where Ford's crews were based, a small museum surveys the film history of the area.

Four Corners Monument – *1mi north of US-160, 11.5mi northeast of Teec Nos Pos.* ▣ The point at which Arizona, New Mexico, Colorado and Utah converge—the only place that four US states meet—is covered by a cement slab bearing each state seal. State flags fly over the isolated Navajo tribal park, surrounded on three sides by Indian vendors selling T-shirts, jewelry and traditional "fry bread."

★★ Canyon de Chelly National Monument – *Tribal Rds. 7 & 64, 3mi east of US-191 at Chinle.* △ ※ & ▣ ☎ *520-674-5500. www.nps.gov/cach.* A place of scenic beauty and cultural history, this 130sq mi park holds two converging canyon net-works framed by sheer cliff walls. In the fertile canyon bottoms lie at least nine major Native American ruins dating from AD 350 to 1300.

The reddish cliffs rise just 30ft above the Chinle Wash at the meeting of the canyons—26mi-long Canyon de Chelly *(SHAY)* to the south, 25mi-long Canyon del Muerto to the north. Miles upstream, they climb as high as 1,000ft above canyon floors that are often covered in water. Modern Navajo farmers plow fields and graze cattle and sheep alongside the ancient ruins.

Perhaps better than any other site, Canyon de Chelly reveals the historical range of Southwestern Indian culture. Archaeologists have unearthed evidence of the earliest Archaic Indians and ensuing Basketmakers. After the Anasazi (11-13C) disappeared around 1,350, their Hopi descendants moved in during the 14-15C. Navajo have been farming here since the 17C.

From the **visitor center** *(Tribal Rds. 7 & 64)*, which offers a small museum and a 22min video presentation, two self-guided drives trace the canyon rims. The 16mi **South Rim Drive★** *(Tribal Rd. 7)* is more traveled. From its White House Overlook, a trail *(1.3mi)* descends 600ft to the multistory **White House Ruin★**, an Anasazi site and the only ruin that may be visited without an official guide. The 15mi **North Rim Drive★** *(Tribal Rd. 64)* overlooks such sites as Antelope House, named for late-7C paintings found near a Basketmaker pit house, and Mummy Cave, continuously occupied by various cultures for 1,000 years. A pair of mummies found here in the late 1880s led to this gorge's being dubbed "Canyon of the Dead." Each drive takes about 2hrs to complete.

Tours by Jeep, horseback or foot, guided by Navajo locals, provide a more in-depth understanding of the canyons' cultural and natural history, as well as the opportunity to visit more ruins and to meet Navajos farming the canyon.

★ Hubbell Trading Post National Historic Site – *Rte. 264, 1mi west of Ganado.* & ▣ ☎ *520-755-3254. www.nps.gov/hutr.* The oldest continually operating trad-ing post on the Navajo Reservation was established in 1878 by John Lorenzo Hubbell. He provided his Navajo clientele with items they couldn't make—food (sugar and coffee) and merchandise (matches, nails and shovels)—in exchange for such craft items as woven rugs and blankets, silverwork and turquoise jewelry.

Visitors today still can buy a good shovel or a cold drink, as well as rugs and saddles, jewelry and carved wooden *kachina* dolls. Navajo weavers demonstrate traditional techniques on looms in a visitor center. Guided tours of the Hubbell home allow the viewing of museum-quality rugs and paintings, displayed in rooms with shades drawn against the desert sun.

Hopi Indian Reservation – *Rte. 264 between Tuba City & Ganado.* △ ✗ ⅋ ▣ ☏ *520-734-2441*. The reservation's 12 principal villages are strung like desert pearls along Route 264 as it climbs over and around three sheer-walled mesas collectively known as Tuuwanasavi, "the center of the earth" in Hopi culture. **Old Orayvi★**, on the more westerly Third Mesa *(50mi east of Tuba City)*, was first occupied about 1100 and is presumed to be the oldest continuously inhabited village in the US. **Walpi**, on First Mesa *(19mi east of Old Orayvi)*, dates from about 1700. Both villages appear today as weathered dwellings of mud-plaster and hand-hewn stone, though pickup trucks and TV antennae are signs of modern influence.

The Hopi Tribal Council meets at **Kykotsmovi**, also known as New Oraibi; but a better place for visitors to get their bearings is the modern **Hopi Cultural Center★** *(Rte. 264, Second Mesa; ☏ 520-734-2401)*, 11mi east of there. The museum has excellent exhibits on Hopi history and lifestyle, and tribal artisans market their distinctive silver jewelry and wood carvings, including *kachinas*. Other craftspeople place signs in windows of their homes, offering goods for sale.

Highly traditional and wary, the Hopi welcome visitors but request that no photography, tape recording or even sketching be done in the villages. Ceremonial dances, always of spiritual significance, may be open to visitors *(inquire locally)*; they are announced only a week in advance, in accordance with ritual practices.

EXCURSION

★**Petrified Forest National Park** – *I-40 Exit 311, 26mi east of Holbrook.* ✗ ⅋ ▣ ☏ *520-524-6228. www.nps.gov/pefo*. An immense and colorful concentration of petrified wood and fossils, more than 225 million years old, is spread over the striated, pastel-hued desert badlands of the Painted Desert.

The main park road runs 28mi between I-40 and US-180, making it an easy detour from the interstate. At its north end, the **Painted Desert Visitor Center** offers a 20min film and exhibits. Two miles up the road is the **Painted Desert Inn**, a national historical landmark, built in 1924. The structure was originally a trading post, then an inn for travelers; it's now a museum and gift shop.

Overlooks on the southbound road pass 13C Anasazi ruins, a sandstone block covered with petroglyphs and a landscape strewn with colorful petrified logs. The terrain is like a moonscape, with pastel bands of pink, yellow and golden sands, blue-and-gray badlands and bleak hills in stark streaks of black and white. There are practically no trees. Several short hikes access off-road areas. Removal of petrified wood or rock specimens is prohibited. The **Rainbow Forest Museum** at the park's south end has fine exhibits on geology and paleontology.

Hawaii

Lei Makers

The very word "Hawaii" evokes romantic and magical images. The chain of 132 volcanic islands, many no more than rocky bird sanctuaries, stretches 1,600mi across the North Pacific Ocean—some 2,500mi southwest of Los Angeles, at a similar latitude to Mexico City. The eight principal islands are clustered at the south-eastern end of the archipelago, across a little more than 500mi.

Seven of the eight—with a total land area of 6,422sq mi—are inhabited. The largest and geologically youngest is the Island of Hawai'i, more popularly known as "The Big Island." Stretching northwest from here, more or less in order, are Maui, Kaho'o-lawe, Lana'i, Moloka'i, O'ahu, Kaua'i and Ni'ihau. Of these, Kaho'olawe is an uninhab-ited former bombing range, and Ni'ihau is a private island where a couple of hundred native Hawaiians live. O'ahu, home of Pearl Harbor and the state capital of Honolulu, is by far the most heavily populated island, with more than 870,000 of the state's 1.1 million people.

Native Polynesians, the first of whom migrated to Hawai'i (hah WHY-ee) from the Marquesas Islands sometime after AD 400, simply called their world 'aina, the land, as opposed to kai, the sea. When British Captain James Cook, the first European to sight the islands, stepped ashore in 1778 with his crew, he named the archipelago the Sandwich Islands—after his sponsor, the Earl of Sandwich.

The Island of Hawaii was the home of King Kamehameha I (c.1758-1819), who united the other islands under his conquering rule. But the monarchy lasted less than a century before pressure from Protestant missionaries, traders, whalers and sugar planters led to wholesale political change. Briefly a republic (1893-98), Hawaii was annexed as a US territory in 1898 during the Spanish-American War.

The single most dramatic 20C event was the 1941 Japanese bombing of Pearl Har-bor, propelling the US directly into World War II. When the war ended, tourism on Waikiki Beach exploded; later other islands, notably Maui and the Big Island, joined in the boom. With sugar and pineapple dominating the economy, Hawaii became the 50th US state in 1959.

Hawaii's mid-Pacific location has given it a rich ethnic mix. Caucasians and Japanese are in the majority, but there also are large numbers of part-Hawaiians, Filipinos and Chinese, as well as Koreans, Samoans, African-Americans and pure Hawaiians. Mixed-race marriages are the rule rather than the exception, and the congenial spirit of aloha—a term that can mean hello, goodbye, love or welcome—persists in the general good will of the people.

Hawaii

171

Please see explanation on p 64.

Staying in Hawaii

Four Seasons Hualalai – *100 Kaupulehu Dr.; Ka'upulehu-Kona (Big Island).*
✗ ♿ 🅿 ⛱ ☎ *808-325-8108. www.fourseasons.com. 243 rooms.* **$$$$** An
intimate, bungalow-style resort on the water, this lush tropical retreat
melts easily into the natural environment. Guests swim in a saltwater pond
or cool off in outdoor rock showers after a round of golf or a full spa
treatment.

Halekulani – *2199 Kalia Rd., Honolulu (O'ahu).* ✗ ♿ 🅿 ⛱ ☎ *808-923-2311.
www .halekulani.com. 456 rooms.* **$$$$** One of the top hotels in the world, the
graceful Halekulani presides over the shores of Waikiki Beach like an aging
grande dame. Spacious rooms overlook the Pacific Ocean from towers as lofty
as the clientele. The service is top-drawer. Both **La Mer** and **Orchid's**, the main
dining room, are worth a visit.

Princeville Resort – *5520 Ka Haku Rd., Princeville (Kaua'i).* ✗ ♿ 🅿 ⛱
☎ *808-826-9644. www.princeville.com. 252 rooms.* **$$$$** This sprawling resort
commands a dramatic view over the rugged cliffs of Hanalei Bay on Kauai's
north side. Every activity under the sun is offered, including sightseeing on the
legendary Na Pali coast. The restaurants are world-class.

Kona Village Resort – *Queen Ka'ahumanu Hwy., Kailua-Kona (Big Island).*
✗ 🅿 ⛱ ☎ *808-325-5555. www.konavillage.com. 125 rooms.* **$$$** Ham-
mocks sway beneath coconut palms beside thatched-roof beachfront cot-
tages. This Polynesian-style resort is a world unto itself. Kids and parents
kayak and windsurf by day and enjoy luaus in the oceanview restaurant by
night.

Lahaina Inn – *127 Lahainaluna Rd., Lahaina (Maui).* ✗ ☎ *808-661-0577.
www.lahainainn.com. 12 rooms.* **$$** Once a whaling town, Lahaina offers a
charming counterpoint to the luxury hotels on much of Maui. This fine old
inn is the jewel of Lahaina, stuffed with antique wooden furniture and more
than a couple of tall tales. Chef David Paul is a master in the kitchen.

Waimea Plantation Cottages – *9400 Kaumualii Hwy., Waimea (Kaua'i).*
✗ 🅿 ⛱ ☎ *808-338-1625. www.waimea-plantation.com. 44 cottages.* **$$**
Charming old sugar workers' bungalows stretch among coconut groves on the
black-sand beach of Kauai's west side. Individual units with full kitchens and
televisions are perfect for families who play croquet, swing on hammocks or
swim in the beachfront pool.

Dining in Hawaii

Roy's Restaurant – *6600 Kalanianaole Hwy. Honolulu (O'ahu).* ☎ *808-396-
7697. www.roys-restaurants.com.* **$$$ Euro-Asian.** Chef Roy Yamaguchi fires up
dishes ranging from Pacific opakapaka smothered in macadamia nut sauce to
roasted duck with passion fruit. The first of Roy's 15 restaurants around
the world, this two-level dining room overlooks the Pacific from the Hawaii-
Kai area of Honolulu.

Merriman's – *Opelo Plaza, Kamuela (Big Island).* ☎ *808-885-6822.* **$$ New
Hawaiian.** The home of Hawaiian regional cuisine, Merriman's boasts locally
grown baby vegetables from the mountain slopes of Waimea, and opaka-
paka from the sea. Wok-charred ahi tuna is the signature dish of chef
Peter Merriman, who draws on the varied cultural palette of the Hawaiian
people.

PacificO's – *505 Front St., Lahaina (Maui).* ☎ *808-667-4341.
www.maui.net/~pacifico/awards.html.* **$$ Pacific Rim.** Delectable cuisine that
ranges from tandoori-spiced seafood to peppered beef is served outdoors
under umbrellas. Selections are tantalizing and artfully prepared—including a
homemade ravioli with saffron coconut sauce.

HONOLULU★★

Map p 174   Hawaiian Standard Time
Population 395,789
Tourist Information ☎ 808-524-0722 or www.visit-oahu.com

Honolulu sprawls across the southeast quadrant of the island of O'ahu. The world's largest Polynesian city is a bustling modern metropolis of skyscrapers and traffic, extending from Waikiki's surf-washed beaches to the 3,000ft crest of the jungle-swathed Ko'olau Range. Here the first missionaries gathered their Hawaiian congregations, the only royal palace in the US was erected, and eight decades of sun-worshipers have spread their beach towels.

Officially, all of O'ahu *(oh-AH-hoo)* is the City and County of Honolulu *(hoh-no-LOO-loo)*. But don't think the 608sq-mi island is entirely urbanized. There are fertile farms, mountain rain forests, and green vistas of pineapple and sugar fields. One-quarter of O'ahu's land is occupied by military bases representing more than 44,000 Army, Navy, Air Force and Marine personnel. Many are based at Pearl Harbor, a deep slot in the south-central coast of the island.

Across the Ko'olaus from Honolulu extends the lush Windward Coast of the island, with its suburban communities of Kailua and Kaneohe. West of Pearl Harbor is the drier Waianae Coast and the big-wave beaches of Makaha. A route through the agricultural center of O'ahu leads to the North Shore, fabled for its country living and renowned surfing venues like Sunset Beach and Waimea Bay.

Waikiki Beach

★★ **Downtown Honolulu** – *Honolulu Harbor to Vineyard Blvd. between Ward Ave. & River St.* While Waikiki, with its beach, hotels, restaurants and nightclubs, may be the traditional center of Hawaii's tourism industry, downtown Honolulu is the hub of history.

★★ **Mission Houses Museum** – *553 S. King St. at Kawaiahao St.* ☎ *808-531-0481.* The modest wood-frame house, oldest Western-style structure in Hawaii, was brought in pieces by ship around Cape Horn and assembled in 1821 by the first American Calvinist missionaries, with Hawaiian assistance. Adjoining coral-block houses were built a short time later.

★★ **Kawaiahao Church** – *957 Punchbowl St.* ♿ 🅿 ☎ *808-522-1333.* Designed by its first minister in 1837, this church was constructed of coral blocks cut and carried from a reef off Honolulu Harbor. The setting for 19C royal coronations, weddings and funerals, and is revered by island residents. Visitors are welcome at the Sunday sermon, still given partly in the Hawaiian language.

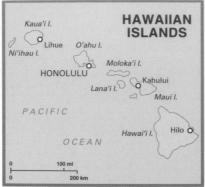

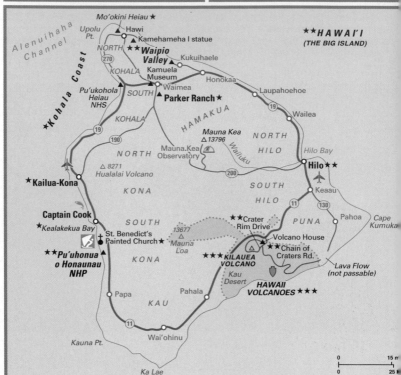

★★ **Iolani Palace** – *S. King & Richards Sts.* ♿ 🅿 ☎ *808-522-0832.* This rococo structure is the only royal palace in the US. King David Kalakaua, back from travels in Europe, erected it in 1882; its last royal occupant was Queen Liliuokalani, whose government was overthrown in 1893. Across King Street is a statue of **Kamehameha the Great** (Kamehameha I). A modern statue of **Liliuokalani** stands on the other side of the palace facing the capitol.

★ **Hawaii State Capitol** – *S. Beretania St. between Richards & Punchbowl Sts.* ♿ 🅿 ☎ *808-586-0146.* Designed and built in 1969, the capitol has pillars that resemble palm trees. The sloping exteriors of the House and Senate chambers project from a pool, reminiscent of volcanoes rising from the sea.

★ **Honolulu Academy of Arts** – *900 S. Beretania St. at Ward Ave.* ✕♿ 🅿 ☎ *808-532-8700. www.honoluluacademy.org.* A few blocks east of the capitol, this airy building has open courtyards and an excellent collection of Asian art, including Japanese woodblocks presented by late author James Michener.

★ **Aloha Tower** – *1 Aloha Tower Dr.* ✕♿ 🅿 ☎ *808-566-2337.* Once Hawaii's tallest building, this 10-story spire has greeted four generations of cruise-ship passengers since 1921. Permanently berthed at the nearby **Hawaii Maritime Center**★ *(Pier 7, Honolulu Harbor;* ☎ *808-536-6373)* is the 19C sailing ship *Falls of Clyde,* a 266ft-

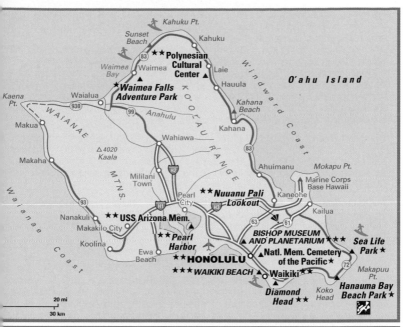

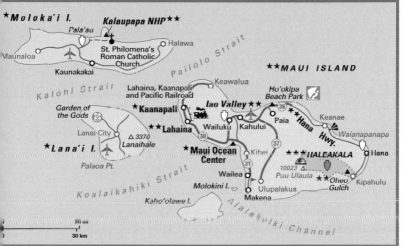

long, four masted square-rigger. Pier 7 is home berth to the *Hokule'a*, a 60ft replica of an ancient Polynesian canoe that has made numerous voyages to and from Tahiti since it was built in 1976.

★★ **Waikiki** – *Ala Wai Canal to Diamond Head, east of the Ala Wai Yacht Harbor.* Once a lounging place for Hawaiian royalty, the 2mi-long suburb of Waikiki (literally, "spouting water") is recognized by the forest of towers created by its hotels. **Waikiki Beach**★★★ remains one of the best places in the world to learn surfing, a sport invented here hundreds of years ago. At Waikiki Beach Center stands a statue of **Duke Kahanamoku** *(Kalakaua Ave. near Kaiulani Ave.)*, Hawaii's three-time Olympic swimming champion (1912-20), who introduced surfing to California and Australia. Non-surfers may ride the waves in an outrigger canoe or take a cruise on a sailboat that casts off right from the shoreline.

Opposite the beach, visitors browse through small shops and stands in the **International Market Place**★ *(2330 Kalakaua Ave.; ☎ 808-923-9871)*, under and around the same giant banyan tree for half a century.

The **Moana Hotel**★ *(2365 Kalakaua Ave.; ☎ 808 922-3111)*, now enshrouded in the Sheraton Moana-Surfrider, has been restored to 1901 Victorian elegance. The **Royal Hawaiian Hotel**★ *(2259 Kalakaua Ave.; ☎ 808-923-7311)*, Waikiki's "Pink Palace," is a Moorish building constructed in 1925, when most visitors came to

Hawaii on ocean liners to stay for a month or longer. The **Halekulani Hotel** *(2199 Kalia Rd.; ☎ 808-923-2311)* also dates from the pre-war years, although a modern structure now surrounds the original main building.

At the east end of Waikiki is 140-acre **Kapiolani Park**. The park encompasses the **Honolulu Zoo** *(151 Kapahulu Ave.; ☎ 808-971-7171)* and **Waikiki Shell**, venue for open-air concerts and the late-morning Kodak Hula Show *(2805 Monsarrat Ave.; ☎ 808-627-3379)*. Denizens of the deep are observed at the compact but well-designed **Waikiki Aquarium**★ *(2777 Kalakaua Ave.; ☎ 808-923-9741)*. The third-oldest aquarium in the US features more than 350 species of Pacific marine life, including the melodically named *humuhumunukunukuapua'a*.

★★ **Diamond Head** – *Diamond Head Rd., .5mi east of Waikiki*. The famous backdrop in pictures of Waikiki Beach is this extinct volcanic crater. The 760ft summit is easily climbed by a **trail** *(.7mi)* that begins on the crater floor. Part of the route tunnels through old World War II fortifications, so a flashlight is advised. Entrance to the crater is through an automobile tunnel.

★ **National Memorial Cemetery of the Pacific** – *Ward Ave. & Prospect Dr.* ☎ *808-946-6383*. Occupying an extinct crater known simply as Punchbowl, this "Arlington of the Pacific" is the final resting place for more than 40,000 US military men and others whom the government has honored. Many visit the graves of World War II correspondent Ernie Pyle and Hawaii astronaut Ellison Onizuka, who died in the *Challenger* space-shuttle disaster of 1986.

★★★ **Bishop Museum and Planetarium** – *1525 Bernice St.* ☎ *808-847-3511. www.bishopmuseum.org*. The premier treasury of the past in Hawaii—and, indeed, in the Pacific—is somewhat off the beaten path in the Kalihi district. Most archaeological and anthropological work done in Polynesia today is based here, and the Bishop Museum's collection of Hawaiiana is unequaled.

■ **Hawaiian Culture**

About 19 percent of Hawaii's population call themselves Hawaiian, although the number with pure Hawaiian blood may be less than 1 percent—perhaps about 10,000. Many Hawaiians died in the 19C from introduced diseases. Over the past 150 years, they intermarried easily, especially with Caucasians (*haoles* in Hawaii) and Chinese. But their influence on isle culture goes far beyond their numbers. Some of the best-known aspects of Hawaiian culture—music, dance, food and the welcoming *aloha* attitude—have been absorbed by all.

For at least 1,000 years, the Polynesian Hawaiians lived alone in the islands. They came in great double-hulled canoes—first from the Marquesas Islands between AD 400 and 750, later from Tahiti about 1100—and built houses of thatched grass. Their lives revolved around fishing, cultivating taro and yams, gathering fruit and raising pigs. They had a sophisticated knowledge of astronomy and an appreciation for the effect of the seasons on farming and harvesting. They imbued birds, fish and inanimate objects with supernatural powers. Things that were sacred were labeled as *kapu*, or forbidden.

As the centuries passed, the Hawaiians ceased to build large ocean-going vessels. Stories of their former lands became mere songs and chants. They retained the basic spoken Polynesian language, adapting it to their own needs; ancestors and ancient gods were remembered through recitation of genealogy.

After 1820, American missionaries transliterated Hawaiian to make it a written language, reducing the number of consonants to just seven—*h, k, l, m, n, p* and *w*. The Hawaiian language today is regularly spoken in daily life only on the private island of Ni'ihau. Hawaii locals speak either standard English or a type of pidgin composed mainly of English words, but with unusual inflection and numerous Chinese, Japanese and Filipino words stirred into conversation.

Many other cultural aspects were developed after contact with the West. Hawaiians embraced the diatonic musical scale and harmonies introduced by missionaries for singing hymns. From Spanish-speaking cowboys (*paniolo*) on the Big Island, Hawaiians learned guitar; they loosened the strings to change the tuning and invented the "slack-key" style of playing. When Portuguese immigrants arrived in the late 19C, Hawaiians learned

A dozen structures make up the museum. The original turreted stone building, the imposing Victorian known as **Hawaiian Hall★**, was built in 1898-1903. Stairways and corridors lead to collections of regalia from the 19C Hawaiian monarchy, including crowns and feathered capes. Icons of gods carved from native koa wood are exhibited with woven pandanus mats and shark-tooth drums. Other items represent the bygone whaling era and Asian cultures. The fine natural-history collection is particularly strong on bird and marine life.

Native arts and crafts—including hula-dancing, lei-making and quilting—are demonstrated daily. The Bishop Planetarium offers star shows and astronomy exhibits in cooperation with observatories atop Mauna Kea, on the Big Island.

★★Nuuanu Pali Lookout – *Nuuanu Pali State Park, Pali Hwy. (Rte. 61).* Not only does Oahu's premier viewpoint offer a wonderful (if windy) vista over the Ko'olau Range and the windward side of the island; it has extreme historical significance. Kamehameha I drove the army of O'ahu up to this point in 1795. When opposing warriors began falling by the hundreds over the 1,000ft-high cliff *(pali,* in Hawaiian), the battle and the island were won.

★Hanauma Bay Beach Park – *Koko Head, Kalanianaole Hwy. (Rte. 72), 12mi east of Waikiki.* ✗ ▣ ☎ *808-396-4229.* An extinct volcanic crater with its seaward side recaptured by surf, this turquoise-hued cove is the single favorite destination in Hawaii for snorkelers to view colorful reef fish and other marine life. Film buffs remember it in *Blue Hawaii* with Elvis Presley (1962).

★Sea Life Park – *Makapuu Point, Kalanianaole Hwy. (Rte. 72), 15mi east of Waikiki.* ✗ ✦ ▣ ☎ *808-259-7933.* A 300,000gal **Hawaiian Reef Tank★★** features a spiral ramp that circles a giant aquarium inhabited by 4,000 marine creatures, including stingrays and sharks. At set times, they are hand-fed by a scuba diver. Other exhibits feature penguins, monk seals, sea lions, dolphins, whales, and the world's only known **wholphin**—a dolphin-whale cross-breed.

Pu'uhonua O Honaunau National Historical Park

to play the four-stringed *braga* and renamed it the ukulele. Along with a drum, it was played to accompany the hula. Performed with fierce rhythms—and only by men in ancient Hawaii, where it was a religious ritual—hula evolved into a graceful dance for women. (Grass skirts were a 20C import from Micronesia; dancers were traditionally clad in ti leaves.)

Traditional tunes are likely to be performed at a luau. This outdoor feast—complete with a *kalua* pig roasted in an *imu* (underground oven)— may be the best way to sample typical Island foods. Expect to be served *poi* (taro-root paste, offered fresh or fermented), *laulau* (steamed meat, fish and taro leaves wrapped in ti leaves), *lomi-lomi* (salted salmon mixed with tomatoes and onions) and *haupia* (coconut pudding).

** Pearl Harbor – *6mi west of downtown via H-1 Freeway & Kamehameha Hwy. (Rte. 90).* It is patriotic for American visitors to make a pilgrimage to Pearl Harbor. Here on December 7, 1941, more than 2,300 servicemen were killed in a surprise early-morning Japanese air attack on the US naval fleet anchored here. Eighteen ships, including six battleships and three destroyers, sank in the greatest US military disaster. President Franklin Roosevelt declared it "a date which will live in infamy" as he plunged the nation into World War II.

Practical Information ....Area code: 808

Getting There – Hawaii's main airports are accessed from the US mainland by major airlines and by regional carriers **Hawaiian Airlines** (☎ *838-1555, www .hawaiianair.com)* and **Aloha Airlines** *(☎ 484-1111, www.alohaair.com)*. **O'ahu**: Honolulu International Airport ☎ 836-6413. **Kaua'i**: Lihue Airport ☎ 246-1400. **Maui**: Kahului Airport ☎ 872-3803. **Big Island**: Hilo International Airport ☎ 934-5838; Kona International Airport ☎ 329-3423. **Shuttle services** connect airports, hotels and tourist attractions.

Getting Around – **Inter-island flight** times average 30min. Aloha and Hawaiian Airlines *(above)*, along with **Island Air** *(☎ 484-2222)*, provide extensive inter-island coverage. **Pacific Wings** *(☎ 873-0877)* has scenic tours and charters. TheBus, Oahu's **mass transit system** *($1/ride)*, covers the full island ☎ 848-4444. Waikiki Trolley ☎ 596-2199 and Aloha Tower Express Trolley ☎ 528-5700 link Waikiki and downtown Honolulu with other attractions.

Accommodations – Lodging options range from world-class resorts to small hotels and bed-and-breakfasts. Package deals may couple hotels with car rentals and airlines. Consult a travel agent to find the best overall value. **Reservation services**: Affordable Paradise Bed & Breakfast ☎ 261-1693; All Islands Bed & Breakfast ☎ 263-2342; Bed & Breakfast Honolulu ☎ 595-7533; Hawaii's Best Bed & Breakfasts ☎ 885-4550, www.bestbnb .com; Go Condo Hawaii ☎ 818-879-5665; Hawaii Condo Exchange ☎ 213-436-0300; Hawaii Connection ☎ 818-879-5665; Places to Stay ☎ 415-372-1700. **Hostels**: Hostelling International Honolulu ☎ 946-0591; Interclub Waikiki Hotel & Hostel ☎ 924-2636; Pineapple Park Hostels, Big Island ☎ 968-8170. **Camping**: For information on permits contact the Hawaiian Trail and Mountain Club, P.O. Box 2238, Honolulu 96804; or call the Sierra Club ☎ 538-6616.

Visitor Information – **Hawaii Convention and Visitors Bureau** ☎ 923-1811, www.gohawaii.com. HCVB **information center**, Royal Hawaiian Shopping Center, Honolulu ☎ 923-1811. Individual islands: **O'ahu Visitors Bureau** ☎ 524-0722, www.visit-oahu.com; **Kaua'i Visitors Bureau** ☎ 245-3971, www.kauaivisitorsbureau.org, **Maui Visitors Bureau** ☎ 244-3530, www.visit-maui.com; **Big Island Visitors Bureau** ☎ 961-5797, www.bigisland.org.

11

★★USS Arizona Memorial – *1 Arizona Memorial Dr.* ♿ 🅿 ☎ *808-422-0561. www.nps.gov/usar.* Perhaps no war memorial is more poignant than this one. Floating over the hulk of a sunken battleship, the concave, 184ft white-concrete bridge marks the permanent tomb of 1,177 sailors killed in the Pearl Harbor attack. Each victim's name is inscribed in white marble on one wall of the memorial. The macabre outline of the ship's hull is visible below. Launches depart on a first-come, first-served basis from a shoreline **visitor center,** where historical exhibits and a documentary film *(23min)* are presented.

★Pacific Fleet Submarine Museum – *11 Arizona Memorial Dr.* ♿ 🅿 ☎ *808-423-1341.* A walk through the *USS Bowfin,* credited with sinking 44 Japanese ships, helps define the claustrophobia of sub missions. Tickets are sold for visits to the nearby **USS Missouri★** *(☎ 808-545-2263),* on which the Japanese surrender was signed in Tokyo Bay on September 2, 1945.

EXCURSIONS

★★Polynesian Cultural Center – *55-370 Kamehameha Hwy. (Rte. 83), Laie, 27mi north of Honolulu.* ✕♿ 🅿 ☎ *808-923-2911 or 808-293-3333. www.polynesia .com.* The Church of Jesus Christ of Latter-day Saints (the Mormons) has had a strong presence in Hawaii since building a temple in tiny La'ie *(LAH-ee-ay)* in 1919. In 1955, the church established a college, now a campus of Utah's Brigham Young University. Students from all over Oceania attend classes, earning tuition by working or performing at the Cultural Center.
Visitors can spend an entire day wandering through the "villages" of Hawai'i, Samoa, Tonga, Tahiti, the Marquesas, Fiji and Aotearoa (Maori New Zealand), capping the evening with a spectacular 90min show of Pacific song and dance. The young staff, in native dress, exhibit and teach skills such as making tapa cloth, weaving pandanus leaves, opening coconuts and learning to play ukulele.

★Waimea Falls Adventure Park – *Kamehameha Hwy. (Rte. 83), 7mi east of Haleiwa & 31mi north of Honolulu.* ☎ *808-638-8511.* Centered on a 45ft waterfall where cliff-diving exhibitions are held, this privately owned nature preserve is filled with indigenous trees, plants and flowers. Demonstrations of Hawaiian arts and crafts take place, and visitors also are treated to games like spear-tossing and some less-historic activities like all-terrain vehicle excursions.

KAUA'I★★

Map p 174   Hawaiian Standard Time
Tourist Information ☎ 808-245-3971 or www.kauaivisitorsbureau.org

Known to locals as "The Garden Island," lush and tropical Kaua'i *(kow-WHY)* seems to have a more genuinely rural landscape than other Hawaiian islands. Centered on a single extinct volcano, **Mt. Waialeale** (5,148ft)- among the wettest spots on earth with an average annual rainfall of 460in—Kaua'i is geologically the oldest inhabited Hawaiian island. It has been eroded to the point where several rivers have been created, the only island so blessed. It also is more separated physically from the other main islands: O'ahu, Kaua'i's nearest significant neighbor, is out of sight over 90mi over the horizon.

Kaua'i was the only island not won in violent conflict by Kamehameha I: It was ceded almost amicably by King Kaumuali'i in 1810. The isle is said to be the home of the *menehune,* a leprechaun-like people who once served the taller Polynesians. Now relegated to legend, they are credited with mythical feats of engineering.

Visitors arrive at Lihue, seat of Kaua'i's county government and its largest town. Two routes circle most of the island. The **Kaumualii Highway** *(Rte. 50)* heads in a westerly direction, with spur roads to Poipu Beach and Waimea Canyon. The **Kuhio Highway** *(Rte. 56)* rounds the island to the north from Lihue, winding past the community of Hanalei. Despite the torrents that deluge the center of the island, many of the beaches get as little as 10in annual rainfall.

SIGHTS

Lihue – The urban hub of Kaua'i is this workaday small town. Its **Kaua'i Museum** *(4428 Rice St.; ☎ 808-245-6931),* which traces early island history, has excellent collections of traditional quilts and gourd calabashes. **Kilohana** *(Kaumuali'i Hwy.; ☎ 808-245-5608)* preserves a 1935 sugar plantation and mansion within an artsy shopping complex.

* **Poipu** – *Poipu Rd. (Rte. 530); 12mi southwest of Lihue.* ☏ *808-742-7444.* A natural tunnel of swamp mahogany trees leads drivers down Maluhia Road *(Rte. 520)* into the 1835 plantation village of Koloa and on to **Poipu Beach**★ on the south coast. A public park adjoins a string of resort hotels. Down the shoreline to the west is a natural feature called **Spouting Horn**★ *(Lawai Beach Rd.).* When ocean waves push through the remains of an ancient lava tube, a spout of water shoots skyward, followed by a low moan.

* **National Tropical Botanical Garden** – *Lawai Beach Rd. opposite Spouting Horn.* ♿ ▣ ☏ *808-332-7361. www.ntbg.org.* The 252-acre **Lawai Garden** has the world's largest collection of native Hawaiian flora, plus other rare Pacific species. Adjacent **Allerton Garden** has more than 80 additional landscaped acres. The National Garden also has a research library and herbarium here. Affiliated gardens are on Kaua'i's north shore (Limahuli Garden and Preserve, near Haena) and on Maui (Kahanu Garden, in black volcanic soil near Hana).

** **Waimea Canyon State Park** – *Koke'e Rd. (Rte. 550) via Waimea Canyon Dr.* Called the "Grand Canyon of the Pacific" by Mark Twain (who never actually saw it), Waimea Canyon's size and depth are startling for a small tropical island. From the principal lookout, about 13mi uphill from Waimea, vivid pinks, greens and browns—or toward twilight, purples, blues and lavenders—accent the contours of three tributary canyons. A distant waterfall tumbles 800ft over a cliff; the ribbon-like Waimea River, draining rainy Waialeale, weaves a course 3,000ft below. Access to the canyon is only by trail.

** **Koke'e State Park** – *Koke'e Rd. (Rte. 550); 19mi north of Waimea.* ☏ *808-335-9975. www.aloha.net/~kokee.* A cool mountain oasis, this forested park boasts a small natural-history museum and access to 45mi of hiking trails, one of which visits the unique bird life of the **Alaka'i Swamp.** At the end of the road, at 4,000ft elevation, a dramatic overlook of the **Kalalau Valley** *(below)* makes it clear why no road will ever completely encircle Kaua'i: The steep mountains and deep valleys of the **Na Pali Coast**★★★ are too rugged to be tamed. The deep blue of the ocean, beyond the lush foliage and spectacular waterfalls, makes this vantage point feel like the very edge of the earth.

* **Fern Grotto** *174 Wailua Rd., Kapaa; off Kuhio Hwy. (Rte. 56) 6mi north of Lihue.* ☏ *808-821-6892.* Live ferns hang naturally from the roof of a cave, reached by boat tours that begin near the mouth of the broad Wailua River. Singing, guitar-playing boatmen favor passengers with renditions of the "Hawaiian Wedding Song" and other melodies.

** **Hanalei** – *Kuhio Hwy. (Rte. 56); 33mi northwest of Lihue.* The road to the north shore passes the expansive **Princeville Resort Kauai**★ *(5520 Ka Haku Rd.,* ☏ *808-826-9644).* Large trucks and tour buses can't get much farther than this, restricted by the load limit on a narrow, rickety old bridge. That suits the residents of sleepy Hanalei just fine. Fishing, swimming and other water sports at **Hanalei Bay**★ seem to be the extent of high-energy activity. Those who enjoy local history can visit the **Waioli Mission House**★ *(Kuhio Hwy.;* ☏ *808-245-3202),* built in 1836 by missionaries and now furnished with period pieces.
A little west of Hanalei is **Lumahai Beach**★, the golden strand where Mitzi Gaynor tried to "Wash That Man Right Out of My Hair" in the 1958 movie *South Pacific.* The end of the road is **Ke'e Beach,** which offers swimming inside its reef.
Though cars can go no farther, this is the beginning of a remarkable 11mi trail along the rugged cliffs of the Na Pali Coast *(above)* into the **Kalalau Valley**★★. For healthy backpackers carrying proper gear, this is a memorable trek. The valley—visible from Koke'e State Park *(above)*—remains an impossible dream to others, except to a few who come into it via sailboat or helicopter.

EXCURSION

Ni'ihau – From various points along the road to Waimea Canyon and Koke'e State Park *(above),* one can see in the mists, 17mi offshore, the outline of the 72sq mi "Forbidden Isle" of Ni'ihau *(NEE-ee-how).* The owners of the island are fiercely protective of the 200-or-so native Hawaiians who still live there without electricity or other conveniences, speaking their ancient language.
Ni'ihau may only be visited on the private helicopter tour *(Niihau Helicopters;* ☏ *808-335-3500)* run by the Robinson family, which has owned the island and its sheep ranch since 1864. The pilot points out things of geological and other natural interest on the island, then lands for a short time near a deserted beach a long way from the tiny village where the residents live.

MAUI★★

Map p 175   Hawaiian Standard Time
Tourist Information ☎ 808-244-3530 or www.visitmaui.com

Maui was named after the demigod Maui *(MAU-ee)*, whose exploits have been celebrated throughout Polynesia for a millennium or longer. On the island that became
his namesake, Hawaiians say he once inaugurated a Stone Age daylight savings time,
ascending the dormant volcano Haleakala (literally, "house of the sun") to capture the
sun itself as it rose from the crater. According to legend, the sun promised Maui that
henceforth it would move more slowly across the sky so that Maui's sister could
thoroughly dry her tapa cloth in its rays.

Two mountain masses dominate Maui, Hawaii's second-largest island (729sq mi).
Haleakala caps east Maui, while the highly eroded West Maui Mountains form the
center of the other section. In ancient geological time they were two separate islands.
Eventually, when the sea level dropped, an isthmus formed between them: Today
much of this fertile central flat area is taken up with fields of sugarcane.

SIGHTS

★**Central Maui** – The twin towns of **Wailuku** and **Kahului**—the latter the site of
Maui's main airport—occupy the north-central coast. At the 1842 **Bailey House**
(2375-A Main St., Wailuku; ☎ *808-244-3326)*, a former schoolmaster's home, the
Maui Historical Society has a museum of artifacts. The **Alexander & Baldwin Sugar
Museum** *(3957 Hansen Rd., Puunene;* ☎ *808-871-8058)*, in a late-19C sugar-mill
superintendent's residence, details the history and future of sugar production in
Hawaii. For a broad agricultural picture, the 120-acre **Maui Tropical Plantation**★
(Honoapiilani Hwy., Waikapu; ☎ *808-244-7643)* offers walking and tram tours of
crops of sugar, pineapple, macadamia nuts, coconuts, guavas, bananas, passion
fruit, Maui onions, Kona coffee and more.

The major resort areas of central Maui, **Wailea** and **Makena**, encompass a group of
charming beaches with fine hotels, golf courses and championship tennis courts.
Offshore, southwest of Makena, is tiny **Molokini** islet, a favorite of snorkelers and
scuba divers. Beyond Molokini, 7mi off Maui, is the barren 45sq-mi wasteland of
Kaho'olawe *(kah-ho-oh-LAH-vay)*, a former US Navy bombing site returned to the state
in 1994 after repeated requests by Hawaiian activists who consider the island sacred.
Its only inhabitants are feral goats.

★★**Iao Valley State Park** – *Iao Valley Rd. (Rte. 320), 5mi west of Wailuku.* ♿ 🅿 Iao is the
reason Maui was nicknamed the "Valley Island." The bright green cliffs and bur-
bling stream at the eroded core of an age-old volcano have made it a popular picnic and hiking venue. Its highlight is **Iao Needle**★★, a basaltic spire that rises 1,200ft
above the 2,250ft valley floor. A 1.5mi trail meanders beneath cliffs that spout
spectacular waterfalls after heavy rains.

★**Maui Ocean Center** – *192 Ma'alaea Rd., Ma'alaea.* ✖♿ 🅿 ☎ *808-270-7000.*
www.mauioceancenter.com. Exhibits in this new aquarium take visitors from
Hawaii's sandy shores to deep ocean trenches, pausing en route to study colorful
reef life. Special exhibits include a touch pool, a whale discovery center and an
acrylic tunnel demonstrating life in the open ocean.

★★**Lahaina** – *Honoapiilani Hwy. (Rte. 30),* ☎ *808-667-9175.* For nearly two centuries, this quaint community has been the center of activity in west Maui. The
town figured prominently in *Hawaii,* author James Michener's novelized history.
Along its waterfront, Lahaina exudes an atmosphere reminiscent of the 19C when
pious missionaries and rollicking whalers vied for the attentions and affections of
the native Hawaiian population.

Whales are still an attraction from November to June. In the 9mi-wide channel
between Lahaina and **Lana'i** *(p 182)*, the great creatures play, mate and give birth
before migrating to northern waters for the summer.

Lahaina walking tours begin under a giant **banyan tree**★ planted April 24, 1873. It
spreads over an entire town square, about two-thirds of an acre. The 1901 **Pioneer Inn** *(658 Wharf St.;* ☎ *808-661-3636)* is one of the oldest hotels still operating in the islands. Facing the inn, a century-old square-rigged sailing vessel, the
Brig Carthaginian *(Lahaina Harbor;* ☎ *808-661-3262)*, is now a whaling museum.
Across Front Street, the former home of Lahaina's medical missionary is the **Baldwin House Museum**★ *(120 Dickenson St.;* ☎ *808-661-3262)*. Dr. Dwight Baldwin is
credited with saving much of the local population in the 1850s when he vacci-
nated hundreds against a smallpox epidemic.

★**Kaanapali** – *Honoapiilani Hwy. (Rte. 30), 3.5mi north of Lahaina.* ☎ *808-661-
3271.* Besides modern shoreline hotels and golf courses, Hawaii's first planned
resort community features a shopping area called **Whalers Village** *(2435 Kaanapali*

Lahaina Harbor

Pkwy.; ☎ 808-661-4567), with a museum based on old-time whaling. The **Lahaina, Kaanapali and Pacific Railroad** *(975 Limahana Pl., Lahaina; ☎ 808-661-0080)*, riding on a late-19C right-of-way, makes the 6mi run between Kaanapali and Lahaina, complete with a singing conductor.

*** **Haleakala National Park** – *Haleakala Hwy. (Rte. 377), 36mi southeast of Kahului.* ✗ ♿ 🅿 ☎ 808-572-4400. www.nps.gov/hale. The dormant volcano Haleakala *(ha-lay-AH-ka-la)* completely dominates east Maui. The spectacular desolation of its enormous crater valley—7.5mi long, 2.5mi wide and 3,000ft deep—has been compared to the mountains of the moon. Pastel hues of red, yellow and orange, as well as gray, purple, brown, black and pink, accent cliff sides and cinder cones. Here and there sprouts a silversword, an agave-like relative of the sunflower that extends a 6ft stalk of small red flowers once a human generation, then promptly dies. Among the lava flows walks Hawaii's state bird, the *nene*, the world's rarest goose. Thirty miles of trails crisscross the crater floor.

The experience of watching the sun rise above the rim can be worth a dark, cold, early-morning drive from a beachside resort to the peak's 10,023ft summit. Sunrise bicycle trips descend the same road. On the often-chilly mountaintop, the **Haleakala Observatory** comprises several scientific and military technical installations. The park headquarters is an 11mi drive downhill from the summit area, around 7,000ft elevation.

** **Hana Highway** – ⚠ *Rte. 360.* Motorized adventurers should get an early start to visit the east end of Maui via this narrow, winding, 53mi road. Three miles past **Paia**—an old sugar-plantation town, 7mi east of Kahului—it passes **Ho'okipa Beach Park**, a famed windsurfing venue. A good picnic stop is **Puohokamoa Falls**, 22mi before **Hana**, a somnolent little village on an attractive bay.

Dedicated explorers may continue to **Oheo Gulch**** *(Pulaui Hwy., 10mi south of Hana; ☎ 808-248-7375)* in the Kipahulu District of Haleakala National Park. A series of small waterfalls tumble from the southeast flank of Haleakala, feeding from one pool to another. These are often referred to as the Seven Sacred Pools—although there are two dozen pools and the ancient Hawaiians, apparently, never regarded them as sacred. The simple marble grave of famed aviator **Charles Lindbergh** (1902-74) rests on a promontory in the churchyard of the 1850 Palapala Hoomau Hawaiian Church, 1.2mi past Oheo Gulch.

EXCURSIONS

* **Lana'i** – ☎ *808-565-7600. www.lanai-resorts.com.* Lana'i *(lah-NAH-ee)* was once known as the "Pineapple Isle." From 1922 until the early 1990s the Dole Company made the 141sq mi island the single largest pineapple plantation in the world. Today the fruit has become more profitable to raise in foreign lands. Two

resort hotels now anchor the economy for the 2,800 isle residents.
Few paved roads cross Lana'i, so visitors must rent a four-wheel-drive vehicle to explore out-of-the-way places. Among them are **Lanaihale** *(Munro Trail east of Lanai City)*, the 3,370ft island summit; and **Garden of the Gods** *(Polihua Rd. northwest of Lanai City)*, dominated by strange volcanic rock formations.

★**Moloka'i** – ☎ *808-553-5221. www.molokai-hawaii.com.* Moloka'i *(MOLE-oak-eye)* also once supported itself with pineapple. Though heavy unemployment now plagues the 6,000 residents, Moloka'i continues to be known as the "Friendly Isle." Its hub is the quiet port village of **Kaunakakai,** whose clapboard main street is reminiscent of a 19C Old West town.

★★**Kalaupapa National Historical Park** – *Kalaupapa.* ☎ *808-567-6802, www.nps .gov/kala.* This unique site encompasses a 13.6sq-mi peninsula separated from the rest of Moloka'i by a 1,600ft cliff. To create an isolation colony for victims of Hansen's Disease (leprosy), native Molokaians were relocated from the beautiful windswept promontory in 1865, to be replaced the following year by banished lepers. In 1873, Father Damien de Veuster, a saintly Belgian priest, arrived to live and work (and die, in 1889) among the infected. His original **St. Philomena's Roman Catholic Church** stands above the ruins of the village of Kalawao. Several dozen elderly leprosy patients, who pose no health threat to adult visitors, continue to live at Kalaupapa. Not permitted to raise children, they shower their affections on scores of dogs and cats.
Access is by small plane or private boat—or for the adventurous, by foot or **mule** *(*☎ *808-567-6088).* A 3.2mi trail with 26 switchbacks begins at **Pala'au State Park** *(Rte. 470, 10mi north of Kaunakakai).* There is no road access between Kalaupapa and the rest of Moloka'i.

HAWAI'I (THE BIG ISLAND)★★

Map p 174   Hawaiian Standard Time
Tourist Information ☎ 808-961-5797 or www.bigisland.org

The Big Island is aptly named. It measures 4,038sq mi—nearly twice as large as all the rest of the Hawaiian Islands combined. And because volcanic eruptions regularly add more lava to the shoreline, it is actually increasing in size. For all its bulk, however, it is sparsely populated, with about 125,000 residents.
Two volcanic mountains dominate the landscape. In the north, Mauna Kea (13,796ft), long dormant, is home to several astronomical observatories. In the south, Mauna Loa (13,677ft) is considered live but is usually sleeping. The active Kilauea Volcano, however, spews lava from the lower slopes of Mauna Loa.
As the birthplace of Kamehameha I, the seminal point of 19C Hawaiian monarchy, and the site of Captain Cook's ill-fated final visit, the Big Island is richer in traditional Hawaiian history than other islands of the archipelago.
The separate coasts of the Island of Hawai'i are readily distinguished by their climates: The drier Kona side is on the west; the much wetter Hilo side is east of the volcanoes. Most major resorts are on the Kona and adjoining Kohala coasts.

SIGHTS

★**Kailua-Kona** – The center of commercial activity in Kona is the sometimes-frenetic town of Kailua, called Kailua-Kona to differentiate it from Kailua, Oahu. Offshore waters provide some of the best deep-sea fishing in the world.
Kailua was the first capital of the Hawaiian Islands: Kamehameha I made his home here. A scaled-down representation of Ahuena Heiau at **Kamakahonu,** the king's final residence *(75-5660 Palani Rd.;* ☎ *808-323-3222),* is on hotel grounds beside the pier. The ruler died there in 1819. The 1838 **Hulihe'e Palace★** *(Ali'i Dr.;* ☎ *808-329-1877)* was a retreat for later monarchs. Opposite is **Mokuaikaua Church★,** Hawaii's first Christian church, built by missionaries in 1837.

Captain Cook – *Mamalahoa Hwy. (Rte. 11), 14mi south of Kailua.* This village is named for the British explorer who introduced the world to Hawaii. A road leads to the **Royal Kona Museum & Coffee Mill** *(83-5427 Mamalahoa Hwy., Captain Cook;* ☎ *808-328-2511),* then downhill to **Kealakekua Bay★,** site of Cook's visit and death in 1779. The road ends near **Hikiau Heiau** *(Napo'opo'o;* ☎ *808-323-2005).* A *heiau* is a stone platform used by ancient Hawaiians for religious purposes, a sort of open-air temple. Cook conducted a Christian burial service here. The bay is now a marine reserve, popular for snorkeling.

★★**Pu'uhonua o Honaunau National Historical Park** – *Rte. 160, Honaunau Bay, 22mi S of Kailua.* ♿ 🅿 ☎ *808-328-2288. www.nps.gov/puho.* Until the early 19C, this walled site was sacred, a sanctuary for Hawaiians who violated the

■ Captain James Cook

No name is more synonymous with exploration in the Pacific Ocean than that of Captain James Cook. He made three voyages between 1767 and 1779, and is credited with discovering nearly all there was to be found in the vast Pacific.

Born in Yorkshire, England, in 1728, Cook escaped a humdrum life by joining the British navy. He gained acclaim as a navigator and cartographer, and at 40, was commissioned to lead an expedition to Tahiti to observe the transit of Venus across the sun. This voyage extended from 1767 to 1771; Cook discovered several islands and mapped the New Zealand and Australian coasts.

On his second voyage (1772-75), Cook circumnavigated the earth while searching vainly for the fabled "great southern continent," a theory popular in Europe. He did discover Tonga, New Caledonia and Easter Island.

Cook failed in his third voyage (1776-79) to find a northern passage from the Pacific to the Atlantic, though he traced the west coast of North America from Oregon to the Arctic Ocean. When he discovered Hawaii, natives initially welcomed him warmly, perhaps mistaking him for the peripatetic god Lono. But Cook and several of his men were killed in a skirmish over a stolen boat at Kealakekua Bay. A white obelisk marks the spot where the navigator is believed to have fallen.

---

kapus of society. If they could gain entry to the *pu'uhonua* (place of refuge), they were safe from capital punishment, as a *kahuna* (priest) would absolve them of their sin. Pacifists and defeated warriors also found refuge here. Today a **trail** *(.5mi)* leads from a visitor center past several archaeological sites, including a reconstructed temple and thatched huts where crafts are demonstrated.

Uphill about 2.5mi from the historical park, a side road leads to **St. Benedict's Painted Church**★ *(follow signs from Rte. 160)*, decorated long ago by its Belgian priest. An amateur *trompe l'oeil*, the wall behind the altar was painted to give his remote congregation an idea of how a grand European cathedral looked.

★**Kohala Coast** – *Queen Ka'ahumanu Hwy. (Rte. 19, South Kohala) & Akoni Pule Hwy. (Rte. 270, North Kohala)*. ☏ *808-886-4915*. North of Kailua, along the edge of a lava desert, is a series of eight impressive resorts. The **Hilton Waikoloa Village** *(425 Waikoloa Beach Dr., Waikoloa;* ☏ *808-886-1234)* has a colony of dolphins that swim and play with guests chosen by lottery for the experience. The Ka'upulehu Cultural Center of **The Four Seasons Hualalai** *(100 Ka'upulehu Dr., Ka'upulehu-Kona;* ☏ *808-325-8000)* has interactive history programs. **Mauna Kea Beach Hotel** *(62-100 Mauna Kea Beach Dr., Kohala Coast;* ☏ *808-882-7222)* was the first resort here, built by Laurence S. Rockefeller in 1966.

Ancient archaeological sites mark the windswept coastline of North Kohala. **Pu'ukohola Heiau National Historic Site** *(.2mi north of intersection of Rtes. 19 & 270, Kawaihae;* ☏ *808-882-7218)* was built as a temple around 1550 and reconstructed in 1791 by Kamehameha I, who treacherously murdered his last Big Island rival here to dedicate the temple and make himself supreme chief.

The **Mo'okini Heiau**★ *(1.5mi on dirt road at Upolu Airport turnoff from Rte. 270)*, dating from AD 480, overlooks the Alenuihaha Channel 19mi north of Kawaihae. Human sacrifices were made here. Nearby is the **King Kamehameha I Birth Site** *(.3mi farther on same road)*. The islands' conqueror may have entered the world on the birthing stones at one end of the compound in 1758, the year of Halley's Comet, as legend tells of a great light in the night sky at his birth.

The old plantation village of **Hawi** is sprucing up with galleries, boutiques and cafes. Outside Kapa'au Courthouse stands a nine-ton, bronze **Kamehameha I statue** *(Rte. 270)*; crafted in Italy in 1879, it sank in a shipwreck off the Falkland Islands but was later recovered. A replica stands in Honolulu *(p 174)*.

★**Parker Ranch** – *Kawaihae Rd. (Rte. 19) & Mamalahoa Hwy. (Rte. 190), Waimea/Kamuela*. ✕ ♿ 🅿 ☏ *808-885-7655. www.parkerranch.com*. With about 350sq mi and more than 55,000 head of cattle, these pasturelands make up one of the largest ranches in the US. The Parker family's original 1840s ranch house, **Mana Hale** *(*☏ *808-885-5433)*, is open for tours; the home of past-owner Richard Smart, **Puopelu**, is now a museum of French Impressionism and Chinese art. Exhibits and a short film at the **Parker Ranch Visitor Center and John Palmer Parker Museum**

(Rte. 19, Waimea) tell the history of the ranch, which began as a land grant from Kamehameha I to Parker, a sailor from Massachusetts who married a Hawaiian princess and stayed. The nearby **Kamuela Museum** *(Rtes. 19 & 250; ☏ 808-885-4724)* is less polished but offers an eclectic collection of artifacts.

★★ **Waipio Valley** – *Overlook at end of Rte. 240, 8mi north of Honokaa off Mamalahoa Hwy. (Rte. 19).* This spectacular wedge-shaped valley—6mi long, 1mi wide, flanked by 2,000ft cliffs that funnel ribbon-like waterfalls into streams emerging on a sandy ocean beach—is accessible only by foot or four-wheel-drive vehicle. Most travelers view it from a dramatic overlook near the small village of **Kukui-haele**. Inhabited for 1,000 years, the lush valley was once home to 4,000 or more Hawaiians. A few dozen pioneers homestead today.

★★ **Hilo** – The island's seat of government is this east-shore city of about 46,000. Rebuilt after disastrous tsunamis (tidal waves) in 1946 and 1960, the community has a hodgepodge look. New homes and businesses have been constructed on higher ground, farther from the water. Early-20C commercial buildings, seemingly frozen in an age of hand-cranked cash registers and creaking wooden floors, mark the original downtown. Here is the **Lyman Mission House and Museum** *(276 Haili St.; ☏ 808-935-5021)*, an 1839 missionary's home restored as a period museum. With 136in annual rainfall, Hilo is a floral center, especially for anthuriums and orchids. The 20-acre **Nani Mau Gardens** *(421 Makalika St., east of Rte. 11, 3.7mi south of downtown; ☏ 808-959-9591)* has a botanical museum.

Many hotels are near the rocky shoreline of Hilo Bay, along tree-lined Banyan Drive and **Liliuokalani Gardens**, named for the last queen. Some have nice views of **Mauna Kea**, the 13,796ft mountain to the northwest, often crowned by snow.

★★★ **Hawaii Volcanoes National Park** – *Mamalahoa Hwy. (Rte. 11), Volcano, 28mi southwest of Hilo. ☏ 808-985-6000. www.nps.gov/havo.* In not many places can casual travelers visit a live volcano. At the **Kilauea Visitor Center**★★, tourists may inspect exhibits and learn from rangers how to view the craters safely. **Volcano House** *(☏ 808-967-7321)*, a rambling wooden hotel first built in 1877, sits on the brink of Kilauea Caldera, at 4,000ft elevation. Steam rises from the caldera's deep **Halemaumau Crater**★★, which erupted most recently in 1982 and likely will again.

The 11mi **Crater Rim Drive**★★ circles the great pit and offers a chance to see (and smell) steam and sulfur fumes emanating from the ground. The drive crosses the moonlike Ka'u Desert, where the **Thomas A. Jaggar Museum**★ *(3mi west of Volcano House)* presents geological exhibits, and continues through a fern forest, where the 450ft-long **Thurston Lava Tube**★ *(2mi east of Volcano House)* beckons visitors.

Although **Kilauea Volcano**★★★ has been in continual eruption since January 3, 1983, it is generally unseen. Magma moves through 7mi of lava tubes under the surface, and only where it breaks out above the island's southern shore is it visible. The 2,000°F molten rock pours into the water, creating a boiling sea and sending steam high into the sky—a plume seen from the end of the 20mi **Chain of Craters Road**★★, extending off Crater Rim Drive 4mi southeast of Volcano House. Park rangers advise which path, if any, is cool enough to approach the lava.

Active Lava Flow

Houston Area

Houston Skyline

The largest city in Texas (fourth largest in the US) sits just inland from the Gulf of Mexico in the bayou country, 90mi west of the state's eastern border with Louisiana. Linked to the Gulf by the Houston Ship Channel—a waterway that has made the city the largest foreign-trade port in the United States—Houston is the hub of a metropolitan area of nearly 4 million people.

Houston is best known for its petrochemical industry. Oil was discovered in 1901, and within five years the city was headquarters for 30 oil companies and seven banks. "Black gold" anchored the economy for most of the 20C, until the price of oil plunged in the mid-1980s; it remains a major player today, along with the medical and aerospace industries.

Industrial areas south and east of the central city are shoulder-to-shoulder with refineries and other petroleum-based manufacturing concerns. Easy to spot on the downtown Houston skyline is the 75-story **Chase Tower** *(600 Travis St.)*. The 700-acre **Texas Medical Center** *(1155 Holcombe St.)*, just south of downtown, is the largest health-care complex in the world.

Houston's industrial wealth has given the city a rich cultural life. One of the few US cities with permanent ballet, opera, symphony and theater companies, Houston is second only to New York in number of theater seats. More than 30 museums are funded by oil fortunes. Professional baseball and basketball franchises are highly successful, and a new pro football team will begin play in 2002. The Houston Astros baseball team played from 1965 to 1999 in the world's first domed stadium, the **AstroDome** *(8400 Kirby Dr. at I-610 Loop South;* ☎ *713-799-9544)*, before moving to a new downtown stadium in 2000.

Galveston, in sharp contrast to Houston, is primarily a resort destination, with little emphasis on industry. The barrier island fills on weekends and summer days with Houstonians getting away from the city. Connected to the mainland by bridge, Galveston Island lies 50mi from Houston via Interstate 45. Much of its activity, from swimming to surf fishing, takes place along the Seawall, constructed to protect the island from storms. The city itself is home to numerous small museums and art galleries, historic homes and The Grand 1894 Opera House, deemed "the official Opera House of the State of Texas."

HOUSTON★★

Michelin map 492 L 14 Central Standard Time
Population 1,786,691
Tourist Information ☎ 713-437-5200 or www.houston-guide.com

Houston embodies much of Texas' mystique, the myth that bigger means better for the largest contiguous US state and everything in it. The city sprawls across 617sq mi of bayou country; the metropolitan area takes in nearly 9,000sq mi and is bound by one of the most intricate highway systems in the nation. As the fourth-largest US city (after New York, Los Angeles and Chicago), Houston is a giant in international shipping, petrochemicals, aerospace and finance. Its varied economy has attracted an equally diverse population; dozens of languages are heard in the metropolitan area.

Historical Notes – In August 1836, two New York land speculators, brothers Augustus and John Allen, navigated the Buffalo Bayou from Galveston Bay. They founded a settlement and named it in honor of Gen. Sam Houston, who had vanquished the Mexican army at San Jacinto four months earlier. The new community became capital of the new Republic of Texas from 1837 to 1839.
Initially beset by yellow fever and mud, Houston grew as a cotton-shipping port. After the Civil War, it developed as a rail center. After the 50mi Ship Channel was dredged in 1914, it became a major port. The discovery of oil in 1901 triggered modern prosperity, exemplified by the location of the Lyndon B. Johnson Space Center east of Houston in 1961. Since the oil crisis of the mid-1980s, Houston has developed a diversified economy that includes biotechnological research.F

PRINCIPAL SIGHTS

Three sectors of Houston are of interest to visitors. Downtown is the hub of commerce and performing arts. The Museum District is the location of most major museums, plus Hermann Park, the city's largest; immediately south is the huge Texas Medical Center. Uptown Houston, on the west side of the city, is the main shopping district, including the huge European-style Galleria complex.

★ **Downtown Houston** – ✗ க் 🄿 *Framed by I-45 & US-59 south of Buffalo Bayou.* Buffalo Bayou, the original corridor of settlement, runs along the north side of downtown. Sam Houston Park *(below)* recalls this first community; above it rises a web of freeways. The commercial district runs east 14 blocks to the George R. Brown Convention Center. The Theater District *(below)* extends north and east of Sam Houston Park. Several 19C buildings have been preserved at **Old Market Square** *(Preston, Travis, Congress & Milam Sts.);* the original **Allen's Landing** *(Commerce & Main Sts.)* is three blocks beyond. More than 50 blocks (about 6mi) of downtown are interconnected by the growing **Houston Underground,** a tunnel system that shelters the working population from summer humidity and winter rain, not to mention year-round street traffic.

★ **Sam Houston Park** 1100 Bagby St. க் 🄿 ☎ *713-655-1912. www .heritagesociety.org.* Seven restored and furnished 19C-early-20C homes, and an 1891 German Lutheran church, have been relocated to this 19-acre park. Oldest is an 1823 pioneer home; most elaborate, a 17-room house built by oil pioneer Henry T. Staiti in 1905. The **Heritage Society Museum** has exhibits on five centuries of history. The Long Row is a reconstructed mid-19C shopping strip.

★ **Theater District** – *Preston Blvd. to Capitol St., both sides of Louisiana St.* Both the Houston Grand Opera and Houston Ballet perform at the **Wortham Theater Center** *(510 Preston Blvd.;* ☎ *713-237-1439),* noted for its six-story grand foyer. The Houston Symphony Orchestra is home in the block-sized **Jones Hall for the Performing Arts** *(615 Louisiana St.;* ☎ *713-227-3974),* identified by its facade of travertine marble. **The Alley Theater** *(615 Texas Ave.;* ☎ *713-228-8431),* whose balcony offers a view of the city skyline, hosts one of the three oldest resident professional theater companies in the US.

★★ **Museum District** – Houston's main cultural neighborhood is 2mi southwest of downtown via Main Street. A half-dozen important art museums, various science and history museums and Houston's children's museum are found here. Although the district extends 1.5mi north-south from the Menil Collection to the Houston Zoo, most facilities are within four blocks north of Hermann Park.

★★★ **Menil Collection** – *1515 Sul Ross St.* க் 🄿 ☎ *713-525-9400. www.menil.org.* One of the world's foremost collections of 20C art, with an emphasis on Surrealism, is presented here. Established in 1987 for the collection of John and Dominique de Menil, the museum exhibits only a small part of more than 15,000 paintings, sculptures, photographs and books. Italian architect Renzo Piano's design has been acclaimed for its use of natural light in display areas.

ADDRESS BOOK

Please see explanation on p 64.

Staying in the Houston Area

The Lancaster – *701 Texas Ave., Houston TX.* ✗ ♿ 🅿 ☎ *713-228-9500. www.slh.com. 93 rooms.* **$$$** More an English country manor than a hotel, the Lancaster is a place of oil paintings and overstuffed chairs. **Bistro Lancaster** is like a London men's club, but the food has a Louisiana flair: A mahogany bar and lanterns shaped like hunting horns mix with Gulf Coast specialties like jumbo lump crabcakes in smoked corn and truffle sauce.

The Tremont House – *2300 Ship's Mechanic Row, Galveston TX.* ✗ ♿ 🅿 ☎ *409-763-0300. www.wyndham.com. 117 rooms.* **$$** Located on the Strand, this bed-and-breakfast inn is hardly modest. Guests on the second and third floors have 15ft ceilings and 13ft windows. From a four-story glass-topped atrium lobby, a piano player sends music filtering to the balconies every night.

Hotel Galvez – *2024 Seawall Blvd., Galveston TX.* ✗ ♿ 🅿 〰 ☎ *409-765-7721. www.grandheritage.com. 231 rooms.* **$** Built in 1911, the "Queen of the Gulf" has endured hurricanes and is listed on the National Register of Historic Places. A restoration has uncovered grand archways and original stencilwork, and yielded rooms in rich gold and sepia. A tropical pool has a swim-up bar.

Sara's B&B – *941 Heights Blvd., Houston TX.* 🅿 ☎ *713-868-1130. www.saras.com. 13 rooms.* **$** Rock in a white wicker chair on the wraparound porch of Sara's romantic clapboard Queen Anne inn. Many of the whimsically themed rooms have iron beds, covered in lace and ruffles. Try the Fort Worth Room (a pine-pole bed, stagecoach lamps and barbed-wire wall decorations).

Dining in the Houston Area

Américas – *1800 Post Oak Blvd., Houston TX.* ☎ *713-961-1492.* **$$$** **Latin American.** With a skylight, trees and exotic flowers, this award-winning spot is like a South American rain forest. The food is appropriately tropical. Pargo Américas is the house version of Gulf snapper, crusted with fresh corn off the cob; sweet soufflé-style rice pudding provides a perfect ending.

Brennan's – *3300 Smith St., Houston TX.* ☎ *713-522-9711.* **$$$** **Creole.** White tablecloths, hardwood paneling and windows overlooking a lanterned courtyard make for an evening of Creole classics and seasonal dishes. Seafood lovers are delighted by shrimp creole, potato-crusted crabcakes and Gulf Coast gumbo.

Gaido's – *3700 Seawall Blvd., Galveston TX.* ☎ *409-762-9625.* **$$** **Seafood.** S.J. Gaido's great-grandchildren still peel shrimp and filet fish the old-fashioned way. The catch of the day is prepared 10 different ways: Locals enjoy the Texas catfish Sapporito style (crusted in crushed crackers and garlic) or Castilla style (blackened, topped with asiago cream sauce).

Benno's on the Beach – *1200 Seawall Blvd., Galveston TX.* ☎ *409-762-4621.* **$** **Seafood.** Most people enter Benno's straight from the sand, in bathing suits and sandals, then eat alfresco on the bustling terrace. Benno's is famed for deep-fried Cajun seafood, its crabs and crawfish spiced with Louisiana heat.

The **Surrealist collection**★★★ features more works by René Magritte and Max Ernst than any other museum in the world. Also represented are paintings by Cézanne, Klee and Matisse; early Cubist work by Braque, Léger and Picasso; Abstract Expressionism by Pollock and Rothko; and late-20C works by Johns, Rauschenberg, Stella and Warhol. Other galleries hold Paleolithic carvings from the eastern Mediterranean; Byzantine and medieval works; and tribal arts of Africa, Oceania and the Pacific Northwest coast. The adjacent **Cy Twombly Gallery** *(1501 Branard St.)* houses 35 works by the noted Expressionist.

One block east, maintained by the Menil, **The Rothko Chapel**★★ *(3900 Yupon St.;* ☎ *713-524-9839)* is as an all-faith ecumenical center. The octagonal Chapel (1971, Philip Johnson), holds 14 paintings (1965-66)—variations on a theme of black—by Mark Rothko. Outside in a reflecting pool stands *Broken Obelisk,* a tributary sculpture (1967) to Martin Luther King Jr. by Barnett Newman.

The Menil's **Byzantine Fresco Chapel Museum**★ *(4011 Yupon St.; ☎ 713-521-3990)* holds the only intact Byzantine frescoes in the Western Hemisphere, rescued from thieves attempting to smuggle the 13C artwork out of Turkish-controlled Cyprus. The frescoes underwent a two-year restoration.

★**Contemporary Arts Museum** – *5216 Montrose Blvd.* ✕&. 𝖯 ☎ *713-284-8250. www.camh.org.* Occupying a distinctive metal parallelogram (1972, Gunnar Birkerts), this cutting-edge museum offers frequently changing exhibits of modern international art in spacious upstairs and downstairs galleries. Rotating every six weeks, major exhibitions in 1999 featured such artists as Maya Lin, Jean-Michel Basquiat, Ernesto Neto and Carrie Mae Weems. Occasional theme exhibitions are organized around questions central to the nature of art.

Le Monde Invisible (1953-54) by René Magritte

Hickery-Robertson/The Menil Collection

★★**The Museum of Fine Arts, Houston** – *1001 Bissonnet St.* ✕&. 𝖯 ☎ *713-639-7300. www.mfah.org* . Founded in 1900 as the first municipal art museum in Texas, the MFAH has a wide-ranging collection of more than 40,000 paintings, sculptures and other objets d'art. Permanent exhibits include the **Glassell Collection**★★ of African gold; Renaissance and 18C art; and Egyptian, Greek and Roman antiquities. The **Beck Collection**★ of Impressionist and Post-Impressionist art has works by Manet, Pissarro, Van Gogh, Renoir, Gauguin, Toulouse-Lautrec, Degas and Matisse, as well as Mary Cassatt. **Western art** features works by Frederic Remington and Indian art of the American Southwest.

The new (March 2000) **Audrey Jones Beck Building** *(5601 Main St.)*, designed by José Rafael Moneo, complements the original Caroline Wiess Law Building (1924) and makes the MFAH the sixth largest art museum in the US. The Beck Building houses European art to 1920 and American art to 1945. Between the Law Building and the museum-operated **Glassell School of Art** *(5101 Montrose Blvd.)* is the **Cullen Sculpture Garden**★ (1986, Isamu Noguchi).

The museum displays American decorative arts at Bayou Bend Collection and Gardens *(p 190)*, and European decorative arts at **Rienzi** *(1406 Kirby Dr.; ☎ 713-639-7800)*, including a fine collection of 18C Worcester porcelain.

★**Houston Zoological Gardens** – 𝗞𝗶𝗱𝘀 *1513 N. MacGregor Way.* ✕&. 𝖯 ☎ *713-523-5888. www.houstonzoo.org.* Spanning 55 acres at Hermann Park, the zoo is home to 5,000 animals of 700 species. The Wortham World of Primates is a 2.2-acre rain-forest habitat for apes and monkeys. The Tropical Bird House is a walk-through jungle aviary for more than 200 free-flying birds. Other denizens include Siberian tigers, pygmy hippos, giraffes, sea lions and vampire bats.

★★★**Houston Museum of Natural Science** – 𝗞𝗶𝗱𝘀 *1 Hermann Circle Dr.* ✕&. 𝖯 ☎ *713-639-4629. www.hmns.org.* This outstanding four-floor museum requires at least two days to see properly. On the main floor are a planetarium and IMAX theater. The **Paleontology Hall** exhibits over 450 fossil specimens chronicled by time and location. Adjacent to the Welch Chemistry Hall is a 63ft-tall Foucault pendulum. The **Wiess Energy Hall**★★ features one of the world's most comprehensive exhibits on oil and natural gas. Unique high-technology displays, using virtual reality and video holography, trace the formation, exploration and recovery of these and other energy resources, as well as the refining and transportation processes.

The **Cockrell Butterfly Center★**, a 25,000sq ft glass pyramid, houses 2,000 free-flying butterflies. The Brown Hall of Entomology showcases the insect world. The **Cullen Hall of Gems and Minerals★** is a major collection of priceless specimens, dramatically illuminated. Lifelike dioramas present wildlife of Texas and Africa's Serengeti Plain; the Strake Hall of Malacology showcases 2,500 rare seashells, mainly from the Gulf of Mexico. The **John P. McGovern Hall of the Americas** focuses on native cultures from the Arctic to the Andes, especially the US and Mexico.

Lower-level exhibits are geared to schoolchildren. The **Arnold Hall of Space Science** incorporates the Challenger Learning Center, where students in a Mission Control mock-up may communicate with others in a remote flight simulator. Beyond a TV weather station is a hands-on science learning center.

★ **Museum of Health & Medical Science** – [Kids] *1515 Hermann Dr.* ⚬ 🅿 ☎ *713-521-1515. www.mhms.org.* As home to the world's largest medical center, Houston makes a natural location for this educational center. In the Amazing Body Pavilion, visitors take a walking tour of the human body, including a 10ft brain, a giant eyeball, a 22ft backbone, and more than 80 interactive exhibits that pose and answer questions about anatomy and health.

★ **The Children's Museum of Houston** – [Kids] *1500 Binz St.* ✗⚬ 🅿 ☎ *713-522-1138. www.cmhouston.org.* Hands-on exhibits in the Technikids Gallery show everyday applications of science through experimentation. The Investigations Gallery teaches where food comes from, beginning with a farm exhibit and continuing through nutrition, shopping and money management. Other displays encourage cross-cultural comparisons and teach respect for natural resources.

★ **Holocaust Museum Houston** – *5401 Caroline St.* ⚬ 🅿 ☎ *713-942-8000. www.hmh.org.* This somber museum (1996, Ralph Appelbaum and Mark Mucasey), designed as an education center and a memorial to victims and survivors of the Holocaust, is unmistakable for the broad, dark, brick cylinder—reminiscent of a Nazi death-camp smokestack—that rises above it. The exhibit traces Jewish history and the roots of anti-Semitism to the World War II-era Holocaust, followed by the Liberation. **The Memorial Room★**, with walls of remembrance, tears and hope, provides a quiet place of reflection.

ADDITIONAL SIGHTS

★★ **Bayou Bend Collection and Gardens** – *1 Westcott St.* ⚬ 🅿 ☎ *713-639-7750. www.mfah.org .* A division of The Museum of Fine Arts, Houston, this spectacular collection showcases 17-19C American decorative arts with 5,000 objects of furniture, ceramics, silver, paper, glass, textiles and paintings. It is located in Bayou Bend (1927, John F. Staub), the Neo-Palladian-style former estate of governor's daughter Ima Hogg (1882-1975). On display are a silver sugar bowl crafted by Paul Revere, colonial portraits by John Singleton Copley and Charles Willson Peale, and furniture by John Townsend. Surrounding the home are 14 acres of woodlands and eight formal gardens.

The Galleria – *5075 Westheimer St. at Post Oak Blvd.* ✗⚬ 🅿 ☎ *713-621-1907.* Several major department stores, two large hotels and an ice rink (beneath an arched glass ceiling) anchor Houston's largest shopping complex. Designed after a plaza in Milan, Italy, the center dominates the Uptown Houston district, west of Loop 610 and north of US-59 (Southwest Freeway). Immediately south of The Galleria, the 64-story Williams Tower *(2800 Post Oak Blvd.;* ☎ *713-850-8841)* offers a vast view from its top floors.

★ **Six Flags AstroWorld** – [Kids] ‖‖‖ *9001 Kirby Dr. at I-610 Loop South.* ✗⚬ 🅿 ☎ *713-799-1234. www.sixflags.com.* The Gulf Coast's preeminent amusement park faces the AstroDome *(p 186)* from across the I-610 freeway. The 75-acre park boasts 10 roller coasters, including the famous Texas Cyclone.

EXCURSIONS

★★★ **Space Center Houston** – [Kids] *1601 NASA Road 1, Clear Lake, 25mi south of downtown Houston off I-45.* ✗⚬ 🅿 ☎ *281-244-2100. www.spacecenterhouston .org.* Official visitor center of the National Aeronautics and Space Administration (NASA), this $70 million facility adjacent to the Johnson Space Center—the mission control, training and research facility for the US space program—offers live shows, presentations and interactive exhibits.

Guided tram tours take visitors for a behind-the-scenes look at the Johnson Space Center to view Mission Control and astronaut training facilities. Live satellite links provide up-to-date information on current space flights. Exhibits include space-

Space Center Houston

craft from early *Mercury, Gemini* and *Apollo* missions; visitors may try on space helmets, touch moon rocks, use a simulator to land a shuttle or take a space walk. Texas' largest IMAX theater showcases large-format films. At Kids Space Place, 40 interactive areas invite exploration as children ride across the moon's surface in a Lunar Rover or command a space shuttle.

★**Battleship Texas State Historical Park** – Kids *3527 Battleground Rd. (Rte. 134), La Porte, 21mi east of downtown Houston via Rte. 225.* ♿ 🅿 ☎ *281-479-2431. www.tpwd.state.tx.us/park/battlesh/battlesh.htm.* Located opposite San Jacinto Battleground State Historical Park *(below),* the USS *Texas* recalls far more recent battles. Commissioned in 1914, the 573ft battleship served in both world wars before it was decommissioned in 1948. Rescued from demolition, the ship is now open for self-guided tours of both its main deck and lower levels.

■ The Republic of Texas

Texans are proud that their state was once the independent Republic of Texas.

Following the victory over Gen. Santa Anna at the Battle of San Jacinto on April 21, 1836, a new government was formed. Sam Houston, hero of San Jacinto, was elected the republic's first president in September 1836. Among his first concerns were the continued threats of attack by Indians and renewed attempts by Mexico to extend its borders across the Rio Grande into Texas.

Houston's initial efforts at establishing diplomatic relations with other countries, including the United States, failed. A breakthrough came when a trade treaty was signed with the United Kingdom. Fearing an alliance between Texas and Britain, the US recognized Texas as sovereign in 1837. Soon France, Belgium, The Netherlands and Germany also recognized the young republic.

In 1839, a permanent capital was established at the frontier village of Waterloo, renamed Austin. A national flag was adopted, featuring a single five-pointed star on a field of blue, flanked by horizontal red-and-white stripes; today, Texas continues to be known as the Lone Star State.

Texas President Houston was reelected to a second term in 1841. Much of his subsequent effort was directed toward achieving statehood within the US for reasons of defense and economy. On October 13, 1845, the people of Texas voted 4,245 to 257 in favor of annexation. US President John Polk signed Texas' admission to the union in December of that year. On February 19, 1846, the flag of the Republic of Texas flew over Austin for the final time.

* **San Jacinto Battleground State Historical Park** – *Battleground Rd. (Rte. 134), La Porte, 21mi east of downtown Houston via Rte. 225.* ⓺ ⓟ ☏ *281-479-2431. www.sanjacinto-museum.org.* This 570ft obelisk (1939) recalls the victory by Texas troops in the 1836 Battle of San Jacinto, establishing their freedom from Mexican colonial rule. The obelisk is covered with fossilized Cordova shellstone; its exterior is presently under renovation. An elevator takes visitors to the top of the monument for a grand view. On the ground floor is the **San Jacinto Museum of History**, documenting Texas' formative years. *Texas Forever! The Battle of San Jacinto* is a 35min multimedia show about the struggle for independence.

GALVESTON★

Michelin map 492 L 9   Central Standard Time
Population 59,567
Tourist Information ☏ 409-763-4311, www.galvestontourism.com

Located 50mi south of Houston, Galveston Island is both a summer getaway and a year-round historic destination. The compact barrier island—32mi long but just 2mi wide—is especially known for its beaches, miles of which were included in Texas' first beach replenishment program. The city, at the eastern end of the island, focuses around a 36-block historic district.

Historical Notes – Home to the Akokisa Indians in the 16C, Galveston Island remained unsettled by Europeans until the early 19C, when pirate Jean Lafitte established the village of Campeche as his base. When he was forced out by the US Navy, the village was renamed, and Galveston slowly developed as a port city. A Confederate base that briefly fell into Union hands during the Civil War, Galveston became the richest city in Texas and home to many state "firsts": post office, hospital, naval base, telephone, private bank, gas and electric lights, and more. At the turn of the 20C, thousands of immigrants made their way through the port, second only to New York's Ellis Island as a US entry point. But Galveston's thriving economy took a blow on September 8, 1900, when the city was struck by one of the worst hurricanes in US history. Known as The Great Storm, it killed more than 6,000 residents and destroyed one-third of the city. To prevent future damage by storms, Galveston constructed a 10mi seawall and raised the level of the island.

SIGHTS

* **The Strand National Historic Landmark District** – *The Strand, 20th-25th St.; visitor center, 2016 The Strand.* ✗⓺ ⓟ ☏ *409-766-1572. www.galvestonhistory.org.* In the late 19C, The Strand was the city's business district. Located a block from the busy seaport, shippers unloaded merchandise from around the world in exchange for cargoes of Texas cotton. Bankers and traders filled the buildings of The Strand, which became known as the Wall Street of the Southwest. Today trolleys clang along the historic streets, transporting visitors through a district filled with specialty shops and restaurants, housed in one of the nation's largest collections of Victorian commercial architecture.
The **Grand 1894 Opera House** *(2020 Postoffice St.; ☏ 409-765-1894)* has been restored to its appearance when it hosted such performers as Sara Bernhardt, John Philip Sousa and Anna Pavlova. The **Galveston County Historical Museum** *(2219 Market St.; ☏ 409-766-2340)* recounts the island's fascinating history. At the **Texas Seaport Museum** *(Pier 21; ☏ 409-763-1877)* is the *Elissa*, a restored 1877 tall ship open for self-guided tours. The museum also has displays on Galveston's shipping history and a database with the names of more than 133,000 immigrants who entered the US here.

Historic Homes – Numerous 19C homes, many along Broadway south of The Strand, are open for tours. The **Bishop's Palace** *(1402 Broadway; ☏ 409-762-2475)*, a castle-like 1886 Victorian, was built for a railroad founder and later belonged to a diocesan bishop. Constructed of Texas granite, white limestone and red sandstone, it features elaborate woodwork, mantels and fireplaces. The 1895 Romanesque-style **Moody Mansion** *(2618 Broadway; ☏ 409-762-7668)* features a French rococo reception room and a Classical Revival library.
Three homes are operated by the Galveston Historical Foundation *(☏ 409-672-3933)*. The 1859 **Ashton Villa** *(2328 Broadway)* is a stately Italianate mansion. The 1838 **Menard Home** *(1605 33rd St.)*, an antebellum estate of Greek Revival style, is furnished with Federal and American Empire antiques. The 1839 **Williams Home** *(3601 Avenue P)* is both a Creole plantation house and a sea captain's home.
Most of Galveston's graceful houses, however, are privately residences not open for tours, including the Carpenter Gothic-style **Sonnenthiel House** *(1826 Sealy Ave.)*.

Sonnenthiel House

★★ Moody Gardens – **Kids** *1 Hope Blvd.; take 81st St. to Jones Rd.* ✕ ♿ 🅿 ☎ *409-744-4673. www.moodygardens.com.* Beginning in 1986 as a therapy center for patients with head injuries, Moody Gardens has expanded into a leading attraction. The glass **Rainforest Pyramid★★** is home to more than 1,700 tropical plants, fish, birds and insects. The **Discovery Pyramid** showcases the world of space through exhibits and interactive displays. The new **Aquarium Pyramid★** contains 1.5 million gallons of water for marine life from the North and South Pacific Oceans, South Atlantic Ocean and Caribbean Sea. *The Colonel,* a re-created 19C paddle-wheeler, is docked at Palm Beach, made of white sand shipped from Florida. Two IMAX theaters complete the offerings.

Kansas City Area

Downtown Kansas City

The mid-American prairie has always been a land of new possibilities. Its rich, fertile soil generates an unlimited bounty of wheat and sorghum, supporting vast herds of cattle. Nary a man-made object obstructs the sun as it rises and sets on wide, sweeping plains that seem to stretch endlessly to the horizons. The land's pristine beauty inspires artists, nature lovers and outsdoorsmen.

Originally inhabited by Kansa (Siouan) Indians and herds of bison as broad as the state of Rhode Island, this region's modern history began with the Lewis and Clark Expedition of 1803-06. Explorers Meriwether Lewis and William Clark identified a site where the Kansas River met the Missouri River as a good place to build a fort; in 1821, fur traders took their advice. By the 1830s, Westport Landing (renamed Kansas in 1850 and Kansas City in 1889) was outfitting westbound travelers with provisions for their long trip, water for their horses, and news of which Indian tribes to avoid. Wagon trains began their journeys on the Oregon, California and Santa Fe Trails from here. Thousands more hopeful settlers headed up the wide Missouri on steamboats and promises.

In the pre-Civil War years, territorial Kansas was caught in the untenable but congressionally ordered position of determining, by popular vote, its position on slave-versus-free state status. Violent confrontations between partisans of both sides of the issue flared for years, even after "Bleeding Kansas" was admitted to the Union as a free state in 1861.

On April 3, 1860, a skinny boy named Johnny Fry galloped out of a stable in St. Joseph, Missouri, just north of Kansas City, on a mare named Sylph. His historic ride was the beginning of the Pony Express, whose legend has lived far longer than the short 18 months it delivered packages, letters and newspapers between St. Joe and Sacramento, California.

Kansas City subsequently developed as a rail center. Thanks to careful planning and foresight, the city has grown in the 20C into a graceful metropolis with beauty, culture and a distinctly European ambience.

Omaha, a 3hr drive north and the largest city in the adjoining state of Nebraska, also grew around the railroad. Today it is a grain- and livestock-shipping center well known for its fine museums and zoo.

Kansas City
KS

KANSAS CITY★★

Michelin map 492 L, 9   Central Standard Time
Population 441,259 (Missouri), 142,654 (Kansas)
Tourist Information ☏ 816-221-5242 or www.gointokansascity.com

Located in the geographical center of the US, Kansas City is a bustling metropolis of 1.4 million that spans two states and serves as a hub for excursions into the heartland. Wide, tree-lined boulevards, more than 200 fountains and myriad parks belie its reputation as a dull city; it isn't flat and it certainly isn't drab, with as many days of sunshine as Miami or San Diego.

Most of Kansas City isn't even in Kansas. Professional sports, jazz clubs, art museums and barbecue restaurants—to name a few of the things for which it's renowned—are all found on the larger Missouri side of town.

US President **Harry S Truman** (1884-1972), painter **Thomas Hart Benton** (1889-1975) and animator **Walt Disney** (1901-66) all considered Kansas City home.

SIGHTS

★★**Arabia Steamboat Museum** – *400 Grand Ave.* ✗ &. ☐ ☏ *816-471-1856. www.1856.com.* On September 5, 1856, a sidewheeler carrying 130 passengers and 200 tons of cargo sank upriver from Kansas City. Not until 1988 did treasure hunters extract the vessel from 45ft of mud and water. The cargo—Wedgwood china, brandied cherries, buggy whips, tobacco, cognac, powderhorns, doorknobs, pickles and other pioneer needs—is now on display. A 14min video tells the *Arabia*'s story. Half the cargo is still in barrels; visitors can watch it being cleaned (the job won't be done before 2025) and chat with the men who recovered it.

The *Arabia* anchors one side of **City Market** *(5th St. between Wyandotte & Grand Aves.)*, a historic district at Kansas City's 19C riverport. Brick buildings contain restaurants, a brewpub and stores selling everything from antiques to avant-garde art to Asian spices. On Saturdays, farmers bring fresh produce to sell.

American Royal Museum and Visitors Center – *Governor's Bldg., 1701 American Royal Court.* ✗ &. ☐ ☏ *816-221-9800.* The century-old American Royal Livestock, Horse Show and Rodeo, held annually in early November, is honored in this interactive museum. Guests may judge livestock, grind grain into flour and dress in rodeo costumes.

Crown Center – *2450 Grand Ave.* ✗ &. ☐ ☏ *816-274-8444. www.crowncenter .com.* Surrounding the world headquarters of Hallmark Cards, this complex has 60 shops, hotels, restaurants and theaters. In the **Hallmark Visitors Center** *(☏ 816-274-5672)*, guests discover the history of the world's largest greeting-card company, begun in 1910 by an 18-year-old Nebraska boy with two shoe boxes of postcards.

Science City at Union Station – **Kids** *30 W. Pershing Rd. at Main St.* ✗ &. ☐ ☏ *816-460-2222. www.sciencecity.com.* A $250 million renovation of this grand train station (1914, Jarvis Hunt)—second in size in the US only to New York's Grand Central Station—was completed in late 1999. Interactive exhibits, on two floors, focus on science and city history; there are live, domed and 3-D film theaters. Many exhibits were relocated from the **Kansas City Museum** *(3218 Gladstone Blvd.; ☏ 816-483-8300)* at Corinthian Hall, a large turn-of-the-20C mansion that still houses permanent history exhibits and temporary displays.

★★**18th & Vine Historic District** – During Prohibition (1919-33), Kansas City officials turned a blind eye to all-night speakeasies. The city became "the place to be" for jazz musicians like native son **Charlie "Bird" Parker** and **Count Basie**, who formed his band here. Some 120 nightclubs prospered, thanks in part to Tom Pendergast—a political boss who later helped launch Harry Truman's career. Liquor flowed freely; gambling, drugs and prostitution thrived.

Famed musicians like Bennie Moten, Jay McShann, Dizzy Gillespie and Big Joe Turner migrated to Kansas City to find work. When the clubs closed for the evening, they retired to the **Mutual Musicians' Foundation** *(1828 Highland St.)*, a hot-pink bungalow that served as a rehearsal hall; today, seven decades later, it remains a second home to jazz musicians. The best time to go is after midnight Friday or Saturday, when musicians gather to jam, sometimes until dawn.

The restored historic district is now home to restaurants, nightclubs, the 500-seat **Gem Theater** (1912), and the **Horace M. Peterson III Visitor Center** *(18th & Vine Sts.)*, where exhibits celebrate Kansas City's African-American community.

★★**Negro Leagues Baseball Museum** – **Kids** *18th & Vine Sts.* &. ☐ ☏ *816-221-1920.* The history of the vaunted Negro Leagues—from post-Civil War origins to Jackie Robinson's admission to the major leagues in the late 1940s—is recounted at this center adjoining the Jazz Museum. Designed around a baseball diamond with real-game sound effects, it features bronzes of such famous players as Satchel Paige, Josh Gibson and "Cool Papa" Bell. Videos, artifacts and souvenirs recall a fascinating era in American sports history.

★ **The American Jazz Museum** – *1616 E. 18th St.* ▣ ☏ *816-474-8463*. Music memorabilia, a jukebox of jazz classics and live music four nights a week in The Blue Room nightclub are features. Special displays honor Louis Armstrong, Duke Ellington, Ella Fitzgerald and Charlie Parker. Exhibits include sound booths and do-it-yourself jazz lessons. The Kansas City Institute for Jazz Performance & History indoctrinates students to nuances of swing and bebop.

© Cameron Davidson/FOLIO, Inc.

Jazz Trumpeter

Westport Historic District – *40th to 43rd Sts. between Main St. & Southwest Trafficway.* ✗ ⴺ ▣ ☏ *816-756-2789*. In 1836, when westbound wagon trains were outfitted here, Westport Landing's small population included John Sutter (central to the 1849 California Gold Rush) and scouts Kit Carson and Jim Bridger. Today, the historic brick buildings are a hip crossroads with specialty shops, boutiques, galleries, restaurants and a slew of nightlife venues.

★★ **The Nelson-Atkins Museum of Art** – *4525 Oak St.; east of Country Club Plaza at Rockhill Rd.* ✗ ⴺ ▣ ☏ *816-561-4000*. With more than 28,000 works in 60 galleries and nine period rooms, this museum is noted for its antiquities and its paintings by European masters. The Asian collection includes a Chinese temple room, 13C BC furnishings and porcelain, and an array of T'ang Dynasty tomb figures. A sculpture park presents the largest US collection of bronzes by British sculptor Henry Moore.

★★ **Kemper Museum of Contemporary Art** – *4420 Warwick Blvd.; one block east of 45th & Main Sts.* ✗ ⴺ ▣ ☏ *816-753-5784*. An art museum for people who think they don't like art, this facility (1994, Gunnar Birkerts) entertains and challenges. Its collection—highlighted by the controversial, 28-watercolor *Canyon Suite* (1916-18), attributed to Georgia O'Keeffe—features such other modern artists as Chihuly, Hockney, Johns, Motherwell, Rauschenberg, Stella and Thiebaud, and photographers Mapplethorpe and Wegman. On the walls of Café Sebastienne is Frederick James Brown's *The History of Art*, a montage of 110 oil paintings that represent important movements in art through the ages.

Country Club Plaza – *450 Ward Pkwy.; between Main, Summit, Brush & W. 46th Sts. at J.C. Nichols Pkwy.* ✗ ⴺ ▣ ☏ *816-753-0100*. Built in 1922 as the first planned shopping center in the US, this unique 14-square-block shopping district features Spanish Moorish architecture of red-tiled roofs, elegant domes, ornate ironwork, romantic courtyards and more than 30 statues and fountains.

★ **Toy and Miniature Museum of Kansas City** – 🅺🅸🅳🆂 *5235 Oak St.* ⴺ ▣ ☏ *816-333-2055. www.umkc.edu/tmm*. More than 100 furnished doll houses, miniatures and antique toys (including model trains) are displayed in this 1911 mansion on the University of Missouri-Kansas City campus.

★ **Kansas City Zoo** – 🅺🅸🅳🆂 *East end of Swope Park, 63rd St. off I-435.* ✗ ⴺ ▣ ☏ *816-871-5701*. A $71 million overhaul has made this 200-acre zoo realistic not only for the 1,500 animals, but for visitors who can wander the plains of Kenya, the rain forest of the Congo or the outback of Australia. Children ride ponies and camels, paddleboats and trains, or watch live animal shows. On summer weekends, visitors can camp out, join a nocturnal safari and enjoy breakfast with the animals. An IMAX theater was the first in any zoo.

★Thomas Hart Benton Home and Studio – *3616 Belleview St.; two blocks west of Southwest Trafficway*. ☎ *816-931-5722*. This Victorian stone mansion (1903) in the graceful Roanoke district is where Benton and his wife, Rita, lived for 36 years. The famous painter died in his studio in 1975 when he was 85, getting ready to sign a 6ft-by-10ft acrylic he had just finished for the Country Music Hall of Fame. The house displays 13 original works; the carriage house-turned-studio still has easels, paintbrushes and other artist's tools.

EXCURSIONS

★Harry S Truman Library and Museum – *US-24 & Delaware St., Independence*. ⚑ 🅿 ☎ *800-833-1225*. A 20min drive from Kansas City, this presidential library and museum tell the story of the plain-speaking haberdasher whose terms in office (1945-53) were a bridge between World War II and the Korean War. A 45min film reviews Truman's life beginning with his boyhood in Lamar, Missouri. In the courtyard are the graves of Harry and his wife, Bess.

Nearby, the house in which the Trumans lived from 1919 onward is preserved as the **Harry S Truman National Historic Site** *(Delaware St. off Truman Rd.; ☎ 816-254-9929)*. Guided tours of the Victorian home, furnished with family heirlooms, depart every 15min *(purchase tickets at 223 N. Main St.)*.

★National Frontier Trails Center – *318 W. Pacific Ave. off Noland Rd., Independence*. ⚑ 🅿 ☎ *816-325-7575. www.frontiertrailscenter.com*. Located in a 19C brick building that once was a flour mill owned by Bess Truman's grandfather, this museum gives a history of the three trails that originated near here: the Oregon, California and Santa Fe. An 18min film details the specifics of crossing the continent; the library exhibits pioneers' letters and diaries.

★★St. Joseph – *I-29 & US-36, 60mi north of Kansas City*. ☎ *816-232-1839. www.stjomo.com*. Tourism in this friendly city of 69,000 thrives on its fame as launch pad for the Pony Express. For 18 months in 1860-61, riders departed from the westernmost US rail station to deliver mail to Sacramento, California. Stopping at some 150 relay stations en route, 80 riders—among them 15-year-old William "Buffalo Bill" Cody and a young James "Wild Bill" Hickok—made the 1,966mi run in only 10 days. The original stables are today the **Pony Express National Memorial★** *(914 Penn St.; ☎ 816-279-5059)*.
Three blocks away, the **Patee House Museum★** *(12th & Penn Sts.; ☎ 816-232-8206)* has exhibits in what was, in 1858, one of the finest hotels in the West. On its grounds is the **Jesse James Home**, restored with period decor. At 34, James, a notorious outlaw, had abandoned his life of crime and lived quietly with his wife and two children in this shuttered clapboard house. But on April 3, 1882, 22 years to the day after the first Pony Express ride, he was shot in cold blood—in this house—by a member of his own gang seeking a $10,000 reward.

■ Kansas City Barbecue

Kansas City is renowned for its barbecued beef, pork and chicken. The Yellow Pages alone list more than 60 BBQ joints. That doesn't begin to include the little roadside stands without phones; restaurants with enough gall to serve "other" dishes beside ribs; and the hundreds of thousands of backyard grills.
Even outsiders are willing to go to a lot of trouble to get a sampling. President Bill Clinton, visiting the city, went back for second, third and fourth helpings. Television personality Bryant Gumbel won a bet with *Today* show co-host Jane Pauley that included ribs from a Kansas City barbecue house. One Milwaukee businessman sent his private jet for $5,000 worth of ribs.
The first documented barbecuer in Kansas City was Henry Perry, who served ribs from an old streetcar barn in 1916. During Prohibition, traveling musicians working the speakeasies spread the word about barbecue. Night or day, ribs, briskets and other cheap cuts of meat were smoked, doused with sauce and served in leftover newspapers. Many of the rib joints didn't even open until midnight. Today, many don't close till well past midnight.

ADDRESS BOOK

Please see explanation on p 64.

Staying in Kansas City and Omaha

The Raphael Hotel – *325 Ward Pkwy., Kansas City MO.* ♿ 🅿 ☎ *816-756-3800. 123 rooms.* **$$** Iron lanterns arch over the driveway and a glass foyer covers the entrance of this brick charmer overlooking Country Club Plaza. As the city's most upscale hostelry, the elegant Raphael offers an old-world touch of marble tiles and wooden ceilings in the lobby, and modern amenities in all rooms.

Southmoorland – *116 E. 46th St., Kansas City MO.* ♿ 🅿 ☎ *816-531-7979. 13 rooms.* **$$** Two blocks from the heart of town, this urban inn feels like a New England B&B. From its cozy Mary Atkins Room, named for a teacher, to the Stover Suite, with a private deck and cannonball bed dedicated to the chocolatier, guests are guaranteed quaint, vintage Americana and gourmet breakfasts.

Redick Plaza Hotel – *1504 Harney St., Omaha NE.* ⨂♿ 🅿 ☎ *402-342-1500. 89 rooms.* **$** Built in 1930 and renovated in 1988, the stucco Redick boasts the largest rooms in Omaha. It is convenient to the Old Market area. The **Redick Grill** offers Omaha strip steak, beef tenderloin and shrimp scampi.

Dining in Kansas City and Omaha

The Golden Ox – *1600 Genessee St., Kansas City MO.* ☎ *816-842-2866. www.goldenox.com/ox.* **$$ American.** Hand-cut steaks at this Stockyards classic are charbroiled over hardwood in the middle of the dining room. Old photographs hang on dark wood-paneled walls, and the carpet boasts the branding iron marks of great cattlemen who have passed through.

Hayward's Pit BBQ – *11051 S. Antioch St., Kansas City KS.* ☎ *913-451-8080.* **$$ Barbecue.** Locals have flocked to this hillside spot for 27 years for plates of barbecue, seasoned and smoked with Hayward sauce. You name the meat, they have it: Beef and pork ribs, turkey, sausage and chicken come separately or combined in a variety plate, with fries and beans.

Johnny's Café – *4702 S. 27th St., Omaha NE.* ☎ *402-731-4774.* **$$ American.** The red leather-back chairs, dim lighting and large mural of cattle in the 220-seat dining room give the oldest steakhouse in Omaha a sense of cowtown history. The wood beams resemble T-bone steaks. Mounted bull heads watch over crowds scarfing down certified Hereford beef (hand-cut on the premises) and fresh rolls.

KANSAS PRAIRIE

Michelin map 493 K, L 9, 10   Central Standard Time
Tourist Information ☎ 785-296-2009 or www.kansascommerce.com

The producers of *The Wizard of Oz* had it all wrong when they depicted Kansas in black and white. This colorful state may not have towering mountains nor rushing ocean waves, but it has a quiet, primal beauty that sneaks up and captivates one's senses.
Until the invention of the steel plow, this state, like others of the Great Plains, was covered with tall-grass prairie. It was a daunting sight—a quarter-billion acres of dancing grasses, many taller than a mounted horse. White man, of course, eventually conquered the prairie, turning it into Kansas City, Lawrence, Wichita and rich farmland where most of America's wheat and corn are grown. But even today, it's not hard to see why Dorothy left Oz convinced there was "no place like home" in Kansas.

SIGHTS

★★ **Lawrence** – *I-70 & US-59, 31mi west of Kansas City.* ☎ *785-865-4499. www. visitlawrence.com.* This college town of 75,000 is a slice of mid-America. A restored 1889 Union Pacific station serves as the **Lawrence Visitor Center** (*N. 2nd & Locust Sts.*). After viewing a 25min film on local history, visitors wander the nearby downtown **historic district** (*Massachusetts St. from 6th to 11th Sts.*).

Two fine museums share the 1,000-acre University of Kansas campus, founded in 1866. The **Natural History Museum**★ *(Dyche Hall, 14th St. & Jayhawk Blvd.; ☎ 785-864-4450)*, features a continuous diorama of more than 250 mounted mammals. Four floors of exhibits feature fossils, life on the Great Plains, and live snakes, fish and insects. The **Spencer Museum of Art**★ *(1301 Mississippi St.; ☎ 785-864-4710)* has 11 galleries that offer a general overview of world art history, including Asian art and contemporary works.

Topeka – *I-70 & US-75, 56mi west of Kansas City.* ☎ *785-234-1030.* The quiet state capital has a limestone **State House** *(Capitol Sq., 10th St. between Jackson & Harrison Sts.; 785-296-3966)*, built in 1866 in French Renaissance style. Among the broad collection of the **Kansas Museum of History** *(6425 SW 6th St.; ☎ 785-272-8681)* is a restored 19C mission.

★**Eisenhower Center** – *SE 4th & Buckeye Sts., Abilene, 147mi west of Kansas City.* ☎ *785-263-4751.* After viewing a 30min orientation film on Gen. Dwight D. Eisenhower (1890-1969), World War II hero and former US president, guests may tour Eisenhower's boyhood home. The Eisenhower Museum displays a lifetime of memorabilia; the Presidential Library houses documents and historical materials from DDE's terms of office (1953-61). The Eisenhower family is entombed at the Place of Meditation.

★**Tallgrass Prairie National Preserve** – *Rte. 177, 2mi north of US-50 near Strong City, 127mi southwest of Kansas City.* 🅿 ☎ *316-273-8494.* Established in 1997, this is the only unit of the National Park System preserving the virgin tall-grass ecosystem that once cloaked the Great Plains. The 10,894-acre national preserve has a hiking trail; in summer there's a 7mi interpretive bus tour and tours of a 19C limestone ranch home, a barn and a one-room schoolhouse.

© Dick Detrich

Old Schoolhouse, Tallgrass Prairie National Preserve

Wichita – *I-35 & I-135 at US-400, 183mi southwest of Kansas City.* ☏ *316-265-2800.* Largest city in Kansas with about 330,000 people, Wichita in the 1860s and '70s was a cattle-drive hub on the Chisholm Trail. Its **Old Cow Town Museum** *(1871 Sim Park Dr.;* ☏ *316-264-0671)* preserves 44 buildings from that era. Sculptures by Rodin, Miró and Moore surround the **Ulrich Museum** at Wichita State University *(N. Hillside & 17th Sts.;* ☏ *316-689-3085).*

★★ **Cosmosphere** – Kids *1100 N. Plum St., Hutchinson, 220mi southwest of Kansas City.* ✗ ⟐ 🄿 ☏ *316-662-2305. www.cosmo.org.* An 83ft-tall *Mercury* rocket greets incoming visitors to this Smithsonian affiliate, one of the premier space exhibits in the US. Dozens of rockets and spacecraft are on display. Numerous Russian items recall the US-Soviet "space race." Also here is the command module from the troubled *Apollo 13* mission: Cosmosphere's Spaceworks made 80 percent of the props for the Hollywood movie. An IMAX theater, daily science shows and five-day space camps are also offered.

OMAHA★

Michelin map 491 K, L 8   Central Standard Time
Population 371,291
Tourist Information ☏ 402-444-4660 or www.visitomaha.com

Named for a Siouan tribe whose appellation means "people upstream," Omaha sits on the banks of the Missouri River not quite 200mi north of Kansas City. The city was founded in 1854 and in 1863 was chosen as the eastern terminus of the transcontinental railroad. Today it has 11 museums, 25 stage groups and 36 golf courses; billionaire investor Warren Buffett makes the city his primary residence. When the nation's only richer man, Microsoft's Bill Gates, was shopping for an engagement ring, he flew to Omaha, where Buffett opened one of his holdings—Borsheim's, the world's largest independent jewelry store—just for Gates.
A highlight is the **Old Market** *(Farnam to Jackson, 10th to 13th Sts.;* ☏ *402-341-1877).* Brick streets, horse-drawn carriages and Victorian storefronts mark this restored district of galleries, boutiques, sidewalk cafes and jazz bars.

SIGHTS

★★ **Joslyn Art Museum** – *2200 Dodge St.* ✗ ⟐ 🄿 ☏ *402-342-3300. www.joslyn .org.* This pink-marble fortress is an outstanding example of Art Deco architecture, built by Sarah Joslyn in 1931 as a memorial to her husband. The collection includes works from the ancient world to the present, emphasizing 19-20C European (Degas, Matisse, Monet, Renoir) and American (Cassatt, Homer, Remington, Benton, Wood, Pollock) art. More than 400 Karl Bodmer watercolors document his 1832-34 journey up the Missouri River with Prince Maximilian of Germany. Art lovers may peruse shelves of art books in several of its 17 galleries.

★ **Durham Western Heritage Museum** – *801 S. 10th St.* ⟐ 🄿 ☏ *402-444-5071.* In its heyday, 64 trains and 10,000 people a day passed through this Union Pacific Railroad station. Now restored, it features a waiting room with gold- and silver-leaf trim, 13ft chandeliers and a classic 1931 soda fountain. A stationary five-car train, complete with steam engine, Pullman car, lounge car and caboose, welcomes passengers. Recorded conversations accompany castings of sailors, lovers and other passengers from the 1930s, 40s and 50s, inviting passersby to eavesdrop.

★★ **Omaha's Henry Doorly Zoo** – Kids *3701 S. 10th St.* ✗ ⟐ 🄿 ☏ *402-733-8401. www.omahazoo.com.* Among the unique features of this 110-acre, world-class zoo is an indoor rain forest, an exhibit that pulsates with life from Asia, Africa and South America. Monkeys howl and macaws screech as visitors duck under vines and waterfalls, walk through caves and swing across rope bridges. The **Cat Complex**, featuring lions and rare tigers, is North America's largest. **Scott Aquarium** displays 20,000 species of fish, 8ft-long sharks, puffins and a large colony of penguins.

★ **Boys Town** – Kids *137th St. & W. Dodge Rd., 10mi west of downtown Omaha.* ✗ 🄿 ☏ *402-498-1140.* In 1917, Father Edward Joseph Flanagan borrowed $90 to rent a downtown Omaha boardinghouse as a home for the city's abused, abandoned and disabled boys. The first Christmas, they had nothing but a barrel of sauerkraut to eat. But in 1921, with many success stories under his belt, Father Flanagan purchased Overlook Farm, the 900 acres that make up today's Boys Town. The **Hall of History** exhibits photos, movies, life-size statues and even the Oscar that actor Spencer Tracy won for playing Flanagan in the 1938 movie *Boys Town*. Cassette tapes in English, French, Spanish and German guide visitors around this national historic landmark, where 550 youths still live today.

EXCURSIONS

Lincoln – *I-80 & US-77, 53mi southwest of Omaha.* ☎ *402-434-5335.* Established as Nebraska's capital in 1867, Lincoln's historic center is the **Haymarket** *(7th & P Sts.;* ☎ *402-434-6900)*, a c.1900 warehouse district revitalized by the National Trust for Historic Preservation. The **State Capitol** *(15th & K Sts.;* ☎ *402-471-0448)*, built in 1922-32 (Bertram Goodhue), features a mosaic dome beneath a 400ft tower and a sculpture of Abraham Lincoln by Daniel Chester French.

At the University of Nebraska, the **State Museum**★ *(14th & U Sts.;* ☎ *402-472-2642)* has a superb collection of fossil mammoths and modern elephants, plus gem, natural-history and Native American artifact displays. The **Sheldon Memorial Art Gallery** *(12th & R Sts.;* ☎ *402-472-2461)* focuses on 20C American art, including paintings by Eakins, Hopper, Sargent, O'Keeffe and Rothko.

Homestead National Monument of America – *Rte. 4, 4mi west of Beatrice, 97mi southwest of Omaha.* ☎ *402-223-3514.* This prairie oasis commemorates the 1862 Homestead Act, which helped open the USA West to pioneer settlement. Displays in a visitor center describe life on the plains; an original cabin and school are open for visits, and a 2.5mi nature trail weaves through the prairie grasses.

■ A Gathering of Cranes

From late February through early April, an 80mi stretch of the Platte River in south-central Nebraska attracts the largest gathering of cranes in the world. Some 50,000 sandhill cranes with 6ft wingspans, bright-red topknots and Mick Jagger-like courtship dances gather to mate and fatten themselves on corn kernels and earthworms before flying 3,000mi to Siberia.

The entire bed of the wide, shallow river from Grand Island to Kearney looks like the *Saturday Night Fever* dance floor. Males and females face off, leap into the air, land with their wings spread and bow gracefully. After a couple of leg lifts and neck jabs, they thrust their long bills into the air and bellow lustily.

Visitor centers in Grand Island (☎ 800-658-3178) and Kearney (☎ 800-805-5305) provide information on early-morning crane watches, films, festivals, workshops and photography seminars.

Las Vegas Area

Casino Slot Machines

L as Vegas is the largest and most distinctive resort destination in the world, a 20C boomtown based on gambling, entertainment and recreation. Boosted by a mild winter climate and an advantageous setting along busy Interstate 15 between the Los Angeles area and Salt Lake City, the once-small railroad town staked its future upon the 1931 legalization of gambling by the state of Nevada. It has developed with unprecedented extravagance. Las Vegas now ranks among the prime tourist and convention destinations in the US, and retains one of the fastest growing residential populations of any US city.

Such prosperity is indeed an anomaly in North America's hottest, driest desert, the Mojave *(mo-HAH-vee)*. Remarkable for its lofty mountains, its high plateaus and the lowest elevatiohs in the Western Hemisphere, the Mojave reaches from western Arizona to the Sierra Nevada, fading north to the Great Basin and south into the Colorado and Sonoran Deserts. Too arid for agriculture, it was sparsely populated by nomadic Shoshonean hunters and gatherers, and infrequently crossed by traders and adventurers. The only permanent settlements were along the lower Colorado River, farmed by Yuman-speaking tribes, and in the Muddy River valley, now a Lake Mead tributary. Here Anasazi clans established isolated farms before AD 1000, to be succeeded in the mid-19C by Mormon emigrants.

The US Army created garrisons along the Mojave Road, but the first large settlements followed late-19C discoveries of gold, silver and especially borax. Mining prompted development of railroads and company towns, as handfuls of pioneers built isolated cattle ranches and service businesses for travelers. Vast empty land lured the military to open training grounds and weapons-testing facilities in the mid-20C, including China Lake Naval Weapons Center, Fort Irwin Military Reservation and Nellis Air Force Range. Federal and state governments set aside scenic tracts as parklands, including Death Valley National Park.

The construction of Hoover Dam on the Colorado River in the 1930s, followed by Parker Dam and Davis Dam, revolutionized settlement patterns in the desert by providing cheap hydroelectricity and abundant reservoir water, enabling new communities to sprout and existing towns to prosper. Las Vegas' booming urban tourism has abetted a parallel growth in recreation in the surrounding desert, engendering the passage of the California Desert Protection Act of 1994, which expanded park lands and set aside millions of acres of designated wilderness.

LAS VEGAS★★★

Michelin map 493 C, D 9, 10   Mountain Standard Time
Population 404,288
Tourist Information ☎ 702-892-7575 or www.lasvegas24hours.com

Internationally renowned for its spectacular casinos, lavish resort hotels, world-class entertainment, lax marriage laws and garish bad taste, Las Vegas is without peer or counterpart on the planet. More than 30 million visitors spent $24.6 billion in 1998, and exponential growth continues, with hotel rooms expected to exceed 141,000 by the end of 2000. Dubbed "Lost Wages" by visiting Californians who regularly invest their paychecks at the gaming tables, Las Vegas is attempting to shed its "adults-only" image and promote itself as a family destination.

Historical Notes

Meadows *(vegas)* at which travelers on the Old Spanish Trail made watering stops distinguished the city's humble beginnings. In 1855, Mormon pioneers established the **Mormon Fort** *(908 Las Vegas Blvd. N.; ☎ 702-486-3511)* but abandoned it three years later to ranchers. The San Pedro, Los Angeles & Salt Lake Railroad, later the Union Pacific, planned its route through here in the early 20C, building a train yard at what became Fremont Street and auctioning off 1,200 lots in a single day in May 1905. The town became a rail-transfer point during construction of Hoover Dam *(p 208)*, but its prosperity and future character owed far more to the state's legalization of gambling in 1931.

Gambling clubs grew up along Fremont Street, which acquired the sobriquet "Glitter Gulch" by virtue of the casinos' brilliant signs. Taking advantage of cheaper land and fewer restrictions beyond the city limits, investors in the 1940s began to build new casinos along the main highway to Los Angeles, a thoroughfare soon dubbed "The Strip." Although the booming gambling business initially attracted organized crime, alarmed state authorities imposed stiff regulations on the industry, driving many shadier interests to sell out to corporate buyers. Among the most acquisitive was reclusive millionaire Howard Hughes, who started his Las Vegas empire by buying the Desert Inn in 1966, followed by the Sands, Frontier, Castaways, Silver Slipper and Landmark.

Las Vegas casinos grew and prospered through the 1970s, attracting a strictly adult clientele. Part of their appeal was sophisticated entertainment by such acts as Elvis Presley, Nat King Cole, Liberace, Jackie Gleason, Jimmy Durante, Frank Sinatra, Sammy Davis Jr., and Dean Martin. By the 1980s, however, pressure to compete with new gaming venues in Atlantic City, New Jersey, and other places prompted owners to focus on casino resorts that catered to families. The trend through the 1990s has produced a plethora of remarkable resorts that offer shows and gambling for adults, but also amusement parks, simulation rides, game arcades and special-effects shows for minors.

SIGHTS

★★ **Fremont Street Experience** – *Fremont St. between Main St. & Las Vegas Blvd.* ☎ *702-678-5777. www.vegasexperience.com.* Suspended 90ft over downtown, a barrel-arched canopy jolts to life several times nightly. The illuminated extravaganza of flashing, rolling images is generated by more than 2 million fiber-optic lights and synchronized to music from a 540,000-watt sound system. Created by a consortium of 11 casinos, the attraction was designed to rejuvenate tourism along five blocks that have been a principal thoroughfare since 1905.

Until eclipsed in the 1960s by Strip developments, Fremont Street was the first focus of Vegas' gaming industry. Patrons were enticed to clubs and casinos like Fitzgerald's, the Four Queens, Jack Gaughan's, the Lady Luck, the Golden Nugget and Benny Binion's **Horseshoe Club.** Illuminated marquees and neon signs were so colossal and flashy that the street was universally known as **Glitter Gulch.** A 60ft-tall talking cowboy, **Vegas Vic★★**, has been an icon since 1951.

★★★ **The Strip** – *2000-4000 blocks of Las Vegas Blvd. S.* This 4.5mi stretch of urban highway—extending from the Stratosphere in the north to Mandalay Bay Resort in the south—embraces Las Vegas' greatest concentration of resorts and casinos, and its most sensational architecture and street-side displays.

When casinos first boomed on Fremont Street, The Strip was a stretch of vacant highway. In 1941, seeking to avoid taxes and restrictions on buildings within city limits, Thomas Hull chose a lonely site to build El Rancho Vegas. Later that year, Guy McAfee—who coined the reference to "The Strip"—opened The Last Frontier. In 1946, Benjamin "Bugsy" Siegel's Flamingo Hotel

■ Strip Casinos

★★ Bellagio, The Resort – *3600 Las Vegas Blvd. S.* ✕⌖ 🅿 ☎ *702-693-7111. www.bellagiolasvegas.com.* An eight-acre lake, scene of twice-hourly **light and fountain shows★★**, graces the foreground of this opulent complex, designed to recall a village on Italy's Lake Como. From a conservatory, visitors may enter the **Bellagio Gallery of Fine Art★★**, a collection of master-pieces by Rembrandt, Van Gogh, Matisse, Manet, Degas, Gauguin, Picasso, Miró and others. Famed for its restaurants, the resort will not admit minors who are not hotel guests.

★★ Caesar's Palace – *3570 Las Vegas Blvd. S.* ✕⌖ 🅿 ☎ *702-731-7110. www.caesars.com/palace/win.* Imperial Rome sets the theme for this vast complex, adorned with majestic fountains and marble statues including a copy of Michelangelo's *David*. The **Forum Shops★★★**, a sumptuous mall in the form of a splendid Roman street, have a sky-like ceiling bedecked with drifting clouds and illuminated to simulate passing days and nights.

★ Circus Circus – *2880 Las Vegas Blvd. S.* ✕⌖ 🅿 ☎ *800-444-2472. www.circus-circus.com.* Famed for the live trapeze artists and tightrope walkers beneath the "Big Top" of the main casino, this enormous circus-themed casino entertains younger guests with indoor roller coasters, water rides, a bungee-cord trampoline, laser tag and other amusements in the five-acre **Adventuredome.**

The Desert Inn Resort – *3145 Las Vegas Blvd. S.* ✕⌖ 🅿 ☎ *702-733-4444. www.thedesertinn.com.* The understated glamour of Palm Beach architecture, complete with pools and lagoons, appeals to guests who shun flashier casinos. Golfers enjoy the only fairway on the Strip, a golf course that hosted the Tournament of Champions from 1953 to 1966.

★ Excalibur – *3850 Las Vegas Blvd. S.* ✕⌖ 🅿 ☎ *702-597-7700. www.excalibur-casino.com.* This sprawling complex suggests a castle bris-tling with battlements, ramparts and bailey towers, from which an auto-mated Merlin periodically emerges to wage magical battle against a mechanical dragon. Keeping with the Camelot theme, the hotel shopping mall is a Medieval village with wandering minstrels. Visitors who enter **King Arthur's Arena** may witness jousting knights, acrobats, fireworks and other sensational entertainment.

Imperial Palace Hotel & Casino – *3535 Las Vegas Blvd. S.* ✕⌖ 🅿 ☎ *702-731-3311. www.imperialpalace.com.* The **Antique & Classic Auto Collection★** dis-plays 200 of a collection of 750 cars, motorcycles and trucks—among them Jack Benny's 1910 Maxwell, Marilyn Monroe's 1955 Lincoln Capri, Elvis Presley's 1976 Cadillac El Dorado, and several Model J Duesenbergs. In the nightly **Legends in Concert** show, entertainers offer uncanny impersonations of Presley, Madonna and other stars.

★★★ Luxor – *3900 Las Vegas Blvd. S.* ✕⌖ 🅿 ☎ *702-262-4000. www.luxor.com.* A 10-story **sphinx** stands sentry before this stunning 36-story **pyramid,** clad in 13 acres of bronze-tinted glass. By night a 315,000-watt laser beam—the **Xenon Light★★**—shoots from the apex of the pyramid into the sky, visible up to 250mi. An huge **atrium★★★** is divided into a ground-floor casino and a terrace level of arcades, food court, IMAX the-ater, simulation rides and the **Tomb and Museum of King Tutankhamen★★**, a copy of the original Egyptian tomb and its artifacts. Stacked into the sloping walls, hotel rooms are reached by unique elevators—"inclinators"—that ride through a shaft angled at 39 degrees.

★ Mandalay Bay Resort & Casino – *3950 Las Vegas Blvd. S.* ✕⌖ 🅿 ☎ *702-632-7777. www.mandalaybay.com.* A tropical theme lends ele-gance to a resort noted not only for its restaurants, theater and events center, but for an artificial wave pool and beach at its 11-acre **Lagoon** complex.

★★ MGM Grand – *3799 Las Vegas Blvd. S.* ✕⌖ 🅿 ☎ *702-891-7777. www.mgmgrand.com.* With 5,034 guest rooms, the world's largest hotel reflects a Hollywood theme in its shops and decor. The principal attraction for youngsters is the attached amusement park, **MGM Grand Adventures★**, which offers shows, food concessions and rides—most remarkably the **Sky-Screamer,** which drops a harnessed rider at 70mph from a 22-story arch.

The Mirage – *3400 Las Vegas Blvd. S.* ✗ Ᏸ 🅿 ☏ *702-791-7111. www.themirage.com.* South Seas flair is bolstered by a tropical "island" embellished by lagoons, waterfalls and a **volcano** that spews fire, smoke and burning coconut-scented oil. Behind the hotel are dolphin pools and a zoo enclosure. The **Secret Garden of Siegfried & Roy*** houses white tigers and other exotic animals appearing in the popular entertainers' nightly magic show (☏ *702-792-7777*).

Monte Carlo Resort & Casino – *3770 Las Vegas Blvd. S.* ✗ Ᏸ 🅿 ☏ *702-730-7777. www.monte-carlo.com.* Patterned after Monaco's Palais du Casino, this elegant hotel sports its own microbrewery and cultivates adult patronage. **Magician Lance Burton*** performs in a theater designed especially for his illusions.

New York-New York Hotel & Casino – *3790 Las Vegas Blvd. S.* ✗ Ᏸ 🅿 ☏ *702-740-6969. www.nynyhotelcasino.com.* This building simulates the Manhattan skyline with 12 apparently distinct skyscrapers, including a 47-story version of the **Empire State Building**. The street-level facade is a tableaux of other familiar New York structures, including a 300ft-long **Brooklyn Bridge and a 150ft-tall **Statue of Liberty****. Fire boats spray over New York Harbor; inside, "street" furnishings include fire hydrants and steaming manhole covers. The casino is ensconced in a pastiche of Central Park. The **Manhattan Express** roller coaster dips through the ceiling en route to its 144ft plunge at 67mph; passengers board at **Coney Island Emporium***, an arcade and boardwalk.

Paris Las Vegas – *3655 Las Vegas Blvd. S.* ✗ Ᏸ 🅿 ☏ *702-946-7000. www.paris-lv.com* Towering over scaled down likenesses of the **Arc de Triomphe, **L'Opéra**, the Champs-Elysées and a Parisian marketplace is a 50-story replica of the **Eiffel Tower****, sporting an observation deck reached by glass elevators. The casino is set amid old Paris streets complete with cobblestones and street lamps.

*Stratosphere – *2000 Las Vegas Blvd. S.* ✗ Ᏸ 🅿 ☏ *702-380-7777. www.stratlv.com.* This 1,149ft tower is a pedestal capped by a 12-story "pod." Four double-deck elevators ascend from the ground-floor casino to the **observation deck** in 30 seconds; **views**** are tremendous. The **High Roller** (coaster) loops giddily around the outside of the pod, while riders of the **Big Shot** ascend 160ft up the building's needle-like mast before free-falling back to the pod with a force four times that of gravity.

Treasure Island at the Mirage – *3300 Las Vegas Blvd. S.* ✗ Ᏸ 🅿 ☏ *702-894-7111.www.treasureisland .com.* In keeping with a buccaneer theme, a well-orchestrated **battle show** between a pirate ship, *Hispaniola*, and a British man-o'-war, *H.M.S. Britannia*—with pyrotechnics and swashbuckling sailors—blasts away periodically in a "Caribbean lagoon" outside the entrance. **Mystère*** (☏ *702-894-7722*), a Cirque de Soleil fantasy, plays twice nightly within.

Showgirl, *Folies-Bergères*

© Robert Holmes

Tropicana Resort & Casino – *3801 Las Vegas Blvd. S.* ✗ Ᏸ 🅿 ☏ *702-739-2222. www.tropicanalv.com.* Noted for the 4,000sq ft **stained-glass ceiling** that curves over the main casino floor, the Tropicana is home to the classic Parisian revue, the **Folies-Bergère***.

The Venetian – *3355 Las Vegas Blvd. S.* ✗ Ᏸ 🅿 ☏ *702-414-1000. www.venetian.com.* An engaging imitation of Venice, Italy, the resort features architectural replicas of the **Doge's Palace, **St. Mark's Square**, the **Campanile** and **Rialto Bridge**. Singing gondoliers pole vessels along the replicated **Grand Canal****, lined by a faux-15C street of shops and restaurants. **Madame Tussaud's*** portrays in wax more than 100 celebrities from sports, film and entertainment

became only the third Strip resort, but ultimately established the upscale tone that set it apart from more conservative downtown casinos. By the 1960s, scores of flashy new casinos and resorts were displacing the downtown venues as visitor favorites. That trend has accelerated. The Strip today is undisputedly the premier attraction of Las Vegas—and, indeed, a prime focus of world tourism.

Nine of the 10 largest US hotels at the turn of the 21C occupied sites along the Strip and its intersecting blocks. The enormous scale of these properties, long a discouragement to pedestrians, has been ameliorated with a growing network

ADDRESS BOOK

Please see explanation on p 64.

Staying in Las Vegas

Also see "Strip Casinos," in this chapter.

Four Seasons Hotel Las Vegas – *3960 Las Vegas Blvd. S.* ✗ & 🅿 ⚓ ☎ *702-632-5000. www.fourseasons.com. 424 rooms.* **$$$$** Hidden behind the glass tower of the Mandalay Bay Resort & Casino is this quiet, elegant retreat from glitter. This non-gaming hotel combines spacious rooms with superb restaurants and an intimate spa. Every element is sublime, from misting devices around the pool to chilled caviar in the **First Floor Grill**, the fine dining restaurant.

The Resort at Summerlin – *221 N. Rampart Blvd.* ✗ & 🅿 ⚓ ☎ *702-869-7777. www.resortatsummmerlin.com. 541 rooms.* **$$$$** Red Rock Canyon forms the backdrop to this sophisticated golf and spa resort. The Regent Grand Spa features a relaxed Southwest setting with world-class water-and-sun treatments. The marble-flanked Regent Grand Palms course is a golfer's dream.

Dining in Las Vegas

Aqua – *3600 Las Vegas Blvd. S. at Bellagio, The Resort.* ☎ *702-693-7223.* **$$$$ Seafood.** Long a San Francisco favorite, the new Aqua stays true to the original's seafood theme. Diners may savor tuna tartare with raw quail egg, toasted pine nuts and garlic; or pan-seared Dover sole with mango-infused basmati rice. Aqua showcases two original paintings by modern artist Robert Rauschenberg.

Aureole – *3950 Las Vegas Blvd. S. at the Mandalay Bay Resort & Casino.* ☎ *702-632-7401.* **$$$$ Creative American.** This high-tech restaurant boasts a four-story, glass-enclosed wine tower crawling with human "wine angels" who retrieve diners' selections from among 10,000 bottles. Also top shelf is the food, such as fruit-wood-grilled salmon with sage ratatouille and fennel, or citrus-braised lobster.

Delmonico Steak House – *3355 Las Vegas Blvd. S. at The Venetian.* ☎ *702-414-3737.* **$$$$ American.** Not a typical steakhouse, this bright, airy restaurant offers an updated version of the dining experience at Emeril Lagasse's famed New Orleans eatery. Diners may relax in the piano bar after chateaubriand for two, or try a double-cut pork chop with caramelized sweet potatoes and tamarind glaze.

Le Cirque – *3600 Las Vegas Blvd. S. at Bellagio, The Resort.* ☎ *702-693-8100.* **$$$$ Continental.** With real monkeys climbing the walls, life is a circus at Le Cirque, perhaps the most exclusive dining venue in Las Vegas. The colorful decor doesn't detract from the serious food. The signature dish is braised rabbit in Riesling with morel mushrooms; leg of lamb (for two) is rolled in garlic, rosemary and thyme.

Piero's Restaurant – *355 Convention Center Dr.* ☎ *702-369-2305.* **$$$ American.** Locals love this celebrity magnet-an old-time Vegas place with tiger-print carpeting and a lively bar crowd. Delicious stone-crab claws and mixed-grill items are served at booths lining the walls. Mick Jagger may strut by just as Frank Sinatra once did.

of elevated walkways and free monorail service between selected casinos. A public conveyance, **The Strip Trolley** *(☎ 702-382-1404)*, makes stops at all major Strip casinos and a detour to the Las Vegas Convention Center.

Liberace Museum – *1775 E. Tropicana Ave.* ♿ 🅿 ☎ *702-798-5595. www.liberace.org.* Filled with flamboyant costumes, ostentatious automobiles and ornate pianos once owned by concert pianist Wladziu Valentino Liberace (1919-87), this museum is a monument to the quintessential Las Vegas showman.

*Nevada State Museum – *700 Twin Lakes Dr.* ☎ *702-486-5205.* Devoted to the history, flora and fauna of Las Vegas and environs, this museum is a fine starting point for exploring nearby deserts and mountains. Displays include plaster-cast Ice Age skeletons of a mammoth and ground sloth, and specimens of modern fauna. Historical exhibits acknowledge Native Americans, Mormon ranchers and gamblers, as well as railroads, Hoover Dam and atomic testing.

EXCURSIONS

**Red Rock Canyon – *W. Charleston Blvd. (Rte. 159), 17mi west of Las Vegas.* ⛺♿🅿 ☎ *702-363-1921. www.redrockcanyon.blm.gov.* A stunning escarpment of banded white, red and gray rock, 20mi long and 3,000ft high, represents the western extent of the Navajo Sandstone Formation prevalent in the Colorado Plateau. It was formed 180 million years ago of sand dunes cemented and tinted by water acting on iron oxide and calcium carbonate.

With more than 30mi of trails, a **visitor center*** and many boulders and sheer walls popular among rock climbers, the 300sq-mi **Red Rock Canyon National Conservation Area**** preserves the northern end of the formation. Among highlights along a 13mi loop road are the old **Sandstone Quarry****, where blocks of red-and-white rock were mined from 1905 to 1912, and the adjacent **Calico Hills***. Hikers explore ancient petroglyphs at **Willow Spring** or escape desert heat via the **Ice Box Canyon Trail*** *(2.5mi round-trip)* into a steep, narrow canyon.

The more recent history of the canyon is preserved at the 528-acre **Spring Mountain Ranch State Park*** *(Rte. 159, Blue Diamond; ☎ 702-875-4141)*, dating from 1876. The ranch was once owned by German actress Vera Krupp and purchased in 1967 by reclusive financier Howard Hughes. A re-created ghost town called **Old Nevada*** *(Rte. 159, Bonnie Springs; ☎ 702-875-4191)* has partly transformed another pioneer ranch. A saloon, restaurant, wax museum, church and other buildings along the dusty main street serve as backdrops for mock shootouts and melodramas.

*Spring Mountains National Recreation Area – *Rtes. 156, 157 & 158, 35mi northwest of Las Vegas.* ⛺♿🅿 ☎ *702-873-8800. www.fs.fed.us/htnf.* A biologically unique island surrounded by the Mojave Desert, Mount Charleston (11,918ft) and other peaks of this 494sq-mi Toiyabe National Forest preserve are home to 23 species found nowhere else, including Palmer's chipmunks. The Spring Mountains are a haven for deer, elk, mountain lions, wild horses and

© Claire Curran

Red Rock Canyon

bighorn sheep. Skiers throng to **Las Vegas Ski and Snowboard Resort** *(Rte. 156)* each winter, while mild summer temperatures draw motorists to enjoy 11 campgrounds and the **Mount Charleston Hotel** *(☎ 702-872-5500)*.

Among hiking trails in the Mount Charleston Wilderness, the **South Loop Trail** *(8.3mi)* climbs to the range's summit from the head of Kyle Canyon Road *(Rte. 157)*. Linking the Kyle and Lee Canyons, the 9mi Deer Creek Road *(Rte. 158)* offers access to **Desert View Trail** *(.1mi)* where views north into the Nevada Test Site range once attracted crowds to witness atomic-bomb tests in 1952-62.

* **Desert National Wildlife Range** – *Mormon Well Rd., 31mi north of Las Vegas off US-95.* △ ☎ *702-646-3401.* The largest US wildlife sanctuary outside of Alaska protects 2,200sq mi of mountainous habitat favored by desert bighorn sheep, Nevada's state mammal. Unpaved roads, suitable for four-wheel-drive vehicles, probe the remote Mojave and Great Basin Desert backcountry. Travel is restricted to designated roads, however, and no all-terrain vehicles are permitted. Information and maps are available from the **Corn Creek Field Station**, a historic oasis that once served as an Indian camp, stagecoach stop and ranch.

LAKE MEAD AREA★

Michelin map 493 D 9, 10   Mountain Standard Time
Tourist Information ☎ 702-293-8907 or www.nps.gov/lame

North America's largest, deepest reservoir is a deep-blue desert lake that adds more than 700mi of shoreline to the Nevada-Arizona border. Created in 1936 on the Colorado River with the construction of the Hoover Dam, highest dam in the Western Hemisphere, Lake Mead has become a recreational showpiece, bringing boating, waterskiing, fishing and other water sports to an arid land. Small resort towns like Laughlin—and, further south in Arizona, Lake Havasu City—have sprung up downstream of Lake Mead in the late 20C.

The region's history, however, goes back far before the 20C. Colonies of Anasazi Indians farmed the fertile valley of the Muddy River, near Overton, as early as AD 800. Their Paiute successors were working the bottomlands when Mormon settlers arrived in the mid-19C. Preceding all of them was the fabulous hand of nature, which sculpted desert landscapes best seen at Valley of Fire State Park.

SIGHTS

* **Clark County Museum** – *1830 S. Boulder Hwy., Henderson, 15mi southeast of Las Vegas.* ㋐ ▣ ☎ *702-455-7955. www.co.clark.nv.us.* This large, pueblo-style exhibit hall highlights southern Nevada history with dioramas of Pleistocene animals, an Anasazi pueblo, Colorado River steamboating, mining and gambling. Outside, on **Heritage Street**★★, are such relocated buildings as a c.1900 desert mining settlement and the 1931 Boulder City rail depot.

* **Boulder City** – *US-93, 25mi southeast of Las Vegas.* ☎ *702-293-2034. www.bouldercitychamber.com.* Tidy and green, Boulder City is the only gambling-free community in Nevada. Constructed in 1931 for 8,000 dam workers, it was the first US city built according to Community Planning Movement principles, integrating social planning into physical design. Saco Reink DeBoer designed greenbelts, schools, parks and separate zones for residential, business, government and industrial uses. The city now has 15,000 residents; its national historic district encourages pedestrian use with shady arcades and Southwest-Art Deco architecture, although the prominent 1933 **Boulder Dam Hotel**★ *(1305 Arizona St.; ☎ 702-293-3510)* strays from the plan with its Colonial Revival facade. The two-story hotel also houses the **Hoover Dam Museum**★ *(☎ 702-294-1988)*, where exhibits and a film provide background on the physical hardships and social conditions prevailing during the Depression-era construction project.

*** **Hoover Dam** – ▥ *US-93, 31mi southeast of Las Vegas.* ㋐ ▣ ☎ *702-294-3524. www.hooverdam.com.* Stretched like a gargantuan wall across the 800ft-deep Black Canyon of the Colorado River, Hoover Dam is a thoroughly practical and intensely dramatic monument to civil .engineering, an almost unrivaled example of creativity, efficiency and workmanship. Designed, built and operated by the federal Bureau of Reclamation for flood control and to provide water for irrigation, municipal use, electricity and recreation, it was the world's largest hydroelectric dam from its completion in 1936 until 1949. Rising 726.4ft from a 660ft-thick base to a 45ft-wide crest, capable of producing nearly 50 million kilowatt-hours daily from 17 massive generators, Hoover Dam is the primary catalyst behind the population and economic boom of Arizona and Nevada.

Conceived to control devastating floods on the lower Colorado, the dam was first planned for Boulder Canyon, upstream from the present site; it remained known as the Boulder Canyon Project after engineers moved it to Black Canyon. Four tunnels were bored through canyon walls to divert the river; after two cofferdams were built, the construction area was pumped dry and excavated to bedrock. The first concrete was poured in June 1933, the last in 1935, two years ahead of schedule. On completion of the power plant, the dam began operation in October 1936. The project (including Boulder City and a nonadjacent canal) was under budget at a cost of $165 million, but 96 construction workers died on the job.

A multistory parking garage on the Nevada side of the dam (RVs must park on the Arizona side) also supplies a **Visitor Center★**, from which there are sensational **views★★** down the front of the dam and Black Canyon. Video and multimedia presentations focus on the dam's construction; an upstairs gallery is devoted to regional natural history, including a dynamic desert **flash-flood demonstration★**. Visitors may choose between two guided tours of the dam, a shorter sightseeing tour and the more comprehensive **Hard-Hat Tour★★★**.

★**Lake Mead National Recreation Area** – *US-93 & Rte. 166, beginning 27mi east of Las Vegas.* △ ※ ⑤ 🄿 🐾 *702-293-8907. www.nps.gov/lame.* Embracing

Hoover Dam and Lake Mead

two vast reservoirs on the Colorado River, this 2,350sq-mi desert preserve was created in 1936. Although 67mi-long **Lake Mohave**—wich was impounded by Davis Dam in 1950—subsequently became an integral part of the park, the centerpiece remains **Lake Mead**. Named for Elwood Mead, Bureau of Reclamation commissioner when Hoover Dam was built, Lake Mead's cold, blue waters contrast brilliantly with the earthtone bluffs, mountains and plateaus of the surrounding desert. With six large, full-service marinas on Lake Mead, and two on Lake Mohave, the recreation area offers superlative opportunities for boating, fishing, water skiing and houseboating. Miles of remote inlets and coves provide privacy and opportunities for exploration. **Sightseeing cruises** of short duration depart from Lake Mead Marina near Boulder Beach, on the lake's western shore. **River-rafting** day trips from below Hoover Dam to Willow Beach are also popular.

The information source is the **Alan Bible Visitor Center★★** *(Lakeshore Scenic Dr. at Rte. 93, 2mi west of Hoover Dam; ☎ 702-293-8990),* with many interactive exhibits on geology and natural history. The **Northshore Scenic Drive** *(Rte. 167)* offers the most impressive desert views on the Nevada shore, including ruddy-colored sandstone formations around the Redstone Picnic Area, where the gentle **Redstone Trail★** *(.5mi loop)* explores the petrified sand dunes.

★★**Valley of Fire State Park** – *Rte. 169, 55mi northeast of Las Vegas.* ☎ *702-397-2088.* Nevada's oldest state park preserves 35,000 acres of desert scenery, including a half-mile-thick layer of Aztec Sandstone Formation, dyed reddish or leached white by chemical erosion and shaped by wind into arches, fins, knobs, domes, ridges and other odd shapes. From the **visitor center★★**, a 7mi spur road leads to the **White Domes Area★★**, a landscape of multihued monuments and smooth, wind-carved sandstone. The intriguing **Petroglyph Canyon Trail★★** (.8mi round-trip) traverses a narrow canyon to **Mouse's Tank★★**, a natural, water-filled basin where a renegade Paiute hid out in 1897. On the west end of the park, a steep metal stairway climbs up to **Atlatl Rock★**, named for a rare petroglyph of an atlatl, or spear-throwing stick, a weapon that predates the bow and arrow.

★ **Lost City Museum of Archaeology** – *Rte. 169 south of Overton, 63mi northeast of Las Vegas.* ♿ 🅿 ☎ *702-397-2193.* This flat-roofed adobe was built in 1935 to preserve archaeological discoveries. On its hilltop site is a reconstructed Puebloan house atop a genuine **pueblo foundation★**. Exhibits document tools, pottery, weapons and other artifacts of the early Desert Culture of sloth and mammoth hunters, as well as the Anasazi (c.300 BC-AD 1150) and nomadic Paiute (after AD 1000). At their cultural peak around AD 800, the Anasazi expanded to farmlands along the Muddy River, built substantial houses, made pottery, traded and practiced a sophisticated religion.

Laughlin – *Rte. 163, 21mi east of US-95, 96mi south of Las Vegas.* ☎ *702-298-2214. www.laughlinchamber.com.* This rambunctious little resort town lines the Nevada side of the Colorado River downstream from Davis Dam and its reservoir, Lake Mohave. Little more than a bait store, bar and motel in 1966 when casino operator Don Laughlin purchased it, the settlement grew as a friendly alternative to booming Las Vegas. Now with 8,500 residents, it boasts a riverside setting with marinas and water sports. Contrary to Las Vegas, where casinos are loath to divert gamblers' attention from the tables, casinos here often sport big picture windows on the river. Jet-boat tours transport passengers down the Colorado River to Lake Havasu City *(below)*.

EXCURSION

Lake Havasu City – *Rte. 95, 19mi south of I-40, 154mi south of Las Vegas.* ☎ *520-855-4115. www.havasuchamber.com.* Sprawling over the Arizona bank of Lake Havasu, a reservoir created by the Parker Dam in 1938, this resort and retirement town of 41,000 is celebrated as the site of the rebuilt **London Bridge★**. Originally built over England's River Thames in 1824, London Bridge was put up for sale in 1962 when it was found to be sinking under the heavy weight of modern traffic. Lake Havasu City founder Robert McCulloch bought the bridge for less than $2.5 million; dismantled it, numbering each of its granite building stones to mark their position; and shipped it to California. It was then trucked to the Arizona desert and reassembled here in 1971. A collection of faux-Tudor-style shops and restaurants, the **English Village** clusters around its eastern pier.

Zabriskie Point

DEATH VALLEY NATIONAL PARK★★★

Michelin map 493 C 9, 10   Mountain Standard Time
Tourist Information ☎ 760-786-2331 or www.nps.gov/deva

At nearly 5,300sq mi, this sun-blasted expanse of mountain, canyon and playa is the largest national park in the contiguous US. Confronting visitors with vast, silent, stark landscapes unobscured by vegetation or scars of human intrusion, Death Valley is a veritable textbook on geology. The enormous basin—130mi long, 5mi to 25mi wide—formed progressively as a block of the earth's crust sagged and sank between parallel mountain ranges, creating an astounding difference in elevations. Altitudes range from 11,049ft at Telescope Peak to 282ft below sea level near Badwater. The mountains are flanked by alluvial fans, delta-like deposits built up as debris washes out of numerous canyons during flash floods.

It's best to visit between late autumn and early spring, as the relentless summer sun heats the bleak valley to some of the highest temperatures on earth. The 134°F recorded at Furnace Creek has been exceeded only in the Sahara Desert.

Historical Notes – For centuries, the Panamint Shoshone made seasonal hunting and gathering forays into the valley during cooler months, spending summers in higher country. Death Valley proved a formidable obstacle to 19C western migration, acquiring its name after an emigrant party was stranded for weeks searching for a way out in 1849. Prospectors combed surrounding mountains in the late 19C and early 20C, striking isolated pockets of gold and other metals, sparking short-lived mining booms and leaving a heritage of abandoned settlements. Industrial exploitation of borax brought commercial operations, including the 20-mule-team wagons required to haul the white mineral to a distant railhead. Death Valley's isolation was considerably eased in the early 20C by the arrival of a railroad (now abandoned). Organized tourism followed after railroad magnates built the Furnace Creek Inn in 1927.

SIGHTS

Park services and lodgings are concentrated at Furnace Creek, Stovepipe Wells and Panamint Springs. Visitors gather information at the **Death Valley Visitor Center** (*Rte. 190; ☎ 760-786-3244*).

Furnace Creek – *Rtes. 190 & 178, 121mi northwest of Las Vegas*. Death Valley's main concentration of lodging and other facilities clusters around an oasis of date palms, planted in 1924 and still producing fruit. **Furnace Creek Ranch** (*☎ 760-786-2361*) occupies the site of the 1874 Greenland Ranch, built among spring-fed meadows to grow produce for miners and alfalfa hay for their mules. Conversion of the ranch to a winter resort began in the 1930s.

On a hill .5mi east of the ranch, the elegantly appointed **Furnace Creek Inn** (*☎ 760-786-2345*), built in 1927, remains the premier hotel in the park. The vaguely Moorish structure towers over a lush **palm grove★★** watered by Furnace Creek, landscaped with grassy terraces and paths, enchantingly lit by night.

© Ric Ergenbright

*Badwater Road – *Rte. 178 south of Furnace Creek.* Following Death Valley's barely perceptible descent to the lowest point in the Americas, the paved road to Badwater *(36mi round-trip)* traverses a spectacularly bleak, sunken salt pan that sprawls westward to the escarpment of the 11,200ft Panamint Range.

From a small parking area west of the road *(2.5mi from Furnace Creek)*, a gently climbing trail *(2mi round-trip)* winds through the badlands of **Golden Canyon****, cut by flash floods through tilted deposits of an ancient alluvial fan. **Artist's Drive*** *(10mi from Furnace Creek)* winds through the steep foothills of the Amargosa Range, where brilliant hues of red, pink, yellow, green and purple climax at the highly mineralized **Artist's Palette****. A picture of exquisite desolation, the **Devil's Golf Course** surrounds its viewing area *(12mi from Furnace Creek, then 1.3mi west)* with a jagged chaos of low salt pinnacles. Reached by a short hike *(.8mi round-trip)* through a narrow, high-walled canyon in the Amargosas *(accessible by a 1.8mi dirt road, 13.5mi from Furnace Creek)*, the **Natural Bridge*** forms a massive, 35ft arch of rock above the canyon floor.

A shallow pool of alkali water at 279.8ft below sea level, **Badwater*** is virtually the nadir of the Western Hemisphere. In fact, two unmarked points some 3ft lower lie 3.3mi and 4.6mi away on the salt flats. Glance up from Badwater to see a sign marking sea level high on the east wall of the valley.

Zabriskie Point – *Rte. 190, 4.5mi east of Furnace Creek.* Overlooking Golden Canyon on the east, this renowned vista point commands splendid views over a bizarre landscape of multicolored badlands, uplifted and tilted by tectonic movements and eroded by wind and rain. Another 1.2mi east, a 2.9mi scenic drive detours through **20-Mule-Team Canyon, where deposits of high-grade borax were once mined.

Dante's View – *Dante's View Rd., 24mi southeast of Furnace Creek via Rte. 190.* From a 5,475ft perch atop the Amargosa Range on Death Valley's eastern wall, this point presents a stunning **view** of the continent's most extreme elevation contrast.

**Stovepipe Wells Sand Dunes – *Rte. 190, 6mi east of Stovepipe Wells.* The park's most accessible sand dunes pile up in billowing hills, reached either by foot from the highway *(park on the shoulder within sight of the dunes)* or via a turnoff 1mi west of the junction of Route 190 and Scotty's Castle Road.

Titus Canyon Road – *98mi round-trip from Furnace Creek. Take Rte. 190 north to Beatty Cutoff, then to Daylight Pass and Nevada Rte. 374. Road ends at Rte. 190, 34mi north of Furnace Creek.* Among the most memorable drives in the park, this one-lane dirt road traverses a landscape of layered cliffs, peaks of tilted and twisted sediments, and remnants of great volcanic eruptions. From a high point of 5,250ft in the Grapevine Mountains, it winds and squeezes into Death Valley past the ghost town of **Leadfield, which experienced a six-month mining boom in the mid-1920s, and through the **narrows**** of Titus Canyon.

*Scotty's Castle – *Rte. 267, 53mi north of Furnace Creek.* ☎ *760-786-2392.* Begun in 1924, this eclectic, Spanish-Moorish complex of house and grounds was commissioned by Albert Johnson, a Chicago insurance magnate and financial backer of Walter Scott, a charlatan who solicited investments for suspect mining operations. "Death Valley Scotty" earned his keep by spinning yarns and adding local color to Johnson family soirees. Guided tours visit the cavernous **Great Hall**, Scott's bedroom and the lavishly appointed **music room**, with its massive 1,121-pipe theater organ and impressive arched-beam ceiling.

EXCURSION

*Mojave National Preserve – *South of I-15 & Rte. 164, 53mi south of Las Vegas; Baker, California is at Rte. 127 & I-15, 113mi south of Furnace Creek.* ☎ *760-733-4040. www.nps.gov/moja.* This pie-shaped area of some 2,500sq mi embraces a stark landscape of precipitous mountain ranges, dry lake beds, lava mesas, sand dunes, limestone caverns, lava tubes and the nation's largest forest of Joshua trees. It is home to some 700 species of plants and nearly 300 species of animals. Largely undeveloped, the preserve allows livestock grazing to continue under a provision of the California Desert Protection Act.

Paved, two-lane roads conduct motorists to many of the scenic areas, though four-wheel-drive enthusiasts, campers, hikers and mountain bikers may enjoy the backroads. Aside from small stores at Cima and Nipton, there are no services. Visitors may gather maps, books and information from three nearby visitor centers. In Barstow is the **California Desert Information Center** *(831 Barstow Rd.;* ☎ *760-255-8760 or 760-255-8801).* There are two **Mojave Desert Information Centers** *(72157 Baker Blvd., Baker,* ☎ *760-733-4040; also 707 W. Broadway, Needles,* ☎ *760-326-6322).*

* **Kelso Dunes** – *Access on foot from a dirt road that turns off Kelbaker Rd., 7.4mi south of Kelso Station.* Billowing up to 600ft above the floor of the Devils Playground, these 45 acres of sand dunes are among the highest in the Mojave. The sands sometimes emit a low-pitched rumbling as people climb or descend their slopes, a phenomenon caused by rose-quartz sand grains rubbing against each other, creating harmonic vibrations.

** **Hole-in-the-Wall**- *26mi from I-40 via the paved Essex & Black Canyon Rds.* ☎ *760-928-2572.* A jumble of volcanic cliffs profusely pocked with clefts and cavities, Hole-in-the-Wall is one of the more bizarre geologic features of Black Canyon. Created 15-18 million years ago by volcanic activity, crags of rhyolite and ash were pitted by uneven cooling and erosion by wind and rain. From the **visitor center**, a footpath *(2mi round-trip)* leads down narrow, twisting **Banshee Canyon**** by means of iron hoops bolted to the steepest sections of rock.

* **Mitchell Caverns** – *22mi north of I-40 via paved Essex Rd.* ☎ *760-928-2586.* Concealed within the Providence Mountains, six limestone caverns were formed by percolating groundwater millions of years ago. **Tours** through the 65°F chambers reveal dripstone and flowstone, including cave shields, "lily pads" and coral pipes. The steep, rugged **Crystal Springs Trail** *(2mi)* introduces hikers to the cacti, wildflowers and piñon forests of these desert mountains.

Los Angeles Area

Skaters, Venice Beach

Filling a vast coastal plain framed by towering mountains, this sprawling, sun-drenched megalopolis is the largest metropolitan area in the US, a collection of once-distinct cities and towns that have grown together. Its enviable climate, its role as an international entertainment center and its remarkable ethnic and cultural diversity contribute to a heady mix of sights and experiences with an ambience so casual that locals refer to their home merely by initials: "L.A."

Greater Los Angeles spills beyond the Los Angeles Basin, a mostly flat plain that runs inland from the Pacific Ocean to the uplands. Skirting the basin to the northwest are the Santa Monica Mountains, which rise from the sea at Oxnard, 70mi northwest of downtown L.A., and create the higher elevations of Beverly Hills, Hollywood and Griffith Park. Other ranges run northeast and southeast.

These mountains are at once a delight and a scourge. They are reminders of geological stress frequently manifested in **earthquakes** and form a natural barrier for **smog**—smoke, automotive exhaust and industrial pollutants transformed by sunlight into a corrosive layer of airborne sludge. Though strict laws have improved air quality in recent years, smog remains oppressive on hot summer days. But pollution is not a uniquely modern issue. Explorer Juan Rodríguez Cabrillo, sailing past the Los Angeles Basin in 1542, was sufficiently moved by the hazy pall from Indian campfires to name it "the Bay of Smokes."

Today the city of Los Angeles covers more than 467sq mi. Almost 10 times that area is embraced by L.A. County, and the metropolitan area stretches to some 34,000sq mi. About 80 incorporated cities are within the county, many completely surrounded by the city of L.A. Population of the city exceeds 3.5 million, county 9.4 million, metropolitan area 13.5 million.

Distinct cities like Santa Monica, Pasadena and Long Beach are part and parcel of Los Angeles County. Adjacent Orange County, home of Disneyland, is within the metropolitan area. Palm Springs and Santa Barbara are farther afield, but both cities are within a two-hour (when traffic permits) drive of downtown L.A., and both are very much a part of the Southern California experience.

214

LOS ANGELES★★★

Map pp 220-221   Pacific Standard Time
Population 3,597,556
Tourist Information ☎ 213-689-8822 or www.lacvb.com

Los Angeles enjoys the benefits and faces the challenges of a major metropolis, though both the pros and cons of life in the city are magnified by its enormous size and its near-mythic reputation. The city's ethnic diversity endows it with rich cultural resources and can make a drive across town seem like a dizzying world tour. In 1990 the population of L.A. County was 49.7 percent Caucasian, 32.9 percent Latino, 8.8 percent Asian and 8 percent African American.

Historical Notes

Anthropologists estimate that 5,000 Gabrieleño Indians lived in this area before the first Spanish colonizing expedition in 1769. The mission town (1781) was named El Pueblo de Nuestra Señora la Reina de Los Angeles de Porciúncula, "The Town of Our Lady the Queen of the Angels by the Porciúncula (River)," later shortened to Los Angeles. By the time the dusty town was designated capital of Mexican California in 1845, it had become the commercial and social center for a region of vast cattle ranches and vineyards.

After the city passed into American hands, the advent of the railroad promoted a population boom. Images of a sun-kissed good life helped create communities like Hollywood, and by 1900 Los Angeles was home to more than 100,000. L.A.'s reputation was further enhanced by the **citrus industry**, as vast orange groves were planted to meet rising nationwide demand for the fruit. Growth, however, was severely limited by a lack of water. To meet this need, the $24.5 million **Los Angeles Aqueduct** opened in 1913, its waters coursing through 142 separate mountain tunnels. Although the controversial project ruined the livelihoods of many farmers, it enabled unprecedented growth for L.A., which soon incorporated the neighboring cities of Beverly Hills, Santa Monica, Long Beach and Pasadena.

The early 20C brought the fledgling motion-picture industry from New York and Chicago to Southern California, whose varied locations and consistently gentle climate encouraging outdoor filming. The studios settled in and around Hollywood. By 1920, 80 percent of the world's feature films were being produced in California, and by the mid-20C, Hollywood's film industry employed more than 20,000 people. Movie stars bought homes in the hills of Hollywood and nearby Beverly Hills, gradually infusing these communities with an aura of fantasy.

After World War II, the halcyon days of the Eisenhower era encouraged still more Americans to head west in search of fortune. Orange groves gave way to housing tracts as population grew. By 1960 more than 6 million people lived in Los Angeles County. The city is still healing from devastating racial riots in 1965 and 1992, yet the efforts of individuals and local and federal organizations are bearing fruit. Groups such as the **Los Angeles Conservancy** dedicate themselves to preserving historic architecture, from the Art Deco masterpieces of Wilshire Boulevard to residences by such architects as Frank Lloyd Wright, Rudolf Schindler and Richard Neutra. The city hosted the **Summer Olympic Games** in 1932 and 1984, and its unquenchable dynamism attracts a variety of international visitors and events.

★DOWNTOWN LOS ANGELES

★El Pueblo de Los Angeles Historic Monument – *Roughly bounded by Arcadia, N. Spring, Macy & N. Alameda Sts.* ✗ ♿ ☎ *213-628-1274.* The city's historic heart is a 44-acre cluster of 27 early-19C buildings. The village was restored as a Mexican marketplace between 1926 and 1930. Shops and wooden stalls along brick-paved **Olvera Street★**, a pedestrian way, sell an assortment of crafts, clothing and food. A zigzag pattern in the pavement marks the path of the city's first water system (1781). The oldest house in Los Angeles, the one-story **Avila Adobe★** *(E-11 Olvera St.),* was built in 1818. The nearby **Sepulveda House** *(W-12 Olvera St.),* a two-story Victorian (1887), blends Mexican and Anglo influences.

The Plaza *(Olvera St. between Main & Los Angeles Sts.)* has occupied its site since about 1825; on its west side is **Our Lady Queen of the Angels Catholic Church** *(535 N. Main St.),* built in 1822 and popularly known as Old Plaza Church.

Union Station – *800 N. Alameda St. opposite El Pueblo.* ☎ *213-683-6875.* A $13 million combined venture of the Southern Pacific, Union Pacific and Santa Fe Railroads (1939, Parkinson & Parkinson), this building gracefully blends Mission Revival, Spanish Colonial, Moorish and Art Deco styles. It is the last of the grand train stations built in the US during the heyday of rail travel.

Chinatown – *Roughly bounded by Sunset Blvd. and Alameda, Bernard & Yale Sts.* This small (15 sq-block) district serves as one of two main centers for the city's residents of Chinese descent. A pagoda-style gateway *(900 block of N. Broadway)* marks the entrance to **Gin Ling Way**; chinoiserie-embellished buildings line this original pedestrian precinct. Herbalists, curio shops and discount stores attract shoppers. The area is well-known for its restaurants.

Little Tokyo – *Roughly bounded by E. 1st, E. 3rd, Los Angeles & Alameda Sts.* Japanese immigrants in late-19C Los Angeles congregated in the area preserved as the **Little Tokyo Historic District** *(1st St. between San Pedro St. & Central Ave.)*. Today, the **Japanese American Cultural and Community Center** *(244 S. San Pedro St.; ☎ 213-628-2725)* and Japan America Theatre host community events. Adjacent is the **James Irvine Garden★**, an 8,500sq-ft garden designed in traditional style by Takeo Uesugi. Overlooking the garden is a brick sculpture plaza designed by L.A. native and internationally acclaimed artist **Isamu Noguchi** (1904-88).

★ **Japanese American National Museum** – *369 E. 1st St.* ✗& ☎ *213-625-0414. www.janm.org.* America's first museum dedicated to Japanese-American history occupies the former Nishi Hongwanji Buddhist Temple (1925) and a new Pavilion (1998), linked by a plaza with a stone-and-water garden.

Civic Center Area – *Roughly bounded by W. 1st, Hope, Temple & Los Angeles Sts.* The largest center for municipal administration in the US, this group of buildings and open plazas, planned and erected between the 1920s and the 1960s, occupies 13 blocks. The random array of structures ranges in style from the monu-

ADDRESS BOOK

Please see explanation on p 64.

Staying in the Los Angeles Area

Hotel Bel-Air – *701 Stone Canyon Rd., Bel Air, Los Angeles CA.* ✗& 🅿 🏊 ☎ *310-472-1211. www.hotelbelair.com. 92 rooms.* $$$$ Ranked among the world's finest hotels, these 12 acres of lush gardens and waterfalls are like a luxurious private estate, hidden from the city near Westwood. Accommodations are in soft pink, Mission-style, tile-floored bungalows. The restaurant serves award-winning cuisine on a bougainvillea-covered terrace.

Ritz Carlton Laguna Niguel – *1 Ritz Carlton Dr., Dana Point CA.* ✗& 🅿 🏊 ☎ *949-240-2000. www.ritzcarltonlagunaniguel.com. 313 rooms.* $$$$ Just south of the seaside enclave of Laguna Beach, this grand hotel perches on a hill above a fine beach and surfers' haven. Inside are crystal chandeliers and tapestry fabrics, oceanfront rooms and restaurants.

Shutters – *1 Pico Blvd., Santa Monica CA.* ✗& 🅿 🏊 ☎ *310-458-0030. www.shuttersonthebeach.com. 198 rooms.* $$$$ A beachside-cottage feel belies the stylish service and dining behind the white shuttered windows. Cozy provincial furnishings line the lobby's piano bar. Guests relax by the pool, in the spa, and over dinner at the award-winning **One Pico** restaurant.

Artists' Inn Bed and Breakfast – *1038 Magnolia St., South Pasadena CA.* 🅿 ☎ *626-799-5668. www.artistsinns.com. 9 rooms.* $$ Each room in this Victorian home reflects a different artist or period—the Gauguin takes guests to Tahiti with a bamboo bed, while bright colors in the Expressionist recall Matisse. Homemade muffins are served on the large front porch overlooking 100 rose bushes.

Hotel Figueroa – *939 S. Figueroa St., Los Angeles CA.* ✗& 🅿 🏊 ☎ *213-627-8971. 285 rooms.* $ This exotic downtown hotel feels like an enclave of Morocco or the Middle East. The arched terra-cotta entrance leads to a lobby of cacti and Spanish tiles, and the pool is surrounded by a lavish garden. The unique Casablanca Suite is painted dark sienna, with mint ceilings and iron lanterns.

The Willows Historic Palm Springs Inn – *412 W. Tahquitz Canyon Way, Palm Springs CA.* & 🅿 🏊 ☎ *760-320-0771. www.thewillowspalmsprings .com. 8 rooms.* $$$$ In a town of new resorts and chain hotels, The Willows stands out. It is a striking Mediterranean villa in Old Palm Springs

mental **Hall of Justice Building** (1925), with its Neoclassical details *(northeast corner of S. Broadway & W. Temple St.)*, to the contemporary structures of the Music Center.

★★ **Los Angeles City Hall** – *200 N. Spring St.* ☎ *213-485-2891*. City Hall's 28-story, pyramid-topped 454ft tower (1928) remains one of downtown L.A.'s most distinctive features and most widely recognized symbols. The 135ft-wide **rotunda**★ reveals French limestone walls and a floor composed of 4,156 inlays cut from 46 varieties of marble. The **observation deck** Kids in the tower *(27th floor)* affords sweeping **panoramas**★★ of the Los Angeles Basin. *Note: Building is closed for seismic retrofitting; scheduled re-opening 2002.*

★ **Music Center of Los Angeles County** – *North of 1st St. between Hope & Grand Aves.* Los Angeles' elegant hilltop mecca for the performing arts (1964, Welton Becket) comprises three white marble structures occupying a seven-acre plaza. Largest and most opulent building in the $34.5 million complex is the 3,197-seat **Dorothy Chandler Pavilion**★ (1964); this imposing composition of towering windows and columns hosts music, opera and dance productions and the annual Academy Awards presentation *(late March)*. Innovative dramatic works are presented at the 752-seat **Mark Taper Forum** (1967), a low, cylindrical structure framed by a reflecting pool and a detached colonnade. The rectilinear 2,071-seat **Ahmanson Theatre** (1967) hosts plays, musicals, dance concerts and individual performing artists. The proposed $170 million, Frank Gehry-designed **Walt Disney Concert Hall** is planned for a site directly across 1st Street from the Center.

★★ **Business District** – *Roughly bounded by Figueroa, 2nd, Spring & 9th Sts.* Anchored by Broadway and Spring Street, Los Angeles' historic business center reveals Beaux-Arts and Art Deco buildings dating primarily from 1890-1930;

Village, with frescoed ceilings and balconies, a waterfall and a backdrop of Mount Jacinto. Rooms feature claw-foot tubs, slate floors and garden patios.

The Venice Beach House – *15 30th Ave., Venice, Los Angeles CA.* ▣ ☎ *310-823-1966. 9 rooms.* **$** With a picket fence and garden, this charming bed-and-breakfast inn recalls the early-20C days of its beach community's founding as an Italian-style artists' community. Some rooms have private entrances; others have cathedral ceilings or rocking chairs.

Dining in the Los Angeles Area

Spago – *176 N. Cañon Dr., Beverly Hills CA.* ☎ *310-385-0880.* **$$$$ European.** Celebrity chef Wolfgang Puck draws a glamorous Hollywood crowd to feast on his "designer pizzas," risottos, fish and duck, or Austrian classics like wiener schnitzel. This super chic restaurant has walls painted in amethyst, green and amber and an exhibition kitchen that started the trend of food as entertainment.

Citronelle – *In the Santa Barbara Inn, 901 E. Cabrillo Blvd., Santa Barbara CA.* ☎ *805-969-2261.* **$$$ California.** With 180-degree beachfront views, a blue and gold interior and a glass-front wine room, the third-floor Citronelle provides a worthy backdrop for its ultra-gourmet blend of France and California. Diners may start with porcupine shrimp, then move on to Chilean sea bass with black trumpet mushroom powder.

Georgia – *7250 Melrose Ave., Los Angeles CA.* ☎ *310-282-8237.* **$$$ Southern.** This open dining room resembles a Southern country home with wrought-iron gates and Spanish moss. Gourmet soul food is the fare: Southern fried chicken comes with macaroni and cheese; crispy catfish tops grits and okra choux. Many diners finish the down-home cookin' with sweet potato pie and whipped cream.

JiRaffe – *502 Santa Monica Blvd., Santa Monica CA.* ☎ *310-917-6671.* **$$$ California.** From the airy storefront of this chic new restaurant, chef Rafael Lunetta—latest darling of the food world—prepares such dishes as duck breast with couscous and black mission figs.

Cedar Creek Inn – *1555 S. Palm Canyon Dr., Palm Springs CA.* ☎ *760-325-7300; www.cedarcreekinnps.com.* **$$ American.** Outdoor patios with striped umbrellas, verandahs with flowered cushions, indoor dining under high ceilings—diners pick their atmosphere at Cedar Creek. Here is served such hearty food as blackened chicken breast, turkey meat loaf, praline ice-cream pie and apricot cake.

Angel's Flight

© David R. Frazier

today it presents a lively Latino street scene. Queen of the district is the **Bradbury Building**★★ *(304 S. Broadway;* ☎ *213-626-1893),* a modest brick building (1893, George H. Wyman) whose marvelous five-story **atrium** was inspired by a futuristic novel of the time, Edward Bellamy's *Looking Backward.* Skylit from the rooftop by diffuse natural light, the atrium has lacey wrought-iron railings and open-cage elevators, red-oak trim and stair treads of Belgian marble.

It is opposite the **Grand Central Market**★ *(315 S. Broadway;* ☎ *213-624-2378),* built in 1897 and converted to a public market in 1917. From the west side of the market on Hill Street, **Angel's Flight**★ *(*☎ *213-626-1901)* climbs Bunker Hill to the hilltop office towers of California Plaza. This two-car funicular railway is a whimsical restoration of a system that ran from 1901 to the early 1960s.

The gleaming commercial skyscrapers of Los Angeles' new downtown commu-

Practical Information

Getting There – Five large airports handle commercial traffic. Largest is Los Angeles International Airport *(LAX)* *(*☎ *310-646-5252, www.lawa.org),* 10mi southwest of downtown. Also: Burbank-Glendale-Pasadena Airport *(BUR)* *(*☎ *818-840-8840, www.bur.com),* 16mi north of downtown; Long Beach Airport *(LGB)* *(*☎ *310-570-2600),* 22mi south of downtown; Orange County/John Wayne Airport *(SNA)* *(*☎ *714-252-5200),* 35mi southeast of downtown; Ontario International Airport *(ONT)* *(*☎ *909-937-2700),* 35mi east of downtown. Rental-car agency branches are at all airports; call for ground transportation information.
Amtrak train: Union Station *(800 N. Alameda St.;* ☎ *800-872-7245, www.amtrak.com).* Greyhound bus: Downtown depot *(E. 7th & Alameda Sts.,* ☎ *800-231-2222, www.greyhound.com).*

Getting Around – Express-bus and Metro rail service provided by Los Angeles County Metropolitan Transit Authority *(MTA)* *(*☎ *213-922-6000 or 213-626-4455, www.mta.net).* Base fare $1.35 with additional 25¢ for transfers. Purchase tickets at stations. The *DASH* (Downtown Area Short Hop) shuttle system *(*☎ *213-808-2273)* runs frequently through downtown L.A. (25¢ with one free transfer) and in other neighborhoods. Taxi: Checker Cab Co. *(*☎ *310-330-3720),* United Independent Taxi Drivers *(*☎ *213-462-1088),* Yellow Cab *(*☎ *213-808-1000).*

Accommodations – The Hotel Reservation Network *(*☎ *214-361-7311, www.hoteldiscount.com)* provides free reservation service. The *Destination L.A.* vacation guide *(below)* contains a lodging directory. Accommodations range from deluxe hotels *(over $250/day)* to budget motels *(as little as $40/day).* Most bed-and-breakfast inns are found in residential sections of the city *($80-$110/day).*

nity are focused around 5th and Grand Streets. They are climaxed by **Library Tower★** *(633 W. 5th St.)*, among the tallest office buildings in the US west of Chicago. Soaring 1,017ft, the 73-story Italian-granite building (1992, I.M. Pei) is topped by an illuminated crown. It stands opposite the **Los Angeles Central Library★** *(630 W. 5th St.; ☎ 323-228-7000)*, a striking building (1926, Bertram Goodhue) conceived as an allegory on "The Light of Learning," expressed through sculptures, murals and tilework.

Around the corner is the **Biltmore Hotel★★** *(506 S. Grand Ave.; ☎ 213-624-1011)*. The 11-story, 700-room inn (1923, Schultze & Weaver), which was once the largest hotel in the West, displays opulent 16C Italian-style brickwork and terra-cotta, and high, hand-painted ceilings, in its Rendezvous Court. Another downtown landmark is **The Westin Bonaventure★** *(404 S. Figueroa St.; ☎ 213-624-1000)*, a 35-story hotel (1976, John Portman) composed of five cylindrical towers of mirrored glass.

★★ Museum of Contemporary Art (MOCA) – *250 S. Grand Ave.* ✖ ♿ 🅿 ☎ *213-626-6222*. An intriguing assemblage of geometric forms clad in red sandstone and green aluminum, this museum showcases late-20C visual art. Arata Isozaki (1986) designed an intimate, low-lying **complex★** of cubes, a cylinder and 11 pyramidal skylights above underground galleries. Changing selections from the permanent collection include pieces by Borofsky, Johns, Nevelson, Oldenburg, Pollock, Rauschenberg, Rothko and Stella. Temporary shows are held here and at **The Geffen Contemporary at MOCA★** *(152 N. Central Ave.; ☎ 213-626-6222)*.

★★ Southwest Museum – 🔳 *234 Museum Dr. (Ave. 43 Exit, Rte. 110), 3mi northeast of downtown.* 🅿 ☎ *323-221-2164. www.southwestmuseum.org.* his 1914 Mission Revival building houses L.A.'s oldest museum, dedicated to Native American cultures. The **Plains Hall** features a fine collection of garments and an 18ft Cheyenne **tepee**. The **Northwest Coast Hall** includes a pair of carved wooden Haida house posts (1860). In **California Hall**, exhibits illustrate the lives of the state's tribes. Collections in **Southwest Hall** include **Clovis points** (10,000 BC), the earliest evidence of human life in the American Southwest. The **Basketry Study Room** presents examples from the museum's 12,000-piece collection.

Entertainment – Consult the "Calendar" section of *The Los Angeles Times* or the *LA Weekly* for a schedule of cultural events and addresses of principal theaters and concert halls. Tickets may be obtained from: Ticketmaster (☎ 213-365-3500, *www.ticketmaster.com*), **A Musical Chair** *(☎ 310-207-7070)* or **Ticket Time** *(☎ 310-445-0900)*.

Visitor Information – Call the **Los Angeles Visitor Information Hotline** *(☎ 800-228-2452)* to obtain *Destination L.A.*, a free vacation-planning guide. **Los Angeles Convention & Visitors Bureau** information centers: **Downtown**, 685 S. Figueroa St. *(☎ 213-689-8822)*; **Hollywood**, 6541 Hollywood Blvd., *(☎ 213-236-2331)*.

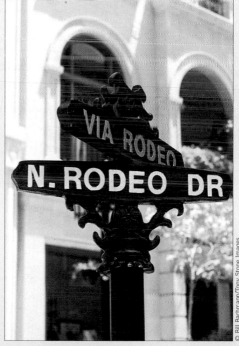

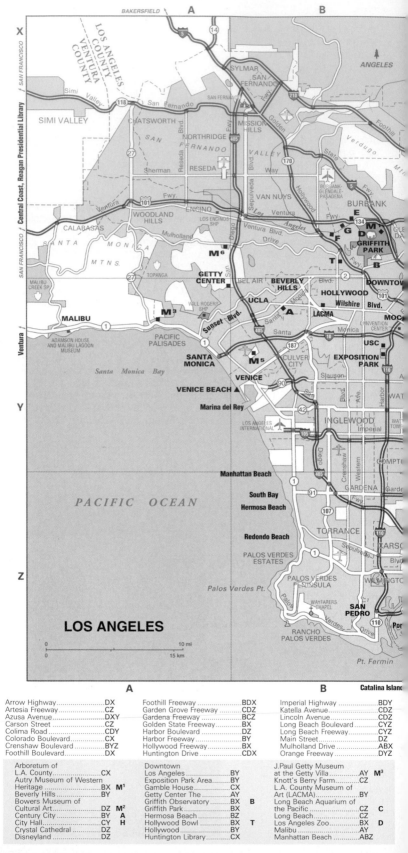

220

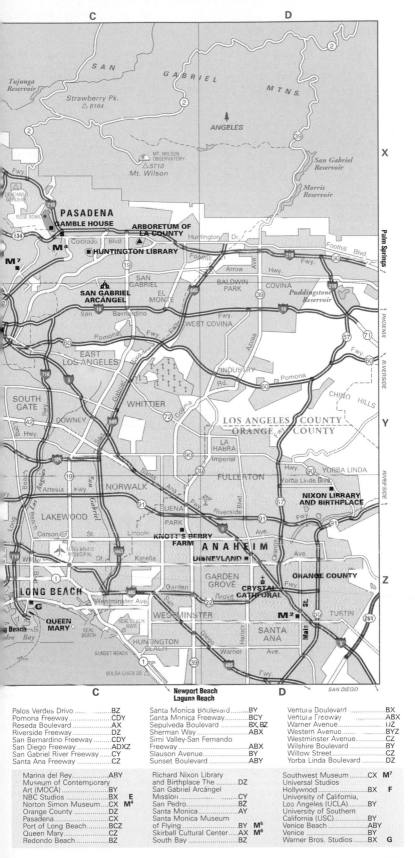

★★ EXPOSITION PARK AREA

This 125-acre park *(bounded by Exposition Blvd., Figueroa St., Martin Luther King Blvd. & Vermont Ave.)* occupies the site of the original (1872) city fairgrounds, 3mi southwest of downtown adjacent to the **University of Southern California** campus. A 1913 civic campaign made it the setting for public museums and exhibit halls, athletic facilities and gardens, laid out in grand Beaux-Arts tradition by landscape architect Wilber D. Cook Jr. Today, a $350 million facelift is in the works, adding greenery, promenades and new facilities.

★★ **Los Angeles Memorial Coliseum** – *3900 block of Figueroa St.* ✕ 🛆 🄿 ☎ *213-748-6131.* This 92,000-seat oval (1923, Parkinson & Parkinson) is Los Angeles' preeminent sports stadium, hosting football, soccer, rock concerts and other outdoor events. Once the world's largest arena, the Coliseum gained renown as the principal venue of the 1932 and 1984 Olympic Summer Games.

★★ **Natural History Museum of Los Angeles County** – Kids *900 Exposition Blvd.* ✕ 🛆 🄿 ☎ *213-744-3466. www.nhm.org.* The third-largest natural-history museum in the US holds more than 35 million specimens and artifacts. The dignified Beaux-Arts structure (1913) once also contained art collections; in 1961 the Los Angeles County Museum of Art *(p 225)* moved to a new facility.
Skeletons of a tyrannosaur and a triceratops poised for battle greet visitors in the main foyer. The **Halls of African and North American Mammals** display animals in natural habitats. The **Hall of Gems and Minerals★** houses more than 2,000 specimens. The **Halls of American History★★** trace the origins and development of the nation from Columbus' discovery to the Industrial Age. The **Discovery Center** offers fossils and bones to touch, live creatures to pet. The **Insect Zoo** includes terrariums crawling with live specimens. The **Hall of Native American Cultures** features a floor-to-ceiling replica of a Pueblo cliff dwelling. The **Hall of Birds★** is filled with interactive displays, including three walk-through habitats. **California and the Southwest: 1540-1940** traces history with replica dwellings, dioramas and historic artifacts.

★ **California Science Center** – Kids *700 State Dr.* ✕ 🛆 🄿 ☎ *323-724-3623. www.casciencectr.org.* The largest and oldest (1951) institution of its kind in the western US, this complex includes the Kinsey Hall of Health (1967) and three 1984 additions—the Aerospace Museum, the Mark Taper Hall of Economics and an IMAX theater. Exhibits in **World of Life** and **Creative World** explore the relationship between science and technology. **World of the Pacific** focuses on Pacific Rim environments; **World Beyond** offers a close look at the solar system and universe.

★★ GRIFFITH PARK

Enter from Los Feliz Blvd., Ventura Fwy. (Rte. 134) or Golden State Fwy. (I-5).

One of the largest urban parks in the US, Griffith Park straddles 4,103 acres (6.4sq mi) of the Santa Monica Mountains northwest of downtown Los Angeles. Wealthy miner Col. Griffith J. Griffith donated the land in 1882, along with money for a park observatory and the **Greek Theatre**, an open-air concert venue. A zoo, two museums and recreational facilities complement those attractions, but Griffith Park remains largely a natural oasis inhabited by deer, opossums, quail and raptors. Miles of hiking and bridle trails weave through the park.

★★ **Griffith Observatory** – Kids *2800 E. Observatory Rd.* ✕ 🄿 ☎ *323-664-1191. www.griffithobs.org.* On the south slope of 1,625ft Mount Hollywood, this Art Deco observatory (1935) is a local landmark. A 240-pound brass Foucault pendulum in the **main rotunda** demonstrates the earth's rotation; murals depict astronomical symbols and the history of science. Exhibit halls extend from the rotunda. Beneath an 84ft copper dome, the **Planetarium Theater** *(☎ 818-901-9405)* offers regular astronomy programs using a massive Zeiss projector, plus laser light shows projected onto the interior of the dome. **Views★★★** sweep to downtown L.A., to the coast and to the nearby Hollywood Sign *(p 226).*

★★ **Autry Museum of Western Heritage** – Kids *4700 Zoo Dr.* ✕ 🛆 🄿 ☎ *323-667-2000. www.autry-museum.org.* Established in 1988 by Western singer-film star **Gene Autry** (1907-98), this collection is presented in spacious galleries. **Spirit of Discovery** highlights North America's early nomadic hunters, 16C Spanish voyagers, 18C Franciscan missionaries and 19C American pioneers. **Spirit of Community★** depicts the formation of social fabric among settlers through family, church, business and politics. **Spirit of Romance** examines the 19C glamorization of the West through art, literature, advertising and Wild West shows. **Spirit of Imagination** traces the portrayal of the West in film, radio and television.

★★ Los Angeles Zoo – Kids *5333 Zoo Dr.* ✗ ♿ 🅿 ☎ *323-666-4000. www.lazoo.org.* Begun in the late 1890s by silent-film producer William Selig to provide animals for motion pictures, the zoo was donated to the city in the early 1920s. In 1966 it moved to 80 acres in northeastern Griffith Park; today it has more than 1,200 creatures of 400 species, including some 70 endangered species. A walkway leads to **Adventure Island**, a children's zoo, then branches into trails that follow hilly terrain to visit aquatic animals, birds, and denizens of Australia, North America, Africa, Eurasia and South America. A documentary display is devoted to the California condor, and the zoo's successful program of breeding this rare species and reintroducing it to the wild.

★WILSHIRE BOULEVARD

Wilshire Boulevard is the city's grandest thoroughfare, extending west 16mi from downtown through central Los Angeles, Beverly Hills and Westwood to Santa Monica. As the main artery of early-20C business and residential development, its architecture (especially from downtown to Fairfax Avenue) chronicles the growth and change of modern Los Angeles. The so-called **Miracle Mile** *(La Brea to Fairfax Aves.)* was named in the 1920s by developers who planned to transform the strip into a grand shopping center. It attracted some remarkable Art Deco buildings. Several museums have located along this stretch.

★ La Brea Tar Pits – *North side of Wilshire Blvd., west of Curson Ave.* Some 38,000 years ago, saber-tooth tigers, mammoths and giant sloths that came here to drink from pools were trapped in a thick, tar-like asphalt *(brea in Spanish)* at the surface. Since 1905, excavations have unearthed more than 100 tons of specimens— the world's largest cache of Ice Age fossils. Asphalt still bubbles through the water beside Wilshire Boulevard. Visitors may view a summer dig at **Pit 91**, behind the Los Angeles County Museum of Art *(below)*.

★★ Page Museum at the La Brea Tar Pits – Kids *5801 Wilshire Blvd.* ♿ 🅿 ☎ *323-857-7243. www.tarpits.org.* Cast-fiberglass friezes of Ice Age animals top this square-sided museum. Skeletons are reconstructed from more than 4.5 million bones of 390 species found at the pits. Displays create the illusion of skeletons—of a **saber-tooth cat** and 9,000-year-old La Brea Woman—transforming into flesh and blood. In a glass-windowed **paleontology laboratory**, scientists clean and examine bones.

© David Hockney

Mulholland Drive: The Road to the Studio (1980) by David Hockney

★★★ Los Angeles County Museum of Art (LACMA) – *5905 Wilshire Blvd.* ✗ ♿ 🅿 ☎ *323-857-6000. www.lacma.org.* This sprawling six-building complex is the nation's largest art museum west of Chicago. LACMA's holdings comprise more than 110,000 works in 11 curatorial divisions. Its **Center for German Expressionist Studies** is the largest and most comprehensive collection of its kind in the world.
In the four-level **Ahmanson Building** are most permanent collections. On the First Level, **Pre-Columbian** works include sculptures, pottery, textiles and gold from Mexico and Mesoamerica, ceramics from Panama and ancient pottery. **American Decorative Arts** reveal pieces from the Arts and Crafts movement as well as a sweep of styles ranging from Queen Anne, William and Mary, Chippendale, Rococo and Federal. **American Painting and Sculpture** (18C-early 20C) includes works by Bierstadt, Keith, Homer and Cole. **African Art** dates mostly from the 20C; many weavings, jewelry, and masks of wood and fiber serve as fertility or funerary objects.
Second Level rooms include ancient Egyptian, Iranian, Greek and Roman art, and **European Art** from Middle Ages to 19C. The adjoining **Hammer Building** displays **Impressionist** and **Postimpressionist** works by such artists as Cézanne, Degas and Gauguin, changing exhibits of photography, and German Expressionist prints and drawings. Third Level galleries highlight **Islamic, Indian, Tibetan and Nepalese art**—3,500 paintings, sculptures, ceramics, textiles and works in silver, jade and crystal, considered one

of the three finest collections in the Western world. In the building's lower level are **Chinese**, **Korean** and **Southeast Asian** works, including bronzes, porcelains, glazed pottery figures, and scroll paintings.

The **Robert O. Anderson Building** (1986, Hardy Holzman Pfeiffer) houses 20C art, with works of Picasso's blue and Cubist periods, and pieces by Magritte, Miró, Hoffmann, Noguchi, Rothko, Stella and Diebenkorn. The four-level structure presents a bold facade of limestone, glass blocks and green-glazed terra-cotta. It is flanked by open-air **sculpture gardens**, one dominated by Rodin bronzes, the second with contemporary works by Alexander Calder, Henry Moore and others.

The **Pavilion for Japanese Art** (1988, Bruce Goff and Bart Prince), a curvilinear structure surrounded by Japanese gardens, highlights the Price Collection of **Shin-enkan**—over 300 scroll paintings and screens created during the Edo period (1615-1868). Also exhibited are textiles, sculptures, ceramics and lacquerware.

One block away is **LACMA West** *(Wilshire Blvd. & Fairfax Ave.)*, a dramatic 1939 Streamline Moderne edifice. The building, used for special exhibitions, has an interactive children's gallery and a satellite to the Southwest Museum *(p 219)*.

** **Petersen Automotive Museum** – 🄺🄸🄳🅂 *6060 Wilshire Blvd.* ♿ 🄿 ☎ *323-930-2277. www.petersen.org.* Imaginative dioramas, photographs and computer stations show how automotive evolution influenced the growth of Los Angeles, the quintessential "car town." More than 200 rare cars, trucks and motorcycles are displayed. The **Streetscape** exhibit sets classic vehicles into dioramas illustrating Los Angeles at various points in history. Exhibits detail civic decisions to build broad boulevards, and eventually freeways, in place of trolley and streetcar lines.

* **Farmers' Market** – *6333 W. Third St. at S. Fairfax Ave.* 🍴 🄿 ☎ *323-933-9211. www.farmersmarketla.com.* In summer 1934, farmers from the valleys surrounding L.A. gathered here to sell produce, engendering construction of a clapboard market complex. The open-air market retains a rustic charm with more than 100 permanent businesses. Greengrocers and butchers serve locals; international food and souvenir stands cater to visitors.

*** HOLLYWOOD

As much a state of mind as a geographic entity, Hollywood is the symbolic and real heart of the movie industry. Part of the city of Los Angeles, it is located 6mi west of downtown and 12mi east of the Pacific coast, sweeping south from the Hollywood Hills (an extension of the Santa Monica Mountains). Prohibitionist H.H. Wilcox founded the suburb in 1883, and by the turn of the 20C the quiet community of 5,000 was most notable for a lack of saloons. It was incorporated in 1903, and seven years later was annexed by L.A. in anticipation of water from the Los Angeles Aqueduct *(p 215)* and the growth that would ensue.

In 1911, filmmaker David Horsely opened Hollywood's first movie studio in an abandoned roadhouse at Sunset Boulevard and Gower Street. By 1912, five large East Coast film companies and many smaller producers had relocated here. Investors in 1923 developed "Hollywoodland," a tract of elegant Mediterranean homes in the hills of Beachwood Canyon. To publicize the venture, the financiers erected what now is known as the **Hollywood Sign★**, of white sheet-metal letters 30ft wide and 50ft tall. It fell into disrepair after 1939, but since the 1950s has been maintained as Hollywood's most visible landmark. *Located in Griffith Park, the sign is best viewed from the Griffith Observatory (p 222)*. Some landmark buildings subsequently deteriorated, but since the 1980s, energetic efforts have restored landmarks along Hollywood and Sunset Boulevards. The **Hollywood Visitors Bureau** *(6541 Hollywood Blvd.; ☎ 323-689-8822)* has tour information.

■ **Television Tapings and Movie Shoots**

To attend the taping of a TV show as a member of the studio audience, phone or write (three weeks in advance) for free tickets (enclose a self-addressed stamped envelope). At Mann's Chinese Theater *(opposite)* and Universal Studios *(p 226)*, representatives circulate offering same-day tickets. **Audiences Unlimited** (all major networks), 100 University City Plaza, Bldg. 153, University City CA 91608; ☎ *818-753-3470* or ☎ *818-506-0067; www.tvtickets.com.* **ABC Tickets,** ☎ *323-575-4321; http://abc.go.com.* **CBS Television City,** 7800 Beverly Blvd., Los Angeles CA 90036; ☎ *323-575-2624 or 323-575-2458; www.cbs.com.* **NBC Tickets,** 3000 W. Alameda Ave., Burbank CA 91523 ☎ *818-840-3537; www.nbc.com.*

Hollywood Hills

★★ Hollywood Boulevard – Hollywood's main thoroughfare Is 4.5mi long. The 1mi stretch between Gower Street and Sycamore Avenue is easily undertaken by foot. Grand movie palaces—including the **Pantages Theater★** *(6233 Hollywood Blvd.)*, **Egyptian Theater★** *(6712 Hollywood Blvd.)* **El Capitan Theater★★** *(6838 Hollywood Blvd.)*—rub shoulders with souvenir stands and theme museums.
Embedded in the sidewalks of the **Walk of Fame★** *(Hollywood Blvd. between Gower St. & La Brea Ave., and Vine St. between Sunset Blvd. & Yucca St.; ☎ 323-469-8311)* are more than 2,500 bronze-trimmed coral-terrazzo stars, conceived in 1958 by the Hollywood Chamber of Commerce as a tribute to entertainment personalities. Some 2,000 stars have been dedicated, at the rate of about 12 per year; names are inset in bronze along with circular plaques bearing symbols that indicate each honoree's field of achievement.
The intersection of **Hollywood and Vine** was immortalized as the hub of Hollywood in the 1930s and '40s. Its landmark is the **Capitol Records Tower★** *(1750 Vine St.)*, a 150ft-tall complex of offices and studios (1954, Welton Becket) that resembles a stack of records surmounted by a phonograph needle.

★★ Mann's Chinese Theater – *6925 Hollywood Blvd.* ☎ *323-464-8111.* An ornate fantasy of chinoiserie, this theater (1926, Meyer & Holler) was commissioned by showman **Sid Grauman.** (It is now owned by Mann Theatres.) Opened in 1927 for the gala premier of Cecil B. deMille's *King of Kings*, "The Chinese" is an eclectic, mansard-roofed pagoda, topped by stylized flames and flanked by white-marble dogs. The U-shaped cement forecourt features footprints and signatures of more than 180 Hollywood stars, with new ones added each year. Mary Pickford and Douglas Fairbanks were the first to leave prints, in 1927.

★ Hollywood Entertainment Museum – *7021 Hollywood Blvd.* ♿ 🅿 ☎ *323-465-7900. www.hollywoodmuseum.org.* This $5.5 million museum preserves the Hollywood mystique. Displays on makeup, costumes and technological innovation dot the rotunda, supplemented with film clips and celebrity sound bites. A **scale model** recreates Hollywood as it was in 1936. "Backlot" tours visit original sets.

★ Sunset Boulevard – Stretching 20mi from El Pueblo to the Pacific Ocean, this thoroughfare runs past the Latino neighborhoods of Elysian Park; the studios and street life of Hollywood; the mansions of Beverly Hills; and the upscale neighborhoods of Westwood, Bel Air, Brentwood and Pacific Palisades. Its most famous stretch is the 1.5mi **Sunset Strip★★** *(Crescent Heights Blvd. to Doheny Dr.)*. Hugging the Santa Monica Mountains, the street transits a once-unincorporated strip (hence its nickname) between Los Angeles and Beverly Hills. It is now part of the city of **West Hollywood,** whose identity as one of L.A.'s largest gay enclaves is more evident on Santa Monica Boulevard. Fashionable nightclubs (Roxbury, Viper Room, Whisky A Go Go) and restaurants (Spago, Nicky Blair's, Diaghilev) define the Strip's character. Giant **billboards** tout the latest Hollywood productions. Major cross streets provide dramatic southward-looking vistas, particularly at night.

* **Melrose Avenue** – Although it stretches 7mi from Hollywood to Beverly Hills, Melrose distills its creativity and craziness into 16 blocks between La Brea and Fairfax Avenues. Once serving adjacent Jewish neighborhoods, stores lining the avenue were taken over in the late 1970s and 80s by boutiques, restaurants and shops specializing in bizarre collectibles and gifts. They draw a swath of humanity that ranges from Versace-clad businesspeople, to pierced-and-tattooed Generation Xers.

* **Paramount Studios** – *5555 Melrose Ave. Visit by guided tour (2hrs) only.* ✗ ♿ ☎ *323-956-5575. www.paramount.com.* This complex of film and television production facilities is the only major studio remaining within the boundaries of Hollywood. The wrought-iron Spanish Renaissance-style **studio gates**, surmounted by "Paramount Pictures" in script, endure as a well-known symbol just north of Melrose at Marathon Street. A walking tour offers glimpses of sound stages.

Hollywood Forever – *6000 Santa Monica Blvd., adjoining Paramount Studios lot.* ☎ *323-469-1181.* The 65-acre cemetery (formerly Hollywood Memorial Park) shelters the grave sites and crypts of such Hollywood legends as Rudolph Valentino, Douglas Fairbanks, Tyrone Power, Peter Lorre and Cecil B. DeMille.

** **Hollywood Bowl** – *2301 N. Highland Ave.* ✗ ♿ ▣ ☎ *323-850-2000. www. hollywoodbowl.org.* Occupying a hollow surrounded by acres of greenery, the world's largest natural amphitheater is a popular concert site and summer home to the Los Angeles Philharmonic Orchestra. It is not just a performance space but a Hollywood icon used since 1919. A series of band shells designed by Lloyd Wright (son of Frank Lloyd Wright) replaced the original concrete stage in 1927; a 100ft white quarter-sphere was finalized in 1929. The shell was acoustically modified by Frank Gehry in 1970 and 1980. Frank Sinatra, the Beatles, Igor Stravinsky and Luciano Pavarotti have all performed here.

*** **Universal Studios Hollywood** – Kids *100 Universal Plaza, Universal City, 3mi northwest of Hollywood Blvd. via US-101.* ✗ ♿ ▣ ☎ *818-622-3801. www. universalstudios.com.* Part film and TV studio, part live-entertainment complex and amusement park, 420-acre Universal Studios sprawls over a hillside above the San Fernando Valley. Silent-film producer Carl Laemmle established a studio here in 1915. In 1964 Universal began to offer tram rides to boost lunchtime revenues at its commissary; visitors were shown makeup techniques, costumes, a push-button monster and a stunt demonstration. The tour's popularity led to the addition of new attractions almost yearly. Today, Universal Studios Hollywood is among the largest man-made tourist attractions in the US, annually welcoming 5 million visitors. Adjoining are the Universal Amphitheatre, a live concert venue; and **Universal CityWalk**, a shopping, dining and entertainment complex designed to appear as a compressed version of Los Angeles.

Live-performance stages in the upper section of the park—the **Entertainment Center**—present regular shows inspired by popular films and TV programs. The **Wild, Wild, Wild West Stunt Show** portrays fist- and gunfights, and the **Animal Actors Stage** presents stunts performed by more than 60 trained animals. **Back to the Future: The Ride** is a rollicking journey through the time-space continuum.

The **Universal Starway**, a .25mi covered escalator, descends to the **Studio Center**, situated in and around actual sound stages and backlots. A comprehensive look at the art and illusion of filmmaking is offered. **The World of Cinemagic** explains special effects. Among film-related rides are **Jurassic Park** (an escape from dinosaurs), **Terminator 2 3-D** (with a live-action story line), **Backdraft** (chemicals burst into flames) and **The E.T. Adventure** (interplanetary flying bicycles).

The **Backlot Tram Tour**** *(45min)* begins at Studio Center. Trams wind through movie sets portraying the Wild West, small-town America, New York City, Mexico, Europe and other locales. En route, they pass the Bates house built for Alfred Hitchcock's *Psycho* (1960); are attacked by the shark from Steven Spielberg's *Jaws* (1975); and encounter a rampaging 6.5-ton, 30ft King Kong. Trams also endure a collapsing bridge, a flash flood, the parting of the Red Sea, an avalanche and an earthquake measuring 8.3 on the Richter scale.

** BEVERLY HILLS

Surrounded by Los Angeles and West Hollywood, Beverly Hills is an independent 6sq mi municipality of 32,400 citizens, founded in 1907. The city's name is synonymous with wealth and elegance, qualities seen in its village-like shopping streets lined with international boutiques, its fashionable restaurants and its luxurious mansions lining gracious, tree-shaded drives. Architect Wilbur Cook laid out the grid; landscape architects John and Frederick Law Olmsted plotted sinuous drives through the foothills. The 1912 **Beverly Hills Hotel** *(9641 Sunset Blvd.)* began to attract stars to the area; Mary Pickford and Douglas Fairbanks built the first mansion, **Pickfair** *(1143 Summit Dr.)*, high on a hill in 1920.

** **Rodeo Drive** – This renowned street is a three-block stretch of mostly two- and three-story buildings north of Wilshire Boulevard. Boutiques and clothiers, jewelers, antique dealers and art galleries cater to expensive tastes. On the northeast corner of Wilshire and Rodeo Drive, the four-story **Via Rodeo** shopping complex (1990) whimsically resembles the street of an Italian hillside town. **Anderton Court** *(328 N. Rodeo Dr.)*, an angular complex with an open ramp that winds around a spire, was built in 1954 from a Frank Lloyd Wright design.

* **Century City** – *Roughly bounded by Santa Monica & W. Pico Blvds., Century Park E. & Century Park W.* ✗ ঠ 🄿 ☎ *310-277-3898*. This 180-acre futuristic complex (1961) of hotels, office buildings, apartments and town houses, live theaters, cinemas and shops occupies the former ranch of Western film star Tom Mix, later the backlot of adjoining **Twentieth Century-Fox Studios.**

WESTSIDE

* **University of California, Los Angeles (UCLA)** – *Roughly bounded by Le Conte, Hilgard & Veteran Aves. and Sunset Blvd.* ✗ ঠ 🄿 ☎ *310-825-8764. www.ucla .edu.* Lodged on a 420-acre foothills campus between Westwood Village and Bel Air, UCLA is the largest member of the University of California's nine-campus system, with more than 35,000 students and a staff of over 5,000. Forty brick-and-stone buildings of the Lombard Romanesque style accommodate the sloping terrain; several encircle **Royce Quadrangle** at the highest point on campus. **Royce Hall** (1929), inspired by the Basilica of San Ambrogio in Milan, houses an 1,850-seat theater. The entrance to **Powell Library** (1928) was modeled after the Church of San Zeno in Verona, its octagonal dome after San Sepolcro in Bologna.
The **Fowler Museum of Cultural History**★ *(☎ 310-825-4361)*, an anthropology museum, is noted for its **Francis E. Fowler Jr. Collection of Silver** from England, Europe and America. Other galleries exhibit artifacts drawn from a worldwide collection of more than 750,000 objects. The tree-shaded **Franklin D. Murphy Sculpture Garden**★★ *(northeast corner of campus; ☎ 310-443-7000)* showcases more than 70 works by such leading artists as Rodin, Matisse, Miró, Moore, Calder and Noguchi.

* **UCLA at the Armand Hammer Museum of Art and Cultural Center** – *10899 Wilshire Blvd., Westwood Village.* ঠ 🄿 ☎ *310-443-7000. www.arts.ucla.edu/hammer.* The **Armand Hammer Collection**, begun by the wealthy industrialist in the 1920s, features paintings and drawings by Old Masters (Tintoretto, Titian, Rubens), Impressionists and Postimpressionists (Degas, Manet, Cézanne, Gauguin, Toulouse-Lautrec). Its highlight is Rembrandt's *Juno* (c.1662), a portrait of the artist's mistress. Also displayed are lithographs, paintings, drawings and woodcuts by 19C French caricaturist Honoré Daumier. The **UCLA Grunwald Center for the Graphic Arts** is one of the top three US collections of works on paper.

*** **The Getty Center** – *1200 Getty Center Dr., just off I-405. Open Tue-Wed 11am-7pm, Thu-Fri 11am-9pm, weekends 10am-6pm. Closed Jan 1, July 4, Thanksgiving Day & Dec 25.* ✗ ঠ 🄿 ☎ *310-440-7300. www.getty.edu.* Perched on a north-south ridge high above the San Diego Freeway, this gleaming cluster of low lying buildings holds one of the nation's most extensive facilities for the study, conservation and presentation of visual art.
Oil millionaire **Jean Paul Getty** (1892-1976) began collecting paintings in 1931. After World War II, he resided in Europe, developing his worldwide oil business while expanding his art holdings and commissioning a new Malibu museum *(p 229)*, inspired by a Roman villa, to display them. The collections quickly outgrew the Malibu space, and in 1989 work began on the Getty Center.
Architect Richard Meier designed the new (1997) facility, a travertine-clad complex melding six buildings on a 110-acre campus with courtyards, walkways, fountains, gardens and stunning views. The **Central Garden** was conceived by artist Robert Irwin. The various branches of the J. Paul Getty Trust, including research and conservation organizations, occupy several of the structures; the **J. Paul Getty Museum**★★★ takes the remainder of the complex.
The museum showcases its founder's superior assemblages of French decorative arts; 17-20C European paintings, including such well-known works as Rembrandt's *St. Bartholomew* (1661) and Van Gogh's *Irises* (1889); and works on paper, encompassing drawings, illuminated manuscripts and photographs. It occupies five pavilions arranged chronologically around an open courtyard and bridged

Central Garden, The Getty Center

by walkways on two levels, allowing visitors to create their own routes through the collections. Paintings are on the upper floors, displayed in natural light augmented as needed by artificial illumination.

Courtyard-level exhibitions in the **North Pavilion** cover 15-16C European bronzes and European ceramics, German and Italian glasswork, and **illuminated manuscripts★★**. Italian Renaissance paintings are presented on the upper level.

In the **East Pavilion** are European sculpture, including works in bronze, alabaster, wood and marble; and drawings from the Renaissance through rococo periods. Exhibits on the upper level begin with Baroque paintings. The influence of post-Dutch Reform art is epitomized by Rembrandt.

Spectacular decorative pieces are in the **South Pavilion,** among them monumental French tapestries from the period of Louis XIV, and an entire gallery of tables, clocks, chests and other items attributed to marquetry master André-Charles Boulle. Four paneled rooms showcase assemblages of French decorative arts.

In the **West Pavilion** are displays of European sculpture, including Neoclassical busts, terra-cotta and plaster sculpture, and Italian decorative arts. The upper level concentrates on early-19C Romantics and on Impressionists, including works by Renoir, Pissarro, Monet, Manet, Van Gogh, Munch and Cézanne.

★★ **Skirball Cultural Center** – *2701 N. Sepulveda Blvd., just off I-405.* ✗ ⅙ ▣ ☎ *310-440-4500.* This West Coast's preeminent Jewish cultural center and museum describes and interprets the beliefs and rites of Judaism, and chronicles the tumultuous history of the faith from its origin to the present. **Visions and Values: Jewish Life from Antiquity to America** tells of cultural influences affecting the Jews and spread by them during migrations. The importance of the flow of time is illustrated in religious holidays; "Sacred Space" explains artistry and symbolism in temples. The **Discovery Center** presents biblical archaeology, inviting young visitors to explore ancient Judaism through artifacts and activities.

EXCURSIONS

★ **Santa Monica** – *14mi west of downtown Los Angeles.* ☎ *310-393-7593. www.santamonica.com.* This seaside city of 89,000 is a center of entertainment and arts, replete with galleries, theaters, fashionable cafes and boutiques. Both visitors and residents throng the **Third Street Promenade★**, a pedestrian mall *(3rd St. between Wilshire Blvd. & Broadway)*, and **Santa Monica Place** *(Broadway between 2nd & 4th Sts.)*, a shopping center designed by Frank Gehry (1979).

Jutting 1,000ft over the ocean, the wooden **Santa Monica Pier★★** 🄺🄸🄳🅂 *(end of Colorado Ave.)* has been a landmark and gathering place since the early 20C. Its 9.5-acre expanse features an antique **carousel★**, fishing docks and an amusement park evoking the carnival spirit of a festive past. The present structure consists of the Municipal Pier (1909) and Pleasure Pier (1916), the latter designed by Coney Island creator Charles I.D. Looff. Both were restored during the 1980s.

** **Santa Monica Museum of Flying** – **Kids** *2772 Donald Douglas Loop N. at the Santa Monica Airport.* ✗ & ▣ ☎ *310-392-8822. www.mof.org/mof.* In a modern steel and glass structure on the first site of Donald Douglas Aircraft Co., this museum has 45 vintage aircraft, many restored to flight condition. Displays, films and models enlighten visitors on airplane construction and aviation history. **AirVenture** includes a mock-up cockpit and a simulated World War I dogfight.

* **Malibu** – *Pacific Coast Hwy. (Rte. 1), bordering Santa Monica to the northwest.* Malibu enjoys the loveliest setting of any Los Angeles-area beachside community. An exclusive residential enclave, the **Malibu Colony,** was established here in 1928, the beachside homesites drawing many celebrities—among them Clara Bow, Barbara Stanwyck, Gary Cooper and Gloria Swanson. Stars still occupy multimillion-dollar homes in the security-gated colony, while others live in luxury aeries clinging to the mountainsides. They are continually threatened by wildfires that denude the slopes and mudslides that follow heavy rains.

J. Paul Getty Museum at the Getty Villa – *17985 Pacific Coast Hwy., between Sunset & Topanga Canyon Blvds. Scheduled reopening 2001.* Sequestered in a lushly landscaped 65-acre canyon, this re-creation of a 1C BC Roman villa overlooks the Pacific. A replica of a villa in Herculaneum buried during the eruption of Mount Vesuvius in AD 79, the building was erected in 1974 to house the Getty art collections—relocated in 1997 to the new Getty Center *(p 227)* in Los Angeles. When the Villa reopens, it will be a museum of comparative archaeology and antiquities, and a showcase for the Getty's collection of Greek and Roman art.

* **Venice and South Bay** – A beachside community just south of Santa Monica, Venice is a lively melting pot. In 1904 tobacco magnate Abbot Kinney began to develop an artists' mecca modeled after Venice, Italy, draining marshlands and dredging a network of canals. Today **Venice Beach**★★ is renowned not only for its sand but for its colorful street life—particularly along **Ocean Front Walk**, a beachside pedestrian way lined with cafes, boutiques and souvenir stalls, plus folksingers and rappers, comedic jugglers and swimsuit-clad skaters and muscle-bound weightlifters.
South along the coast is **Marina del Rey,** the world's largest artificial harbor for 10,000 private yachts and sailboats. Farther south, beyond the international airport, is the area known as **South Bay.** Its three distinctive communities are upscale **Manhattan Beach,** bohemian **Hermosa Beach** and surfside **Redondo Beach.**

** **Pasadena** – *9mi northeast of downtown Los Angeles.* ☎ *626-795-9311.* A city of 134,000, Pasadena boasts architectural and cultural attractions worthy of a larger community. A winter resort in the 1880s (many socialites' lavish mansions survive today), its early prosperity is reflected in the Spanish Baroque and Renaissance buildings of the **Civic Center,** erected in the 1920s.
In 1889 Pasadena's elite Valley Hunt Club marked New Year's Day with a parade of flower decked coaches. Over the years the carriages evolved into elaborate floats covered with flowers, and in 1916 the parade was coupled with a championship college football game. Today the **Rose Parade**★★ and the **Rose Bowl Game** are televised across North America.

*** **Norton Simon Museum** – *411 W. Colorado Blvd.* & ▣ ☎ *626-449-6840. www .nortonsimon.org.* Elegantly displayed in a stark contemporary building are 1,000 works from a private art collection spanning seven centuries of European painting and sculpture and 2,000 years of Asian sculpture. Entrepreneur Norton Simon (1907-93) began collecting paintings in 1954, beginning with canvases by Gauguin, Bonnard and Pissarro. Before he died, Simon had amassed more than 11,000 pieces, with particular strengths in 14-18C European art, French Impressionist paintings, the works of Edgar Degas, and Indian and Southeast Asian sculpture. Immediately recognizable are Renoir, Monet and Van Gogh, as well as Degas' famous sculpture, *The Little Fourteen-Year-Old Dancer* (1878-81). Also presented are Picasso *(Woman with a Book,* 1932), Daumier, Manet, Toulouse-Lautrec, Cézanne, Matisse, Modigliani, Braque, Klee and Kandinsky.

** **Gamble House** – *4 Westmoreland Pl., paralleling 300 block of N. Orange Grove Blvd. Visit by guided tour only.* ☎ *626-793-3334.* A masterpiece of the Arts and Crafts movement (1908, Charles and Henry Greene), this house was the winter residence of David Gamble, heir of the Procter & Gamble soap company. Covered in redwood shingles, the sprawling, two-story gabled "bungalow" and its contents show a dedication to craftsmanship and integrated design. Decorative masterworks include furnishings and intricate woodwork.

*** **Huntington Library, Art Collections and Botanical Gardens** – *1151 Oxford Rd., San Marino, off E. California Blvd. 2.3mi southeast of downtown Pasadena* ✗ & ▣ ☎ *626-405-2141. www.huntington.org.* The Huntington comprises one of the world's finest research libraries of rare books and manuscripts; a world-class collection of 18-19C British art, French and American works; and renowned botanical gardens. Secluded in the upscale Pasadena suburb of San Marino, it occupies the ranch of rail tycoon Henry E. Huntington (1850-1927).

The stately **Library★★** houses 3.5 million manuscripts and 357,000 rare books, with emphasis on British and American history, literature and art from the 11C to the present. Displays include the **Ellesmere Chaucer,** an exquisitely illustrated manuscript (c.1410) of *The Canterbury Tales,* and a **Gutenberg Bible** (c.1450), one of only three vellum copies in the US. Other highlights are a **First Folio** of William Shakespeare's plays, noteworthy handwritten letters and manuscripts.

The **Huntington Art Gallery★★** is housed in the Beaux-Arts-style former residence. Its collection of **British art★★★** is considered outstanding, particularly for its 20 full-length portraits. Among them are Gainsborough's *Jonathan Buttall: "The Blue Boy"* (c.1770) and Lawrence's *Sarah Barrett Moulton: "Pinkie"* (1794). The small **Virginia Steele Scott Gallery** features works of 18C—early-20C American art. Covering 150 acres, the **Botanical Gardens★★** include 14,000 species. The 12-acre **desert garden** presents more than 5,000 types of mature cacti and succulents. The terraced **Japanese garden★** encompasses a koi pond, moon bridge, Zen rock garden and bonsai. Rose and camellia gardens have more than 1,400 cultivars. Others display herbs, palms, Australian plants and tropical species.

★**San Gabriel Arcángel Mission** – *537 S. Mission Dr., San Gabriel, 7mi southeast of Pasadena via I-210, Sierra Madre Blvd. & Junipero Serra Dr.* ⛬ ⯐ ☏ *626-457-3035.* The mission was established in 1771 and moved here in 1775. The impressive **church** (1779-1805), still active, was inspired by the Moorish cathedral in Cordova, Spain. A cemetery dates from 1778. On the grounds are remnants of a water cistern, an aqueduct, soap and tallow vats, a kitchen and a winery.

★★**Arboretum of Los Angeles County** – *301 N. Baldwin Ave. at I-210, Arcadia, 5mi east of Pasadena.* ⛾⛬ ⯐ ☏ *626-821-3222.* These 127-acre grounds showcase 30,000 plants of more than 7,000 species, including 150 species of eucalyptus and 2,299 species of orchids. A spring-fed lake was once a location for Hollywood films. South of the lake are historic buildings furnished in period style: reconstructed Gabrieleño wickiups; the rustic, three-room **Hugo Reid Adobe** (1840); and the ornately decorated **Lucky Baldwin Cottage** (1885).

★**Warner Bros. Studios** – *4000 Warner Blvd., Burbank, off Rte. 134 (Ventura Fwy.) at Hollywood Way, 14mi west of Pasadena. Visit by guided tour (3hrs) only; reservations required.* ⛬ ⯐ ☏ *818-954-8687. www.studio-tour.com.* This 108-acre complex has been Warner Bros. headquarters since 1928. Today its 33 sound stages are in constant use for movies, TV programs, commercials and sound recordings. Visitors are transported via golf cart to the backlot for a no-frills walk through sets, prop rooms, construction shops and other areas revealing the practical, working aspects of production.

NBC Studios – Kids *3000 W. Alameda Ave, Burbank, off Rte. 134 (Ventura Fwy.), 14mi west of Pasadena. Visit by guided tour (1hr) only.* ⛬ ☏ *818-840-3537.* Housing the largest color television studio in the US, this complex offers a look at simple static and videotaped displays. Tours include demonstrations of special effects, sound effects, makeup, costumes and sports broadcasting.

★**Long Beach** – *25mi south of Los Angeles.* ☏ *562-436-3645. www.golongbeach.org.* Long Beach's growth began in earnest with the 1921 discovery of oil at Signal Hill. World War II brought a naval port and shipbuilding facilities; today the 2,807-acre **Port of Long Beach** ranks first in foreign-trade

---

■ **Earthquakes**

Although severe earthquakes are infrequent, they are also unpredictable, making preparedness a fact of life in California. If you are outside when an earthquake occurs, stay clear of trees, buildings and power lines. If you are in a vehicle, pull to the side of the road and stop. Do not park on or under bridges; sit on the floor of the vehicle if possible. If you are in a building, stand inside a doorway or sit under a sturdy table; stay away from windows and outside walls. Be alert for aftershocks. If possible, tune to local radio or TV stations for advisories. For further information, call the **Earthquake Preparedness Hotline** (☏ *818-908-2671*).

value and total liner-cargo tonnage among all US ports. Together with the adjacent Worldport L.A., it is the largest, busiest waterborne shipping center in the US. The sprawling city now has a population of 430,000.

***Queen Mary – **Kids** *1126 Queens Hwy.* ✗ ☎ *562-435-3511*. Dominating Long Beach Harbor, this renowned passenger ship was permanently docked after 31 years in England's Cunard White Star line. The 81,237-ton vessel is 1,019ft long. Built in Scotland in 1930-34, the *Queen Mary* made her maiden voyage in May 1936. Converted for military use during World War II, she carried more than 750,000 troops over 550,000mi, earning the nickname "Gray Ghost" for her camouflage paint and zigzag routes. The ship returned to civilian use in July 1947 and became a favorite of such celebrities and socialites as Greta Garbo, Clark Gable, Elizabeth Taylor, Bob Hope and the Duke and Duchess of Windsor. By the mid-20C, air travel had eclipsed the era of the great passenger ships, and the *Queen Mary* completed the last of her 1,001 transatlantic voyages in 1967.

Visitors may explore the bridge, officers' quarters and other operational centers; passenger suites and dining rooms; the engine room, with its massive propeller box; and a display of model ships. Guided tours penetrate luxuriously furnished staterooms; guides may also tell tales of purported ghosts. Display cases and documentary photographs illustrate life aboard the *Queen Mary* and showcase some of her celebrated passengers. A hotel occupies three of the 12 decks.

*Scorpion Submarine – **Kids** *1126 Queens Hwy.* ☎ *562-435-3511*. The 3,000-ton *Scorpion*—more officially, the Soviet Foxtrot-class submarine Povodnaya Lodka B-427—is moored next to the *Queen Mary*. Nearly all of this 1972 diesel-electric sub (decommissioned in 1994) is open for tours.

Long Beach Aquarium of the Pacific – **Kids *100 Aquarium Way (off Shoreline Dr. south of Ocean Blvd.).* ✗ ✆ ▣ ☎ *562-590-3100. www.aquariumofpacific.org.* The flowing wave shapes of this $117 million shoreside aquarium (1998) contain a fine marine exhibition. Its canvas is the Pacific Ocean, represented by more than 10,000 creatures—from the icy arctic waters off Russia and northern Japan, the temperate waters of the California and Mexico coasts, and the tropical islands and lagoons of the Palau archipelago in Micronesia. These three marine ecozones are divided into 17 major habitats and 30 smaller exhibits with more than 550 species of fish, birds, marine mammals, turtles and other denizens of the Pacific.

*Catalina Island – *By passenger ferry from Long Beach, San Pedro or Newport Beach (45min-2hrs one way).* ☎ *310-510-1520. www.catalina.com.* Catalina's only town (of 3,000), **Avalon** is packed with pastel-colored houses and bungalows, hotels and restaurants. As autos are restricted, streets throng with pedestrians, bicycles and rented golf carts. The stately **Wrigley Mansion** (1921), now a country inn, overlooks the town 350ft above crescent-shaped Avalon Bay—not far from the adobe **Zane Grey Hotel** (1929), former home of the Western novelist. From the **Pleasure Pier**, glass-bottomed boats depart to view undersea life along the coastline; other tours visit sea lion colonies and track schools of flying fish.

The old **Casino Building** ** *(1 Casino Way;* ☎ *310-510-2444)*, a 140ft-tall, circular Art Deco building (1928-29) with Spanish and Moorish flourishes, dominates Avalon Bay's north end. In the 1930s and 40s, such big-band legends as Benny Goodman and Kay Kyser performed in its **Avalon Ballroom**, with the world's largest circular dance floor. Murals adorn the box-office loggia and 1,184-seat Avalon Theatre, whose elliptical ceiling is covered with 60,000 squares of silver leaf.

The 38-acre **Wrigley Memorial and Botanical Garden** *(1400 Avalon Canyon Rd., 1.3mi inland from Avalon Bay,* ☎ *310-510 2288)* highlights Catalina's native plants, including cacti and succulents. Exhibits at the nearby **Santa Catalina Island Interpretive Center** *(Avalon Canyon Rd.,* ☎ *310-510 2514)* examine isle flora and fauna, marine ecology, geology and native history.

San Pedro – *Rtes. 47 & 110, 6mi west of Long Beach & 22mi south of downtown Los Angeles.* Linked to Long Beach by the stately **Vincent Thomas Bridge**, San Pedro's vast **Worldport L.A.** is one of the nation's busiest ports and the West Coast's leading passenger terminal. Harbor history is told at the **Los Angeles Maritime Museum** **Kids** *(Berth 84, foot of 6th St.;* ☎ *310-548-7618)*, a collection of nautical memorabilia in the historic Art Deco Municipal Ferry Building. Housed in an innovative gray structure (1981, Frank Gehry) designed to evoke maritime images, the **Cabrillo Marine Aquarium** * **Kids** *(3720 Stephen White Dr. off Pacific Ave.;* ☎ *310-548-7562)* offers an introduction to California marine life.

ORANGE COUNTY★★
Michelin map 493 B 10, 11 and map p 221   Pacific Standard Time
Population 2,642,300
Tourist Information ☎ 714-765-8888 or www.anaheimoc.org

Sprawling east and south of Los Angeles, once-rural Orange County has become a metropolitan extension of its large neighbor. Its broad plain, formerly cloaked with the orange groves for which the county is named, extends 22mi from the 5,687ft crest of the Santa Ana Mountains to Pacific beaches. Population has nearly doubled since the 1960s, especially in the inland region surrounding Anaheim and Santa Ana, which burst at their seams with suburban housing and shopping malls.

In the mid-1950s, a cartoonist from Missouri bought 180 acres of citrus groves for a theme park that he named Disneyland. When Walt Disney purchased the land, Anaheim's population stood around 15,000. Today it is close to 300,000.

SIGHTS

★★★ **Disneyland** – Kids ‖‖‖ *Between Katella Ave., West St., Ball Rd. & Harbor Blvd., Anaheim. Open year-round 10am-8pm (9am-midnight summers and holidays). $39 (child under 12, $29).* ✗ ♿ 🅿 *($7)* ☎ *714-781-4560. http://disney.go.com/Disneyland.* Since its opening in 1955, the Magic Kingdom has been America's ultimate fantasy land. Though larger Disney theme parks have opened around the world, California's 90-acre Disneyland embodies the original vision of its creator. Roughly elliptical in shape, it has eight distinct sections—Main Street USA, Tomorrowland, Fantasyland, Mickey's Toontown, Frontierland, Critter Country, New Orleans Square and Adventureland—which radiate from a Central Plaza. Visitors with limited time can see the main attractions in one day; however, a two- or three-day visit is recommended, particularly for families with young children.

Walter Elias Disney (1901-66) began working in animation before he headed for Hollywood at age 22. He and his brother, Roy, established a studio and scored their first big success with the 1928 debut of *Steamboat Willie*, starring a character named **Mickey Mouse** and combining animation with sound. The first Technicolor cartoon, *Flowers and Trees*, won Disney his first of 32 Oscars. The first animated feature film, *Snow White*, opened in 1937 to rave reviews.

In the early 1950s, Disney purchased a 180-acre tract of orange groves for an amusement park—a "Magic Kingdom." The park opened in July 1955 to national fanfare and 90min of live television coverage, hosted by then-actor Ronald Reagan. Technology for **Audio-Animatronics**®, lifelike robotic figures, was developed for the 1964 New York World's Fair and put to widespread use in the park. Soon after, Disney conceived Walt Disney World and an adjacent Experimental Prototype Community of Tomorrow (Epcot) in Orlando, Florida. Today the vast Disney enterprises include theme parks abroad in Tokyo (1983) and Paris (1992), and Disney Studios is a major force in the US film industry.

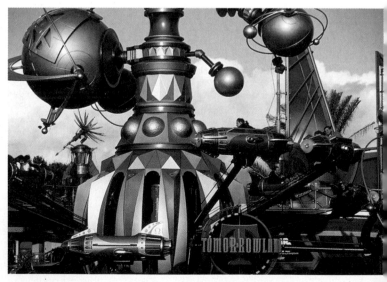

Astro Orbiter, Tomorrowland

Ground was broken in 1998 in Anaheim on the Disneyland Resort, scheduled to open in 2001 with a second theme park, **Disney's California Adventure**; a shopping, dining and entertainment complex, **Downtown Disney**; new hotels and gardens.

Main Street, USA – Tidy Victorian storefronts, horse-drawn trolleys and a double-decker omnibus accent this idyllic re-creation of early-20C, small-town America. Evenings bring **Fantasy in the Sky** fireworks, featuring a Tinker Bell fly-by. **The Walt Disney Story** traces the construction of Disneyland and the Disney empire. A theater features Disney's crowning Audio-Animatronics® success, **Great Moments with Mr. Lincoln**. At the **Main Street Cinema**, animated black-and-white classics from the 1920s and '30s, including *Steamboat Willie*, are continuously screened.

Passengers can board the **Disneyland Railroad** here to circle the park, making stops at New Orleans Square, Mickey's Toontown and Tomorrowland.

Tomorrowland – **Space Mountain** is a roller coaster enclosed in a futuristic mountain. **Star Tours**, conceived by *Star Wars* creator George Lucas, take travelers to the Moon of Endor by means of special effects. **Rocket Rods** is the fastest (3min at 35mph) ride in Disneyland. The **Astro Orbiter** is both a 64ft-high kinetic sculpture and a spinning ride. **Honey, I Shrunk the Audience** is a 3-D film presentation (viewers wear special glasses) based on the hit film *Honey, I Shrunk the Kids*. **Innoventions** showcases emerging technologies in electronics and computer applications.

An overview of the park can be achieved from the **Disneyland Monorail**, which since 1959 has whisked passengers between here and the Disneyland Hotel.

Fantasyland – Fantasyland was Walt Disney's personal favorite. The main entrance is through **Sleeping Beauty Castle**, a renowned icon with gold-leafed turrets and a moat. At the **King Arthur Carrousel**, Disney movie tunes are pumped from a calliope as antique horses take their riders in continual circles. **It's a Small World** boats float visitors past 500 Audio-Animatronics® children and animals representing nearly 100 nations, all singing a repetitive theme song.

Rides transport visitors past storybook images of Peter Pan, Snow White, Pinocchio and Alice in Wonderland. Carnival-style rides include the **Mad Tea Party**, a tilt-a-whirl of colorful cups and saucers. For the very young, **Dumbo the Flying Elephant** soars up and down in gentle circles; **Storybook Land Canal Boats** glide past a series of scale-model miniatures. Bigger kids prefer the **Matterhorn Bobsleds**, which speed downhill through ice caves and past an abominable snowman.

Mickey's Toontown – An exclusive residential address for Disney characters, Toontown features curving streets and buildings with the garish colors and the skewed perspective of animated cartoons. At **Mickey's House**, the celebrity mouse may pose for a photo. His loyal sweetheart invites friends to check on what's cooking at **Minnie's House**. Donald Duck's boat, the **Miss Daisy**, offers a bird's-eye view of Toontown from its bridge, adjacent to **Goofy's Bounce House**, an inflatable dwelling for the younger set. A spiral staircase invites exploration of **Chip 'n Dale's Tree House**. Older children follow skid marks to **Roger Rabbit's Car Toon Spin**.

Frontierland – The **Golden Horseshoe Stage** features Old West musical revues. **Big Thunder Mountain Railroad**, a runaway mine train, scales the crags and caves of an impressive reddish mountain. Plying the **Rivers of America** are the **Mark Twain Steamboat**, an elegant Mississippi River paddle wheeler, and the **Sailing Ship Columbia**, a three masted windjammer. Coonskin-capped guides paddle voyageurs in **Davy Crockett's Explorer Canoes**. At night, visitors crowd the riverbank to see **Fantasmic!**, a fiber-optic show *(22min)* that presents Disney animation at its pyrotechnic best.

Critter County – At the **Country Bear Playhouse**, the playful "Bear-itones," a troupe of Audio-Animatronics® bears, sing, tell jokes and delight the crowds. Riders float through the swamps and bayous within **Splash Mountain**, at the top of which awaits a 52ft flume that hurtles down a 47° slope to a drenching splash.

New Orleans Square – Jazz artists stroll this French Quarter, a narrow, twisting street of stuccoed shop facades and wrought-iron balustrades. In **Pirates of the Caribbean**, visitors float through a swamp and enter a village of buccaneers, imperiled damsels, parrots, dogs and pigs. Ghosts and ghouls spook the **Haunted Mansion**; "doom buggies" travel eerily among holographic specters.

Adventureland – The **Enchanted Tiki Room** stars funny, fantastical tropical birds and flowers with enough charisma to inspire the audience to sing along with them. **Jungle Cruise** safari boats travel through a forest populated by mechanized crocodiles, hippos, elephants and tigers. In the **Indiana Jones Adventure**®, rugged transport vehicles make a harrowing journey through an archaeological site—replete with spiders, snakes and skulls—to the Temple of the Forbidden Eye.

★ **Knott's Berry Farm** – Kids ▦ *8039 Beach Blvd., Buena Park, off I-5.* ✗ ♿ ▣ ☎ *714-220-5200. www.knotts.com.* In the 1920s, Walter Knott established a berry farm and roadside stand on 20 acres of rented land here. During the Great

Depression, his wife, Cordelia, began selling chicken dinners. A popular restaurant resulted, and in 1940 Knott constructed an Old West town to amuse hungry patrons waiting to get in. Today Knott's Berry Farm features many relocated or replicated historic structures along with 165 rides and shows.

Visitors may pan for gold in **Ghost Town** and try out GhostRider, a long wooden roller coaster; Bigfoot Rapids, a wet trip through wilderness whitewater; or Mystery Lodge, a 20min special-effects show based on Indian legends. At **The Boardwalk**, old-fashioned rides recall seaside amusement parks and boardwalks. The waterworks show in **Fiesta Village** features musically choreographed jets of water, as well as frightening high-tech roller coasters. Areas designed specifically for children include **Kingdom of the Dinosaurs**, **Indian Trails** and **Camp Snoopy**—whose *Peanuts*-theme rides are suited to the very young.

* **Crystal Cathedral** – *12141 Lewis St., Garden Grove, off I-5 via Harbor Blvd. & Chapman Blvd.* %& P @ 714-971-4000. www.crystalcathedral.org. In 1961 evangelist Robert Schuller commissioned architect Richard Neutra, a practitioner of the International style, to design a "drive-in church" with 1,400 parking spaces for visitors to attend the service in their cars. In 1980, Philip Johnson conceived a glass-walled sanctuary, seating 3,000 and accommodating drive-in worshipers via a large video screen. The awe-inspiring interior has a lacelike framework of white steel trusses sheathed in more than 11,000 individual window panes.

** **Bowers Museum of Cultural Art** – *2002 N. Main St., Santa Ana; off I-5.* %& P @ 714-567-3600. www.bowers.org. Dedicated to indigenous fine art of the Americas, Africa and the Pacific Rim, this collection comprises 85,000 artifacts dating from 1500 BC to the mid-20C. In the **Gallery of Oceanic Art** are bark paintings by Australian aborigines. The **African collection** features objects in wood, metal, textiles and ivory. Architectural elements and ceramics from the **pre-Columbian collection** are set into context by photo backgrounds. **Native American art** includes baskets, beadwork and pipes. Artifacts from California's mission and rancho periods are in another gallery.

* **The Richard Nixon Library & Birthplace** – *18001 Yorba Linda Blvd., Yorba Linda, 3.5mi east of Rte. 57 (Orange Fwy.).* & P @ 714-993-3393. www.nixonfoundation.org. Letters, papers, memorabilia and interactive exhibits illustrate and commemorate the life of Richard Nixon (1913-94), 37th US president (1969-74). Innovative exhibits chronicle his political career, including his 1960 campaign debates with John F. Kennedy and the Watergate scandal that forced his resignation.

* **Newport Beach** – *Pacific Coast Hwy. (Rte. 1) & Newport Blvd. (Rte. 55).* The maritime roots of this resort and residential community are evident on the **Balboa Peninsula**, a large pleasure-craft anchorage. The **Balboa Pavilion**★ *(400 Main St.)*, a charming Victorian structure (1904) topped by a jaunty cupola, was a popular dance hall in the 1940s big-band era. Extending east is the **Fun Zone** Kids of arcades and carnival rides. Private companies operate **harbor cruises**.

The respected **Orange County Museum of Art**★ *(850 San Clemente Dr., Fashion Island, off Jamboree Rd.; @ 949-759-1122)* focuses on modern and contemporary work, especially 20C California art.

* **Laguna Beach** – *Pacific Coast Hwy. (Rte. 1) & Laguna Canyon Rd. (Rte. 133).* A magnificent sea-cliff **setting**★ has attracted artists since 1903. Several artistic movements were spawned here, notably "Plein Air," a variant of American Impressionism. Today more than 90 studios and galleries share the community of 25,000. The **Laguna Art Museum**★ *(307 Cliff Dr.; @ 949-494-6531)* is a center for modern California art, including American Impressionism, installation art and photography. The **Festival of the Arts** *(Jul-Aug)* attracts 200,000 visitors to its "Pageant of the Masters," in which models pose as famous paintings.

** **San Juan Capistrano Mission** – *Ortega Hwy. (Rte. 74) & Camino Capistrano, San Juan Capistrano, off I-5.* @ 949-248-2048. www.missionsjc.com. The seventh California mission was among the most beautiful and prosperous. Founded in 1776 by Padre Junípero Serra, its **Great Stone Church** (1806) was a cross-shaped edifice with a 65ft-high roof topped by seven domes, and a bell tower that could be seen from 10mi away. An 1812 earthquake collapsed the ceiling, killing 40 neophytes; the original four bells now hang in a wall near the ruins. Three rooms in the west wing display items from Native American, mission and rancho periods. Behind lies a factory area where workers pressed olives and grapes, tanned leather, forged metal and made soap from tallow. In the east wing is the original mission chapel (1777), believed to be the only remaining building in California in which Padre Serra offered Mass. Restoration is scheduled for completion in 2002.

Both the town of San Juan Capistrano and the mission are famous for the swallows that return each year on March 19 from their winter nesting grounds in Argentina; their arrival is celebrated with a popular festival.

PALM SPRINGS★★

Michelin map 493 C 11   Pacific Standard Time
Population 43,942
Tourist Information ☎ 760-770-9000 or www.desert-resorts.com

Palm Springs is the most celebrated of a string of resort and retirement towns in the Coachella Valley east of Los Angeles. The area annually welcomes 2 million visitors and part-time residents, among them celebrities who come to play golf (80 courses dot the valley) and browse the upscale galleries and boutiques.

Natural hot springs and dry climate made Palm Springs a small health resort in the early 20C. In the 1930s, Hollywood stars discovered the attractions of desert living; business executives followed. Strict zoning maintains an elegant character: Garish signs and tall buildings are prohibited, and new houses must be constructed to avoid casting shadows on existing ones.

SIGHTS

★★★ **Palm Springs Aerial Tramway** – **Kids** *Tramway Rd. west off Rte. 111, 2mi north of downtown Palm Springs.* ✗ & 🅿 ☎ *760-325-1391.* Bus-size gondolas ascend the face of Mount San Jacinto *(ha-SIN-toe)* on cables suspended from towers anchored in the rocky slope. The 5,900ft climb *(14min)* to the 8,516ft summit crosses five biotic zones, from barren desert to alpine forest where snow lies through the winter. Spectacular **views**★★ stretch over the crags below.

★★ **Palm Springs Desert Museum** – *101 Museum Dr., adjacent to Desert Fashion Plaza at N. Palm Canyon Dr. and Tahquitz Way.* ✗ & ☎ *760-325-0189.* This museum offers a survey of the natural history, anthropology and art of California's deserts. Exhibits in the **Central Gallery** include Native American basketry, Asian art (collected by actor William Holden), and furniture and bronze sculptures by actor George Montgomery. The **Natural Science** wing introduces geology, flora and fauna, while the **Art Collections** focus on 20C California art. On the upper level is the 15ft glass sculpture *End of the Day #2* by master artist Dale Chihuly *(p 353).*

★ **Indian Canyons** – *S. Palm Canyon Dr., 4mi south of downtown Palm Springs, off Rte. 111.* 🅿 ☎ *760-325-3400. www.aguacaliente.org.* The Agua Caliente Band of Cahuilla Indians retains ownership of three canyons in the lower San Jacinto Mountains with groves of **fan palms**, California's only native species of palm. **Palm Canyon**★★ shelters a grove of 3,000 fan palms. Trails lead into smaller but equally lush **Andreas Canyon**★ *(.8mi)* and more remote **Murray Canyon** *(1mi).* The **Tahquitz Canyon Visitors Center** has interpretive displays on Cahuilla artifacts and culture.

La Quinta Golf Course

© Tim Thompson

★★ **Living Desert Wildlife & Botanical Park** – **Kids** *Portola Ave., 1.3mi south of Rte. 111, Palm Desert, 15mi east of Palm Springs.* ✗ & 🅿 ☎ *760-346-5694. www .livingdesert.org.* This 1,200-acre botanical garden and zoo offer a survey of 1,500 plants and 152 species of animals from arid lands. A path connects gardens representing each main subdivision of North American deserts, including the Upper Colorado Desert, the Yuman Desert and the arid Baja Peninsula. Guided tram tours *(50min)* offer an introduction; live animal shows are presented twice daily.

EXCURSIONS

Joshua Tree National Park – *North entrance at Twentynine Palms (Rte. 62), 52mi northeast of Palm Springs & 140mi east of Los Angeles via I-10.* ⚠ ☎ 760-367-7511. *www.nps.gov/jotr.* Named for a tree-like member of the Yucca genus whose strangely contorted branches made early Mormon travelers think of Joshua pointing to the promised land, this 1,240sq-mi park contains two very distinct deserts—the high (Mojave) and low (Colorado). The transition can be experienced in a short drive. From **Keys View** *(26mi from Oasis Visitor Center, off Rte. 62 at Twentynine Palms, via main park road and turnoff at Ryan Campground),* on the crest of the Little San Bernardino Mountains at 5,185ft, a sweeping **view** extends from Palm Springs to the Salton Sea.

The **Joshua tree** *(Yucca brevifolia)* is common in the high, cool Mojave Desert (above 3,000ft) and is distinguished from other yuccas by its height (it can grow as tall as 40ft). The trees propagate both by seed and by sending out long underground runners, and colonize broad areas to form sparse "forests." The park's distinct, picturesque rounded hills formed 135 million years ago.

Rim of the World Drive – *Rte. 18 from San Bernardino to Big Bear City (40mi), 85mi northwest of Palm Springs via I-10.* The rugged San Bernardino Mountains dominate the landscape north of their namesake city. Snow-dusted in winter—rising to 11,499ft at San Gorgonio Mountain—the range harbors jewel-like lakes that invite four seasons of recreational use. Best known is **Big Bear Lake*, 6mi long with a crenellated 24mi shoreline. This drive links Big Bear with other resort areas, including **Lake Arrowhead**, a summer-home colony.

CENTRAL COAST*

Michelin map 493 A, B 10   Pacific Standard Time
Tourist Information ☎ 916-322-2881 or www.gocalif.ca.gov

The Central Coast region balances a vital agricultural economy with a robust tourist industry. Natural beauty, historic Spanish roots, and a blend of cultural sophistication with casual friendliness contribute to its popularity.

Juan Rodríguez Cabrillo claimed this coast for Spain in 1542. But not until the missions of San Luis Obispo de Tolosa (1772), San Buenaventura (1782), Santa Bárbara (1786), La Purísima Concepcion (1787), San Miguel Arcángel (1797) and Santa Inés (1804) were built did the Spanish exert a hold. Santa Bárbara became the headquarters of the mission chain in 1803; unlike many of the old missions, it has continued to serve an active parish for more than two centuries.

SIGHTS

Ventura – *Pacific Coast Hwy., US-101 & Rte. 126, 62mi west of Los Angeles.* ☎ 805-648-2075. This low-key coastal city of 98,000 grew up around San Buenaventura Mission. Modern commerce has blossomed at busy **Ventura Harbor** *(access via Spinnaker Dr.),* replete with shops, restaurants and pleasure boats.

San Buenaventura Mission – *225 E. Main St.* ☎ 805-643-4318. Padre Serra set his ninth mission halfway between San Diego and Carmel. Laborers spent 15 years building the large stone-and-brick structure (1809) that serves as parish church. The reredos inside, painted to resemble marble, was made in Mexico City. A single-room **museum** displays a variety of religious relics, including vestments and the only wooden bells used in any of the 21 California missions.

*Channel Islands National Park – *Headquarters, 1901 Spinnaker Dr., Ventura.* ⚠ ☎ 805-658-5730. *www.nps.gov/chis.* Encompassing the northern five of eight islands that extend along the coast south of Santa Barbara, this unique park nurtures a rich plant, animal and marine life. Public access is tightly controlled. Late-18C fur traders exploited the bounty of otters, seals and sea lions and relocated Chumash Indians, who had lived here 6,000 years, to mainland missions. Anacapa and Santa Barbara Islands became a national monument in 1938; all five islands were made a national park in 1980 (though part of Santa Cruz remains in private ownership). Six-mile bands around each island are marine sanctuaries.

Anacapa Island, 14mi west of Ventura, comprises three islet seabird colonies. Large **Santa Cruz Island** has beach-fringed cliffs and wooded slopes populated by diverse animal species. Sea lions inhabit **Painted Cave***, California's largest sea cave, reached by boat on the northwest shore. **Santa Rosa Island** has grassy hills with oaks and

Torrey pines. Windswept **San Miguel Island** harbors a caliche forest, the calcium-carbonate castings of ancient trees. Tiny **Santa Barbara Island**, 33mi south of Anacapa, is a breeding ground for sea lions and elephant seals.

Information on transportation and activities such as camping, hiking, kayaking and scuba diving can be obtained from the **Robert J. Lagomarsino Visitor Center** at park headquarters. Boats depart from Ventura with **Island Packers** *(☎ 805-642-1393)*, from Santa Barbara with **Truth Aquatics** *(☎ 805-962-1127)*.

★★**Santa Barbara** – *US-101, 94mi west of Los Angeles. ☎ 805-966-9222. www.santabarbaraca.com.* Red-tile roofs, whitewashed stucco buildings and palm-fringed beaches create a Mediterranean ambience in this chic yet easygoing city of 86,000, arrayed along a coastal ledge and extending into hills between the Pacific Ocean and Santa Ynez Mountains. Appearing as a New England coastal town at the end of the 19C, Santa Barbara began its architectural transformation to Spanish Colonial Revival after a severe 1925 earthquake leveled the business district. The showpiece is the 1929 **Santa Barbara County Courthouse★★** *(1100 block of Anacapa St.; ☎ 805-962-6464)*, a Moorish castle surrounding a sunken garden.

A white-sand beach edged with stately palms, the city's **waterfront★** extends from the **Santa Barbara Yacht Harbor** *(W. Cabrillo Blvd.)* to **Stearns Wharf★** *(foot of State St.)*—a .5mi pier, lined with shops and restaurants, that is the oldest working wooden wharf (1872) in California. The **Nature Conservancy Visitor Center** *(☎ 805-962-9111)* has displays on the Channel Islands; the **Sea Center** 🄺🄸🄳🅂 *(☎ 805-962-0885)* is an aquarium devoted to marine life and geology. Clifftop **Shoreline Park** provides a vantage point to watch whales during the migrating season *(Nov-Apr)*.

★**Santa Barbara Museum of Art** – *1130 State St.* ✕ ♿ ☎ *805-963-4364. www.sbmuseart.org.* Thirteen galleries showcase 4,500 years of Asian, European and American art. **Greek and Roman antiquities,** dating from the 4C BC, include the famed Lansdowne Hermes (AD 2C). **French and British art** of the 19C-early 20C features Chagall, Matisse and Monet. Galleries of 18-19C **American art** include works by Bierstadt, Chase, O'Keeffe and Sargent. The Davidson Gallery of **20C art** has pieces by Hofmann, Tamayo and Marin. Rotating exhibitions of contemporary **California art, Asian art** and **photography** round out the museum's collections.

★★★**Santa Bárbara Mission** – *2201 Laguna St.* 🄿 ☎ *805-682-4713.* Its twin towers rising against the foothills of Mission Canyon, California's 10th mission dominates the city physically and spiritually. Dedicated in 1786, the first church was replaced three times by larger structures. Near the main quadrangle stood 250

Santa Barbara Mission, Front Facade

single-room adobe dwellings for neophytes. The complex was rebuilt after an earthquake in 1812. The present church (1820) serves not only as a parish church, but as a research library and archive for the entire chain.

Designers of the regal **facade** borrowed freely from 1C BC Roman architecture. Six Ionic columns are crowned by pink-domed towers. The thick-walled **padres' quarters** contain mission artifacts from the late 18C to early 19C, including vestments and musical instruments. The **interior** of the church is adorned with bright motifs; the painted canvas reredos (1806) formed the basis for the detailed design scheme.

* **Santa Barbara Museum of Natural History** – *2559 Puesta del Sol. From the mission turn right on Los Olivos St.* ⏐ ⏐ ☎ *805-682-4711. www.sbnature.org.* Exhibits in this complex display flora, fauna, geology and ethnography of the West Coast. The **Chumash Indian Hall** contains artifacts from this tribe.

Solvang – *Rte. 246 east of US-101, 34mi northwest of Santa Barbara.* Founded as a Danish farm colony near Santa Inés Mission in 1911, charming Solvang is a popular tourist stop. A Danish provincial architectural style is applied at **Elverhøj Museum** *(1624 Elverhoy Way;* ☎ *805-686-1211),* which resembles an 18C Jutland farmhouse. Elsewhere in the town of 5,000 are timbered houses and windmills.

* **Santa Inés Mission** – *1760 Mission Dr., Solvang.* ⏐ ⏐ ☎ *805-688-4815. www .missionsantaines.org.* Founded in 1804, Santa Inés was the final link in the chain between San Francisco and San Diego. An 1824 neophyte revolt left much of it burned to the ground; an early-20C restoration created the present complex. In the **museum** are handmade **vestments*** from as far back as the 16C. The **church*** features *trompe l'œil* painting, a 17C polychromed wood statue of St. Agnes, and Stations of the Cross modeled after 18C Italian woodcuts.

** **La Purísima Mission** – *2295 Purisima Rd., via Mission Gate Rd., 1.8mi off Rte. 246 near Lompoc, 53mi northwest of Santa Barbara via US-101 and Hwy. 1.* ⏐ ☎ *805-733-3713.* Mission la Purísima Concepción de María Santísima was built near present-day Lompoc in 1787, but moved 3mi northeast after extensive earthquake damage. The Civilian Conservation Corps began restoration in 1934. Designed without a formal facade, the long, narrow **church** (1818) was built to provide easy access to travelers on El Camino Réal. The **shops and quarters building** housed soldiers and contained weaving, candle-making, leather-working and carpentry workshops. The 318ft-long **residence building*** housed padres' quarters, a library, office, wine cellar, guest quarters and chapel. Plants raised for food and medicine are cultivated in the restored **mission garden***.

Oklahoma

Southern Plains Indian Museum, Anadarko

It's fitting that Oklahoma's name means "red people" in the Choctaw language. The human history of this state revolves around its native population, largest in the US. Long before Coronado traipsed through the region in 1541, Osage, Kiowa, Commanche and Apache tribes had outposts in the short grass plains. Wichitas and other sedentary tribes built mound homes in the green mountains of the east.

After the Louisiana Purchase of 1803, the burgeoning population of the eastern US began eyeing the plains as a "remedy" for what they, in their push for development, perceived as "the Indian problem." Despite previous treaties with the US, huge numbers of Native Americans were forcibly evacuated from their homelands. Most tragic was the Cherokee Nation's "Trail of Tears": In 1838-39, 15,000 were compelled at gunpoint to march to Oklahoma.

Oklahoma became known as the Indian Territory. For a time, the "Five Civilized Tribes"—Cherokees, Choctaws, Seminoles, Chicasaws and Creeks—lived peacefully in their new home, setting up tribal governments, schools and farms. At the conclusion of the Civil War, however, the US government took from the Indians the western part of what is now Oklahoma as "punishment" for siding with the Confederacy and opened it to settlement. Cattle barons began driving their herds of longhorns up the Chisholm Trail through these western lands.

The first of several well-publicized land runs took place on April 22, 1889. A gun sounded at noon and 50,000 landowners-to-be raced to stake out their 160-acre plots on a 2 million acres. The run impelled cheaters to stake early claims, earning the state a nickname: the Sooner State. About 100,000 more showed up for the Cherokee Outlet land run in September 1893, when 6 million acres were offered.

Soon Oklahoma City became the largest stockyard in the US. Oil was discovered as early as 1901, and the territory became a magnet for oil prospectors the world over. In 1907, Oklahoma became the 47th state admitted to the Union.

Today these various elements are integral parts of the patchwork quilt of Oklahoma history. Indian festivals and museums can be found all over the state. Oil money has given Oklahoma City and Tulsa world-class art galleries and other cultural facilities. A cowboy ambience pervades the state in art, music and wardrobe, reflecting the famous Rodgers and Hammerstein musical *Oklahoma!*

OKLAHOMA CITY★

Michelin map 492 K 11   Central Standard Time
Population 472,221
Tourist Information ☎ 405-297-8912 or www.visitokc.com

Oklahoma City has grown from a land-grab tent city of 10,000 to a bustling urban hub with more than a million residents in its metropolitan area. Resting on the banks of the North Canadian River, it stretches across three counties and 650sq mi, ranking it as one of the largest cities, geographically, in the US.

Oil was discovered in 1928; oil wells still can be found all over the city, seven on the grounds of the state capitol. Western heritage is apparent in everything from museums and restaurants to the locals' favorite garb: cowboy boots and shirts.

In 1993, residents voted more than $300 million to urban revitalization. Two years later, the shocking terrorist bombing of the city's federal building took 168 lives; the Oklahoma City National Memorial is contributing to the recovery process.

SIGHTS

★**Oklahoma State Capitol** – *NE 23rd St. & Lincoln Blvd.* ✗ ᕲ ᐅ ☎ *405-521-3356.* This is the only capitol building in the world with working oil wells on its grounds. "Petunia," erected in the middle of a flower bed in 1941, and six sister wells have generated more than $8 million in revenue since they were first drilled. With 650 rooms, the Greco-Roman building of limestone, granite and marble features history murals and portraits of famous Oklahomans.

★**Oklahoma Historical Society & State Museum of History** – *2100 N. Lincoln Blvd.* ᕲ ☎ *405-521-2491. www.ok-history.mus.ok.us.* Opposite the capitol, this museum presents a overview of Oklahoma history, from early Indians to oilfield wildcatters to Oklahoma's role in the space program. Unique exhibits include a bison-hide tepee, a wagon used in two land runs, Indian murals and historic quilts.

★**Oklahoma City National Memorial** – *NW 5th & Harvey Sts.* ᕲ ☎ *405-235-3313. http://connections.oklahoman.net/memorial/.* With its two massive gates, reflecting pool and 168 empty glass-and-granite chairs, this memorial stands as a solemn reminder of the April 19, 1995, terrorist bombing of the Alfred P. Mur-

ADDRESS BOOK

Please see explanation on p 64.

Staying in Oklahoma

McBirney Mansion – *1414 S. Galveston St., Tulsa OK.* ᕲ ᐅ ☎ *918-585-3234. www.McBirneyMansion.com. 9 rooms.* **$$** Situated on a crest overlooking the Arkansas River is this quiet three-story landmark on the National Register of Historic Places. Stone pathways wind through three acres of gardens and ponds. Breakfast comes in a basket to rooms filled with fresh flowers.

The Waterford – *6300 Waterford Blvd., Oklahoma City OK.* ✗ᕲ ᐅ ☎ *405-848-4782. 197 rooms.* **$$** Rooms at this modern brick luxury hotel are equipped with the latest amenities. Live music is served with gourmet regional specialties in the **Garden Terrace;** the athletic club offers massage therapists and squash courts.

Dining in Oklahoma

Cattlemen's Steakhouse – *1309 S. Agnew St., Oklahoma City OK.* ☎ *405-236-0416.* **$$ American.** Right in the heart of Stockyards City, guests can enjoy hand-cut steaks cooked over hot coals—just as cowboys have done since 1910, when they stopped in after a roundup. The name changed in 1945 when the restaurant was lost in a craps game, but the menu has always featured the best meat in town.

Metro Diner – *3001 E. 11th St., Tulsa OK.* ☎ *918-592-2616.* **$ American.** Waitresses in poodle skirts swirl past the tables of this classic Route 66 diner, where patrons still can get a great 50s-style burger, a chocolate malt and a slice of apple pie as the jukebox pumps out "Rock Around the Clock."

rah Federal Building that killed 168 men, women and children. The design, by Hans Butzer, Torrey Butzer and Sven Berg, was selected from 624 entries that came from 50 states and 23 countries. Dedicated on the fifth anniversary of the bombing, the memorial was built around the "Survivor Tree" that withstood the blast. Each year, its seeds are gathered and planted in other cities to aid in psychological healing. Pilgrims from all over the world leave photos, children's toys and other memorabilia at the site where the nine-story building once stood.

* **Bricktown** – *Main St. & Sheridan Ave. between E.K. Gaylord & Stiles Sts.* ✗ ૐ ▣ ☎ *405-236-8666. www.okccvb.org/special/bricktown.htm.* Cafes, nightclubs, boutiques and antique shops mark this restored warehouse district. It incorporates the **Southwestern Bell Bricktown Ballpark** *(Mickey Mantle Dr. & Sheridan Ave.),* home of minor-league baseball's Oklahoma RedHawks. Paths flank the picturesque, 1mi **Bricktown Canal**; water taxis run past cafes, fountains and waterfalls.

** **Myriad Botanical Gardens** – *Reno & Robinson Sts.* ૐ ▣ ☎ *405-297-3995. www.OKC-cityhall.org/botanicalgarden.* Conceived by architect I.M. Pei, this 17-acre garden was modeled after Copenhagen's Tivoli Gardens. It features rolling hills, a lake and the Crystal Bridge Tropical Conservatory—a suspended, translucent bridge, seven stories high and 224ft long. Inside this architectural wonder are exotic plants from around the world, a skyway and a 35ft waterfall.

** **Stockyards City** – *Agnew & Exchange Sts., just south of I-40.* ☎ *405-235-7267.* The world's largest cattle market, this historic district has been restored to early-20C glory. More than 102 million cattle have been herded through here. Visitors can see a live cattle auction, Monday and Tuesday at the **Oklahoma National Stock Yards Company** *(2501 Exchange Ave.),* or watch craftsmen making saddles, boots and other Western wear. The "3-3" brand in the **Cattlemen's Steakhouse** *(1309 S. Agnew St.;* ☎ *405-236-0416),* an institution since 1910, represents the "hard six" that rancher Gene Wade threw to win the restaurant in a 1945 dice game.

* **Oklahoma City Art Museum** – *3113 General Pershing Blvd., Oklahoma State Fairgrounds.* ૐ ▣ ☎ *405-946-4477. www.okcartmuseum.com.* In 1968, when the Washington Gallery of Modern Art merged with the Corcoran Gallery of Art, this museum (Oklahoma's oldest) purchased the full Washington collection. Now the cornerstone of a 3,500-piece collection, these 153 pieces highlight such artists as Claes Oldenburg, Roy Lichtenstein, Helen Frankenthaler and Ellsworth Kelly. Also featured are works by Gauguin, Picasso, Cassatt, Magritte, Warhol and Calder. In 2001, the museum is to move downtown *(400 block of Couch Dr.).*

** **Omniplex** – 🄺🄸🄳🄢 *2100 NE 52nd St.* ✗ ૐ ▣ ☎ *405-602-6664. www .omniplex.org.* This 10-acre complex contains three museums, the OmniDome theater, a planetarium, botanical gardens, art galleries and more than 350 interactive exhibits. **Kirkpatrick Gardens and Greenhouse** has herb, rose and Japanese gardens as well as seasonal plantings. The **Kirkpatrick Science and Air Space Museum**★ *(*☎ *405-602-6664)* takes visitors on a journey from the Wright Brothers to the space shuttle with vintage aircraft and NASA artifacts. The **Red Earth Indian Center**★ *(*☎ *405-427-5228)* features a collection of Native American cradle boards and other artifacts. The **International Photography Hall of Fame and Museum**★★ *(*☎ *405-424-4055)* showcases the world's largest photo-mural, a 360-degree "laserscape" of the Grand Canyon; hundreds of antique cameras; and a hall of fame featuring George Eastman, Ansel Adams and Margaret Bourke-White.

* **Oklahoma City Zoo and Botanical Garden** – *2101 NE 50th St.* ✗ ૐ ▣ ☎ *405-424-3344. www.okczoo.com.* This 110-acre park is set on a lake and features more than 2,100 animals. Highlights include dolphin and sea-lion shows, a pride of lions, and the "Great EscApe" primate habitat, where visitors view gorillas, chimpanzees and orangutans in a rain forest. There's a butterfly garden, aviaries, an "endangered species carousel" and a safari tram that circles the zoo.

*** **National Cowboy Hall of Fame & Western Heritage Center** – *1700 NE 63rd St.* ✗ ૐ ▣ ☎ *405-478-2250. www.cowboyhalloffame.org.* Collections from saddles and barbed wire to contemporary Western and Native American art are presented in this fine museum. There are rodeo and cowboy exhibition galleries, a museum devoted to Western history, an art collection with works by Bierstadt, Remington and Russell, and a "corral" where children dress up and learn about ranch life. Prosperity Junction re-creates a late-19C cattle town. Western States Plaza, which flies 17 state flags, flanks botanical gardens. In summer, the museum hosts the Prix de West, a prestigious exhibition and sale of modern Western art.

Norman – *I-35, US-77 & Rte. 9 on south boundary of Oklahoma City.* ✗ ♿ ☐
☎ *405-366-8095. www.ncvb.org.* This city of 93,000 people has several
museums on or near its University of Oklahoma campus. The **Jacobson House
Native American Cultural Center** *(609 Chautauqua St.; ☎ 405-366-1667)* was the
home of Oscar Jacobson, who as first director of the university's School of Art
initiated a renaissance in Native American painting on the Southern Plains. The
Fred Jones Jr. Museum of Art *(410 W. Boyd St.; ☎ 405-325-3272)* also has a
strong Indian focus in its collection of 20C American art. The new **Sam Noble
Museum of Natural History** *(2401 Chautauqua St.; ☎ 405-325-4712)* is the largest
university-based natural-history museum in the US; in 1999 its paleontologists
discovered the world's tallest dinosaur, the giraffe-like Sauroposeidon, in
southeastern Oklahoma.

EXCURSIONS

**Guthrie – *US-77 & Rte. 33, 32mi north of Oklahoma City via I-35.* ✗ ♿ ☐
☎ *405-282-1947. www.guthrieok.com.* Founded in the land run of 1889,
Guthrie immediately established itself as the capital of Indian Territory. For 21
years, the territorial and state governments met here, until June 1910, when
the governor—engaged in a feud with the local newspaper editor—had the state
seal stolen during the night and moved to Oklahoma City. Now with 10,000 citizens, Guthrie has the largest National Historic Landmark District in the US—
400 city blocks, with 2,169 buildings. **First Capital Trolley** *(2nd & Harrison Sts.;
☎ 405-282-6000)* offers hourly tours of the city and its distinctive Victorian
architecture.

Anadarko – *US-62 & Rte. 9, 60mi southwest of Oklahoma City.* ✗ ♿ ☐ ☎ *405-
247-6651.* Anadarko calls itself the "Indian Capital of the Nation." The **National
Hall of Fame for Famous American Indians*** *(US-62; ☎ 405-274-5555)* displays bronze
busts of 41 Indians—including Chief Joseph, Cochise, Pocahontas, Sacagawea,
Sitting Bull, Tecumseh and Jim Thorpe—accompanied by descriptive plaques.
Within the **Southern Plains Indian Museum** *(US-62; ☎ 405-247-6221)* is the **Oklahoma
Indian Arts and Crafts Cooperative***. The well-known **Indian City USA** *(Rte. 8, 2.5mi
south; ☎ 405-247-5661)*, with replica tribal villages, is tourist-oriented.

*Fort Sill Military Reservation – *I-44 Exit 41 (Key Gate), Lawton, 87mi southwest of Oklahoma City.* ✗ ♿ ☐ ☎ *580-442-5123. http://sill-www.army.mil.* A
frontier post during the Indian Wars, Fort Sill contains more than 50 original
stone buildings from the 1870s, erected by the Buffalo Soldiers of the 10th
Cavalry. Among them are the guardhouse where Geronimo was prisoner, the
commanding general's house, a commissary, a chapel and post headquarters,
now the **Fort Sill Museum** *(437 Quanah Rd.; ☎ 580-442-5123)*.

*Chickasaw National Recreation Area – *Rte. 7, Sulphur, 84mi south of Oklahoma City via I-35.* ⛺ ♿ ☐ ☎ *580-622-3165. www.nps.gov/chic.* Ancient Indians called this area of mineral springs, streams and lakes "the peaceful valley of
rippling waters." Today's visitors fish, swim, camp or hike 20mi of trails. The
Travertine Nature Center has exhibits on history, geology and fauna. The park's centerpiece is **Lake of the Arbuckles**, created by the damming of Rock Creek.

TULSA*

Michelin map 492 L 10   Central Standard Time
Population 381,393
Tourist Information ☎ 918-585-1201 or www.tourism.tulsachamber.com

Tulsa dates its history from a Creek Indian conclave in 1836. The city grew as a cattle-ranching center in the 1870s but wasn't incorporated until 1898. After oil was
discovered in nearby Red Fork in 1901, Tulsa boomed. Another big strike in 1905—
the Glenn Pool, at that time the world's largest—made this city on the banks of the
Arkansas River a center of oil exploration. Between 1907 and 1920, Tulsa's population increased tenfold to 72,000. Today it has some 1,000 petroleum-related businesses, ranging from drilling contractors to wildcatters to refining operators.
A fixture on fabled Route 66 in its 1930s-1960s heyday, Tulsa has gorgeous Art
Deco architecture, nationally acclaimed art museums and notable opera, ballet and
symphony companies. *Fortune* magazine has ranked it as one of the nation's top 15
cities in quality of life.

SIGHTS

⋆⋆ Downtown Art Deco District – *Between 1st & 8th Sts., Cheyenne & Detroit Sts.* ✗ ⬤ 🅿 ☎ *918-583-2617.* The legacy of the early oil barons and a $1 million-a-month construction boom in the 1920s can be seen on a walking tour of the historical central business district. Only New York and Miami claim to have more Art Deco buildings.

The 1927 **Philtower Building** *(5th & Boston Sts.),* with its green-and-red tiled roof, monogrammed door knobs, brass elevator doors and 25ft vaulted ceilings, was once the tallest building in Oklahoma. Opposite, the 1930 **Philcade Building** *(5th & Boston Sts.)* conceals carved-stone birds, reptiles and mammals in the stylized foliage above its ground-floor windows.

Union Station Facade, Art Deco District

⋆⋆⋆ Gilcrease Museum   *1400 Gilcrease Museum Rd., off US 64 west of downtown.* ✗ ⬤ 🅿 ☎ *918-596-2700. www.gilcrease.org.* The world's largest collection of art of the American West, the Gilcrease exhibits paintings, drawings, prints and sculptures by more than 400 artists—among them Remington, Russell, Moran and Catlin. It features outstanding Native American art and artifacts; an interactive exhibit on Mexican art, history and culture; and myriad historical manuscripts, documents and maps.

Local oilman Thomas Gilcrease (1890-1962) began collecting in 1922 when few others were interested in Western art. In 1949, he built this museum on his estate. The 460-acre grounds contain theme gardens, outdoor sculpture, natural meadows and woodlands. From pleasant walking paths there are panoramic views of the Osage Hills.

⋆⋆ The Philbrook Museum of Art – *2727 S. Rockford Rd.* ✗ ⬤ 🅿 ☎ *918-749-7941. www.philbrook.org.* Set in 23 acres of English-style gardens, this castle-like Italian villa was once the home of oilman Waite Phillips. Today it is a renowned museum of fine and decorative arts of the Americas and Europe, Asia and Africa. The collection ranges from classical antiquities to 20C pieces, including Italian Renaissance oils and sculptures. Bouguereau's *The Shepherdess* (1890s) highlights the 19C French Salon. The lower level has Native American art and artifacts, and Taos-style furniture.

⋆ Oral Roberts University – *7777 S. Lewis Ave.* 🅿 ☎ *918-495-6807. www.oru.edu.* Banners from 60 nations and a 60ft, 30-ton pair of praying hands (by Leonard McMurry), the largest bronze sculpture on earth, greet visitors to this 500-acre Christian campus. The centrally located, 200ft Prayer Tower serves as the ORU visitor center; a self-guided tour of the modern campus begins on its observation deck.

★Tulsa Zoo and Living Museum – *5701 E. 36th St. N.* ✕ ♿ 🅿 ☎ *918-669-6600. www.tulsazoo.org.* The highlight of this zoo is the North American Living Museum Complex of four primary ecosystems—Arctic tundra, Southwest desert, Eastern forest and Southern lowlands—with animals, plants and cultural displays. The Tropical American Rainforest has jaguars and howler monkeys; at the Elephant Encounter, guests watch large pachyderms at work and play. Researcher Jane Goodall has acclaimed the Chimpanzee Connection. A zoo train circles the park's 70 acres, providing access to its 1,500 animals.

★Discoveryland – *5mi west of Rte. 97 on W. 41st St. S.* ✕ ♿ 🅿 ☎ *918-245-6552. Open June–Aug.* Although most visitors go only for the outdoor production of Rodgers and Hammerstein's *Oklahoma!,* Discoveryland also offers an Indian dance show, a Western musical revue, a barbecue and lots of kids' activities. There's an authentic Plains Indian village and trading post, and a country store. *Oklahoma!*—a delightful performance of the 3hr musical—features a cast of 50 with horses and a real surrey with a fringe on top.

EXCURSIONS

★J.M. Davis Arms & Historical Museum – *Rte. 66, Claremore, 29mi northeast of Tulsa.* ☎ *918-341-5707. www.state.ok.us/~jmdavis/.* Hotelier John Monroe Davis began to amass guns when he was 7 years old. When his collection of 20,000 guns, 1,200 steins, 70 saddles and 600 World War I posters began to consume the old Mason Hotel, the state took it over. This 40,000sq-ft building now displays everything from a Chinese cannon to elephant and whaling guns.

★★Will Rogers Memorial – *Rte. 88, Claremore, 25mi northeast of Tulsa via Rte. 66.* ⚠ 🅿 ☎ *918-341-0719. www.willrogers.com.* Overlooking Tiawah Valley, this limestone memorial, with nine galleries and a children's museum, tells the compelling story of Will Rogers' homespun life. The "Cowboy Philosopher" was a trick roper, movie star, radio commentator and newspaper columnist. Rogers (1879-1935) originally bought the 20-acre spread to build his retirement home prior to his death in an air crash. The museum that frames the family tomb has statues, paintings, celebrity photos, playbills, saddles, dioramas, video kiosks and six theaters showing films in which Rogers starred. **Will Rogers Birthplace,** a log-walled, two-story house at Dog Iron Ranch on Lake Oologah *(EW 38 Rd., Oologah, 12mi north of Claremore),* has an airstrip, an oak barn and friendly farm animals for petting.

Courtesy Will Rogers Memorial

Will Rogers

★Five Civilized Tribes Museum – *Agency Hill, Honor Heights Drive, Muskogee.* ♿ 🅿 ☎ *918-683-1701. www.fivetribes.com.* Housed in the former Union Indian Agency Building, built of native stone in 1875, this museum tells of the five tribes—Cherokee, Chickasaw, Choctaw, Creek and Seminole—who were forcibly moved to Indian Territory (now Oklahoma) in the 19C. The museum has an art collection of more than 800 items of traditional Native American art and sponsors four major art competitions annually. It also has an education division known as the **Center for the Study of Indian Territory.**

★The Cherokee Heritage Center – *Willis Rd., 1mi east of US-62, Tahlequah.* ♿ 🅿 ☎ *918-456-6007. www.leftmoon.com/cnhs.* Tahlequah was the end of the "Trail of Tears" for the Cherokees. The Heritage Center, established in 1963, is located on 44 wooded acres south of town. It has an authentic re-creation of a pre-European Cherokee settlement; the Adams Corner Rural Village, a typical 1880s Cherokee community; and the Cherokee National Museum. Craftspeople reenact the activities of their ancestors and demonstrate practices such as flint-knapping, basketry, pottery and cooking.

■ The Trail of Tears

Despite the US treaty of 1791, which recognized the Cherokee Nation and its right to ancestral lands in the Southeast, Congress in 1830 passed the **Indian Removal Act** *(p 29)*. The US militia rounded up 15,000 Cherokees, along with Chickasaws, Choctaws, Creeks and Seminoles, and in 1838 moved them to a camp in Tennessee, many in chains and shackles. In the treaty, the Cherokees had agreed to give up hunting; but they had built homes, farms and other businesses and even published a newspaper. Yet now they were forced to abandon their property, their livestock and their ancient burial grounds.

From Tennessee, in severe winter weather, they were marched at gunpoint 800mi to Indian Territory, now the state of Oklahoma. It took six months and cost more than 4,000 lives. Those who resisted were either forcibly removed or shot on sight. Over 25 percent of the Cherokee population perished.

The trail became a national monument in 1987, standing as a symbol of the wrongs suffered by the Indians at the hands of the US government.

★★**Woolaroc Ranch** – *Rte. 123, 12mi southwest of Bartlesville via US-60.* ✗ 㐧 ▣ ☏ *918-336-0307. www.woolaroc.org.* Established in 1925 as the country estate of Frank Phillips, founder of Phillips Petroleum, this 3,600-acre ranch and wildlife preserve has a museum with a world-class collection of Western art, artifacts and special exhibits, a spectacular lodge and a Native American Heritage Center. There is also an oil history area and a traders' camp that regularly does frontier reenactments. More than 700 animals, including buffalo, elk, deer and longhorn cattle, graze freely in the natural surroundings of the Osage Hills.

Phoenix-Tucson Area

Saguaro National Park, Sonoran Desert

To some, southern Arizona's Sonoran Desert is hell. Its average annual rainfall is less than 10in and temperatures spend a good part of the year in excess of 100°F. Bleached-out coyote skulls and 200-year-old saguaro skeletons are continual reminders to most visitors that this is an alien climate.

But others find heaven in these climes. A brief, sudden thunderstorm can cause the desert to erupt in color—the ocotillo's flaming orange, the palo verde's yellow, the prickly pear's peach, the saguaro's crimson. And Phoenix, seventh-largest city in the US, has more major golf and spa resorts than anywhere else between Florida and Southern California. Thanks to air-conditioning—invented here, claim Arizonans, by Oscar Palmer in his father's sheet-metal shop, two decades before it became commercially available—the desert is a highly livable place.

Thousands of years ago, this land of stark beauty was home to Tohono O'odham and Hohokam Indians, who designed an elaborate canal system for irrigating fields of squash, beans and corn. In the 16C, Spaniards dispatched from Mexico tramped through the dry mountains searching for gold, and although they came away with no riches, the conquistadors paved the way for priests and soldiers who established missions and walled forts called presidios.

Most of this rugged country (south of the Gila River) didn't become US territory until the 1853 Gadsden Purchase. Soon after, folks came to mine or ranch. Phoenix was founded in the 1860s and boomed after Roosevelt Dam, the world's largest masonry dam, was built in 1911. Tucson, a couple of hours' drive south, has even more sunshine than Phoenix, if not quite as many golf courses.

In the early days of settlement, the most prosperous communities in the Arizona Territory were in the southeast. The copper town of Bisbee had opera, money and Victorian architecture. Tombstone's silver mine was prolific, its citizens wealthy, its restaurants "the best between New Orleans and San Francisco." Its citizenry was also trigger-happy, solving petty arguments with the smoke of a pistol. Settlers also had to worry about raids from hostile Apache Indians. Led by Cochise and his successor, Geronimo, the Apaches heisted wagon trains and played hide-and-go-seek with the US Cavalry.

PHOENIX★

Map pp 254-255   Mountain Standard Time
Population 1,198,064
Tourist information ☎ 602-254-6500 or www.arizonaguide.com/phoenix

Located in the heart of the Sonoran Desert, greater Phoenix is known as the Valley of the Sun. This desert oasis stretches across more than 2,000sq mi and takes in Scottsdale, Tempe, Mesa and other communities surrounding the relatively young urban center of Phoenix. Main streets are laid parallel in 1mi-by-1mi grids, making orientation and navigation simple.

Historical Notes – When a mid-1860s hay camp was built atop a Hohokam site, it was dubbed "Phoenix," intimating that a new city might rise from ancient ruins just as the mythical bird rose from its ashes. A town site was laid out in 1870. By the end of that decade the village was a supply center for central Arizona mines and ranches; by 1900 it was territorial capital. Its transition from frontier town was assured in 1911, one year before Arizona became the 48th US state, when the Salado (Salt) River was dammed 60mi east of Phoenix. Roosevelt Dam and Theodore Roosevelt Lake provided plentiful water for farm irrigation and personal consumption, and electric power for industrial development.

The Southern Pacific arrived in 1926, just as air-conditioning grew popular. Chewing-gum magnate William Wrigley Jr., industrialist Cornelius Vanderbilt Jr. and architect Frank Lloyd Wright established second homes in the valley, which became known for its moderate winter climate. With more northerners wintering in Arizona, the Valley of the Sun began a boom that continues today.

DOWNTOWN

The city hub is **Patriots Square**, a park block flanked on its north and south by Washington and Jefferson Streets, respectively, and on its east by Central Avenue. A $1 billion revitalization east of the square has made **Civic Plaza** a major cultural center; a modern convention center, **Phoenix Symphony Hall** *(225 E. Adams St.; ☎ 602-262-7272)* and the **Herberger Theater** *(222 E. Monroe St.; ☎ 602-252-8497)* are located here. **Heritage and Science Park** *(between N. 5th, N. 7th, E. Washington & E. Monroe Sts.)* contains Heritage Square, the Arizona Science Center and the Phoenix Museum of History *(all below)*.

Arizona Center *(E. Van Buren St. between N. 3rd & N. 5th Sts.; ☎ 602-271-4000)*, a shopping complex with fountains and sunken gardens, is just north. A few blocks west is the **Orpheum Theatre** *(203 W. Adams St.; ☎ 602-252-9678)*, built in the Spanish Colonial Revival style in 1929 and recently restored. Bank One Ballpark *(below)* and **America West Arena** *(201 E. Jefferson St.; ☎ 602-379-2000)* are a short walk south; Phoenix is one of eight US cities with major-league baseball, basketball, football and ice hockey teams.

Several museums are on or near North Central Avenue, a boulevard lined with palm, mesquite and palo verde trees, running north from Patriots Square.

Heritage Square – *Between E. Monroe & E. Adams, N. 5th & N. 7th Sts.* ⚒ ♿ 🅿 ☎ 602-261-8948. The six remaining homes from the original Phoenix townsite, built 1895-1902, now house museums or restaurants. Oldest is the **Rosson House** *(113 N. 6th St.; ☎ 602-262-5071)*, an 1895 Queen Anne. Devonshire teas are served at the **Teeter House** *(622 E. Adams St.; ☎ 602-252-4682)*. A doll and toy museum is in the **Stevens House** *(602 E. Adams St.; ☎ 602-253-9337)*.

★**Arizona Science Center** – 🅺 *600 E. Washington St., Heritage and Science Park.* ⚒ ♿ 🅿 ☎ 602-716-2000. www.azscience.org. This concrete monolith (1997, Antoine Predock) has 350 hands-on exhibits, a five-story theater and cutting-edge planetarium. Visitors monitor activity at Sky Harbor International Airport, measure how much energy their bodies use, and experience virtual reality. **The World Around You** focuses on such themes as geology, hydrology and space sciences, **Networks** compares the likes of an ant colony and a ham radio operation with the internet.

★**Phoenix Museum of History** – *105 N. 5th St., Heritage and Science Park.* ♿ 🅿 ☎ 602-253-2734. Displays in this sleek, modern building give a good history of Phoenix's evolution from a dusty desert town to a modern metropolis. Interactive exhibits enable visitors to do everything from design a Victorian mansion to load a wagon for a cross-country trek.

★**Bank One Ballpark** – *401 E. Jefferson St.* ⚒ ♿ 🅿 ☎ 602-462-6799 *(tours) or* 602-462-6500. www.azdiamondbacks.com/bob/index.html. This "field of dreams" is a $356 million natural-grass baseball stadium with a retractable roof and a center-field swimming pool (rent: $4,300 per game) where home runs make a big splash. "The Bob," as locals know it, is home to the Arizona Diamondbacks. A restaurant and microbrewery are built into the stadium. A museum, **Cox Clubhouse★** Kids, displays Hall of Fame memorabilia, and features high-tech video productions and interactive games.

Arizona State Capitol Museum – *W. Washington St. & 17th Ave.* & ☎ *602-542-4675. http://dlapr.lib.az.us.* Built in 1900 as the Territorial Capitol, this tuff-and-granite structure became the state capitol in 1912. Displays included memorabilia of the USS *Arizona (p 179)*, sunk at Pearl Harbor in 1941.

★★★**The Heard Museum** – *2301 N. Central Ave.* & 🅿 ☎ *602-252-8840. www.heard.org.* Devoted to Native American culture and art, especially Southwest tribes, this fine museum contains 10 exhibition galleries and 32,000 works of art. Arches, colonnades and courtyards are hallmarks of Spanish Colonial architecture. The story of its 1929 founding is told in the **Sandra Day O'Connor Gallery.** The **Kitchell Gallery,** near the entrance, provides an orientation to baskets, jewelry, pottery and textiles.

A multimedia program introduces the impressive **Native Peoples of the Southwest Gallery★★★**. The traditions of Arizona's various tribal cultures—the Hohokam, O'odham and Pima of the Sonoran Desert, the Mogollon and Apache of the Uplands, the Pai, Navajo, Pueblo, Hopi and Zuni of the Colorado Plateau—

■ Kachina Dolls

A real Hopi kachina *(kat-SEE-na)* is a valued treasure. A kachina made by a well-known carver can fetch $10,000, although the average price ranges from $500 to $1,000. Originally carved by Hopi men and given to their female children to ensure fertility, these dolls (*tihu* to the Hopi) represent the 250 kachina spirits who intercede with the gods in the growing season. Children are given kachinas not as toys but to educate and inspire spiritual values.

Nineteenth-century kachinas were rudimentary and posed in static positions, arms and legs implied by bulges carved from the torso. Today, with a growing demand from collectors, kachinas are more artistic and detailed. Hopi religion forbids certain masked dolls to be produced for anyone outside the tribe. But many figures—such as Mud Head Clown and Morning Kachina—are found in abundance in museums and shops around the state.

No kachina is considered authentic unless it is carved from the root of a cottonwood tree, is anatomically correct and bears the artist's signature.

Cloud Messengers: Hopi Kachina Dolls Exhibit

are examined within the context of their unique geographical environs. Visitors can view a Navajo hogan, an Apache wickiup and a Hopi corn-grinding room, as well as talk with artisans working in the artist-in-residence program. The offshoot **Katsina Doll Gallery**★★ displays nearly 500 hand-carved Hopi kachinas.

★★ **Phoenix Art Museum** – *1625 N. Central Ave.* ✗ ⚕ 🅿 ☎ *602-257-1222. www.phxart.org.* An **orientation theater** introduces the 14,000-work collection, which includes a rare reproduction of Gilbert Stuart's 1796 *George Washington.* Arguably the most famous US portrait, it's the basis for the picture on the $1 bill. Featured is American art of the 19-20C and Western Americana, such as Maxfield Parrish's *Arizona* (1950). European artists include Renoir, Pissarro, Monet and Rousseau. Latin American art is represented by Rivera, Tamayo, Orozco and Kahlo. "Art of Our Time" features O'Keeffe, Picasso, Rothko and Calder. Further collections offer Asian art, miniature interiors and fashion.

PAPAGO SALADO

Southeast Phoenix, between Scottsdale and Tempe north of the Salt (Salado) River, is dominated by 1,200-acre **Papago Park.** 16C Spanish explorers, who at Pueblo Grande *(below)* found remains of a Hohokam civilization, labeled these vanished desert farmers *papago*, or "bean eaters." They left a complex system of aqueducts. Several major attractions are scattered among the buttes.

★★ **Desert Botanical Garden** – *1202 N. Galvin Pkwy., Papago Park.* ✗ ⚕ 🅿 ☎ *602-941-1225.* With more than 20,000 desert plants, this unique garden has won awards for environmental education. Four trails snake through the natural landscape. The brick-paved **Desert Discovery Trail** weaves past plants from around the world; a guide pamphlet identifies 20 unique cacti and succulents. The **Sonoran Desert Nature Trail** focuses on regional plants and animals. The **Plants & People of the Sonoran Desert Trail** provides a window on how Indian and Hispanic residents used native plants in their traditional lifestyles. The **Center for Desert Living Trail** displays a modern house and garden with exhibits on water and energy conservation. There's a plant shop, herbarium and research library. Workshops are offered on such topics as botanical sketching, desert landscaping and saguaro harvesting.

★ **Phoenix Zoo** – Kids *455 N. Galvin Pkwy., Papago Park.* ✗ ⚕ 🅿 ☎ *602-273-1341. www.phoenixzoo.org.* A motorized **Safari Train** runs a 30min narrated loop through the four habitat areas of this 125-acre nonprofit zoo. Some 1,300 animals are resident. On the Tropics Trail, the **Forest of Uco** simulates a Colombian rain-forest outpost with native animals. The **Arizona Trail** visits a desert home for coyotes, mountain lions, Mexican wolves and other Southwest wildlife. White rhinos, Sumatran tigers, South American spectacled bears and a breeding colony of Arabian oryxes are among 150 endangered animals.

Hall of Flame Museum of Firefighting – Kids *6101 E. Van Buren St., Papago Park.* ⚕ 🅿 ☎ *602-275-3473. www.hallofflame.org.* With more than 90 fully restored fire engines dating back to 1725, this museum lures anyone who runs to their window at the sound of a siren. Retired firefighters share tales of their profession as visitors operate alarms and see 3,000 pieces of equipment.

Pueblo Grande Museum and Archaeological Park – *4619 E. Washington St.* ⚕ 🅿 ☎ *602-495-0901. www.pueblogrande.com.* In the 14C, 1,000 people lived at this Hohokam ruin beside the head gate of the canal system. Homes, storage rooms, cemeteries and ball courts are easily discernible. Now a National Historic Landmark, the site has a museum with a theater and exhibits.

SCOTTSDALE

Founded as a farm village in 1888, Scottsdale *(☎ 800-805-0471; www .scottsdalecvb.com)* is nearly synonymous with "the good life." Resorts, golf courses and shopping districts of this city of 195,000 are world famous; there are more art galleries per capita than any other US city. Creative architecture and early zoning ordinances have allowed Scottsdale to preserve the desert's natural beauty in spite of the fast pace of urban development.

Downtown Scottsdale – *Camelback Rd. south to 2nd St., 68th Ave. east to Civic Center Blvd.* ✗ ⚕ 🅿 ☎ *480-947-6423.* This arts district embraces Main Street, Marshall Way and Fifth Avenue. Thursday nights for more than 20 years, galleries have scheduled new exhibits, artist appearances, demonstrations and music to coincide with **Scottsdale ArtWalk.** A free trolley shuttles those who prefer to ride.

Among Scottsdale's famed **shopping centers**★★ is glitzy **Scottsdale Fashion Square** *(Camelback & Scottsdale Rds.; ☎ 480-994-2140)*. **The Borgata** *(61661 N. Scottsdale Rd.; ☎ 480-998-1822)* re-creates a walled 14C Italian village. **El Pedregal Festival Marketplace** *(Scottsdale Rd. & Carefree Hwy.; ☎ 480-488-1072)* is a posh north Scottsdale center at the base of a 250ft boulder formation; its tenants include **The Heard Museum North** *(34505 N. Scottsdale Rd.; ☎ 480-488-9817)*, a satellite to the Indian art museum in downtown Phoenix.

★ **Old Town Scottsdale** – *Scottsdale Rd. north and south of First Ave.* ✗ ♿ 🅿 A mock strip of the 19C West in the heart of swank Scottsdale, Old Town has wooden sidewalks, cigar-store Indians, rustic storefronts, and Mexican and Western art. To some, its highlight is a pink ice-cream parlor called the **Sugar Bowl** *(4005 N. Scottsdale Rd.; ☎ 480-946-0051)*, an institution since 1958.

Old Town borders **Scottsdale Mall**, an emerald fantasyland of gurgling streams and fountain pools. It includes the striking new **Scottsdale Museum of Contemporary Art**★ *(7374 E. 2nd St.; ☎ 480-994-2787)*, with changing exhibits of architecture, art and design. Also here: **Scottsdale Center for the Arts** *(7380 E. 2nd St.; ☎ 480-994-2787)* and **Scottsdale Historical Museum** *(7333 Scottsdale Mall; ☎ 480-945-4499)*.

Other attractions perpetuate the Old West theme. The quirky **Buffalo Museum of America** 🄺🄸🄳🅂 *(10261 N. Scottsdale Rd.; ☎ 480-951-1022)* pays tribute to the American bison with eclectic memorabilia, from a family of singing buffaloes to buffalo banks made of cast iron. **Rawhide Western Town** 🄺🄸🄳🅂 *(23023 N. Scottsdale Rd.; ☎ 480-502-5600)* re-creates an 1880s community with stagecoach rides, mock gunfights, Indian dances, camel and burro rides for kids, and a steakhouse for all.

Cosanti – *6433 Doubletree Ranch Rd.* ♿ 🅿 ☎ 480-948-6145. *www.cosanti.com.* Italian architect Paolo Soleri showcases "arcology," which he defines as the integration of architecture and ecology in new urban habitats. A prototype is under construction an hour's drive north: **Arcosanti** *(off I-17 Exit 262, Cordes Junction; ☎ 520-632-7135)* will combine compact structure with large solar

ADDRESS BOOK

Please see explanation on p 64.

Staying in the Phoenix-Tucson Area

The Boulders Resort – *34631 N. Tom Darlington Rd., off Rte. 74, Carefree AZ.* ✗ ♿ 🅿 🏊 ☎ 602-488-9009. *www.grandbay.com. 208 rooms.* **$$$$** The eponymous red rocks in front of this world-class New Age resort are just part of the allure of The Boulders, a mecca for spa, golf and tennis lovers just northeast of Phoenix. At night, guests search for wildlife with infrared glasses.

Tanque Verde Ranch – *14301 E. Speedway Blvd., Tucson AZ.* ✗ ♿ 🅿 🏊 ☎ 520-296-6275. *www.tanqueverderanch.com. 73 rooms.* **$$$$** Rates at this plush dude-ranch retreat beside Saguaro National Park include unlimited riding, cowboy barbecues and Mexican fiestas. Cacti and pink-stucco casitas surround the main house, where guests linger over rustic communal tables.

Arizona Inn – *2200 E. Elm St., Tucson AZ. 86 rooms.* ✗ ♿ 🅿 🏊 ☎ 520-325-1541. **$$** Little has changed since Franklin Roosevelt came here to "rough it" in the 1930s, except that Tucson has now enfolded this 14-acre hacienda-style hotel. It sprawls with coral-pink casitas, log-pole trellises and mock-orange trees. Velvet lawns surround sunny patios, and the pool is enclosed by rose-covered walkways.

Hermosa Inn – *5532 N. Palo Cristi Rd., Paradise Valley AZ.* ✗ ♿ 🅿 🏊 ☎ 602-955-8614. *www.hermosainn.com. 35 rooms.* **$$** Cowboy artist Lon Megargee built this hacienda in the 1930s as his home and studio. It remains a peaceful resort of casitas spread over six acres of prickly pear and barrel cactus. Aged chaps on the wall, alongside original Megargee paintings, create a ranch feel.

Bisbee Inn – *45 OK St., Bisbee AZ. 23 rooms.* 🅿 ☎ 520-432-5131. **$** In 1920, it cost $2 to stay at this basic hotel, and it remains a bargain to this day. Guests get history rather than luxury—colorful quilts, pedestal sinks and softly patterned wallpaper. Once a wooden building catering to miners, the Inn is now solid brick, touched with old maps and photos.

Hotel San Carlos – *202 N. Central Ave., Phoenix AZ.* ✗ 🅿 🏊 ☎ 602-253-4121. *www.hotelsancarlos.com. 133 rooms.* **$** A yellow-brick downtown classic since 1928, the San Carlos is a historic anomaly in a region

greenhouses to house 6,000 people on 25 acres. Cosanti's wind bells, cast of bronze or fired in ceramic kilns, hang everywhere and are sold in great numbers at a gift shop.

★★ Taliesin West – *12621 Frank Lloyd Wright Blvd., via Taliesin Dr. off Cactus Rd. Visit by guided tour (13hrs) only.* ⚹ 🅿 ☎ *480-860-2700. www.franklloydwright .org.* Frank Lloyd Wright, perhaps the greatest architect of the 20C, built this

Taliesin West

© Dave G. Houser

of spa resorts and golf haciendas. The lobby's chandeliers and period wallpaper give an Old World ambience; the rooftop pool is a modern amenity.

The Sunburst Resort – *4925 N. Scottsdale Rd., Scottsdale AZ.* ✕⚹ 🅿 ⌇ ☎ *602-945-7666. www.sunburstresort.com. 210 rooms.* **$** Southwest resort life in the heart of Scottsdale features an oasis-like aquatic courtyard with bridges, lagoons, waterslides and a torch-lit main pool. Rooms have hand-painted adobe walls and open-beam ceilings.

Dining in the Phoenix-Tucson Area

RoxSand – *2594 E. Camelback Rd., Phoenix AZ.* ☎ *602-381-0444.* **$$$ Creative American.** Global influences at this Biltmore Fashion Park restaurant range across five continents, but produce is local and organic. The house specialty is air-dried duck with pistachio onion marmalade in buckwheat crepes.

Alice Cooper'stown – *101 E. Jackson St., Phoenix AZ.* ☎ *602-253-7337. www.alicecooperstown.com.* **$$ American.** Two halls of fame—baseball and rock 'n' roll—coexist at this lively sports bar and grill near Bank One Ballpark. Servers wear black eye makeup in tribute to owner Alice Cooper, a Phoenix native famed as a rock musician, while delivering barbecue and "fields of greens."

Café Roka – *35 Main St., Bisbee AZ.* ☎ *520-432-5153.* **$$ Italian.** The exterior of this local favorite looks as it did in 1908, but the inside has changed with the times. The main floor, with a central bar, features paintings by local artists. The second floor overlooks an open kitchen where chefs prepare pastas.

Fuego Restaurant Bar and Grill – *6958 E. Tanque Verde Rd., Tucson AZ.* ☎ *520-886-1745. www.snnewpages.com/fuego.* **$$ Southwestern.** *Fuego* (Spanish for "fire") is the fashion here. Dishes may be finished off with a flame of tequila, either on the patio or inside the earth-toned dining room. The namesake appetizer contains chef Alan Zeman's own chorizo; trademark dishes are prickly-pear pork and ostrich or emu specials.

Café Poca Cosa – *88 E. Broadway, Tucson AZ.* ☎ *520-622-6400.* **$ Mexican.** Suzana Davila's daily-changing menu has imaginative food from all regions of Mexico, including 26 varieties of moles and her own plum salsa. Decor is colorful and festive, with Mexican art hanging beside Mayan masks. Locals often crowd on the patio around the fountain to the tune of folk music.

complex of low-lying buildings by gathering desert rocks and sand from washes, assembling them by hand to blend with 600 surrounding acres. Taliesin West, a National Historic Landmark, served as his winter home, studio and architectural canvas from 1937 until his death in 1959. Tours showcase Wright's talent for linking indoor and outdoor spaces with dramatic terraces, gardens and walkways. The site still holds a residence, archives, the Frank Lloyd Wright School of Architecture, and Taliesin Architects, a working design firm.

✱Fleischer Museum – *17207 N. Perimeter Dr. at Pima & E. Bell Rds.* ♿ 🅿 ☎ *480-585-3108. www.fleischer.org.* The first museum dedicated to American Impressionism (1890-1930), this museum—cornerstone of an office building—features a skylit sculpture court and more than 250 pieces from such painters as Franz Bischoff, Donna Schuster, Guy Rose and Joseph Raphael. Another gallery focuses pre-World War II Soviet Realism.

ADDITIONAL SIGHTS

✱South Mountain Park Preserve – *10919 S. Central Ave.* ♿ 🅿 ☎ *602-495-0222.* Once a Hohokam hunting ground, later a mining camp and a Depression-era work camp, this municipal park offers impressive city views from **Dobbins Lookout** and 58 trails for hiking, biking and riding across its 25sq mi.
At its foot is **Mystery Castle** 🧒 *(800 E. Mineral Rd., end of S. 7th St.; ☎ 602-268-1581)*, an 8,000sq-ft, 18-room manse hand-built of everything from desert rocks to Bing Crosby's golf club. Mary Lou Gulley, whose father built the "castle" for her in 1930-45, still lives there and gives tours.

Tempe – *US-60 & Loop 202, 9mi east of Phoenix.* ☎ *480-894-8158. www.tempecvb .com.* ✗♿ 🅿 Founded in 1871 at a crossing of the Salt River, this bustling city of 167,000 is home to 44,000-student Arizona State University. The Tempe *(tem-PEE)* historical district extends along six blocks of Mill Avenue. On the fringe of Papago Park, the **Arizona Historical Society Museum** *(1300 N. College Ave.; ☎ 480-929-0292)* has exhibits that focus on water's role in developing the Valley of the Sun.

Arizona State University – *South bank of Salt River east of Mill Ave.* ✗♿ 🅿 ☎ *480-965-9011. www.asu.edu.* The campus highlight is **Grady Gammage Auditorium✱** *(Apache Blvd. & Mill Ave.; ☎ 480-965-4050)*; the circular structure, Frank Lloyd Wright's last major nonresidential design (1959), is famed for acoustics. The **J. Russell and Bonita Nelson Fine Arts Center✱** *(10th St. & Mill Ave.)*, designed by Antoine Predock (1989), is a grayish-purple complex of colliding boxes, triangles and terraces that at once resembles a Hopi pueblo and a desert mountain range.

Guadalupe – *Avenida del Yaqui, south off Baseline Rd. at I-10 Exit 155.* Founded in 1904 as a camp for Yaqui Indians fleeing Mexico, this settlement between Tempe and South Mountain Park is a suburban anomaly. It looks like a small village in Mexico but has a **farmers' market** *(9210 W. Avenida del Yaqui; ☎ 480-730-1945)*, a Mexican bakery and a *mercado* with bargains on pottery, ceramics, curios and even piñatas.

Mesa – *US-60 & Rte. 87, 15mi east of Phoenix.* ✗♿ 🅿 ☎ *480-827-4700. www.mesacvb.com.* Fast-growing Mesa, its population having more than doubled to 360,000 in 20 years, was founded by Mormon pioneers in 1878. The faith's **Arizona Temple** *(525 E. Main St.; ☎ 480-964-7164)* remains a landmark. The **Mesa Southwest Museum** *(53 N. Macdonald St.; ☎ 480-644-2230)* features Hohokam and pioneer history. At municipal Falcon Field *(Greenfield & McKellips Rds.)*, the **Champlin Fighter Aircraft Museum** *(4636 Fighter Aces Dr.; ☎ 480-830-4540)* has a collection of vintage fighter aircraft; the **Confederate Air Force Museum-Arizona Wing** *(2017 N. Greenfield Rd.; ☎ 480-924-1940)* displays World War II aircraft.

EXCURSIONS

✱✱Apache Trail – *Rte. 88 & US-60.* ⛺ ✗♿ 🅿 This 164mi loop has little to do with Apaches, although the US Cavalry combed the area for renegade bands in the late 19C. Formally, the Trail is the 78mi stretch of Route 88 between Apache Junction and Globe, connecting at either end with US-60. The road crosses the dramatic **Superstition Mountains,** skirts ghost towns and **Weaver's Needle Lookout,** and passes three exquisite lakes—Canyon, Apache and Roosevelt—created by the **Roosevelt Dam.** The 25mi from **Tortilla Flat,** a ghost town of six residents that began as a stage stop, to Roosevelt is a narrow, winding gravel road. Most travelers treat the Trail as a loop drive, returning to Phoenix via US-60 through Superior.

✱Tonto National Monument – *Rte. 88, 4mi east of Roosevelt Dam.* 🅿 ☎ *520-467-2241. www.nps.gov/tont.* For 300 years, the Salado Indians, descendants of the Hohokam, lived along the Salt River. This preserve holds the remains of 13C cliff dwellings. A .5mi trail climbs to the 20-room Lower Dwelling where the Salado slept, cooked and stored crops. Rangers conduct tours of the 32-room Upper Dwellings *(Nov–Apr; reservations required)*.

★**Boyce Thompson Arboretum** – *37615 Rte. 60, Superior*. ♿ 🅿 ☎ *520-689-2811. http://arboretum.ag.arizona.edu*. Mining magnate William Boyce Thompson turned this site beneath Picketpost Mountain into a 300-acre public park in the 1920s. The 1.5mi main trail provides an overview; other trails take in a variety of vegetation that attracts a year-round colony of colorful birds. A hidden canyon, desert lake and interpretive center with two greenhouses are on site.

★**Casa Grande Ruins National Monument** – *1100 Ruins Dr., Rte. 87, Coolidge. 52mi southeast of Phoenix; take Rte. 387 at I-10 Exit 185 and follow signs*. ♿ 🅿 ☎ *520-723-3172. www.nps.gov/cagr*. Dominating an ancient village along the Gila River, this four-story, 60ft-long structure—named *casa grande*, or "big house," by Spanish discoverers—was among the last and largest constructions of the 12C Hohokam. Built of sand, clay and limestone mud, it may have been used in astronomical observations for farming and ritual. It became the first US archaeological preserve in 1892; a canopy has sheltered it since 1903.

South along the interstate is **Picacho Peak State Park** *(I-10 Exit 219)*, a solitary peak rising 1,500ft above the desert. The Butterfield Stage Road skirted the mountain, site of an 1862 Civil War tiff in which 12 Union troops defeated 17 Confederate forces.

TUCSON★★

Map pp 254-255   Mountain Standard Time
Population 460,466
Tourist Information ☎ 520-624-1817 or www.visittucson.org

Unlike Phoenix, which has conquered the desert with massive irrigation projects, Tucson embraces dry land as its child. With little or no agriculture, the city has come to consider green lawns a waste of time and water. Most residents focus on enjoying the sunshine (350 days a year) and high Sonoran Desert. Five mountain ranges surround this city that sprawls across 500sq mi and includes the University of Arizona, an inspiring campus with a palm-flanked pedestrian mall.
Tucson's night skies have inspired astronomers, both professional and amateur, to set up telescopes of all sizes and shapes. Tucson has a greater concentration of observatories within a 50mi radius than anywhere else on earth.

Historical Notes – The first stargazers, the Hohokam, left petroglyphs, ball courts and pit houses that may be seen in parks, canyons and excavations around the city. Pima and Tohono O'odham tribes later took up residence. The name "Tucson" was not applied until 1694, when Spanish missionaries had trouble pronouncing *stjukshon*, an Indian word that means "spring at the foot of a black mountain." The city was founded in 1775 by Irishman Hugh O'Connor, an explorer for the Spanish crown. The walled **Presidio San Agustín del Tucson** was built under his direction; its ruins may be seen in El Presidio Historic District.
Tucson became part of newly independent Mexico in 1821, then was transferred to the US with the Gadsden Purchase in 1853. A wild-and-woolly frontier town, it became capital of the Arizona Territory in 1867. The seat of government was later moved north to Prescott, then to Phoenix, but the land-grant university, founded in 1885, helped establish Tucson's role as a cultural center.

DOWNTOWN AREA

Though the hub of a metropolitan area of 725,000 people, Tucson's downtown core is rather small, condensed within a few square blocks east of Interstate 10. Most historic buildings have been replaced by modern structures, although some old adobes and Spanish Colonial edifices remain. A downtown walking tour takes in the 1896 **St. Augustine Cathedral** *(192 S. Stone Ave.;* ☎ *520-623-6351)*. Across a skywalk, on the original presidio site, Tucson's government complex includes the **Pima County Court House** *(Church Ave. between Alameda & Pennington Sts.)* with its tiled Spanish-style dome. **El Presidio Historic District** preserves numerous 19C and early-20C homes and shops, including **Old Town Artisans** *(p 254)* and **La Casa Cordova** *(Meyer & Telles Sts.)*, believed to be Tucson's oldest (c.1850) surviving building.

★**Tucson Museum of Art & Historic Block** – *140 N. Main Ave.* 🍴♿ 🅿 ☎ *520-624-2333. www.tucsonarts.com*. This incongruously bold, colorful, contemporary museum has an intriguing collection of avant-garde art and photography in a series of descending galleries, plus fine 19-20C American works (Thomas Moran, Arthur Dove, Anton Refreigier, Marsden Hartley). The museum owns and maintains the adjacent Historic Block, which includes La Casa Cordova *(p 253)* and four other buildings.

Old Town Artisans – *186 N. Meyer Ave.* ✗ ⚘ 𝗣 ☎ *520-623-6024. www.oldtownartisans.com.* This restored 1850s adobe in El Presidio is home to six shops selling Latin American folk art, Native American tribal art, imports from Mexico and regional crafts, plus a pair of restaurants. Over the years, this adobe—its ceilings supported by saguaro ribs, barrel staves and packing crates—has been used as everything from a grocery store to a distillery.

★ **University of Arizona** – *Between Euclid & Campbell Aves., 6th & Elm Sts.* ✗ ⚘ 𝗣 ☎ *520-621-2211. www.arizona.edu.* Nearly 35,000 students attend this 352-acre campus 1mi northeast of downtown. A top research institution in optics and computer software, it has several museums. Dendrochronology (tree-ring dating) and garbology (the study of cultures by analyzing refuse) were developed here.

West of campus, a six-block stretch of **Fourth Avenue** *(University Blvd. to 9th St.)* bustles with eccentric shops, unusual restaurants and colorful murals. Two old-time trolley cars are under restoration in a **trolley-car barn** *(4th Ave. & 8th St.);* on weekends, the Old Pueblo Trolley runs between there and the UA Main Gate.

★ **Arizona State Museum** – *1013 E. University Blvd. at Park Ave.* ⚘ 𝗣 ☎ *520-621-6302. www.statemuseum.arizona.edu.* This anthropology museum specializes in cultures of the Southwest and Mexico. In the north building, the **Paths of Life**★★ exhibit interprets origins, history and modern lifestyles of 10 desert cultures —the Seri, Tarahumara, Yaqui, Tohono O'odham, Yuman, Paiute, Pai, Apache, Navajo and Hopi. A **Mexican mask** exhibit in the south building contains more than 350 colorful folk-art masks. Museum archives hold over 100,000 artifacts.

★ **UA Museum of Art** – *1031 N. Olive St.; E. 2nd St. & Speedway Blvd.* ⚘ 𝗣 ☎ *520-621-7567. http://artmuseum.arizona.edu.* Paintings by Rembrandt, Picasso and O'Keeffe, and Jacques Lipchitz sculptures, highlight a collection of 4,000 works.

★★ **Center for Creative Photography** – *Olive St. between E. 2nd St. & Speedway Blvd.* ⚘ ☎ *520-621-7968. www.creativephotography.org.* Founded in 1975 by Ansel Adams and then-university president John P. Schaefer, the center highlights 20C photography as an art form. Changing exhibitions draw from the work of Adams, Richard Avedon, Louise Dahl-Wolfe, Philippe Halsman, Edward Weston and 2,000 other photographers whose prints are archived in one of the world's finest photo research centers. Talks, lectures and presentations are regularly scheduled.

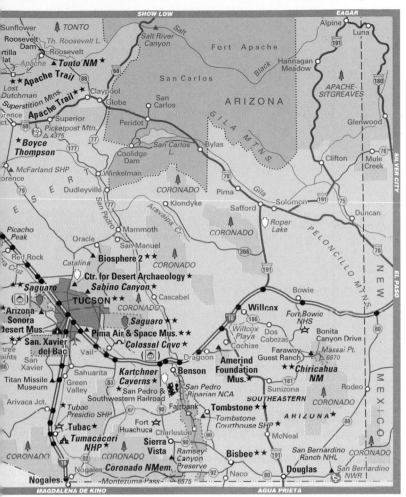

★**Flandrau Science Center and Planetarium** – 🏷Kids *Cherry Ave. & University Blvd. mall, east side of campus* ♿ ☎ 520-621-4515. *http://www.flandrau.org.* Interactive exhibits deal with mirrors, vacuums, holograms, kinetics and other basic physics. Visitors touch rare stones, including moon rocks, in an extensive mineral exhibit. An observatory offers stargazing through a 16in telescope.

★**Arizona Historical Society Museum** – *949 E. 2nd St., across Park Ave. from UA campus.* ♿ 🅿 ☎ 520-628-5774. *http://w3.arizona.edu/~azhist.* Exhibits include re-created O'odham, Mexican and Anglo-American homes of the 1870s and a replica of El Presidio. The Arizona Mining Hall features an underground copper mine that illustrates mining, smelting and production processes.

NORTH SIDE

Tucson Botanical Gardens – *2150 N. Alvernon Way, south of Grant Rd.* ♿ 🅿 ☎ 520-326-9686. *www.azstarnet.com/~tbg/.* This 5.5-acre urban oasis, founded in 1931, features a series of intimate gardens with cacti, wildflowers and Native American crops. There are also a children's garden and sensory garden. A xeriscape garden demonstrates landscaping in an arid climate.

★**Center for Desert Archaeology** – *3975 N. Tucson Blvd.* ⚠ 🅿 ☎ 520-885-6283. *www.cdarc.org.* Archaeologists lead half-day tours to such prehistoric sites as Catalina State Park, where in a 2.5sq-mi area the center has uncovered 42 different sites—including Hohokam petroglyphs, a mesquite bean-grinding site, and a 1,500-year-old village covered with pottery shards and containing two ball courts. Center membership allows participation in future excavations.

*Sabino Canyon – *5900 N. Sabino Canyon Rd. at Sunrise Dr.* ♿ 🅿 ☎ *520-749-2861.* A shuttle bus offers 45min tours through this Coronado National Forest canyon in the Santa Catalina Mountains of northeast Tucson. Once visited by mammoths and soldiers, who rode from Fort Lowell to swim, the canyon was "civilized" in the 1930s when Civilian Conservation Corps workers built bridges and 3.8mi of roads. Today locals enjoy hiking, biking, picnicking and swimming.

Tohono Chul Park – *7366 N. Paseo del Norte.* ✗♿ 🅿 ☎ *520-575-8468. www.tohonochulpark.org.* Nature trails wind through 49 acres of desert flora—home to a variety of wildlife—surrounding the adobe Exhibit House. Devonshire teas are served on a plant-filled patio of the West House. Events include concerts, art shows and a summer tribute to the night-blooming cereus.

WEST SIDE

Overlooking downtown is **"A" Mountain** *(Sentinel Peak Rd., off Congress St.),* so nicknamed for a big "A" whitewashed on the side of Sentinel Peak in 1915 by rabid fans of the university football team, and annually reapplied since. **Views**** are excellent from atop the peak, once used as a Spanish lookout.

Much of west Tucson is embraced within **Tucson Mountain Park** *(Gates Pass & Kinney Rds.),* 27sq mi of arid mountain and mesa lands speckled with saguaro cacti and other desert vegetation. There are impressive views of the western desert from Gates Pass, 8mi west of downtown via Speedway Boulevard.

The International Wildlife Museum – 🄺🄸🄳🅂 *4800 W. Gates Pass Rd.* ✗♿ 🅿 ☎ *520-617-1439. www.thewildlifemuseum.org.* More than 400 species of stuffed and preserved animals are displayed in galleries and dioramas. About half are antelope, sheep and deer heads in the Comparative Species Gallery. Sections on animal anatomy and on insects, including Africanized "killer bees," emphasize learning. The museum offers nature films and education programs.

*Old Tucson Studios – 🄺🄸🄳🅂 *201 S. Kinney Rd.* ✗♿ 🅿 ☎ *520-883-0100. www.oldtucson.com.* Hollywood in the desert, this 1880s Western town has been the location for more than 350 movies and TV shows since it was built in 1939 by Columbia Pictures as the set for *Arizona,* starring William Holden. The Old West as perceived by video drones was largely shaped by this village. John Wayne *(Rio Lobo,* 1966; *McClintock,* 1962) did several films here; Clint Eastwood *(The Outlaw Josey Wales,* 1976) and Paul Newman *(Hombre,* 1966) were among other stars.

With keen attention to authenticity, the dusty frontier town was turned into an entertainment park in 1959, but has continued to operate as a film venue. Visitors can saunter by jails and corrals or swagger into saloons and dance halls for a drink of root beer or sarsaparilla. **Town Hall** is a museum of film history; there are stunt shows, stagecoach rides, gunfights, theaters, even a spooky and thrilling **Iron Door Mine Ride.**

**Arizona-Sonora Desert Museum – 🄺🄸🄳🅂 *2021 N. Kinney Rd.* ☎ *520-883-2702. www.desert.net/museum.* A combination zoo and botanical park with natural-history exhibits, this "museum" is best seen by walking 2mi of trails through 21 acres of desert. More than 300 animal and 1,300 plant species, all indigenous to the Sonoran Desert, include ocelots and jaguarundi in a red-rock canyon, mountain lions and black bears in a mountain woodland, bighorn sheep climbing rock ledges, javelina rooting among prickly pears. Visitors come nose to snout or beak with Gila monsters, prairie dogs and red-tailed hawks.

A limestone cave with stalagmites and stalactites contains an **Earth Sciences*** display on geology. In the **Hummingbird Aviary****, seven species of native hummingbirds hover frightlessly around their visitors. Nocturnal desert dwellers are active by day in **Life Underground.** Native **basket weavers** seasonally demonstrate their craft beneath a mesquite ramada.

**Saguaro National Park – ⚠♿ 🅿 ☎ *520-733-5100. www.nps.gov/sagu.* The giant saguaro, symbol of the American Southwest, grows only in the Sonoran Desert of Arizona and northern Mexico. This park protects thriving communities of the cacti, which can grow to 50ft in height, 8 tons in weight and 200 years in age. Saguaros anchor diverse communities of animals and smaller plants.

The park has two units. In the 37sq mi **Tucson Mountain District** *(2700 N. Kinney Rd.;* ☎ *520-733-5158),* saguaros are thicker and younger. Beginning from the Red Hills Visitor Center, 1mi north of the Desert Museum, 41mi of trails and the **Bajada Loop Drive** *(9mi)* offer fine views of cacti climbing mountain slopes.

The 103sq-mi eastern unit of the national park, the **Rincon Mountain District** *(3693 S. Old Spanish Trail;* ☎ *520-733-5153),* extends on the east side of Tucson, 15mi from downtown. The **Cactus Forest Drive** *(8mi)* loops from the visitor center through a saguaro forest; 128mi of hiking and horse trails climb over 7,000ft ridges into a woodland shared by scrub oak and ponderosa pine.

■ The Giant Saguaro

The giant saguaro, an appropriate icon for the state of Arizona, is found only in the highly specialized Sonoran Desert climate. The largest species of cactus in the US grows slowly: After three years, a young saguaro is barely half an inch high. It will be 50 before it flowers and 75 before it sprouts its first arm.

An individual saguaro produces some 40 million seeds, but generally only one develops into a mature plant. For germination, heavy summer rains must fall; of those that sprout, only about 1 percent survive.

It's illegal to damage saguaros or remove them from the desert, living or dead, without a permit. But poaching has long been a problem. Investigators for the Arizona Department of Agriculture, sometimes called "Cactus Cops," patrol the desert in search of violators. The ultimate revenge was exacted several years ago on a Phoenix man who began blasting a saguaro with a 16-gauge shotgun. A spiny 4ft arm fell off the cactus, crushing the vandal.

Saguaro Cactus Blooms

SOUTH SIDE

★★ **Mission San Xavier del Bac** – *1950 W. San Xavier Rd.* ♿ 🅿 ☎ *520-294-2624.* The oldest US Catholic church still in use, San Xavier del Bac has been called the Sistine Chapel of the US by the man who restored Michelangelo's master work in Rome—and who supervised work on this San Xavier Indian Reservation mission. Founded in 1692 by Father Eusebio Kino, the mission wasn't finished until 1797. With bricks, stone and limestone mortar, Tohono O'odham Indians created an exquisite white-domed building of Mexican Renaissance, Moorish and Byzantine styles. The walls and ceilings of the sanctuary, entered through mesquite-wood doors, are beautifully painted in historical frescoes. Throughout are statues and carvings. Small handmade objects with ribbons, *milagros,* are left by people who are seeking a miracle or are giving thanks for one already granted.

Pima Air and Space Museum – 🄺🄸🄳🅂 *6000 E. Valencia Rd. at I-10 Exit 267.* 🗙 ♿ 🅿 ☎ *520-574-0462. www.pimaair.org.* With more than 200 aircraft, this museum displays everything from a full replica of the Wright Brothers' 1903 Flyer to the SR-71 Blackbird, capable of speeds over 2,000mph. Visitors see military, private and commercial planes, including the Air Force One used by Presidents Kennedy and Johnson. Tours visit the **Aerospace Maintenance and Regeneration Center (AMARC) on Davis-Monthan Air Force Base, where thousands of retired aircraft are stored in various stages of air readiness.

Pima operates the **Titan Missile Museum*** *(1580 W. Duval Mine Rd., Sahuarita, at I-19 Exit 69, 25mi south of Tucson; ☎ 520-574-9658),* a chilling reminder of the Cold War. For two decades, the US kept 54 nuclear-warhead missiles ready to be launched at a moment's notice from various sites. All except this one were dismantled in the mid-1980s. Guided tours *(1hr)* include the launch control center, the rocket engine that propelled a 330,000-pound missile to an altitude of 47mi in just 2 1/2 min, and the reentry vehicle.

EXCURSIONS

**Biosphere 2 – *Milepost 96.5, Rte. 77, Oracle, 40mi north of Tucson.* 🗙 ♿ 🅿 ☎ *520-896-6200. www.bio2.edu.* Science fiction meets fact at this surrealistic outpost. From 1991 to 1993, eight researchers lived within a three-acre glass-enclosed terrarium, a self-sustaining laboratory sealed off from the outside world. Visitors now may tour "the whole world" in a single afternoon: There's a million-gallon ocean, a tropical rain forest, a savanna, a desert and other environments and life forms of Biosphere 1, also known as Planet Earth. New York's Columbia University owns and operates the $150 million facility, which includes a 250-acre research campus, hotel and conference center. At the visitor center, a film, narrated by actor Alan Alda, offers an overview.

*Colossal Cave – 🄺🄸🄳🅂 *Old Spanish Trail, 6mi north of I-10 Exit 279, Vail, 25mi southeast of Tucson. ☎ 520-647-7275. www.colossalcave.com.* Tours of this large dry cave follow a .5mi route planned by the Civilian Conservation Corps in the mid-1930s. Visitors walk up and down the equivalent of 6 1/2 stories, framed by flowstone, boxwork and helictites. The cave has concealed whisky stills, train robbers and the cast of TV's *Sesame Street.*

Kitt Peak National Observatory – *Rte. 86, Tohono O'odham Reservation, 46mi west of Tucson.* ♿ 🅿 ☎ *520-318-8726. www.noao.edu.* Atop 6,875ft Kitt Peak is the world's largest collection of optical telescopes, funded by the National Science Foundation and managed by a consortium of 29 universities. Tours *(1hr)* begin at the visitor center and canvass a mind-boggling array of observatories, one of them 18 stories tall. An evening stargazing program *(by reservation)* includes dinner and a 3hr astronomy program.

Biosphere 2

*Organ Pipe Cactus National Monument – *Rte. 85, 140mi west of Tucson via Rte. 86.* △ & 🄿 @ *520-387-6849. www.nps.gov/orpi.* This 516sq-mi preserve on the Mexican border is the only place in the US to see wild organ-pipe cacti—huge, vertical arm-sprouting cousins of saguaro. In late spring and early summer, they open their lavender-white, night-blooming flowers. Within the park are 25 other types of cacti and an abundance of wildlife, from javelinas to Gila monsters. Both of the monument's scenic loops are meandering dirt roads. **Ajo Mountain Drive** *(21mi)* winds along the foothills of the 4,800ft Ajo Range through impressive stands of cacti. **Puerto Blanco Drive** *(53mi)* circles past Quitobaquito Spring, a historic waterhole that attracts more than 260 species of birds.

SOUTHEASTERN ARIZONA*

Map pp 254-255   Mountain Standard Time
Tourist Information @ 602-230-7733

Hollywood may have made it a legend, but the Old West's heart and soul belong to southeast Arizona. Here the Apache Indians—led by Cochise and his successor, Geronimo—battled the US Cavalry and sowed fear in the hearts of settlers. Here Wyatt Earp and Doc Holliday got into a little disagreement with the Clanton Gang at the O.K. Corral. Today, with rugged mountains, sweeping desert vistas and superb bird-watching, this frontier land bordering Mexico offsets its nefarious past with some of the most mouth-dropping scenery in the Southwest.

SIGHTS

*Tubac – *I-19 Exit 34, 45mi south of Tucson.* ✗ 🄿 @ *520-398-2704. www.tubacaz .com.* A 1691 mission farm (since vanished) and 1752 Spanish presidio made Tubac the first European settlement in Arizona. **Tubac Presidio State Historic Park*** *(Presidio Dr. & Burreul St.;* @ *520-398-2252)* offers a film and exhibits that recount the 250-year history of the fortress. Juan Bautista de Anza, second commander (1760-74) of the Tubac Presidio, led two expeditions to California and discovered San Francisco Bay in 1776.
Tubac's economy now focuses around 80 **artists' studios*** and galleries that line the half-dozen streets of the historic village, selling everything from handmade fabrics and Indian jewelry to Mexican pottery and southwestern rugs.

*Tumacácori National Historical Park – *I-19 Exit 29, 50mi south of Tucson.* & 🄿 @ *520-398-2341. www.nps.gov/tuma.* Construction of Tumacácori's Franciscan mission, designed to replace a small 1757 Jesuit church, began in 1800; but the bell-tower dome was uncapped (it remains incomplete) when missions were secularized in 1828. Walking tours of the mission ruins begin at a visitor center and include the sanctuary, cemetery, granary, convent and fiesta grounds.

Nogales – *Rte. 82 at I-19, 63mi south of Tucson.* ✗ & 🄿 @ *520-287-3685.* Visitors park in Arizona and walk across the US-Mexico border, through international customs and immigration, to **Nogales, Sonora.** It's only three blocks to **Avenida Obregón,** the city's main shopping and dining thoroughfare. Merchants speak good English and encourage negotiating prices for a wide range of items.

Sierra Vista – *Rte. 90, 69mi southeast of Tucson via I-10 Exit 302.* △ ✗ & 🄿 @ *520-458-6940.* The economy of this town of 38,000 is tied to 114sq-mi **Fort Huachuca,** a 19C cavalry post now headquarters for US Army information systems and intelligence. Here is based the **San Pedro Riparian National Conservation Area** *(1763 Paseo San Luis;* @ *520-458-3559),* enclosing a 40mi stretch of the San Pedro River as it flows northward toward the Gila River. A rare desert oasis, the 58,000-acre preserve supports over 350 species of birds, 80 species of mammals, 40 species of amphibians and reptiles, and several species of fish. Inhabited since 11,000 BC, the preserve has many historic sites, including the late-19C ghost town of **Fairbank** *(Rte. 82, 19mi northeast of Sierra Vista).*
The Nature Conservancy's **Ramsey Canyon Preserve** *(Ramsey Canyon Rd. off Rte. 92, 9mi south of Sierra Vista;* @ *520-378-2785)* is a 380-acre parcel in the Huachuca Mountains, designated a National Natural Landmark. It is famed for hummingbirds (14 species), coatimundi, rare frogs and flowering plants. Steep but scenic Hamburg Trail offers a good overview of this gorgeous canyon.

Coronado National Memorial – *5mi west of Rte. 92, 22mi south of Sierra Vista.* & 🄿 @ *520-366-5515. www.nps.gov/coro.* In February 1540, Francisco Vásquez de Coronado left west-central Mexico with 336 soldiers and four priests to find and conquer the fabled Seven Cities of Cibola, their "streets lined with goldsmith

Gunfight Reenactment, Tombstone

shops ... and doorways studded with emeralds and turquoise." Coronado's party found only desert, grassland and rock pueblos inhabited by Native Americans. Spain regarded the two-year expedition as a failure, but it opened the way for missionizing and colonizing the Southwest.

This 4,750-acre reserve offers a scenic drive to the top of 6,575ft **Montezuma Pass** just north of the Mexican border, as well as hiking trails and a 600ft cave. Coronado and his men never set foot here, however; they viewed the Huachuca Mountains from the San Pedro River valley 10mi to the east.

★★ **Tombstone** – *US-80 between Benson & Bisbee, 67mi southeast of Tucson via I-10 Exit 303.* ✗ ♿ 🅿 ☎ *520-457-9317.* "The Town Too Tough to Die" hasn't changed much since 1881, when Sheriff Wyatt Earp, his brothers and Doc Holliday vanquished the cattle-rustling Clanton Gang in the legendary "Gunfight at the O.K. Corral." Many original buildings still stand from the silver- and gold-mining halcyon years of 1877-85. Wooden sidewalks line **Allen Street★★**. Horse-drawn stagecoaches offer mood-provoking town tours, shops sell Western clothing and souvenirs, and saloons like Big Nose Kate's persist like *Gunsmoke* stage sets.

On any given day, dozens of gunslingers, gamblers and dance-hall hostesses wander the town, giving visitors pause to think they've entered a time warp.

Several gunfights are reenacted daily in different parts of town, one at the original **O.K. Corral** *(Allen St. between 3rd & 4th Sts.; ☎ 520-457-3456).* The Clantons were among 250 rowdy characters who "died with their boots on" and were buried in **Boothill Cemetery** *(US-80 at north city limits).* Visitors may tour the 19C newsroom and print shop of the *Tombstone Epitaph (5th St. between Allen & Fremont Sts.; ☎ 520-457-2211)*, the oldest continuously published newspaper in Arizona, and see the original stage fixtures of the bawdy 1881 **Bird Cage Theatre** *(6th & Allen Sts.; ☎ 520-457-3421)*. The **Rose Tree Inn** *(4th & Toughnut Sts.; ☎ 520-457-3326)* has a rosebush noted as the world's largest by the *Guinness Book of World Records.* **Tombstone Courthouse State Historic Park★** *(219 E. Toughnut St.; ☎ 520-457-3311)*, built in 1882 as the Cochise County Courthouse with sheriff's offices and a county jail, has been a museum since 1959.

★★ **Bisbee** – *US-80 & Rte. 92, 96mi southeast of Tucson.* △ ✗ ♿ 🅿 ☎ *520-432-4321. www.arizonaguide.com/bisbee.* This historic copper-mining town, its buildings swaggering up the sides of the Mule Mountain canyons, was the largest and most prosperous settlement between St. Louis and San Francisco at the turn of the 20C. Immigrants from Britain, Ireland, Germany, Italy, Serbia and Croatia came to mine ore discovered in 1880. When the Phelps Dodge company closed its Copper Queen Mine in 1975—after $2 billion in copper, gold, lead, silver and zinc had been taken—real-estate prices plummeted. Artists of all persuasions snatched up homes available for as little as $80. Today a visible number of Bisbee's 6,500 people are former hippies turned entrepreneurs. Their galleries, funky shops and coffeehouses are lodged in dozens of late-19C and early-20C buildings of Italianate Victorian architecture, including the saloons and brothels of Brewery Gulch. The red brick **Bisbee Mining and Historical Museum** *(5 Copper Queen Plaza; ☎ 520-432-*

7071) once served as the Phelps Dodge general office. Overlooking the museum, the four-story **Copper Queen Hotel** *(11 Howell St.;* ☎ *520-432-2216)* has dominated the town since it was built in 1902.

Retired miners guide **Queen Mine Tours**★★ *(118 Arizona St.;* ☎ *520-432-2071),* 75min underground excursions into a mere fragment of the 2,500mi of shafts surrounding Bisbee. Participants don yellow slickers, helmets and headlamps, and travel on old mine trains. A 13mi bus tour visits the **Lavender Pit**, a stunning open-pit mine that produced 94 million tons of copper ore.

Douglas – *US-80 & US-191, 119 miles southeast of Tucson.* ⚠ ╳ ♿ 🅿 ☎ *520-364-2478. www.discoverdouglas.com.* This old copper town on the US border opposite Agua Prieta, Mexico, has 335 buildings on the National Historic Register. The 1907 **Gadsden Hotel** *(1046 G Ave.;* ☎ *520-364-4481)* has a neo-Renaissance lobby with a marble staircase and a 42ft stained-glass mural. The **San Bernardino Ranch National Historic Landmark** *(Geronimo Trail;* ☎ *520-558-2474),* 15mi east, recalls turn-of-the-20C cattle ranching. The 300-acre site has an adobe ranch house, ice house, wash house, granary and commissary.

Benson – *I-10 Exits 302-306, 45mi east of Tucson.* ⚠ ╳ ♿ 🅿 ☎ *520-586-2842.* Founded in 1880 on the Southern Pacific line, Benson grew as a copper-smelting center. The **Benson Railroad Historic District** *(E. 3rd St.)* preserves late 19C buildings. Rail heritage persists with the historic **San Pedro & Southwestern Railroad**★ *(796 E. Country Club Dr. off US-80, 1mi south;* ☎ *520-586-2266),* whose *Frontier Flyer* offers a 4hr run through the San Pedro Riparian National Conservation Area *(p 259)* to the ghost town of Fairbank.

★**Kartchner Caverns State Park** – ⛺ *Rte. 90, 8.7mi south of Benson.* ♿ 🅿 ☎ *520-586-2283. www.pr.state.az.us. Tours by reservation only.* This huge "wet" limestone cave in the Whetstone Mountains was discovered in 1974 but kept secret until 1988. Unveiled to the public in late 1999, the stunning cave, home to 2,000 bats, is actively dripping stalactites and growing stalagmites. Visitors enter via the **Discovery Center**, with exhibits and videos on cave geology, natural history and spelunking. A 1.2mi trail passes two main galleries, the largest known (21ft-by-.25in) soda straw, and a 58ft column called Kubla Khan. About 2.4mi have been explored; the cave may rival New Mexico's Carlsbad Caverns *(p 146)* in size.

★**Amerind Foundation Museum** – *1mi east of I-10 Exit 318, Dragoon, 16mi east of Benson.* 🅿 ☎ *520-586-3666. www.amerind.org.* A nonprofit archaeology institute, Amerind is devoted to studying native cultures from Alaska to Patagonia. Exhibits include beadwork, costumes, pottery, basketry, ritual masks, weapons, children's toys and clothing, and cover everything from Cree snowshoe-making tools to the finest 19C Navajo weavings. Its Spanish Colonial Revival-style buildings (1931-59, H.M. Starkweather) blend dramatically with the boulder-strewn landscape of Texas Canyon.

Willcox – *Rte. 186 at I-10 Exit 340, 81mi east of Tucson.* ╳ ♿ 🅿 ☎ *520-384-2272. www.willcoxchamber.com.* The halfway point for travelers between Phoenix and El Paso, Willcox boasts an 1880 railroad depot and the **Rex Allen Museum** *(150 N. Railroad Ave.;* ☎ *520-384-4583).* The museum commemorates the life and times of favorite son Allen (b.1920), "last of the singing cowboys."

★★**Chiricahua National Monument** – *Rte. 186, 37mi southeast of Willcox.* ⚠ 🅿 ☎ *520-824-3560. www.nps.gov/chir.* Chiricahua Apaches called this the "Land of the Standing-up Rocks," a name befitting the fantastic wilderness of sculptured columns, spires, grottoes and balanced rocks that climaxes this preserve. The region became a national monument in 1924 after promotion by the Swedish-immigrant owners of the **Faraway Guest Ranch** ("so god-awful far away from everything"), now a historic property open for guided tours.

From the entrance station, beautiful **Bonita Canyon Drive** rises 8mi, past a small visitor center, to spectacular Massai Point at 6,870ft atop the Chiricahua Range. More than 20mi of hiking trails extend to such unusual rock formations as Duck on a Rock and Totem Pole. Believed to have been formed 27 million years ago in the wake of a nearby volcanic eruption, the Chiricahuas harbor unique flora and fauna, including numerous rare birds.

About 21mi northwest via Rte. 186, gravel Rte. 181 and a 1.5mi trail, **Fort Bowie National Historic Site** *(*☎ *520-847-2500)* preserves the ruins of a fort that played a key role in the late-19C subjugation of the Chiricahua Apaches. Built in 1862 after an ambush by Cochise, Fort Bowie was a headquarters for US military operations until Geronimo surrendered in 1886.

Portland Area

Pioneer Courthouse Square, Portland

The metropolitan center of the state of Oregon, Portland commands a prominent position at the confluence of the Willamette and Columbia Rivers. The 1 million people who inhabit the city and its surrounding area have spread their homes across a verdant landscape of fields, rolling hills and forested ridges about 100mi upriver from the Pacific Ocean. A friendly city of unpretentious charm, Portland boasts a handsome downtown core, some 200 parks and gardens, and lively neighborhoods on both sides of the Willamette.

The greater state of Oregon *(OAR-a-gun)*—bordered by California on the south and Washington state on the north—embodies the West of big dreams, sweeping ranchlands, sky-thrusting mountains and a cherished independence. The snow-topped spine of the volcanic Cascade Range divides the wet maritime region of a spectacular 362mi Pacific coastline and the lush Willamette *(will-AM-it)* Valley from the sparsely populated deserts of the east. Created by magma released during tectonic plate movement beginning 36 million years ago, the Cascades were subsequently chiseled and scoured to their present form by the series of ice ages that left the highest elevations still glaciated.

Early nomads first settled in eastern Oregon and along the Columbia River thousands of years ago. By the time Spanish and English navigators began exploring the coast in the late 1700s, Native Americans had penetrated most corners of the vast Oregon Country. The Lewis and Clark Expedition passed through in 1805-06, describing the Pacific coast near Astoria in glowing terms even though the weather was "wet, cold and disagreeable." Fur traders followed in their footsteps and established the Oregon Country, which comprised nearly the whole of the northwestern US and southwestern Canada. By 1846 a treaty with Britain established America's right to the land south of the 49th parallel; the state of Oregon was carved from the southwestern part of this new territory. Throughout the 20C, Oregon has been at the forefront of social reform, struggling most recently with the clash between environmentalism and the traditional pioneer spirit of independence and resource exploitation. In the more populous western part of the state, timber and fishing have given way to high-tech industries, metal processing and tourism, the latter drawing visitors to dramatic beaches, snow-crusted peaks, serene lakes and gorges.

PORTLAND★★

Michelin map 493 B 4   Pacific Standard Time
Population 503,891
Tourist Information ☎ 877-678-5263 or www.travelportland.com

The Willamette River, spanned by a dozen distinctive bridges, is deep enough to make Portland one of the West Coast's largest inland ports and a Pacific Rim gateway. The river acts as a natural dividing line between the city's hilly, forested west side and flatter eastern neighborhoods. Less trendy than Seattle (three hours' drive north), Portland maintains a relaxed atmosphere, yet holds numerous cultural venues, noteworthy buildings, fine restaurants and hip coffeehouses.

Historical Notes – Well before the 1842 opening of the Oregon Trail, American Indians and then trappers and homesteaders had settled around the confluence of the Willamette and Columbia Rivers. Although Oregon City, 12mi south, was the first population center, Portland burgeoned with the arrival of the railroads in the 1880s: The city's river-junction location gave it a clear advantage as a shipping port and trade center. Masted schooners and steam-driven sternwheelers crowded the waterfront as trade extended to China and other distant lands. Immigrants sought their fortunes in shipping, farming, lumber and gold. The war years created a huge demand for shipyard workers, swelling Portland's population.

Portland's reputation as an urban model dates from its 1972 Downtown Plan, which laid out guidelines for development, architecture and public transportation. Today the pedestrian-friendly downtown is suffused with trees, public art and fountains, and the surrounding countryside is relatively free of suburban sprawl.

Built around a manufacturing base, the diversified economy has been greatly bolstered by high-tech companies, yet Portland remains an important trade and transportation center. Tourism added $1.9 billion to the local economy in 1998.

SIGHTS

★**Oregon History Center** – *1200 SW Park Ave.* & ☎ *503-222-1741. www.ohs .org.* Eight-story trompe l'oeil murals of Lewis and Clark and the Oregon Trail rise beside the entrance plaza of this archival museum. Filled with interactive displays, the "**Portland!**"★ exhibit traces city history, beginning with the 1840s and 1850s—when the first white settlers were arriving—and touching on the influential 1905 Lewis and Clark Exposition, the population boom of World War II and the rise of the car culture of the 1950s. A "cyber-walk" through city neighborhoods is offered at computer terminals; a small maritime gallery holds models of 18C ships.

★**Portland Art Museum** – *1219 SW Park Ave.* ✗& 🅿 ☎ *503-226-2811. www.pam.org.* Presenting outstanding collections of Native American and regional art as well as top-notch traveling exhibitions, this museum, founded in 1892, is the oldest art museum in the Pacific Northwest. Highlights include its collection of **French Impressionism**★, with works by Monet, Manet, Cézanne and Pissarro; and its **East Asian Galleries**★, with sculpture, ceramics and furniture. The museum occupies a low brick building with travertine trim, designed in the 1930s by modernist Pietro Belluschi (1899-1994) and now undergoing a $30 million expansion.

★**Governor Tom McCall Waterfront Park** – *Bordering SW Naito Pkwy. & the Willamette River between Marquam Bridge & Steel Bridge.* The grassy 23-acre park that stretches along a 1.5mi esplanade beside the Willamette was once a raucous river port. As part of its 1970s urban-renewal scheme, Portland reclaimed the land and named the park for Tom McCall (1913-83), who as governor (1967-75) was a proponent of land-use planning. The park is a venue for concerts and the **Rose Festival** in June. Among eight bridges that may be seen from the esplanade is Portland's first, the **Morrison Bridge** (1887). The buff-colored **Hawthorne Bridge** (1910) is the oldest operating vertical-lift bridge in the world, while the **Steel Bridge** (1912) is the world's only telescoping double-deck vertical-lift bridge.

★★**Oregon Museum of Science and Industry** – **Kids** *1945 SE Water St.* ✗& 🅿 ☎ *503-797-4000. www.omsi.edu.* This striking brick-and-glass building (1992, Zimmer Gunsul Frasca), beside the Willamette on the site of a former power plant, harbors OMSI—a two-floor galaxy of hands-on exhibits, an OMNI theater, a planetarium and even a submarine. First-floor exhibits allow children to build bridges, launch boats and design and test aircraft. Upstairs in the Life Sciences Hall, an eerily beautiful collection of human **embryos**★ depicts stages of prenatal development. In the Earth Sciences Hall, the **Earthquake Room**★ offers the jolting experience of a major quake. Computer-oriented displays in the Technology Hall focus on recent advances in electronic technology.

ADDRESS BOOK

Please see explanation on p 64.

Staying in Oregon

The Benson Hotel – *309 SW Broadway, Portland OR.* ✗ ♿ ✆ *503-228-2000. www.westcoasthotels.com/benson. 286 rooms.* **$$$** Simon Benson, lumber baron and philanthropist, completed this grand hotel in 1912, and its opulence has endured since. Elaborate Austrian crystal chandeliers illuminate the marble floors and walnut walls of the lobby, and the rooms have an equally lavish ambience.

The Governor Hotel – *611 SW 10th Ave., Portland OR.* ✗ ♿ ✆ *503-224-3400. www.govhotel.com. 100 rooms.* **$$** Murals recall the early-19C expedition of Lewis and Clark; the original stained-glass dome and tiled floor remain from 1909 construction. This classic hotel combines turn-of-the-20C touches of mahogany detailing with large and contemporary rooms, all within a grand shell.

Jacksonville Inn – *175 E. California St., Jacksonville OR.* ✗ ♿ ✆ *541-899-1900. www.jacksonvilleinn.com. 8 rooms.* **$$** Occupying a gold rush-era building with glints of gold visible in its mortar, the inn and its striped awning have been around since 1861. Guests select from 1,500 wines to accompany venison or hazelnut chicken at the **Dinner House**, then retreat to cheerful, country-style rooms.

Stephanie Inn – *2740 S. Pacific Hwy., Cannon Beach OR.* ✗ ♿ ✆ *503-436-2221. www.stephanie-inn.com. 50 rooms.* **$$** The secluded Stephanie is only six years old, but with wood beams and local stone it has settled comfortably into its beachside site. Every window looks out to sea, and guests step off a porch onto the beach. Fresh seafood is a dinnertime staple.

Dining in Oregon

Fiddlehead's – *6716 SE Milwaukie St., Portland OR.* ✆ *503-233-1547.* **$$ Native American.** With traditional masks and colorful cedar collages, the atmosphere here matches the menu of indigenous food, including organic produce and plenty of Indian fry bread. Three Sisters stew is a hearty blend of corn, fresh beans and chayote squash; Tygh Valley *tatonka* is a braised buffalo stew with corn dumplings.

Jake's Famous Crawfish Restaurant – *401 SW 12th Ave., Portland OR.* ✆ *503-226-1419.* **$$ Seafood.** Jake Freiman cooked up his first crawfish in 1892, and his place has offered an orgy of seafood ever since. Alaskan Copper River salmon, Hawaiian striped marlin and Quilcene oysters are just the beginning. They may be roasted on cedar planks, grilled with papaya salsa or battered in beer.

Pine Tavern – *967 NW Brooks St., Bend OR.* ✆ *541-382-5581.* **$$ American.** At 64, the Tavern is central Oregon's oldest and best-known restaurant, built around a 200ft-tall Ponderosa pine that extends through the roof. Known for beef purchased from local ranchers, the food fits this timber town: Pan-fried trout, meatloaf and barbecue ribs all were served by the original owners.

Wildwood – *1221 NW 21st Ave., Portland OR.* ✆ *503-248-9663. www .wildwood.citysearch.com.* **$$ Regional.** An open kitchen adds activity to this warm, bright space, with its floors of Douglas fir and ceramic mural of crabs and fish. The menu changes daily, but there are always fresh dishes such as salmon with sugar-pea vinaigrette or portabello mushroom-and-potato lasagna, all with Northwest hints.

Moored in the river behind the museum, the **USS Blueback**, a diesel-electric sub built in 1959 and decommissioned in 1994, is open for guided tours of the officers' quarters, command center, torpedo room, bunkroom and mess hall.

⋆⋆**Washington Park** – *Entrances south of W. Burnside Rd. & west of SW Vista Ave.* ✆ *503-823-7529.* Flanked on its north by the exclusive Portland Heights neighborhood, this urban oasis winds south along the ridge that limns the west side of the city. Within its boundaries are a handful of notable attractions.

The **International Rose Test Garden**⋆⋆ *(400 SW Kingston Ave.;* ✆ *503-823-3636)* provides a dazzling display of 8,000 roses of 525 species, in fragrant, formal terraces that overlook downtown. New strains of roses are exhibited; those chosen by the American Rose Selections organization are given fanciful names and moved to the Gold Award Gardens. Just uphill, the immaculately tended 5.5-acre **Japanese Garden**★★ *(611 SW Kingston Ave.;* ☎ *503-223-1321)* uses plants, rocks and water to mold a serene and contemplative beauty. Highlights include a picturesque moon bridge, a ceremonial teahouse and a Zen-inspired sand-and-stone garden.

In the 173-acre **Hoyt Arboretum** *(4033 SW Fairview Blvd.;* ☎ *503-228-8733)* are 900 species of trees from around the world. Trails wind through well-established stands of magnolia, oaks and maples. The **World Forestry Center**★ **Kids** *(4033 SW Canyon Rd.;* ☎ *503-228-1367)* is a storehouse of information and exhibits about the world's forests; a multilingual talking tree greets visitors and explains how a tree grows. The **Oregon Zoo**★ **Kids** *(4001 SW Canyon Rd.;* ☎ *503-226-1561)* keeps more than 1,300 animals from 215 species, including one of the world's largest breeding herds of **Asian elephants**★.

★★ **Pittock Mansion** – *3229 NW Pittock Dr., off NW Barnes Rd.* ✗ 🅿 ☎ *503-823-3624.* The largest and most opulent home in Portland perches on a 940ft crest in Imperial Heights, looking east over the city, the river and Mount Hood. Built in 1914 (Edward T. Foulkes) for Henry Pittock, publisher of *The Oregonian* newspaper, the manse is a French Renaissance Revival-style château with exterior sandstone walls. Guided and self-guided tours take in magnificent marble and woodwork and luxurious early-20C furnishings.

★★ **Elk Rock Gardens at the Bishop's Close** – *SW Military Lane, 6mi south of downtown Portland via SW Macadam Ave.* ☎ *503-636-5613.* Estate owner Peter Kerr, a prosperous grain merchant, made his blufftop 1916 Scottish manor home the focal point for an English landscape garden designed by John Olmsted. Kerr supplemented it with plants he collected during world travels. Both house and gardens now belong to the Episcopal church.

EXCURSIONS

★★ **Mount Hood** – *US-26, 50mi east of Portland.* ☎ *888-622-4822. www.mthood.org.* The familiar snow-cloaked cone of Mount Hood, Oregon's highest peak, pierces the sky at 11,239ft. The mountain draws visitors throughout the year to its forested trails, alpine glaciers, challenging ski areas, scenic roads and rustic lodges. In 1805, explorers Lewis and Clark were the first white Americans to clap eyes on the volcanic peak, previously named by British sailors. It became a beacon of road's end to thousands of weary Oregon Trail travelers in the mid-19C. Their wagon ruts remain visible just west of **Barlow Pass** *(Rte. 35 east of US-26).*

Nearby **Timberline Lodge**★ *(off US-26, 6mi north of Government Camp;* ☎ *503-272-3311),* built by the Works Progress Administration in 1936-37, shows off fine examples of American craftsmanship with its carved wood, inlaid marquetry and stained glass. From here, hikers can attack the spectacular 40mi **Timberline Trail**★★ for mountain scenery. Trail conditions are best in late summer.

★★ **Columbia River Gorge** – *I-84 from Troutdale to The Dalles, 17 to 84mi east of Portland.* ☎ *800-984-6743.* Extending from suburban Portland to the mouth of the Deschutes River, the 455sq-mi Columbia River Gorge National Scenic Area encompasses 11 major waterfalls, 25 state parks and dramatic 700ft-high

Multnomah Falls

© Tim Thompson

cliff-edge vistas. The Columbia, second-largest river in the US (after the Mississippi), creates a gentle grandeur as it slices through volcanic basalt along the Oregon-Washington border. Almost 3 million visitors come annually to admire the falls, photograph, hike, fish, mountain-bike and windsurf.

Providing a leisurely and scenic alternative to the interstate is the **Historic Columbia River Highway**★★ (US-30). Completed in 1915, it now may be driven only in two distinct sections linked by I-84: 22mi from Troutdale *(Exit 17)* to Ainsworth State Park *(Exit 40)* and 16mi from Mosier *(Exit 69)* to The Dalles *(Exit 84)*. Some of the best views are closest to Portland, including those from **Portland Women's Forum State Park** *(Mile 10)* and the **Vista House at Crown Point** *(Mile 11;* 🅿 ☎ *503-695-2230)*. Another highlight is **Multnomah Falls**★★ *(I-84 Exit 31;* ☎ *503-695-2376)*, a mesmerizing 620ft plunge of water.

US Army Corps of Engineers visitor centers at **Bonneville Locks and Dam**★ *(I-84 Exit 40;* ☎ *541-374-8820)* and **The Dalles Lock and Dam**★★ *(I-84 Exit 87;* ☎ *541-298-7650)* show how the river has been harnessed. The region's geography and human history are well interpreted at the **Columbia Gorge Discovery Center**★★ *(Wasco County Historical Museum, 5000 Discovery Dr., The Dalles;* ☎ *541-296-8600)*, where visitors can toy with a windsurfing simulator.

■ Windsurfing the Gorge

Skipping the waves like multicolored flying fish, sailboarders have found a paradise at the Columbia River Gorge town of **Hood River** *(I-84 Exit 63)*. Here at a natural break in the Cascade Mountains, steady currents from the east meet strong winds from the west, so that summer winds average 20-25mph. Windsurfing enthusiasts had discovered the gorge by the mid-1980s, and Hood River, a cozy hillside town of about 5,000 people, witnessed an adrenaline shot to its economy.

Although windsurfing competitions are not as frequent as they once were, the town's streets remain packed in summer with shiny sports-utility vehicles driven by neoprene-clad wind worshipers, the most dedicated of whom carry pagers that beep when the wind is best. The US Windsurfing Association has chosen Hood· River as its home base, as have more than three dozen sailboard retailers, distributors, and custom-board and accessory manufacturers.

© David R. Frazier

★Oregon City – *12mi south of Portland on Rte. 99E at I-205.* ☎ *503-655-5511. www.clackamas-oregon.com.* Established in 1844 at the end of the 2,000mi Oregon Trail, this town of 21,000 is the oldest settlement in the Willamette Valley. It was the first capital of the Oregon Territory.

★End of the Oregon Trail Interpretive Center – *1726 Washington St.* & ▣ ☎ *503-657-9336. www.endoftheoregontrail.org.* Sprawling across 8.5 acres of Abernathy Green, the main arrival area for Oregon Trail travelers, the center is housed in three 50ft-high buildings shaped like covered wagons. Tour guides in pioneer costume recount the hardships of the six-month overland journey, and a multi-media show traces the lives of three fictional emigrants.

McLoughlin House – *713 Center St.* ▣ ☎ *503-656-5146. www.mcloughlinhouse.org.* Dr. John McLoughlin, the "father of Oregon," built this two-story clapboard home in 1845. Territorial head of the Hudson's Bay Company, McLoughlin earned the disapproval of the British by assisting American pioneers. Original furnishings are visible on 30min tours.

★Oregon Wine Country – *Via Rte. 99 West off I-5, 20-40mi SW of Portland.* ☎ *503-228-8336.* Situated on the same latitude as France's Burgundy region, the northern Willamette Valley has developed into one of the finest wine regions in the world, its wines noted for their delicate flavor, crisp finish and low alcohol content. Established in the 1960s, the Oregon wine industry remained relatively unknown until a Pinot Noir from Eyrie Vineyards did the unimaginable in a French-sponsored tasting in 1979: It outperformed several esteemed French wines.

Favorable soils and a long growing season moderated by the Pacific Ocean—dry summers, cool autumns and wet winters—produce ideal conditions not only for Pinot Noir, but also for Pinot Gris, Chardonnay, Merlot, Cabernet Sauvignon and other varietals. Dozens of wineries and more than 100 vineyards cluster among the undulating green hills of this valley. Most are small, family-run operations; many are open for tours and tastings.

Driving the region is a delight. Uncrowded country roads lead past neat rows of vineyards, fruit orchards and roadside stands. At the heart of the wine country is the pleasant Linfield College town of **McMinnville**, whose biggest attraction is still undergoing restoration. The *Spruce Goose*, built and flown in 1947 by billionaire aviator Howard Hughes as the world's largest wood-frame aircraft, previously was displayed alongside the *Queen Mary* in Long Beach, California.

★Vancouver National Historic Reserve – *750 Anderson St. off Mill Plain Blvd., Vancouver WA, 8mi north of Portland.* & ▣ ☎ *360-992-1820.* Several historic sites along the Columbia River make up this reserve, located where the Hudson's Bay Company had its headquarters in 1825-46 and where the first US military post in the Pacific Northwest was founded in 1849. Visits usually begin in the 1878 Victorian **O.O. Howard House Visitor Center★**. Just north is **Officers Row★**, a parade of 22 impressive 19C houses, including the 1886 **Marshall House★** *(☎ 360-693-3103)*, a turreted Queen Anne that was home to General George C. Marshall, the US secretary of state and Nobel Peace Prize winner who commanded the Vancouver Barracks from 1936-38.

North of Officers Row, **Fort Vancouver National Historic Site★** [Kids] (& ▣ ☎ *360-696-7655)* offers guided tours of the reconstructed Hudson's Bay Company stockade, fur warehouse, carpenter's shop and chief factor's residence. A visitor center has a museum and audiovisual program.

WILLAMETTE VALLEY
AND SOUTHERN OREGON★

Michelin map 493 A, B 4, 5, 6   Pacific Standard Time
Tourist Information ☎ 541-928-0911 or 541-779-4691

If Portland is the face that Oregon shows to the world, the broad, fertile Willamette Valley is its heart. Running 110mi south from Portland to Eugene and 30mi between the Cascades and the Coast Range, this lovely valley began attracting pioneers in the 1840s. Settlers spread out after their 2,000mi Oregon Trail journey and began patching the region with farms, vineyards, sheep ranches and little towns. Today, despite being the state's most populated area outside of metropolitan Portland, most of the valley retains a rural feel: Motorists cruise a landscape of farmland, tulip fields, hazelnut orchards and covered bridges.

Further south via Interstate 5, the Southern Oregon highlands extend about 100mi north of the California border, from the wheat fields of the Klamath Basin to the white waters of the Rogue and Umpqua Rivers. Dormant volcanoes, thick forests, rugged canyons and alpine lakes make this a haven for outdoors lovers. A short-lived gold rush in the mid-19C brought settlers, many of whom stayed on despite a failed 1870s attempt by the Klamath and Modoc Indians to retake their native lands. The area's best-known attractions today are Crater Lake, Oregon's only national park, and one of the top Shakespeare festivals in the US, in Ashland.

SIGHTS

★**Salem** – *I-5 & Rte. 99 East, 44mi south of Portland.* ☏ *503-581-4325. www .scva.org.* The capital of Oregon and the state's third-largest city with about 126,000 residents, Salem traces its founding to 1840, when Jason Lee moved the headquarters of his Methodist mission to this mid-Willamette Valley location.

Lee's home and several other early buildings still stand at the **Mission Mill Museum**★★ *(1313 Mill St.;* ✗ ♿ 🅿 ☏ *503-585-7012),* a five-acre historical park that includes the 1889 Thomas Kay Woolen Mill. Anchoring downtown, the domed **Oregon State Capitol**★ *(900 Court St. NE;* ✗ ♿ 🅿 ☏ *503-986-1388),* built in 1938 (Francis Keally) in the Greek Revival style, is topped by a 23ft bronze-and-gold-leaf statue of a pioneer. The city's small but highly regarded **Willamette University**★ *(900 State St.;* ☏ *503-370-6300)* was founded by the Methodists in 1842 as the first institution of higher learning in the American West.

A half-hour's drive east of Salem is **Silver Falls State Park**★★ *(Rte. 214, Sublimity;* ☏ *503-873-8681),* Oregon's largest state park at 8,700 acres. Its highlight, in addition to a historic lodge and a variety of recreational facilities, is the **Trail of Ten Falls**★★, a 7mi loop along Silver Creek that takes hikers through deep forest to 10 cascading falls, ranging in height from 27ft to 178ft.

★**Eugene** – *Rtes. 99 & 126 just west of I-5, 108mi south of Portland.* ☏ *541-484-5307. www.cvalco.org.* Oregon's second-largest city—its population of 128,000 is about half the greater urban area—still has ties to its agricultural and timber-industry roots. But the **University of Oregon**★ *(18th Ave. to Franklin Blvd., Agate to Alder Sts.;* ☏ *541-346-3201)* is today the pacesetter. Founded in 1876 (original **Deady Hall** still stands) and now enrolling more than 17,000 students, this university is largely accountable for Eugene's thriving counterculture, evident in its casual dress, health-food stores and environmental organizations. The UO **Museum of Art**★★ *(Memorial Quadrangle near Kincaid St.;* ☏ *541-346-3027)* is a fantasy of intricate brickwork whose treasures include a fine collection of Asian art. The **Museum of Natural History**★ *(1680 E. 15th Ave.;* ♿ 🅿 ☏ *541-346-3024)* is devoted mainly to indigenous peoples, including the local Kalapuya culture.

Elsewhere in Eugene, the **Hult Center for the Performing Arts**★★ *(7th Ave. & Willamette St.;* ♿ 🅿 ☏ *541-682-5087)* has been acclaimed as one of the finest performing-arts centers in the world; the dramatic, multipeaked building (1982, Norman Pfeiffer & Lutes Amundson) hosts hundreds of events annually.

★★★ **Crater Lake National Park** – *Rtes. 62 & 138 west of US-97, 145mi southeast of Eugene.* ☏ *541-594-2211. www.nps.gov/crla.* The deepest lake in the US at 1,932ft rests in the crater of a collapsed volcano once more than 12,000ft high. Spectacularly ringed by mountains that are tinged with snow most of the year, this crystal-clear sapphire lake, 6mi in diameter, attracts hikers, geologists and those compelled by the mysterious eye-like blue caldera. A cataclysmic eruption 7,700 years ago hurled more than 18 cubic miles of pumice and ash into the air and surrounding valleys. The collapsed mountain created a bowl-shaped caldera that eventually filled with pure rainwater; although it has no inlet nor apparent outlet, precipitation and evaporation keep it at a fairly constant level.

A 33mi Rim Drive circles the lake and offers a series of spectacular **views**★★. Among the best are those from **Sinnott Memorial Overlook** *(Rim Village, south side of lake)* and **Cloudcap**, highest point on the Rim Drive (7,865ft). Better yet is the perspective from atop 8,929ft **Mount Scott**★★, requiring a strenuous 5mi round-trip hike to the park's highest summit. A 7mi spur road off Rim Drive leads to **The Pinnacles**★★, hollow fossilized fumaroles that spire up to 80ft tall.

★**Ashland** – *Rte. 99 at I-5 Exit 14, 180mi south of Eugene.* ☏ *541-482-3486.* This attractive town of 18,000 on the eastern flank of the Siskiyou Mountains has turned itself into a premier cultural center. Surrounded by orchards, vineyards and Arabian horse farms, Ashland began as a 19C trading post. After failing to turn its lithium-rich springs into a world-class spa, the town capitalized on the dreams of a drama professor and converted an old bandshell into an outdoor amphitheater.

Crater Lake

There, in 1935, the city kicked off the first **Oregon Shakespeare Festival★★★** *(15 S. Pioneer St.; ☎ 541-482-4331)*. Now running from February to October, the festival stages about a dozen plays a year in its three theaters, featuring works by Shakespeare and a host of other playwrights. On fun **backstage tours★★**, visitors watch the production staff creating costumes, painting portraits and marbleizing floors; see the room where lighting and sound cues are controlled; and hear a wealth of amusing behind-the-scenes anecdotes.

★★ **Jacksonville** – *Rte. 238, 14mi northwest of Ashland.* ☎ *541-899-8118. www.jacksonvilleoregon.org.* Enveloped by rolling hills and by pear and apple orchards, Jacksonville claims more than 80 well-preserved mid-19C wooden buildings—so many that the entire, once-forgotten 1850s gold-rush town is a National Historic Landmark District. A visitor center at the old railway depot *(Oregon & C Sts.)* has walking-tour maps. The summer-long **Britt Festivals★★** fill the hills with classical, blues, jazz and rock music.

★★ **Oregon Caves National Monument** – *Rte. 46, 20mi east of Cave Junction & 92mi west of Ashland via I-5 & US-199.* ✗ 🅿 ☎ *541-592-2100. www.nps.gov/ orca.* Folded into the southwestern corner of Oregon is this web of marble and limestone chambers, bejeweled with stalactites, stalagmites and other wondrous calcite formations. The caves were created millions of years ago when acidic water trickled through faults, dissolving the stone and carving out a cavern with 3mi of known passageways. On 75min tours, visitors climb 500 stairs, duck through low-ceilinged tunnels and enter chambers like Watson's Grotto and the Ghost Room.

OREGON COAST★★

Michelin map 493 A, B, 4 A 5, 6   Pacific Standard Time
Tourist Information ☎ 541-574-2679 or www.oregon-coast.org

Civilization falls lightly on the 362mi Oregon coastline, a wild and scenic blend of wave-swept rocks and sandy beaches. Even the few places where homes and businesses border the shore are nature's province: A 1967 act of the state legislature made all Oregon beaches public. Though much of the forest just inland has been heavily logged, a tall border of spruce and cedar presses up to the shore, forming a key part of the coastal ecosystem.

This lush landscape has encouraged human settlement for thousands of years. The bounty of the sea and forest, coupled with a mild climate, enabled numerous tribes to establish permanent villages. Baskets, carvings and other fruits of the Indians' creative labors are on view in many small coastal museums.

Even after white settlement began in the 1840s, the small seaside communities remained isolated until the completion of the coast highway in the 1930s. Today visitors come to view cliffs and sea, to watch birds and whales, and to roll up their cuffs and stroll a wave-whipped beach.

SIGHTS

* **Astoria** – *US-26, 30 & 101, 96mi northwest of Portland.* ☎ *503-325-6311.* Founded as a fur-trading post in 1811, Astoria was the first US settlement west of the Rocky Mountains. By the 1850s it was a thriving port at the mouth of the Columbia River. Despite crashes in the local salmon and timber industries in recent decades, the town of 10,000 remains a busy port. Exhibits at the **Columbia River Maritime Museum** * *(1792 Marine Dr.;* ☎ *503-325-2323)* capture the long seafaring heritage. **Fort Clatsop National Memorial** ** *(6mi southwest off US-101;* ☎ *503-861-2471)* preserves the site where Lewis and Clark spent the winter of 1805-06, in a re-created fort redolent of smoked meat, dried skins and wet wood.

* **Cannon Beach** – *US-101, 22mi south of Astoria & 80mi west of Portland.* ☎ *503-436-2623.* This village of 1,400, on a long curve of sandy beach, caters to artist-residents and well-heeled travelers. **Haystack Rock** rises 235ft at water's edge. **Ecola State Park** ** *(2mi north of Cannon Beach;* ☎ *503-436-2844)* embraces 9mi of old-growth forest and coastline documented by Lewis and Clark.

** **Three Capes Scenic Drive** – *40mi from Tillamook to Pacific City, west of US-101; 63mi south of Astoria. From Tillamook, take Third St. west & follow signs.* ☎ *503-842-7525.* This delightful spin takes in dairy farms, bays of diving pelicans, coastal forest, seaside hamlets, dunes and vistas of the open Pacific from state parks at Capes Meares, Lookout and Kiwanda. For a sample, drive out to **Cape Meares**, where an 1890 lighthouse perches on a high cliff and the Pacific breaks far below against dark seastacks.

■ **Whale Watching**

Though nearly harpooned to extinction by 19C whalers, more than 20,000 gray whales now migrate along the Oregon coast each winter and spring on a 6,000mi journey between the Bering Sea and Mexico. Whale-watching trips runs from several coastal towns. On calm days, from numerous headlands that jut into the sea, observers may scan the sea's surface for the 12ft-high blow made by whales as they surface. Around Christmas and in late March, tens of thousands of whale-watchers seek out the best vantage points up and down the coast.

---

* **Newport** – *US-101, 136mi south of Astoria & 88mi west of Salem.* ☎ *541-265-8801.* Midway along the coast, this town of 8,500 has a tradition of agriculture, fishing, logging and—unlike most of its neighbors—tourism. The bayfront sports a lively jumble of commercial fishing boats, art galleries and knickknack shops. Across the Yaquina Bay bridge stands the noteworthy **Oregon Coast Aquarium** ** **Kids** *(SE Ferry Slip Rd., .25mi east of US-101;* ☎ *541-867-3474).* The orca whale Keiko, star of the movie *Free Willy* (1993), lived here until 1998, when it was relocated to its home waters off Iceland. The aquarium displays 200 marine species, most of them native to Oregon waters, in five major indoor galleries and six acres of outdoor exhibits. About .25mi north, the **Hatfield Marine Science Center** * **Kids** *(2030 S. Marine Science Dr.;* ☎ *541-867-0100),* headquarters for Oregon State University's marine-research program, offers intriguing interactive exhibits founded in oceanography and marine sciences.
Four miles up the coast, the **Yaquina Head Outstanding Natural Area** ** *(NW Lighthouse Dr., .5mi west of US-101;* ☎ *541-574-3100)* occupies an ancient finger of lava that protrudes into the Pacific. An interpretive center has high-quality exhibits on natural and human history; the adjacent **Yaquina Head Lighthouse** (1873) is, at 93ft, the tallest lighthouse in the state.

* **Yachats** – *US-101, 159mi south of Astoria & 88mi west of Eugene.* ☎ *541-547-3530. www.yachats.org.* The village of Yachats *(YA-hots)* sits on a marine terrace embraced by towering hills and husky headlands. It's the gateway to **Cape Perpetua Scenic Area** ** *(US-101, 3mi south;* ☎ *541-547-3289),* which combines fine coastal forest and rocky shoreline in its 2,700 acres.

Ecola State Park

★★Oregon Dunes National Recreation Area – *West side of US-101 for 48mi from Florence (186mi south of Astoria & 61mi west of Eugene) to Coos Bay.* △ & 🅿 ☎ *541-271-3611.* This strand of coastal dunes, some as high as 200ft, leaves a memorable impression. Visitors may explore a fascinating ecosystem of sand, tree islands, wetlands, estuaries and beaches via trails, viewpoints and roads. From the **Oregon Dunes Visitor Center** *(US-101, north end of Reedsport)*, rangers will direct travelers to trails and overlooks. The **Siltcoos Recreation Area★** *(Siltcoos Beach Rd. off US-101, 7mi south of Florence)* has a 1mi boardwalk that loops along a lagoon loud with frogs and wood ducks. Hikers on the **Umpqua Scenic Dunes Trail★★** *(US-101, 11mi south of Reedsport)* top off a .5mi forest walk by ascending the highest dunes in the area for panoramas of the sand hills, beach and ocean.

★Coos Bay – *US-101, 234mi south of Astoria & 109mi southwest of Eugene.* ☎ *541-269-8921.* The largest natural harbor between Puget Sound and San Francisco Bay is been a major shipping center for forest products. Once home to thousands of Coos Indians, this deep estuary first attracted European settlement in the 1850s. Today, with 25,000 inhabitants, the adjoining towns of Coos Bay and North Bend form the largest Oregon coastal community. A waterfront boardwalk, shops and galleries attract tourists. Several state parks are visitor lures—notably **Cape Arago State Park★** *(Cape Arago Hwy., 14.5mi southwest of Coos Bay; ☎ 541-888-3778)*, from whose 150ft bluffs one may sight whales, seals and sea lions.

CENTRAL AND EASTERN OREGON★

Michelin map 493 B, C, D 4, 5, 6   Pacific Standard Time
Tourist Information ☎ 541-382-8334 or 541-523-9200

Oregon divides dramatically along the spine of the Cascades. West is a green land of farms, orchards and lush forest. East is higher, drier land, more open and less populated. There are grassy valleys, timbered mountains, deep canyons, badlands and high desert. Uplifted by tectonic forces, piled higher with deposits of lava and ash, the region was born of volcanic cataclysm and shaped by erosion.

Long an Indian home, central and eastern Oregon were passed up by early white pioneers en route to the fertile Willamette Valley. Later arrivals found this country excellent for ranching and mining. Natural resources still provide an economic foundation, but the region remained sparsely populated until tourism took root in outdoor recreation in the 1960s and 70s. Fishing and hunting always were passions for visitors; but with the growth in popularity of snow skiing, mountain biking and white-water rafting, to name a few, the area has attracted more permanent residents fleeing big-city pressures for a laid-back lifestyle.

SIGHTS

★Bend – *US 20 & 97, 163mi southeast of Portland.* ☎ *541-382-3221.www .bendchamber.org.* This city of 35,000—largest in Oregon east of the Cascades—sprawls along the banks of the Deschutes River. The Three Sisters mountains and other snow-capped peaks provide a stirring backdrop to the west. Early-20C buildings downtown hold restaurants, coffeehouses, galleries and antique stores.

★★ High Desert Museum – Kids *US-97, 3.5mi south of Bend.* ☎ *541-382-4754. www.highdesert.org.* Both a small zoo and a museum of regional history, culture and art, this facility is nestled in a pine forest. In several life-size dioramas, sound effects vividly depict a colorful history. A "Desertarium" highlights dry plateau ecosystems; river otters frolic in a stream near a center for birds of prey.

★★ Newberry National Volcanic Monument – *Lava Lands Visitor Center, US-97 13mi south of Bend.* ☎ *541-593-2421.* Extending from the Deschutes River 24mi southeast to 7,987ft Paulina Peak, this 55,000-acre site embraces lava caves and tubes, cinder cones, fields of volcanic glass, ancient archaeological sites and two crater lakes of remarkable beauty—all within a scarred and blistered landscape built by successive lava flows. The Newberry Volcano's last eruption occurred only 1,300 years ago, and hot springs still bubble beneath lake surfaces.

At the **Lava Cast Forest★** *(Forest Rd. 9720, 12mi southeast of visitor center)*, a 1mi trail loops through molds made 6,000 years ago when molten lava encased a grove of ponderosa pine, then cooled to rock. The 18sq mi **Newberry Crater★★** *(Rte. 21, 25mi southeast of visitor center)* contains twin, deep-blue, spring-fed Paulina and East Lakes. The only break in the steep 700-1,700ft walls of the caldera is at **Paulina Falls**, which drop dramatically 80ft off the outer face. Ancient Paiute Indians quarried glassy black obsidian from within the crater for tools and weapons.

Obsidian Flow, Newberry Crater

★★ Cascade Lakes Highway – *West on Rte. 372, south on Forest Rd. 46, east on Forest Rd. 42.* ☎ *541-388-5664.* This delightful 91mi drive passes scores of tree-fringed lakes, rustic fishing camps and mountain trailheads. Alpine **views★★★** are stunning from atop 9,065ft **Mount Bachelor★** *(☎ 541-382-2442)*, considered the Northwest's best ski resort. A chairlift operates to the summit year-round.

Warm Springs Indian Reservation – *US-26, 108mi southeast of Portland & 55mi north of Bend.* The largest of eight native reservations in Oregon was created in 1855 from 10 million acres of Wasco and Sahapto tribal land. In addition to a casino hotel, its highlight is the **Museum at Warm Springs★★** Kids *(US-26, Warm Springs; ☎ 541-553-3331).* The architecturally acclaimed museum contains one of the largest collections of tribal heirlooms and photographs in the US, as well as a history timeline and a model village of various domicile types.

** **Smith Rock State Park** – *NE Crooked River Dr., Terrebonne, 23mi north of Bend.* ⚠ 🅿 ☎ *541-548-7501*. Internationally renowned for its challenging rock climbing, this spectacular set of multicolored cliffs frames the Crooked River Canyon. Outcroppings of solidified magma, eroded by aeons of wind and water, tower more than 550ft above the river.

** **John Day Fossil Beds National Monument** – *Sheep Rock Unit, Rte. 19, 2mi north of US-26, 115mi northeast of Bend. Painted Hills Unit, Burnt Ranch Rd., 7mi north of US-26, 88mi northeast of Bend. Clarno Unit, Rte. 218, 101mi northeast of Bend.* ☎ *514-987-2333. www.nps.gov/joda.* Preserving a small portion of the 10,000sq mi of fossil beds covering north-central Oregon, the monument holds fossilized plants and animals that lived here 50 million to 10 million years ago. The **Sheep Rock Visitor Center**★ displays fossils of some of the unusual creatures that lived then, including bear-dogs, saber-tooth cats, rhinoceroses and entelodonts (bison-sized pigs). A few miles north, interpretive trails lead to **Blue Basin**★, a natural amphitheater loaded with fossils.

* **Baker City** – *US-30 & Rte. 7 at I-84, 302mi east of Portland.* ☎ *541-523-3356. www.neoregon.com/visitBaker.html.* The discovery of gold in the Blue Mountain foothills in 1861 brought a rush of prospectors to Baker City, and the arrival of the railroad two decades later cemented the town's place on the map. The red-brick and volcanic-tuff historic district, centered on Main Street, is anchored by the 1889 Italian Renaissance-style **Geiser Grand Hotel**, restored and still operating.

** **National Historic Oregon Trail Interpretive Center** – *Rte. 86, 5mi east of I-84 at Baker City.* ♿ 🅿 ☎ *541-523-1843. www.or.blm.gov/NHOTIC.* Perched atop Flagstaff Hill, the museum overlooks ruts made by covered wagons on the Oregon Trail. Hands-on exhibits and full-scale dioramas render indelible images of the travails of early pioneers.

■ The Tragedy of the Nez Percé

For 8,000 years, Hells Canyon and the Wallowa Mountains were the homeland of the Nez Percé and their ancestors. Traveling with the seasons to hunt, fish, trade and gather the wild camas root, they were renowned as horsemen and breeders of the Appaloosa. In 1805, the tribe assisted Lewis and Clark; three generations later, after prospectors found gold on tribal land, they were asked to make room for white settlement. Some Nez Percé, living near Idaho's Clearwater River, signed an 1863 treaty that established a reservation in those precincts. Others, who would have been forced to abandon ancestral lands, balked at the agreement.

Among the latter was **Chief Joseph** (c.1840-1904), a Wallowa tribal leader who for years had cooperated with federal authorities to resolve conflicts. He asked only that he be left "a free man. Free to travel, free to choose my own teachers, free to follow the religion of my fathers, free to talk and think and act for myself, and I will obey every law or submit to the penalty."

In June 1877, Joseph led 750 men, women and children, with 2,000 horses and cattle, from the Wallowas across Hells Canyon to Idaho. An impetuous raid on white settlers by members of another Nez Percé band led to a skirmish with the US cavalry. Anticipating retribution, Joseph and Chief Looking Glass fled east with their bands across the Continental Divide, through Yellowstone Park, then north almost to Canada—a 1,200mi odyssey. In Montana's Bear Paw Mountains, Looking Glass was killed and Joseph surrendered his surviving 417 followers to the army, which had pursued him for 15 weeks with more than 5,000 troops.

Joseph's surrender speech is among the most poignant in the annals of the West: "I want to have time to look for my children and see how many of them I can find; maybe I shall find them among the dead. Hear me, my chiefs. I am tired. My heart is sick and sad. From where the sun now stands, I will fight no more, forever."

In 1885, after exile in Oklahoma, Joseph's band returned to the Nez Percé Reservation in Idaho. Joseph himself, however, was forever separated from his people. He died on Washington's Colville Reservation.

✶✶ Hells Canyon National Recreation Area – *Extending about 80mi on either side of the Oregon-Idaho border, 350mi east of Portland. Headquarters: Rte. 82, Enterprise.* ☏ *541-426-5546.* The Snake River carves the boundary between Oregon and Idaho through the deepest canyon in North America. Isolated from development, overlooked by casual travelers, Hells Canyon is a vertical landscape whose dark cliffs and grassy foothills tumble headlong 6,000-8,000ft. from the Wallowa Range and Seven Devils Mountains to the swift, north-flowing river at its heart. Covering more than 1,000sq mi, nearly one-third of it rugged wilderness, the recreation area sprawls across the canyon and adjacent rim country.

The **canyon floor✶✶** may be reached below Hells Canyon Dam *(via Rte. 86, 91mi east of Baker City)*. From here, the only way to proceed is by boat or on foot. With modern inflatable rafts and jet boats, running the river has become almost routine, if still challenging. Outfitters such as River Odysseys West *(P.O. Box 579, Coeur d'Alene ID 83816;* ☏ *208-765-0841)* put in at the dam and take out several days later at Pittsburg Landing, a 34mi passage, or farther downstream. Jet boats run upriver about 100mi from Lewiston, Idaho.

The best canyon overlooks are from Oregon's 208mi **Wallowa Mountains Loop✶✶** *(from LaGrande, on I-84, drive northeast on Rte. 82 through Enterprise and Joseph to Rte. 350, south on Rte. 39, then west on Rte. 86 through Halfway to Baker City;* ☏ *541-426-5546)*. This glorious though demanding drive combines paved and unpaved byways, offering spectacular vistas and opportunities to see bighorn sheep, mountain goats, elk, deer, black bears and other wildlife.

✶ Nez Percé National Historical Park – The park comprises 38 sites in four states, including the 1877 battlefields and locations important to tribal legend. The tribe's story is documented at the main visitor center and museum *(US-95, Spalding, Idaho, 14mi east of Lewiston;* ☏ *208-843-2261; www.nps.gov/nepe)*, along with the **Spalding-Allen Collection✶✶**, a fabulous sampling of artifacts and hide clothing adorned with dentalia shells, porcupine quills and elk teeth dating from 1836.

Pendleton – *US-395 & Rte. 11 at I-84, 209mi east of Portland.* ☏ *541-276-7411. www.pendleton-oregon.org.* Tucked beneath high bluffs on the banks of the Umatilla River, this city of 16,000 has stayed true to its cowboy roots. History is tangible in the Victorian homes north of the river and in the compact business district, location of saddleries and antique shops. Pendleton is renowned for its wool shirts and blankets; guided tours of the **Pendleton Woolen Mills✶** *(1307 SE Court Pl.;* ☏ *541-276-6911)* offer an inside look at the whole production process, from sheep to store.

The **Pendleton Round-up**, a high-spirited, week-long pageant held every September since 1910, is one of the world's biggest rodeos. The **Round-Up Hall of Fame✶** *(Round-up Grounds, I-84 Exit 207;* ☏ *541-278-0815)* commemorates the event and its participants.

✶ Tamastslikt Cultural Center – *Rte. 331, Mission, 7mi east of Pendleton.* △ ✕ ♿ ▣ ☏ *541-966-9748.* Located on the Umatilla Indian Reservation, this excellent new museum tells the story of the area's indigenous people—Cayuse, Umatilla and Walla Wallas—with skillfully presented artifacts, dioramas and native storytelling.

Salt Lake City Area

Historic Temple Square and Salt Lake Temple

Scott T. Smith/DPA

Set between the dramatic Wasatch Mountains and the saline sprawl of the Great Salt Lake and Desert, Salt Lake City is unique. Founded in the 1840s by persecuted religious refugees from the east and midwest US, it grew as the world capital of the Church of Jesus Christ of Latter-day Saints (Mormons), a distinction that still dominates social, cultural and political life throughout the region and beyond the boundaries of the state of Utah. Yet Salt Lake City is more than a spiritual enclave: It is a thriving modern city, firmly rooted in its heritage but looking well into the future as a leading center of the high-technology and biomedical industries.

The Great Salt Lake itself, fewer than 15mi west of the city, spreads across 2,500sq mi when filled to capacity, but nowhere is it deeper than 42ft. The inland sea is a remnant of ancient Lake Bonneville, which covered an area eight times this large in the later ice ages. Twice as salty as any ocean (with a saline content that typically is in the 20 percent range), it draws water and dissolved minerals from mountain streams ... yet it has no outlet and precious little aquatic life. As water evaporates in the high desert heat of summer, salinity increases markedly in the Great Salt Lake.

Some 800,000 people live today in Salt Lake County. Many more live a short drive south in Provo and north in Ogden, for a metropolitan population of nearly 1.5 million. Outdoor recreation is paramount to many of these area residents. Within an hour's drive of these three urban hubs, in fact, are 10 downhill and six cross-country ski resorts—an unparalleled concentration that helped earn Salt Lake the honor of hosting the 2002 Winter Olympic Games.

Many of the competitions will be held in the mountains around Park City, a historic mining town high in the Wasatch Range 30mi east of Salt Lake City. Not only is this sophisticated resort center surrounded by three world-class ski areas and the Utah Winter Sports Park, where Olympic ski-jumping and sledding will be contested; it is home to the renowned annual Sundance Film Festival.

SALT LAKE CITY★★

Michelin map 493 E, F 7, 8 Mountain Standard Time
Population 174,348
Tourist Information ☎ 801-521-2822 or www.visitsaltlake.com

Historic Temple Square, with its concentration of buildings tied to Mormon religion and history, is the central attraction of Salt Lake City, certainly worthy of several hours' exploration by anyone with a desire to understand this important modern world religion. Other sights include museums and, especially, scenic attractions. *Note: Because of the strong presence of the Mormon church, few sights (except natural ones) are open Sundays. Call ahead to check.*

Historical Notes

Salt Lake City was founded on July 24, 1847, by 148 Mormon pioneers led by Brigham Young. *(See "The Mormon Faith," p 278)* The first non-Indians to settle permanently in the valley, these 143 men, three women and two children almost immediately began tilling the soil, planting crops and platting their town. More emigrants joined them the following year. But a late frost, a drought and a plague of crickets nearly destroyed the harvest until flocks of seagulls descended upon the insects and enabled the settlers to survive that winter. The seagull was later designated Utah's state bird.

Ownership of the Salt Lake Valley transferred from Mexico to the US in 1848, and in 1850 the Utah Territory was formed, with Brigham Young as its first governor. To the Mormons, however, their home was the State of Deseret. A *deseret* honeybee is acknowledged in *The Book of Mormon* for its industriousness; bee-like hard work and a sense of community, coupled with extensive irrigation, enabled the Mormons to succeed. Today, Utah's state symbol is a beehive.

Utah's isolation ended in 1869 with the completion of the first transcontinental railroad and the driving of the Golden Spike at Promontory Point, 80mi northwest of Salt Lake City. Through World War I, hundreds of copper, silver, gold and lead mines opened in the canyons east and west of Salt Lake City. Wealthy mine owners built luxurious manors in the city, a stark contrast from modest Mormon homes.

ADDRESS BOOK

Please see explanation on p 64.

Staying in the Salt Lake Area

Stein Eriksen Lodge – *Royal St. W., Deer Valley Resort, Park City UT.* ✂ ♿ P 🏊 ☎ *435-649-3700. www.steinlodge.com. 127 rooms.* **$$** *(summer),* **$$$$** *(winter).* Skiers pay top dollar to experience the Stein's Scandinavian alpine decor, prime service and ski-in, ski-out privileges. Summer guests get a massive stone fireplace, courtyard waterfall and plush terry-cloth robes without all the snow.

Alta Lodge – *Rte. 210, Alta UT.* ✂ ♿ P 🏊 ☎ *801-742-3500. www.altalodge.com. 57 rooms.* **$$$** Beds are narrow, and there are no TVs, but that's part of the charm. Opened in the late 1930s by the Denver & Rio Grande Railroad, the Lodge is an institution for the skier's skier. Unpretentious regulars come for family-style dining and floor-to-ceiling windows looking out to the Wasatch Mountain peaks.

Homestead Resort – *700 N. Homestead Dr., Midway UT.* ✂ ♿ P 🏊 ☎ *435-654-1102. www.homesteadresort.com. 152 rooms.* **$$** A Swiss-born farmer discovered mineral "hot pots" here over a century ago, and buggy-loads of visitors convinced him to create a resort. Now, lodgings range from cottages and condos to The Virginia House, a Victorian B&B; decor is Southwestern or New England. Guests may snorkel in the warm Homestead Crater even in the middle of winter.

Peery Hotel – *110 W. 300 South, Salt Lake City UT.* ✂ ♿ P ☎ *801-521-4300. www.citysearch.com/slc/peeryhotel. 73 rooms.* **$$** All rooms in the newly renovated Peery, built in 1910 and listed on the National Register of Historic Places, are reached by a classic grand staircase from the expansive lobby. A casual pub and bistro serve up chilled pastas that change daily.

Largely because of early Mormon adherence to polygamy, Congress was slow to grant statehood to Utah. Only after the church withdrew its sanction of multiple-spouse marriages was Utah admitted to the union (in 1896, as the 45th state), with its capital at Salt Lake City.

The distinctive Mormon city-grid plan persists today, not only in Salt Lake City but in most towns around the state. Broad streets—"wide enough for a team of four oxen and a covered wagon to turn around"—radiate in 10-acre squares from a central hub, in Salt Lake City's case Temple Square. Addresses and street names, confusing to visitors, reveal their direction from the hub. Thus 201 E. 300 South Street is two blocks east and three blocks south of Temple Square; 201 S. 300 East Street is two blocks south and three east of the square.

SIGHTS

***Historic Temple Square** – *50 W. South Temple St. (between North, South & West Temple Sts. & Main St.).* ♿ ☎ *801-240-2534. www.lds.org.* This pleasantly landscaped 10-acre plot is the hub of downtown Salt Lake City and the heart of the Mormon faith. Here are the six-spired temple, the silver-domed tabernacle, the beautiful Assembly Hall and several noteworthy statues and monuments. Pairs of young Latter-day Saint missionaries from all over the world conduct **free tours**★★ and discuss elements of their faith in 30 languages, leaving every few minutes from a flagpole at the center of the complex.

Although no one not baptized into the church is permitted to enter the **Salt Lake Temple**★ (or any other temple), audiovisual presentations in the **North and South Visitors Centers** show some of its highlights. The red-sandstone foundation was laid in 1853-55, but the capstone was not put into place until 1892. The stunning structure has granite walls 9ft thick at ground level, 6ft thick at top, and a statue of the angel Moroni, cast in copper (by sculptor Cyrus E. Dallin) and covered with 22-karat gold, trumpeting from a 210ft spire.

The **Salt Lake Tabernacle**★ took just three years to construct; it opened in 1867 as the first building on Temple Square. Seating 6,000 people, it contains a remarkable 11,623-pipe, 32ft-tall **organ**★★ that accompanies the world-famous

The Inn at Temple Square – *71 W. South Temple St., Salt Lake City UT.* ✗♿ 🅿 ☎ *801-531-1000. www.theinn.com. 90 rooms.* **$** Erected in 1930, this stately, restored brick hotel has a prime spot opposite the central Mormon temple. The rooms have four-poster beds; wallpaper and fabric bloom with floral patterns.

1904 Imperial Hotel – *221 Main St., Park City UT.* ♿ 🅿 ☎ *435-649-1904 www.1904imperial.com. 10 rooms.* **$** Each room in this historic inn is named after a local silver mine – Little Belle, Bluebird, Anchor. Built to house miners in 1904, the hotel lures modern visitors with huge breakfasts and down comforters. It has survived a fire and a stint as a bordello.

Dining in the Salt Lake Area

Log Haven Restaurant – *4mi up Millcreek Ave. from S. Wasatch Blvd., Salt Lake City UT.* ☎ *801-272-8255. www.log-haven.com.* **$$$ Creative American.** Built in 1920 from Oregon logs hauled up Millcreek Canyon by horse-drawn wagon, this forest cabin nestles at the base of the Wasatch Range. Walls glow with rustic warmth, and the food is gourmet: coriander-rubbed ahi tuna with lemon-guava sauce is a house favorite.

Market Street Grill – *48 W. Market St., Salt Lake City UT.* ☎ *801-322-4668.* **$$$ Seafood.** This loud and crowded restaurant works hard to get food on the table. Fresh fish is flown in daily: moonfish and mahimahi from Hawaii, orange roughy from New Zealand, lobster tails from Canada, six kinds of oysters on the half shell. As many as 250 diners can be seated under mock palm trees.

Zoom – *660 Main St., Park City UT.* ☎ *435-649-9108.* **$$ American & Continental.** Its venue is a century-old former train station, but the cuisine at Zoom is anything but old-fashioned. Cornmeal-crusted Utah trout and Mediterranean lamb kabobs share the menu with sea scallops, served with jicama and black-bean salad.

Mormon Tabernacle Choir. There is no charge to the public to attend weekly broadcast choir performances *(9:15am Sun)* or rehearsals *(8pm Thu)*. Daily organ recitals are also offered *(noon Mon-Sat, 2pm Sun)*.

Also on the grounds is the semi-Gothic **Assembly Hall*** (1880), a miniature cathedral that now hosts free concerts and lectures. Nearby is **The Miracle of the Gulls Monument** (1913, Mahonri Young), honoring the seagulls that saved the first pioneers' crop. The **Nauvoo Temple Bell**, a 782-pound bronze bell transported by wagon from Illinois in 1846-47, rings hourly on the square. Outside the southeast corner of Temple Square is the **Brigham Young Monument**, erected in 1897 to honor the founding father of Salt Lake City.

Opposite Temple Square to the west are two important facilities.

** Museum of Church History and Art – *45 N. West Temple St.* ♿ ☎ *801-240-3310 (recording) or 801-240-2299*. This well-presented museum is an essential stop for any visitor seeking to understand the roots of The Church of Jesus Christ of Latter-day Saints, its evolution and its doctrines. Interpretive exhibits delineate the history of the religion, from its seminal revelation in upstate New York through the westward trek to modern growth. There are galleries of 19-20C Mormon and American Indian art and portraits of historic church leaders. An orientation film, demonstrations by costumed docents, and audio tours enhance its value.

* Family History Library – *35 N. West Temple St.* ♿ ☎ *801-240-2331. www .familysearch.org.* The world's largest collection of genealogical materials—on microfilm, on microfiche and in books—offers free public access for research. Church staff are available to assist. Established in 1894, this is the hub of more than 3,400 Family History Centers in 65 countries and territories. An introduction is offered at the FamilySearch Center *(below)*.

Across Main Street east of Temple Square is another block of church buildings.

■ The Mormon Faith

Foundations of The Church of Jesus Christ of Latter-day Saints, as the Mormon Church is properly known, rest on covenants, sacred promises made with God. In 1823, as young Joseph Smith (1805-44) knelt in prayer in a grove near his family farm in Palmyra, New York, God and Jesus appeared to him and told Smith that, through him, the original church of Jesus would be restored to earth. Some time later, the angel Moroni appeared to Smith, revealing the burial place of metal tablets inscribed with sacred writings of an ancient civilization. Smith translated and published this text, which relates the ministry of Jesus in North America after His resurrection in Jerusalem, as *The Book of Mormon* in 1829.

Library of Congress

Brigham Young

Having established the new church in New York in 1830, Smith and his fellow believers tried to escape persecution by moving west, first to Ohio, then to Missouri and Illinois, until Smith and his brother Hyrum were shot and killed by an armed mob. His successor, Brigham Young (1801-77), led the exodus west in 1846-47 and established Salt Lake City, where the Mormons prospered.

Mormons regard as scriptural the *Holy Bible, The Book of Mormon,* later oracles to Smith and ongoing revelation by God to prophets of the Church, including Young and 20C leaders. God is seen as a real spiritual being who once was mortal, who lived and died on earth, was resurrected, and evolved to become the supreme intelligence. His son Jesus

★ **Joseph Smith Memorial Building** – *15 E. South Temple St.* ⸙ ♿ 🅿 ☎ *801-240-1266. www.jsmb.com*. The former Hotel Utah (1911), restored in 1987, reopened as a community center. Its elegant lobby features an original stained-glass ceiling, marble pillars and grand staircase. **"Legacy"** (☎ *801-240-4383*), a 53min film telling the saga of the pioneers' westward trek, is shown in a theater. The **FamilySearch Center** (☎ *801-240-4085*) introduces visitors to genealogical research by means of computers that access the names of hundreds of millions of deceased all over the world.

Church Administration Building – *47 E. South Temple St*. A stately Greek Revival-style building of gray granite with polished interior marble walls, this structure represented stability and respectability for the Mormon faith when it opened in 1917. The world headquarters for The Church of Jesus Christ of Latter-day Saints and its nearly 11 million members, it houses the offices of the president and his counselors, the Twelve Apostles and other church leaders.

★ **The Beehive House** – *67 E. South Temple St.* ⸙ ♿ ☎ *801-240-2681.* The official home of Brigham Young and his large family from 1854 to 1877, this beautifully restored National Historic Landmark is filled with period furnishings. Guided tours take in family rooms, several bedrooms, kitchen and office of the two-story New England Colonial-style home, named for the state symbol that appears in decorative motifs.

Adjoining, multigabled 1856 **Lion House** *(63 E. South Temple St.)*, named for the stone lion sculpted for the front porch, was part of the original residence. It is not open for tours. At the southeast corner of Beehive House is **Eagle Gate** (1859), former entrance to Young's homestead. It is topped by a 6,000-pound eagle with a 20ft wingspan, a symbol of strength, patriotism and integrity.

Young's gravesite, and those of several members of his family, are a block east of here in the tiny **Mormon Pioneer Memorial Cemetery** *(140 E. First Ave.)*.

---

was the only perfect man; His other son, the Holy Ghost, someday will take a mortal body. The Gospel has existed since the beginning of time, long predating Jesus' mortal ministry. Jesus someday will reign personally over Zion, the New Jerusalem, a communal paradise of holy saints in North America.

Baptism by immersion symbolizes the remission of one's sins, and acceptance of Christ's death and resurrection. Deceased ancestors are invited through proxy baptism to accept the Gospel and thereby gain everlasting life in Zion. Church emphasis on tracing genealogy has resulted from a desire to offer eternal life to all ancestors. Missionary work (all young Mormons are asked to contribute two years of field-work) reflects an interest in bringing the Gospel to all.

The family is the most important unit of temporal and sacred society. Marriages are "for time and all eternity," not "'til death do you part." Couples are "sealed" into the afterlife; their children, also, are spiritually bound to them for eternity.

The gender roles are well defined: Fathers, by proclamation, "are responsible to provide the necessities of life and protection for their families. Mothers are primarily responsible for the nurture of their children." Although the Church withdrew its sanction from the practice of polygamy (multiple wives) in the 1890s, an underground movement persists.

The Church places a high value on welfare for poverty and disaster relief, both in the US and abroad. Mormons are asked to fast for two meals, one day of each month, and donate the money they would have spent on those meals to a fund for the needy. In addition, they tithe 10 percent of their income for church construction, education, missionary service and other programs.

Acknowledging the body as the temple of God, members adhere to a strict code of behavior that includes abstaining from alcohol, tobacco, harmful drugs, coffee and tea, as well as sex outside of wedlock.

The Mormon church is run by a well-defined bureaucratic and spiritual hierarchy. The Church president (chosen as a prophet "by God" upon the death or incapacity of his predecessor) and two counselors are supported in policy-making and administration by the Quorum of the Twelve Apostles.

Church Office Building – *50 E. North Temple St.* ☎ *801-240-1000*. Lovely plaza gardens surround this 26-story building, Salt Lake's tallest. The general administrative offices of The Church of Jesus Christ of Latter-day Saints are housed here. From the top-floor observation deck, there are superb **views**★★ of the greater Salt Lake area.

★★ **Utah State Capitol** – *North end of State St.* ♿ 🅿 ☎ *801-538-3000 or 801-538-1563 (tours). www.utah.com*. Completed in 1915 (Richard Kletting) at a cost of $2.74 million, this fine example of Renaissance Revival-style architecture—with its Corinthian columns and copper dome—was patterned after the US Capitol in Washington DC. The interior of the dome, 165ft above the foyer, is adorned with seagulls and historic murals. Guided tours are offered half-hourly on weekdays.

Facing the State Capitol on 300 North Street is **Council Hall** *(☎ 801-538-1030)*, built downtown in the 1860s, dismantled brick-by-brick in 1963 and moved to Capitol Hill. It now houses state tourism offices.

Pioneer Memorial Museum – *300 N. Main St.* ♿ 🅿 ☎ *801-538-1050*. Located opposite the State Capitol to the west, this eclectic and extensive collection of pioneer artifacts—on four floors and in an adjacent carriage house—includes an enormous range of sacred and sectarian items, especially from 1847-69.

★ **Maurice Abravanel Concert Hall** – *123 W. South Temple St.* ♿ ☎ *801-355-2787. www.arttix.org*. Home of the Utah Symphony Orchestra, this 1993 hall, catercorner from Temple Square, is renowned for its acoustics.

Salt Palace Convention Center – *100 S. West Temple St.* ♿ 🅿 ☎ *801-534-4777. www.saltpalace.com*. This 415,000sq-ft space also includes **The Visitor Information Center** *(90 S. West Temple St.; ☎ 801-521-2822)*.

★ **University of Utah** – *Presidents Circle & University St., 2mi east of downtown via 2nd South St.* ✗♿ 🅿 ☎ *801-581-6515. www.utah.edu*. Founded in 1850 as the University of Deseret, this 1,494-acre campus is Utah's oldest. Opening and closing ceremonies of the 2002 Olympic Winter Games will be at its Rice-Eccles Stadium; Olympic Village, providing athlete housing, also will be here.

★ **Utah Museum of Natural History** – Kids *1390 E. Presidents Circle (east end of 2nd South St.).* ♿ 🅿 ☎ *801-581-4303 (recording) or 801-581-6927. www.umnh.utah.edu*. Paleontology exhibits highlight this museum, including several dinosaur skeletons. The Geology Hall emphasizes the Utah mining industry. The Barrier Canyon Mural re-creates pictographs from cliffs in Canyonlands National Park.

★ **Utah Museum of Fine Arts** – *370 S. 1530 East St. (S. Campus Dr. opposite Rice-Eccles Stadium).* ♿ 🅿 ☎ *801-581-7332. www.utah.edu/umfa*. This wide-ranging collection features paintings and decorative arts from all over the world; the permanent collection of 15,000 objects includes 5,000-year-old Chinese antiquities. Emphasis is on 17-19C European and American art, including works by Jan Brueghel, Francesco Solimena, Gainsborough, Stuart, Corot and Cole. *In summer 2000, the museum will relocate to a new building at 1650 E. South Campus Dr.*

★ **Red Butte Garden and Arboretum** – *300 Wakara Way off Foothill Dr.* ♿ 🅿 ☎ *801-581-4747. www.redbutte.utah.edu*. Spread across a semi-arid hillside above the university, extending through a snowmelt-fed canyon, these gardens preserve wildflowers, shrubs and trees (300 species), and cultivated gardens.

★ **This Is The Place Heritage Park** – Kids *2601 Sunnyside Ave. east of Foothill Dr.* ♿ 🅿 ☎ *801-584-8392. www.thisistheplace.org*. It is said that as Brigham Young and his party crested the Wasatch Range and descended Emigration Canyon in 1847, Young gazed upon the Salt Lake Valley and said, "This is the place." On the centennial of that occasion, **This Is The Place Monument** was erected to honor the passage from Illinois on the 1,300mi Mormon Pioneer National Historic Trail. Mormon pioneer lifestyle (c.1847-69) is re-enacted in **Old Deseret Village**★★ in summer. In three dozen reconstructed buildings—homes, shops, farms, schools and churches—villagers demonstrate how to make quilts, candles and adobe bricks, spin and color wool, tend domestic animals, and cook.

Utah's Hogle Zoo – Kids *2600 Sunnyside Ave. east of Foothill Dr.* ✗♿ 🅿 ☎ *801-582-1631. www.hoglezoo.org*. More than 1,000 animals, both exotic and regional, are displayed at this community zoo. Children are delighted by a working scale-model railroad.

Tracy Aviary – Kids *Liberty Park, 589 E. 1300 South St.* ♿ 🅿 ☎ *801-596-8500*. Established in 1938, this is one of the oldest public bird parks in the US. Some 500 birds of 150 species, including exotics and 21 threatened or endangered species, live here. Bird shows are scheduled May-September.

EXCURSIONS

*Big Cottonwood Canyon – *Rte. 190, extending 15mi east from I-215 Exit 6.*
△ ╳ ⅙ ▣ Old mining claims and impressive scenery mark this canyon that
extends into the Wasatch Range from southeast Salt Lake City. Two popular ski
areas, both rising above 10,000ft, nestle at its end. Village expansion is ongoing
at powder-rich **Solitude** *(28mi from downtown;* ☎ *801-534-1400).* Less than 2mi
up the road, family-oriented **Brighton** *(30mi from downtown;* ☎ *801-532-4731)*
entices snowboarders.

*Little Cottonwood Canyon – *Rte. 210, extending 14mi south & east from I-215
Exit 6.* △ ╳ ⅙ ▣ The primary lures of this gorge, shorter and narrower than Big
Cottonwood, are its two vaunted resorts. Nearest to Salt Lake City is **Snowbird***
(25mi from downtown; ☎ *801-742-2222),* whose 11,000ft summit and 3,240ft
vertical surpass all other Wasatch resorts. A 125-passenger aerial tramway climbs
from base to summit in 8min and provides a contemporary European-style ambience. **Alta**** *(27mi from downtown;* ☎ *801-359-1078)* opened in 1938 as the
second (after Idaho's Sun Valley) destination ski resort in the western US. Famed
for relaxed, old-fashioned atmosphere and deep powder snow (over 500in per
year), Alta steadfastly refuses to install high-capacity or high-speed lifts or to permit snowboarding, and daily lift rates are kept lower than other top resorts. In
the village library, the **Alta Historical Society** *(*☎ *801-742-3522)* maintains a permanent exhibit on Alta's silver-mining boom days of 1864-78.

**Kennecott's Bingham Canyon Mine – *4.5mi southwest of the intersection of
Rtes. 48 & 111 near Copperton, and 29mi from downtown Salt Lake City via Rte.
48, west off I-15 Exit 301.* ⅙ ▣ ☎ *801-252-3234.* The largest open-pit mine on
earth is more than 2.5mi in diameter and nearly 4,000ft deep—more than twice
the height of the world's tallest buildings. It is one of only two man-made objects
that can be seen from outer space, the other being the Great Wall of China. Since
mining operations began in 1906, 6 billion tons of earth have been removed from
what was once a mountain. The Bingham Canyon Mine has yielded more wealth
than the California, Comstock and Klondike rushes combined: 15 million tons (30
billion pounds) of copper ore, 700 million pounds of molybdenum, 175 million
ounces of silver and 20 million ounces of gold.

Exhibits in the Kennecott Utah Copper Corporation **visitor center***, on the east side
of the pit, tell the history of company and mine, and describe the process of concentrating, smelting and refining to produce copper from ore. The best panoramas of the mine are from an outside observation area.

*Great Salt Lake State Park – 🔲 *I-80 Exit 104, 17mi west of Salt Lake City.*
☎ *801-250-1898.* A marina and beach provide access to the largest US lake west
of the Mississippi River. Only the Dead Sea has a higher salt content. Waterbirds
of all varieties thrive here—more than 257 species inhabit the shores and island.

WASATCH FRONT*

Michelin map 493 E, F 8 – Mountain Standard Time
Tourist Information ☎ 801-538-1030 or www.utah.com

A startling backdrop to the Salt Lake area, the Wasatch Mountains rise like a 7,000ft
wall east of the metropolis, 150mi from Logan south to Nephi, climbing over
11,000ft elevation. Once an obstacle to exploration, they were pierced by silver miners in the late 19C. Today the range is a leading source of white gold—the downy
powder into which winter-sports lovers cast skis and snowboards. Utah's vehicle
license plates even declare: "The Greatest Snow on Earth." Park City, largest of the
resort communities and a mere 35mi east of Salt Lake City, will be the hub of mountain activities during the 2002 Olympic Winter Games.

Utah's population base extends south and north from Salt Lake City, along the west
face of the Wasatch Range and around its north end. Known as the Wasatch Front,
this region includes Provo, 45mi south, Utah's second largest city and the home of
Brigham Young University; and Ogden, 35mi north.

SIGHTS

**Park City – *Rte. 224, 5mi south of I-80 Exit 145.* △ ╳ ⅙ ▣ ☎ *435-649-6100.*
www.parkcityinfo.com. A rich mining district in the late 19C, producing more than
$400 million in silver, Park City was founded in 1872. In its heyday, nearly
10,000 residents supported theaters, dance halls, saloons and brothels. An 1898
fire destroyed three-quarters of the city; the surviving 19C structures now are

part of the **Main Street National Historic District★★**, which entices visitors with galleries, boutiques and restaurants. Walking tours begin from the **Park City Museum** *(528 Main St.; ☎ 435-645-5135)*, in the territorial jailhouse.

Park City established itself as a year-round resort in the 1960s. Modern sprawl (in anticipation of the Winter Olympics) has it approaching its halcyon size. Three major ski areas are a short shuttle-bus run from Main Street; one, family-oriented **Park City Mountain Resort★** *(Lowell Ave.; ☎ 435-649-8111)*, is mere steps away. Elegant, celebrity-conscious **Deer Valley Resort★** *(Deer Valley Dr.; ☎ 435-649-1000)* is 1mi east. Flush with new development is **The Canyons★** *(The Canyons Dr.; ☎ 435-649-5400)*, 3mi north off Route 224. Between them, the three similarly sized resorts offer 9,290ft of vertical (at least 3,000ft each) served by 44 lifts.

■ XIX Olympic Winter Games

From February 8-24, 2002, about 3,500 athletes and officials from 80 countries will gather to test their skills in eight winter sports and 78 events at the XIX Olympic Winter Games *(☎ 801-212-2002; www.slc2002.org)*.

The University of Utah will be the hub of activity, providing housing in a 70-acre Olympic Village and hosting opening and closing ceremonies in **Rice-Eccles Stadium** *(S. Campus Dr.)*. Events will be spread throughout the Wasatch Front.

Downtown Salt Lake City will host figure skating and short-track speed skating at **The Delta Center** *(301 W. South Temple St.)*. Men's ice hockey will be played at **The 'E' Center** *(West Valley City, 8mi southwest)*, women's ice-hockey at the **Peaks Ice Arena** in Provo *(51mi south)*. Long-track speed-skating will be at the **Oquirrh Park Oval** *(Kearns, 11mi southwest)*. **The Ice Sheet at Ogden** *(33mi north)* hosts curling.

Skiing will be divided among three resorts. **Deer Valley Resort** *(37mi east of Salt Lake City)* will see men's and women's slalom, freestyle moguls and

aerials. **Park City Mountain Resort** *(35mi east)* will have giant-slalom races and snowboarding. **Snowbasin Resort** *(52mi north)* will provide downhill and super-G courses. Ski jumping, bob-sledding and luge are scheduled for **Utah Winter Sports Park** *(33mi east)*. **Soldier Hollow** *(Wasatch State Park, 45mi east)*, near Heber City, will be the venue for 23 nordic events, including cross-country skiing and biathlon.

© Dusan Smetana/DPA

Two weeks after the conclusion of the Olympic Winter Games, another 1,100 athletes and officials from 35 nations will arrive in Salt Lake City (March 7-16) for the **VIII Paralympic Winter Games** for superior disabled athletes.

Near The Canyons is the **Utah Winter Sports Park**★ *(Bear Hollow Dr. off Rte. 224;* ☎ *435-658-4200),* where several Olympic events will be held. A training facility for US national teams, it has four jumping hills of 18m-120m, four ramps for freestyle aerial jumps and a 1,335m (4,331ft) bobsled/luge track. The public may watch athletes perform, take a bobsled ride or invest in a 2hr ski-jumping lesson.

The arts calendar is highlighted by the **Sundance Film Festival**★★ *(*☎ *801-328-3456 or 435-645-0110)* in January. The world's best independent filmmakers premiere new works at this Robert Redford-produced event, held in Park City since 1986.

Heber Valley Historic Railroad – 〚Kids〛 *450 S. 600 West St., Heber City, 18mi southeast of Park City.* 🅿 ☎ *435-654-5601. www.hebervalleyrr.org.* Restored vintage coaches and a 1907 steam locomotive take passengers on an excursion around Deer Creek Reservoir, to Vivian Park in Provo Canyon.

Sundance Resort – *Rte. 92, Sundance, 15mi north of Provo via US-189.* ✗⛇ 🅿 ☎ *801-225-4107. www.sundance-utah.com.* Purchased in 1969 by actor-director Robert Redford and named for the Utah-born character he played in *Butch Cassidy and the Sundance Kid,* this enclave is devoted to recreation, environment and the arts. In winter a modest ski area serves a flank of 11,750ft Mount Timpanogos. In summer, Sundance is a hiking and riding center with outdoor musical theater.

★**Timpanogos Cave National Monument** – ⸾⸾⸾ *Rte. 92, American Fork, 9mi east of I-15 Exit 287.* ✗ 🅿 ☎ *801-756-5238. www.nps.gov/tica. Advance ticket purchase recommended weekends.* Three limestone caverns, linked by man-made tunnels, are located on the northern slope of Mount Timpanogos. Reached by a steep 1.5mi, 1,065ft uphill hike from the canyon-floor visitor center, its impressive features are still in formation: dripstone, helictites, stalagmites and stalactites. The cave is a cool 43°F year round.

Provo – *US-89 & US-189 at I-15 Exit 268.* △✗⛇ 🅿 ☎ *801-379-2555. www.thechamber.org.* The second-largest city in Utah, with more than 110,000 people, Provo nestles midway down the eastern shore of large freshwater Utah Lake. Besides Brigham Young University, the city boasts the gold-spired **Provo Mormon Temple** *(N. Temple Dr. off N. 900 East St.),* on a hill above the university, and the **Utah County Courthouse** *(Center St. & University Ave.),* built in the 1920s of limestone.

★**Brigham Young University** – *Campus Dr. off E. 1230 North St.* ✗⛇ 🅿 ☎ *801-378-4678. www.byu.edu.* The educational center of Mormonism was established in 1877 by Brigham Young. One of the largest private universities in the US, the 634-acre campus has several museums. The **Museum of Art** *(*☎ *801-378-8256)* features 19C American and European works and a collection of primitive musical instruments. The **Earth Science Museum**★ *(*☎ *801-378-3680)* boasts an outstanding research collection of Jurassic dinosaurs. The **Monte L. Bean Life Science Museum** *(*☎ *801-378-5051)* explores natural history. The **Museum of Peoples and Cultures** *(*☎ *801-378-6112)* focuses on Southwest Indian, Mexican and Mayan artifacts.

★**Springville Museum of Art** – *126 E. 400 South St., Springville, 6mi south of Provo.* 🅿 ☎ *801-489-2727. http://www.shs.nebo.edu.* Perhaps the best collection of Utah art and artists, this small museum has 11 exhibition galleries presenting works by painters, sculptors and printmakers since 1862.

★**Antelope Island State Park** – 〚Kids〛 *Rte. 127; 7.5mi west of I-15 Exit 335 via Rte. 108; 40mi northwest of Salt Lake City.* △✗⛇ 🅿 ☎ *801-773-2941 or 801-322-3770 (camping reservations).* A long causeway crosses the shallow flats of the Great Salt Lake to this 28,000-acre wildlife refuge, largest island in the lake. From a new **visitor center** *(4528 W. 1700 South St., Syracuse),* guests can hike, bike or ride horses on 40mi of trails. Besides antelope, the island is home to mule deer, bighorn sheep, coyotes, bobcats, upland game birds, waterfowl, and 500 bison descended from a late-19C herd.

Hill Aerospace Museum – 〚Kids〛 *7961 Wardleigh Rd., Hill Air Force Base.* ⛇ 🅿 ☎ *801-777-6818. www.hill.af.mil/museum.* One of the largest collections of vintage aircraft and ordnance in the US includes more than 50 bombers, cargo planes, helicopters and other vessels. Engines, missiles, bombs and other weapons are displayed, along with a variety of military flight memorabilia.

Ogden – *US-89 east of I-15 Exit 344.* ✗⛇ 🅿 ☎ *801-627-8290. www.ogdencvb .org.* Established as a railroad town, Ogden—now with about 67,000 residents—echoes its past in restored buildings along its historic **25th Street**. In the

Great Salt Lake and Antelope Island

former depot, the **Utah State Railroad Museum** *(2501 Wall Ave.; ☎ 801-629-4444)* has historic exhibits and a model-railroad room. Also here are car and firearms museums, mineral exhibits, and Ogden's Visitor Information Center.

★ **Ogden River Scenic Byway** – *Rte. 39 east from Ogden to Huntsville.* △ This scenic 62mi route follows Ogden River Canyon upriver past Pineview Reservoir and across the crest of the Wasatch Range. Leaving Ogden, it skirts the **George S. Eccles Dinosaur Park** Kids *(1544 E. Park Blvd.; ☎ 801-393-3466)*, whose 98 replicas of tyrannosaurs, pterodactyls and their ilk are depicted in a realistic outdoor setting. A southbound turnoff from the reservoir, 17mi east of Ogden, climbs to **Snowbasin Resort** *(Rte. 226, Huntsville; ☎ 801-399-1135)*, slated to host downhill and super-G ski racing during the Winter Olympics. About 11mi north is another resort, **Powder Mountain** *(Rte. 158, Eden; ☎ 801-745-3772)*.

EXCURSION

★ **Golden Spike National Historic Site** – *32mi west of I-15 Exit 368, Brigham City, via Rtes. 13 & 83. ☎ 435-471-2209. www.nps.gov/gosp.* This site recalls the completion of the transcontinental railroad with the driving of a symbolic "golden spike" connecting Central Pacific and Union Pacific lines on May 10, 1869. Although trains have long since chosen a different route across the Great Salt Lake Desert, working replicas of the two **steam locomotives** that first met here are on display May to October. Costumed reenactments of the original ceremony are often staged. A **visitor center** *(open year-round)* displays artifacts and photos.

GREEN RIVER COUNTRY

Michelin Map p 493 F 7   Mountain Standard Time
Tourist Information ☎ 801-538-1030 or www.utah.com

Largely isolated from population centers and major highways, northeastern Utah has developed in relative seclusion on either side of the lofty Uinta Mountains and along the Green River and its tributaries. Its principal interest to tourists today revolves around water sports, especially river rafting, and its deposits of dinosaur bones, among the richest on earth. Backpackers and mountain climbers strive for the summits of 13,528ft **Kings Peak**, Utah's highest, and a raft of other 12,000ft-plus pinnacles. Sprawling through the heart of the region is the **Uinta and Ouray Indian Reservation** *(Fort Duchesne; ☎ 435-722-5141)*, home to 1,600 members of four related tribes.

SIGHTS

Price – *US-6 & 191 and Rte. 10, 118mi southeast of Salt Lake City.* △ ※ ☎ *435-637-3009. www.castlecountry.com.* A late-19C coal town that boomed with the coming of the railroad in the 1880s, Price still produces large quantities of coal and other minerals. The **College of Eastern Utah Prehistoric Museum** *(*Kids* 155 E. Main St.; ☎ 435-637-5060)* displays several full-size dinosaur skeletons and a remarkable collection of 12C Fremont Indian figurines of unbaked clay. Curators provide self-guiding tour information to the **Cleveland-Lloyd Dinosaur Quarry★** *(BLM 216 Rd., 11mi east of Cleveland & 30mi southeast of Price via Rtes. 10 & 155)*, where the bones of at least 70 species of prehistoric animals have been unearthed and provided to museums around the world. **Nine Mile Canyon Road★** *(60mi from Wellington, US-6/191, to Myton, US-40/191)*, a backcountry route beginning 7mi east of Price, leads to prolific ancient Indian petroglyphs and pictographs.

Vernal – *US-40 & 191, 176mi east of Salt Lake City.* ☎ *435-789-6932. www .dinoland.com.* Western gateway to **Dinosaur National Monument★★** *(p 106)* and southern gateway to Flaming Gorge National Recreation Area *(below)*, Vernal is in an area of extreme geological interest. Its **Utah Field House of Natural History State Park** *(*Kids* 235 E. Main St.; ☎ 435-789-3799)* re-creates prehistoric ecosystems and populates them with 18 life-size dinosaur figures. An adjacent museum displays fossils, gems and Indian artifacts.

★**Flaming Gorge National Recreation Area** – *US-191 & Rte. 44, 43mi north of Vernal. ☎ 435-784-3445. www.fs.fed.us/r4/ashley.* Straddling the Utah-Wyoming border, this recreation area surrounds a 91mi-long reservoir that backs up through colorful canyons carved through the Uinta Mountains by the Green River. Several marinas provide access for boating and other water sports. The **Red Canyon Visitor Center and Overlook★★** *(Rte. 44; ☎ 435-889-3713)* offers a bird's-eye view of the reservoir, in summer, from 1,400ft above Red Canyon. Guided tours of a 502ft concrete-arch dam are provided at the **Flaming Gorge Dam Visitor Center** *(US-191, Dutch John; ☎ 435-885-3135)*.

San Antonio Area

The Alamo

Any attempt at understanding Texans must begin in the San Antonio area, for here is the very soul of Texas history and culture.

Originally inhabited by Indians of the warlike Comanche tribe, the region was settled by Spanish missionaries at the end of the 17C. In 1836 one mission, converted to military use and known as The Alamo, became a stronghold for 189 Texas patriots who gave their lives defending the bastion against the vast forces of Mexico's president, General Antonio López de Santa Anna. Their sacrifice became a rallying cry—"Remember The Alamo!"—for other rebels who soon defeated Santa Anna and won Texas independence.

The Hispanic presence remains strong in central and south Texas, an area that claims San Antonio as its cultural, spiritual and economic hub. The Spanish language is heard as often as English. Gondolas ply the waters of the Rio San Antonio, passing strollers on the cypress-shaded River Walk, which meanders past row after brightly lit row of atmospheric restaurants. The new Rockefeller Center for Latin American Art, in the San Antonio Museum of Art, is a showcase in a city rife with fine museums. From atop one of the city's newer buildings, the 750ft Tower of the Americas, you can gaze down upon some of its oldest, the quartet of 18C missions that make up San Antonio Missions National Historical Park.

An hour's drive northeast is Austin, the lively state capital. The University of Texas, the political ambience and an influx of high-tech industry have engendered a spirit of intellectual and cultural excitement. Scores of nightclubs have led Austin to become known as the "Live Music Capital of the World."

Topographical and cultural diversity is showcased through this expansive region, its geography ranging from rugged hills to verdant pine forests to sandy beaches. The fault line of the Balcones Escarpment divides the limestone hills and juniper-clad valleys of the European-flavored Hill Country from the coastal plain, which gradually flattens and slopes toward the Gulf of Mexico.

SAN ANTONIO★★★

Map p 291   Central Standard Time
Population 1,114,130
Tourist Information ☎ 210-207-6700 or www.SanAntonioCVB.com

No city in Texas is as appealing to visitors as San Antonio. Its historic sites and world-class museums, semitropical climate, multicultural ambience and manageable size—many leading attractions are within walking distance of downtown hotels—combine to make it a shining star of tourism.

Before Franciscan priests founded missions in the 1690s, Coahuiltecan Indians dominated the region. Two decades later, San Antonio de Bejar became a military garrison for the Viceroy of Spain; it was a fulcrum of the Texas Revolution when The Alamo fell to Santa Anna in 1836. Following the Civil War, San Antonio became a cattle center and population boomed. After a devastating flood in 1921 led the city to consider covering its river and turning it into a storm sewer, the San Antonio Conservation Society raised funds to redesign the eyesore into a tourist attraction. Robert H. H. Hugman's park-like first phase was constructed in 1939-41. In the 1960s, when the city spruced up for its HemisFair 1968 world's fair, Hugman's dream of a festive shopping and dining promenade was realized.

SIGHTS

★★★ **The Alamo** – *300 Alamo Plaza at Crockett St.* ♿ ☎ *210-225-1391. www.TheAlamo.org.* The symbolic "Cradle of Texas Liberty" fronts a busy plaza in the heart of downtown. Mission San Antonio de Valero—known as The Alamo (Spanish for "cottonwood")—is an enduring symbol of Texas and one of the most photographed buildings in the US. It was built in 1718, secularized in 1793 and occupied as a Spanish, then Mexican military garrison in the early 1800s. In December 1835, rebellious Texans drove oppressive Mexican troops from San Antonio and consolidated their defenses within The Alamo. But Gen. Santa Anna, the Mexican president, led thousands of troops in an assault on the former mission two months later. The 13-day siege (February 23-March 6, 1836) was not over until every last one of The Alamo's 189 defenders—including commander William B. Travis, renowned knife fighter Jim Bowie and the legendary Davy Crockett, who had left Congress to explore Texas' new frontier—had perished. "Remember The Alamo!" became the battle cry of the war of Texas Independence, which climaxed less than two months later when Gen. Sam Houston defeated Santa Anna at San Jacinto, near Houston.

Although surrounded by hustle, bustle and numerous tourist traps, the site commands quiet respect. The Alamo is an apt memorial to the courage of the men who fought for Texas in the face of insurmountable odds. Its centerpiece is **The Shrine★★★**, the former mission church, where exhibits canonize the men who died here. Further exhibits in the **Long Barrack Museum★★** describe historic events leading to the siege and its aftermath. The Gift Museum has more exhibits; the entire complex is contained within a park-like courtyard.

★★★ **River Walk** – *Bridge entrances at Losoya and Commerce Sts.* 🍴♿ ☎ *210-227-4262.* Also called Paseo del Rio, this verdant promenade meanders below street level through 2.5mi of downtown, weaving along both banks of a horseshoe-shaped bend in the slow-flowing San Antonio River.

© Greg Proost/Tony Stone Images

River Walk

ADDRESS BOOK

Please see explanation on p 64.

Staying in the San Antonio-Austin Area

The Fairmount Hotel – *410 S. Alamo St., San Antonio TX.* ☒ ♿ ♲ ☎ *210-224-8800. www.wyndham.com. 37 rooms.* **$$$** The Italianate Fairmount is a small jewel of dark-red brick, carved limestone and elaborate pediments. In 1985, the entire structure was moved six blocks and across a bridge. All the marble finishes and soft colors survived, as did the deluxe **Polo's Restaurant.**

Driskill Hotel – *604 Brazos St., Austin TX.* ☒ ♿ ♲ ☎ *512-474-5911. 205 rooms.* **$$** Double balconies, columns and arched windows make Austin's grandest and most historic hotel into an elegant frontier palace. Ongoing restorations ensure that Colonel J.L. Driskill's 1886 vision of granite floors and original artwork lives on. Lobster-and-corn enchiladas are a menu feature at **The Grill.**

Havana Riverwalk Inn – *1015 Navarro St., San Antonio TX.* ☒ ♿ ♲ ☎ *210-222-2008. 27 rooms.* **$$** Individual room decor is unique at this Mediterranean Revival-style inn. Room 300 boasts an armoire from a palace in India and a bed with posts from a French estate. Room 104 has an iron-haloed convent bed. Throughout are exposed brick walls and hardwood floors.

The Menger Hotel – *204 Alamo Plaza, San Antonio TX.* ☒ ♿ ♲ ☒ ☎ *210-223-4361. www.mengerhotel.com. 317 rooms.* **$$** A glazed iron canopy and intricate railings form the facade of the elegant Menger, built in 1859. Leaded skylights in a grand three-story lobby guide guests to opulent rooms of dark wood trim. Wild-game dishes have been on the **Colonial Room** menu for 100 years.

Dining in the San Antonio-Austin Area

Boudro's – *421 E. Commerce St., San Antonio TX.* ☎ *210-224-8484. www.boudros.com.* **$$$** **Mexican & Cajun.** The best restaurant on the River Walk offers a bistro blend of France and Louisiana with south-of-the-border cuisine. Diners may choose blackened prime rib at a cozy inside table or prickly-pear margaritas on the patio. River-barge dining cruises feature guacamole made tableside.

Guero's – *1412 S. Congress Ave., Austin TX.* ☎ *512-447-7688.* **$$** **Mexican.** This Tex-Mex spot, occupying a converted feed store, is a big part of the hip South Austin scene. The kitchen serves up shrimp *fajitas*, *huachinango* (broiled red snapper with garlic or jalapeño), and chicken prepared three ways: *chipotle* (smoky jalapeño), *tampiqueño* (salsa and jack cheese) or *guanajuato* (guacamole).

Altdorf Biergarten – *301 W. Main St., Fredericksburg TX.* ☎ *830-997-7865.* **$** **German.** In a town of German heritage, this may be the single best place to absorb Deutsch culture. Up to 150 people sit outside with steins of beer listening to oom-pah bands. Bavarian specialties include bratwurst, knockwurst, wiener and zwiebel schnitzel, all served with sweet-and-sour potatoes, red cabbage or sauerkraut.

La Margarita – *120 Produce Row, San Antonio TX.* ☎ *210-227-7140.* **$** **Mexican.** Strolling mariachi bands and sizzling *fajitas* create a fiesta-like atmosphere at this Market Square restaurant, fueled by margaritas that sell by the liter. Very popular is the Queso Flameado, a flaming combination of cheese and sausage; the usual Mexican fare also features burritos, tacos and enchiladas.

Stubb's Bar-B-Q – *801 Red River St., Austin TX.* ☎ *512-480-8341.* **$** **Barbecue.** C.B. Stubblefield once promised diners "Cold Beer and Live Music," and his legacy lives on with soul food and live rhythm-and-blues every night. Diners may start with Texas fries or onion rings, then try a Stubb's Major BBQ plate of smoked beef brisket, sausage and ribs, ladled with C.B.'s original sauce.

Sidewalk cafes, small shops and nightclubs are wedged between the arched bridges of this cypress-shaded walkway. Strollers snake like a conga line through busy areas; other stretches have a quiet, park-like atmosphere.

Work Projects Administration crews built the cobblestone and flagstone path in 1939-41 under the direction of architect Robert Hugman and engineer Edwin Arneson. The plan included the **Arneson River Theatre**, an open-air amphitheater with a stage on one side of the stream, terraced seating on the other.

The best way to view River Walk without joining the pedestrian crowds is aboard gondola-style **Yanaguana Cruises★** 〔Kids〕 ‖‖‖ *(315 E. Commerce St.; ☎ 210-244-5700)*. Taking the name "refreshing waters" given the river by indigenous Payaya Indians, the 60min open-air cruises feature lighthearted historical narratives by informative guides.

La Villita – *418 Villita St., between S. Alamo & S. Presa Sts.* ⸾& ☎ *210-207-8610. www.lavillita.com.* At the time The Alamo was a military outpost, "The Little Village" developed as a temporary community of people without land title. The Mexican surrender climaxing the Texas Revolution was signed here. Today this is a National Historic District. Early 19C structures house artisans in 26 studio shops; there are two restaurants and a museum exhibit.

★**Market Square** – 〔Kids〕 *514 W. Commerce St. at Santa Rosa St.* ⸾& ▣ ☎ *210-207-8600.* This traditional Mexican marketplace, extending across several blocks, began as an early-19C farmers' market. Later, pharmaceutical items were sold at **Botica Guadalupana**, oldest continuously operated drugstore in central and south Texas. Today a Latin flavor persists in the shops and restaurants, including **El Mercado**, largest Mexican mall in the US. At two long-standing restaurants, **La Margarita** and **Mi Tierra**, troupes of mariachi musicians serenade diners. **El Centro de Artes**, a cultural arts center, is scheduled to reopen in December 2000 with traveling exhibits from the Smithsonian Institution.

> ■ **Cradle of Con Carne**
>
> Market Square was the birthplace of chili con carne, the spicy meat-and-bean mixture that today is generally considered the state dish of Texas. Young girls known as "chili queens" first sold the concoction from small stands in the San Antonio market.

Spanish Governor's Palace – *105 Plaza de Armas.* ☎ *210-224-0601.* This National Historic Landmark near Market Square is Texas' sole surviving example of a colonial aristocrat's home. It was completed in 1749 (as the date on its massive door indicates) and restored in 1931. Self-guided tours wind through an enclosed fountain courtyard and chambers furnished with 18C antiques.

Casa Navarro State Historic Park – *228 S. Laredo St.* ☎ *210-226-4801.* The three refurbished buildings on this site—an adobe-and-limestone house, kitchen and office—come to life on curator-led tours. Home builder José Antonio Navarro (1795-1871) was a lifelong San Antonio rancher and statesman whose life spanned the key events of Texas' dramatic history.

★**Tower of the Americas** – 〔Kids〕 *600 HemisFair Park.* ⸾& ▣ ☎ *210-207-8615.* The city's finest **views★★★** are from this 750ft tower overlooking the grounds of HemisFair 1968. Visitors are whisked day and night to the 500ft level on a 1min ride in a glass-enclosed elevator. This is one of the tallest free-standing structures in the Western Hemisphere—67ft higher than the Washington Monument.

★**Institute of Texas Cultures** – 〔Kids〕 *801 S. Bowie St.* & ▣ ☎ *210-458-2300, www.texancultures.utsa.edu.* Twenty-seven distinct ethnic and cultural groups are profiled at this HemisFair Park heritage museum. An outdoor interpretive area replicates a 19C pioneer village.

★★**San Antonio Missions National Historical Park** – *2202 Roosevelt Ave.* & ▣ ☎ *210-534-8833. www.nps.gov/saan.* The Alamo was not the only mission in the valley of the Rio San Antonio. Four others were erected in 1720-31 near the river, which supplied water for drinking and crop irrigation by means of an *acequia* (aqueduct). The park comprises these Franciscan missions, which portray the size and scope of traditional compounds—typically including a church and chapel, convent, Coahuiltecan living quarters, farmland, a granary to store crops and a blacksmith to produce and repair tools. All four still support active parishes.

The chain begins at **Mission Concepción★** *(807 Mission Rd. at Felisa St., 2.3mi south of The Alamo via S. St. Mary's St.; ☎ 210-534-1540)*. Of special note are traces of geometric designs painted by Coahuiltecans on the interior walls of the magnificent mission church (c.1731) and convent.

Mission San José y San Miguel de Aguayo★★ *(6701 San Jose Dr., 2.2mi south of Mission Concepción; ☎ 210-932-1001)* was once "Queen of the Texas Missions." At its peak, San José was a major social and cultural center and home to 300 people; it remains an impressive fortress today. A bilingual Sunday-morning Mariachi Mass, featuring religious music by mariachi musicians in its 1720 chapel, highlights a visit. The national historical park's primary **visitor center** is nearby.

Structures within the agricultural compound of **Mission San Juan Capistrano** *(9101 Graf Rd., 2.5mi south of Mission San José; ☎ 210-534-0749)* have been extensively restored, including the 1772 chapel, rectory and Indian quarters. Priests rescued precious icons from the 1740 church at **Mission San Francisco de la Espada** *(10100 Espada Rd., 1.5mi south of Mission San Juan; ☎ 210-627-2021)* during a 1997 fire. A small museum focuses on vocational education.

★★San Antonio Museum of Art – *200 W. Jones Ave.* ✖ ♿ 🅿 ☎ *210-978-8100. www.sa-museum.org.* This large, bright, thoroughly remodeled museum, housed in the 1904 Lone Star Brewery Company building, has impressive collections of Egyptian, Greek and Roman antiquities in its west wing; Asian works include ancient Chinese tomb figures. Among 17-18C European masters exhibited in the Great Hall are Steen, Hals and Bosch; 18-20C American works include oils by Copley, Stuart, Sargent and Homer.

Courtesy San Antonio Museum of Art

Mexican Lacquered Dish (19C), Rockefeller Center for Latin American Art

The $11 million **Nelson A. Rockefeller Center for Latin American Art★★** opened as a three-story east wing in 1998. It traces 4,000 years of Indian and Hispanic culture—pre-Columbian, Spanish Colonial, folk and modern art. An interactive education center introduces cultural history of Mexico, Central and South America. Exhibits feature Mesoamerican culture from Olmec, Mayan, Aztec, Toltec and other periods, as well as Andean ceramics and gold work. Spanish Colonial works are primarily religious in nature, encompassing more than 100 paintings and objects. Folk art includes utilitarian and ceremonial pieces plus decorative items in wood, metal, ceramics, paper and textiles. Modern art features such 20C masters as Rivera, Tamaya, Torres-Garcia and Siqueiros.

Brackenridge Park – 🄺🄸🄳🅂 *2800 N. Broadway.* ✖ ♿ 🅿 ☎ *210-207-7275.* Brackenridge sprawls across 343 riverside acres shaded by majestic live oaks. A popular picnic destination, the park is also home to the **San Antonio Zoological Garden and Aquarium** *(3903 N. St. Mary's St.; ☎ 210-734-7183)*, lodged in a former rock quarry. Nearby, the **Japanese Tea Gardens** *(3800 N. St. Mary's St.)* offer lush flowers, climbing vines and tall palms alongside koi-filled pools.

★Witte Museum – 🄺🄸🄳🅂 *3801 Broadway.* ♿ 🅿 ☎ *210-357-1900. www.wittemuseum .org.* The Witte showcases human and natural history and culture, from anthropology to fashions and decorative arts. Exhibits in the main building (1926, Robert M. Ayres) include **Texas Wild★**, whose depiction of the state's ecological zones includes a walk-through diorama of sticky thornbush. **Ancient Texans★★** focuses on the Lower Pecos culture of the Rio Grande Valley. A half-dozen relocated pioneer homes share grounds behind the museum. The new **H-E-B Science Treehouse★** (1997, Lake/Flato) is an ingenious four-level series of interactive science exhibits, perched over the San Antonio River on concrete oak trees created by sculptor Carlos Cortes.

★San Antonio Botanical Gardens and Halsell Conservatory – *555 Funston Pl.* ✖ ♿ 🅿 ☎ *210-207-3255. www.sabot.org/bg.* Separate areas for roses, herbs and native plants are found within these 33-acre gardens. The centerpiece is the **Lucile**

Halsell Conservatory★★, a 90,000sq-ft cluster of individual glass houses tucked into the earth around a courtyard sunk 16ft underground to escape the hot Texas summers. Beneath the conical and triangular roofs, conceived by architect Emilio Ambasz, are special collections of tropical, desert, alpine and aquatic plants.

★★**Marion Koogler McNay Art Museum** – *6000 N. New Braunfels Ave.* ⟨ ⟩ 📶 ☎ *210-824-5368. www.mcnayart.org.* A world-class collection of 19C and 20C European and American art occupies this 24-room Spanish Mediterranean-style manor (1926, Atlee B. & Robert M. Ayres), former home of oil heiress and art collector Marion McNay. Galleries surround a landscaped garden patio or overlook the courtyard from balconies. The collection is strong in Post-Impressionist French art, including Cézanne, Manet, Renoir, Monet *(Water Lilies)*, Van Gogh, Gauguin and Rousseau. Five decades of Picasso's works are in three rooms; 20C paintings by Braque, Matisse, Modigliani and Chagall also are presented. American Modernist works include O'Keeffe and Dove, with later pieces by Pollock, Hockney and Motherwell. Among sculptures are casts of Rodin's *Five Burghers of Calais*.

EXCURSIONS

★**Fiesta Texas** – 🅺🅸🅳🆂 〽〽 *17000 I-10 West.* 🍴⟨ 📶 ☎ *210-697-5050. www.sixflags.com.* This popular theme park showcases the music of Texas, from 50s rock 'n' roll to *tejano* to German polka. Shows are interspersed with thrill rides, which include one of the world's tallest wooden roller coasters. One section is devoted to water rides, especially popular in summer.

★★**SeaWorld San Antonio** – 🅺🅸🅳🆂 〽〽 *Rte. 151 at Ellison Dr. & Westover Hills Blvd.* 🍴⟨ 📶 ☎ *210-523-3611. www.seaworld.com.* Sprawled across 250 acres northwest of the city is the world's largest marine park. Displays and shows feature dolphins, beluga whales, sea lions, seals and otters. The star is Shamu, a 2.5-ton orca who gracefully leaps and dives with human partners before as many as 1,500 spectators. Indo-Pacific fishes cavort in a simulated coral reef near North America's largest display of hammerhead sharks. New additions include "The Steel Eel" and "The Great White" roller coasters.

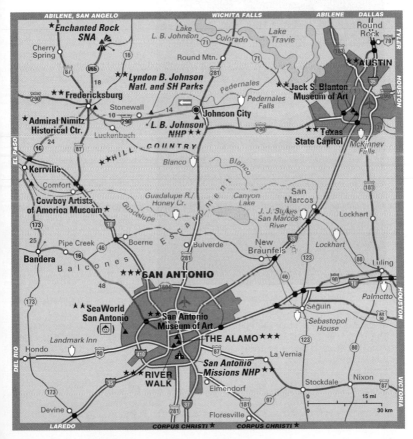

AUSTIN★★

Map p 291   Central Standard Time
Population 552,434
Tourist Information ☎ 512-478-0098 or www.austintexas.org

The Texas capital, located between the rolling Hill Country and fertile farmland, has a vibrant cultural life and a young population that includes 50,000 University of Texas students. Founded in 1835 as Waterloo, it became the seat of government upon independence, changing its name to honor statesman Stephen F. Austin. Austin experienced steady growth that included construction of a new state capitol, dedicated in 1888. The city was plagued by flooding along the Colorado River until a series of flood-control dams were constructed in 1938, forming the chain of Highland Lakes that includes Town Lake and Lake Austin.

Today Austin balances its serious role as seat of state government with the youthful exuberance of the university, known locally as UT. The **Sixth Street Entertainment District**, extending seven blocks from I-35 to Congress Avenue, is home to dozens of clubs that have built Austin's reputation as a mecca for musicians in all genres, including blues, country, rock and jazz.

The nation's largest urban **colony of bats** nestles beneath downtown Austin's Congress Avenue bridge from March to October between migrations to Mexico. Ensconced in Austin since 1980, they have even bestowed their name upon Austin's minor-league hockey team: the "Ice Bats."

SIGHTS

★★**Texas State Capitol** – *Congress Ave. at 11th St.* ✗ ♿ 🅿 ☎ *512-463-0063. www.tspb.state.tx.us*. Dominating Austin's skyline, the Renaissance Revival-style capitol was built in 1888 (Elijah E. Myers) of red granite and limestone. Over

302ft in height, it is taller by more than 14ft than the US Capitol. A four-year building renovation was completed in 1995. Guided tours, departing from the south foyer every 15min, visit the chambers of the state legislature, which meets in odd-numbered years from January through May. In the foyer, statues by 19C sculptor Elisabet Ney memorialize founding fathers Stephen Austin and Sam Houston; paintings by W. H. Huddle portray Davy Crockett at The Alamo and the surrender of Santa Anna at San Jacinto. A terrazzo floor—depicting the Lone Star of the Republic of Texas surrounded by the coats of arms of other nations whose flags have flown here— is the centerpiece of the rotunda.

Texas State Capitol Rotunda, Interior

© Tim Thompson

The **Capitol Complex Visitors Center** *(112 E. 11th St.;* ☎ *512-305-8400)* is at the southeast corner of the exquisite, 22-acre grounds. The center is housed in the former General Land Office Building (1857), oldest surviving state building in Texas. Inside, a theater shows *A Lone Star Legacy: The Texas Capitol Complex*, a 23min film narrated by famed Texas newsman Walter Cronkite.

★★**Lyndon Baines Johnson Presidential Library and Museum** – *2313 Red River St.* ♿ 🅿 ☎ *512-916-5136*. Located on the UT campus, this monumental facility honors the Hill Country's most famous native son. Lyndon Johnson (1908-73)

served as US president following John F. Kennedy's assassination; his turbulent term (1963-69) was marked by the Vietnam War and the civil-rights movement. The eight-story library (1971, Skidmore, Owings and Merrill), constructed of travertine marble, is the repository for all presidential documents produced during the LBJ administration—more than 36 million pieces of paper. Archival files, contained in red, acid-free boxes stamped with the gold presidential seal, are opened only for scholars and researchers.

Three floors—the first, second and eighth—are open to the public. Tours begin with a 23min film on LBJ's childhood in the Hill Country, his political life in the House and Senate, and finally his White House years. Accompanying exhibits place his life in the context of US history. Display cases showcase handmade gifts from US citizens and bejeweled keepsakes from foreign heads of state. On the eighth floor, Johnson's Oval Office at the White House is replicated in seven-eighths scale.

★★ **Jack S. Blanton Museum of Art** – *Harry Ransom Center, University of Texas, 21st & Guadalupe Sts.* ♿ 🅿 ☎ *512-471-7324. www.utexas.edu/cofa/hag.* The Blanton's permanent collection of more than 13,000 works ranges from ancient to contemporary art. The ground floor features the **Mari & James Michener Collection** of 20C American art; donated by the late novelist and his wife, it offers hundreds of modern masterworks, from Cubist to Abstract Expressionist. The **C.R. Smith Collection** of 19C American art includes Henry Farny's 1899 portrait of *Sitting Bull* and works by Bierstadt, Moran and Russell. The **Suida-Manning Collection** on the second floor has important Renaissance and Baroque art, including works by Rubens and Veronese. The **Latin American Art** gallery presents contemporary work from artists in Central and South America. An original 15C **Gutenberg Bible**, one of only five copies in the US, is displayed on the ground floor of the Ransom Center.

Also in the city are the **Austin Museum of Art at Laguna Gloria** *(3809 W. 35th St.; ☎ 512-458-8191)*, with a collection of 20C American art; the **Elisabet Ney Museum** *(304 E. 44th St.; ☎ 512-458-2255)*, 19C studio of Texas' first sculptor; and the **Umlauf Sculpture Garden and Museum** *(605 Robert E. Lee Rd.; ☎ 512-445-5582)*, showcasing the work of 20C sculptor Charles Umlauf.

★ **Lady Bird Johnson Wildflower Research Center** – *4801 La Crosse Ave.* ✕ ♿ 🅿 ☎ *512-292-4100. www.wildflower.org.* Created by the former First Lady in 1982 as part of a national beautification project, this facility is the only one in the US dedicated exclusively to conserving and promoting the use of indigenous plants, including 400 species native to Texas. The 42-acre site includes 23 separate research, display and botanical theme gardens—ablaze with color particularly in April and May—as well as natural grasslands and woodlands, an observation tower, stone cisterns, aqueducts, courtyards and nature trails.

HILL COUNTRY★★

Map p 291   Central Standard Time
Tourist Information ☎ 830-997-6523 or www.traveltex.com

The scenic Hill Country northwest of San Antonio was shaped 30 million years ago by a violent earthquake that buckled the earth and kicked up strata of limestone and granite into rugged hills and steep cliffs. Rivers, lakes, limestone caves and other natural attractions mark the region's 25,000sq mi.

The Hill Country was originally home to several Indian tribes, including Apache, Tonkawa and Comanche. Republican (1836-45) and early statehood periods were marked by immigration from the eastern US, France, Denmark, Sweden, Czechoslovakia and especially the German Rhine states. Today the Hill Country's distinctive character is largely the legacy of a German small-landholder tradition. Life in the region remains predominantly agrarian and somewhat isolated.

DRIVING TOUR *2 days, 226mi*

The best times to visit are spring, when the region is painted with fields of bluebonnets, and autumn, when Spanish oak and sumac infuse the plateau with color. Summer days are hot and humid, winter often chilly and overcast.

Take US-281 from San Antonio 63mi north, or US-290 from Austin 48mi west, to Johnson City.

Johnson City – Though named for Sam Ealy Johnson, grandfather of former US President Lyndon Baines Johnson, attractions in this small community of just over 1,000 people today focus on "LBJ," its most famous son.

Bluebonnets and Indian Paint Brushes, Lyndon B. Johnson National Historical Park

** **Lyndon B. Johnson National Historical Park** – *Ave. G & Ladybird Lane.* ♿ 🅿 ☎ *830-868-7128*. The life and family heritage of LBJ (1908-73) is portrayed in exhibits at the **Visitor Center**. The **LBJ Boyhood Home** *(Elm St. & Ave. G; guided tour only)* has been restored to its 1920 appearance and furnished with family heirlooms. The **Johnson Settlement** *(west end of Ladybird Lane)* preserves the tiny log home and outbuildings of cattle rancher Sam Johnson and his brother, Tom, in the 1860s.

Continue 14mi west on US-290.

** **Lyndon B. Johnson National and State Historical Parks** – *US-290, Stonewall.* ♿ 🅿 ☎ *830-644-2252*. LBJ's "Texas White House"—the president's sprawling ranch beside the Pedernales River—is the featured attraction at these combined parks, which span 1,200 acres. Buses depart from the State Park Visitor Center; those awaiting a **tour** 🚶 can view a film and displays on Johnson's life. The 90min National Park Service tour travels to the **LBJ Ranch**, stopping at the one-room Junction School where Johnson began his education. The bus slows for photos of the Texas White House, then continues past an airstrip and cattle barns to LBJ's reconstructed birthplace home and the family cemetery where he is buried. Private vehicles are permitted on the ranch only between 5pm and sunset.

Within the state-park boundary is the 1918 **Sauer-Beckmann Living History Farm**, furnished in period style and manned by costumed interpreters who perform the daily chores of a c.1900 Texas-German farm family.

Continue another 16mi west on US-290 to Fredericksburg.

** **Fredericksburg** – This community of 8,350 was settled in 1846 by 120 German pioneers who ventured to Texas in response to a land-grant program. Their heritage persists along wide streets lined with picturesque homes of native limestone, *Fachwerk* and Victorian gingerbread. Signs on guest houses, restaurants and gift shops invariably declare, *"Wir sprechen Deutsch."* Such annual festivals as Oktoberfest pack the lanes with revelers, and oom-pah music carries the day.

Historical artifacts are displayed in the **Vereins Kirche Museum** *(Marktplatz; ☎ 830-997-2835)* and the **Pioneer Museum Complex** *(309 W. Main St.; ☎ 830-997-2835)*. Eighty-three buildings are designated sites in Fredericksburg's 30-block historic district; many have been converted to charming bed-and-breakfast inns.

* **Admiral Nimitz Historical Center** – *340 E. Main St.* ♿ 🅿 ☎ *830-997-4379. www.tpwd.state.tx.us/parks/nimitz*. Honoring Admiral Chester Nimitz, a World War II hero and Fredericksburg native, this site comprises a museum—housed in a curiously shiplike 1852 hotel built by the admiral's seafaring grandfather—

and nine acres of adjacent grounds. Nimitz became Commander-in-Chief of US Pacific forces on December 25, 1941, and directed 2.5 million troops until the Japanese surrender in August 1945. Highlights of the Pacific war, featured in the George Bush Gallery, include a B-25 aircraft preparing to take off from the deck of the *USS Hornet (p 318)* and a midget submarine captured off Hawaii. The Plaza of the Presidents honors 10 US presidents, from Franklin Roosevelt through Bush, and their World War II experiences. Behind the museum lies the Garden of Peace, a classic Oriental garden presented in respect of Nimitz by the people of Japan.

Drive 18mi north on Ranch Rd. 965.

*Enchanted Rock State Natural Area – ⅢⅢ *16710 Ranch Rd. 965.* △ ▣ ☎ *915-247-3903.* This state park features one of the largest stone formations in the West, a 640-acre granite outcropping. The ascent takes about an hour, and hikers are rewarded with a magnificent **view**★★ of the Hill Country. In warm weather *(Apr-Oct)*, it's wise to begin the hike early in the morning, as a visitor limit may close the park to crowds until 5pm on weekend days.

Return to Fredericksburg and take Rte. 16 for 24mi south.

Kerrville – The Hill Country's largest town, with over 20,000 residents, Kerrville was the hub of Alsatian immigrant Charles Schreiner's Y.O. Ranch. At its peak in 1910, the Y.O. covered about 940sq mi, extending northwest in an 80mi strip.

*Cowboy Artists of America Museum – *1550 Bandera Hwy. (Rte. 173).* ♿ ▣ ☎ *210-896 2553. www.caamuseum.com.* This hilltop museum features work by 26 contemporary Western artists—including Gordon Snidow of New Mexico and Robert Scriver of Montana—whose paintings and sculptures capture the spirit and traditional lifestyle of the plains. The building (1982, O'Neill Ford), constructed in Mexican style of 18 brick domes, surrounds an open sculpture garden. Visitors may take in special programs on the folklore, music and history of the Old West.

Continue on Rte. 173 for 25mi south.

Bandera – Bandera claims to be "The Cowboy Capital of the World." Rodeos are scheduled weekly from late May to early September. Local dance halls—such as the sawdust-floored **Arkey Blue's Silver Dollar**—are filled with two-steppers, clad in jeans and cowboy hats, dancing to country-and-western music most nights. The country surrounding Bandera is dotted with family-oriented guest or "dude" ranches where rates typically include all meals and horseback-riding programs.

Return to San Antonio on Rte. 16, about 48mi.

CORPUS CHRISTI★

Michelin map 492 K 15   Central Standard Time
Population 281,453
Tourist Information ☎ 361-561-2000 or www.corpuschristi tx cvb.org

Where the South Texas plains meet the Gulf of Mexico, the thriving harbor city of Corpus Christi nestles beside broad Corpus Christi Bay. Its calm waters, shielded from the wind-whipped gulf by the sandy, reef-like barrier of Mustang and Padre Islands, have made "Corpus" one of the busiest ports in the US and the home of one of its largest naval air bases.

Spanish explorer Alonzo Alvarez de Piñeda gave the bay its "body of Christ" name as he charted the coast in 1519. The area remained largely unattended, however, except by pirates who found refuge behind the islands through the 16C and 17C; legends of their buried treasures and sunken galleons of gold persist today. There was no settlement until a frontier trading post was founded in the Republic of Texas in 1839.

Today the bayfront is a combination fishing village and tourist hub. Modern hotels overlook piers lined with brimming shrimp boats. Ocean Drive begins at the gates of the **Corpus Christi Naval Air Station** and winds northwest past grand mansions on bluffs facing the bay. The avenue becomes Shoreline Boulevard as it follows **The Seawall**, designed by Mt. Rushmore sculptor Gutzon Borglum and constructed in 1939-41 to contain a landfill on which downtown was built. Of special note is the **Mirador de la Flor**, a memorial to Selena Quintanilla-Pérez, the young *tejano* singer tragically slain in 1995. (Her name also has been given to the city's new performing-arts center, Selena Bayfront Auditorium.)

SIGHTS

★ World of Discovery – [Kids] *1900 N. Chaparral St.* ♿ 🅿 ☎ *361-883-2862*. Comprising a museum and authentic re-creations of Christopher Columbus' fleet, this complex explores everything from dinosaurs to sunken treasure. Highlights of the **Museum of Science and History** are a 17ft scale model of an offshore oil rig and a multimedia exhibit on Spanish galleons shipwrecked off Padre Island. "Seeds of Change" commemorates the 500th anniversary of the European discovery of America. Outside stand the **Ships of Columbus★**, life-size replicas of the *Pinta* and *Santa María* constructed by the Spanish government to commemorate the explorer's 1492 voyage. Knowledgeable docents describe life aboard the surprisingly small ships. A **xeriscape demonstration garden** highlights water and energy conservation in arid climates.

South Texas Institute for the Arts – *1902 N. Shoreline Blvd.* ☎ *361-825-3500*. This bayside art museum is as often noted for its stark white architecture (1972, Philip Johnson) as for its collection. Changing fine-art exhibits feature traditional and contemporary works, mainly by Texas artists.

★ Texas State Aquarium – [Kids] *2710 N. Shoreline Dr.* ♿ 🅿 ☎ *361-881-1200*. *www.txstateaq.com*. More than 350 species of Gulf of Mexico marine life are at "home" in a series of ecosystem exhibits, including marsh and shoreline, pier and estuary. Islands of Steel replicates an offshore oil platform surrounded by nurse sharks and amberjack. The Flower Gardens re-create a coral reef 115mi off this coast, blooming with colorful aquatic life and inhabited by moray eels and angelfish. Outdoors are touch tanks of small sharks and stingrays, as well as river otters, sea turtles and a rare white alligator.

■ Padre Island National Seashore★★

Padre Island National Seashore (△♿ 🅿 ☎ *361-949-8068; www.nps .gov/pais*) is 70mi of undeveloped beach stretching south from Corpus Christi to Port Mansfield, the southern 55mi of it off-limits to all but four-wheel-drive vehicles. There are few more enticing places for beach and nature lovers.

Bird-watchers train binoculars on the barrier island's 350 recorded species of native birds. Endangered Kemp's Ridley sea turtles dig their nests and lay eggs along these shores. Rare seashells wash ashore daily, piling in largest number at aptly named Big Shell and Little Shell beaches. Park Road 22—an extension of South Padre Island Drive *(Rte. 358)*, which crosses the JFK Bridge and Causeway 25mi east of Corpus Christi—ends just past **Malaquite Beach Visitor Center** *(20420 Park Rd.)*. Even for visitors driving standard vehicles, these northern 10mi of national seashore offer a taste of the vast sand-and-shell beaches, dunes, tidal flats and grasslands beyond. Spur roads lead to **North Beach**, on the Gulf, and to **Bird Island Basin** on Laguna Madre, South Padre's sheltered leeward side, favored by windsurfers.

Laguna Madre—the "Mother Lagoon"—bustles in fall and winter with thousands of migrating bird species. From November to March, look for rare whooping cranes, which makes their homes at the Aransas National Wildlife Refuge north of Padre Island. These statuesque birds, 5ft long with 7ft wingspans, once numbered fewer than 20 worldwide. White and brown pelicans, killdeer, meadowlarks, sandhill cranes, laughing gulls, black skimmers, Caspian terns, great blue herons, sanderlings and long-billed curlews are also common.

The **Grasslands Nature Trail** *(off Park Rd. 22 north of Malaquite Beach)* is a .75mi loop through grasslands and past freshwater marshes and stabilized dunes, home to many native species. Brochures are available at the trailhead.

The Great Texas Coastal Birding Trail eventually will extend more than 600 miles from the Lower Rio Grande Valley to the Texas-Louisiana border. Signs illustrated with "black skimmer" logos mark the best observation points. Many are on **South Padre Island**, a resort community in far south Texas, 170mi from Corpus Christi, that in 1964 became a separate island with the completion of the Port Mansfield Gulf Channel.

★★ USS Lexington Museum on the Bay – [Kids] *2914 N. Shoreline Blvd.* ♿ 🅿
☎ *361-883-8087. www.usslexington.com*. This mammoth World War II aircraft carrier, berthed near the aquarium across the Harbor Bridge from downtown, was the most decorated carrier in US Navy history. Reported sunk four times, the ship was nicknamed "The Blue Ghost" both for its color and its resurrections. Today "The Lex," its main deck larger than three football fields, offers self-guided tours. Visitors spend hours weaving through corridors past captain's and enlisted men's quarters, the mess and sick bay, navigation and flag bridges. Numerous aircraft sit on the flight deck and hangar deck.

EXCURSION

★ King Ranch – *King Ave., Kingsville; take US-77 to Rte. 141, turn right (west) onto King Ave., proceed 3mi to blinking light; follow signs from ranch gate (on left) to visitor center.* 🅿 ☎ *361-592-8055. www.kingranch.com*. King Ranch sprawls across 1,300sq mi of acacia and mesquite grassland 39mi south of Corpus Christi. It was founded in 1853 by steamboat pilot Richard King, whose sixth-generation descendants still own the ranch. Two breeds of cattle and the first registered American quarter horse were developed here in the 20C. Today one of the largest cattle ranches in the US, King Ranch is home to 60,000 cattle (including 60 longhorns) and 300 working quarter horses.

Highlights of a 90min bus tour include the grave of horse-racing's 1946 Triple Crown winner, Assault, and a weaver's cottage where dozens of Texas ranch brands—including King's own distinctive "running W"—are on display. Tours pass but do not enter the white, castle-like Santa Gertrudis manor (built in 1912-15), the ranch headquarters and primary residence.

In nearby Kingsville, the **King Ranch Museum** *(405 N. Sixth St.; ☎ 361-595-1881)* provides visitors with a look at ranch history, including a photographic essay on King Ranch in the 1940s. Collections of saddles, guns, historic Texas flags, antique carriages and vintage cars round out the exhibits.

San Diego Area

Mission San Diego de Alcala

California began in San Diego. Hunter-gatherer Indians of the Kumeyaay tribe probably watched a trio of Spanish ships under Juan Rodríguez Cabrillo enter San Diego Bay in 1542 before sailing north. The next flotilla visited on November 12, 1601, feast day of St. Didacus of Alcalá. Spanish commander Sebastián Vizcaíno christened the region San Diego, honoring the saint, before he sailed away.

It was another century before Europeans came to stay. Jolted by English land claims from Point Reyes to Canada, Spain launched its own colonists, led by Capt. Gaspar de Portolá and Padre Junípero Serra. The pair established California's first mission and Spanish garrison at San Diego on July 16, 1769. The mission was eventually moved 6mi to the San Diego River; both church and state prospered in the remote outpost, albeit slowly.

Following Mexican independence in 1821, a town, or *pueblo*, now called Old Town San Diego, grew below the garrison. The pueblo became a center for *Californios*, ranchers of Spanish and Mexican descent who owned parcels of California land. An American corvette captured San Diego during the Mexican American War in 1846. Mexican Governor Pío Pico surrendered near San Diego a year later, completing the US conquest of California.

Hispanic culture remains strong throughout the area. The Mexican metropolis of Tijuana is a short trolley ride south of downtown San Diego. English is the dominant language north of the border, but Mexican is the dominant element in arts, architecture, crafts, culture and food.

Just north of San Diego is La Jolla, an upscale enclave famous for its boutiques, coastal scenery and burgeoning biomedical community. Beyond the urban area, San Diego County's 4,255sq mi encompass numerous towns, pleasant beaches and rural climes. An inland jumble of mountains and valleys climaxes at Anzo-Borrego Desert State Park, vanguard of a vast desert that runs east into Arizona and south into Mexico.

The city of San Diego enjoys a mild coastal climate, with more than 300 sunny days most years. But east of the first range of hills that blocks the daily sea breeze, temperatures may soar into triple digits in summer.

SAN DIEGO★★★

Michelin map p 493 B 11   Pacific Standard Time
Population 1,220,666
Tourist Information ☏ 619-232-3101 or www.sandiego.org

Its gleaming high-rises overlooking a vast, bustling bay, cosmopolitan San Diego is California's second-largest city and the sixth-largest in the US. Balboa Park's cultural institutions share the verdant mesas and canyons north of downtown with Spanish-style mansions. San Diego Bay was Pacific Fleet headquarters during both world wars and remains an important naval center.

Charming residential communities, lively business districts and efficient public transportation contribute a sense of relaxed well-being. So do renovations of Old Town, the Gaslamp Quarter and Victorian-era houses. In San Diego's sunny, mild climate, where daily temperatures average 70°F, outdoor and spectator sports are of prime importance to many residents. World-class tourist attractions and the enticing Mexican border less than 20mi south have earned San Diego a reputation as one of the most livable cities in the nation.

★★★OLD SAN DIEGO

Sights preserving and commemorating the birth of San Diego and the beginning of the European presence in Alta California lie in the vicinity of Interstate 8 as it stretches east to west, roughly following the course of the San Diego River.

★★ **Old Town San Diego State Historic Park** – *2645 San Diego Ave.; exit I-5 at Old Town Ave.* ✗ ⌖ 🄿 ☏ *619-220-5422.* A broad plaza surrounded by restored adobe and wooden structures lies at the foot of Presidio Hill. Colorful shops and eateries re-create Mexican and early American periods. The 13-acre park was set aside in 1968; seven buildings were restored and stabilized, others reconstructed. The 1853 **Robinson-Rose House**, at the plaza's west end, has a diorama of Old San Diego in its visitor center. **La Casa de Machado y Silvas★** (1830-43), restored as a period restaurant, once was a boardinghouse, a brothel and a church. **La Casa de Machado y Stewart★** (1833) is an outstanding example of adobe restoration. **La Casa de Estudillo★★** (1829), largest and most impressive of the original adobes, has 13 rooms connected by a veranda; it offers a glimpse of upper-class lifestyle. The first floor of **La Casa de Bandini★**, a popular Mexican restaurant, was built by Peruvian Juan Bandini in 1829; in 1869, a second floor was added and the establishment became a hotel.

★ **Presidio Park** – *Presidio Dr.; from Old Town, take Mason St. north to Jackson St.; turn left and follow signs.* Highlight of this beautifully landscaped park is the **Junípero Serra Museum** (☏ *619-297-3258*), a stately white Mission Revival building (1929, William Templeton Johnson). Its five galleries of early San Diego history include a remarkable collection of Spanish Renaissance furniture and an exhibit interpreting the effect of colonization on local Indians. Downhill from the museum, ruins of the original 1769 presidio complex—first European settlement on the West Coast—are being excavated behind a protective wall.

★★ **Mission San Diego de Alcalá** – *10010 San Diego Mission Rd.; from Old Town, take I-8 east 7mi to Mission Gorge Rd. and follow signs.* 🄿 ☏ *619-283-7319.* California's first mission occupies a secluded site on the north slope of Mission Valley. Padre Junípero Serra's 1769 Presidio Hill mission was relocated here by Padre Luis Jayme in 1774. The mission was restored between 1895 and 1931 and designated a Minor Basilica by Pope Paul VI in 1976.

An original white-stucco, buttressed facade and five-bell campanario herald the entrance to the complex. The sparsely furnished **Casa del Padre Serra**, where the friar resided during frequent visits, is all that remains of the original monastery. The narrow 139ft-by-34ft church **interior** is restored to its 1813 appearance; early hand-carved wooden statues are in the sanctuary.

★★★BALBOA PARK

San Diego's cultural focal point is a 1,200-acre park immediately north of downtown. Lawns, gardens and century-old shade trees harbor the world-renowned San Diego Zoo, as well as theaters and museum buildings created for two world's fairs. The 1915 Panama-California Exposition was a city of stylized pavilions surrounding two central plazas—Plaza de Balboa and Plaza de Panama—linked by El Prado, a broad pedestrian thoroughfare. Architecture was Spanish Colonial Revival, a rich hybrid of Moorish, Baroque and Rococo ornamentation contrasting with colorful tiles and unadorned walls. The 1935 California Pacific International Exposition added new pavilions surrounding Pan-American Plaza in Art Deco, Mayan-Aztec and Southwestern styles.

Please see explanation on p 64.

Staying in the San Diego Area

La Costa Resort and Spa – *Costa del Mar Rd., Carlsbad CA.* ✗ & 🅿 ⤵ ☎ *760-438-9111. www.lacosta.com. 479 rooms.* **$$$$** Sprawled across 450 hilltop acres along the coast north of San Diego, this utopian escape boasts two golf courses, 21 tennis courts, five heated pools and five restaurants, as well as spirulina wraps and shiatsu massage. La Costa is a true splurge for recharging body and mind.

Hotel del Coronado – *1500 Orange Ave., Coronado CA.* ✗ & 🅿 ⤵ ☎ *619-435-6611. www.hoteldel.com. 692 rooms.* **$$$** This seaside gingerbread castle is a massive white Victorian of whimsical turrets and red-shingled roofs. "The Del" has hosted 14 presidents and countless celebrities since 1888. Guests stroll the resort's 26 oceanfront acres and indulge in flaky pastry topped with beluga caviar in the **Crown Coronet Room**, with its 33ft-high, rib-vaulted, ceiling.

La Valencia – *1132 Prospect St., La Jolla CA.* ✗ & 🅿 ⤵ ☎ *858-454-0771. 101 rooms.* **$$$** On a bluff overlooking the Pacific, this landmark pastel-pink stucco palace is a statement of opulent American beachside style. Surrounded by palms, topped by Spanish tile and a domed tower, mere steps from La Jolla Cove, La Valencia has witnessed more than 70 years of California sunsets.

Horton Grand Hotel – *311 Island Ave., San Diego CA.* 🅿 ☎ *619-544-1886. www.hortongrand.com. 132 rooms.* **$$** This historic Victorian-era hotel has been fully restored to its 1886 glory—when it shone above the brothels, saloons and opium dens of young San Diego's red-light district. Period decor—including an Austrian grand staircase—recaptures Gaslamp District charm.

Crystal Pier Hotel – *4500 Ocean Blvd., San Diego CA.* 🅿 ☎ *858-483-6983. 29 rooms.* **$** On a dock that juts into the ocean at Pacific Beach, a series of blue-and-white cottages provide unique over-the-water lodging. The 1927 bungalows have kitchenettes and wicker-chair furnishings, plus patios with umbrellas and deck furniture. Guests may rent rods and fish from the pier, or close the shutters of their cottages and fall into bed to the sounds of rumbling surf and incoming tides.

Dining in the San Diego Area

George's at the Cove – *1250 Prospect St., La Jolla CA.* ☎ *619-454-4244. www.georgesatthecove.com.* **$$$ Seafood.** All three stories of this seaside showplace have views of La Jolla Cove, whether inside the formal modern dining room or out on the terrace, under canvas umbrellas. George's is famous for fish—including sautéed Arctic char, dusted in anise seeds, and ahi sashimi—and for its signature soup of smoked chicken, broccoli and black beans.

Croce's – *802 5th Ave., San Diego CA.* ☎ *619-233-4355. www.croces.com.* **$$ Creative American.** This shrine to folk-rock singer Jim Croce was opened by his wife, Ingrid, after Jim died in a 1973 plane crash. Its bars offer live music every night—often from A.J. Croce, a child when his father passed on. The walls are decorated with photos, original lyrics and guitars. Seafood specialties (pan-seared sturgeon or grilled sea bass with a wild-rice pepper crust) are fine dining choices.

Casa de Bandini – *Calhoun & Mason Sts., Old Town, San Diego CA.* ☎ *619-297-8211.* **$ Mexican.** Mariachis and guitar players stroll around the fountain in this 1829 adobe hacienda's courtyard, once a home and social center in Old San Diego. Throngs of diners now guzzle massive margaritas in the lush gardens, and feast on such *pescados mexicanos* as fish tacos, crab enchiladas and shrimp fajitas.

Corvette Diner – *3946 5th Ave., San Diego CA.* ☎ *619-542-1476.* **$ American.** A disk jockey plays requests at this classic 1950s diner, as pink-and-black poodle-skirted waitresses carry burgers, fries and shakes to crowded tables. Photos of Elvis and Sinatra adorn the walls, alongside neon signs and 50s kitsch. Soda jerks mix cherry Cokes at the fountain as cooks sling hash behind the counter.

The **Visitors Center** in the House of Hospitality *(1549 El Prado; ✗ & 🄿 ☎ 619-239-0512; www.balboapark.com)* offers books, maps and general information. Parking is free, as are trams between attractions.

***San Diego Zoo** – Kids ⅢⅢ *2920 Zoo Dr.; Open year-round daily 9am-4pm (grounds close at 6pm during school vacations); closed major holidays. $16; children (3-11) $7. ✗ & 🄿 ☎ 619-234-3153. www.sandiegozoo.org.* One of the largest and most celebrated zoological parks in the world, the San Diego Zoo occupies 100 acres of hillsides and ravines at the northern end of Balboa Park, lushly landscaped with some 6,500 botanical species. Habitats disguise moats and fences used to separate, protect and display 4,000 animals of 800 species, divided into 10 bioclimatic zones.

Guided bus tours *(30-40min)* orient visitors to the undulating terrain. Moving sidewalks climb steep hills to assist those who wander the network of pathways by foot. Kangaroo Bus Tours allow hop-on, hop-off access to major points of interest. The Skyfari aerial tram carries visitors to Horn & Hoof Mesa. Animal shows *(25min)* are staged in Wegeforth Bowl and Hunte Amphitheater.

Ituri Forest is the zoo's newest theme area (1999): The Central African rain forest displays hippopotamuses, okapi, forest buffalo, spot-necked otters, monkeys and birds. Residents of **Gorilla Tropics** include troops of western lowland gorillas and pygmy chimpanzees. Adjoining is the **Scripps Aviary**, a multilevel enclosure with more than 200 species of African birds.

A winding trail descends **Tiger River** into a misty rain forest, passing crocodiles, Chinese water dragons, fishing cats, tapirs, pythons and mouse deer, ending at a Sumatran tiger habitat. In **Bear Canyon** is the Giant Panda Research Station, housing a pair of pandas on loan from China. Paths atop **Horn & Hoof Mesa** pass giraffes, Przewalski's horses and endangered Mhorr's gazelles, finally reaching the **Polar Bear Plunge**, with an underwater viewing area on a 14ft-deep moat.

***San Diego Natural History Museum** – Kids *1788 El Prado. ☎ 619-232-3821. www.sdnhm.org.* This imposing building (1933) fronting Plaza de Balboa uses multimedia dioramas and live animals to convey the region's natural wonders. It is scheduled to reopen in October 2000 after expansion.

***Reuben H. Fleet Science Center** – Kids *1875 El Prado. ✗ & 🄿 ☎ 619-238-1233. www.rhfleet.org.* Five galleries, a dome screen Space Theater for planetarium shows and IMAX films, and a 23 rider SciTours motion simulator for "space voyages" share this Spanish Colonial style building.

***Casa de Balboa** – *1649 El Prado. ✗ & 🄿.* This richly ornamented structure (1914) is based on the Federal Government Palace in Queretaro, Mexico. The **Museum of San Diego History** *(☎ 619-232-6203)* looks at the city's development since 1850. The **Museum of Photographic Arts** *(☎ 619-238-7559)* is scheduled to reopen in 2000 after a renovation and expansion.

Balboa Park

© David R. Frazier

★★Timken Museum of Art – *1500 El Prado.* ♿ 🅿 ☏ *619-239-5548.* *www.gort.ucsd.edu/sj/timken.* Clad in Italian travertine marble, the museum (1965) displays a collection of 50 European and American paintings and tapestries, and 17 remarkable **Russian icons★★** of the 14-19C. Works by Hals, Rubens, Rembrandt, Bierstadt and Copley are among those on exhibit.

★★San Diego Museum of Art – *1450 El Prado.* ✗♿ 🅿 ☏ *619-232-7931.* *www.sdmart.com.* The ornate Plateresque facade of this building (1926) was inspired by Spain's University of Salamanca. Depicted are Spanish Baroque masters; replicas of Donatello's *Saint George* and Michelangelo's *David;* and heraldry of Spain, America, California and San Diego.

Highlights of the wide-ranging collection include such Medieval European art as Luca Signorelli's *Coronation of the Virgin* (1508) and El Greco's *The Penitent Saint Peter* (c.1600). Impressionism is represented in works by Monet, Degas, Matisse and Pissarro. Acclaimed 20C works include Modigliani's *Le Garçon aux Yeux Bleux (The Boy With Blue Eyes)* and Georgia O'Keeffe's *White Trumpet Flower* (1932). An extensive collection of contemporary art features Deborah Butterfield, Bruce Conner, David Hockney and Wayne Thiebaud.

★Mingei International Museum of Folk Art – *1439 El Prado.* ♿ 🅿 ☏ *619-239-0003. www.mingei.org.* Rotating exhibits of traditional and contemporary folk art, crafts and design are presented. A collection of Japanese Shinto and American Shaker furniture and decorative arts share space in the Founder's Gallery.

★★San Diego Museum of Man – 🄺🄸🄳🄎 *1350 El Prado.* 🅿 ☏ *619-239-2001.* *www.museumofman.org.* Exhibits on human evolution (including a cast of "Lucy," among the oldest protohuman skeletons yet found), anthropology and ethnology are drawn from a collection of more than 70,000 artifacts. Emphasis is placed on the cultures of Egypt and pre-Columbian Mayas and Incas. The museum occupies the **California Building,** a Spanish Colonial structure (1915) with a massive Moorish-tile dome and three-belfry, 180ft campanile that rings on the quarter-hour.

★★San Diego Aerospace Museum – 🄺🄸🄳🄎 ‖‖‖‖ *2001 Pan American Plaza.* ♿ 🅿 ☏ *619-234-8291. www.aerospacemuseum.org.* The white and blue, ring-shaped, Art Moderne structure (1935) displays six dozen vintage aircraft from biplanes to space capsules, 14,000 scale models, and 10,000 aviation-related items.

Next door is the **San Diego Automotive Museum** 🄺🄸🄳🄎 *(2030 Pan American Plaza;* ♿ 🅿 ☏ *619-231-2886),* with classic automobiles and motorcycles.

DOWNTOWN SAN DIEGO

Civic leaders and developers restored the Gaslamp Quarter's Victorian treasures in the 1970s and 80s, spurring further revitalization along Broadway. A waterfront redevelopment soon followed, including Seaport Village, the San Diego Convention Center and numerous luxury hotels.

San Diego Skyline from Shelter Island (Point Loma)

★**Gaslamp Quarter** – *4th & 5th Aves. between Broadway & Harbor Dr.* ☎ *619-233-4692. www.gqhf.com* . Sixteen blocks of restored late-19C and early-20C Victorian buildings have become San Diego's trendiest restaurant and nightlife district. Walking tours begin from a neighborhood visitor center in the 1850 saltbox **William Heath Davis House** *(410 Island Ave.).*

★**Broadway** – Shopping and office complexes of cutting-edge architectural distinction reign here. **Horton Plaza★** *(bordered by Broadway & G St., 1st & 4th Aves.;* ☎ *619-238-1596)* is a mall (1985, Jon Jerde) with twisting post-Modern passageways and a 50-color crazy-quilt of design styles. The **U.S. Grant Hotel★** *(326 Broadway;* ☎ *619-232-3121)* is a stately, 11-story Italian Renaissance Revival inn (1910); its interior boasts 107 chandeliers and 150 tons of marble. **Emerald Plaza★** *(402 W. Broadway;* ☎ *619-239-7000)* is perhaps the most memorable building (1990, C.W. Kim) on the skyline, a 30-story cluster of eight hexagonal glass office towers lit at night with emerald-green neon.

★**Waterfront** – One of the city's first modern harborside projects was **Seaport Village** *(West Harbor Dr. at Kettner Blvd.;* ☎ *619-235-4014),* a 14-acre shopping-and-dining complex of New England- and Mediterranean-style buildings linked by cobblestone pathways and a boardwalk. Its centerpiece is an 1890 carousel. Not far away is the huge **San Diego Convention Center** *(111 W. Harbor Dr.;* ☎ *619-236-1212),* its open-air rooftop plaza surmounted by a giant white tent that resembles a futuristic sailing vessel.

★**Maritime Museum of San Diego** – Kids *1306 N. Harbor Dr.* ☎ *619-234-9153. www.maritime.com.* Three historic ships make up this floating museum. The **Star of India★★**, oldest iron merchant ship afloat (launched from Britain's Isle of Man in 1863), circumnavigated the globe 21 times in the late 19C. The **Berkeley** (1898), second propeller-driven ferry on the Pacific coast, was built in San Francisco. Moored alongside is the **Medea** (1904), a 140ft iron-hulled luxury steam yacht that once plied the lochs of Scotland. All three ships have extensive onboard exhibits. *Plans are under way to move the museum permanently to Broadway Pier, just south of its present site.*

ADDITIONAL SIGHTS

★**Coronado** – *Take I-5 south to Rte. 75; cross westbound toll bridge.* This affluent enclave of residences, hotels, restaurants and boutiques is serenely sheltered on a peninsula .5mi across the bay from downtown San Diego. Its landmark structure is the **Hotel del Coronado★★** *(1500 Orange Ave.;* ☎ *619-522-8023),* California's sole surviving Victorian seaside resort. Its white wood and red shingles, sweeping balconies and graceful spires rising beside Coronado's southern shore are immortalized in books and film.

★★**Cabrillo National Monument** – *Cabrillo Memorial Dr., Pt. Loma; from downtown San Diego, drive 7mi north on Harbor Dr., then left on Rosecrans St., right on Canon St. & left on Catalina Blvd.* ♿ 🅿

© Claire Curran

☎ *619-557-5450. www.nps.gov/cabr.* Located on the crest of a sandstone ridge 400ft above the sea, this park commemorates the Spanish discovery of the California coast in 1542. From the foot of a **statue** of explorer Juan Rodríguez Cabrillo, visitors may watch the passage of Navy ships, planes and submarines. A short uphill walk from the **visitor center**—whose exhibits interpret exploration and early local history—is the **Old Point Loma Lighthouse** (1855), one of the oldest lighthouses on the coast.

★★**SeaWorld San Diego** – Kids ▮▮▮▮ *500 SeaWorld Dr.; take I-5 to SeaWorld Dr. Exit.* ✗♿🅿 ☎ *619-226-3901. www.seaworld.com.* The first (1964) of four US SeaWorlds, this Mission Bay marine park mixes education and entertainment in five live shows and 25 exhibits and aquariums.

Highlight of the animal shows *(25min)* is the **Shamu Adventure**, featuring a family of trained orcas (killer whales). Other shows feature dolphins, sea lions, walruses and birds. **Rocky Point Preserve** invites visitors to touch and feed bottle-nosed dolphins. **Wild Arctic** mimics an arctic research station with polar bears, walruses, seals and beluga whales. **Penguin Encounter** re-creates the icy conditions of Antarctica. **Shark Encounter** offers a close-up look at these marine predators. **Manatee Rescue** is the only non-Florida venue with the endangered sea cows.

The revolving **SkyTower** provides bird's-eye views of the park and San Diego skyline from a 265ft observation point. **Guided tours** (90min), offer a behind-the-scenes look at SeaWorld's animal-rescue, training and medical facilities.

EXCURSIONS

★★ La Jolla – *12mi northwest of downtown San Diego via I-5 and Ardath Road.* ☏ *619-454-1444.* An upscale, sun-kissed suburb, La Jolla *(la-HOY-ya)* hugs a breathtakingly beautiful shoreline. The community is noted for posh shopping; important national research enclaves lie at its fringes. Rugged coastal beauty beckons swimmers and snorkelers to cliff-fringed **La Jolla Cove★★**, downslope from Prospect Street.

★ Museum of Contemporary Art, San Diego – *700 Prospect St.* ✗ ♿ ☏ *619-454-3541. www.mcasandiego.org.* San Diego's premier venue for contemporary art occupies the remodeled home of publishing baroness Ellen Browning Scripps (1916, Irving Gill). Exhibits rotate from a permanent collection of 3,000 Minimalist and Conceptual paintings, photographs, video and mixed-media pieces. A sculpture garden with native plants overlooks the Pacific.

★★ Birch Aquarium at Scripps – Kids *2300 Expedition Way, off Torrey Pines Rd. south of La Jolla Village Dr.* ✗ ♿ 🅿 ☏ *619-534-3474. www.aquarium.ucsd.edu.* The contemporary Mission-style complex, atop a bluff above the Scripps Institution of Oceanography, encompasses a modern aquarium and the largest US museum of oceanography. Marine life from the Pacific Northwest, Southern California, Mexico and tropical seas is displayed in 33 tanks housing some 3,500 fish of 280 species. Exhibits in the Hall of Oceanography cover the history and future of marine science, the physics of seawater, and the ocean's effect on climate and weather.

★ Salk Institute for Biological Studies – *10010 N. Torrey Pines Rd.* ♿ 🅿 ☏ *619-453-4100. www.salk.edu.* This striking Louis Kahn structure (1960) features two identical six-story buildings of reinforced concrete, teak and steel, facing each other across a travertine courtyard bisected by a narrow channel of water. Some 400 scientists conduct research here in neuroscience, molecular-cellular biology and genetics.

★ Torrey Pines State Reserve – *N. Torrey Pines Rd., 2mi north of Genesee Ave., 1mi south of Carmel Valley Rd.* 🅿 ☏ *619-642-4200. www.torreypine.org.* This 1,750-acre blufftop preserve was established in 1921 to preserve one of the world's rarest

---

■ Catching a Wave

Although Malibu's Surfrider Beach claims to be the birthplace of surfing in California, every beach with predictable waves, from La Jolla north to Santa Barbara and beyond, has a loyal band of surfers. Most sit patiently just beyond the surf line, waiting for the next perfect wave, then paddle madly to catch the crest and ride to shore. The artistry and grace on display—as surfer after surfer skims the face of a breaking wave—is breathtaking.

There may be as many surf shops as fast-food outlets along San Diego County beaches, which have bigger waves in winter but bigger crowds in summer. Most surfers wear wet suits all year to ward off a chill. Watching surfers is even more popular than surfing itself; bring a light jacket in winter, plenty of drinking water in summer, and sunblock all year. Binoculars bring the action closer.

Favorite surfing beaches include Swami's, in Encinitas, named for a meditation center on the cliffs above the beach; and the entire beachfront of Oceanside. The latter town also has one of the nation's finest surfing museums: the **California Surfing Museum** *(223 North Coast Hwy.; ☏ 760-721-6876).*

evergreens. Fewer than 4,000 Torrey pines *(Pinus torreyana)* remain from an ancient forest; they grow naturally only here and on Santa Rosa in the Channel Islands.

San Diego County Coast – North of La Jolla, scenic beaches and beach towns are strung like pearls along Route S21, the commercial artery that parallels Interstate 5. It passes through **Del Mar**, home of the renowned Del Mar Racetrack, and **Encinitas**, world-famous for its poinsettias, before reaching **Carlsbad**, a spa town whose local waters are chemically identical to those of Karlsbad, Germany.

Carlsbad's newest attraction is **LEGOLAND California** 🄺🄸🄳🄸 *(1 LEGO Dr., off Cannon Rd. east of I-5;* ✗ ♿ 🅿 ☎ *760-918-5379).* The first US theme park for the Danish-designed children's building blocks uses 30 million signature LEGO bricks in 5,000 models of animals, buildings and famous sights. Childhood stories are rendered along Fairy Tale Brook; life-size African beasts lurk on Safari Trek; an Adventurers Club Walk penetrates the Pyramids, an Amazon rain forest and an arctic icescape.

*** San Diego Wild Animal Park – 🄺🄸🄳🄸 ⅢⅡ *15500 San Pasqual Valley Rd., Escondido, 30mi northeast of San Diego; take I-15 to Via Rancho Parkway Exit and follow signs north and east.* ✗ ♿ 🅿 ☎ *760-747-8702 or 619-234-6541. www.sandiegozoo.org.* Exotic and endangered animals find safe haven in this 2,200-acre park of rolling grasslands and botanical gardens operated by the San Diego Zoo, created as a breeding facility to ensure the survival of species.

Visitors enter through **Nairobi Village**, a replica Congo fishing village with exotic-bird aviaries. Animal shows demonstrate natural behaviors and abilities of birds of prey, North American animals and Asian elephants. The **Wgasa Bush Line** monorail *(5mi, 50min)* departs from here to traverse six principal biogeographical areas: East and South African savanna, North African desert, Asian plains and waterholes, and Mongolian steppe. Roaming freely are herds of giraffes, wildebeests, gazelles, oryxes and the largest collection of southern white rhinoceroses in the US.

San Diego Wild Animal Park

© David Falconer/FOLIO, Inc.

Walking exploration is encouraged in **Heart of Africa**. Warthogs, duikers, bonteboks, elands, giraffes, cheetahs and vultures are among free-roaming denizens. Several smaller habitats feature success stories from zoo breeding programs, including Sumatran tigers, Przewalski's wild horses, okapi and pygmy chimpanzees.

** San Luis Rey de Francia Mission – *4050 Mission Ave., San Luis Rey, 40mi north of San Diego via I-5 & Rte. 76.* ♿ 🅿 ☎ *760-757-3651. www.sanluisrey.org.* A bridge between the distant missions of San Diego and San Juan Capistrano, the "King of the Missions" was founded in 1798 and named for 13C crusader King Louis IX of France. It became one of the most successful outposts of Catholicism in California, with 2,800 neophytes in residence. The mission housed a Franciscan monastery in the late 19C and now serves an active parish.

A domed bell tower crowns the right front corner of the large cruciform mission church. A two-story cloister once extended 500ft on each side; 12 arches remain of the 32 that formerly graced the front wall. Within the mission is a rare collection of old Spanish **vestments** and the only extant mission-era walking staff and padre's hat.

Tijuana, Mexico – *16mi south of downtown San Diego.* ☎ *619-299-8518. Visitors may walk across the border from the San Diego Trolley terminus at San Ysidro.* Home to nearly 1 million people, Tijuana is the most visited Mexican border city. Long considered a bawdy town of inexpensive pleasures, "TJ" has been transformed by tourist dollars into a commercial center with high-rise hotels, shopping areas, two bull rings and a jai alai arena. **Avenida Revolución** is the main artery for shopping, dining and bar-hopping. The rooftop **Mexitlán** *(Avenida Ocampo at Calle 2)* displays exact scale models of 150 Mexican architectural landmarks. **Centro Cultural** *(Paseo de los Héroes at Avenida Mina)* has a permanent exhibit on Mexico's pre-Columbian era and regional history.

ANZA-BORREGO DESERT★★

Michelin map 493 C, D 11   Pacific Standard Time
Tourist Information ☎ 760-767-4205

Inland San Diego County is a jumble of mountains and valleys that climax at Anza-Borrego Desert State Park, the largest state park in the western US. West of the mountains are the charming hamlet of Julian and the Palomar Observatory atop 6,126ft Palomar Mountain. East of the state park is the agriculturally rich Imperial Valley, with the Salton Sea at its north end.

SIGHTS

★★ **Anza-Borrego Desert State Park** – *80mi northeast of San Diego via Rte. 78.* △ ᰔ ☎ *760-767-5311. www.anzaborrego.statepark.org.* Named for Juan Bautista de Anza, the Spanish military explorer who traversed the region in 1774, and for endemic *borregos,* or bighorn sheep, this 939sq-mi preserve contains rocky mountains, sculptured badlands, hidden palm groves and historic pioneer trails. Check at the **visitor center** *(1.5mi west of traffic circle on Palm Canyon Dr., Borrego Springs;* ᰔ 🄿 ☎ *760-767-4205),* quarried into natural rock, for road conditions in areas accessible only by four-wheel-drive vehicle. A Wildflower Hotline *(☎ 760-767-4684)* estimates spring bloom dates.

The **Erosion Road Auto Tour,** running east along Route S22 from Borrego Springs, traverses rolling plains below the Santa Rosa Mountains. Markers describe geologic forces that shaped the landscape. At Mile 29.3, a sandy side road leads 4mi to Font's Point and panoramic **views**★★ over the Borrego Badlands.

Popular hiking trails include the 3mi **Borrego Palm Canyon Trail** *(trailhead at campground 2mi north of visitor center),* a moderately difficult canyon trail that ascends an alluvial fan to a hidden fan-palm oasis; and the .5mi **Narrows Earth Loop Trail** *(trailhead 12.2mi south of Borrego Springs on Rte. S3, then 4.7mi east on Rte. 78),* which offers an extended look at canyon geology.

■ Finding a Date

Many of the gracious palms adorning the San Diego area are date palms, first imported into the semi-arid region for their sweet, sticky fruit. Most city palms are now strictly ornamental, but dates remain an important agricultural crop elsewhere. The Imperial Valley town of Calipatria—now best known for a 184ft flagpole that brings the center of the sunken town up to sea level—originally was called Date City. Most of California's date crop now comes from groves near Indio, north of the Salton Sea.

★ **Julian** – *57mi northeast of San Diego via I-8 & Rte. 79.* At 4,200ft, this village is a popular weekend getaway spot known for apples, peaches, pears and 19C-style storefronts along Main Street. Eight miles northwest is the **Santa Ysabel Asistencia Mission** *(Rtes. 79 & 78;* ☎ *760-765-0810),* established in 1818 as an outpost of the San Diego de Alcalá Mission.

Palomar Observatory – *Rte. S6, 55mi northeast of San Diego via I-15 & Rte. 76.* 🄿 ☎ *760-742-2119. www.astro.caltech.edu.* Located near the peak of 6,126ft Palomar Mountain, this California Institute of Technology observatory

Wildflowers, Anza-Borrego Desert State Park

boasts the largest optical telescope in the US. The celebrated **Hale Telescope**★, with its 200in Pyrex lens, has a range surpassing 1 billion light years. An adjacent gallery explains the development and use of the huge telescope, as demonstrated by stunning photographs of Milky Way stars, distant galaxies, quasars, nebulae and other celestial wonders.

★**Imperial Valley** – *117mi east of San Diego via I-8, Rte. 111 (north) & Rte. 78 (east)*. Fields of lettuce, melons, tomatoes, carrots and other vegetables cluster around El Centro, main town of this sub-sea-level valley. Its east side is part of the **Imperial Sand Dunes Recreation Area** *(Rte. 78; ☎ 760-344-3919)*, whose dunes crest up to 300ft. Eighty percent of these hills, once known as the Algodones Dunes, are open to off-road vehicles (ORVs), but the Imperial Sand Dunes National Natural Landmark remains a protected area. Hugh Osborne Overlook, 3mi east of Gecko Rd, off Rte. 78, offers the best viewpoint.

★**Salton Sea** – *168mi east of San Diego via I-8 & Rte. 86*. This accidental sea was formed when the Colorado River flooded an ancient lake bed in 1905, creating an inland sea 35mi long by 15mi wide but just 20ft deep. The **Salton Sea National Wildlife Refuge** *(Rte. 86; ☎ 760-348-5278)* protects migratory bird habitat on the marshy southern shore. The **Salton Sea State Recreation Area** *(Rte. 111)* and other north-shore areas offer swimming beaches.

San Francisco Area

View from Alamo Square

From the redwood forests of the north to the towering cliffs of Big Sur, the seaboard and coastal hinterlands of Northern California possess an unparalleled variety of scenic and natural beauty. The cosmopolitan city of San Francisco and its surrounding Bay Area form the hub of a region that embraces the Wine Country of the Napa and Sonoma Valleys, the charming and historic Monterey Peninsula, the remote coves and beaches of the rocky Pacific coast, historical mission settlements and the deep forest solitude of the Redwood Empire.

The rugged mountains that run the length of California's northern coast once formed part of the Pacific Ocean floor. Over 25 million years ago, the continuing tectonic collision of the Pacific and North American plates gradually warped and folded the seabed to form the Coast Ranges. Thick fogs that shroud the coast during summer nourish the famous redwood forests and grape vineyards along the ridges. The San Andreas Fault, running mostly parallel to this continental collision zone, is the largest of many earthquake faults that periodically shake the region.

In ancient times, northern California's varied landscapes and rich natural resources supported the densest native population of any American region north of Mexico. Spanish soldiers and churchmen, building a network of isolated mission settlements in the 18C, decimated this original population in their attempts to colonize and convert the tribes. The structured mission society, which never extended farther north than the Bay Area, ended with Mexican secularization of the missions in 1834, whereupon rancho life and trade in hides and tallow became the mainstays of California's economy and day-to-day culture. After the US seized California in 1846, and especially with the gold rush of 1849, waves of US and international immigrants flooded into the state, shifting economic and political power from the Spanish capital of Monterey and concentrating it in the San Francisco Bay Area. Development of the North Coast—a region virtually ignored by the Spanish though historically claimed by both England and Russia—accelerated in the late 19C as redwood forests were harvested for timber to build San Francisco and other burgeoning cities and towns.

San Francisco

CA

SAN FRANCISCO★★★

Map pp 314-315   Pacific Standard Time
Population 745,774
Tourist Information ☎ 415-391-2000 or www.sfvisitor.org

Founded as Mission Dolores (by priests) and the Presidio (by soldiers) in 1776, San Francisco grew from the pueblo of Yerba Buena. In 1835, English sailor William Richardson, married to the daughter of the Presidio *comandante*, set up a tent where Grant Avenue now runs. Yerba Buena grew modestly on trade, changing its name to San Francisco after the US claimed California in 1846.

The discovery of Sierra gold in 1848 put San Francisco in the fast lane toward the future. Word of the strike spread like wildfire as ships from all over the world arrived with hopeful miners. The tiny village exploded into a boomtown serving 90,000 anxious transients. Abandoned ships were winched ashore to serve as hotels and warehouses. New buildings rose daily (and burned with alarming frequency). Another burst of fortune came with the discovery in 1859 of a vein of Nevada silver known as the Comstock Lode. Its investors' profits flooded San Francisco with fabulous wealth. Ostentatious and high-living new millionaires funded a wide range of civic improvements and construction—factories, offices, theaters, wharves, hotels, ferries and the famous cable cars.

With a population of nearly 400,000 at the turn of the 20C, San Francisco was the largest American city west of the Mississippi River. A terrible earthquake and fire in 1906 virtually destroyed the city center, leaving 250,000 people homeless and 674 dead or missing. The plucky city reconstructed with phenomenal speed, riding its progressive momentum through the first half of the 20C with a host of epic civil-engineering projects that included two of the largest bridges in the world.

After World War II, faced with the rise of Los Angeles and the separate growth of its own suburbs, San Francisco began to lose its claim as the premier banking and manufacturing (and some would say cultural) center of the West Coast. By the 1970s, tourism had become the city's biggest business, as it remains today.

SIGHTS

★**Union Square** – *Roughly bounded by Sutter, Taylor, Kearny & O'Farrell Sts*. San Francisco's most prestigious urban shopping district boasts fine luxury department stores. Facing pleasant 2.6-acre **Union Square Park** are Saks Fifth Avenue, Macy's and Nordstrom. **Neiman-Marcus** has a stunning **rotunda**★ topped by an elaborate art-glass dome. The **Westin St. Francis Hotel**★★ *(335 Powell St.; ☎ 415-397-7000)* commandeers the block west of the square, an elegant Renaissance and Baroque Revival pile completed in 1904 and rebuilt after 1906. A small but active theater district fans out to the west, embracing the **Geary Theater**★ *(415 Geary St.; ☎ 415-749-2228)*, home of the American Conservatory Theater, and the **Curran Theater**★ *(445 Geary St.; ☎ 415-551-2000)*, distinguished by its mansard roof.

★★**Financial District** – *Bounded by Market, Kearny & Jackson Sts. and The Embarcadero*. The city's banking, commodities-trading and corporate-business center is concentrated in a triangular district around California and Montgomery Streets, the latter called "Wall Street of the West." Until Bank of America merged with NationsBank in 1998, **Bank of America Center**★★ *(555 California St.)* was world head quarters of an institution that financed much of the development of San Francisco and the West; a grand **view**★★★ extends from its 52nd-floor Carnelian Room restaurant *(☎ 415-433-7500)*. Wells Fargo Bank recalls its Old West roots (it started as a transport business in 1852) at the **Wells Fargo History Museum**★ 🧒 *(420 Montgomery St.; ☎ 415-396-2619)*. The city's grandest bank edifice is the Neoclassical **Bank of California**★★ *(400 California St.)*, which displays mid-19C gold and currency in the **Museum of Money of the American West** 🧒 *(☎ 415-765-3213)*.

San Francisco's tallest building, the 48-story **Transamerica Pyramid**★★ *(600 Montgomery St.)*, rises 853ft from street level to the tip of its 212ft hollow lantern; built in 1972, the slender pyramid is a symbol of the city. **Embarcadero Center**★ *(bounded by Sacramento, Battery & Clay Sts. & the Embarcadero)*, an ambitious series of four slablike office towers (1967-72), incorporates a three-level, open-air shopping center. Its **SkyDeck**★★ *(One Embarcadero Center; ☎ 415-772-0555)* offers views of the city and bay from the 41st floor.

★★★**Chinatown** – *Bounded by Montgomery, California & Powell Sts. and Broadway*. A teeming fusion of Cantonese market town and Main Street USA, Chinatown spreads along the lower slope of Nob Hill. With 30,000 residents in its 24-block core, it is one of the most densely populated neighborhoods in North America. The main thoroughfare, **Grant Avenue**★★, starts with a flourish at **Chinatown Gate** on Bush Street and runs eight blocks north to Broadway. Exotic ambience is provided by distinctive architectural chinoiserie: painted balconies, curved-tile rooflines, and red, green and yellow color schemes. Shops selling souvenirs, jewelry, artwork,

Please see explanation on p 64.

Staying in the San Francisco Area

Campton Place Hotel – *340 Stockton St.; San Francisco CA.* ✗ ♿ ☎ *415-781-5555. www.camptonplace.com. 110 rooms.* **$$$$** An intimate Union Square hotel once popular with the white-gloved "carriage trade" set, the Campton Place is the epitome of elegance and fine service. Asian-inspired decor squares off with a French-style restaurant to provide a rarefied experience in a discreet location.

Meadowood Napa Valley – *900 Meadowood Lane, St. Helena CA.* ✗ ♿ ▣ ⚊ ☎ *707-963-3646. www.meadowood.com. 85 rooms.* **$$$$** Just off the Silverado Trail, this resort is a perfect perch for Wine Country adventurers. Rustic cottages dotting a cool wooded grove bring guests down to earth, but service is top-flight. The resort offers golf, tennis, a full spa and an award-winning dining room.

Post Ranch Inn – *Hwy 1, Big Sur CA.* ✗ ♿ ▣ ⚊ ☎ *831-667-2200. www .postranchinn.com. 30 rooms.* **$$$$** Exquisite views of the Pacific Ocean at Pfeiffer Point extend from the inn's steel-roofed redwood cottages. Guests may recline under skylights on the denim bedspreads in their minimalist rooms, or walk the 98-acre ranch through oak and madrone forest. At night, they may join the stargazing class or dip in the warm-water basking pool.

Hotel Monaco – *501 Geary St., San Francisco CA.* ✗ ♿ ☎ *415-292-0100. www.hotelmonaco.com. 201 rooms.* **$$$** Situated near Union Square, this boutique hotel offers the warmth and comfort of home in a much grander setting. Baroque plaster fireplaces and sumptuous striped armchairs invite conversation in the lobby; Provençal fabrics drape over the beds in guest rooms. Downstairs, the **Grand Café** offers a bistro-style lunch and dinner.

Hotel Bijou – *111 Mason St., San Francisco CA.* ☎ *415-771-1200. www.sftrips .com. 65 rooms.* **$$** This Art Deco building feels like a 1920s movie palace. It is adorned with deep-gold walls and black-and-white photos of San Francisco's old movie houses, and every guest room is named for a film shot in San Francisco. Visit the small theater in the lobby and don't forget the popcorn.

Dining in the San Francisco Area

Chez Panisse – *1517 Shattuck Ave., Berkeley CA.* ☎ *510-548-5525.* **$$$$ California.** California cuisine was born here, near the "Cal" campus, under the watchful eye of culinary doyenne Alice Waters. Organic greens and baby vegetables pair up with free-range poultry and meats to create prix-fixe meals at this mecca of gastronomy. Try the guinea hen with smoked bacon and zucchini pancakes.

Jardinière – *300 Grove St., San Francisco CA.* ☎ *415-861-5555.* **$$$$ California French.** Behind the French name, a real American garden grows at this elegant Civic Center restaurant, a great place for pre- or post-theater dining. Hundreds of bubbles sparkle on the ceiling of the Champagne Rotunda. House specialties of chef Traci Des Jardins include the duck confit salad and foie gras.

Lark Creek Inn – *234 Magnolia Ave., Larkspur CA.* ☎ *415-924-7766.* **$$$$ American.** Just over the Golden Gate Bridge sits this charming restaurant. Situated in a wooden glen in Marin County, the countrified inn serves classic fare, from grilled king salmon to barbecued, glazed pork medallions.

The Slanted Door – *584 Valencia St., San Francisco CA.* ☎ *415-861-8032.* **$$$ Asian fusion.** This trendy Mission District cafe offers Vietnamese-inspired food in a bustling atmosphere. Crowds arrive early for the exotic cuisine: crispy imperial rolls, "shaking beef" with garlic, grilled Muscovy duck with plum sauce.

Gordon's House of Fine Eats – *500 Florida St., San Francisco CA.* ☎ *415-861-8900.* **$$ American.** In the Potrero Hill neighborhood, this hip techno-industrial restaurant serves up hearty fare with a trendy twist: The menu is divided into sections for "Comfort," "Health," "Luxury" and "Local Showcase." Recommended: asparagus spring rolls or Angus rib-eye steak with skinny french fries.

The Ramp – *855 China Basin St. at Pier 64, San Francisco CA.* ☎ *415-621-2378.* **$ American.** Locals queue up Saturday afternoons for live music and salsa dancing at this burger-and-sandwich shack beneath Potrero Hill. Any sunny day is a reason to enjoy these simple pleasures while looking out at the boats on San Francisco Bay.

furniture, cameras and electronics share the street with tourist restaurants, hardware stores, banks, poultry and fish markets, herbalists' shops, tea stores and cafes that cater to local residents. **Old St. Mary's Cathedral★** *(660 California St. at Grant Ave.; ☎ 415-288-3800)*, dedicated in 1854, was built of brick and iron shipped from New England, laid upon a foundation of granite quarried in China. **Portsmouth Square★** *(between Clay & Washington Sts., one-half block below Grant Ave.)*, the original plaza of Yerba Buena, is now a social gathering point for Chinatown residents. A few blocks away, the **Chinese Historical Society of America** *(644 Broadway, 4th floor; ☎ 415-391-1188)* offers a historical perspective on the Chinese experience.

Tin How Temple

© Robert Holmes

A less commercialized neighborhood of markets surrounds **Stockton Street**, a full block uphill from Grant, and a maze of narrow alleys between. **Waverly Place★** is noted for its temples and brilliantly decorated balconies. The 1852 **Tin How Temple** *(125 Waverly Pl., 4th floor; ☎ 415-421-3628)* is Chinatown's oldest.

★★ **North Beach** – *Columbus Ave. and adjacent streets from Pacific Ave. to Bay St.* The erstwhile heart of the Italian community, North Beach inspires dawdling at coffeehouses by day and restaurants by night. The Beat Generation—"beatniks"—flocked here in the 1950s seeking relaxed Mediterranean attitude along with the cheap food and drink of family-run trattorias, bars and cafes. A traditional Latin flavor persists at **Washington Square Park★**, backed by the twin spires of **SS Peter and Paul Church★** *(666 Filbert St.; ☎ 415-421-0809)*, known as the Italian Cathedral. On the east side of North Beach, 274ft **Telegraph Hill★** is capped by fluted-concrete **Coit Tower★★★** Kids *(☎ 415-362-0808)*, which rises an additional 212ft to an observation deck offering fine city **views★★**. Built in 1934 during the Great Depression, the tower has a lobby decorated with **murals★★** painted by 26 local artists as part of the Public Works of Art Project. Blatantly critical of social and political conditions, the murals sparked heated controversy.

★ **Russian Hill** – *Roughly bounded by Columbus Ave., Bay & Polk Sts., Broadway & Mason St.* Apartment dwellers covet this district for its stupendous views of the northern waterfront. From the lofty crossroads of Hyde and Lombard Streets, visitors gaze north down **Hyde Street Hill★★**, following the precipitous line of the Powell-Hyde Street Cable Car tracks toward the historic ships of Hyde Street Pier, and beyond to Alcatraz. Turning east, **Lombard Street★★★** Kids ||||| undulates down through flower gardens to Leavenworth Street; the one-block stretch is nicknamed "The Crookedest Street in the World." The eight switchbacks were built in 1922, taming the hillside's natural gradient of 27 percent to a manageable 16 percent.

★★ **Nob Hill** – *Roughly bounded by Broadway and Stockton, Bush & Polk Sts.* Nob Hill achieved its reputation as an abode of the rich and influential in the late 1860s, when millionaires built on its summit and slopes. Construction of a cable-car line in 1873 made the hilltop more accessible, and by the 1880s the roster of resident "nabobs" included railroad potentates and silver barons. With the exception of James Flood's mansion, now the exclusive **Pacific-Union Club★** *(1000 California St.)*, all original mansions were destroyed in the 1906 fire.

Prestigious hotels now dominate. The opulent **Fairmont Hotel**★★ *(950 California St.; ☏ 415-772-5000)* is famed for glorious **views**★★★ from its Crown Room restaurant. The **Mark Hopkins Inter-Continental Hotel** *(999 California St.; ☏ 415-392-3434)* offers stunning **vistas**★★★ from its swank bar, the Top of the Mark.

The most dynamic site on Nob Hill is the **Cable Car Museum**★★ Kids *(1201 Mason St.; ☏ 415-474-1887)*, which doubles as the powerhouse for the clanging cars that move up and down San Francisco's steep hills, gripping a moving cable that loops continuously through a slot in the city streets. From the balcony of the museum, visitors may gaze upon the humming engines and whirling sheaves that drive the cable through its winding course.

★★**Civic Center** – *Bounded by Market St., Van Ness & Golden Gate Aves.* San Francisco's governmental center comprises one of the nation's finest groupings of Beaux-Arts-style buildings. The design was inspired by the 1905 Burnham Plan, prepared by Chicago architect Daniel Burnham at the behest of businessmen and politicians who sought civic improvements along design guidelines of the City Beautiful Movement. Although the leveling of the city by the 1906 earthquake and fire provided a prime opportunity to implement the plan, the urgency of reconstruction precluded its adoption anywhere except Civic Center.

Buildings are arranged along a central axis running three blocks west from Market and Leavenworth Streets to City Hall. At the eastern head of this pedestrian mall, **United Nations Plaza**★ commemorates the founding of the UN at Civic Center in 1945. After passing the **San Francisco Public Library**★ *(100 Larkin St.; ☏ 415-557-4400)*, the axis opens up to the formal gardens and reflecting pool of **Civic Center Plaza**, foreground for the imposing dome of **City Hall**★★ *(facing Polk St.)*. Rising to 307ft above a massive, four-story colonnaded building, the black and gold dome is 13ft taller than that of the US Capitol building in Washington DC. Inside, a grand staircase ascends to a 181ft open rotunda, flanked by city government offices.

On the west side of City Hall, the **San Francisco War Memorial and Performing Arts Center**★★ *(Van Ness Ave. between McAllister & Grove Sts.; ☏ 415-552-8338)* comprises the War Memorial Opera House and the Veterans Building, site of a theater and art gallery. Immediately south is **Davies Symphony Hall**★ *(Grove St. & Van Ness Ave.)*, home of the San Francisco Symphony Orchestra.

★**Mission Dolores** – *16th & Dolores Sts.* ☏ *415-621-8203.* Officially named Mission San Francisco de Asis, the city's oldest extant structure dates from 1791, when it replaced the original (1776) mission chapel staked out by Juan Bautista de Anza near the shores of a lake he called *Nuestra Señora de los Dolores* (Our Lady of Sorrows). The 4ft-thick adobe walls of the sturdy **chapel**★★ are covered with stucco and roofed by a beamed ceiling painted with Ohlone Indian designs. The marked graves of Catholic pioneers adorn the chapel and **cemetery**★, where thousands of Ohlone neophytes lie in unmarked plots.

★★**Yerba Buena Gardens** – *Bounded by Mission, Howard, 3rd & 4th Sts.* Uniting an outdoor garden with cinemas, galleries, playgrounds, museums and the **Moscone Convention Center**, Yerba Buena Gardens is the city's most ambitious entertainment and cultural complex of the late 20C. At the 5.5-acre **Esplanade**, visitors loll on grassy terraces and visit a memorial to Dr. Martin Luther King Jr., curtained by an exhilarating waterfall. Adjacent are the theaters, gallery and forum of the **Yerba Buena Center for the Arts**★ *(3rd & Mission Sts.; ☏ 415-978-2787)*, and the new **Rooftop at Yerba Buena Gardens** Kids *(750 Folsom St.; ☏ 415-777-3727)*, a children's complex with a high-tech studio-theater and year-round ice-skating rink. The four-story **Sony Metréon**★ Kids *(4th & Mission Sts.; ☏ 415-537-3400)* houses 15 cinemas, a 600-seat IMAX theater, "virtual" amusements, restaurants and retail shops.

★★**San Francisco Museum of Modern Art** – *151 3rd St.* ☏ *415-357-4170. www.sfmoma .org.* This premier showcase for contemporary art occupies an innovative building (1995, Mario Botta) opposite Yerba Buena Gardens. The huge **atrium**★★ resembles an urban piazza, sheathed in bright woods and polished granite. A grand staircase rises through the building's heart, culminating in a narrow steel **catwalk**★ five stories above the rotunda floor. Permanent holdings include 1,200 paintings, 500 sculptures, 9,000 photographs and 3,000 works on paper, representing major artists and schools of Europe, North America and Latin America. Noteworthy artists include Matisse, Picasso, Braque, Míro, Rivera, Kahlo, Pollock, Rothko, Dalí, Still, Kandinsky, O'Keeffe, Warhol, Rauschenberg, Lichtenstein and Johns.

★**The Embarcadero** – *Along San Francisco Bay from China Basin to Fisherman's Wharf.* The waterfront was once a clamorous district of piers and warehouses. Today most structures have either been torn down or converted into offices, shops and restaurants. A promenade known as **Herb Caen Way ...★**, named for a local newspaper columnist famed for his "three-dot" style of writing, offers **views★★** across San Francisco Bay to the hills of East Bay (p 318).

Lumbering across the bay are the towers, two-tiered roadway and twin suspension spans of the western part of **San Francisco-Oakland Bay Bridge★★**. Joining the eastern cantilever section at Yerba Buena Island, the 5.2mi bridge is one of the world's longest high-level steel bridges. When opened in 1936, it ended the golden age of bay ferries and their terminus, the 1898 **Ferry Building★★** (foot of Market St.), until then the nation's busiest transport center. The distinctive 253ft clock tower was the city's only high-rise undamaged by the 1906 quake and fire.

★★★ **Fisherman's Wharf** – Kids ▮▮▮▮ North of Bay St. between The Embarcadero & Van Ness Ave. The Wharf draws throngs to its colorful docks, carnival amusements and multitudinous seafood eateries. Although fishermen still bring in their catch during early-morning hours, tourism now dominates the economy. Most popular of the diversions is **Pier 39★** Kids, a marketplace of shops, restaurants, aquarium and theater; it is famed for the pod of wild sea lions that slumber off its west side.

Cruise Boat, Fisherman's Wharf

Pier 45 visitors may tour the World War II submarine **USS Pampanito★★** Kids (☎ 415-441-5819), one of several ships maintained by the **National Maritime Museum★** (Beach St. at Polk St.; ☎ 415-556-3002), itself housed in a 1939 Streamline Moderne building above **Aquatic Park Beach.** Other ships are moored at the **Hyde Street Pier★★** Kids (☎ 415-556-3002), including the three-masted, steel-hulled square-rigger, **Balclutha★★**, and the 1890 passenger and car ferry, **Eureka★**, one of the largest wooden vessels afloat.

Terminus for **bay cruises★** (Pier 39, ☎ 415-705-5555; or Pier 43 1/2, ☎ 415-447-0597) and ferry excursions to Marin County (Pier 39 1/2), Alcatraz (below) and Angel Island (p 320), Fisherman's Wharf also lures shoppers in search of unique souvenirs. T-shirts and knickknacks dominate the shops of **Jefferson Street,** while a more eclectic array fills the refurbished warehouses at **The Cannery★★** (2801 Leavenworth St.) and the old chocolate factory of **Ghirardelli Square★★** Kids (Larkin, Beach, Polk & North Point Sts.).

★★★ **Alcatraz** – Kids ▮▮▮▮ Ferry departs from Pier 41. ☎ 415-705-5555. Known as "The Rock," this barren 12-acre island, buffeted by strong winds and cold currents, began as an army fortress and prison in 1850, incarcerating renegade soldiers, Indians and Confederate sympathizers. It became famous as a maximum-security penitentiary for "desperate and irredeemable criminals" after being transferred to the US Department of Justice in 1933. Among its notorious inmates were Al Capone, George "Machine Gun" Kelly, Alvin "Creepy" Karpis and Robert Stroud, the "Birdman of Alcatraz." Worsening conditions, and the possible success of a 1962 escape attempt, prompted the government to close the prison. Today part of the Golden Gate National Recreation Area, the

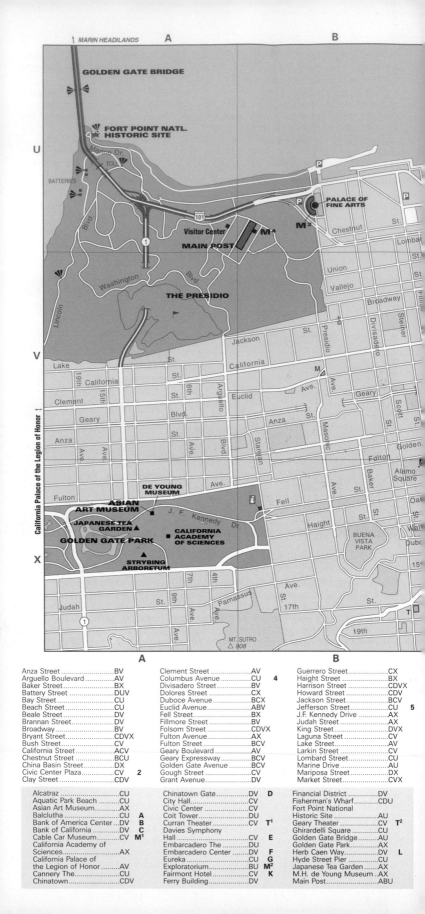

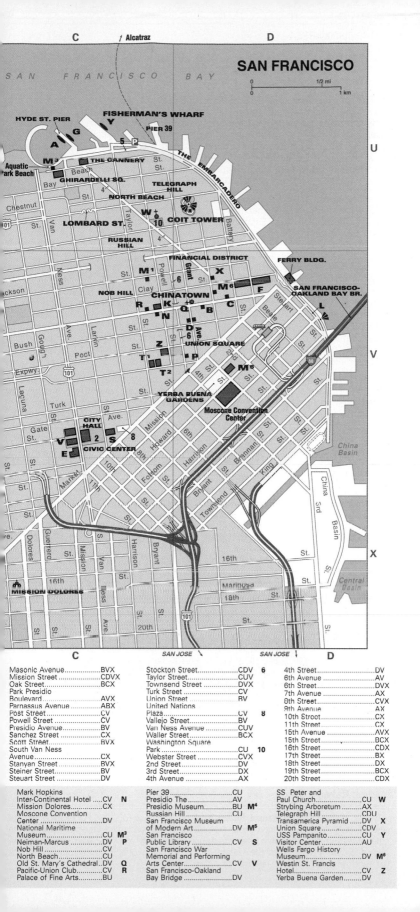

island is open to tourists who watch an **orientation video** and take a self-guided audio tour of the bleak **cellhouse**★★, the recreation yard, the cafeteria and the bunker-like control center.

★★ **Palace of Fine Arts** – *Baker & Beach Sts.* The sole remaining structure from the celebrated Panama-Pacific International Exposition of 1915, the Palace of Fine Arts was designed by Bernard Maybeck as a fanciful Roman ruin. The wood-and-plaster building was spared demolition by citizens who admired its hauntingly beautiful rotunda, peristyle and reflecting pond. Rebuilt in concrete, the Palace now houses the **Exploratorium**★★ Kids *(3601 Lyon St.; ☎ 415-397-5673)*, a hands-on science museum with more than 60 exhibits in physics, electricity, life sciences, thermodynamics, sensory perception, weather and other subjects.

★★ **The Presidio** – *West of Lyon St. & south of the Golden Gate Bridge. ☎ 415-556-0560.* This 1,480-acre former military reservation is now part of the Golden Gate National Recreation Area. Established in 1776 to guard the entrance to San Francisco Bay, it remained an army base through the Mexican and most of the US eras, though an angry shot was never fired. As the Park Service and local interest groups debate the future of rows of onetime offices, enlisted housing and comely officers' homes, a brick barracks on the historic **Main Post**★★ has been converted to a **Visitor Center** *(Montgomery St.; ☎ 415-561-4323)*. The 1857 Post Hospital is now the **Presidio Museum**★ *(Funston Ave. at Lincoln Blvd.; ☎ 415-561-4331)*.

An imposing brick bastion built in 1861 to guard the Golden Gate from Confederate attack during the Civil War, **Fort Point National Historic Site**★★ *(end of Marine Dr.; ☎ 415-556-1693)* sits planted beneath a giant arch of the Golden Gate Bridge. Visitors may explore its courtyard, powder magazine, barracks rooms, three tiers of arched casements, and an upper terrace with astounding **views**★★ of the southern pier and underbelly of the famous bridge.

★★★ **Golden Gate Bridge** – Kids *US-101 north of the Presidio. ☎ 415-921-5858.* Painted a vibrant "international orange," this graceful Art Deco suspension bridge spans the channel via twin 746ft towers and an intricate tracery of cables that support a 1.6mi roadway. Despite treacherous tidal surges, strong winds, bone-chilling fogs and the deaths of 10 workers in a scaffolding collapse, the bridge opened in 1937 to great fanfare. Some 130,000 vehicles cross it daily. Astounding **views**★★ of the city, the Marin Headlands and the vertiginous 220ft drop to the surface of San Francisco Bay are reserved for pedestrians and bicyclists.

★★ **California Palace of the Legion of Honor** – *Legion of Honor Dr. & El Camino del Mar, Lincoln Park. ☎ 415-863-3330. www.thinker.org.* Situated on a hillside overlooking the west side of the Golden Gate, this stately edifice (1924) is a replica of Paris' Palais de la Légion d'Honneur. A square-based glass pyramid was added to the outdoor Court of Honor in the 1990s, serving as a skylight for new underground galleries while paying homage to I.M. Pei's larger pyramid at the Louvre in Paris. A showcase of European decorative and fine arts, the Legion's permanent holdings include Medieval stained glass, carvings, panels and tapestries, Rodin sculptures, and paintings from the early Italian Renaissance through the French Impressionist period.

★★★ **Golden Gate Park** – *Stanyan St. to Ocean Beach, between Fulton St. & Lincoln Way. ☎ 415-831-2700.* Sprawling over 1,017 acres of meadows and gardens, the largest cultivated urban park in the US stretches 3mi from Haight-Ashbury to the Pacific. One-half-mile wide, it is large enough to accommodate 27mi of footpaths and 7.5mi of horse trails—linking the Pacific with an enchantingly natural, yet entirely artificial, scenery of lakes, woods and waterfalls.

Most visitors concentrate on the eastern third of the park, especially its museums, and on the gardens surrounding its Music Concourse. **Strybing Arboretum**★★ *(Martin Luther King Jr. Dr.; ☎ 415-661-1316)* covers 70 acres of rolling terrain with 6,000 species of plants from all over the world, arranged according to region of origin. The **Japanese Tea Garden**★★ Kids *(west of Music Concourse; ☎ 415-831-2700)* harbors a delightful maze of winding paths, ornamental ponds swarming with *koi*, potted bonsai, stone lanterns, a wooded pagoda and a Zen rock garden. Near the center of the garden is a 10.5ft-tall Buddha image; cast in Japan in 1790, it is the largest bronze statue of the spiritual figure outside of Asia.

★★ **California Academy of Sciences** – Kids *Music Concourse. ☎ 415-750-7145. www.calacademy .org.* Founded in 1853, the oldest scientific institution in the West comprises three distinct divisions. The **Natural History Museum**★★ is one of the 10 largest in the world, with access to more than 14 million specimens. The **Steinhart Aquarium**★ is the oldest in the US, and presents more than 185 exhibits. **Morrison Planetarium** *(☎ 415-750-7141)* takes the theme of development over time beyond the limits of earth and into the far reaches of space.

Practical Information

Getting There – The Bay Area has two major airports: **San Francisco International Airport (SFO)** (☎ *650-876-7809, www.ci.sf.ca.us/sfo)*, 11mi south of downtown, and Oakland International Airport (OAK) (☎ *510-577-4000, http://oaklandairport .com)*, 22mi southeast of downtown San Francisco. From both airports, taxi service to downtown averages $40; commercial shuttles range from $9 to $14. There are also numerous rental-car branches *(p 409)*.
Amtrak train: 5885 Land Regan St. (☎ *800-872-7245, www.amtrak.com)*.
Greyhound bus: 101 7th St. (☎ *800-231-2222, www.greyhound.com)*.

Getting Around – Visitors can access route and fare information on all Bay Area transportation systems by calling Bay Area Traveler Information (☎ *415-817-1717; www.transitinfo.org)*. Most public transportation in San Francisco is operated by the San Francisco Muncipal Railway **(Muni)**. Lines operate daily 5:30am-12:30am; a limited number of routes operate 24hrs/day. Fare for buses and streetcars is $1; transfers are free, exact fare required. **Cable cars** operate daily 6am-12:30am; fare $2. Purchase tickets on-board, at selected hotels or at the Visitor Information Center (below). Muni Passports are good for one *($6)*, three *($10)* or seven *($15)* days. **BART** (Bay Area Rapid Transit), a light-rail system, is convenient for trips to Berkeley and Oakland (☎ *510-464-6000)*. **Taxi:** National *(☎ 415-648-4444)*, Pacific *(☎ 415-776-7755)*, Yellow Cab *(☎ 415-626-2345)*.

Cable Car, Hyde Street

© Dave G. Hauser

Accommodations – The San Francisco Lodging Guide is available *($3)* from the San Francisco Convention & Visitors Bureau (below). Reservation services: San Francisco Reservations (☎ *800-677-1500, www.hotelres.com)*. Bed & Breakfast San Francisco (☎ *479-1913 or 800-452-8249)*.

Entertainment – Consult the arts and entertainment sections of local newspapers (particularly the weekly Bay Guardian) for listings of current events, theaters and concert halls, or call the Cultural Events Hotline (☎ *415-391-2000)*. Obtain event tickets from BASS Ticketmaster (☎ *510-762-2277)* or Tix Bay Area, which offers half-price tickets for selected events on the day of the show (☎ *415-433-7827)*.

Visitor Information – The San Francisco Convention & Visitors Bureau operates an information center on the lower level of Hallidie Plaza (900 Market St.; ☎ *415-391-2000, www.sfvisitor.org)*.

★★ **M.H. de Young Museum** – *Music Concourse.* ☎ *415-863-3330. www.thinker.org*. With collections of historical American art, African and Oceanic art, pre-Columbian American art, and textiles, the De Young also hosts important traveling exhibitions. Its **American Collection**★★, which is deep in portrait, landscape and genre painting, is displayed with contemporary furniture, silver, glass, porcelain and other decorative arts. Among US painters represented are Bierstadt, Eakins, Sargent, Homer, Remington, Hill and Keith.

★★★ **Asian Art Museum** – *Music Concourse; enter through De Young Museum.* ☎ *415-379-8880. www.asianart.org.* Possessing the finest US collection of Asian art, this museum was spawned by Avery Brundage (1887-1975), longtime president of the International Olympic Committee. The collection of **Chinese art**★★★ numbers 3,100 ceramics, bronzes, paintings, sculptures and decorative arts dating from prehistory to the present. Highlights include scroll paintings from the Yuan, Ming and Qing dynasties; the largest assemblage of ritual bronzes on public display outside of China; the oldest-known dated Chinese Buddha (AD 338), and more than 1,200 jade objects. The **Korean art**★ collection comprises 350 items, including hanging scrolls and stoneware from AD 5-9C. The most comprehensive US collection of **Japanese art**★★ features screens and scroll paintings, a set of iron armor and 1,800 *netsuke* (kimono toggle) miniatures of bone and ivory. The museum also hosts impressive sculptures, bronzes and Mughal miniatures in its **Indian Gallery**★, as well as significant holdings of **Southeast Asian, Himalayan** and **Near Eastern** artwork.

EAST BAY★

Map opposite   Pacific Standard Time
Tourist Information ☎ 510-208-4646

Directly across the bay from San Francisco, Oakland and Berkeley nestle on the flanks of steeply wooded hills. **Oakland,** incorporated in 1852, prospered after its selection in 1868 as the western terminus of the transcontinental railroad. When the 1906 earthquake and fire devastated San Francisco, Oakland sheltered more than 150,000 refugees, many of whom remained. In 1931, the Art Deco **Paramount Theatre**★★ *(2025 Broadway;* ☎ *510-465-6400)* opened with a towering exterior tile mosaic. The San Francisco-Oakland Bay Bridge (1936) ushered in a new era for the city, whose population grew by a third during World War II as its shipyards attracted thousands of workers.

Although severe economic decline and social unrest set in after World War II, the reestablishment in 1989 of passenger ferry service between San Francisco and **Jack London Square** *(south end of Broadway at Embarcadero;* ☎ *925-426-5420)* brought new life to the waterfront. Stretching along the Inner Harbor, this once-gritty dock area boasts an attractive complex of shops, restaurants, hotels, cinemas, a farmers' market and a yacht harbor. The expanded, modernized Port of Oakland ranks among the top 20 in the world. A city of 365,000, Oakland is among the most ethnically diverse of any in the US.

Berkeley, named for early-18C Irish bishop-philosopher George Berkeley, grew up around its university—founded in 1861 as the flagship campus of the **University of California**. Campus life continues to dominate Berkeley, a city of 108,000 famed for its intellectual and cultural vitality, political turmoil and social experimentation.

SIGHTS

★★ **Oakland Museum of California** – 🅺🅸🅳🆂 *1000 Oak St., Oakland.* ☎ *510-238-2200. www.museumca.org.* Architect Kevin Roche designed this treasury of art, culture and natural history (1969) as a series of horizontal glass and concrete tiers around a landscaped courtyard. The **Hall of California Ecology** *(1st level)* simulates a walk eastward across California, with detailed dioramas of flora and fauna re-creating eight distinct biotic zones. The **Cowell Hall of California History** *(2nd level)* traces human history with tableaux and displays of 6,000 artifacts, from native basketry and stone tools to the lifestyles of contemporary board and Web surfers. Devoted to artists who have lived, worked or studied in California, the **Gallery of California Art** *(3rd level)* displays paintings, sculptures, drawings, prints, photographs and mixed-media works from the early 19C to the present. It features the works of California Impressionists, the Oakland-based Society of Six landscapists, and the Bay Area Figurative movement.

★★ **USS Hornet** – 🅺🅸🅳🆂 *Pier 3, Alameda.* ☎ *510-521-8448.* Decommissioned and docked near Oakland, this Essex-class aircraft carrier had one of the most heroic combat records of World War II. The 894ft-long ship served in the Pacific for 18 months and destroyed 1,420 enemy aircraft, 42 cargo ships, 10 destroyers, a carrier, cruiser and battleship without once sustaining a hit in return. In May 1969, the *Hornet* retrieved the crew of *Apollo 11* after splashdown from the first manned lunar landing. Exhibits on the vast **Hangar Deck** highlight this mission. Visitors may then climb to the sprawling **Flight Deck** and the massive **Island** (control tower), or take a self-guided tour below decks.

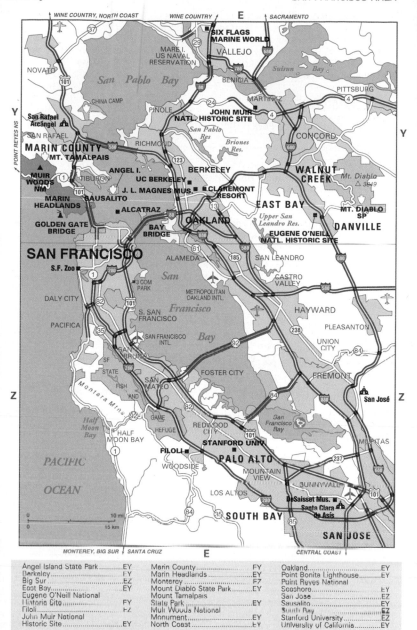

** **University of California** – *Roughly bounded by Bancroft Way, Oxford St. & Hearst Ave., Berkeley.* ☎ *510-549-7040. www.berkeley.edu.* The 178-acre "Cal" campus boasts 30,000 students and a variety of architectural styles. John Galen Howard set the theme for this "Athens of the West" with stately Neoclassical buildings of white granite walls and red-tile roofs, a look complemented by other architects.

Sproul Plaza★ *(Bancroft Way & Telegraph Ave.)* served as Ground Zero for protests during the Vietnam War, and today remains a lively gathering place. The filigreed bronze gateway at the plaza's north end, **Sather Gate★**, has marked the ceremonial entrance to campus since 1910. At its opposite end, the bookstores, coffeehouses and eateries of **Telegraph Avenue** throng with a continuous stream of students, bibliophiles, crafts-sellers and street people.

Designed to recall a Roman temple, **Doe Library★** oversees 8 million bound volumes and 90,000 periodicals. Adjacent **Bancroft Library** *(☎ 510-642-3781)* stores rare books, manuscripts, archival materials and the largest collection of Mark Twain's manuscripts and papers.

Modeled on the bell tower at St. Mark's Square in Venice, Italy, 307ft Sather Tower, known as **The Campanile**★★ **Kids** (☎ *510-642-5215*), supports four clock faces and a carillon of 61 English and French bells played in a fascinating, if deafening, performance three times daily (once on Sunday). On the eighth floor, arched windows frame panoramic **views**★★ of the surrounding campus.

EXCURSIONS

★**Mount Diablo State Park** – *North Gate Rd., 3mi east of Walnut Creek via Oak Grove Rd.* ☎ *925-837-2525. www.mdia.org.* The 360-degree **view**★★ from Diablo's 3,849ft summit encompasses more than 40,000sq mi, a panorama said to be surpassed only from atop Africa's Mount Kilimanjaro.

★★**Eugene O'Neill National Historic Site** – *Shuttles from Railroad Ave. & Church St., Danville.* ☎ *925-838-0249. www.nps.gov/euon. Visit by reservation only.* Modest **Tao House** was home for more than six years to playwright Eugene O'Neill (1888-1953), who wrote four of his greatest plays here, including *The Iceman Cometh* and *A Long Day's Journey into Night*. The only American to win the Nobel Prize for drama, O'Neill overcame tuberculosis, alcoholism and depression to transform American theater with his powerful, autobiographical dramas.

★**John Muir National Historic Site** – *Rte. 4, Martinez.* ☎ *925-228-8860. www.nps.gov/jomu.* This Italianate frame residence was home to legendary conservationist John Muir (1838-1914) from 1890 until his death. Muir wrote many influential books in the second-floor "scribble den," which still contains his chair and desk. A film on his life is shown in the visitor center.

MARIN COUNTY★★

Map p 319   Pacific Standard Time
Tourist Information ☎ 415-499-5000 or www.visitmarin.org

Roughly divided by a mountainous spine into an eastern corridor of upscale suburbs and bayside towns, and a far larger western portion of dairy farms, rural villages and extensive parklands, Marin County is conveniently situated for day trips at the north end of the Golden Gate Bridge.

The county is most celebrated for its federal, state and municipal parks. Among them is **Angel Island State Park**★ (☎ *415-435-1915*), San Francisco Bay's largest island, accessible by private boat or passenger ferry.

SIGHTS

★★**Marin Headlands** – *Alexander Ave. exit from northbound US-101; turn left, then right onto Barry Rd.* ☎ *415-331-1540.* These windswept coastal cliffs and hills anchor the northern end of the Golden Gate. Of strategic importance, the area was long owned by the US Army and thus was spared commercial development. Today part of Golden Gate National Recreation Area, the headlands are reached by **Conzelman Road**, which offers astounding **views**★★★ of San Francisco and the Golden Gate. The road passes abandoned military installations and ends near **Point Bonita Lighthouse**★. The **Marin Headlands Visitor Center**★ mounts excellent exhibits on natural history and human habitation of the headlands. Hiking trails thread the grassy slopes, connecting with others to Mount Tamalpais and Point Reyes.

★**Sausalito** – *4mi north of San Francisco via US-101.* ☎ *415-332-0505.* Developed as a resort in the 1870s, Sausalito has quaint, winding streets, attractive hillside neighborhoods and fine views. Thousands of visitors arrive on sunny days and weekends—many by ferry from San Francisco—to wander, window-shop and relax in boutiques and restaurants along **Bridgeway Boulevard**, the waterfront commercial district. The docklands of **Marinship** *(1mi north on Bridgeway)*, a shipbuilding center during World War II, now shelter a houseboat community. One converted warehouse contains the **Bay Model Visitor Center**★ *(2100 Bridgeway Blvd.;* ☎ *415-332-3870)*, a two-acre hydraulic scale model of the San Francisco Bay and Delta. The US Army Corps of Engineers uses it to study the effects of dredging, shoreline development and other projects on currents and ecology.

★★**Muir Woods National Monument** – **Kids** *Muir Woods Rd., 19mi north of San Francisco.* ☎ *415-388-2595. www.nps.gov/muwo.* Named for conservationist John Muir, this 560-acre plot of virgin forest is the largest unlogged grove of

© Robert Holmes

Point Bonita Lighthouse, Marin Headlands

coast redwoods within an hour's drive of San Francisco. Saved from the ax by its rugged canyon, the park contains 6mi of trails that wind along Redwood and Fern Creeks, and up the slopes of Mount Tamalpais. The level, paved **Main Trail** *(1mi)* loops from the visitor center through giants more than 1,000 years old, including the park's tallest tree, an unmarked 253ft specimen in **Bohemian Grove.**

★★**Mount Tamalpais State Park** – *Panoramic Hwy., 20mi north of San Francisco.* ☎ *415-388-2070.* The serpentine ascent of the 2,572ft east peak of Mount Tamalpais *(tam-ul-PIE-us),* locally known as "Mount Tam," is rewarded with sweeping **views**★★ embracing San Francisco, its bay and the Pacific Ocean. Hundreds of miles of trails lace the mountain's flanks, leading to reservoirs, remote cascades and the Pacific shore by way of adjacent open space preserves.

★★**Point Reyes National Seashore** – **Kids** *Bear Valley Rd. off Hwy. 1 at Olema, 40mi north of San Francisco.* ☎ *415-663-1092. www.nps.gov/pore.* This 102sq-mi park embraces white sand beaches, rocky headlands, windswept moors, salt marshes, lush forests and abundant wildlife. A product of tectonic shift, the cape is located where the Pacific Plate meets the North American Plate along an active San Andreas rift zone clearly marked by Bolinas Bay, Olema Valley and Tomales Bay.

The **Bear Valley Visitor Center**★ *(west of Hwy. 1 intersection)* contains exhibits on local ecology and history. Hikers on the adjacent **Earthquake Trail**★ *(.6mi)* can see a fence line that was shifted 16ft by the 1906 earthquake. A 22mi drive from the visitor center is **Point Reyes Lighthouse**★★, clinging to a rocky shelf on a 600ft precipice, 300 steps from a parking lot. Equipped with a Fresnel lens imported from France in 1870, the lighthouse offers sweeping **views**★★ of the Farallon Islands to the southwest and of magnificent winter whale migrations.

WINE COUNTRY★★

Michelin map 493 A 8   Pacific Standard Time
Tourist Information ☎ 707-226-7459 or www.insiders.com/winecountry

Within a two-hour drive north from San Francisco, Napa and Sonoma Counties thrive on the abundant sunshine, occasional fogs and fertile soil that produce grapes for some of North America's finest wines. A Hungarian immigrant, Agoston Haraszthy (1812-69), planted California first varietals for commercial vintages and founded the **Buena Vista Winery**★ *(18000 Old Winery Rd., Sonoma; ☎ 707-938-1266)* in 1857. Other vintners followed Haraszthy's lead, expanding the acreage under cultivation, experimenting with new varietals and production methods. The industry recovered from a plague of phylloxera that devastated vineyards in the late 19C, but a heavier blow fell when Prohibition (1919-33) curtailed production of all alcoholic beverages except sacramental or medicinal wines. Not until the early 1970s did the wine industry recover completely.

California wines have since experienced an enormous boom in popularity. Greatly improved quality has brought international fame to many vintages. More acreage is under the vine than ever before, as established wineries share the territory with hundreds of newer vintners. Following in their wake are fine restaurants, refined hotels and bed-and-breakfast inns, gourmet grocery stores (providing first-rate picnic supplies), and other tourist shops and services.

■ Napa Valley Wineries

From south to north, these are some popular stops for Napa Valley visitors:

The Hess Collection *(4411 Redwood Rd., Napa; ☎ 707-255-1144)*, in a 1903 stone winery, has an outstanding collection of modern US and European art.

Domaine Chandon *(1 California Dr., Yountville; ☎ 707-944-8844)* offers guided tours describing the *méthode champenoise* used in producing sparkling wines.

Robert Mondavi Winery *(7801 St. Helena Hwy., Oakville; ☎ 707-259-9463)*, a striking 1966 complex, set the tone for later wineries by emphasizing art, architecture and music.

St. Supéry *(8440 St. Helena Hwy., Rutherford; ☎ 707-963-4507)* houses a comprehensive **Wine Discovery Center** with in-depth displays on seasonal viticulture, the winemaking process, soil types and appellations.

Niebaum-Coppola *(1991 St. Helena Hwy., Rutherford; ☎ 707-968-1161)*, a massive chateau owned by Francis Ford Coppola, contains a museum of movies by the director of *The Godfather* trilogy.

Beringer Vineyards *(2000 Main St., St. Helena; ☎ 707-963-7115)*, the Napa Valley's oldest (1876) continuously operating winery, has extensive wine caves and the stately **Rhine House**, 17-room manse of founder Frederick Beringer.

Sterling Vineyards *(1111 Dunaweal Ln., south of Calistoga; ☎ 707-942-3344)*, a hilltop winery reached via aerial tramway, complements tours with fine views.

Clos Pegase *(1060 Dunaweal Ln., south of Calistoga; ☎ 707-942-4981)* was designed by Michael Graves (1987), who conceived a temple to wine and art.

© Robert Holmes

Grape Harvest, Domaine Chandon Winery

SIGHTS

** **Sonoma** – *Rte. 12.* ☎ *707-996-1090.* The Wine Country's most historically sig-nificant town, now with about 8,800 residents, Sonoma is built around the largest Mexican-era plaza in California. On June 14, 1846, the eight-acre public square was the scene of the **Bear Flag Revolt,** when American settlers raised a flag emblazoned with a bear, proclaiming California an independent republic; the future state was claimed as a US possession a month later. Around the plaza stand a venerable array of buildings under the auspices of **Sonoma State Historic Park***** (☎ *707-938-1519).* They include **San Francisco Solano Mission***** (1826), California's northernmost and final mission; **Sonoma Barracks*****, (1841), built for Mexican troops; the **Toscano Hotel,** a general store in the 1850s; and the 1840 **Blue Wing Inn,** a two-story adobe saloon and hotel. Also managed by the park is **Lachryma Montis***** *(north end of 3rd St. W.;* ☎ *707-938-9559),* retirement home of Mariano Vallejo (1807-90), founder of the pueblo of Sonoma. Briefly jailed during the Bear Flag Revolt, Vallejo later served in California's first state senate.

** **Jack London State Historic Park** – *2400 London Ranch Rd., Glen Ellen.* ☎ *707-938-5216. www.parks.sonoma.net.* Sprawling among peaceful hills, 80-acre Beauty Ranch was the Sonoma Valley home of writer Jack London (1876-1916) in his later life. London planned a four-story mansion of hewn red boulders and redwood logs that he called Wolf House; it burned just a few days before he and his wife, Charmian, were to move in. Charmian later built and resided at the **House of Happy Walls*****, now a museum furnished with memorabilia and furniture custom-made for Wolf House. A wooded trail leads to the Londons' hilltop graves and the impressive ruins of **Wolf House*****.

* **St. Helena** – *Rte. 29.* An excellent base for exploring the Napa Valley, this charm-ing town of 5,400 boasts fine restaurants along a picturesque main street. The **Robert Louis Stevenson Silverado Museum***** *(1490 Library Ln.;* ☎ *707-963-3757)* is devoted to the life and works of the Scottish author of *Treasure Island* and *Kid-napped,* whose Napa Valley honeymoon in 1880 is described in *The Silverado Squatters.* The **Culinary Institute of America at Greystone** *(2555 Main St.;* ☎ *707-963-7115)* occupies a massive stone building erected in 1889.

* **Calistoga** – *Rtes. 29 & 128.* ☎ *707-942-6333.* Founded in 1859, this resort town of 4,600 is famed for hot-spring spas. Tourists "take the waters," enjoy mud baths, ride hot-air balloons or simply enjoy the town's ambience. Privately owned **Old Faithful Geyser***** *(Tubbs Ln.;* ☎ *707-942-6463),* one of only three large geysers in the world to erupt on a dependable and frequent schedule, spews a superheated column of water 60ft in the air about every 40min.

NORTH COAST**

Michelin map 493 A 6, 7, 8   Pacific Standard Time
Tourist Information ☎ 415-394-5991 or www.redwoodempire.com

As early as 10,000 BC, tribes of Coast Miwok, Pomo and Yuki Indians hunted and fished along the densely wooded coast of Northern California. In spite of early English and Spanish claims, the first Europeans to colonize this coast were Russians—at Fort Ross, in 1812. The fort was abandoned in the 1830s. Gold was discovered on the Klamath and Smith Rivers in 1848; after the mid 19C, logging dominated the economy. As log-ging camps leveled vast tracts of coast redwoods from Marin County north to Oregon, sawmills and port facilities sprang up in the coastal towns of Mendocino, Arcata, Eureka and Crescent City. Since 1918, however, thousands of acres of old-growth redwoods, the tallest living things on earth, have been preserved in state and federal parks.
From the Golden Gate, scenic **Highway 1**** follows the coast north for 205mi, mostly via a winding, well-paved, two-lane road. In Humboldt County, it meets US-101, a route known from San Francisco to Oregon as the **Redwood Highway.**

SIGHTS

** **Fort Ross** – *Hwy. 1, 97mi north of San Francisco.* ☎ *707-847-3437.* Built high on a grassy promontory above a sheltered cove, flanked by forested mountains, Fort Ross reigned as Russia's easternmost outpost for nearly three decades after its founding in 1812. Russian and Aleut colonists hunted sea otters for their pelts and farmed to support Alaskan colonies. The stockaded fort was abandoned after the sea-otter population declined in the mid-1830s. Deeded to the State of Cali-fornia in 1906, it has been partially restored with an Orthodox chapel, officials' quarters and two blockhouses.

★★ Mendocino – *Hwy. 1, 72mi north of Fort Ross.* ☎ *707-961-6300.* Seated on a foggy headland where the Big River meets the Pacific, this picturesque Victorian village appears little changed from its heyday as a lumber town in the late-19C. Favoring New England-style architecture, it has a "skyline" of clapboard houses with steep gabled roofs, wooden water towers, a Gothic Revival-style **Presbyterian church** (1868) and the false-fronted **Mendocino Hotel** (1878). Mendocino's prosperity declined in the 1920s; in the 1960s artists discovered the tranquil atmosphere and idyllic setting. Hollywood directors have shot numerous films here. Enveloping the town, **Mendocino Headlands State Park★★** *(☎ 707-937-5397)* preserves marvelous **views★★** of fissure-riddled rocks and sea caves.

★★ Humboldt Redwoods State Park – *South entrance on US-101, 6mi north of Garberville.* ☎ *707-946-2409.* Established along the Eel River in 1921, this 80sq-mi park contains a spectacular reserve of coast redwoods best seen along the **Avenue of the Giants★★**, which runs 29mi through its heart, paralleling US-101 and the Eel River. A nature trail through **Founder's Grove★★** begins at the Founder's Tree, once considered the world's tallest (364ft before the top 17ft broke off). The world's largest remaining virgin stand of redwoods is the **Rockefeller Forest★★**, encompassing 16sq mi of the Bull Creek watershed west of the Eel River. Hiking trails probe the sublime depths of these venerable groves.

★ Eureka – *US-101.* ☎ *707-443-5097.* The largest Pacific coastal community in the US north of San Francisco, this town of 25,600 grew as a shipping hub for minerals and lumber in the mid- to late 19C. Buildings in its 10-block waterfront **historic district** *(2nd & 3rd Sts. between E & M Sts.)* include the ornate Victorian **Carson Mansion★★** *(2nd & M Sts.),* a three-story redwood mansion built in 1886 for a lumber magnate.

★★ Redwood National and State Parks – *Mainly along US-101 between Orick & Crescent City.* ☎ *707-464-6101. www.nps.gov/redw.* With majestic redwood groves and 33mi of beaches, this 165sq-mi expanse joins three venerable state parks—**Prairie Creek Redwoods** *(☎ 707-488-2171),* **Del Norte Coast Redwoods** *(☎ 707-458-3310)* and **Jedediah Smith Redwoods** *(☎ 707-458-3310)*—within the jurisdiction of Redwood National Park. The parks are cooperatively managed and casually linked by a network of highways and roads, few of them designed for sightseeing. There are two visitor centers: the **Redwood Information Center** *(US-101, 1mi south of Orick;* ☎ *707-488-3461)* and **Park Headquarters** *(1111 2nd St., Crescent City;* ☎ *707-464-6101).*

Highlights include the **Lady Bird Johnson Grove★★** and **Tall Trees Grove★**, both in the Redwood Creek watershed. The latter contains a 367.8ft-high **tree★**, discovered by a National Geographic Society scientist in 1963 and determined to be the world's tallest. The Newton B. Drury Scenic Parkway passes through **Prairie Creek Meadows** with its herds of grazing Roosevelt elk. Home Creek debouches into the Pacific through **Fern Canyon★**, a narrow ravine walled with lush ferns.

Chandelier Drive-Thru Tree (1942) Near Leggett, Redwood Highway

SOUTH BAY★

Map p 319 Pacific Standard Time
Tourist Information ☎ 408-283-8833 or www.sanjose.org

California's third-largest city, center of the high-tech industry in the US, **San Jose** sprawls southward from San Francisco Bay. Founded as a farming pueblo in 1777, the city was state capital for several months in 1849; but agriculture remained the chief industry until electronics factories began to replace orchards in the mid-20C. The change was so pervasive that by the late 1960s, San Jose began to define itself as the "capital of Silicon Valley." Such computer giants as IBM, Apple and Hewlett Packard developed facilities in the city and in neighboring communities.

San Jose's revitalized downtown, bustling with high-tech prosperity, retains a mix of stately old buildings and modern skyscrapers, while its suburban neighborhoods overspread the valley floor along tree-lined streets. Today with a population of 861,284, San Jose ranks as the 11th-largest city in the US.

Silicon Valley extends north through suburbs like Santa Clara, Sunnyvale, Palo Alto and Menlo Park. Its academic hub is Stanford University, snug against the foothills of the Coast Range.

SIGHTS

★★ Filoli – *Cañada Rd., Woodside, 13mi north of Palo Alto.* ☎ *650-364-8300. www.filoli.org.* Built in 1916 for Empire Mine owner William Bourne (1857-1936), this elegant 700-acre estate derives its name from a credo Bourne admired: *Fight for a just cause; love your fellow man; live a good life.* The modified Georgian Revival **mansion★★**, designed by Willis Polk, is furnished with 17-18C Irish and English furniture. The 16-acre **gardens★★★**, designed by Bruce Porter and Isabella Wood in Italian and French style, are a marvel of horticultural ingenuity. Several distinct theme gardens blend formal and natural elements to create an ever-changing progression of scenery, with colorful blooms through every season. Volunteers guide tours of the house and gardens.

★★ Stanford University – *Main Quadrangle on Serra St., Palo Alto.* ☎ *650-723-2560.* Railroad magnate Leland Stanford (1824-93) and his wife, Jane, established this private institution in memory of their late son. Now a leading academic and research center with an enrollment of 14,000, the campus—a creation of architect Charles Allerton Coolidge and landscape architect Frederick Law Olmsted—is noted for gracious Romanesque buildings shaded by eucalyptus, bay and palm trees.

The historic heart of campus is the **Main Quadrangle★**, a tiled, cloistered courtyard bordered by colonnaded buildings. Its **Memorial Church★★**, built in 1903 by Jane Stanford, is famed for its Byzantine-style mosaics, stained glass and 7,777-pipe organ. **Hoover Tower★** (☎ 650-723-2053), a 285ft landmark campanile with a 35-bell carillon, offers views over campus from its observation deck.

Iris & B. Gerald Cantor Center for Visual Arts★ *(Lomita Dr. & Museum Way;* ☎ *650-723-4177)* houses 20,000 pieces of ancient to contemporary sculpture, paintings and crafts from six continents. The adjacent **Rodin Sculpture Garden★** contains 20 large-scale bronze casts by famed French sculptor Auguste Rodin, whose works also stand freely around campus.

★★ The Tech Museum of Innovation – Kids *201 S. Market St., San Jose.* ☎ *408-294-8324.* This interactive exhibition of cutting-edge technology encourages curiosity characteristic of Silicon Valley's techno-tinkerers. Housed in a domed, mango-colored building, the Tech entertains all ages, but mainly courts young people with playful participatory exhibits in such fields as space exploration, communications, microelectronics, robotics and biotechnology.

★ Rosicrucian Egyptian Museum – *1342 Naglee Ave., San Jose.* ☎ *408-947-3636.* Set amid a complex of Egyptian and Moorish-style buildings in Rosicrucian Park, this treasury of artifacts is modeled after the Temple of Amon at Karnak. Among the 5,000 pieces displayed are pottery, jewelry, glass, mummified human and animal remains, sarcophagi, painted coffins and a full-scale reproduction of a **Middle Kingdom Rock Tomb★**.

Winchester Mystery House – Kids *525 S. Winchester Blvd., San Jose.* ☎ *408-247-2101.* This rambling, 160-room mansion is the legacy of Sarah Winchester, heir to the Winchester arms fortune. In superstitious hope of prolonging her life by appeasing ghosts of people killed with Winchester rifles, she compulsively expanded the house from 1884 to her death in 1922, creating a hodgepodge of rooms and hallways, secret passages, and doors and stairways that go nowhere.

MONTEREY AND BIG SUR★★★

Michelin map 493 A 9   Pacific Standard Time
Tourist Information ☎ 831-626-1424 or www.GoMonterey.com

Sebastián Vizcaíno sailed into Monterey Bay in 1602, his enthusiastic response to the harbor enhanced by the lack of anchorages along the Big Sur coastline that he had just traversed. Not until 1770 did Spain found the presidio, chapel and pueblo that became its California capital. Padre Junípero Serra subsequently moved his mission a few miles south to Carmel, away from the influence of Monterey.

On July 7, 1846, a few weeks after the Bear Flag Revolt in Sonoma *(p 323)*, the US officially seized California at Monterey. But after Sierra gold was discovered in 1848, Monterey's political and economic preeminence gave way to San Francisco.

In the 1880s, Chinese and Italian fishermen discovered the wealth of Monterey Bay and built a port and cannery town of national significance, until harvests were depleted in the 1950s. In its heyday, industry was focused at Cannery Row, a raucous industrial strip described by author John Steinbeck as "a poem, a stink, a grating noise." Tourism is now the mainstay of the economy of Monterey, a city of 31,000; Cannery Row has been reborn with shops, restaurants and an aquarium.

Carmel, which developed as an artists' community near the old mission in the early 20C, is a genteel resort town. It is a perfect foil to historic Monterey and rugged Big Sur, whose primeval beauties extend 90mi down the California coast to the imposing hilltop estate known as Hearst Castle.

SIGHTS

★★ **Monterey State Historic Park** – *Headquarters at Pacific House, Custom House Plaza.* ☎ *831-649-7118. www.mbay.net/~mshp.* Monterey's compact central district is ideally explored on the **Path of History Walking Tour★**, a 2mi route blazed by bronze discs embedded in sidewalks, and described in maps and pamphlets available at an information center at **Pacific House.** This two-story adobe, built in 1847 to house US troops, also contains a history museum.

Fisherman's Wharf★ is lined with shops and cafes. Adjacent is broad **Custom House Plaza★★.** At **Stanton Center,** a theater presents a film outlining Monterey history. The **Maritime Museum of Monterey★** *(☎ 831-373-2469)* exhibits model ships, navigational devices and nautical paraphernalia from 300 years of seafaring. The adobe **Custom House★** served port authorities from 1827 to 1867.

The two-story **Larkin House★★** *(Calle Principal & Pearl St.),* built in 1834, melded elements of New England architecture—including high ceilings, a hipped roof and central hallway—with the local adobe motif, giving rise to the Monterey Colonial style of architecture. The **Cooper-Molera Complex★★** *(Pearl St. at Munras Ave. & Polk St.)* features a large home whose separate wings—an adobe section and a two-story Victorian—contrast Hispanic and Anglo cultures.

★★ **Monterey Bay Aquarium** – ▣ Kids ▥ *West end of Cannery Row.* ☎ *831-648-4800. www.mbayaq.org.* Built out over the water in a revamped cannery building, this modern aquarium presents the rich marine life of Monterey Bay—focal point of the **Monterey Bay National Marine Sanctuary,** North America's largest offshore natural preserve. With more than 300,000 animals and plants of nearly 600 species, the aquarium represents the full range of Monterey Bay habitats, from coastal wetlands and tide pools to deep sea.

The west wing houses the **Nearshore Habitats** exhibits, including a touch pool for fast-gliding bat rays, an open-air aviary and the 28ft-high **kelp forest★** tank, where swaying seaweed provides a rich marine home. **Outer Bay★** habitats in the east wing showcase the inhabitants of the open ocean, highlighted by an enormous **ocean tank★★** where tuna, green sea turtles, sharks, barracudas and other species swim. **Mysteries of the Deep★★** displays up to 60 species collected from the dark waters of Monterey Canyon, 3,300ft deep.

★ **17-Mile Drive** – *Access via the Carmel Gate (N. San Antonio Ave. off Ocean Ave.) or the Pacific Grove Gate (Sunset Dr., Pacific Grove).* ☎ *831-624-6669.* Celebrated for exquisite coastline views, this private toll road winds through exclusive estates and the 8,000-acre Del Monte Forest. Turnouts offer spectacular vistas, including **Lone Cypress,** a classic landmark of the Monterey Peninsula. Golfers from around the world play the renowned links at Pebble Beach and Spyglass Hill.

★★ **Carmel** – *Hwy. 1, 5mi south of Monterey.* ☎ *831-624-2522.* A delightful square mile of carefully tended cottages beneath a canopy of pine, oak and cypress, Carmel began to attract artists and writers in the very early 20C. While strict ordinances preserve residential charm, a painstakingly quaint commercial district of upscale boutiques, galleries, inns and restaurants nestles around Ocean, 6th and 7th Avenues *(between Junipero Ave. & Monte Verde St.).* Steep Ocean Avenue meets the turquoise waters of Carmel Bay at **Carmel City Beach★★**, a wide sweep of white sand bounded on the south by rocky Point Lobos and on the north by the clifftop greens of the Pebble Beach Golf Club.

★★ **San Carlos Borromeo de Carmelo Mission** – *Rio Rd. & Lasuen Dr.* ☎ *831-624-3600.* Headquarters of the mission chain in its expansive early years, the Carmel Mission resonates with the vision of Padre Junípero Serra, whose remains are interred in the sanctuary. Founded in 1771 when Serra moved his neophytes from Monterey, this mission prospered under his care and that of his successor, Padre Fermin Lasuén, who rebuilt the original adobe chapel with sandstone in 1782. Upon Lasuén's death in 1803, mission headquarters were transferred to Santa Barbara. Restored in 1931, the chapel preserves original 18C paintings and a statue of the Virgin Our Lady of Bethlehem that Serra brought from Mexico in 1769. The rebuilt padres' quarters include a period library, kitchen and residence halls.

★★ **Tor House** – *Stewart Way off Scenic Rd., 1.2mi south of Ocean Ave.* ☎ *831-624-1813.* Overlooking Carmel Bay, this enchanting stone complex embodies the spirit of its builder, poet Robinson Jeffers (1887-1962), who settled in Carmel in 1914. Guided tours offer a peek at the furnished rooms, including the whimsical Hawk Tower, which contains Jeffers' desk and chair, and the bedroom where he died.

★★ **Point Lobos State Reserve** – *Hwy. 1, 3.5mi south of Carmel.* ☎ *831-624-4909.* This small but dramatic peninsula defines the southern end of Carmel Bay. Early Spanish explorers named the site *Punta de Los Lobos Marinos* ("point of the sea wolves") because of the "howling" of resident sea lions. Deeded to the state in 1933, the site comprises 1,250 acres, including 750 submerged acres of the first US underwater reserve, and several miles of coastal trails.

★★★ **Big Sur** – *Hwy. 1 between Carmel and San Simeon.* This rugged coastline, extending 90mi south from Carmel, is celebrated for its charismatic, wild beauty. A precipitous coastal wall, plunging 4,000ft to the sea, thwarted settlement by the Spanish, who called it *El Pais Grande del Sur*—"the Big Country to the South." Mid-19C homesteaders trickled into narrow valleys to ranch and log redwoods. Completion of the highway in 1937 opened the area to visitors. Small resorts and state parks now employ many residents; artists and writers still seek their muses.

Traveling south from Carmel, the concrete-arch **Bixby Creek Bridge**, built in 1932, is one of the 10 highest single-span bridges in the world. **Point Sur State Historic Park** preserves an 1889 stone lighthouse built 272ft above the surf on a volcanic rock connected to the mainland by a sandbar. Near the **village of Big Sur** *(23mi south of Carmel)*, in the forested Big Sur River valley, **Andrew Molera State Park** and **Pfeiffer Big Sur State Park★** offer coastal vistas and access. Four miles south, the venerable **Nepenthe★** bar and restaurant boasts sweeping **views★★★** from its cliffside terraces 800ft above the ocean.

Roman Pool, Hearst Castle

***Hearst Castle** – *Rte. 1, 98mi south of Monterey. Visit by reservation only.* ☎ *805-927-2020. www.hearstcastle.org.* Overlooking the Pacific Ocean from atop a Santa Lucia Mountain crest near the village of San Simeon, this 127-acre estate and the opulent mansion crowning it embody the flamboyance of William Randolph Hearst. It was eclectically designed and lavishly embellished with the newsman's world-class collection of Mediterranean art and antiques. Hearst's father, George, purchased this ranch in 1865. In 1919, William hired architect Julia Morgan to create a "bungalow" that over 28 years grew from a modest residence to "The Enchanted Hill." Morgan designed a Mediterranean Revival-style main house, **Casa Grande**, and three guest houses. From twin Spanish Colonial towers with arabesque grillwork and Belgian carillon bells, to Etruscan colonnades that complement the Greco-Roman temple facade of the **Neptune Pool★**, and gold-inlaid Venetian glass tiles of the indoor **Roman Pool★**, the design emerged as a mélange that defies categorization.

The 65,000sq-ft main house contains 115 rooms, including 38 bedrooms, 41 bathrooms, two libraries, a billiards room, beauty salon and theater. All feature Hearst's art holdings, including silver, 16C tapestries, terra-cotta sculpture and ancient Greek vases that line the shelves of a 5,000-volume library.

Five different tours are offered, all lasting 2hrs and departing from a visitor center at the foot of the hill. Shuttle buses climb 10min to the castle, with spectacular views en route. As they wait, visitors may take in a 40min film.

EXCURSIONS

National Steinbeck Center – *1 Main St., Salinas, 17mi east of Monterey.* ☎ *831-796-3833. www.steinbeck.org.* Multimedia exhibits, written excerpts and film clips depict themes and settings of John Steinbeck's novels, stories, scripts and journalistic dispatches. More than 30,000 manuscripts, letters, first editions, photos, oral histories and other mementos are preserved.

Born in Salinas, Steinbeck (1902-68) grew up amidst the communities and characters that animated his greatest stories and novels, including *Tortilla Flat* (1935), *The Grapes of Wrath* (1939), *The Red Pony* (1945), *Cannery Row* (1945) and *East of Eden* (1952). Although he won Pulitzer and Nobel prizes, his sympathetic depiction of local brothels, labor organizers and ne'er-do-wells embarrassed and antagonized the Salinas establishment.

*★**Pinnacles National Monument** – *Rte. 146, 22mi south of Salinas.* ☎ *831-389-4485. www.nps.gov/pinn.* The distinctive ridgetop rock formations of this 37sq-mi park are the remnants of a volcano formed 23 million years ago by tectonic plate movement in the San Andreas rift zone. Several trails, including the **Juniper Canyon Trail★** *(2.4mi round-trip),* climb steeply into the Pinnacles.

Santa Fe Area

Taos Pueblo

Known as the "Land of Enchantment," northern New Mexico is a cultural mélange of ancient and modern Indian and Spanish, American pioneer and high-technology influences. The chosen home of painter Georgia O'Keeffe and author D.H. Lawrence delivers stark adobe architecture in brilliant contrast to strikingly blue skies, towering mountains and precipitous gorges.

Though not the largest city, the state capital of Santa Fe is considered New Mexico's cultural and tourism hub. The former Spanish capital, founded in 1609, is home to outstanding museums, galleries, restaurants and summer opera. Santa Fe's closely monitored adobe architecture nestles around a central plaza that sees a year-round commerce between native artisans and international visitors.

Santa Fe is an hour's drive north of modern Albuquerque, an hour's drive south of the rustic mountain art town of Taos. East is the historic Santa Fe Trail town of Las Vegas. West is the domain of the Navajo, Zuni and Jicarillo Apache tribes, where Gallup and Farmington are the largest towns.

New Mexico is isolated by extreme geography. The Rocky Mountains begin here, dividing the Great Plains from the southern desert and extending thousands of miles north into Canada. Seven life zones exist in the state, at elevations ranging from 2,800ft in the Rio Grande valley to 13,161ft at Wheeler Peak, near Taos.

A thousand years ago, the ancient pueblo civilization of the Anasazi Indians spawned a sophisticated trade network. Ruins of their culture can be seen at such far-flung sites as Bandelier, Pecos and Aztec Ruins National Monuments and Chaco Culture National Historical Park. Today's nearest equivalents are the primitive pueblo cultures at Acoma Pueblo, west of Albuquerque, and at Taos Pueblo, still occupied by 200 residents who live without electricity or running water. Nineteen Indian pueblo communities call New Mexico home today.

Spanish explorers first visited in 1540 when Francisco Vasquéz de Coronado and his expedition searched for gold from the legendary Seven Cities of Cibola. Although they failed to find riches, the resourceful Spanish left Catholic missionaries who helped assert a claim to what is now New Mexico by the end of the 16C. Long-distance Spanish control extended well into the 19C. The region was ceded to the US at the conclusion of the Mexican War in 1848.

ADDRESS BOOK

Please see explanation on p 64.

Staying in the Santa Fe Area

Inn of the Anasazi – *113 Washington Ave., Santa Fe NM.* ✗ ♿ 🅿 ☎ *505-988-3030. www.innoftheanasazi.com. 59 rooms.* **$$$** With traditional beamed ceilings of peeled log, sculpted stairways and intricately patterned pillows, the inn is a rich blend of Southwestern culture. Indian baskets and cacti adorn a lobby with a warm fireplace. The library houses books on local history and artwork.

The Bishop's Lodge – *Bishop's Lodge Rd, Santa Fe NM.* ✗ ♿ 🅿 🏊 ☎ *505-983-6377. www.bishopslodge.com. 90 rooms.* **$$** Although just 3.5mi north of downtown Santa Fe, this resort is secluded in a private valley. Within its 400 acres of piñon-juniper forest, guests may enjoy horseback riding, hiking, tennis and skeet-shooting. Lodges have bright interiors and Southwestern touches.

Fechin Inn – *227 Paseo del Pueblo Norte, Taos NM.* ♿ 🅿 ☎ *505-751-1000. www.fechin-inn.com. 85 rooms.* **$$** Inspired by Russian-born painter Nikolai Fechin (1881-1955), this new inn is a gallery of his prints and lithographs, and a tribute to his whimsical wood carvings. Window frames, mantels and beams recall the sunbursts and vines of the artist's own home, now the adjacent Fechin Institute, on the six-acre estate.

Hotel Santa Fe – *1501 Paseo de Peralta, Santa Fe NM.* ✗ ♿ 🅿 🏊 ☎ *505-982-1200. www.hotelsantafe.com. 128 rooms.* **$$** Owned by the Picuris Pueblo, the only Native American hotel in Santa Fe features native artwork and architecture. The three-story, pueblo-style building features ceremonial dance performances and storytellers who immerse guests in Picuris culture.

The Historic Taos Inn – *125 Paseo del Pueblo Norte, Taos NM.* ✗ ♿ 🅿 🏊 ☎ *505-758-2233. www.taosinn.com. 36 rooms.* **$** Beginning in 1895, Dr. T. Paul Martin, Taos County's first (and, for a time, only) physician, rented many of the small adobe houses in this complex to artists and writers. Rooms showcase kiva fireplaces and bedspreads loomed by Indian weavers. **Doc Martin's** restaurant, once his waiting room, serves plates of tamales and blue-corn enchiladas.

Las Palomas – *119 Park Ave., Santa Fe NM.* ♿ 🅿 ☎ *505-988-4455. www.laspalomas.com. 33 rooms.* **$** Guests at the casitas of Las Palomas also are welcome at the nearby Eldorado Hotel, a large resort with such amenities as a rooftop pool. But Las Palomas' rambling courtyards, trickling fountains and gardens are much more intimate. Odd-sized doorways and uneven walls add genuine adobe charm, and breakfast is delivered to each room in a basket.

La Posada de Albuquerque – *125 2nd St. NW, Albuquerque NM.* ✗ ♿ 🅿 ☎ *505-242-9090. www.placestostay.com/albq-laposada. 101 rooms.* **$** The only historic hotel in Albuquerque has a two-story lobby of arches, balconies and wall murals, centered on a tiled fountain. New Mexico's tallest building when it opened in 1939 on the site of a livery stable, it has been fully restored.

Dining in the Santa Fe Area

Coyote Cafe – *132 W. Water St., Santa Fe NM.* ☎ *505-983-1615.* **$$$ Creative Southwestern.** Most folks agree, the original Coyote Cafe is worth the hype. Here in Mark Miller's kitchen, dishes like duck-confit tacos and *chipotle*-grilled quail were first concocted. Prices are lower at the rooftop cantina, where prickly-pear margaritas are the drink of choice. A shop sells sauces, stews and T-shirts.

Fred's Place – *223 Paseo del Pueblo Sur, Taos NM.* ☎ *505-758-0514.* **$$ Mexican.** This tiny hangout is always busy. A ceiling mural depicts aspects of heaven and hell. The menu offers burritos, enchiladas and tacos.

Maria's New Mexican Kitchen – *555 W. Cordova Rd., Santa Fe NM.* ☎ *505-983-7929.* **$$ Mexican.** Strolling mariachi troubadours serenade diners as cooks craft handmade tortillas on an open grill. Servers carry platters of burritos and tacos with Spanish rice; the tamale plate is a pork and vegetable combo served in a cornhusk. The menu lists more than 100 varieties of margaritas.

The Shed – *113 1/2 E. Palace Ave., Santa Fe NM.* ☎ *505-982-9030.* **$ Southwestern.** Classic New Mexican fare—rice, beans and blue-corn tortillas—is served in the rooms and patio of a 1692 hacienda, its walls painted with multicolored flowers on a rich purple background.

SANTA FE★★★

Map p 335   Mountain Standard Time
Population 67,879
Tourist Information ☎ 505-984-6760 or www.santafe.org

Home to Pueblo Indians for more than 1,000 years, Santa Fe was a Spanish territorial capital at the beginning of the 17C, an American frontier city in the 19C, a state capital and center for high-tech research in the mid-20C. Now, as the 21C begins, it has coalesced into a world-renowned center for the arts, cuisine and shopping, its diverse elements and heritage maintaining their unique characters while providing a compelling cultural blend.

Distinctive adobe and Mission-style architecture spread across the foothills of the Sangre de Cristo Mountains at 7,000ft elevation. Five remarkable collections are administered by the Museum of New Mexico, there are several more museums and a wealth of historic churches and other buildings. Art galleries and shops surround the historic Plaza and wind down Canyon Road, once a trail leading to the Pecos Indian pueblos. Visitors make special trips for the annual Santa Fe Opera and impressive Indian Markets.

Historical Notes – Colonists from Spain, including missionaries, founded the first territorial capital in the Española Valley, north of Santa Fe, in 1598. Eleven years later, Don Pedro de Peralta established Santa Fe as the Spanish Crown's seat of power north of the Rio Grande. By 1610, the Plaza and Palace of the Governors had been constructed; the city would become the oldest continuous seat of government in the US. That same year, the Mission Church of San Miguel was built. By 1617, 14,000 "heathen" Indians had been converted to Catholicism and the church was reckoned a political force.

With the opening of the Santa Fe Trail in 1821, US westward expansion led adventurous Americans from Missouri to the trade hub of Santa Fe, though many continued to California. Briefly occupied by the Confederacy during the

Indian Market, Palace of the Governors

Civil War, Santa Fe rebounded strongly. It was attracting artists as early as 1878-81, when Territorial Governor Lew Wallace scribed his novel, *Ben Hur*, while ensconced in the Palace of the Governors.

Since 1909, the "Palace" has been run as a history museum by the **Museum of New Mexico** *(113 Lincoln Ave.; ☎ 505-476-5060; www.nmculture.org)*. Four other Santa Fe museums are under the same umbrella. The Museum of Fine Arts and Georgia O'Keeffe Museum are downtown near the Palace of the Governors, adjacent to the Plaza. The Museum of Indian Arts and Culture and Museum of International Folk Art are 2mi southeast, on Museum Plaza *(Camino Lejo)*.

SIGHTS

★★ **The Plaza** – *Flanked by Palace Ave., Old Santa Fe Trail, San Francisco St. & Lincoln Ave.* ✗ ♿ 🅿 *www.santafe.org.* Faced on its north by the Palace of the Governors, this National Historic Landmark was the original city center of Santa Fe as a Spanish colonial outpost in the 1600s. It was the focus of a Pueblo Indian revolt in 1680 and of the recapture of the city by the Spanish in 1692-93. Later, it was the end of the Santa Fe Trail for American travelers heading west in the 19C. Preservation laws today protect surrounding historic adobe and Mission-style architecture; these buildings are home to shops, galleries, restaurants and hotels.

★★★ Palace of the Governors – *105 W. Palace Ave., north side of Plaza.* ✕ ♿ 🄿 ☎ *505-476-5100. www.nmculture.org.* This low, flat-roofed hacienda was the original home and seat of power for early Spanish governors. Built in 1610, it is one of the oldest occupied buildings in the US. A collection of 17,000 objects is displayed in rooms surrounding a courtyard. Exhibits depict Santa Fe history, from Spanish Colonial through the Anglo frontier era and up to today. Outside beneath the portico, Indian craftsmen and artisans spread wares for sale.

★★ The Museum of Fine Arts – *107 W. Palace Ave., opposite the Palace of the Governors.* ♿ ☎ *505-476-5072. www.nmculture.org.* In a Pueblo Revival-style building a block northwest of the Plaza, the museum has a collection of 20,000 pieces. Contemporary and historic New Mexican art is presented, including works of the Taos Society and Cinco Pintores. The museum also has an extensive photography exhibit.

★★ Georgia O'Keeffe Museum – *217 Johnson St., three blocks northwest of Plaza.* ✕ ♿ ☎ *505-995-0785. www.okeeffemuseum.org.* Here is the largest collection of paintings, pastels, watercolors and sculptures by Georgia O'Keeffe (1887-1986). O'Keeffe was fascinated by the textures created by light and color in the landscape of New Mexico, her adopted home from 1949 until her death. Works displayed include her signature flowers and bleached bones, as well as abstracts, nudes, landscapes, cityscapes and still lifes.

Jimson Weed (1932) by Georgia O'Keeffe

© Wendy McEahern/The Georgia O'Keeffe Foundation

★★ Cathedral of St. Francis of Assisi – *Cathedral Place, one block east of Plaza.* ♿ ☎ *505-982-5619.* The first church between Durango, Mexico, and St. Louis, Missouri, to attain cathedral status was intended to resemble great cathedrals of Europe. Unlike other local churches, it is not built in adobe style. Archbishop Jean-Baptiste Lamy recruited Italian masons to assist in the 1869-86 construction of the French Romanesque structure, which overlooks the east side of the Plaza.

In a niche in the north chapel wall is a wooden statue, "La Conquistadora," believed to be the oldest representation of the Madonna in the US. Brought to Santa Fe in 1625, it was rescued from an earlier church during the 1680 Pueblo Rebellion and returned 12 years later as a symbol of Spain's reconquest of the city.

★ The Institute of American Indian Arts Museum – *108 Cathedral Pl., opposite St. Francis Cathedral.* ♿ ☎ *505-988-6211. www.iaiancad.org.* Home of The National Collection of Contemporary Indian Art, this provocative museum presents works of Indians and native Alaskans. Some 6,500 works—paintings, sculptures, ceramics, jewelry, costumes, graphics and photographs—express modern lifestyles.

★★ Loretto (Our Lady of Light) Chapel – *211 Old Santa Fe Trail, one block south of Plaza.* ♿ ☎ *505-982-0092.* Modeled after the Sainte-Chapelle church in Paris and dedicated in 1878, this chapel is noted for its famous spiral staircase. Leading to the choir loft, this staircase makes two complete 360-degree turns with no nails or other visible support. Legend claims it was built by a mysterious carpenter who appeared astride a donkey, in answer to the prayers of the Sisters of Loretto.

■ The Eight Northern Pueblos

Ancestral Pueblo people first occupied northern New Mexico more than 1,000 years ago. Today, eight independent pueblos are well known for their distinctive, traditional, handmade arts and crafts. Several offer glimpses of their historic past to visitors; the public is generally welcome to view special feast days, including traditional Indian dances scheduled annually at some pueblos. At other times, ceremonial activities are planned with shorter notice to take advantage of natural astronomical, weather or climatic cycles. Often, however, pueblo communities keep their spiritual practices entirely private, with no visitors allowed.

The **Eight Northern Indian Pueblos** have a formal council *(San Juan Pueblo; ☎ 505-852-4265; www.indianpueblos.org)* that provides information on the following pueblo villages:

Tesuque Pueblo – *US 84/285, 10mi north of Santa Fe; ☎ 505-983-2667.* Listed on the National Register of Historic Places, Tesuque has adobe structures dating from AD 1250. The main enterprise is a three-pronged business venture comprised of a casino and flea market adjacent to the Santa Fe Opera.

Pojoaque Pueblo – *US-84/285, 12mi north of Santa Fe; ☎ 505-455-3460.* The tribe operates the **Poeh Cultural Museum** *(☎ 505-455-3334)*, a shop offering crafts by 800 Native American artisans, and a casino-hotel.

Nambe Pueblo – *Rte. 503, 20mi north of Santa Fe; ☎ 505-455-2036.* Inhabited since 1300, this village is known for its stone sculptures, black-and-red carved pottery, textiles and beadwork.

Buffalo Dance Performer, San Ildefonso Pueblo

© Robert Frerck/Odyssey

San Ildefonso Pueblo – *Off Rte. 502, 24mi northwest of Santa Fe; ☎ 505-455-3549.* The village is known for its black-on-black matté pottery, as well as for the black, red and polychrome pottery sold by individual artisans.

Santa Clara Pueblo – *Rte. 30, 2mi south of Española; ☎ 505-753-7326.* Descended from ancestral cliff dwellers, villagers are known for their weaving, black pottery and beadwork. Several structures dating from AD 1250-1577 can be seen 11mi west of here at the **Puye Cliff Dwellings**—reached by descending staircases and ladders from a 7,000ft mesa top. A tribal permit is required.

San Juan Pueblo – *US-84/285, 5mi north of Española; ☎ 505-852-4400.* The largest Tewa-speaking pueblo has over 2,000 members. The village operates a casino and the **O'ke Oweenge Arts and Crafts Cooperative** *(☎ 505-852-2372)*.

Picuris Pueblo – *Rte. 518, 33mi south of Taos; ☎ 505-587-2519 or ☎ 505-587-2957.* Visitors need a permit to visit the San Lorenzo Mission and nearby pueblo ruins, including a 700-year-old kiva.

Taos Pueblo – *2mi north of Taos Plaza; ☎ 505-758-1028.* The oldest and best-known northern New Mexico pueblo is described on p 340 .

Mission of San Miguel de Santa Fe – *401 Old Santa Fe Trail at E. De Vargas St., 3 blocks south of Plaza.* ☎ *505-983-3974.* Established in 1610, this old church has been oft-remodeled since it was rebuilt in 1710. A Mexican sculpture of its patron saint, St. Michael, dates from the 17C.

New Mexico State Capitol – *Paseo de Peralta & Old Santa Fe Trail.* ⓗ 🅿 ☎ *505-986-4589. www.legis.state.nm.us.* The only round capitol building in the US was built in 1966 in the shape of a Pueblo *zia*, or Circle of Life. It symbolizes the four directions, four winds, four seasons and four sacred obligations. Some 6.5 acres of gardens surround the building.

El Santuario de Guadalupe – *Agua Fria & Guadalupe Sts., four blocks west of Plaza.* ☎ *505-988-2027.* The church dates from 1776 and is the oldest US shrine to the Virgin of Guadalupe, patroness of Mexico. A famous oil painting, *Our Lady of Guadalupe,* signed by José de Alzíbar in 1783, is inside.

Cristo Rey Church – *Canyon Rd. & Camino Cabra.* ⓗ 🅿 ☎ *505-983-8528.* This imposing adobe church was built only in 1940. Stone reredos or altar screens, dating from 1761, were taken from St. Francis Cathedral.

Museum of Indian Arts and Culture – 🄺🄸🄳🅂 *710 Camino Lejo.* ⓗ 🅿 ☎ *505-827-6344. www.nmculture.org.* Some 70,000 Pueblo, Navajo and Apache artifacts, including pottery, basketry, jewelry, clothing and rugs, highlight the cultural history and lifestyles of New Mexican tribes. The museum was established to showcase the research of the adjoining Laboratory of Anthropology, founded in 1931 by John D. Rockefeller Jr.

Museum of International Folk Art – 🄺🄸🄳🅂 *706 Camino Lejo.* ⓗ 🅿 ☎ *505-476-1200. www.moifa.org.* Traditional arts from over 100 countries on six continents represent the largest folk collection in the world—more than 120,000 objects. They include historical and contemporary religious art, folk art, traditional costumes and textiles, silver and gold work, ceramics and glass, and children's toys and dolls. Miniature dioramas in the Girard Wing depict international lifestyles.

Wheelwright Museum of the American Indian – *704 Camino Lejo.* ⓗ 🅿 ☎ *505-982-4636. www.wheelwright.org.* This small independent museum is built in the eight-sided shape of a Navajo hogan, its door facing east toward the rising sun. Founded in 1937 by a Boston scholar and a Navajo medicine man to preserve ritual beliefs and practices, the museum focuses on living arts in rotating exhibits. In the basement is a replica of a Navajo trading post; outside is a sculpture garden.

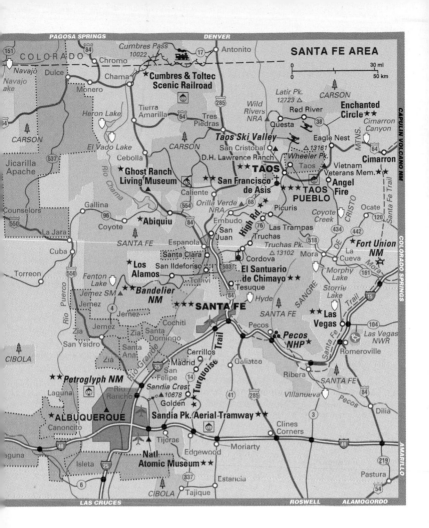

The Santa Fe Opera – *US-84 & 285, 7mi north of Plaza.* ⚐ 🅿 ☎ 505-986-5900. *www.santafeopera.org.* Works by European composers like Verdi, Mozart and Richard Strauss follow on the heels of 20C American premieres at this hilltop amphitheater. The opera company, ranked by many as second in the US only to New York's Metropolitan Opera, was established in 1957. Famed conductors and performers guest-star during a nine-week, 37-performance season, which extends from late June to late August. Year-round tours let visitors appreciate the soaring curves of the 2,128-seat theater, which in 1998 added a roof to deflect desert storms and an Electronic Libretto System for individual translation of opera lyrics.

EXCURSIONS

⭐ **Los Alamos** – *Rte. 502, 35mi northwest of Santa Fe.* ✗⚐ 🅿 ☎ 505-662-8105. *www.losalamos.com.* Unique among world cities, Los Alamos perches atop a series of isolated finger canyons lined by the cottonwoods *(alamos)* for which it was named. The town of 18,000 was founded in 1942 as a top-secret community devoted to the creation of atomic weapons. It is the home of the **Los Alamos National Laboratory**, which employs 7,000 in scientific research for national security and economic strength. Unlike other towns in northern New Mexico, the architecture is not predominantly adobe; most homes are of the simple wood-frame variety.

⭐⭐ **Bradbury Science Museum** – *15th St. & Central Ave.* ⚐ 🅿 ☎ 505-667-4444. *www.lanl.gov./external/ museum.* This high-tech museum offers exhibits on the historic development of the atomic bomb. More than three dozen hands-on displays educate visitors on current technology and science development at Los Alamos National Laboratory, including biomedical and energy research.

■ Developing the Bomb

A 1939 letter from scientist Albert Einstein to President Franklin Delano Roosevelt, alerting him to the destructive wartime potential of atomic energy, sparked a technological revolution that changed the world forever. A first step was the creation of the cyclotron, a Flash Gordon-style device that on September 10, 1942, energized atoms to create plutonium, a necessary bomb component. Because copper was scarce during the Second World War, resourceful engineers appropriated millions of dollars worth of pure silver from the US Treasury for wiring to assist in the quest to build an atomic bomb.

Oak Ridge, Tennessee, housed a city of 10,000 workers focused on creating the necessary uranium. Thousands more were employed manufacturing plutonium in Hanford, Washington. In New Mexico, the Los Alamos Ranch School outside Santa Fe was chosen as the site for Project Y of the Manhattan Engineer District, or "The Manhattan Project." Los Alamos' remoteness assured that secrecy and safety could be maintained for the 100 scientists who assembled and tested the bomb.

The first bomb was exploded on July 16, 1945, at the Trinity Site *(p 143)*, a forlorn stretch of the White Sands Missile Range about 200mi southeast of Los Alamos. (Tours are offered twice annually, the first Saturdays of April and October.) Enrico Fermi, instrumental in the project, wrote of the detonation: "The temperature at its center was four times that at the center of the sun. The pressure was over 100 billion atmospheres. The radioactivity emitted was equal to 1 million times that of the world's total radium supply.... A huge pillar of smoke with an expanded head like a gigantic mushroom rose rapidly beyond the clouds, probably to a height of 30,000ft."

Three weeks after the Trinity test, atomic bombs were exploded over the Japanese cities of Hiroshima and Nagasaki. Japan capitulated shortly thereafter, putting an end to World War II.

** **Bandelier National Monument** – *Rte. 4, 15mi south of Los Alamos.* △ ♿ 🅿 ☎ *505-672-3861. www.nps.gov/band.* This 50sq-mi park preserves cliffside dwellings and other sites occupied by ancient Puebloans for 500 years starting in AD 1050. From a visitor center and museum, a 1.5mi paved trail along Frijoles Creek leads to the main, partially reconstructed ruins. Wooden ladders allow visitors to climb 140ft to a ceremonial *kiva*. Surrounding the ruins, more than 70mi of foot trails lead to extensive canyon-and-mesa backcountry and designated wilderness areas.

* **Abiquiu** – *US-84, 47mi northwest of Santa Fe.* A village that provided scenic inspiration for her work, Abiquiu was home to artist Georgia O'Keeffe *(p 332)* for nearly 40 years. The **Georgia O'Keeffe Foundation** *(☎ 505-685-4539)* allows small groups to visit her home and studio by reservation, several times weekly.

* **Ghost Ranch Living Museum** – 🅺🅸🅳🆂 *US-84, 12mi northwest of Abiquiu.* ♿ 🅿 ☎ *505-685-4312.* This US Forest Service sanctuary harbors wildlife indigenous to New Mexico. Most animals were orphaned, abandoned or raised as pets. Exhibits feature geology, range management, an aspen woods and a fire lookout tower.

** **El Santuario de Chimayo** – *Rte. 76, Chimayo, 25mi north of Santa Fe.* ♿ 🅿 ☎ *505-351-4889.* A National Historic Landmark, this Spanish adobe church is the most important pilgrimage site in the Southwest. Some 30,000 pilgrims walk here every Good Friday from as far away as Albuquerque. Many take home soil from the anteroom beside the altar, believed to be holy and hold miraculous healing powers. Leg braces, crutches and canes discarded by believers provide testimony. The chapel contains five sacred reredos and a number of religious carvings.

** **High Road to Taos** – *Rte. 76 east from Chimayo to Rte. 518 near Vadito.* Traditional 19C lifestyles persist in a string of villages along this intriguing and mountainous 25mi route. Beginning in the weaving center of Chimayo, it extends through the wood-carving village of **Cordova**, where crafts are often sold from roadside stalls. The farming hamlet of **Truchas**—where Robert Redford filmed his

1987 movie, *The Milagro Beanfield War*—sits atop a mesa beneath snow-capped 13,102ft Truchas Peak, the state's second-highest elevation. In the village of **Las Trampas**, founded in 1751, is the José de Gracia Church, an oft-photographed Spanish Colonial adobe structure listed on the National Register of Historic Places.

* Pecos National Historical Park – *Rte. 63, 4mi north of I-25 Exit 307, 27mi east of Santa Fe.* & ▯ ☏ *505-757-6414. www.nps.gov/peco.* Coronado, in 1540, wrote that Pecos Pueblo was "feared through the land." Within 300 years, however, the 17 survivors of an original tribe of 2,000 had abandoned their home. This site preserves the ruins of the 14C village and a 1625 mission church. A self-guided 1.25mi paved loop trail leads past the sites, beginning at the **Fogelson Visitor Center**. Ranger-guided tours lead visitors to the Santa Fe Trail and the Civil War battlefield at Glorieta Pass.

** Las Vegas – *I-25 Exit 345, 66mi east of Santa Fe.* ✗ & ▯ ☏ *505-425-8631. www.lasvegasnewmexico.com.* With 900 buildings listed on the National Historic Register, a classic plaza and no pretensions, Las Vegas—no relation whatsoever to its Nevada namesake—epitomizes old New Mexico. The friendly charm of this city of 16,500 may be discovered in nine historic districts. Structures represent many styles of the Victorian era, as well as a downtown core consisting of adobe buildings in the Old Town Plaza Park district.

* Fort Union National Monument – *Rte. 161 off I-25 Exit 366, 28mi northeast of Las Vegas.* & ▯ ☏ *505-425-8025. www.nps.gov/foun.* Established in 1851, Fort Union was a base for military operations on the Santa Fe Trail, the chief quartermaster depot for the Southwest. Campaigns against the Jicarilla Apaches in 1854, the Utes in 1855 and the Kiowas and Comanches in 1860-61 were launched from here. After a railroad replaced the trail in 1879, Fort Union's role decreased, and it was abandoned in 1891. Today's visitors tour its sprawling brick-and-adobe remains. A small museum focuses on the history of the fort and the Santa Fe Trail.

ALBUQUERQUE*

Map p 335   Mountain Standard Time
Population 419,311
Tourist Information ☏ 505-842-9918 or www.abqcvb.org

Albuquerque is an intriguing stew of old and new, of 14C Indian pueblos, 18C Spanish village and 21C high-technology center. Its architecture is liberally sprinkled with reminders of its mid-20C fling as a prime stop on cross-country Route 66, in the days before the interstate highway system. By far New Mexico's largest city, one of seven US cities to receive federal funds to preserve its classic roadside architecture; Pueblo Revival architecture, neon-lit cafes and motor courts speckle its cultural corridors.

More than 10 percent of hot-air balloons in the US are registered in Albuquerque. Balloonists relish the calm air and predictable high desert weather. Mornings are generally windless, and on weekend dawns many of the colorful aircraft may be seen floating above the 100sq mi of the city. In October, the city's Balloon Fiesta is the world's largest gathering of hot air. But the biggest blowout of the year is mercifully less explosive than its atomic predecessors.

Historical Notes – Paleo-Indian artifacts ascribed to Sandia Man, discovered in the mountains overlooking Albuquerque, have been dated from 25,000 years ago. Ancestral Indian farmlands, longtime homes of stationary tribes, are still inhabited pueblo communities. Spanish colonists established a villa on the Old Chihuahua Trail in 1706 and named it after the regional governor—Don Francisco Cuervo y Valdez, the 13th Duke of Alburquerque. Anglos (non-Hispanic whites) arrived en force in the 1880s when the Santa Fe Railroad bypassed a costly mountain crossing at Santa Fe and came through this site instead. Sleepy Albuquerque was transformed into a rail boomtown, later to become a high-tech hub on the coattails of Los Alamos *(p 335)*.

SIGHTS

** Old Town – *Northeast of Central Ave. & Rio Grande Blvd. NW.* ✗ & ▯ Some 150 shops and galleries face hidden gardens and cobbled walkways around a tree-shaded 18C plaza. The modern city has grown from this traditional central core. Today, restored adobes share the plaza with Pueblo Revival architecture, some structures painted in bold colors that suggest an adobe-Deco hybrid. The **Church of**

San Felipe de Neri★ was built on the west side of the plaza in 1706; reconstructed on the north side in 1793, it has been in continuous use since. Pueblo and Navajo artisans display wares at the small **Indian market** on Romero Street.

★ **New Mexico Museum of Natural History and Science** – Kids *1801 Mountain Rd. NW.* ✗ ⌖ ▣ ☎ *505-841-2800. www.museums.state.nm.us/nmmnh.* A block from Old Town, this lively museum offers a ramble through geologic time. Interactive exhibits place visitors in the middle of a live volcano and an Ice Age cave. Displays describe the paleontology, zoology and botany of the region from a time when dinosaurs were local residents. Other features include the giant-screen **Dynamax Theater** and the **Lodestar Astronomy Center.**

★★ **The Albuquerque Museum of Art and History** – *2000 Mountain Rd. NW.* ⌖ ▣ ☎ *505-242-4600. www.cabq.gov/museum.* The evolution of the Rio Grande valley, from Coronado to the present, is chronicled at this plaza-area museum. An extensive collection of Spanish Colonial artifacts includes religious tapestries, maps, coins, arms and armor. A gallery of contemporary art, a sculpture garden and an extensive photo archive also are featured.

★★ **Indian Pueblo Cultural Center** – Kids *2401 12 St. NW, 1 block north of I-40.* ✗ ⌖ ▣ ☎ *505-843-7270. www.indianpueblo.org.* The arts of New Mexico's 19 Pueblo communities are exhibited at this important nonprofit center a mile from Old Town. Modeled after 9C Pueblo Bonito in Chaco Culture National Historical Park *(p 344)*, this is the one place to get an overview of cultures as presented by the Indians themselves, not interpreted by Anglos.

Ancient artifacts and contemporary weavings, jewelry, pottery and paintings— each piece individually chosen for display by tribal members—trace the development of Pueblo cultures. Pottery designs are unique to each pueblo. Traditional dancers perform weekends on an outdoor stage, and artisans demonstrate various crafts.

Pottery and Weavings, Indian Pueblo Cultural Center

★★ **Petroglyph National Monument** – Kids *4735 Unser Blvd. NW, 3mi north of I-40 & 4mi west of Old Town.* ⌖ ▣ ☎ *505-839-4429. www.nps.gov/petr.* More than 20,000 petroglyphs, scratched or chipped into basalt along a 17mi lava escarpment beneath five ancient volcanoes, chronicle the lives of countless Native American generations. The carvings—human, animal and ceremonial forms—are found in concentrated groups accessed by hiking trails. Most date from AD 1300-1650, although some may be over 3,000 years old. Paved trails run through **Boca Negra Canyon**, 2.5mi north of the **visitor center** *(Unser Blvd. & Western Trail Rd.).*

★ **Rio Grande Zoological Park** – *903 10th St. SW.* ✗ ⌖ ▣ ☎ *505-764-6200. www.cabq.gov/BioPark.* Sixty acres of riverside cottonwood bosque are home to more than 900 animals of various species. Especially strong in New Mexico species, the zoo includes open-habitat areas of African savanna, Amazon rain forest and Australian outback. Rhinoceroses and elephants, Bengal tigers and Komodo dragons, lowland gorillas and vampire bats are among the denizens.

The zoo is part of Albuquerque Biological Park, which includes **Rio Grande Botanic Garden & Albuquerque Aquarium** *(2601 Central Ave. NW;* ☎ *505-764-6200).*

University of New Mexico – *Yale Blvd. NE at Central Ave.* ✗ ♿ 🅿 ☎ *505-277-5813. www.unm.edu.* About 24,000 students attend the main campus of this state institution, 2mi east of Old Town. Oldest of six museums is the **Maxwell Museum of Anthropology**★ *(Redondo Dr. at Ash St. NE;* ☎ *505-277-4405),* whose exhibits highlight world cultures, especially those of the Southwest and Latin America; Asian textiles and African culture are other strengths. It has achieved acclaim for its regional finds and programs.

The **University Art Museum** *(Cornell St. north of Central Ave.;* ☎ *505-277-4001),* in the Center for the Arts, focuses on 19-20C American and European art. The **Jonson Gallery** *(1909 Las Lomas Blvd. NE;* ☎ *505-277-4967)* presents shows by community and campus artists, plus works by early-20C modernist painter Raymond Jonson. In Northrup Hall *(200 Yale Blvd.)* are the **Meteorite Museum** *(*☎ *505-277-2747),* which displays one of the largest meteorites ever found, and the **Geology Museum** *(*☎ *505-277-4204).* The adjacent Biology Annex *(190 Yale Blvd.)* contains the **Museum of Southwestern Biology** *(*☎ *505-277-4225),* featuring regional species and the US Geological Survey biological collection.

★★ **National Atomic Museum** – *Bldg. 20358, Wyoming Blvd., Kirtland Air Force Base; courtesy shuttle from Gibson & Wyoming gates.* ♿ 🅿 ☎ *505-284-3243. www.atomicmuseum.com.* Many exhibits in this hangar-sized building are devoted to the development of the atomic and hydrogen bombs. There are replicas of Fat Man and Little Boy, nicknames given the world's first two nuclear bombs, and an actual B-29 bomber similar to the planes that dropped them. A 50min film, *Ten Seconds That Shook the World,* chronicles the history of "The Manhattan Project." Other exhibits include robotics, nuclear medicine and arms control.

★★ **Sandia Peak Aerial Tramway** – [Kids] *10 Tramway Loop NE.* ✗ ♿ 🅿 ☎ *505-856-7325. www.sandiapeak.com.* The world's longest jig-back aerial tramway covers 2.7mi from the northeastern city limits to 10,678ft **Sandia Crest**. Climbing from urban desert to alpine terrain in just 15min, the tram affords panoramic views of 11,000sq mi, across the entire Albuquerque area and other parts of northern New Mexico. Hikers and mountain bikers in summer, skiers in winter, also exit the tramway here. Sandia Crest *(*☎ *505-281-3304)* also can be reached by a 35mi drive from Albuquerque *(east 16mi on I-40, north 6mi to Sandia Park on Rte. 14, then northwest 13mi on Rte. 536).*

EXCURSION

★★ **Turquoise Trail** – *Rte. 14, Tijeras (16mi east of Albuquerque at I-40 Exit 175) to Santa Fe.* This 52mi back road avoids I-25 and runs along the scenic eastern edge of the Sandia Mountains, which show a fertile, forested side not apparent from the desert-like west slope. The route passes dry washes and arroyos and visits a trio of revived "ghost towns"—artsy villages suitably weather-beaten but colorfully painted—before opening into a broad, arid, high plain south of Santa Fe.

Turquoise, gold, silver, lead and coal were once mined in great quantities in **Golden** *(16mi north of I-40),* **Madrid** *(12mi north of Golden)* and **Cerrillos** *(3mi north of Madrid).* When the last coal mines closed in the mid-1950s, the communities went into decline until rediscovered by artists and craftspeople, who found them perfect places to make the 1960s live on. Madrid, largest of the three hamlets, invites visitors to descend into the **Old Coal Mine Museum**, now a crafts collective, and attend performances at the **Madrid Opera House,** which boasts a built-in steam locomotive on-stage.

TAOS★★

Map p 335   Mountain Standard Time
Population 4,100
Tourist Information ☎ 505-758-3873 or http://taoswebb.com

Taos Pueblo has been occupied for at least 1,000 years. The rustic, Spanish colonial town of Taos is perhaps 300 years old. Built around a cozy plaza that remains the heart of the modern community, it is today a center for the arts, much smaller than Santa Fe but equally alluring to aficionados of Southwest art.

Taos found its niche in the world of art in 1915 when Ernest Blumenschein, Bert Phillips and friends founded the **Taos Society of Artists**. The society focused world attention on the unique light that falls on the northern New Mexico landscape; its reputation laid a foundation for today's prolific, tricultural art community.

Taos sits on a plateau between the Rio Grande and the Sangre de Cristo Range. The Rio Grande gorge is crossed by a three-span, continuous-truss bridge 650ft above the river, 8mi northwest of Taos on US-64. San Francisco de Asis Church, 4mi south, is one of the most distinctive adobe structures of the Southwest.

SIGHTS

★★★ **Taos Pueblo** – Kids *2mi north of Taos Plaza.* ☎ *505-758-1028.* The oldest and best-known New Mexico pueblo has been designated a World Heritage Site, of enduring value to mankind, by the United Nations. A visit is a step back in time. Although Pueblo Indian ruins are found throughout the Southwest, here the site is intact, occupied and used daily, which makes it unique.

The pueblo contains a multistory adobe structure with ladders leading to upper floors. Some 200 residents live here year-round without running water or electricity. Other villagers live outside the pueblo in modern homes, but sell mica-flecked pottery, silver and turquoise jewelry, moccasins and drums from homes on the pueblo's ground floor that have been converted to small shops.

Ruins of the **Mission San Geronimo de Taos**★ are near the pueblo entrance. Part of the original bell tower and an outer wall can be seen. The church was established in 1598, burned during the Pueblo Rebellion of 1680, and rebuilt a quarter-century later, only to be burned once again by US troops during an 1847 Indian uprising.

★★ **Kit Carson Home and Museum** – Kids *E. Kit Carson Rd., 1 block east of Taos Plaza.* ☎ *505-758-4741. http://taosmuseums.org.* Carson, a famous frontier scout and Indian agent (1809-68), lived in this 1825 house from 1843 until his death. The museum, in a part of the original house, illustrates Carson's career and frontier life of that era through displays featuring guns, clothing, saddles, furniture and period equipment used by mountain men and Indians.

★ **Ernest L. Blumenschein Home & Museum** – *222 Ledoux St., 2 blocks west of Taos Plaza.* ▯ ☎ *505-758-0505. http://taosmuseums.org.* A founder of the Taos Society, painter Blumenschein (1874-1960) first visited Taos in 1898; he moved here in 1919. His adobe home, built in 1797, is maintained to demonstrate the early-20C artist's lifestyle. The collection includes works by Blumenschein and other Taos Society artists, accented by European and Spanish Colonial antiques.

★★ **The Harwood Museum** – *238 Ledoux St.* ⅙ ▯ ☎ *505-758-9826. www.nmculture.org.* Works by 20C Taos artists—paintings, drawings, prints, sculptures and photography—are displayed at this museum, founded here in 1923. There are works by Taos Society artists, noted American Modernists including Marsden Hartley, and a Hispanic folk-art collection with 80 19C retablos (religious paintings on wood).

★ **The Fechin House and Studio** – *227 Paseo del Pueblo Norte.* ▯ ☎ *505-758-1710. www.fechin.com.* Before he moved to Taos in 1927, Nikolai Fechin (1881-1955) had secured a reputation in his native Russia and in New York as a renaissance man. Securing a huge adobe home, Fechin embellished it with hand-carved doors, furniture, and wood trim to reflect a Russian country home. His paintings, sculptures and drawings are on display inside.

★★ **Martinez Hacienda** – *Ranchitos Rd., 2mi west of Taos.* ▯ ☎ *505-758-1000. http://taosmuseums.org.* One of the few Spanish Colonial "great houses" open to the public, the fortress-like hacienda was built in 1804 by merchant Don Antonio Severino Martinez. Its windowless adobe walls rise above the west bank of the Rio Pueblo de Taos. Twenty-one spartan rooms, built around two courtyards, provide a look at frontier life. Period pieces furnish bedrooms, servants' quarters, stables, the kitchen and a large fiesta room. Weavers, blacksmiths and other skilled workers often give living-history demonstrations.

★★ Millicent Rogers Museum – *4mi north of Taos Plaza.* ♿ 🅿 ☏ *505-758-2462.* *www.millicentrogers.org.* Founded by Standard Oil heiress Millicent Rogers, this museum exhibits collections of silver and turquoise Indian jewelry, Navajo and Rio Grande weavings. It has been expanded to include Hispanic religious and domestic arts, paintings, photography and graphics. Also featured are crafts from all over northern New Mexico, Hopi and Zuni kachina dolls, ceramics, textiles and jewelry.

★★ San Francisco de Asis Church – *Rte. 68, 4mi south of Taos Plaza.* ☏ *505-758-2754.* The exterior of this heavily buttressed adobe church is probably the most painted and photographed in New Mexico. Georgia O'Keeffe and Ansel Adams are among artists who have immortalized its stark, 120ft-long form. The two-story church was built between 1710 and 1755; its only door and three small windows are not visible from the highway. In the chapel are images of saints, a large Christ figure and reredos dating to the church's founding.

A painting on the wall of an adjacent building is shrouded in mystery. In ordinary light, *The Shadow of the Cross* (1896) shows a barefoot Christ at the Sea of Galilee. In darkness, the portrait luminesces and the perfect shadow of a cross appears over Jesus' left shoulder. Even artist Henri Ault was shocked.

San Francisco de Asis Church

EXCURSIONS

★★ Enchanted Circle – *Rtes. 522 & 38 and US-64, north and east of Taos.* ❌ 🅿 *www.enchantedcircle.org.* This 85mi US Forest Service Scenic Byway circles 13,161ft **Wheeler Peak**, New Mexico's highest point, and connects Taos with several small resort towns. A first stop for northbound motorists, traveling clockwise around the loop, is the **D.H. Lawrence Ranch and Shrine** *(County Rd. 7, San Cristobal, 6mi east of Rte. 522, 15mi north of Taos;* ☏ *505-776-2245).* Lawrence (1885-1930) lived at this ranch sporadically in the early 1920s; when the author died of tuberculosis in southern France, his ashes were returned for burial. Literary pilgrims, who decorate the shrine with personal momentos, have made the guest book an anthology of heartfelt letters and poetry. The shrine is a short uphill walk from the Lawrence Ranch, now a University of New Mexico retreat center.

The town of **Questa** *(Rte. 522, 24mi north of Taos;* ☏ *505-586-0694)* is a starting point for white-water trips on the upper Rio Grande. **Red River** *(Rte. 38, 12mi east of Questa;* ☏ *505-754-2366)* and **Eagle Nest** *(US-64 & Rte. 38, 17mi east of Red River & 31mi northeast of Taos;* ☏ *505-377-2420),* both 19C gold-mining towns, serve primarily as bases for outdoor excursions into pine forests shadowed by Wheeler Peak. Activities include skiing at **Red River Ski Area** *(*☏ *505-754-2223)* and fishing for trout and salmon in Eagle Nest Lake.

Angel Fire *(Rte. 434, just south of US-64;* ☏ *505-377-6661),* a tiny village in the Moreno Valley of the Sangre de Cristo Range, is a year-round ski and golf resort. The **Vietnam Veterans Memorial★** *(US-64, Angel Fire;* ♿ 🅿 ☏ *505-377-6900),* a father's tribute to his martyred son, is a white curved structure perched on a serene hillside, offering broad views of the Moreno Valley and the Sangre de Cristo. Inside are a small museum and thick bound books bearing the names of American GIs who died in the Vietnam conflict of the 1960s and 70s.

Cimarron – *US-64, 55mi east of Taos.* 🅿 ☎ *505-376-2417.* Once home to Jicarilla Apaches and Ute Indians, Cimarron became a stop on the mountain branch of the Santa Fe Trail. Mining and ranching prospered. Between 1865 and 1880, a slew of famous and infamous Western characters passed through, including Wyatt Earp, Clay Allison, Billy the Kid and the outlaw James brothers, Jesse and Frank. An Old Town walking tour weaves past **St. James Hotel** *(US-64;* ☎ *505-376-2664)*, where "Buffalo Bill" Cody contracted Annie Oakley to join his Wild West Show, and the **Old Mill Museum** *(*☎ *505-376-2417)*. Outside the village, the Boy Scouts of America maintain their nationally acclaimed, 214sq-mi **Philmont Scout Ranch** *(Rte. 21, 5mi south;* ☎ *505-376-2281)*.

Capulin Volcano National Monument – *Rte. 325, Capulin, 125mi east of Taos via US-64.* ♿ 🅿 ☎ *505-278-2201. www.nps.gov/cavo.* This cinder cone was created 60,000 years ago from piled ash and cinders arranged in a nearly cylindrical form. A 2mi paved road winds to the summit of the 8,182ft peak; trails descend into the crater *(.2mi)* and around the rim *(1mi)*.

GALLUP-GRANTS AREA★

Map p 334   Mountain Standard Time
Tourist Information ☎ 505-863-3841 or www.gallupnm.org

In decades past, both Gallup and Grants "got their kicks on Route 66." Both have seen better days but are on the rebound. Gallup is a gateway to the Navajo and Zuni reservations and a center for Indian arts and crafts. Free dances are regularly presented, and fine trading posts invite shoppers and browsers. So lucrative is the native-art market that Gallup claims the highest percentage of millionaires of any community on earth: 200 of them, or 1 percent of its population of 20,000.

Grants, once a uranium boomtown, is near the fascinating Pueblo community of Acoma, the strange badlands of volcanic El Malpais National Monument, and the inscriptions of early travelers carved in rock at El Morro National Monument.

SIGHTS

★ **Gallup** – *US-666 at I-40 Exit 20, 139mi west of Albuquerque.* 🍴♿ 🅿 ☎ *505-863-3841. www.gallupnm.org.* Gallup is filled with trading posts, Indian shops and galleries along its fabled Route 66 corridor and in its 12-block historic district. The surrounding desert terrain features red mesas to the north and east, mountains, the striated pastel hues of the Painted Desert to the west.

Each August for more than 75 years, the Intertribal Indian Ceremonial has been held at **Red Rock State Park** *(Rte. 66 at I-40 Exit 26, 4mi east of Gallup; 505-722-3829)*. Members of 30 tribes—from New Mexico and Arizona to Mexico and Canada—engage in parades, dances, rodeo events and arts competitions.

Zuni Indian Reservation – *Rte. 53, 37mi south of Gallup via Rte. 602.* △ 🍴♿ 🅿 ☎ *505-782-4481. http://zuni.k12.nm.us/tribe/main.html.* The arts and ambience of an ancient Pueblo community are very much alive in modern Zuni, largest (with 10,000 residents and 259sq mi of land) of New Mexico's pueblos. Scouts sent by Coronado in 1540 believed Zuni to be one of the Seven Cities of Cibola; its gold turned out to be sunlight reflecting golden straw mixed with mud, used in adobe construction. The style still predominates in Zuni; outdoor clay ovens seem to be fixed in every backyard.

A mural at the **Pueblo of Zuni Visitor Information Center**★ *(1222 Rte. 53)* depicts the Zuni origin story. Silversmiths, fetish carvers, potters and jewelers are considered among the most skilled in the Southwest. Their detailed work is seen at the **A:shiwi A:wan Museum and Heritage Center**★★ *(1220 Rte. 53;* ☎ *505-782-4403)*, where other exhibits describe traditions of gardening, herbal and medicinal plant use and cooking. Murals in the nearby **Old Zuni Mission**★ depict a complex spiritual life blending tribal and Catholic traditions. Special permission is required to visit the crumbling ruins of **Hawikuh** *(Tribal Rd. 2, 12mi south of modern Zuni)*, where Coronado first encountered the Zuni.

★★ **El Morro National Monument** – *Rte. 53 near Ramah, 54mi southeast of Gallup.* △♿ 🅿 ☎ *505-783-4226. www.nps.gov/elmo.* For at least 1,000 years, names and messages have been carved into a sandstone monolith that rises 200ft above the valley floor. **Inscription Rock** is in a narrow catchment basin, the only water source for many miles. Pueblo Indians, Spanish explorers and frontier travelers camped here, leaving petroglyphs (AD 1000-1400) and other inscriptions. The earliest non-Indian words were written in 1605 by Don Juan de Oñate, New Mexico's first Spanish colonial governor. Emigrants and Army personnel left later inscriptions. A .5mi trail leads to the base of the rock; a steep 2mi trail climbs to Indian ruins on the mesa top.

* **El Malpais National Monument and Conservation Area** – *Rte. 53, 23mi south of I-40 at Grants.* 🅿 ☎ *505-783-4774. www.nps.gov/elma.* A volcanic landscape whose name is Spanish for "The Badlands," this park attracts adventurous hikers and outdoors lovers. Forty different volcanoes, including cinder cones, spatter cones and shield volcanoes, produced a vast lava field, part of it a mere 2,000 years old. Lava tubes, trenches, tree molds and other preserved flow-top features can be seen in the dense and rugged terrain. Puebloan and Navajo Indians continue a tribal tradition of visiting El Malpais to pay respects and gather herbal medicines.
The **Northwest New Mexico Visitor Center** *(1900 E. Santa Fe Ave., Grants; ☎ 505-876-2783)* dispenses information on all federal lands in this part of the state.

** **New Mexico Museum of Mining** – 🅺🄸🄳🅂 *100 Iron Ave., Grants, 61mi east of Gallup and 72mi west of Albuquerque.* ♿ 🅿 ☎ *505-287-4802. www.grants.org.* Designed to fit beneath the office of Grants' chamber of commerce visitor center, accessed via elevator through a small mining museum, is a replica of a uranium mine. Uranium was discovered in the Grants area in 1950. This replica mine includes real drilling equipment and passages for mine cars to remove rocks. It is the only underground uranium-mining museum in the world.

Acoma Pueblo – *Rte. 23, 12.5mi southwest of I-40 Exit 108, 30mi southeast of Grants and 64mi west of Albuquerque.* 🅿 ☎ *505-470-4966.* Native Americans say the clifftop **Sky City***** has been inhabited "since the beginning of time." Archaeologists verify that this 70-acre, Medieval looking, walled adobe village—perched atop a sheer mesa, 367ft above the valley floor—has been lived in at least since the 11C, making it one of the oldest communities in the US. In 1598, Indians repelled a Spanish army during a three-day siege by raining rocks upon soldiers. Little more than three decades later, Spanish priests formed the continent's oldest parish here. Between 1629 and 1640, they built the **San Esteban del Rey Mission****, now (like Sky City itself) a National Historic Landmark.

Sky City

One-hour guided tours depart every 20min from a visitor center near the foot of the mesa. Today, only a handful of the 6,000 Acoma *(ACK-uh-ma)* tribal members reside year-round in Sky City without running water or electricity. Others set up shop in some of the mesa-top homes to sell their distinctive brown-and-black-on-white pottery to tourists. (Only those pieces with rough interiors are handmade.) Photography is not allowed on church grounds.

© Robert Holmes

FARMINGTON AREA★

Farmington is the gateway to several of the world's unique and ancient Indian ruins, as well as mountain and desert recreational sites. A business hub for the Four Corners region, the city of 39,000 anchors the northeastern corner of the 250,000sq-mi Navajo Indian Reservation.

SIGHTS

★**Aztec Ruins National Monument** – *84 Ruins Rd., .5mi north of US-550, Aztec.* ♿ 🅿 ☎ *505-334-6174. www.nps.gov/azru.* Parts of a 400-room Anasazi pueblo from AD 1100-1300 remain at this site beside a modern-day trailer park. In its heart is the largest reconstruction anywhere of a great kiva, a round chamber believed to have been used for ceremonies and other gatherings. This community was significant as a farming center beside the Animas River, a fertile location midway between the much larger Pueblo communities at Chaco Canyon and Mesa Verde. The ruins are easily accessible from short paved walkways.

★**Salmon Ruins & Heritage Park** – *US-64, 11mi east of Farmington & 2mi west of Bloomfield.* ♿ 🅿 ☎ *505-632-2013. www.more2it.com/salmon.* Excavation has partially exposed this 150-room Anasazi site beside the San Juan River. It was originally settled by Chacoans between AD 1088 and 1130, then added onto with Mesa Verde-style techniques around AD 1185, before being abandoned about AD 1250. Visitors today can explore the site and adjacent Heritage Park, which contains re-created traditional homes of various Four Corners-area tribes.

★★★**Chaco Culture National Historical Park** – *Rte. 57, Nageezi, 73mi south of Farmington via US-64 & US-550.* ⛺ 🅿 ☎ *505-786-7014. www.nps.gov/chcu.* Preserving one of the foremost cultural and historical areas in the US, Chaco Canyon was a major center of ancestral Anasazi (Puebloan) culture from AD 850-1250. A hub of ceremony, trade and government for the prehistoric Four Corners area—a city of thousands whose trade network extended into Mexico—it was unlike anything before or since.

Remarkable for its multistoried public buildings, ceremonial structures and distinctive architecture, Chaco's monumental masonry structures were oriented toward solar and lunar astronomical cycles observed over centuries. Primitive apartment complexes of hundreds of rooms were tied, by carefully engineered roads, to outlying communities such as those at the Salmon and Aztec ruins.

There are 13 major excavated archaeological sites in Chaco Canyon, and hundreds of smaller sites. **Pueblo Bonito** (c.AD 850-1200) was the largest "great house"—four stories high, with 600 rooms and 40 kivas. Adjacent to it, **Chetro Ketl** (c.AD 1020-1200) contained 500 rooms, 16 kivas and an immense, elevated earthen plaza. **Pueblo del Arroyo** (280 rooms) and **Kin Kletso** (100 rooms)

Pueblo Bonito, Chaco Culture National Historical Park

were built in stages in the late 11C and early 12C. **Casa Rinconada**, built in the 12C as one of the largest kivas in the Southwest, may have served a community purpose.

Situated in an isolated desert canyon, Chaco can be reached only by dirt roads. The preferred 21mi route is from the north, via County Road 7900 off US-550, 3mi southeast of Nageezi. An alternative 69mi route from the south begins off Tribal Road 9, 4mi north of Crownpoint. Roads are well maintained but may become impassable during heavy rains, so it's wise to phone ahead.

* **Cumbres & Toltec Scenic Railroad** – Kids *Rte. 17, Chama, 110mi east of Farmington via US-64.* ✗ ☈ ◨ ☏ *505-756-2151.* The longest remaining example of the original Denver & Rio Grande narrow-gauge line was built in the 1880s to haul miners and ore from the steep, mineral-rich western slope of the Rockies. It covers 64mi between Chama, New Mexico, and Antonito, Colorado, over trestles and through tunnels in the San Juan Mountains above the Los Piños River. Round-trip passage in vintage rail cars takes six to eight hours.

Seattle Area

Mount Rainier National Park

Wedged into the far northwest corner of the contiguous 48 states, the booming metropolis of Seattle possesses a low-key, youthful flavor different from anywhere else in the US. Here, high-tech entrepreneurs mingle easily with grunge-rock and cafe society, and a futuristic skyline plays warm-up to snow-draped peaks only a couple of hours' drive away.

The surrounding state of Washington is one of the most scenically diverse in the nation. Its Pacific coast is filigreed by beautiful Puget Sound, surrounded by dense evergreen forests. The volcanic domes of Mounts Rainier and St. Helens define the craggy central spine of the sky-scraping Cascade Mountain range. The Columbia River spells most of the state's southern boundary with Oregon and traverses the wheat fields of its eastern plains to the foothills of the Rocky Mountains.

Long before the incursion of Europeans, coastal Indians basked in the region's riches. Their elaborately carved canoes, totems and masks attested to a culture that took advantage of abundant forests and teeming waterways. The first important exploration by white men came in 1792 with the expedition of British Capt. George Vancouver, who made detailed charts of the Puget Sound area. By the early 1800s, the region was included in the vast Oregon Country, hotly contested by British and American fur-trading interests. With the steady arrival of more and more American settlers, the territory became US soil, and towns soon grew along the coast at Seattle and Port Townsend.

The establishment by William Boeing in 1916 of an aircraft industry in Seattle assured the city's space-age future, an inevitability celebrated in a 1962 world's fair. Another fair 12 years later in Spokane trumpeted the more cautionary message of environmental conservation. Nature staged its own exposition in 1980 when Mount St. Helens erupted and captured the world's attention. Seattle, and indeed all of Washington, had arrived center stage. While the state scrambles with the rest of the Northwest to slow the exploitation of natural resources, yet accommodate an expanding population, visitors continue to discover scenic splendors and urban pleasures. Hip Seattle nightclubs and swank restaurants vie for attention with sea kayaking in the San Juan Islands, hiking on Mount Rainier and day-tripping to quaint seaside villages.

SEATTLE★★★

Maps p 350 and p 353   Pacific Standard Time
Population 536,978
Tourist Information ☎ 206-461-5840 or www.seeseattle.org

Blanketing high hills that overlook Puget Sound, Seattle has grown from a hard-working lumber town to one of the nation's cultural trendsetters. Noted for its livability and natural beauty, the city is surrounded by spectacular vistas—Mt. Rainier and the Cascade Range on the east, the Olympic Mountains on the west. In the city, ubiquitous street-corner coffee bars have encouraged a cafe society, and an abundance of Northwest seafood and produce has resulted in a distinctive regional cuisine and world-class restaurants. In the late 20C, Seattle became a leader in high-technology, thanks to local software giant Microsoft. Though light rains fall on the city much of the year, they rarely dampen its youthful spirit.

Historical Notes

Though Vancouver sailed into Puget Sound and anchored within sight of Alki Point (now West Seattle) in the late 18C, he found the area unworthy of exploration. No serious white settlement arrived until the 1850s, when disappointed 49ers from the California gold fields and homesteaders from the Olympia area filtered north. On a typically chilly and gray November day in 1851, two small pioneer parties—one traveling overland, the other by schooner—met at Alki and subsequently established a community on Elliott Bay. Named for Chief Sealth, respected Duwamish Indian leader, the new town was platted in 1853, with commerce centering upon a sawmill built by new arrival Henry Yesler.

Growing pains beset the city for the rest of the 19C. It was held back by lack of a major rail connection (until 1887), Indian unrest, harsh anti-Chinese sentiment and a great fire that gutted the business district and waterfront. But when a steamship arrived in 1897 laden with Klondike gold from Canada's Yukon Territory, Seattle was galvanized overnight into a supply point for a new gold rush. By the turn of the 20C, lumber barons Frederick Weyerhaeuser and William Boeing had set up shop in Seattle, the latter soon turning to the new technology of flight. These two industrial giants would fuel the area's economy for a full century to come.

Seattle suffered its ups and downs through the first half of the 20C. Yet the economy stabilized after World War II. The 1962 world's fair endowed the city with one of its most treasured attractions—the futuristic Seattle Center, home of the Space Needle, the Monorail and a wealth of cultural venues. Grassroots efforts in the late 1960s helped to preserve historic districts including Pioneer Square and Pike Place Market, and a building boom in the central business district punctured the skyline with new high-rises.

Now a casually cool style-maker, the once-gritty lumber town has given the country a zest for coffee, grunge-rock music and youthful entrepreneurship. And the Port of Seattle continues to prosper from Pacific Rim and Alaska trade.

DOWNTOWN

★**Pioneer Square**   *Generally bounded by Alaskan Way, S. King St., Fourth Ave. S. & Cherry St.* ☎ *206-622-6235.* The Pioneer Square National Historic District, surrounded by a modern skyline, anchors downtown with 18 blocks of restored turn-of-the-20C commercial buildings. Site of Seattle's first permanent settlement, Pioneer Square retains the nostalgic appeal of an older and less refined city. Tracing roots to mid-19C logging days, the area is still cut by the long incline of Yesler Way, the original Skid Road down which logs were slid to the sawmill. A great fire destroyed most of downtown in 1889; in spite of rebuilding, the town pushed north and east, letting Pioneer Square lapse into a neglected "skid row" notorious for its bawdy houses and gambling dens. Proclaimed a historic district in 1969, the area now boasts galleries and restaurants, parks and squares, where street people lounge side-by-side with young professionals.

The site of the city's first intersection, **Pioneer Place★★** *(First Ave. & Yesler Way)* holds a 1909 streetcar pergola, erected to shield passengers from weather, and a 1930s Tlingit Indian totem pole. The six-story **Pioneer Building** *(610 First Ave.)* was completed in 1892 in the Romanesque Revival style with a heavy ashlar entryway; it was once considered the finest building west of Chicago. The popular, humorous **Bill Speidel's Underground Tours★** *(☎ 206-682-4646)* depart from here, descending into defunct sewage tunnels that lie at the original street level, where visitors see storefronts that existed before the great fire and learn about Seattle life from the mid-19C through Prohibition.

About two blocks south, the Seattle unit of **Klondike Gold Rush National Historical Park** *(117 S. Main St.; ☎ 206-553-7220)* holds artifacts and photographs detailing the Yukon gold rush and its impact on the city. When the steamship *Portland* arrived in

Please see explanation on p 64.

Staying in the Seattle Area

The Sorrento – *900 Madison St., Seattle WA.* ⚔️♿ 🅿️ 🚐 *206-622-6400. www
.hotelsorrento.com. 76 rooms.* **$$$** Beginning with its canopied carriage
entrance and lighted Italianate fountain, the Sorrento is intimate and elegant.
Seattle's oldest hotel (1909) boasts rich mahogany throughout. In **The Hunt Club**
restaurant, salmon and scallops share the menu with New York steak.

Hotel Edgewater – *2411 Alaskan Way, Pier 67, Seattle WA.* ⚔️♿ 🅿️ 🚐 *206-
728-7000. 236 rooms.* **$$** Ferries, tall ships and sea lions cruise past Seattle's
only waterfront hotel, built atop a pier. When the Beatles stayed here back in
1964, they fished from the windows of Room 272. Plaid comforters and
hand-peeled pine tables create the feeling of a rustic mountain-lake lodge.

Inn at the Market – *86 Pine St., Seattle WA.* ⚔️♿ 🅿️ 🚐 *206-443-3600. www
.innatthemarket.com. 70 rooms.* **$$** Built within the famed Pike Place Market
complex, the inn's ivied courtyard and fifth-floor deck overlook Puget Sound
and the Olympic Range. Most rooms have natural-pine furniture and floor-to-
ceiling bay windows; room service arrives from the **Campagne** restaurant.

The Captain Whidbey Inn – *2072 W. Captain Whidbey Inn Rd., Coupeville,
Whidbey Island WA.* ⚔️ 🅿️ 🚐 *360-678-4097. www.captainwhidbey.com. 32
rooms.* **$$** This island retreat captures the romance of the sea with feather
beds inside a weathered log cottage. The rustic dining room affords views of
Penn Cove and plates of ginger-steamed Penn Cove mussels. The innkeeper-
captain launches his classic 52-foot ketch as guests trim the sails.

Rosario Resort – *1 Rosario Wy., Eastsound, Orcas Island WA.* ⚔️♿ 🅿️ 🏊
🚐 *360-376-2222. 127 rooms.* **$$** This is a great base from which to explore
the San Juan archipelago. The historic mansion, with dark-wood paneling and
a working 1,972-pipe organ, is surrounded by eight bayside acres. Guests
enjoy whale-watching, sailing, yoga, tennis or kayaking.

Lake Quinault Lodge – *345 South Shore Rd, Quinault WA.* ⚔️♿ 🅿️ 🏊 🚐 *360-
288-2900. www.visitlakequinault.com. 92 rooms.* **$** On the shores of a moun-
tain lake in a temperate rain forest, the Lodge—with its grand brick fire-
place—has been a haven for rain-soaked travelers since 1926. A totem pole
on the wooden porch measures the 17ft of annual rainfall.

Dining in the Seattle Area

The Herbfarm – *195 N.E. Gilman Blvd., Issaquah WA.* 🚐 *206-784-2222. www
.theherbfarm.com.* **$$$$ Continental.** The Northwest's most elusive reservation,
this ultimate indulgence is a five-hour, nine-course, six-wine dining experience.
For the lucky few who get a candlelit table next to old wine casks, the oft-
changing menus are unbeatable: lavender-steamed rabbit, wild mushroom pud-
ding, foie gras ravioli with sage.

Elliott's Oyster House – *Pier 56, Seattle WA.* 🚐 *206-623-4340.* **$$$ Seafood.**
Fresh Northwest seafood is the *raison d'être* for this fine restaurant on a pier
jutting into Elliott Bay. Oyster selections change daily, and the Pike Place Market provides produce to accompany such dishes as Pacific king salmon cooked
on alder planks and Dungeness crab with three dipping sauces.

Flying Fish – *2234 First Ave., Seattle WA.* 🚐 *206-728-8595.* **$$$ Pacific Rim.**
The factory-gallery decor is bright and loud: aqua chairs, curvaceous lamps.
The menu, which changes daily, puts Pacific Rim accents on fresh seafood. A
popular dish is the whole fried snapper platter, sold by the pound and served
in lemon-grass marinade with bean sprouts and purple basil.

Salish Lodge and Spa – *6501 Railroad Ave. SE, Snoqualmie WA.* 🚐 *206-888-
2556. www.salish.com.* **$$$ American.** A steady, watery roar persists outside this
dramatic restaurant, perched on the crest of 268ft Snoqualmie Falls in a mist-
cloaked forest 30 minutes from Seattle. While famed for its four-course
breakfasts and its luxurious spa facilities, the Lodge also serves fine dinners.

Wild Ginger – *1400 Western Ave., Seattle WA.* 🚐 *206-623-4450.* **$$ Pan-Asian.**
Chefs grind their own spices at this minimalist restaurant. Satays—skewers of
lemon-grass chicken, mahimahi or scallops—are served from a center-stage
grill ringed by padded chairs.

Seattle on July 17, 1897, laden with two tons of Klondike gold, gold fever struck the city. Films and exhibits convey the excitement of those heady days. Many residents grew rich outfitting prospectors; others shipped out for the Yukon via Skagway, Alaska *(p 365)*, where most of this historical park is located.

Smith Tower *(Second Ave. & Yesler Way;* ☎ *206-682-9393)* has anchored the northwest corner of Pioneer Square since 1914. The 42-story edifice, with its terracotta facade, reigned as the tallest building west of the Mississippi River for nearly half a century.

Pike Place Fish Vendor's Stall

© Tim Thompson

★★★ **Pike Place Market** – Kids *First Ave. & Pike St.* ✗ 🅿 ☎ *206-682-7453.* *www.pikeplacemarket.org.* Epitomizing the soul of Seattle, this "public market center" has been a revered city institution since 1907. Fun, feisty and infinitely appealing, the market has maintained its earthy egalitarianism while a modern city has grown up around it. An abundance of farm-fresh vegetables, seafood and flowers dazzles the eye and tempts many a traveler to take bags of market produce aboard homebound planes.

Despite depressions, wars and urban flight, Pike Place has persisted, welcoming respectable housewives and street people alike. An urban renewal program nearly killed the market in the early 1960s, one plan calling for it to be demolished and replaced by a giant hotel. But Seattleites in 1971 voted overwhelmingly to preserve the market and surrounding blocks. Today a nine-acre parcel and a dozen buildings are protected in a national historic district that extends from First to Western Avenues, Union to Virginia Streets.

Hundreds of food vendors, eateries and small shops line boisterous, crowded streets and alleys and fill a multilevel labyrinth of building interiors. The market's original building, the **Main Arcade** *(Pike Place between Pike & Stewart Sts.)*, remains the hub of activity, its street-level stalls vibrant and colorful with seasonal vegetables, stands of fresh and dried flowers, and fish shops where salmon, halibut and Dungeness crabs glisten on beds of ice. A crowd often collects around **Pike Place Fish**, where mongers loudly chant the daily specials and throw fish to one another over customers' heads. Nearby **Post Alley**, an Old World-style walkway, runs between market buildings and offers more shops and several top-notch restaurants. Leading down to the waterfront, the **Hillclimb Corridor** is a landscaped series of stairs flanked by shops and cafes.

★★ **Seattle Art Museum** – *First Ave. & University St.* ✗ ♿ ☎ *206-654-3100. www.seattleartmuseum.org.* The extensive permanent holdings at this well-rounded repository (1991, Robert Venturi) include porcelains, carved screens and textiles from Korea, Japan and China; African ceremonial masks and headdresses; and Northwest Coast basketry and wood and stone sculpture. Western art, exhibited on the fourth floor, includes works by Rubens, Van Dyck, Lucas Cranach the Elder and Jackson Pollock. Opposite the museum's Second Avenue entrance, **Benaroya Hall★★** *(Third Ave. & University St.;* ☎ *206-215-4800)*, state-of-the-art home of the Seattle Symphony, opened in 1998.

★★ **Odyssey: The Maritime Discovery Center** – Kids *Pier 66.* ✗ ♿ ☎ *206-374-4000. www.ody.org.* This innovative addition to the Seattle waterfront rises in glass-walled modernism on renovated Bell Street Pier. Its wide range of imaginative exhibits explore facets of Seattle's maritime life, including ocean trade, environmental safety and the daily life and work of salmon fishermen.

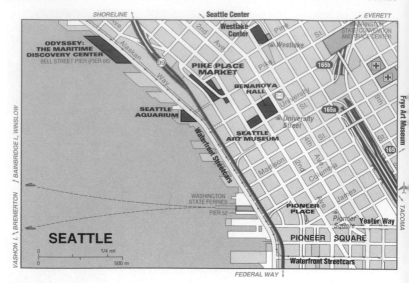

South of Odyssey, the **Seattle Aquarium★** Kids *(Pier 59; ☎ 206-386-4320)* is home to some 380 species of fish, birds, plants, marine invertebrates and mammals native to the Puget Sound area.

★★**Frye Art Museum** – *704 Terry Ave. at Cherry St.* ✗⛛🅿 ☎ *206-622-9250. www.fryeart.org.* A small gem set among the medical centers of First Hill, this facility showcases 19C and 20C representational works by American, French and especially German artists. The galleries, lit by natural light, offer an appealing, intimate space for the quiet appreciation of art. The core collection of Munich School painters of the late 19C and early 20C is the most complete in the US; the movement's leaders included Franz Seraph von Lenbach and Wilhelm Leibl. American paintings in the permanent holdings (not always displayed) include works by Albert Bierstadt, Winslow Homer, John Singer Sargent and Thomas Eakins.

ADDITIONAL SIGHTS

★★★**Seattle Center** – Kids *Generally bounded by Denny Way, Broad St., Fifth Ave. N., Mercer St. & First Ave. N.* ☎ *206-684-8582. www.seattlecenter.com.* The location for the world's fair of 1962, this 74-acre campus northwest of downtown has flourished in the decades since. It now harbor theaters, museums, an amusement park and a sports arena, the whole complex drawing more than 8 million visitors a year. Already an entertainment hub with a stadium, civic auditorium and ice arena before the 1960s, the sector was a natural site for the Century 21 Exposition. Taking modernism as its theme, this fair was responsible for such futuristic landmarks as the Space Needle and Monorail. Several new buildings were constructed, while others took on new uses. The auditorium, for instance, became the brick-facade **Opera House**. The 1990s have seen more renovations and improvements: A sculpture garden was added to the 20 acres of landscaped grounds, and the **International Fountain** was revamped and outfitted with a sound-and-light system that turns it into a showy nighttime spectacle.

★★**Space Needle** – Kids *Off Broad St. opposite Fourth Ave. N.* ✗⛛🅿 ☎ *206-443-2100. www.spaceneedle.com.* Time has not robbed the Space Needle of its modern appearance. Embodying a 1960s vision of the future, the graceful metal tripod (1962, Victor Steinbrueck & John Graham Jr.) rises 602ft, with a revolving, saucer-like observation room and restaurant beneath its acme. Glass-walled elevators whoosh guests to a gift shop and encircling outdoor deck. Panoramic **views**★★ take in the city skyline, Elliott Bay, the Olympic Mountains and the Cascades.
Just north of the Space Needle entrance, the Swedish-designed **Monorail**★★ *(departs every 15min; ☎ 206-441-6038)* quietly traverses the 1.3mi from Seattle Center to downtown's Westlake Center in less than 2min.
Opened in June 2000 at the foot of the Space Needle, the **Experience Music Project** is dedicated to rock and other forms of American popular music, highlighting such Seattle artists as Jimi Hendrix, Kurt Cobain and jazz saxophonist Kenny G. Architect Frank Gehry's psychedelically colored building, a tribute to the ever-changing dynamic of rock'n'roll, will feature interactive exhibits and live performances.

** **Pacific Science Center** – *Second Ave. N. at Denny Way.* ✗ ♿ 🅿 ☎ *206-443-2001.*
www.pacsci.org. Dominating the south end of Seattle Center, this U-shaped facility
of six interconnected buildings with striking arches operates with the support of
such Seattle corporate behemoths as Boeing and Microsoft. Interactive exhibits
range from a virtual meteorology center and a hall of robotic dinosaurs to a tropical butterfly house and a "tech zone," outfitted with smart computers that enable
visitors to compose music, create art or try virtual hang gliding. Laser and IMAX
theaters enhance the wealth of learning centers.

** **Seattle Asian Art Museum** – *1400 E. Prospect St., Volunteer Park.* ♿ 🅿
☎ *206-654-3100. www.seattleartmuseum.org.* Ranked as one of the top 10 collections outside Asia, this Art Moderne museum (1933, Carl Gould) holds more
than 7,000 objects of Asian art, only a quarter of them on display at any one
time. Among the artifacts exhibited in the quietly meditative space are South Asian
Buddhist and Hindu sculpture, 4,000-year-old Chinese vessels and finely wrought
Japanese ceramics and temple art.

* **University of Washington** – *Generally bounded by 15th Ave. NE, NE 45th St.,
Union & Portage bays.* ☎ *206-543-2100. www.washington.edu.* This respected
university sprawls across nearly 700 acres above the northeast bank of the Lake
Washington Ship Canal. It educates some 35,000 students a year, making it one
of the largest institutions of higher learning on the West Coast. Two excellent
museums are located on the campus grounds, designed in the early 20C by landscape architect John Olmsted.

* **The Burke Museum of Natural History and Culture** – *17th Ave. NE & NE 45th St.,* ✗ ♿ 🅿
☎ *206-543-5590. www.washington.edu/burkemuseum.* The diverse geology,
archaeology and ethnology of the Pacific Rim are celebrated on two floors of
exhibits. On the lower level are artifacts and photographs that highlight cultures
of the Northwest Coast, the Pacific Islands, and East and Southeast Asia. The
main floor examines geologic history through dinosaur skeletons, mineral specimens and an exhibit on plate tectonics.

** **Henry Art Gallery** – *15th Ave. NE & NE 41st St.* ✗ ♿ ☎ *206-616-8674. www
.henryart.org.* One of the most progressive small museums in the US, the Henry
(1927, Carl Gould) is known for encouraging and exhibiting cutting-edge art. Permanent holdings, which may be stored in favor of temporary exhibitions, focus on
20C movements in French and American art. The contemporary collection includes
works by Robert Motherwell, Max Weber and Robert Rauschenberg. Among photographers represented are Man Ray, Ansel Adams and Imogen Cunningham.

** **Washington Park Arboretum** – *2300 Arboretum Dr. E., between Union Bay & Lake Washington Blvd. E.* 🅿 ☎ *206-543-8800. weber.u.washington.edu/~wpa.* Preserving
230 acres of woodlands just south of the campus, the arboretum is largely the
legacy of landscape architect brothers John Olmsted and Frederick Law Olmsted
Jr., who laid out its curving roadway and various gardens between 1909 and the
early 1930s. Trails lace the preserve, winding past 5,500 different trees, flowers
and other plants, past a Japanese garden and through a rhododendron glen, a
rock garden and an avenue of azaleas.

Seattle Skyline and Space Needle

■ **Bill Gates and Microsoft**

The youngest billionaire ever, Microsoft mogul Bill Gates (b.1955) made his first billion dollars by the age of 31. A scrappy and highly competitive entrepreneur, William Henry Gates III grew up in Seattle, his father a lawyer, his mother an educator. In his early teens he discovered computers and began teaching himself to program. With a small group of like-minded friends, Gates developed marketable computer programs that did everything from handling payrolls to monitoring highway traffic. As a high-school senior-to-be, Gates was offered a position at TRW, Inc., with an annual salary of $20,000, and took a year off from his studies to work. He attended Harvard University for two years but dropped out to pursue programming full-time. Gates correctly anticipated a coming revolution that would "put a computer in every home."

In 1975 Gates and childhood friend Paul Allen established a programming company called Microsoft in Albuquerque, New Mexico. The firm relocated to suburban Seattle in 1979. A year later Microsoft was hired by IBM to develop a disk-operating system for personal computers, and MS-DOS was born.

The rest is corporate history. For well over a decade Microsoft has dominated the software industry, often incurring the wrath of competitors and the scrutiny of the Federal Trade Commission. At time of publication, Gates and his company had emerged from most disputes victorious. He and his family live in a 37,000sq-ft house on the shores of Lake Washington.

* **Museum of History and Industry** – *2700 24th Ave. E., off Montlake Blvd. NE.* ☎ *206-324-1126. www.seattlehistory.org.* Multi-sensory exhibits explore Seattle's colorful past. Full-scale displays re-create an 1880s street scene, detail the fishing and maritime industries, recall the influence of the great 1889 fire and subsequent Klondike gold rush, and peer into the worlds of Native Americans and immigrant populations.

** **Hiram M. Chittenden Locks** – Kids *3015 NW 54th St.* ☎ *206-783-7059. www.nws.usace.army.* The US Army Corps of Engineers maintains this site on the Lake Washington Ship Canal, linking the lake on Seattle's eastern flank with Puget Sound. Two navigational locks, a dam and spillway, botanical garden and visitor center make up the project, which opened in 1917. Each year, 100,000 boats— pleasure and fishing craft, freight and research vessels—are "locked through," providing amusement for spectators who line the north side of the canal. A **fish ladder** on the south side enables spawning salmon to swim upstream while human visitors watch them through a submarine window.

** **Woodland Park Zoological Gardens** – Kids *Phinney Ave. N. between N. 50th & N. 59th Sts.* ✗ & ⯊ ☎ *206-684-4800. www.zoo.org.* Highly acclaimed for habitats that reflect the native environments of its 1,100 animals of 280 species, this fine zoo includes 65 acres of savanna, tundra, marshland, tropical rain forest and other terrain. The largest space is an open African savanna; Asian elephants roam through a Thai village as wolves and elk graze in an Alaskan taiga. John Olmsted designed most original zoo buildings in 1909; the park was improved during the 1930s and fully renovated with cageless spaces in the late 1980s.

** **Museum of Flight** – Kids *9404 E. Marginal Way S. at Boeing Field.* ✗ & ⯊ ☎ *206-764-5720. www.museumofflight.org. 5mi northwest of I-5 Exit 158.* The largest air-and-space museum in the western US features interactive exhibits that re-create the adventure of flight. The steel-and-glass central building contains a diverse collection of aircraft, from early gliders and biplanes to space capsules. One simulator gives visitors a feel for flying and air-traffic control; a theater has a live link to NASA satellite reception. The 1909 "Red Barn" relocated to this site was the hub of William Boeing's original Pacific Aero Products Company. Exhibits within outline The Boeing Company history.

EXCURSIONS

** **Bloedel Reserve** – *7571 NE Dolphin Dr., Bainbridge Island (35min crossing via Washington State Ferry from Pier 52, Alaskan Way, Seattle).* & ⯊ ☎ *206-842-7631. www.bloedelreserve.org. Call for advance reservations & specific directions.* This 150-acre reserve encapsulates the meadowlands, forests and glens representative of the natural beauty of the Northwest. Native flora thrives in its own setting, amid deft and subtle landscaping. Trails visit a marsh habitat for migratory and native waterfowl, a wetland forest, a grove of flowering shrubs, a Zen rock garden and a moss garden. The visitor center is housed in **Collinswood**, a classic French château-style home built in 1932.

★**Tillicum Village** – Kids *Tours (about 4.5hrs) depart Piers 55 & 56, Alaskan Way, Seattle.* ✗ ⅙ ☎ *206-443-1244. www.tillicumvillage.com.* A commercialized but sincere attempt to celebrate the native cultures of the Northwest, the "village"—actually a single longhouse of Kwakiutl style—was built in the 1960s on small Blake Island in Puget Sound. Visitors are treated to a traditional salmon bake, with the whole fish splayed open on cedar stakes and cooked over an alder-wood fire. Native performers offer a stage presentation based on Northwest myths, then demonstrate such traditional crafts as wood carving. Adjacent **Blake Island Marine State Park** encompasses 476 acres of trees and shrubs, 15mi of trails and 5mi of beaches. Deer, bald eagles and other wildlife inhabit the preserve.

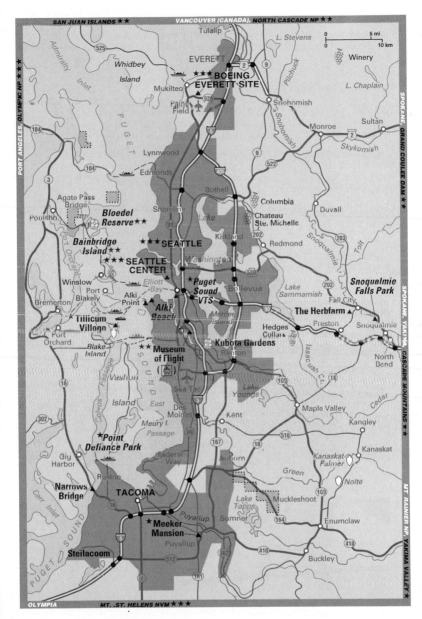

PUGET SOUND AREA★

Map p 353   Pacific Standard Time
Tourist Information ☎ 360-753-5600

Puget Sound funnels through northwest Washington state, spilling around myriad islands and into bays, inlets and straits created by long-gone glaciers. The fingers of water that extend south encompass the ever-expanding Sea-Tac megalopolis. Tacoma, once a rival to Seattle, now positions itself as a more-sedate alternative to the big city, with its own appealing museums, restaurants and theaters. Dominated by the grand dome of the state capitol, small-town Olympia lives quietly apart from the hub-bub of its northern neighbors.

The commercial center of Bellingham, hard by Canada, also maintains a relaxed, welcoming atmosphere. In the middle of the sound, the scores of isles and islets of the San Juan archipelago have for decades been the haunt of artists and craftsfolk. Summer visitors now descend upon these enchanting islands to savor their unsullied natural beauty from kayaks, bicycles and hiking trails.

SIGHTS

Tacoma – *32mi south of Seattle via I-5 (Exit 133).* ☎ *253-627-2836. www.tpctourism.org.* The 19C port and railroad town of Tacoma recently has spruced up its aging-industrial-town image and reinvented itself as a livable modern city of 180,000 people, complete with worthy museums, galleries and a new University of Washington branch campus. Nice parks, a lively theater district and fine old neighborhoods add to the city's friendly charm.

★★**Washington State History Museum** – *1911 Pacific Ave.* ✕ 🚻 📂 ☎ *253-272-3500. www.wshs.org.* In nine thematic exhibit areas, life-size dioramas and voice-overs dramatize the growth of the state from earliest European-Indian encounters, through 19-20C industrialization, to modern high-tech and environmental challenges. Upper-level galleries are devoted to stimulating temporary exhibits.

★**Tacoma Art Museum** – *1123 Pacific Ave.* 🚻 ☎ *253-272-4258. www.tacomaartmuseum.org.* Highlight of this museum, which exhibits the work of numerous Northwest artists, is an exquisite collection of **glass art**★★ by renowned Tacoma native **Dale Chihuly**.

★**Point Defiance Park** – **Kids** *Pearl St. at N. 54th St., 3mi north of Rte. 16 Exit 132.* ☎ *253-305-1000.* This 700-acre park sprawls on bluffs above Puget Sound. Features, in addition to gardens and woodsy trails, include **Fort Nisqually Historic Site**★★ *(Five Mile Dr.;* ☎ *253-591-5339)*—a living-history museum within a re-created 1855 Hudson's Bay Company fort—and the small but well regarded **Point Defiance Zoo and Aquarium**★ *(5400 N. Pearl St.;* ☎ *253-591-5337).*

© Robert Holmes

Glass Art by Dale Chihuly

Olympia – *60mi south of Seattle via I-5 (Exit 105).* ☎ *360-357-3362. www.olympiachamber.com.* Washington's modest capital centers around the striking state capitol building and the workings of state government. As far back as the 1840s, the town boasted the first US customs house in the Northwest; in 1856, a wooden territorial capitol was built. Though Olympia's early economic steam disappeared with a lack of railroad commerce, it became established as the permanent state capital in 1889. It now has a population approaching 40,000.

★★ **Washington State Capitol** – *Capitol Way between 11th & 16th Aves.* ☏ *360-664-2700*. The white-domed capitol makes a grand statement, rising 287ft above its base. Built between 1893 and 1928, the Neoclassical building sports six massive bronze doors embossed with scenes symbolizing state history and industry. Inside, a five-ton crystal Tiffany chandelier is centered above a marble floor in the vast rotunda. Public areas include the State Reception Room and the House and Senate legislative chambers.

Three blocks away, exhibits at the **State Capitol Museum★** *(211 W. 21st Ave.; ☏ 360-753-2580)* focus on construction of the capitol and the political and cultural history of the city and state. The museum is housed in a 1920s Italian Renaissance-style mansion.

★★★ **Boeing Everett Site** – *Rte. 526, Everett. Take I-5 north 24mi from Seattle to Exit 189; then turn west 3.5mi.* ♿ 🄿 ☏ *425-544-1264. www.boeing .com/companyoffices/aboutus/tours.* At its plant on the south side of the city of Everett, aeronautical giant Boeing assembles its wide-body commercial jetliners—747s, 767s and 777s. Since William Boeing founded Pacific Aero Products Company in 1916, the aircraft industry has been a bulwark of the regional economy. Thousands of people work here in one of the company's largest factories. Free 1hr **tours★★** take in the cavernous Main Assembly Building, where guides describe the work teams and assembly stations. Just outside, on Paine Field, completed jets are flight-tested before being delivered to customers worldwide.

Whidbey Island – *Coupeville, on Rte. 20, is 58mi north of Seattle via I-5 (Exit 182) & Rte. 525.* ☏ *360-675-3535.* A popular weekend getaway for Seattleites, Whidbey Island arcs in a narrow 60mi curve along the mainland coast, its bucolic tumble of hills, small towns and verdant fields interrupted only in the north by Whidbey Island Naval Air Station and the commercialism of Oak Harbor. The waterfront town of **Coupeville★**, dating from the 1850s, harbors gift shops and seafood restaurants, as well as Victorian homes built by 19C sea captains. The town is the locus of the sprawling 27sq-mi **Ebey's Landing National Historical Reserve★**, which preserves the land and spirit of an entire rural community and encompasses a museum and two state parks. Headquarters are in the **Island County Historical Museum** *(23 Front St.; ☏ 360-678-3310)*.

On the north end of the island, **Deception Pass State Park★** *(Rte. 20, 23mi north of Coupeville; ☏ 360-675-2417)* occupies both sides of Rosario Strait. Turnouts and a pedestrian walkway enable sightseers to cross the 976ft **Deception Pass Bridge★** and admire the surrounding rocky cliffs and turbulent tidal rush below.

Skagit Valley – *La Conner, on Rte. 534, is 66mi north of Seattle via I-5 Exit 221.* ☏ *360-466-4778.* This lush and often misty valley, drained by the Skagit *(SKA-jit)* River flowing westward from the Cascades, is especially colorful in spring when thousands of acres of **tulips, daffodils and irises★★** bloom in farms around Mount Vernon, its commercial hub. One of the largest commercial bulb-cultivation districts in the world, the valley hosts special tours and the Skagit Valley Tulip Festival *(☏ 360-428-5959)* in April. In fall, bird-watchers flock upstream to observe a bevy of bald eagles that roost and fish near Rockport.

The picturesque village of **La Conner★**, on the National Register of Historic Places, edges the Swinomish Channel off Skagit Bay. Founded in the 1860s, the artists' community boasts waterfront galleries, crafts shops, three museums and a charming ambience that make it an attractive weekend destination for urbanites. The **Museum of Northwest Art★★** *(121 S. First St.; ☏ 360-466-4446)* has acquired a strong reputation for its focus on Northwest masters, including Guy Anderson, Morris Graves and glass-artist Dale Chihuly.

★ **Bellingham** – *91mi north of Seattle via I-5 (Exit 256).* ☏ *360-671-3990.* A pleasant, well-heeled city of 62,000 in the Mount Baker foothills, Bellingham wraps itself around a bay of the same name. Early mid-19C settlements were based on coal mining and sawmills. Today the town is both a maritime hub, as southern terminus of the Alaska State Ferry System, and a college town focused around **Western Washington University** *(south of downtown via Bill McDonald Pkwy.; ☏ 360-650-3424)*, noted for its outdoor sculpture.

The **Fairhaven Historic District★** *(between 13th & 20th Sts.)* dates to the 1870s but burgeoned in the 1890s during speculation that the Great Northern Railroad would locate its western terminus here. That honor went instead to Tacoma, leaving this neighborhood a delightful mix of red brick storefronts housing cafes, galleries, bookshops and charmingly restored Victorian homes.

Preserving the region's cultural and artistic history, the **Whatcom Museum of History and Art★** *(121 Prospect St.; ☏ 360-676-6981)* has collections of West Coast Indian

■ Building a Boeing

The Boeing Company is the world leader in the manufacture of commercial jetliners, from commuter planes to long-distance carriers—including the 737, the world's most widely used large plane.

Boeing's largest factory, a half-hour's drive north of Seattle in Everett, includes the world's most spacious building: At 472 million cubic feet, the Main Assembly Building is larger even than the Vehicle Assembly Building at Florida's Kennedy Space Center. Its 11 stories cover 98.3 acres, room enough for four fully assembled jets. All three Boeing wide-bodies—the 747, 767 and 777—are made in Everett, each one taking four to five months to produce. These planes have logged 72 million flight hours on 18 million flights.

The largest, the 747-400, made its debut flight in 1988. It has a wingspan of 211ft 5in and a length of 231ft 10in. Fully loaded with 568 passengers, the double-aisle aircraft can fly 610mph at 35,000ft. With a lighter load of 400 passengers, it can fly more than 8,400mi nonstop. In May 1998, Boeing celebrated the production of its 2,000th wide-body.

Courtesy The Boeing Company

747s on Factory Floor, Boeing Everett Site

art, pioneer artifacts and natural-history specimens. It is lodged in a distinctive, turreted Victorian city hall, built in 1892 of red brick and topped by a bell tower. Adjoining the complex is a children's museum.

** **San Juan Islands** – *90-105mi north of Seattle; take I-5 north 65mi to Exit 230 at Burlington, then Rte. 20 west 15mi to Washington State Ferry terminal at Anacortes.* ☎ *360-468-3663*. Floating between the mainland and Vancouver Island like a fog-wrapped armada, this 172-island archipelago was once a range of mountains, covered by glaciers during the ice ages. Lummi Indians hunted on the islands; settlers farmed and tended orchards. Now the quiet San Juans attract artists, craftspeople, writers and summer vacationers who come for the bird-watching, whale-watching, beach-combing and general relaxing.

** **San Juan Island** – The most westerly of the three islands that offer visitor accommodations is also the most populous. Here the two units of **San Juan Island National Historical Park★** *(☎ 360-378-2240)* preserve coastal swatches of land associated with the joint occupation (1859-72) of the island by British and US troops following the Pig War, a tense two-month standoff resulting from the shooting of a swine. In the main town of Friday Harbor, the grassroots-style **Whale Museum** *(62 First St. N.; ☎ 360-378-4710)* has exhibits on echolocation, mating, calving and other cetacean topics.

★★ **Orcas Island** – Largest of the San Juans, horseshoe-shaped Orcas bends around long and beautiful East Sound. Its forested low mountains provide panoramas of the San Juans, the Cascade and Olympic Ranges, the Canadian Coast Range and Vancouver Island. More than 5,000 acres of the island are contained within **Moran State Park★** *(Horseshoe Hwy.; ☎ 360-376-2326)*, which has five lakes and 30mi of hiking trails.

★ **Lopez Island** – Relatively undeveloped, Lopez is a haven for artisans and seekers of solitude, its peaceful beaches and rocky inlets offering numberless seascapes. Tiny Lopez Village is the commercial center.

OLYMPIC PENINSULA★★★

Michelin map 493 B 2, 3   Pacific Standard Time
Tourist Information ☎ 360-452-8552 or www.olympicpeninsula.org

Northwestern Washington's Olympic Peninsula extends like a thumb, separating the jigsaw puzzle of Puget Sound islands and waterways from the Pacific Ocean. The glacier-sheathed Olympic Mountains rise in the north-central part of the peninsula, trapping wet Pacific air and creating a rain shadow to the east. This has made for a remarkable difference in rainfall between the Sequim-Dungeness Valley area on the east, which averages 16in a year, and the Pacific coastal valleys, which get 150in or more. Those western valleys harbor some of the few remaining stands of old-growth rain forest in the contiguous US. Shoreward of the forests lies a strand of wonderfully wild and log-tossed Pacific beach.

Historical Notes – Although early Spanish voyagers first laid claim to these northwestern shores, the presence of the Hudson's Bay Company in the early 19C helped firm up Great Britain's dominance of the area. White settlement, mostly concentrated along the Strait of Juan de Fuca, did not begin until the 1850s when farming, logging, fishing and sea trade became an entrenched way of life. Depletion of salmon runs and clear-cutting of forests in recent decades have forced local economies to rely more and more upon tourists, who flock here from urban areas for the varying wonders of Olympic National Park and the Victorian charms of Port Townsend.

SIGHTS

★★★ **Olympic National Park**   *Access via US-101 south and west of Port Angeles.*
△ ⚒ ♿ 🅿 ☎ *360-452-4501. www.nps.gov/olym. Visitor center, 3002 Mt. Angeles Rd. (south of US-101), Port Angeles; ☎ 360-452-0330.* Designated an International Biosphere Reserve and World Heritage Site, the 1,440sq-mi park is highly regarded for its exceptional natural beauty and the remarkable diversity of its three distinct wilderness ecosystems—glaciated mountain ranges, temperate rain forests and primitive coastal habitats. Within the park's boundaries live more than 300 types of birds and 70 species of mammals, among them some 5,000 Roosevelt elk, the largest herd in the world.
US Highway 101 runs around the perimeter of the national park on its east, north and west. Among its most accessible attractions is **Lake Crescent★★** *(18mi west of Port Angeles)*, one of three large lakes in the park. Cupped within steep, forested hillsides, the deep glacial lake is popular with outdoor recreation lovers, who often base themselves at the 1915 **Lake Crescent Lodge★** *(416 Lake Crescent Rd.; ☎ 360-928-3211)*. From here, a 2mi trail leads through old-growth forest to **Marymere Falls★**, a beautiful 90ft cascade.

★★★ **Hurricane Ridge** – *17mi south of visitor center on Heart O' the Hills/Hurricane Ridge Rd. ☎ 360-452 0329. Snowfall may close portions of the road Oct late Apr.* The winding road that climbs to the 5,230ft summit passes through dense forest and skirts lush alpine meadows, unfolding magnificent vistas of crenellated, snow-crusted peaks and the distant sea. Views from the top feature unobstructed perspectives on peaks, ridges and deep valleys. A network of trails traverses subalpine meadows covered in early summer with low-lying sedges, grasses and wildflowers.

★★★ **Hoh Rain Forest** – *91mi southwest of Port Angeles; entrance station 12mi east of US-101. Visitor center ☎ 360-374-6925.* On the western side of the park, this lush, dripping, primordial world of giant spruce and hemlock is draped with soft green club mosses and floored by shaggy, moldering logs. Shafts of sunlight angle into these ancient woods, casting a mystical glow and creating scenery that is eerily reminiscent of a pre-human earth, rank with life. Three short interpretive trails meander among the arboreal giants, many of them 20 stories tall, 12ft in diameter and 500 years old.

Hoh Rain Forest

Not far west of here, the **beaches**★★ around Kalaloch feature offshore sea stacks and shorelines that vary from narrow and rocky to wide and sandy. The ocean waters are part of the 3,300sq-mi **Olympic Coast National Marine Sanctuary,** where protected animals include sea otters, seals, gray whales and the world's largest species of octopus.

Port Angeles – *US-101, about 80mi northwest of Seattle.* ☎ *360-452-8552.* Situated on the Strait of Juan de Fuca about midway along the northern shoreline of the Olympic Peninsula, Port Angeles is the peninsula's largest town with about 19,000 people. It functions as a gateway to the national park. A ferry service links the town to Victoria, British Columbia, directly across the strait. Nearby **Dungeness National Wildlife Refuge**★ *(15mi northeast via Kitchen Dick Rd.;* ☎ *360-457-8451)* encompasses serene, 6mi-long Dungeness Spit, a sandy hook of land that is home to a cornucopia of seabirds and marine life.

★★ **Port Townsend** – *Rte. 20, 58mi northwest of Seattle.* ☎ *360-385-2722.* One of the best-preserved late-19C seaports in the US, Port Townsend is chockablock with grand houses and commercial buildings with ornate touches and high ceilings. Sited at the entrance to Puget Sound, the town of 8,000 traffics in its maritime flavor and heritage, yet manages to feel sophisticated and authentic rather than commercial. Fine two- and three-story stone edifices cluster along Water Street; many of them house bookshops, restaurants and boutiques. On the bluff above stands a trove of Victorian homes, some converted to bed-and-breakfast inns.

Port Townsend remains a center for the marine trades: Boat-building, sail-making and rope-making are all practiced and taught here. The entire town is a designated National Historic Landmark District, and its colorful past is well documented at the **Jefferson County Historical Museum**★ *(210 Madison St. at Water St.;* ☎ *360-385-1003).* Visitors may partake of both history and scenery at **Fort Worden State Park**★ *(W St. at Cherry St.;* ☎ *360-385-4730),* where the parade ground of a decommissioned fort is lined with a smart row of Victorians that once quartered officers. Beaches frame views north to the San Juans.

★ **Neah Bay** – *Rte. 112, 70mi northwest of Port Angeles.* Archaeological research indicates that Makah Indians have inhabited the Olympic Peninsula's extreme northwestern coastal region for at least 4,000 years. Carved totem poles rise above the gravestones in the small cemetery at Neah Bay, their modern reservation's only town. The history and culture of the tribe, which in 1999 inspired controversy when it resumed hunting whales after a self-imposed seven-decade moratorium, are brought into focus at the **Makah Museum**★★ *(Bay View Ave.;* ☎ *360-645-2711).* Displays include well-preserved remains and artifacts from a coastal village buried in a 15C mudslide and exposed by tidal erosion in 1970. Seven miles west of Neah Bay, **Cape Flattery**★, named by Captain James Cook in 1788, is the northwesternmost point of the contiguous US.

© Robert Holmes

Long Beach Penin-sula – *Rtes. 100 & 103 via US-101, 165mi southwest of Seattle.* ☏ *360-642-2400.* Stretching from the Columbia River to the mouth of Willapa Bay, the Long Beach Penin-sula fronts 28mi of surf-pounded coastline. Originally inhabited by Chinook Indians, the area is famous as the place where Lewis and Clark reached the shores of the Pacific in 1805. The **Lewis & Clark Interpretive Center**★ *(Fort Canby State Park, Rte. 100, 2mi southwest of Ilwaco;* ☏ *360-642-3029)* outlines their journey of exploration and provides a view of the ironically named Cape Disappointment, where the explorers had their first, awe-inspiring look at the tumultuous Pacific. A tour of nearby **North Head Lighthouse** *(*☏ *360-642-3078)* offers outstanding **views**★ of wave-lashed shore. North of this rocky headland, the peninsula narrows to a flat, 2mi-wide strip of land between the Pacific Ocean and **Willapa Bay**, a tidal estuary whose oyster beds are regarded by connoisseurs as among the finest in North America. A handful of small towns offer historic sites, miles of sandy (and windy) beach and lots of seaside ambience.

CASCADE MOUNTAINS★★

Michelin map 493 C 2, 3   Pacific Standard Time
Tourist Information ☏ 360-753-5600

Separating the wet coastland from the high, dry, eastern portion of Washington state, the jagged spine of the Cascades runs the entire length of Washington, from Canada to the Columbia River, and down through Oregon into northern California. Several volcanoes distinguish the Cascades, including its highest peak, Mt. Rainier (14,410ft), and Mt. St. Helens (8,363ft), which blew up as the world watched in 1980. These and other major Washington volcanoes—Mt. Adams (12,276ft), Mt. Baker (10,778ft) and Glacier Peak (10,568ft)—origi-nated only about 1 million years ago, although the Cascades began rising at least 25 million years earlier.

Native Americans and frontier settlers found the Cascades a highly effective bar-rier to east-west travel. Not until 1972, in fact, did the North Cascades Highway (Route 20) traverse the rugged terrain just south of the Canadian border. Even today few adventurers make their way deep into these craggy, glaciated strong-holds. A patchwork of national park and forest land blankets most of these moun-tains, helping to protect a rich chain of wildlife and providing myriad opportuni-ties for outdoor recreation. Thousands of miles of trails weave across highland meadows, streams and woodlands, past old mining camps and gorgeous alpine lakes, up to prime mountain viewpoints. Drawing steady visitation from the urban areas of Puget Sound, the range still manages to feel larger than life, its cold heights and remote valleys providing restorative power to those who seek it.

SIGHTS

★★★ **Mount St. Helens National Volcanic Monument** – *164mi south of Seattle.* ☏ *360-274-2100. Main access via Rte. 504, 48mi east of I-5 (Exit 49) at Castle Rock.* One of the world's most famous volcanoes, St. Helens erupted in 1980 with the intensity of several atomic bombs, destroying its northern flank and reducing its elevation by more than 1,300ft. Today the eviscerated mountain, surrounded by a 172sq-mi preserve, has become a leading visitor attraction. Youngest of the major Cascade volcanoes, St. Helens was known to ancient Native Americans as Fire Mountain. Quiet through most of the 20C, the conical mountain rumbled slowly awake in spring 1980, for several weeks giving off warning quakes and hisses, allowing time for locals to evacuate and news media and scientists to gather. The sudden explosion on May 18 sent a column of ash 15mi into the atmosphere; poured hot rock and pumice over the countryside; devastated 250sq mi of forest; caused severe flooding, and left 57 people dead. When the eruption was over, the 9,677ft peak measured only 8,363ft, and the landscape was forever changed.

The **Mount St. Helens Visitor Center**★★ *(Rte. 504, 5mi east of I-5;* ☎ *360-274-2100)* offers a fascinating live-footage film, a slide show and other worthy exhibits. From here, the 43mi drive along Spirit Memorial Highway leads to the **Johnston Ridge Observatory**★★★ *(Rte. 504;* ☎ *360-274-2140),* within 5mi of the volcano's crater. The devastation is still vividly apparent. Acres of scorched trees, interspersed with newly planted trees, give way to the blowdown zone, where the forest was leveled by the blast. Other interpretive centers offer different perspectives on the destruction and regrowth.

★★★ **Mount Rainier National Park** – *Rtes. 410 & 706, about 70mi southeast of Tacoma.* ☎ *360-569-2211. www.nps.gov/mora.* Highest volcano and fifth-highest peak in the contiguous US, Rainier is a majestic backdrop to the Puget Sound megalopolis. An arctic island in a temperate zone, the summit is covered in more than 34sq mi of ice and snow. Melt-water from its 25 glaciers filigrees the terrain with fast-running rivers and streams, while volcanic steam vents have created a labyrinth of ice caves. Though its last major eruption occurred 2,000 years ago, scientists believe it could come roaring to life again soon.

The **Nisqually-Paradise Road** *(Rte. 706, open all year; other roads closed late Oct-late May, depending upon snowfall)* enters the park at its southwest corner, twisting 19mi past streams, waterfalls and grand viewpoints to the meadows of **Paradise Valley**★★★. A visitor center and observatory at 5,400ft provide overviews of park wildlife and geologic features. Hikes vary from the Nisqually Vista Trail *(1.2mi)* to the challenging Skyline Trail *(5mi)*. **Sunrise**★★★ *(14mi from White River entrance, Rte. 410)* is the highest point attainable by car (6,400ft) and boasts breathtaking views of Rainier (west), Sunrise Lake (east) and conical Mt. Adams (south).

★ **Northwest Trek** – 🅺🅸🅳🅾 *Rte. 161, 6mi north of Eatonville.* ☎ *360-832-6117.* This 635-acre wildlife park displays animals native to the Pacific Northwest region. Tram tours *(5.5mi, 1hr)* enable visitors to see grizzly and black bears, caribou, elk, moose, bison, bighorn sheep, great blue herons, wild turkeys and other creatures. Walk-through habitats, several miles of nature trails and a children's discovery center are additional offerings.

Mount St. Helens from Johnston Ridge Observatory

** **North Cascades National Park** – *Approximately 120mi northeast of Seattle. Main access from Rte. 20, 50-100mi east of I-5 (Exit 230), or from Rte. 542 at Mt. Baker, 55mi east of Bellingham.* ☎ *360-856-5700. www.nps.gov/noca.* Old-growth forests, hidden waterfalls, jewellike lakes, alpine meadows and glaciated peaks of 7,000ft to 9,000ft fill this park's 1,069sq mi, most accessible only by foot. Its 300 glaciers account for half of the icefields in the US outside Alaska. Endangered animals such as grizzly bears and mountain lions inhabit the backcountry, generally far from human eyes. In 1988, Congress designated 93 percent of the park's lands as wilderness, affording the highest degree of federal protection. The 2,600mi **Pacific Crest National Scenic Trail** traverses the park.

Just off Route 20, which divides the park into northern and southern units, the **visitor center** *(Rte. 20, 1mi west of Newhalem)* offers films and information on fishing, hiking and backpacking. A short boardwalk trail ends at a viewpoint looking north to 6,805ft Pinnacle Peak in the Picket Range.

* **Ross Lake National Recreation Area** – *Rte. 20, 50-75mi east of I-5 (Exit 230).* ☎ *360-856-5700. www.nps.gov/rola.* Bordering both sides of Route 20 as it slices North Cascades National Park, then angling north, this 183sq-mi preserve encompasses three dams, three lakes and two small towns. Between 1924 and 1939, Seattle City Light built the dams across the upper Skagit River for hydroelectric power; the largest, Ross Dam, measures 540ft high by 1,300ft long. Since the mid-20C, the power company has conducted popular **tours** outlining the purpose, construction and operation of its dams. Tours include a film, powerhouse tour, boat cruise and ride on a 1920s incline railway built to carry dam workers 570ft up the 47 percent grade of Sourdough Mountain. Foot trails lace the backcountry around Ross Lake, largest of the three reservoirs.

** **Lake Chelan National Recreation Area** – *Accessible via boat or small plane from Chelan, 182mi east of Seattle on US-97A.* △ ✗ ⚕ ☎ *360-856-5700. www.nps.gov/lach.* This narrow, 55mi-long lake nestles in a glacially gouged trough in the rain shadow of the Cascades. Its lower end is surrounded by arid hills and apple orchards; its upper end snakes among sawtooth peaks that soar 8,000ft above the water's surface. Abutting North Cascades National Park, the recreation area centers on the charming and serene village of **Stehekin**. Narrated shuttle-bus tours ply the gravel Stehekin Valley Road, which follows the Stehekin River north from the head of the lake.

EASTERN WASHINGTON

Michelin map 493 C, D 3, 4   Pacific Standard Time
Tourist Information ☎ 360-753 5600

Open, dry and rugged, the vast expanse of eastern Washington stretches from the foothills of the Cascades to the Idaho border, and from Walla Walla north to the Okanogan highlands. Rivers cut deep, meandering canyons across the arid land, punctuated here and there by irrigated fruit orchards and vineyards.

Over the centuries, a parade of Plateau Indians, explorers, ranchers and farmers came through and left their respective marks. Modern visitors who explore this grand landscape will find a variety of appealing natural areas, parks, museums and historic sites.

SIGHTS

* **Spokane** – *276mi east of Seattle via I-90.* ☎ *888-776-5263. www.visitspokane.com.* An 1880s transportation hub and trading center, Washington's second-largest city (184,000 residents) sprawls along the wooded slopes of the Spokane River near the state's eastern border. Its downtown encompasses dozens of historic buildings and a spectacular stretch of river where waterfalls crash over basalt lava cliffs. Elsewhere, residential neighborhoods line tree-shaded bluffs with well-kept Victorian mansions and Craftsman-style cottages. Exhibits in the **Cheney Cowles Memorial Museum*** *(2316 W. First Ave.; ☎ 509-456-3931)* provide a concise overview of the history of Spokane and eastern Washington, from prehistory to the present day.

** **Riverfront Park** – *Spokane Falls Blvd. between Post & Washington Sts.* ✗ ⚕ ☎ *509-456-4386.* Occupying both banks of the Spokane River, this outstanding park was developed for the Expo '74 world's fair. It offers rolling lawns shaded by ponderosa pines, landscaped walkways, a splendidly restored 1909 **carousel***, a **gondola ride** to the base of Lower Spokane Falls, a small amusement park and an IMAX theater.

* **Manito Park** – *Grand Blvd. & 18th Ave.* ♿ 🅿 ✆ *509-625-6622.* This delightful park, 2mi south of downtown, presents a Japanese garden, an immense rose garden, a perennial garden and a European Renaissance-style garden.

** **Grand Coulee Dam** – *Rte. 155, Coulee Dam, 228mi east of Seattle via US-2. Visit interior of dam by guided tour only.* ♿ 🅿 ✆ *509-633-9265.* This mammoth, 55-story-high wall of sloped concrete stretches across the Columbia River for nearly a mile, spanning the cliffs of a deep desert canyon. Built by the Civilian Conservation Corps in the 1930s, it generates a tremendous amount of electricity and provides irrigation for thousands of square miles of farmland. Lake Roosevelt, its 151mi-long reservoir, is contained within **Lake Roosevelt National Recreation Area** *(1008 Crest Dr., Coulee Dam;* ✆ *509-633-9441).*

* **Yakima Valley** – *141mi southeast of Seattle via I-90 & I-82.* ✆ *509-575-3010.* A verdant river corridor, the Yakima Valley stretches in a long southeasterly arc nearly 100mi from Ellensburg to the Horse Heaven Hills. Settled in the 1860s by cattle ranchers, the valley today ranks as one of the richest fruit-growing regions in the US, its orchards, vineyards and farms yielding apples, wine grapes, winter pears, sweet cherries and more.

The city of Yakima itself, a commercial hub of 65,000 people, offers an attractive riverside greenbelt and two interesting museums. The **Yakima Valley Museum** *(2105 Tieton Dr.;* ✆ *509-248-0747)* focuses on regional history and personalities, including native sons US Supreme Court Justice William O. Douglas (1898-1980) and world-champion skier twins Phil and Steve Mahre (b.1957). The **Yakima Electric Railway Museum** *(306 W. Pine St.;* ✆ *509-575-1700)* is a depot for vintage electric trolley cars that take passengers on 2hr rides through the city and countryside.

South of Yakima, the story of the native Yakama Indian tribe and its struggle to endure is presented through dioramas, paintings and petroglyphs at the excellent **Yakama Nation Cultural Center Museum*** 🄺🄸🄳🄴 *(100 Spilyiy Loop off US-97, Toppenish;* ✆ *509-865-2800).*

North, in Ellensburg, the **Chimpanzee and Human Communication Institute**** 🄺🄸🄳🄴 *(400 E. 8th Ave.;* ✆ *509-963-2244)* is located on the Central Washington University campus. Unique in the world, the facility offers 1hr guided tours that include interaction with a family of chimpanzees trained to converse with humans, and among themselves, in American Sign Language.

Tri-Cities Area – *Approximately 220mi southeast of Seattle via I-90, I-82 & I-182.* ✆ *509-946-1651.* Including the adjacent communities of Richland, Pasco and Kennewick, poised at the confluence of the Yakima, Columbia and Snake Rivers, this remote area came to sudden life in 1942 as a major site for the Manhattan Project. Plutonium produced at the **Hanford Site** north of Richland powered the atomic bomb dropped on Nagasaki in 1945. Production continued until 1988; a cleanup of the toxic waste is expected to pump more money into the local economy than did plutonium-making itself.

Today a center for technology industries, the Tri-Cities constitute one of the largest metropolitan areas in Washington state: The three communities have a combined population of 115,000.

Displays at the **Columbia River Exhibition of History, Science and Technology** *(95 Lee Blvd.;* ✆ *509-943-9000)* detail the history of the Hanford Site with historical photos and interactive models. **Columbia River Journeys*** *(Columbia Park Marina, 1229 Columbia Dr. SE, Richland;* ✆ *509-943-0231)* offers half-day jet-boat excursions through part of the site. Off-limits since World War II, Hanford's desert lands are still rugged, largely roadless, and rich in wildlife.

Walla Walla – *273mi southeast of Seattle via I-90, I-82 & US-12.* ✆ *509-525-0850.* An appealing agricultural hub and college town, Walla Walla stands amid rolling hills and farmland at the foot of the Blue Mountains. Wheat, wine grapes and vegetables grow here in prodigious quantities. **Whitman Mission National Historic Site*** *(7.7mi west on Rte. 12;* ✆ *509-522-6360)* preserves the grounds of an 1836 Presbyterian mission to the Cayuse Indians that operated until 1847, when missionaries Marcus and Narcissa Whitman and 11 workers were massacred.

Sierra Nevada

Emerald Bay, Lake Tahoe

The mountains that arc along California's eastern and northern boundaries, separating the state from the rest of the country, historically have served both as barriers to, and magnets for, emigrant populations. The granite bulwark of the Sierra Nevada marches 400mi from Tehachapi Pass, south of Bakersfield, to the Cascade Range near Lassen Peak, walling off the fertile Central Valley from the desert of the Great Basin. From Lassen north to Mt. Shasta and beyond, the volcanic Cascade Range presents a barrier generally lower, though similarly rugged, punctuated with isolated volcanic peaks of great height. These ranges traditionally divided the homelands of various Native American peoples, many of whom nevertheless engaged in summer trade over their crests. It was the presence of gold in these mountains that inspired the massive influx of wealth-hungry prospectors to California during the Gold Rush of 1849.

Mining heritage remains strong in the mountains and foothills today. But the Sierra now are better known for their recreational opportunities. Some of the nation's largest and most sublime national parks, wilderness areas and outdoor resorts abound throughout these ranges, preserving landscapes and natural curiosities of extraordinary character. Here are the giant forests of Sequoia National Park, the deep canyons and jagged peaks of Kings Canyon, the polished walls and glistening waterfalls of Yosemite. Here, too, are Mt. Shasta's soaring white dome and the deep blue waters of Lake Tahoe as well as remnants of a recent volcanic past that still smolder at Lassen Peak.

West of the Sierra sprawls the Central Valley, created by silt carried in rivers from the mountains over the millennia. The burgeoning California state capital of Sacramento is located here. To the east, in the rain shadow of the great ranges, lies a high desert of stark mountains and deep valleys. The Great Basin, highly mineralized with ores that spawned their own repeated gold and silver rushes, has left a colorful legacy of boom towns, ghost towns and a unique, free-wheeling attitude toward gambling that epitomizes the modern state of Nevada.

363

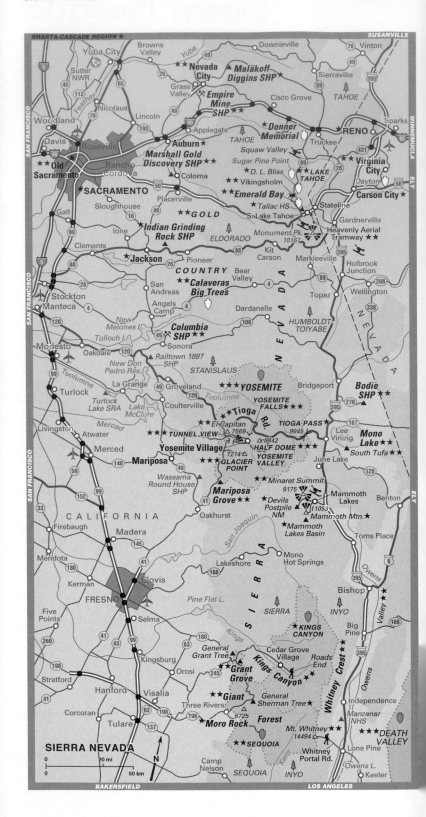

LAKE TAHOE★★

Encircled by a ring of lofty ridges and peaks, this deep blue lake straddling the California-Nevada border at 6,225ft elevation is the most popular and complete vacation resort in the Sierra. The lake basin was once the summering grounds of the Washoe people. It was rapidly claimed and developed after the 1859 discovery of the Comstock Lode, when its broad surface was used by steamboats that transported its timber to shore up the mines.

Subsequent developers recognized the lake's rare beauty, staking shoreline claims for early resorts, summerhouses and vacation mansions. The federal government set aside most of the hinterlands as national forest in the late 19C; some lakeside properties became California state parks in the 20C. But most of the lakefront remains privately owned.

South Lake Tahoe, a small city of motels, shops and restaurants, serves vacationers who flock for summer recreation, winter skiing and year-round casino and celebrity entertainment in the adjacent Nevada community of Stateline. Highways encircle the lake, linking numerous ski resorts and smaller, rustic settlements geared for summer visits. Trailheads offer access to excellent hiking, including the 150mi Tahoe Rim Trail, designed to encircle the lake near the ridgeline (two sections are still under construction).

By riding the spectacular cable car at Squaw Valley (☎ 530-583-6955), visitors to the north side of Lake Tahoe can enjoy splendid views from the 8,200ft-elevation sundeck at High Camp★. Skiing and snowboarding provide winter sport at Squaw Valley, site of the 1960 Winter Olympic Games; an ice-skating rink, swimming pool, restaurants and spa are open year-round. Another splendid view of Lake Tahoe, this one from the south, rewards riders who ascend the flanks of 10,167ft Monument Peak on the Heavenly Aerial Tramway★★ (☎ 530-586-7000).

SIGHTS

★Taylor Creek Visitor Center – 870 Emerald Bay Rd. (Rte. 89), 2.5mi northwest of South Lake Tahoe CA. ▲ & 🄿 ☎ 530-573-2674. www.r5.fs.fed .us/tahoe. This US Forest Service center provides a comprehensive overview of Tahoe's human and natural history. Several trails approach the lakeshore, though only the hardiest swimmers brave its frigid waters. The Rainbow Trail (.5mi) follows the fringe of an aspen-ringed meadow to the Stream Profile Center★, where subterranean plate-glass windows provide a fish's-eye view of life in a Sierra brook. This walk is most sensational in October, when spawning kokanee salmon fill Taylor Creek with thousands of wriggling, flaming-red fish. The trail to Tallac Historic Site★ leads to the remains of a fashionable 19C resort hotel and casino built by mining speculator Lucky Baldwin. Other private estates farther east from Baldwin's are now likewise owned by the Forest Service, which maintains the Pope-Tevis Estate (1899) and Valhalla mansion (1924), and opens the Baldwin-McGonagle House★ (1921) in summer as a museum.

★★Emerald Bay State Park Emerald Bay Rd. (Rte. 89), 8mi northwest of South Lake Tahoe CA. ▲ ☎ 530-525-7232. Embracing a glacier-carved fjord acclaimed as the loveliest corner of the lake, this park provides majestic alpine views, beautiful hiking trails and guided tours of a strikingly eccentric mansion, Vikingsholm★★ (1929), designed to resemble an AD 9C Nordic castle. The 5.3mi lakeshore Rubicon Trail leads across the northern edge of Emerald Bay to Lester Beach in D.L. Bliss State Park★.

EXCURSION

★Donner Memorial State Park – Off I-80 at Rte. 89, 2.3mi west of Truckee CA. ▲ 🄿 ☎ 530-582-7892. Commemorating the Donner Party disaster of the winter of 1846-47, the centerpiece of this ironically peaceful park on the shore of Donner Lake is a cast-bronze statue of a family in the desperate straits of starvation. When caught by early snows while attempting to cross the 7,239ft ridge now known as Donner Pass, the party of 87 emigrants, stranded without adequate provisions, erected makeshift cabins and settled in to await rescue as a smaller party set out for help. Before their rescuers returned in mid-February, the survivors were forced to cannibalize their dead; only 47 survived the ordeal. Their story is related in exhibits and film at the park's Emigrant Trail Museum★★.

Please see explanation on p 64.

Staying in the Sierra Nevada and Central Valley

The Ahwanee Hotel – *Yosemite National Park CA.* ⏹ ♿ 🅿 ☎ *559-252-4848. 126 rooms.* **$$$$** A National Historic Landmark, this towering timber-and-stone hotel has hosted famous guests from Winston Churchill to Charlie Chaplin. Nature lovers sit around a granite fireplace and conjure the spirit of John Muir. After hiking the Yosemite Valley, they recline on twig furnishings in The Great Lounge or **The Indian Room**, decorated with Indian crafts.

Gold Hill Hotel – *1540 Main St., Virginia City NV.* ⏹ 🅿 . ☎ *775-847-0111. 15 rooms.* **$$** Nevada's oldest operating hotel was established in 1859 atop the Comstock Lode. Period antiques—from guest rooms to the cozy brick-walled bar—help maintain its historical appeal. An intimate dining room overlooking Gold Hill Canyon serves country French cuisine. Historical programs include cowboy poetry readings.

Riverboat Delta King – *1000 Front St., Sacramento CA.* ⏹ ♿ 🅿 ☎ *916-444-5464. www.deltaking.com. 44 rooms.* **$$** During the Prohibition era, this "floating pleasure palace" ran between Sacramento and San Francisco. These days, the red paddlewheeler remains in one place, on the Sacramento River in Old Town. Guests stroll on the promenade deck, listen to Dixieland jazz and dine in the **Pilothouse Restaurant.** Cabins are cozy, with solid oak and brass fixtures.

The Shore House – *7170 North Lake Blvd., Tahoe Vista CA.* ⏹ 🅿 ☎ *530-546-7270. www.tahoeinn.com. 9 rooms.* **$$** Each room has a private entrance that overlooks Lake Tahoe. The Moon Room has a Tahoe sky painted on the ceiling; the Tree House is framed by Ponderosa pines. Log beds and knotty pine walls are a rustic complement to the dining room, which features a large, river-rock fireplace.

Sorensen's Resort – *14255 Hwy. 88, Hope Valley CA.* ⏹ ♿ 🅿 ☎ *530-694-2203. www.sorensensresort.com. 33 rooms.* **$** After taking a resort class in fly-fishing, watercolor painting or astronomy, guests may steam in the wood-fired sauna or retire to a miniature log cabin in a grove of aspen. Lodgings range from dormitory-style bunkhouses to a replica Norwegian farmhouse for six.

Dining in the Sierra Nevada and Central Valley

Erna's Elderberry House – *Rte. 41, Oakhurst CA.* ☎ *559-683-6800. www.elderberryhouse.com.* **$$$ Creative Continental.** Just 20 minutes south of Yosemite Park, this restaurant feels like a country estate with three dining rooms of French provincial furnishings and impressive views of the Sierra. Prix-fixe menus of simple, natural ingredients change daily-perhaps including salads of field greens with nectarine vinaigrette or pan-seared scallops topped by saffron aioli.

Slocum House – *7992 California Ave., Fair Oaks CA.* ☎ *916-961-7211.* **$$ Creative International.** This elegant manor, some 13mi east of Sacramento, offers dining in a classically appointed indoor setting or in a large outdoor garden with free-roaming fowl. The eclectic menu ranges from California French to spicy Southwestern and Caribbean, with Asian influences.

Sunnyside Restaurant – *1850 West Lake Blvd., Tahoe City CA.* ☎ *530-583-7200. www.hulapie.com/sunnyside.* **$$ American.** Diners moor their boats at the Sunnyside Marina on Lake Tahoe before grabbing a dinner of barbecued pork ribs with Western "giddy-up" sauce and crispy zucchini. The building doubles as a comfortable mountain lodge, with beautiful views of the surrounding High Sierra.

Louis' Basque Corner – *301 E. Fourth St., Reno NV.* ☎ *775-323-7203.* **$ Basque.** Many Basques came to the US from their European homeland in the late 19C, lodging in family boardinghouses. The tradition lives on at Louis', where unacquainted diners share large tables. All-inclusive meals include soup, salad, beans, potatoes and hearty entrées like chicken Basquaise or oxtails Bourguignon.

SACRAMENTO AND THE GOLD COUNTRY★★

Map p 364   Pacific Standard Time
Tourist Information ☎ 916-264-7777 or www.sacramentocvb.org

California's green and sprawling state capital was founded during the Gold Rush at the confluence of the American and Sacramento Rivers, a port of disembarkation for steamboat passengers. The site lay 2mi west of Sutter's Fort, a spacious rancho founded on a Mexican land grant by Swiss adventurer John Sutter in 1839. Ironically, the mining stampede sparked by his own workman's discovery of gold on the American River ultimately cost Sutter both his property and his mercantile advantages.

Despite terrible floods and fires, Sacramento's waterfront commercial district thrived as a vital link between trans-Sierra highways and Sacramento River shipping. A protective levee and new brick buildings brought prosperity and stability, prompting California to relocate its capital here in 1854. The city's destiny as a transportation hub was boosted when the Central Pacific line was leveraged eastward across the Sierra Nevada, completing the first transcontinental rail link in 1869. Today sitting astride two major interstate highways, Sacramento, with a population of approximately 404,000, remains a primary agricultural distribution center in addition to its role as state capital.

In recognition of James Marshall's discovery of gold in early 1848, the Sierra Nevada foothill region to the east of Sacramento is known as the Gold Country. The region counted nearly 90,000 miners at the peak of the Gold Rush in 1852, and some 106 million troy ounces of gold were extracted before "gold fever" subsided in 1867. While many settlements were quickly depopulated, others developed into commercial centers, setting the stage for a regional economy that depends today more on ranching, tourism and timber production than on mining. Route 49 links the principal communities along a winding 326mi route from Sierra City in the north to Mariposa in the south.

★SACRAMENTO

★★**California State Capitol** – *10th St. between L & N Sts.* ✗ ☎ 916-324-0333. Surrounded by Capitol Park, a 40-acre rectangle of stately trees and lawn, and crowned by a 210ft Neoclassical dome, the 1860 capitol rises grandly at the head of the Capitol Mall behind a colonnaded facade of granite and white-painted brick. Tours begin from a basement visitor center. When the legislature is in session, visitors may observe the Senate and Assembly at work from third-floor balcony seats; both chambers are decorated to appear c.1900.

★**Golden State Museum** – *1020 O St.* ✗ ▣ ☎ 916-653-7524. *www.ss.ca.gov/museum/.* Through multimedia exhibits, this sleek treasury of archival documents, artifacts and newsreels attempts to illuminate the qualities of geography, history, politics and population that make California unique. Specific exhibits portray the impact of water on the state's economy, the procedures of creating successful legislation, and the power of such cultural touchstones as the movie industry to create the "image" of California.

★★**Old Sacramento** 〔Kids〕 *I to L Sts., between Sacramento River & I-5. Self-guided walking tour brochure from visitor center (Front & K Sts.).* ✗ ▣ Sacramento's original downtown is the nation's largest assemblage of Gold Rush-era buildings. Springing up in the early 1850s beside Sutter's embarcadero, the brick and wood buildings, fronted by covered wooden sidewalks, now house a lively collection of souvenir shops, museums and eateries. Permanently docked as a floating hotel along the waterfront levee is the *Delta King*, a sternwheeler that once shuttled passengers from here to San Francisco. Historic addresses include the **B.F. Hastings & Co. Building** *(2nd & J Sts.)*, western terminus of the Pony Express (as commemorated by a bronze equestrian statue across the street); today it houses Gold Rush paraphernalia in a snug **Wells Fargo Museum** *(☎ 916-440-4263).*

Old Sacramento's high point is the **California State Railroad Museum**★★ 〔Kids〕 *(125 I St.; ☎ 916-445-6645)*, where 21 meticulously restored locomotives, a railway post office, a sleeping car, a luxurious private car and other stock illustrate the impact of local and trans-Sierra railroading. Mining and agricultural history, and pioneer domestic life, are dynamically illustrated in exhibits in the **Discovery Museum**★ 〔Kids〕 *(101 I St.; ☎ 916-264-7075)*.

★**Sutter's Fort State Historic Park** – 〔Kids〕 *2701 L St.* ▣ ☎ 916-445-4422. Founded in 1839 as headquarters of a 76sq-mi land grant known as New Helvetia, Sutter's Fort welcomed early pioneers and explorers with legendary hospitality. John Sutter's prosperity was in sharp decline by the 1850s, however. The state acquired the abandoned and dilapidated fort in 1890, renovating and furnishing it. Visitors may explore the living quarters, bakery, and blacksmith's and other work rooms. Costumed docents often enliven the tour with historical reenactments.

★★ GOLD COUNTRY

★★ **Nevada City** – With scores of handsome Victorian houses on its forested hills above Deer Creek, this picturesque town of 3,200 has long been known as the graceful "Queen City" of the northern mines. Elegant shops and restaurants in the picturesque commercial district today cater to overnight visitors.

★★ **Empire Mine State Historic Park** – 🄺🄸🄳🄸 *5mi south of Nevada City via Empire St., near Grass Valley.* 🄿 ☏ *530-273-5762.* California's largest and richest deep mine boasts 367mi of tunnels that produced 5.8 million troy ounces of gold in a century of operation (1856-1956). Visitors may tour the home and gardens of mine owner William Bourn, Jr., and descend 30ft to gaze down the main winze, or diagonal shaft, extending 10,000 feet to a depth of nearly a mile.

★ **Malakoff Diggins State Historic Park** – *27mi northeast of Nevada City. Take Rte. 49 north 11mi; turn on Tyler Foote Crossing Rd., left on Cruzon Grade Rd. and follow signs.* △ 🄿 ☏ *530-265-2740.* California's largest hydraulic mining pit is a lurid example of the disastrous effects on hillsides wrought by miners armed with high-pressure streams of water. The gaping gulch of the Malakoff Pit was eroded from 1855 until 1884, when hydraulic mining was banned by the state because it caused such destructive silting and flooding of downstream farm-lands. A handful of Gold Rush-era buildings survive in the pleasant, tree-shaded village of North Bloomfield, site of the park visitor center.

★ **Auburn** – The Gold Country's largest town, with over 12,000 people, Auburn is a rail and highway junction with a charming 19C Old Town and an informa-tive **Gold Country Museum** *(1273 High St.; ☏ 530-889-6500).*

★★ **Marshall Gold Discovery State Historic Park** – *Rte. 49, 8mi northwest of Placerville.* 🄿 ☏ *530-622-3470. www.coloma.com.* This park preserves two-thirds of the historic village of **Coloma,** built where James Marshall discovered gold on January 28, 1848. A reconstructed sawmill and visitor center com-memorate the events that touched off the California Gold Rush.

★ **Jackson** – Founded in 1849, Jackson today displays handsome 19C Main Street architecture. The **National Hotel** (1863) claims to be the oldest continually operating hotel in the state. In a historic brick home (1859) atop a small knoll overlooking downtown, the **Amador County Museum★** *(225 Church St.; ☏ 209-223-6386)* displays numerous Gold Rush artifacts including working mine models.

★ **Indian Grinding Rock State Historic Park** – 🄺🄸🄳🄸 *Volcano Rd., 12mi east of Jackson via Rte. 88.* △ ♿ 🄿 ☏ *209-296-7488.* Pitting a flat limestone outcrop are hun-dreds of mortar holes once used by native Miwok Indians to grind acorns into meal. Re-created Miwok bark dwellings and a ceremonial roundhouse stand near a small regional museum.

Panning for Gold, Columbia State Historic Park

★★ Calaveras Big Trees State Park – *Rte. 4, 24mi east of Angels Camp.* △ ▣
☏ *530-795-2334.* The first grove of giant sequoias to be developed for
tourism was discovered in 1852 by a bear hunter. Visitors see giants along the
well-groomed, self-guided nature trail *(1mi)* through the **North Grove.** Fewer hike
the more remote trail *(4.7mi round-trip)* to the **South Grove,** although it leads to
the park's largest specimens, including the massive Agassiz tree.

★★ Columbia State Historic Park – [Kids] *Rte. 49, 4mi north of Sonora.* ✗ ▣
☏ *209-532-0150.* Founded in 1850, the boomtown of Columbia survived several fires and a lengthy decline before the state acquired it in 1945. Cars are
banned from downtown, where costumed park employees re-create daily life in
1850-70 at shops and businesses. Visitors may pan for gold or tour an operating hard-rock tunnel, the **Hidden Treasure Mine★** *(*☏ *209-532-9693),* on a hillside
beyond town.

Mariposa – A gateway to Yosemite National Park, Mariposa is home to the
California State Mining and Mineral Museum★★ [Kids] *(Mariposa County Fairgrounds;*
☏ *209-742-7625),* one of the West's most informative displays of mining history. With about 20,000 specimens, the collection offers eye-catching displays
of California gold, a working model of the 1904 Union Iron Works stamp mill,
and a walk-through model of a Gold Country mine.

SEQUOIA AND KINGS CANYON NATIONAL PARKS★★

Map p 364   Pacific Standard Time
Tourist Information ☏ 559-565-3134 or www.nps.gov/seki

The world's largest forests of giant sequoia trees are found in these impressive
twin parks, which—together with adjacent national-forest wilderness areas—preserve the second-largest roadless area in the continental US.

This is a rugged land of plunging canyons, deep forests, ranging wildlife and mountain crests soaring above 14,000ft. Formed in 1890 to protect uncut sequoia
groves, Sequoia National Park was soon tripled in size when Congress established
General Grant National Park to protect the Grant Grove. In 1940, the new Kings
Canyon National Park absorbed the Grant Grove. Among many superlative features
are the Sherman Tree, earth's largest living thing; Kings Canyon, one of the deepest canyons in the US; and Mt. Whitney, highest peak in the continental US.

No road traverses the Sierra here. Visitor facilities lie on the parks' western edge,
separated from the east boundary by a broad wilderness open only to hikers and
packers. (The eastern slope is accessible by trail from roadheads near the Owens
Valley, p 373.) Most visitors arrive by the General's Highway *(Rtes. 198 & 180),* a
fine, two-lane loop road that links the Central Valley cities of Fresno and Visalia.
Lodging is available in Sequoia at Wuksachi Village *(*☏ *559-565-3301),* or at Grant
Grove and Cedar Grove Villages in Kings Canyon *(*☏ *559-335-5500).* Campground
reservations are available five months in advance *(*☏ *800-436-7275).* In Sequoia
Park, a shuttle bus carries visitors between Wuksachi Village, Lodgepole, the Giant
Forest Museum, Moro Rock and Crescent Meadow roughly every half-hour on summer days. Winter brings heavy snows to the parks, but the General's Highway is
kept plowed for snowshoers and cross-country skiers.

★★ SEQUOIA NATIONAL PARK

★★ Giant Forest – *30mi southeast of Big Stump entrance, 16mi northeast of Ash
Mountain entrance.* ▣ Containing 8,000 mature sequoias, the sprawling Giant
Forest is the second largest of 75 sequoia groves in the Sierra Nevada; only the
remote Redwood Mountain Grove in the Grant Grove section of Kings Canyon is
larger. The largest living thing on earth—the **General Sherman Tree★**—grows near
the forest's northern end, adjacent to the General's Highway. With a circumference of 102.6ft and a height of 275ft, it forms a conspicuous starting point for
several trails that fan out into the Giant Forest. The **Congress Trail** *(2mi)* loops
through some of the forest's largest and most spectacularly homogeneous
stands of *Sequoiadendron giganteum,* including the House and Senate groups.

Crescent Meadow – Described by John Muir as the "Gem of the Sierra," this curving glade—lush with wildflowers and fenced by giant sequoias—lies on the
southern edge of the Giant Forest. A .8mi trail winds through meadow and
woods to **Tharpe's Log,** a cabin made in the 60ft-hollow of a single log. The 8ft
open end was closed off in the 1860s with a chimney, door and window, by a
cattleman who also built the table and bed from the log's wood.

Trail of the Sequoias

★**Moro Rock** – *South of Giant Forest via Crescent Meadow Road.* 🅿 An ingenious trail *(.5mi round-trip)* climbs some 400 steps to the top of this sheer-faced dome, providing spectacular **views**★★ 4,000ft down the Kaweah River Canyon, west to the Central Valley, and 12mi east to the jagged wall of the Great Western Divide. Built in 1931, the stairway was added to the National Register of Historic Places in 1978 in recognition of its harmonious integration with natural rock clefts.

★KINGS CANYON NATIONAL PARK

★★**Grant Grove** – *1mi west of Grant Grove Village.* A short loop trail *(.5mi)* passes among several noteworthy giants, including the **General Grant Tree**, officially named the "Nation's Christmas Tree" in 1926. Ranked as the world's third-largest sequoia, this massive specimen is the broadest, with a circumference of 107.6ft.

★★**Kings Canyon** – Hugging the southern wall of what is claimed to be the deepest gorge in the US, the Kings Canyon Highway (Rte. 180) winds 30mi and descends 2,000ft from Grant Grove Village to **Cedar Grove Village** on the canyon floor. At its deepest, 11mi downstream from the park boundary, the gorge is about 8,200ft deep—at 1,850ft elevation, overlooked by 10,051ft Spanish Mountain. Most popular of many canyon-floor trails is **Roads End** *(5mi beyond Cedar Grove)*, where lush Zumwalt Meadows lies 3,500ft beneath North Dome, on the north wall, and Grand Sentinel, on the south. Winter snows typically close this highway from November to mid-June.

YOSEMITE NATIONAL PARK★★★

Map p 364   Pacific Standard Time
Tourist information ☎ 209-372-0265 or www.nps.gov/yose

Sheer-walled Yosemite Valley stands at center stage of this sprawling national park, which encompasses 1,170sq mi of pristine forests, groves of giant sequoias, alpine lakes, abundant wildlife and awe-inspiring peaks. Ice Age glaciers grinding down the Merced River canyon scooped out Yosemite's distinctive U-shaped trough, 7mi long and in places more than 4,000ft deep, sculpting monumental rocks and polishing cliffs where tributary streams now plummet as waterfalls.

The native Ahwahneechee people were forced to surrender Yosemite to European and American pioneers in 1851; just 13 years later, the federal government set aside Yosemite Valley and the Wawona Grove as a natural preserve. The effusive writings of naturalist John Muir prompted Congress in 1890 to preserve the surrounding wilderness as Yosemite National Park. Today, millions of visitors a year come to hike, backpack, bicycle, fish, ride horseback, camp, ski or simply drink in the magnificent scenery.

Though it constitutes less than 6 percent of the park's land area, Yosemite Valley remains the principal attraction. Lodging, dining facilities, shops and other amenities are found at rustic Camp Curry, motel-style Yosemite Lodge and magnificent **Ahwahnee Hotel** *(lodging reservations ☎ 209-252-4848)*. Campsites may be reserved up to five months in advance *(☎ 800-436-7275)*. Visitors may tour the east end of the valley aboard a free shuttle bus. Outside the valley, a more modest array of park facilities exists at Crane Flat, Tuolumne Meadows, White Wolf and Wawona in summer, and at Badger Pass Ski Resort in winter.

YOSEMITE VALLEY

Yosemite Village – The administrative and commercial center of the park includes a post office, the **Ansel Adams Gallery** and a Wilderness Office where hikers obtain backcountry information and permits. Staffed by rangers, the **Visitor Center** presents exhibits on geology and natural history. Evening performances in the adjacent **Yosemite Theater** dramatize the life of John Muir, as impersonated by Lee Stetson. The **Yosemite Museum** houses a collection of native artifacts, changing art exhibits and the snug Yosemite Library. Behind the museum, the reconstructed Ahwahneechee Village displays bark dwellings and a sweat lodge still used for tribal rites.

★★★**Yosemite Falls** – Plunging 2,425ft in three stages down the valley's north wall, the highest waterfall in North America appears most spectacularly as a billowing plume on windy spring days. It may dry up completely by late summer. From parking lots near Yosemite Lodge, a short path *(.2mi)* leads to the thundering base of the **lower fall**★★ (320ft). The strenuous Yosemite Falls Trail *(7mi round-trip)* switchbacks up a cleft in the north wall, passing above the middle cascade (675ft) to a ledge near the lip of the **upper fall**★ (1,430ft).

 ★**Happy Isles** – At the mouth of the Merced River Canyon, a cluster of small islands splits the roaring cataract into smaller channels. A delightful picnic spot at 4,050ft elevation, Happy Isles is the start of the often-spectacular **John Muir Trail**. Very popular is the short, steep jaunt to **Vernal Fall Bridge**★★ *(.7mi)*; from here, the Mist Trail climbs to the brink of 317ft **Vernal Fall**★★ *(1.5mi)*. Ambitious hikers may proceed to the top of 594ft **Nevada Fall** *(3mi)*. A farther trail continues to the summit of **Half Dome**★★★ *(8.2mi)*, a massive rock that rises 4,800 vertical feet above its base (to 8,842ft elevation) at the eastern head of the valley. This hike is not for the faint-hearted nor weak of limb, as the final assault of the summit mounts a 45-degree granite slab with the aid of an exposed cable ladder.

★★★**Tunnel View** – From this stupendous viewpoint at the east end of the Wawona Tunnel, visitors gaze eastward into Yosemite Valley. Its portals are framed on the south by **Cathedral Rocks** and on the north by the massive, 3,593ft face of **El Capitan**★★, the world's largest unbroken cliff. Graceful Bridalveil Falls hangs in the foreground, as do ephemeral Ribbon and Silver Strand Falls in early spring. The distinctive, sheer face of Half Dome peers round the shoulder of Glacier Point from the eastern end of the valley.

EXCURSIONS

★★★**Glacier Point** – *30mi south and east from Yosemite Village; 0.2mi walk from parking area.* ♿ ♿ *Road may be closed Nov-late May.* Jutting 3,000ft above the valley floor, this majestic clifftop perch offers an unforgettable view of the toy like Yosemite Valley below. To the northwest, Yosemite Falls hang at full length; to the east, Vernal and Nevada Falls can be seen in one glimpse, pouring out of Little Yosemite Valley. Half Dome looms in the foreground, while the jagged Clark and Cathedral ranges punctuate the Yosemite high country.

★★**Mariposa Grove of Big Trees** – *34mi south of Yosemite Village.* ♿ ♿ *Tours by foot (loop trips 1mi-7mi) or 1hr tram tour (daily mid-Apr-mid-Nov).* The largest of the park's three groves of giant sequoias spreads over 250 acres of a steep hillside. Most massive of nearly 400 mature sequoias is the **Grizzly Giant**, a 2,700-year-old specimen with a base circumference of 96ft and a pronounced lean of 17 degrees. The adjacent **California Tunnel Tree** was bored in 1895 to allow coaches to pass through it, a fashionable novelty of Victorian tourism.

Yosemite Valley from Tunnel View

★★Tioga Road – *62mi one-way north and east from Yosemite Village to Tioga Pass. Last 45mi (past Crane Flat) closed Nov-late May*. Route 120 snakes 14mi through thick evergreen forests before opening to broad views of the high country. **Olmsted Point★** provides striking vistas down Tenaya Canyon to Half Dome and Clouds Rest (9,926ft). Passing subalpine **Tenaya Lake,** the largest natural body of water in the park, the road enters **Tuolumne Meadows★★**, an alpine grassland at 8,600ft elevation. The heart of the high country, Tuolumne Meadows has rustic lodging and dining, a visitor center and access to miles of backcountry trails. A marvelous short trail climbs to the glacier-polished summit of 9,450ft **Lembert Dome★** *(3mi round-trip)*. Beyond 9,945ft **Tioga Pass★**, highest point on a continuous roadway in California, Rte. 120 descends 13mi to the junction of US-395 near Mono Lake.

EASTERN SIERRA★

Map p 364   Pacific Standard Time
Tourist information ☎ 760-934-8006

The eastern escarpment of the Sierra Nevada rises abruptly from the sagebrush flats of the Great Basin, sere by virtue of the rain shadow cast by the Sierra crest. Running parallel, US-395 is among the most spectacular highways in the US, with continuous views of towering granite peaks and awesome volcanic scenery. Side roads probe narrow canyons to lakes and trailheads in rugged alpine regions. The highway reaches its climax in the broad, deep Owens Valley.

SIGHTS

★Bodie State Historic Park – *Rte. 270 east from US-395; final 3mi unpaved. Road may be closed by snow in winter* ☎ *760-647-6445*. This stark, windswept, unrestored ghost town rambles along dirt streets in the sagebrush hills of the high desert. Although the discovery of gold in 1859 brought a rush of prospectors, not until 1874 did corporate investment shape Bodie into a mining city of 10,000 people. The town had a nasty reputation, the "bad man from Bodie" being a standard bogey of Western lore. Population dwindled when mining waned in 1882; the town was eventually abandoned. It was acquired in 1962 by the state, which has maintained its 150 buildings in a state of "arrested decay" with no restoration. The **Miners Union Hall** on Main Street functions as museum and visitor center.

★★Mono Lake – Remnant of a prehistoric lake five times larger than its present 60sq mi, Mono Lake is three times saltier than the ocean and 80 times more alkaline. Dubbed "the Dead Sea of California" by Mark Twain, Mono in fact supports a wealth of brine shrimp and alkali flies that attract migratory birds

© Ric Ergenbright

and waterfowl. The flies were valued by the native Paiutes, who ate the shelled pupae and traded them across the Sierra Nevada to the Yokuts; the Yokut word *mono*, meaning "fly eaters," was attached to the lake itself.

The **US Forest Service Visitor Center** *(north end of Lee Vining, off US-395;* ☎ *760-647-3044)* serves as a museum of the region's natural and human history. Foremost among lakeshore sights are the grotesque limestone spires of **South Tufa**★★ *(6mi south of Lee Vining on US-395, then 4.5mi east on Rte. 120 to gravel access road),* formed between AD 1100 and 1900 as calcium deposits from submerged springs combined with lake-water carbonates.

★**Mammoth Region** – A 19C mining town transformed into a four-season resort community, **Mammoth Lakes** *(information* ☎ *760-934-8006)* lies restlessly beneath the massive dormant volcano of 11,053ft **Mammoth Mountain**★. Camping, fishing and hiking in the nearby **Mammoth Lakes Basin**★ and the surrounding high country dominate the snow-free season from late May to October. Winter brings skiers to the **Mammoth Mountain Ski Center** *(*☎ *760-934-2571);* the thaw attracts brash mountain bikers; and a year-round gondola climbs to the summit for magnificent views over the eastern Sierra. Summer trams shuttle hikers over panoramic **Minaret Summit**★★ to **Devils Postpile National Monument**★ *(Rte. 203;* ☎ *760-934-2289).* An easy trail *(.4mi)* leads to the monument's namesake, a 60ft wall of six- to eight-sided basalt columns at the face of a 100,000-year-old lava flow.

★★**The Whitney Crest** – The 60mi stretch of the **Owens Valley**★★ from Bishop to Lone Pine, bounded by the Sierra Nevada on the west and the White-Inyo Range on the east, ranks among the most dramatic valleys in North America. The valley floor at Lone Pine lies two vertical miles beneath the 14,494ft summit of **Mt. Whitney**★★, highest point in the contiguous US. The most sublime view of the jagged Whitney crest is from the **Alabama Hills**★★, west of Lone Pine; scores of Hollywood films and TV shows have been shot among these fantastic boulder formations. The **Eastern Sierra Interagency Visitor Center** *(US-395, 1mi south of Lone Pine;* ☎ *760-876-6222)* provides maps. The steep and winding but well-paved **Whitney Portal Road** climbs to a lovely mountain canyon (8,360ft), trailhead for the rugged **Mt. Whitney Trail** *(21.4mi round-trip; permit required from Inyo National Forest office in Lone Pine;* ☎ *760-876-6200).*

RENO AREA★

Map p 364   Pacific Standard Time
Tourist information ☎ 800-367-7366 or www.playreno.com

Straddling the Truckee River where the Sierra Nevada meet the Great Basin, Reno enjoys a reputation as a center for outdoor recreation, although casino gaming is its foremost tourism draw. The city was founded around a toll bridge in the 1860s and named for a Civil War general. It achieved an economic boost when Central Pacific rail construction crews passed through in 1868, and grew as a distribution center after the transcontinental line was completed in 1869. The prosperity of nearby Virginia City in the 1870s, and later mining rushes to Tonopah and Goldfield, bolstered its role. Reno became a county seat in 1870, home of the University of Nevada in 1886, and the banking and population center of Nevada early in the 20C.

Although gambling and other vices had always thrived in Reno, casino gaming underwent a revolution when Raymond "Pappy" Smith opened **Harold's Club** on Virginia Street in 1935 and began courting a "respectable" clientele through widespread advertising. Attracted by this new image, gambling trips to Reno became a favorite weekend pastime of Californians. They increased in popularity after William Harrah opened **Harrah's** in 1946; by the 1950s, new casinos filled the downtown area with pulsating neon lights, establishing Reno as the supreme gaming destination of Nevada. In the 1960s, however, the frantic development of the Las Vegas Strip wrested that reputation away from Reno; by the 1980s, Las Vegas had also surpassed Reno in population.

The Reno area nevertheless experienced unprecedented growth at the end of the 20C. The city, now with a population of 163,334, offers peerless recreational opportunities—especially with its proximity to Lake Tahoe (*p 365*)—and a broad-based economy as the banking center, transportation hub and entertainment dynamo of northern Nevada.

★RENO

★**North Virginia Street** – *Between I-80 & the Truckee River.* ✗ ♿ 🅿 This seven-block "Strip" contains Reno's greatest concentration of gambling casinos, flamboyantly celebrated in the **Reno Arch**★ *(Virginia & Commercial Sts.)*, which arcs over the street and proclaims Reno "The Biggest Little City in the World."

Rectangular city blocks compel casinos, many of them linked by sky bridges, to conform to regular architectural footprints. Conventional, high-rise facades rely on extravagant **lighting displays**★ and open shopfronts to attract pedestrians to their slot machines and gaming tables, highly visible and audible just inside their doors. Harrah's, Fitzgerald's, the Cal-Neva, the Eldorado and other casinos established before the 1990s likewise abstain from the fantastic themes that pervade recent casino-hotels of the Las Vegas Strip. The most notable exception is the **Silver Legacy Resort Casino** *(407 N. Virginia St.; ☎ 775-329-4777)*, where a re-created 120ft mining scaffold ignites an hourly light show, complete with lightning, beneath a central dome that mimics celestial changes. The casino strip ends at the Truckee River, where wooded promenades trace the banks of the cold mountain stream through downtown Reno.

© Robert Holmes

Blackjack Table

★★ National Automobile Museum (The Harrah Collection) – *10 Lake St. S.* ♿ 🅿
🕾 *775-333-9300. www.automuseum.org.* With over 225 antique, classic and custom automobiles displayed in imaginative period settings, this collection ranks among the West's most interesting. Visitors watch a high-tech multimedia history of the auto industry, then stroll among indoor "streets" lined by vintage autos and facades that represent the turn of the 20C, the 1930s, the 1950s and contemporary times. Exceptional displays include an 1892 steam-driven Philion carriage, the 1907 Thomas Flyer that won the New York-to-Paris Automobile Race in 170 days, Al Jolson's 1933 Cadillac V-16, and the 1949 Mercury driven by James Dean in *Rebel Without a Cause.*

★ W.M. Keck Museum – *1664 N. Virginia St., Mackay School of Mines, University of Nevada.* ♿ 🕾 *775-784-6052.* The Mackay School of Mines (1908), north of the UN's tree-lined quadrant, is a preeminent school of mining engineering. Specimens of Nevada minerals and fossils line the walls of its Keck Museum, illustrating Nevada's historic and continuing role as a leader in this field. The Mackay silver collection in the basement recalls the role of John Mackay (1831-1902) as one of the Comstock "Bonanza Kings."

EXCURSIONS

★ Carson City – *30mi south of Reno on US-395.* 🕾 *775-687-7410. www.carson-city.org.* Founded in 1858, the city was named for the Carson River, itself named by adventurer John C. Frémont for scout Kit Carson. The town became the Nevada territorial capital, then the state capital in 1864, acquiring a US Mint. Today it has a population approaching 50,000.

The **Kit Carson Trail** winds past historic residences, passing the 1895 home of famed Washoe basket-weaver Datsolalee, the 1909 Governor's Mansion and a house built in 1864 by Orion Clemens. Clemens, the first and only secretary of the Nevada Territory, accompanied his brother Samuel ("Mark Twain") Clemens from Missouri in a journey described by the author in *Roughing It.*

The dignified **Nevada State Capitol Complex** *(Carson Ave.;* 🕾 *800-638-2321)* gathers numerous government buildings in a handsome parklike setting. Capped by a silvery cupola, the sandstone capitol (1871) still houses the offices of the governor and other officials, the Senate and Assembly, however, now meet in the Nevada State Legislature (1970) across the adjacent plaza.

★★ Nevada State Museum – *600 N. Carson St.* 🕾 *775-687-4811.* Housed in the 1869 Carson City Mint, this institution provides an engaging overview of Nevada's flora, fauna, geology and human history, with a special emphasis on the state's mining heritage. The **Mint History Gallery★** surveys the process that produced more than 56 million coins from Nevada gold and silver between 1870 and 1895; workers on occasion still strike medallions on Coin Press No 1. Beyond an archetypal **ghost town★**, natural-history galleries display mounted birds and mammals from the Great Basin. The **Earth Sciences Gallery** features a walk-through exhibit of Devonian Nevada, 35 to 40 million years ago, when these precincts were on the ocean floor. Anthropology galleries illustrate the cultures of native peoples. Of extensive displays on Nevada's more recent history, none is more compelling than the model **mine★★** in the basement.

★★ Virginia City – *14mi northeast of Carson City, 23mi southeast of Reno, on Rte. 341.* 🕾 *775-847-0311.* Preserved as a National Historic Landmark, this bustling old mining town—perched on the steep slopes of Mount Davidson—ranks among the most fascinating in the West. Built atop the fabulously rich Comstock Lode, Virginia City played a crucial and colorful role in US history. Today it is a fascinating and picturesque example of an archetypal boom-and-bust mining city.

Two prospectors working in Six Mile Canyon in 1859 discovered the Comstock Lode, extracting a bluish clay that assayed at $875 per ton in gold and $3,000 in silver. As word leaked out, miners flooded in. Traditional techniques proved inadequate to extract the ore, however, so prospectors sold their claims to San Francisco corporations that developed such ventures. Virginia City was rapidly transformed from a rough settlement into the West's first industrialized city.

In the early 1870s, miners struck the richest lode of ore in American history, and Virginia City reached its peak of prosperity with a population of 25,000 and another 10,000 in adjacent Gold Hill. It boasted all the amenities of any great city and eagerly hosted such world-class performers as Helena Modjeska, Ignacy Paderewski and Harry Houdini. By the early 1880s, though, the mines began to play out, condemning the city to a long decline.

© Catherine Ursillo/FOLIO, Inc.

Virginia City

By 1900 Virginia City was taking on characteristics of a dilapidated ghost town. Not until tourism boomed after World War II did its fortunes reverse. Tourism so thoroughly reinvigorated the downtown that its fantasized image of the Old West threatened to besmirch the integrity of true history. Some locals even faced old brick buildings with wooden facades to make them look like the Virginia City depicted in *Bonanza*, a popular TV series of the 1960s and 70s.

Visit – Virginia City is built on steep terraces, its downtown concentrated along C Street. Few buildings predate a devastating 1875 fire, but about half were built before 1890. Linked by uneven wooden sidewalks with overhanging roofs and porches, four densely packed blocks of wood and brick buildings are occupied by stores, restaurants, saloons and several private collections of curios optimistically labeled "museums." Among the historic sites is the office of the *Territorial Enterprise*, where young Mark Twain worked in the 1860s. Even children are free to enter any of the colorful saloons on C Street, the **Best and Belcher Mine**★ (☎ 775-847-0757) behind the Ponderosa Saloon, or the **Choller Mine**★ (☎ 775-847-0155) on the south edge of town.

Among old mansions seasonally open for tours are **The Castle** (B Street; ☎ 775-847-0275) and the **Mackay Mansion** (D Street; ☎ 775-847-0173). Built in 1875, **Pipers Opera House**★ (B & Union Sts.; ☎ 775-847-0433) still offers dramas on the boards where Jenny Lind and Edwin Booth once performed. One of the city's better historical collections occupies the four-story, 1876 **Fourth Ward School**★ (☎ 775-847-0975). The **Virginia & Truckee Railroad** (☎ 775-847-0380), built to transport silver to Carson City, and Tahoe Basin timber to shore up Virginia City's mines, still offers rides from its F Street station.

SHASTA-CASCADE REGION★

Michelin map 493 A, B 6, 7   Pacific Standard Time
Tourist information ☎ 530-225-4100

At the northern end of the Sierra Nevada, the mountains meet the Cascade, Trinity and Klamath ranges in an arc of peaks arrayed at the head of the Sacramento Valley. These highlands embrace and define a region of extraordinary beauty, with the agricultural center of **Redding** at its hub.

Dominating the landscape for hundreds of miles around is the volcanic cone of Mt. Shasta (14,162ft), which presents an enchanting, and potentially dangerous, symbol of this highly volcanic region. Lassen Peak (10,457ft) erupted violently from 1914 to 1917 and today forms the nucleus of a serene, though still smoldering, national park. A trio of large man-made lakes are preserved within the **Whiskeytown-Shasta-Trinity National Recreation Area**. Beyond the Cascades, the high Modoc Lava Plateau covers 26,000sq mi of California's northeastern corner, a vast desert upland noted for its lava tubes and stark, craggy scenery.

SIGHTS

** **Lassen Volcanic National Park** – *47mi east of Redding via Rte. 44.* ☎ *530-595-4444. www.nps.gov/lavo.* Anchoring this 106,000-acre natural preserve, Lassen Peak erupted on May 30, 1914, the first of 298 eruptions over several years. Congress established the national park in 1916 to allow visitors the opportunity to witness the spectacular effects of volcanism.

The scenic Park Road *(Rte. 89)* makes a winding 30mi arc around Lassen Peak. From the **Manzanita Lake Visitor Center** *(Loomis Museum;* ☎ *530-335-7373),* the road passes through the **Devastated Area,** blasted at the height of Lassen's 1915 eruptions, though now recovering with new forests of aspen and pine. At the road's closest approach to Lassen Peak, at 8,500ft, a strenuous trail *(5mi)* begins climbing to the summit. The highlight of current volcanic activity is **Bumpass Hell★★.** Accessible only by a 3mi round-trip hike from the roadhead, its sulfuric fumaroles, boiling springs and bubbling mudpots are visible from a boardwalk that passes safely over the soft ground.

* **McArthur-Burney Falls Memorial State Park** – *65mi northeast of Redding via Rtes. 229 & 89.* △ & 🄿 ☎ *916-335-2777.* Highlight of this popular park is **Burney Falls★★,** where the combined flows of Burney Creek and an underground stream tumble enchantingly over a 129ft cliff of basalt. Springs amid the ferns in the face of the cliff engorge the falls with ribbons of water, so that the flow is visibly greater at the bottom than the top.

** **Lava Beds National Monument** – *170mi northeast of Redding via Rtes. 299, 139 & 10.* ☎ *530-667-2282. www.nps.gov/labe.* This desolate stretch of the Modoc Lava Plateau contains more than 300 lava tubes, several of which penetrate as far as 150ft below the earth's surface, while others extend horizontally for thousands of feet. Rangers provide flashlights, hard hats, books and maps for exploring tubes along **Cave Loop Road** and farther afield.

In 1872, 53 Modoc warriors and their families held off the US Army for five months at a natural fortress now called **Captain Jack's Stronghold★★.** The Modoc leader, Kientpoos (known to settlers as Captain Jack), opted to fight rather than endure exile on a reservation controlled by traditional enemies. Outnumbered by as much as 20 times, the Modocs used the crags and caves for hiding and ambushes. Captain Jack finally led the Modocs out of the lava beds after fatally shooting an Army general during peace negotiations. He was later captured and hanged; the remainder of the tribe was exiled to Oklahoma.

* **Mt. Shasta** – Visible for hundreds of miles around northern California, this glacier-clad, 14,162ft volcano is second in height in the Cascades only to Mt. Rainier in Washington. Sacred to native tribes, who thought it was inhabited by the Chief of Sky Spirits, it is a popular symbol to New Age devotees and a year-round recreational area. Around its massive base, 17mi in circumference, are numerous trailheads. Many hikes start from the **Everitt Memorial Highway,** a scenic route that ascends through Shasta-Trinity National Forest.

Backpackers near Mount Shasta

Yellowstone Region

Grand Canyon of the Yellowstone

America's first national park, and arguably the best known in the world, Yellowstone National Park was established by the US Congress in 1872. Much of the park sits astride an ancient collapsed volcanic caldera, 28mi wide and 47mi long. Within the borders of this 3,472sq-mi preserve (roughly the size of the eastern state of Connecticut) are great rivers and lakes; the largest free-roaming wildlife population in the lower 48 states; the world's greatest concentration of thermal features and its largest petrified forest. A designated World Heritage Site, Yellowstone is one of man's greatest environmental success stories.

One of the pleasures of a visit to Yellowstone is that its awe-striking attractions are so accessible. More than 370mi of paved road weave a figure-eight course through the park, introducing such renowned features as Old Faithful and its surrounding geysers, the travertine terraces of Mammoth Hot Springs and the spectacular chasm of the Grand Canyon of the Yellowstone. Majestic elk, bison, moose and other large animals range widely through this realm of steamy beauty, often visiting campgrounds and lodges, and causing traffic jams whenever they wander close to a main road.

Immediately south of Yellowstone is Grand Teton National Park, enclosing a small but dramatic mountain range that rises high above the Snake River and a series of pristine lakes, themselves created by glacial moraines. The gateway to the Tetons is Jackson, which has grown from a small ranching center to become the leading resort community of the northern Rocky Mountains. Jackson cashes in on its cowboy persona and is home to major ski resorts, the National Elk Refuge and the National Museum of Wildlife Art.

East of Yellowstone is Cody, founded by the redoubtable William F. "Buffalo Bill" Cody himself in the late 19C. The "Rodeo Capital of the World," Cody lures visitors to its Buffalo Bill Historical Center, an unrivaled museum of Western art and history.

Each of Yellowstone's three Montana entrance routes has a character of its own, from remarkable alpine scenery (the Beartooth Highway) to outdoor recreation (West Yellowstone) to culture and urbanity (Bozeman). Throughout the region are evocative ghost towns and remarkable geological phenomena. The Snake River Valley runs west from Yellowstone through southern Idaho, and here, too, are a plethora of worthy stops, including the classic resort facilities of Sun Valley and the roof-of-the-world scenery of Sawtooth National Recreation Area.

YELLOWSTONE NATIONAL PARK***

Map p 384   Mountain Standard Time
Tourist information ☎ 307-344-7381 or www.nps.gov/yell

The earth is a living force in Yellowstone, its dynamic natural features laid bare. Set aside primarily for its geological features—the brilliant, multicolored hot pools and lively geysers, and the dramatic Grand Canyon of the Yellowstone—the park's role as a haven for wildlife has assumed paramount importance. This vast wilderness is one of the last remaining strongholds of the grizzly bear; in recent years it has gained additional attention with the reintroduction of wolves into its ecosystem. While visitors can count on Old Faithful to erupt every 88min or so, their chance encounters with the park's large mammals are most endearing—and enduring.

Located on a high plateau bisected by the Continental Divide and bounded to the north, east and south by mountains, Yellowstone occupies the northwest corner of the state of Wyoming, with small portions spilling over into adjacent Montana and Idaho. Five highways (from west, north, northeast, east and south) provide access to its main Grand Loop Road, which dissects the forested landscape in a large figure eight between the principal scenic attractions. Visitors may choose from the paved roads and 1,200mi of hiking trails, traversing elevations from 5,282ft at Reese Creek to 11,358ft at the summit of Eagle Peak.

Yellowstone boasts more than 10,000 individual thermal features—more than all other such earthly collections combined. These are the result of a rare, migrating hot spot in the earth's crust that originated near the southern border of Oregon and Idaho, 300mi to the southwest, about 17 million years ago. The lava flows of the Snake River Plain trace the "movement" of this hot spot as the continental plate slides southwesterly above the source of heat, a stationary magma plume only 1-3mi beneath the earth's surface. The Yellowstone Caldera was created 600,000 years ago by a volcanic blast dwarfing that of Mount St. Helens in 1980.

Park roads are generally open to motor vehicles May through October, and for over-snow vehicles mid-December to early March. Winter comes early and doesn't release its grip until June. Snow may fall at any park elevation any time of year.

Historical Notes

Nomadic tribes hunted here for thousands of years, but may never have lived in the Yellowstone basin, out of respect for spirits they believed spoke through the rumblings of the earth. They named the canyon *Mi-tse-a-da-zi*, "Rock Yellow River." The first white man to explore the area was probably John Colter, who left the Lewis and Clark party in 1806 to spend several months trapping. His descriptions of Yellowstone's wonders fell on deaf ears back East, where they were regarded as tall tales or the hallucinations of someone who had spent too much time alone in the wilderness.

Generations and rumors came and went before the private Washburn-Langford-Doane party braved the wilds in 1870 to finally separate fiction from fact. Stunned to discover there was little fiction, and ample awesome fact, this party convinced the US Geological Survey to investigate. In June 1871, Survey director Dr. Ferdinand Hayden explored Yellowstone with 34 men, including painter Thomas Moran and photographer William Henry Jackson; the following year, armed with Hayden's 500-page report and with Moran's and Jackson's visuals, Congress proclaimed this wilderness the world's first national park.

Tourists weren't far behind, especially when a rail link from Livingston, Montana, to Gardiner, near the north entrance, eased access. The park's early civilian administrators couldn't handle the poaching and vandalism, so the US Army took over. From 1886 to 1918, 400 soldiers were stationed at Mammoth Hot Springs, enforcing park regulations and guarding primary scenic attractions.

SIGHTS

The following attractions are best seen by driving Yellowstone's 172mi **Grand Loop Road** in a clockwise direction around the park, beginning and ending at any of the five park entrances. The greatest traffic comes through the West Entrance (from West Yellowstone, Montana), gateway for this tour.

** **Norris Geyser Basin** – *Left (west) off the Grand Loop Road at Norris Junction, 14mi north of Madison Junction, then .25mi to parking area.* ♿. The oldest and hottest thermal area in the park is also its most dynamic. While temperatures of 459°F have been recorded just 1,000ft underground, the features of this basin have undergone regular fluctuations in temperature and activity. The major geysers are in **Back Basin***, where thermal features are scattered among trees. **Steamboat Geyser** is the world's tallest active geyser. Its rare major eruptions (it is dormant for years at a time) can reach heights of 400ft. **Echinus Geyser**★★, the largest acid-water geyser, puts on an entertaining show every 40-80min, filling, erupting and draining like a toilet bowl.

ADDRESS BOOK

Please see explanation on p 64.

Staying in the Yellowstone Region and Southern Idaho

Jenny Lake Lodge – *Grand Teton National Park WY.* ✗ ⅋ ▯ ☎ *307-733-4647. www.gtlc.com. 37 rooms. $$$$ Closed Oct-late May.* Surrounding the main lodge, where guests gather in front of a stone fireplace or relax in rockers on the porch, are 37 secluded log cabins. Guests at this former dude ranch are unburdened by phones, radios or TVs as they repose beneath country-quilt bedspreads. A formal six-course meal is included in the room rate.

Spring Creek Resort – *1800 Spirit Dance Rd., Jackson WY.* ✗ ⅋ ▯ ☎ *307-733-1524. www.springcreekresort.com. 120 rooms. $$$$ (summer), $$$ (winter).* Views of the Teton Range are spectacular from this sprawling modern 1,000-acre ranch-resort, located atop East Gros Ventre Butte in the heart of Jackson Hole. Horseback riding, tennis and the gourmet **Granary** restaurant tempt guests, whose lodgings come with pine furniture and stone fireplaces.

Rusty Parrot Lodge – *175 N. Jackson St., Jackson WY.* ⅋ ▯ ☎ *307-733-2000. www.rustyparrot.com. 31 rooms. $$ (summer), $$$$ (winter).* Rustic touches like peeled-pine furniture, antler chandeliers and rawhide lampshades complement the luxury of down comforters and whirlpool tubs this modern spa hotel. Gourmet breakfasts, cooked to order, may be enjoyed on private balconies.

The Irma Hotel – *12th & Sheridan Sts., Cody WY.* ✗ ▯ ☎ *307-587-4221. www.irmahotel.com. 40 rooms. $* Most of Cody is dedicated to Buffalo Bill, who built this basic Victorian, full of tales and personalities, and named it for his daughter in 1902. Some of the high-ceilinged rooms still display bullet holes from past revelry. The cherry-wood bar was a present from Queen Victoria.

Old Faithful Inn – *Yellowstone National Park WY.* ✗ ⅋ ▯ ☎ *307-344-7311. www.ynp-lodges.com. 327 rooms. $$ Closed mid-Oct-early May.* As the largest log cabin in the world, the Old Faithful Inn was a model for other national-park lodges in the West. Architect Robert Reamer used twisted lodgepole pine in the 85ft-high lobby to create a forest of balconies and stairways under a massive gable roof. Rooms, while small, capture the rustic natural spirit.

Sun Valley Lodge – *Sun Valley Resort, Sun Valley ID.* ✗ ⅋ ▯ ☎ *208-622-4111. www.sunvalley.com. 579 rooms. $$* The Union Pacific Railroad opened this resort in 1936, enabling East Coast society to "rough it" in style alongside Hollywood stars. The tradition continues today in the oak-paneled lodge, which attracts well-heeled visitors for winter skiing and summer golf.

The Wort Hotel – *50 N. Glenwood St., Jackson WY.* ✗ ▯ ☎ *307-733-2190. www.worthotel.com. 60 rooms. $$* Log beds, plaid blankets and barbed-wire wallpaper are in keeping with the cowboy-rancher atmosphere of Jackson. This Swiss-style hotel, opened in 1941, is famous for its **Silver Dollar Bar**, an S-curve embedded with 2,032 uncirculated 1921 silver dollars.

Dining in the Yellowstone Region and Southern Idaho

Desert Sage – *750 W. Idaho St., Boise ID.* ☎ *208-333-8400. $$$ Creative Regional.* Chef David Root uses local organic produce in his creations, transforming Alaskan halibut, fennel, apples, lobster and maybe a jasmine rice cracker into a work of art. Warm colors, tumbleweed chandeliers and paintings by regional artists help make this restaurant a Snake River Valley standout.

The Range – *225 N. Cache St., Jackson WY.* ☎ *307-733-5481. $$$ Regional.* A stainless-steel exhibition kitchen is the stage for "gourmet theater." The core menu focuses on regional specialties—homemade wild-game sausages, Rocky Mountain trout and elk medallions. The decor features modern lines of leather, rich woods and copper.

Gun Barrel Steak and Game House – *862 W. Broadway, Jackson WY.* ☎ *307-733-3287. www.gunbarrel.com. $$ Regional.* This warehouse once was a wildlife museum, but now the game is saved for the plate. Velvet elk with sun-dried tomatoes, venison bratwurst and caribou tortillas head a menu heavy on steaks and chicken. Double Barrel home brew tempts bar patrons.

Jedediah's Original House of Sourdough – *135 E. Broadway, Jackson WY.* ☎ *307-733-5671. $ American.* Housed in one of the oldest log cabins in town, Jedediah's is famous for its sourdough pancake breakfasts. At lunch and dinner, crowds file in for grilled steaks, chicken and trout, served with sourdough bread amid photos of Jackson old-timers and faded newspaper articles.

★★★ **Mammoth Hot Springs** – *North Entrance & Grand Loop Rds.* ♿ 🅿. Perched on a hillside with multicolored terraces above, Mammoth is the park's command post. Headquarters are located in the complex's historic buildings. The green lawns and orderly appearance recall Mammoth's early history as an army post.

Change, constant throughout Yellowstone, is most obvious at Mammoth. Each day, two tons of travertine are deposited by the relatively cool (170°F) hot springs. The water mixes with carbon dioxide to form carbonic acid, which dissolves underlying limestone to produce the travertine, similar to that found in limestone caves. As this solution reaches the surface, it cools rapidly and releases carbon dioxide, leaving behind deposits of calcium carbonate. Brilliant color is added to this three-dimensional "canvas" by algae and tiny living bacteria. Color relates to the temperature and pH level of the water; no organisms can survive in water hotter than 175°F at this elevation. Cooler alkaline (high-pH) water attracts cyanobacteria, which can be yellow, orange, green, red or brown, depending upon temperature variations.

Elevated boardwalks climb and descend the ornate flows of the Main Terrace and the **Minerva Springs**★★★. Impressive from a distance, this formation is truly remarkable when viewed up close, where the elaborate collection of minute cascades and multicolored terraces resemble a still photo of a waterfall. The most visibly active feature is **Opal Terrace**★★, which sprang to life in 1926 after years of dormancy. Popular with elk, which recline here like living sculptures, it is growing rapidly. A couple of hundred yards north, the distinctive **Liberty Cap**★ juts from the earth like a massive Christmas tree. This extinct hot-spring cone was named for its resemblance to the hats worn by colonial patriots.

Mammoth's red-roofed buildings, many of stone, were built as part of Fort Yellowstone in the 1890s and early 1900s. Today they shelter administration, staff housing and the **Horace M. Albright Visitor Center and Museum**★★ (☏ *307-344-2263*). Named for a longtime director of the National Park Service and early park superintendent, the museum traces the human and natural history of the park, highlighting Thomas Moran paintings and William Henry Jackson photographs from the 1871 Hayden expedition. The facility also serves as the primary Yellowstone information center and backcountry permit office.

The most interesting aspect of the 1937 **Mammoth Hot Springs Hotel** (☏ *307-344-5400*) is a US map, assembled on a wall like a large puzzle, the states carefully cut from 15 different woods of nine countries.

★ **Specimen Ridge** – *Access by trail 2.5mi east of Tower Junction, 19mi east of Mammoth Hot Springs.* 🅿 This 8,442ft crest and 40sq mi of surrounding uplands constitute the largest petrified forest in the world. Remnants of more than 100 different plants, including redwoods similar to those of California, are found here. Ash and mudflows buried the trees as they stood 50 million years ago; weathering agents reversed the process. The **Specimen Ridge Trail** (*17.5mi*) ascends the ridge.

© Ric Ergenbright

Minerva Springs

★★Tower Fall – *2mi south of Tower Junction*. 🅿. This impressive waterfall on squeezes between namesake stone "towers" and plunges 132ft to join the Grand Canyon of the Yellowstone at its narrowest point. A steep **trail** *(.5mi)* descends 300ft to the base of the fall. The dramatic **gorge★★** is best viewed from a turnout at **Calcite Springs**, from which basaltic columns—similar to those overhanging this very road—may be seen rimming the 500ft bluffs beneath which the river flows.

★Dunraven Pass – *14mi south of Tower Junction*. High point of the Grand Loop Road, 8,859ft Dunraven Pass offers the park's best perspective on the contours of the ancient Yellowstone Caldera, along with spectacular **views★★** of the Absaroka and Beartooth ranges to the east. Looming over the pass is 10,243ft **Mount Washburn**.

★★★Grand Canyon of the Yellowstone – *Canyon Village, 19mi south of Tower Junction*. ⚠♿ 🅿. After Old Faithful, this magnificent canyon is probably the park's best-known feature, roughly 20mi long, 800-1,200ft deep and 1,500-4,000ft wide. The brilliant color of its rhyolite rock is due to iron compounds "cooked" by hydrothermal activity. Weathering resulted in the oxidation of the iron, producing the yellow, orange, red and brown colors. At the end of the last ice age, scientists believe ice dams formed at the mouth of Yellowstone Lake. When breached, they released tremendous amounts of water down the Yellowstone River course, carving the canyon.

The one-way loop **Inspiration Point Road** visits several perspectives on the canyon. **Lookout Point** offers a classic view of the 308ft **Lower Fall★★**—most impressive in spring, when 63,500gal of water (at peak run-off) surpass its crest each second. A little farther west, a trail leads to the brink of the 109ft **Upper Fall★**, where a railing is all that separates viewers from the surging water.

Upstream, a 2.5mi spur road crosses the Yellowstone River to the South Rim. **Artist's Point★★** offers perhaps the best views of the canyon and Lower Fall. **Uncle Tom's Trail** descends steeply on metal stairs to an impressive vantage point of the Upper Fall. Osprey nest in the rocky cliffs.

★★Hayden Valley – *5-10mi south of Canyon Village*. 🅿. An abruptly placid contrast to the dramatic canyon, this lush valley of meadow and marsh may be the best place in the park to observe wildlife. Hayden Valley is home to large herds of bison, plus moose and elk, and in spring is a good place to catch a glimpse of grizzly bears. Coming across even a portion of the bison herd is as close as one can come to viewing life in the West before European settlement. Bears are often seen in spring and early summer, when they feed on newborn bison and elk calves.

In summer, traffic backs up for miles when bison decide to cross the road. Turnouts, situated in key positions for viewing, may be occupied by a ranger with a spotting scope happily shared with visitors.

Fishing Bridge – *East Entrance & Grand Loop Rds*. 🅿. Until 1973, fishermen stood shoulder-to-shoulder here, angling for abundant cutthroat trout. Fishing was terminated to protect the spawning of the fish and to allow grizzly bears to forage unmolested. **Fishing Bridge Visitor Center★** *(☎ 307-242-2450)* has fine exhibits of the birds of the national park near the shore of Yellowstone Lake.

★★Yellowstone Lake – ⚠♿ 🅿. At 7,733ft altitude, the largest natural high-elevation lake in North America has 136sq mi of surface area, 110mi of shoreline and depths of nearly 400ft. Although the surface is frozen half the year, lake-bottom vents produce water as warm as 252°F. The Yellowstone River flows into the lake from the southeast, and exits at Fishing Bridge through the Grand Canyon of the Yellowstone, continuing 671mi to its confluence with the Missouri River. It is the longest river still undammed in the lower 48 states.

The stately, three-story **Lake Yellowstone Hotel★** *(1.5mi south of Fishing Bridge; ☎ 307-242-3700)* faces eastward on the lakeshore. Yellow clapboard with white trim, it was built in 1891; the exterior received its first major facelift in 1903 when architect Robert Reamer added Ionic columns and 15 false balconies. The dining room, sun room and porte cochere were added by 1929.

At **Bridge Bay** *(3mi south of Fishing Bridge)*, a marina offers boat tours and supplies anglers. **Lake tours** last 90min and skirt the pine-cloaked shoreline.

West Thumb – ♿ 🅿. This small collapsed caldera within the big Yellowstone Caldera includes the **West Thumb Geyser Basin★** on its western shore. It extends beneath Yellowstone Lake where hot springs and even underwater geysers mix their boiling contents with the frigid lake water. A boardwalk winds through the land-based thermal features, among which are 53ft-deep, cobalt-blue **Abyss Pool★**, and **Fishing Cone Geyser★**. Until prohibited for safety reasons (such as unexpected 40ft eruptions), anglers could catch a trout in the lake and, without taking a step, dip it into Fishing Cone to cook it while still on the line.

Grant Village – *2mi south of West Thumb.* ♿ ⊞. Named to honor US President Ulysses S. Grant, who signed the legislation that created Yellowstone in 1872, this full-service park community includes the **Grant Village Visitor Center★** *(☎ 307-242-2650)*. Exhibits and a 20min film explain the natural benefits of wild fires.

★★★ **Old Faithful** – 🚸 *18mi northwest of West Thumb & 16mi south of Madison Junction.* ♿ ⊞. The world's most famous geyser has been spouting with uncanny regularity since it was discovered by the Washburn-Langford-Doane party in 1870. Averaging 135ft in height when it erupts, sometimes reaching 180ft, Old Faithful puts on a show approximately every 88min. (Park officials can predict within 10min when the next "blow" will occur.) Eruptions last 90sec to 5min and spew between 3,700gal and 8,400gal of boiling water.

Old Faithful

A semicircular boardwalk with benches surrounds the geyser. During the high season of July and August, thousands of people wait patiently for an eruption, then scurry to other activities, creating a phenomenon locals refer to as a "gush rush." Restaurants fill immediately after an eruption and clear out just before.

The village flanking Old Faithful is the park's most commercial, with massive parking lots and numerous buildings facing the geyser. Chief among them is **Old Faithful Inn★★** *(☎ 307-545-4600)*, the world's largest log building. This National Historic Landmark was designed by Robert Reamer and constructed in 1903-04. It is the definitive structure of "parkitecture"—six stories high, its steep roof capped by a widow's walk, its massive lobby featuring whole log columns, a stone fireplace and tortured lodgepole-pine railings.

Old Faithful Lodge *(☎ 307-545-4900)*, another large log-and-stone building, was completed in 1928. Predicted times for geyser eruptions are posted on a huge clock behind a tour desk. The large plate-glass windows of the **Old Faithful Visitor Center** *(☎ 307-545-2750)*, sandwiched between the Inn and Lodge, enable visitors to watch Old Faithful erupt without leaving the building.

■ Geysers

Geysers are created by constrictions in the subterranean plumbing of a hot spring. Steam bubbles, like commuters at rush hour, create immense pressure as they force their way through the water above them, erupting with even more superheated water and steam from the depths.

Two-thirds (about 300) of the world's geysers are located in Yellowstone. "So numerous are they and varied," wrote naturalist John Muir, "nature seems to have gathered them from all over the world as specimens of her rarest fountains to show in one place what she can do."

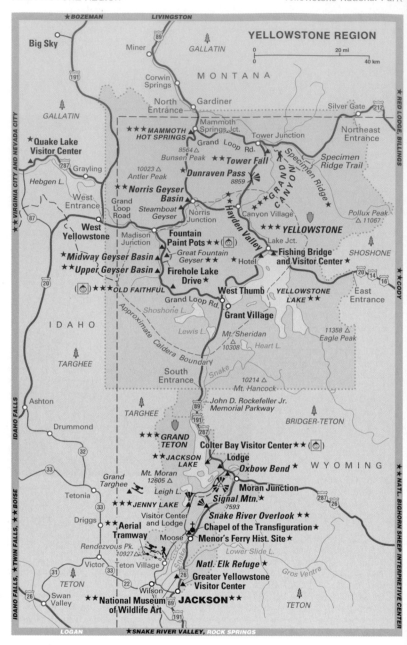

★★Upper Geyser Basin – ♿ 🅿 . Surrounding Old Faithful is the world's single largest concentration of geysers. Few of them, however, approach Old Faithful in predictability. Among the better known are **Grand Geyser★**, which unleashes a 200ft fountain every 7-15hrs; **Riverside Geyser★**, whose stream spurts up to 80ft over the Firehole River at 5-6hr intervals; and **Castle Geyser★**, which explodes to 90ft twice daily from an ancient 12ft cone.

The varied colors and shapes of the Upper Geyser Basin's hot springs offer clues to their creation and composition. Because no organism can survive in water 161°F or warmer (at this altitude), the hottest pools typically reflect the color of the sky. The best-known spring, **Morning Glory Pool★★**, is not as blue as it once was, however: Its hot-water vent has been clogged by coins and other objects thrown into the pool by visitors, leading to gradual cooling.

* **Midway Geyser Basin** – *6mi north of Old Faithful*. 🅿 . Mist from the wide **Excelsior Geyser** envelops visitors who cross the footbridge and climb past a multicolored bank of the Firehole River. Runoff from acidic **Grand Prismatic Spring★★** has created terraced algae mats, often decorated with hoof prints from bison. At 370ft across and 120ft deep, Grand Prismatic is the second-largest hot spring in the world. Its rainbow colors were created by dissolved iron and other minerals, manifesting in red, orange and black hues.

* **Firehole Lake Drive** – *8mi north of Old Faithful*. 🅿 . A quiet 3mi, one-way circuit east of the Grand Loop Road, this route winds past **Great Fountain Geyser★★**, the **White Dome** and **Pink Cone** geysers, and **Firehole Lake**, with runoff in every direction. Between Great Fountain's 45-60min eruptions at intervals of 8-12hrs, the still water of its broad, circular pool mirrors the sky in myriad terraces. Firehole Lake's thermal waters flow through the forest here, giving trees a skeletal appearance of stark white stockings and gray trunks. The absorption of sinter (dissolved minerals) kills the trees but acts as a preservative, delaying their decay.

** **Fountain Paint Pots** – 🆔 *9mi north of Old Faithful*. ♿ 🅿 . Visitors may view all four types of Yellowstone thermal features on a short tour of this area. A boardwalk leads past colorful bacterial and algae mats, hot pools and the namesake bubbling "paint pots." Adults as well as children revel in the implied messiness, oozing and rotten-egg stench of the spring's hydrogen sulfide gas. The perpetually active **Clepsydra Geyser★** is especially scenic in winter, when bison wander in front of its plume of steam. It is best viewed from the Grand Loop Road north of the Paint Pots, backlit in afternoon light.

GRAND TETON NATIONAL PARK★★★

Map opposite   Mountain Standard Time
Tourist information ☎ 307-739-3600 or www.nps.gov/grte

North America's most spectacular mountains, the Teton Range, rise dramatically above a broad valley near the headwaters of the Snake River, immediately south of Yellowstone National Park. Cresting atop 13,770ft **Grand Teton**, the Tetons, which extend about 40mi from south to north, are the highlight of Grand Teton National Park—485sq mi of rugged peaks, alpine lakes, streams, marshland and sage-and-aspen plains.
The Tetons are the result of a continuing cycle of mountain building and erosion. Geologic youngsters at 5 to 9 million years, they are still growing along a north-south fault line. As the valley floor—once a flat layer of sediment left by an ancient inland sea—has subsided, the blocks of rock that form the Tetons have risen, tilting westward. Erosion has shaved soft sandstone from the caps of the peaks, gradually filling the valley several miles deep with sediment.
The high peaks attract significant precipitation, especially as snow in winter. As snowfall rates exceed melting, glaciers form, chiseling singular peaks like the Grand Teton. Twelve active glaciers flow as many as 30ft each year around several of the peaks, especially the Grand Teton and 12,605ft **Mount Moran**. Glacial debris, deposited at the base of the mountains, has formed lateral and terminal moraines that act as natural dams, capturing melt-water to form lakes.

Historical Notes – Known to Native Americans as *Teewinot*, "many pinnacles," the Tetons' modern name came from early 19C French trappers, who saw them as *Les Trois Tétons*, "the three breasts," as they approached from the west.
Although Native Americans used Jackson Hole as a summer hunting ground for thou sands of years, few chose to endure the harsh winters. Cattle ranchers eventually established an economic presence, but they were gradually supplanted by tourism following the establishment of Yellowstone Park in 1872.
Grand Teton's transition to national park was not a smooth one. Early settlers proved as stubborn as the winter weather when it came to turning the land over to federal jurisdiction. Fearing development, philanthropist John D. Rockefeller Jr. secretly bought up ranchland and deeded it to the government. The original park boundaries were established in 1929; they were expanded to their present margins in 1950. The **John D. Rockefeller Jr. Memorial Parkway**, a corridor of land linking Grand Teton and Yellowstone parks, was created in 1972.

SIGHTS

Park headquarters are adjacent to the **Moose Visitor Center** *(Teton Park Rd., 0.5mi west of Teton Junction & 12mi north of Jackson;* ☎ *307-739-3399)*, at the southern end of the park. A driving tour from here is best done in a counterclockwise direction, heading northeast along the Snake River to Jackson Lake, returning south at the foot of the mountain range.

★★ Snake River Overlook – *US-26/89/191, 8mi north of Moose Junction.* ♿ 🅿 . Immortalized by photographer Ansel Adams, this is the most popular vista point in the park. Adams created a definitive black-and-white image of the ragged

Fly Fisherman

Tetons with the silvery Snake River in the foreground. The view is especially pretty at sunrise, when the peaks light up with the rosy glow of dawn and the canyon is filled with mist.

Moran Junction – *18mi north of Moose Junction.* This is the east entrance station for Grand Teton National Park.

★ Oxbow Bend – *US-89/191/287, 4mi northwest of Moran Junction.* ♿ 🅿 . The Snake River almost doubles back on itself at this bulbous elbow made up of an abandoned river meander. This is one of the most dependable spots in the park to spy moose, which often feed in the shallows.

★★ Jackson Lake – ⛺ ✗ ♿ 🅿 . The largest of seven natural morainal lakes in the park, Jackson Lake—16mi long and 8mi wide—was enlarged by a succession of dams built at its Snake River outlet. Of the lake depth of 438ft, only the last 39ft were added when the dams raised the water level. **Boat tours** (90min) are offered daily in summer.

Jackson Lake Lodge – *US-89/191/287, 6mi northwest of Moran Junction.* ⛺ ✗ ♿ 🅿 ☎ *307-543-2811.* Designed by Gilbert Stanley Underwood, architect of the Ahwahnee Hotel in California's Yosemite National Park, this concrete, steel and glass structure was built above the beaver ponds of Willow Flats. The lobby features massive, 60ft-tall picture windows framing a classic view of the Tetons.

★★ Colter Bay Visitor Center – **Kids** *1mi west of US-89/191/287, 11mi northwest of Moran Junction.* ⛺ ✗ ♿ 🅿 ☎ *307-739-3594. Open summers only.* The center holds the **Indian Arts Museum,** whose display of native crafts—beadwork, weaponry, moccasins, shields and pipes—is among Wyoming's best.

★ Signal Mountain – *Off Teton Park Rd., 16mi north of Moose Junction & 5mi south of Jackson Lake Lodge.* ♿ 🅿 . Rising above **Signal Mountain Lodge** *(Teton Park Rd.; ☎ 307-543-2831)* on the east side of Jackson Lake, 7,593ft Signal Mountain provides great **views★★** of the Tetons and Jackson Hole. The **Signal Mountain Summit Road** is a narrow, winding, 5mi, 800ft climb with few turnouts.

★★★ Jenny Lake Scenic Drive – *Off Teton Park Rd., beginning 11.5mi north of Moose Junction.* ♿ 🅿 . This 4mi loop weaves along the eastern shore of gem-like **Jenny Lake★★★** before reconnecting with Teton Park Road. En route are numerous impressive views of the high Tetons. From the **Cathedral Group Turnout★**, the peaks crowd together like church steeples.
Little **String Lake** ties Jenny Lake to more northerly **Leigh Lake.** Beyond here, the two-way road becomes a narrow, one-way southerly drive. A cluster of 37 log cabins surrounds rustic **Jenny Lake Lodge** *(☎ 307-543-2811),* the park's top-end accommodation. From the **Jenny Lake Overlook★★**, lake waters reflect the Tetons rising abruptly from the water's edge. The **Jenny Lake Visitor Center** at South Jenny Lake has a set of geology exhibits. From here, Teton Boating Company operates boat tours and shuttles to the Cascade Canyon trailhead.

* **Menor's Ferry Historic Site** – *Teton Park Rd., 1.5mi north of Moose Junction.* &. ▣. An interpretive trail *(.5mi)* leads to a replica of a flat-bottomed ferry that Bill Menor operated from 1894 to 1927. Interpreters reenact the Snake River crossing in summer. Menor's white log cabin is decorated as the country store he also ran from the home.

* **Chapel of the Transfiguration** – *0.5mi east of Teton Park Rd., 1.5mi north of Moose Junction.* &. ▣. The window behind the altar of this rustic little chapel, built in 1925, frames the Tetons. Services are offered summer Sundays.

* **Moose-Wilson Road** – *Moose Visitor Center to Rte. 22 (1.6mi east of Wilson).* &. ▣. This scenic drive to the small community of Wilson, at the base of Teton Pass, skirts groves of aspens and a network of willow-clogged beaver ponds. Moose are often spotted from **Sawmill Ponds Overlook.** The road—all but about 2mi of it paved—accesses several popular trailheads, especially to emerald **Phelps Lake** *(2mi).* In winter, closed to vehicles, it makes for an enjoyable cross-country ski.

JACKSON★★

Map p 384　　Mountain Standard Time
Tourist information ☎ 307-733-3316 or www.jacksonholechamber.com

The resort town of Jackson sits at 6,350ft altitude near the south end of the 45mi-long valley known as Jackson Hole, between the Tetons and the Gros Ventre Mountains. Existing in relative obscurity until Yellowstone and Grand Teton National Parks were established, the town's economy has gradually shifted away from cattle ranching in favor of tourism and outdoor recreation. It is now a year-round paradise both for wildlife and the wild life. River rafting, fishing, hiking, horseback riding and mountain climbing are among its offerings, and in winter, Jackson is one of the finest ski destinations in the world. Three ski areas, famed for light and ample powder snow, are within a short drive; the **Jackson Hole Ski Area★★** *(Rte. 390, Teton Village, 12mi west of Jackson;* ☎ *307-733-4005)* has the greatest vertical rise (4,139ft) of any ski area in the US.

Jackson is crowded with fine restaurants, high-end Western-wear boutiques and fine-art galleries that occupy hard-core shoppers for days, and its proliferation of modern condominium developments has attracted many well-heeled part-time residents. But it has retained a firm grip on its Western heritage.

Town Square *(Broadway & Cache Dr.)* is the hub of this community of 5,000. An arch of elk antlers frames each of its four corners—a tiny fraction of what is collected at the end of each winter on the National Elk Refuge. Prior to 1957, the antlers were offered as souvenirs. Today they are auctioned by Boy Scouts in mid-May. Of the $90,000 typically raised, 80 percent goes to augment the elk-feeding program at the refuge; the remaining revenue supports Scouting.

Summer nights at Town Square, actors re-create a stagecoach robbery and **Jackson Hole Shootout** Kids—even though no such incident ever took place in Jackson. Facing the Square is the **Million Dollar Cowboy Bar** *(25 N. Cache Dr.; ☎ 307-733-2207),* with saddles for stools and silver dollars inlaid into its bar.

SIGHTS

Greater Yellowstone Visitor Center – *532 N. Cache Dr. ☎ 307-733-9212. www.jacksonholechamber.com.* This contemporary sod-roofed building, an interagency visitor center, features a platform with spotting scopes for viewing the adjacent elk refuge and marsh, and interpretive exhibits on fire management and wildlife migration.

* **National Elk Refuge** – *Elk Refuge Rd. off E. Broadway. ☎ 307-733-9212.* Between 7,000 and 9,000 elk spend their winters in this 24,700-acre refuge after migrating from higher elevations in the national parks and Bridger-Teton National Forest. November to April, this herd resembles swaths of dark brown earth on the otherwise white landscape. The refuge was established after cattle ranching and development disrupted normal migration patterns.
  Sled tours★★ Kids *(45min)* are offered daily in winter. Draft horses pull sleighs to herds, where most animals graze sedately—although bull elk may joust with their immense racks. The refuge is also a popular winter range for bighorn sheep, coyotes, deer, wolves and, occasionally, pronghorn and mountain lions. Tickets are sold by the National Museum of Wildlife Art *(below).*

** **National Museum of Wildlife Art** – Kids *2820 Rungius Rd., off US-89, 2.5mi north of Jackson.* ✗&. ▣ ☎ *307-733-5771. www.wildlifeart.org.* Tucked into a hillside overlooking the National Elk Refuge, this sandstone complex (1994) is nearly invisible. Its rough-hewn exterior resembles Anasazi ruins. Within are 12 exhibition galleries, an interactive children's gallery, a 200-seat auditorium, classrooms, and a library and archive.

Sled Tour, National Elk Refuge

Covering five centuries, the collection of more than 2,300 works includes John J. Audubon, Robert Bateman, Albert Bierstadt, George Catlin, John Clymer, Bob Kuhn and Charles M. Russell. Media range from oil, pastel, acrylic and watercolor to bronze, stone, pencil, charcoal, lithography and photography.

The American Bison Collection explores man's relationship with buffalo since the 18C. Also featured is the largest body of work in the US by Carl Rungius.

★★**Teton Village Aerial Tramway** – *Rte. 390, Teton Village.* ☎ *307-733-2292. www.jacksonholechamber.com.* A gondola whisks sightseers skyward on a brisk ride, climbing over 4,000ft in 12min to the 10,450ft ridge of Rendezvous Peak at the Jackson Hole Ski Area. Spread to the east is Jackson Hole, bisected by the Snake River. Many hikers descend Rendezvous Peak on foot via the steep 10mi **Granite Canyon Trail**.

EXCURSIONS

Grand Targhee Ski & Summer Resort – *Targhee Rd., Alta, 5mi east of Driggs, Idaho, & 32mi northwest of Jackson via Rtes. 22 & 33.* ✗ 🄿 ☎ *307-353-2300. www.grandtarghee.com.* Nearly 40ft of light, dry snow falls on the "back side" of the Teton Range each winter, making this a mecca for powder hounds. In summer, music festivals and ecology classes complement outdoor recreation and scenic chairlift rides.

★★ **National Bighorn Sheep Interpretive Center** – *907 W. Ramshorn St., Dubois, 85mi east of Jackson via US-26/287.* ♿ 🄿 ☎ *307-455-3429.* Located in the frontier logging-town-turned-recreational-center of Dubois *(DEW-boys)*, this facility's interactive exhibits offer insight into wildlife management. Visitors may "manage" a herd of wild sheep, balancing reproduction rates, expected mortality and forage requirements with a variety of management techniques including hunting, culling the herd and non-intervention. Staff direct visitors on a self-guided tour of lower **Whiskey Mountain**, home to the largest wintering herd of Rocky Mountain bighorn sheep in the US.

CODY★★

Michelin map 493 G 6   Mountain Standard Time
Tourist Information ☎ 307-587-2777 or www.codychamber.org

William F. "Buffalo Bill" Cody founded this town as his own in 1896, two decades after he first scouted the region. Cody envisioned a place where the Old and New West could meet; this site, 50mi east of Yellowstone National Park, was ideal. Cody poured the profits from his popular Wild West Show into the town's growth. By 1901, rail service was established; by 1905, construction was under way on the ambitious Shoshone (now Buffalo Bill) Dam. When the national park opened its gates to automobiles, access via Cody became the most popular route.

Tourism remains the major industry; Yellowstone-bound guests still drive the economy. The **Cody Country Chamber of Commerce** *(836 Sheridan Ave.; ☎ 307-587-2777)* has information on walking tours of the historic town, including **The Irma** *(1192 Sheridan Ave.; ☎ 307-587-4221)*. This 1902 hotel, built by Buffalo Bill and named for his youngest daughter, features an ornate cherry backbar hand-crafted in France and shipped to Cody as a gift from Queen Victoria of England.

The summer **Cody Night Rodeo**★ Kids *(W. Yellowstone Hwy.; ♿ P ☎ 307-587-5155; www.comp-unltd.com/~rodeo/rodeo.html)* is a lively introduction to the sport of rodeo. Contestants vie in bronco and bull riding, calf roping, team roping, bulldogging and barrel racing, as an announcer explains with deadpan humor the events and their rules. A nightly highlight is the Calf Scramble, in which children pursue a calf with a yellow ribbon tied to its tail.

`Buffalo Bill' Cody

More than any other individual, Colonel William F. "Buffalo Bill" Cody (1846-1917) bridged the gap between old and new, East and West. An icon of the exploration and settlement of the US West, this articulate and visionary man tied his experiences into a neat package and delivered them in theatrical form to eager audiences in the eastern US and Europe.

Cody at 15 distinguished himself by completing a 322mi Pony Express ride in 21hrs 40min, using 20 different horses. Following service as a Union scout in the Civil War, he was hired for $500 per month to provide buffalo meat for workers laying track for the Kansas Pacific Railroad. He reportedly killed 4,280 bison in just eight months; his nickname, "Buffalo Bill," was bestowed after he won a competition with another hunter.

After the Civil War, Cody became a US cavalry scout, helping to resolve conflict between Indians and settlers who disregarded government treaties. His knowledge and endurance became legendary. Back East, dime novelists were looking for a Western hero, and young Cody fitted the bill. His exploits, both real and imagined, became household conversation. Hundreds of thousands of words about Buffalo Bill were spewed by Ned Buntline and other writers.

Cody retired from the Army in 1872, after he was awarded the Congressional Medal of Honor for bravery in combat. He moved to New York to pursue an acting career, portraying himself in Buntline's *Scouts of the Prairie*. He took to the stage as naturally as he did to the saddle. Cody launched his famed Wild West Show in 1883, depicting historic events with actual participants, including Chief Sitting Bull. Cody's climb to stardom was meteoric and he enjoyed a long ride at the top of his profession as his show toured for 30 years, some 10 of those in Europe.

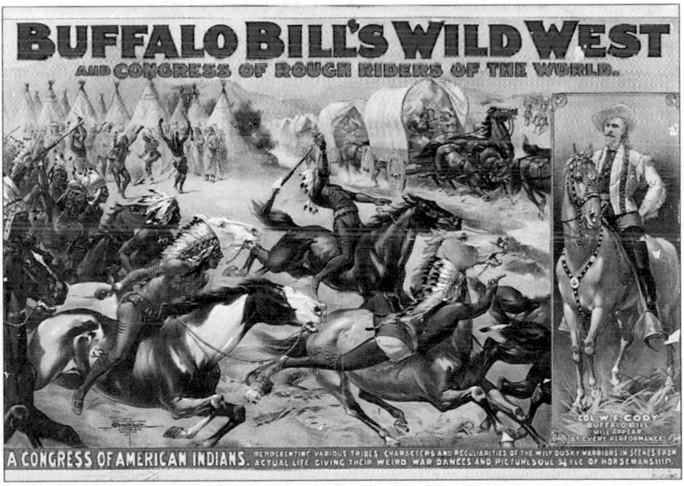

Library of Congress

Buffalo Bill's Wild West Poster by Courier Lithographic Co. 1899

SIGHTS

***Buffalo Bill Historical Center** – **Kids** *720 Sheridan Ave. at 8th St.* ✗ ♿ 🅿
☎ *307-587-4771. www.bbhc.org.* Four internationally acclaimed galleries and a
research library, occupying three levels of this fan-shaped complex, explore
aspects of the history of the American West. Also on the site is the boyhood home
of William F. "Buffalo Bill" Cody, shipped by train from Iowa in 1933.

The **Whitney Gallery of Western Art★** presents a broad spectrum of paintings and sculpture, including oils by Catlin, Bierstadt and Russell, and bronzes by Remington,
Fraser and Rumsey. Artists-in-residence work in public view. The wing is named
for sculptor Gertrude Vanderbilt Whitney, whose dynamic *The Scout*, situated
north of the complex, depicts a mounted William F. Cody.

The **Buffalo Bill Museum★★** chronicles the storied life of "Buffalo Bill," man and myth.
Much of the collection focuses on his Wild West Show and its relationship to public perception of the West. Displays include firearms, clothing, silver-studded saddles, and film gathered from Cody's private and public lives.

The **Plains Indian Museum★★** was scheduled to reopen in June 2000 with a new inter-
pretation of the cultural history and artistry of the Arapaho, Blackfoot, Cheyenne,
Comanche, Crow, Gros Ventre, Kiowa, Pawnee, Shoshone and Sioux.

The **Cody Firearms Museum★★**, which traces the evolution of guns, is the world's most
comprehensive collection of post-16C American and European firearms—nearly
4,000 in all. Also presented are world-record big-game mounts.

*★**Trail Town** – *1831 DeMaris Dr. off W. Yellowstone Hwy.* 🅿 ☎ *307-587-5302.*
More than 100 wagons and 25 buildings dated 1879-1901, moved from a
150mi radius, are arranged on the original surveyed site for Cody City.

EXCURSIONS

★★Bighorn Canyon National Recreation Area – *Via Rte. 37 northeast of Lovell. Visitor center on US-14A, Lovell, 48mi northeast of Cody.* ⚠ ✗ ♿ 🅿 ☎ *307-548-2251.
www.nps.gov/bica.* Bighorn Lake, a 60mi-long reservoir created by Montana's 525ft-
high Yellowtail Dam, is wedged between 2,200ft cliffs. It entices boaters and fishermen. Flanking the national recreation area on its west is the expansive **Pryor Mountain
Wild Horse Range**. Between 100 and 200 wild horses roam freely in bands.

*★**Hot Springs State Park** – **Kids** *US-20 & Park St., Thermopolis, 83mi southeast of
Cody.* ⚠ ✗ ♿ 🅿 ☎ *307-864-2176. www.thermopolis.com.* Shoshone and Arapaho
Indians sold these springs to Wyoming in 1896 with the stipulation that they remain
free for public use. Today 3.6 million gallons of 135°F water flow daily from Monument Hill, piped through the center of two 20ft travertine terraces created over a
century by the continual deposit of 27 different minerals. The free Wyoming State
Bathhouse sits between two commercial facilities at the foot of the springs.

MONTANA GATEWAYS★

Michelin map 493 F, G 5   Mountain Standard Time
Tourist Information ☎ 406-444-2654 or http://visitmt.com

Although less than 8 percent of Yellowstone National Park falls within Montana,
three of its five entrances are in the "Big Sky" state. The West Yellowstone entrance
is the busiest, capturing one-third of park visitors. Mammoth Hot Springs is near
Gardiner, at the north entrance. The magnificent northeastern-approach road climbs
nearly to 11,000ft at Beartooth Pass.

SIGHTS

West Yellowstone – *US-20 & 287.* ⚠ ✗ ♿ 🅿 ☎ *406-646-7701. www
.westyellowstonechamber.com.* The Union Pacific Railroad built a spur line to the
park's border in 1907. Today this town has about 1,000 year-round residents;
in winter, it calls itself the "Snowmobile Capital of the World." In the former
Union Pacific Depot—designed in "park rustic" style by Gilbert Stanley Underwood—the **Museum of the Yellowstone** *(Yellowstone & S. Canyon Sts.; ☎ 406-646-
7814)* offers wildlife dioramas and a highly regarded display of Indian beadwork
and quillwork.

★★Grizzly Discovery Center – **Kids** *201 S. Canyon St.* ♿ 🅿 ☎ *406-646-7001. www
.grizzlydiscoveryctr.com.* The habitats and behavioral tendencies of grizzly bears
and gray wolves are the focus of this educational facility. A pack of 10 wolves

with a clear social hierarchy shares a den in one fenced enclosure. Nearby, eight grizzlies enjoy an enclosure with two ponds and a flowing stream. Released two or three at a time, the bears are encouraged to use their natural abilities tearing logs apart, digging up the earth and flipping rocks to forage for insects. An interpreter discusses behavior, from eating habits to intelligence and mating.

★**Quake Lake Visitor Center** – *US-287, 25mi northwest of West Yellowstone.* ☏ *406-646-7369. www.fs.fed.us/r1/gallatin.* Just before midnight on August 17, 1959, a magnitude-7.5 earthquake, with an epicenter near **Hebgen Lake**, triggered a landslide that buried 19 people at a Madison River campground and destroyed miles of highway. Soon the Madison was backing up behind a natural-earth dam, as cracks developed in the manmade dam at Hebgen Lake. Had either dam broken, the flooding would have destroyed several communities. The story of the tragedy, and of how a secondary disaster was averted, is told at this Forest Service visitor center. It is perched on a hillside overlooking the slide scar and natural dam; a quickly engineered spillway; and **Quake Lake**, 190ft deep and 6mi long.

★★**Virginia City and Nevada City** – *Rte. 278, 84mi northwest of West Yellowstone.* ⚠ ✗ 🄿 ☏ 4 *06-843-5555. www.virginiacitychamber.com.* These sister villages, 1.5mi apart in Alder Gulch, feature Wild West architecture embellished with vigilante legends. Both prospered during an 1863 gold rush; Virginia City survived to become the capital of the Montana Territory, while Nevada City became a ghost town. Today **Nevada City**★★ is a restored mining camp with more than 90 period buildings—some originals, some reconstructions, some moved from other sites. **Virginia City**★★ is a living museum, the entire town being listed on the National Register of Historic Places. The Main Street boardwalk is fringed with current-day businesses alongside storefronts that display 19C wares.

★**Three Forks Area** – *I-90, 28mi west of Bozeman.* ⚠ ✗ 🄿. Lewis and Clark named the three rivers that merge to form the Missouri—the Madison, Jefferson and Gallatin—for statesmen of their day. **Missouri Headwaters State Park**★ *(Rte. 286, 5mi north of Three Forks;* ☏ *406-994-4042)* marks the start of North America's longest river system, the Missouri-Mississippi. **Lewis and Clark Caverns State Park**★★ 🄺🄸🄳🅂 *(Rte. 2, 19mi west of Three Forks;* ☏ *406-287-3541)*, named by Theodore Roosevelt after the caves' discovery by miners, boast 3-million-year-old stalactites and stalagmites as well as a colony of bats.

★**Bozeman** – *Rte. 84 at I-90 Exit 309, 92mi north of West Yellowstone.* ✗ ♿ 🄿 ☏ *406-586-5421. www.bozemanchamber.com.* Home to **Montana State University**, this town of 30,000 was named for wagonmaster John Bozeman. A railroad spur to West Yellowstone was completed in the early 20C. Today restaurants, bookshops, galleries and boutiques occupy the historic brick buildings on either side of **Main Street**, and nearby **Wilson Avenue**★ is lined with beautiful c.1900 homes.

★★**Museum of the Rockies** – 🄺🄸🄳🅂 *600 W. Kagy Blvd.* ♿ 🄿 ☏ *406-994-2251. www .montana.edu/wwwmor.* Exhibits in this outstanding museum trace the geologic history of life, with emphasis on the Rockies. In the **Life Sciences Exhibits**★★, a dinosaur display showcases the prominent role played by Montana and Wyoming in modern paleontology. Moving models of the great lizards are popular with children. At a working lab, a technician engages visitors in conversation while cleaning an authentic fossil. The **Taylor Planetarium** features star and laser shows. Outside, the **Tinsley Homestead** is the venue for living-history demonstrations depicting an early Gallatin Valley farm.

Big Sky – *Rte. 64, 3mi west of US-191, 45mi south of Bozeman & 47mi north of West Yellowstone.* ⚠ ✗ ♿ 🄿 ☏ *406-995-5000. www.bigskyresort.com.* Originally developed by TV newsman Chet Huntley, Big Sky is a summer-winter resort with 15 lifts that access 3,650 acres of ski terrain in winter. In summer, there is golf, horseback riding, biking and fishing; **gondola rides** go part way up 11,150ft Lone Peak and take in wide-ranging views.

Livingston – *US-89 at I-90 Exit 332, 60mi north of Mammoth Hot Springs.* ⚠ ✗ ♿ 🄿 ☏ *406-222-0850. www.yellowstone-chamber.com.* Founded in 1882 by the Northern Pacific, Livingston was the point at which rail tourists boarded a spur line to Yellowstone National Park's north entrance. The town of 7,000 has preserved 436 buildings from its heyday.

★**Red Lodge** – *US-212, 115mi east of Mammoth Hot Springs.* ✗ ♿ 🄿 ☏ *406-446-1718. www.redlodge.com.* Red Lodge began as a coal town. After the mines died, tourism brought new life. Main Street is lined with brick buildings, most constructed around the turn of the 20C. Oldest is the 1893 **Pollard Hotel** *(2 N. Broadway;* ☏ *406-446-0001)*, a National Historic Register site.

★★ **Beartooth Highway** – *US-212 from Red Lodge to Cooke City. Open May-Oct depending upon snow conditions.* △. CBS television correspondent Charles Kuralt called this 67mi route "the most beautiful road in America." Precipitous switchbacks climb from Red Lodge, ascending nearly 4,000ft in 5mi. **Views**★★★ are spectacular from an overlook at 10,947ft **Beartooth Pass**; an interpretive trail is frequented as often by mountain goats as by humans. The broad summit plateau is carpeted with wildflowers in summer; ragged peaks jut upward on every horizon. A gentle downward grade passes a series of picturesque lakes.

Billings – *US-87 at I-90 Exit 450.* ✗ ♿ 🅿 ☎ *406-252-4016. www .billingscvb.visitmt.com.* Montana's largest city (92,000 people) sprawls across a floodplain of the Yellowstone River. Its most compelling sight is the **Moss Mansion**★ *(914 Division St.; ☎ 406-256-5100)*, a 1903 banker's home built by Henry Janeway Hardenbergh, architect of New York's Waldorf-Astoria Hotel. A castle-like, 1901 library of Romanesque design houses the **Western Heritage Center** *(2282 Montana Ave.; ☎ 406-256-6809)*, a history museum. The **Yellowstone Art Museum** *(401 N. 27th St.; ☎ 406-256-6804)*, built around the old county jail, features such Montana artists as cowboy painter Will James and sculptor Deborah Butterfield.

SNAKE RIVER VALLEY★

Michelin map 493 D, E, F 6   Mountain Standard Time
Tourist Information ☎ 208-334-2470 or www.visitid.org

Rising in Wyoming and flowing through Yellowstone and Grand Teton National Parks, the Snake River arcs across southern Idaho, carving deep canyons and nourishing rich agricultural lands. A series of dams have turned this high lava plain into productive land, supporting cities and towns of moderate size.

Once an inland sea that drained westward as the land mass uplifted, the region was covered by lava that oozed through faults to cloak the rich marine silt. To the south, great Lake Bonneville, 340mi long and 140mi wide, covered much of modern Utah and eastern Nevada. When the lake breached a volcanic plug 15,000 years ago, a flood of biblical proportion raged for eight weeks at a rate three times that of the modern Amazon River, sweeping millions of tons of rocks and debris and carving the magnificent Snake River and Hells Canyons.

SIGHTS

Idaho Falls – *US-20 & 26 at I-15 Exit 118, 90mi west of Jackson.* ✗ ♿ 🅿 ☎ *208-523-1010.* This agricultural center of 48,000 is the gateway to the **Idaho National Engineering & Environmental Laboratory**. Spread across 890sq mi of lava rock are 52 nuclear reactors, the largest concentration on earth. Experimental Breeder Reactor 1 was the first in the US, having operated 1951-64; free tours of the facility, known as **EBR-I**★ *(Van Buren Blvd., Atomic City, 48mi west of Idaho Falls; ☎ 208-526-0050)* are offered summers.

★ **Twin Falls** – *US-93, 6mi south of I-84 Exit 173, 110mi west of Pocatello.* ✗ ♿ 🅿 ☎ *208-733-3974. www.twinfallschamber.com.* This town of 33,000 boasts the **Herrett Center for Arts & Science**★ *(315 Falls Ave. W., College of Southern Idaho; ☎ 208-733-9554)*, whose anthropology collection, emphasizing Native American cultures, is highly regarded and whose planetarium is the largest in the Pacific Northwest. Interstate 84 travelers enter Twin Falls via the **Perrine Bridge**, 486ft above the **Snake River Canyon** and the longest span bridge in the USA West. The ramp from which motorcycle daredevil Evel Knievel unsuccessfully attempted to leap 1,500ft across the canyon in 1974 can still be seen.

The main attraction here is **Shoshone Falls**★★ *(3300 East Rd., 5mi east of Twin Falls via Falls Ave.; ☎ 208-736-2265)*. Nicknamed "the Niagara of the West," these 212ft falls are 52ft higher than the eastern US cataract. In spring, before upriver irrigation diversions steal much of the thunder, this is an impressive sight, a 1,000ft-wide wall of water that drops into its own cloud of mist.

★★ **Thousand Springs Scenic Route** – *US-30 between Buhl (18mi west of Twin Falls) and Bliss (I-84 Exit 141).* ♿ 🅿 www.nps.gov/hafo. The **Thousand Springs**★★ seep or gush from the opposite (north) wall of the Snake canyon, an outflow from the Lost Rivers that disappear into the porous Snake River Plain, emerging through gaps or fractures in the rock. Numerous **fish hatcheries** and trout farms in the valley take advantage of the pristine water.

Perched on a bluff on the southwest side of the Snake is **Hagerman Fossil Beds National Monument★** *(W. 2700 South Rd.; visitor center at 221 N. State St., Hagerman;* ☎ *208-837-4793).* The richest trove of Pliocene fossils in North America, the beds were first excavated in the 1930s when Smithsonian Institution scientists unearthed a zebra-like horse extinct for more than 3 million years. There are overlooks and trails but no on-site facilities; tours are offered from the visitor center on summer weekends.

★**Bruneau Dunes State Park** – ᴷⁱᵈˢ *Rte. 78, 18mi south of Mountain Home at I-84 Exit 95.* 🛆 ⚹ 🅿 ☎ *208-366-7919. www.idahoparks.org.* The highest (470ft) free-standing sand dunes in North America occupy a 600-acre depression in an ancient bend of the Snake. Hiking trails climb the stationary dunes, composed mainly of quartz and feldspar particles. A small observatory attracts weekend stargazers; a larger complex is planned.

Snake River

★★**Boise** – *US-20/26/30 at I-84 Exit 53, 120mi northwest of Twin Falls.* ✕ ⚹ 🅿 ☎ *208-344-7777. www.boise.org.* The Boise *(BOY-see)* River lends a unique character to this city of 157,000, Idaho's capital and the state's commercial and cultural center. High-tech office workers on their lunch hours wade into the stream and cast flies for trout, as Boise State University students drift by on rafts and inner tubes within sight of the Neoclassical **Idaho State Capitol★** *(700 W. Jefferson St.;* ☎ *208-334-2470).* Built of native sandstone in 1905-20 and patterned after the US Capitol in Washington DC, the capitol is the beneficiary of the modern world's first urban geothermal heating system. Since 1892, 700,000gal of 172°F water have been pumped daily from an aquifer adjacent to the **Warm Springs Historic District.** Four hundred private residences and eight government buildings are so heated.

Activity downtown centers around **The Grove** *(8th Ave. & Grove St.),* a broad pedestrian plaza. Nearby, the **Basque Museum and Cultural Center** *(607 Grove St.;* ☎ *208-343-2671)* pays tribute to the European minority that has made Boise the largest Basque community outside the group's native Spain and France.

The **Boise River Greenbelt★★,** a mostly paved 35mi network of walking and biking paths, links a series of riverside parks through the heart of the city. Nearest to downtown, **Julia Davis Park** *(Julia Davis Dr. & Capitol Blvd.)* is home to the **Idaho State Historical Museum** ᴷⁱᵈˢ *(*☎ *208-334-2120),* the **Boise Art Museum** *(*☎ *208-345-8330)* and the hands-on **Discovery Center of Idaho** ᴷⁱᵈˢ *(*☎ *208-343-9895).* Also in the park is **Zoo Boise** ᴷⁱᵈˢ *(355 N. Julia Davis Dr.;* ☎ *208-384-4260).* East of the park is the **M-K Nature Center★** ᴷⁱᵈˢ *(600 S. Walnut St.;* ☎ *208-334-2225),* which re-creates the life cycle of a mountain stream.

Two miles east, the **Old Idaho State Penitentiary★** *(2445 Old Penitentiary Rd., off Warm Springs Blvd.;* ☎ *208-368-6080)* is one of only four US territorial prisons still in existence. The fortress-like sandstone edifice was built by convict labor in 1870 and used until 1973.

Peregrine Falcon
© Tim Thompson

★★World Center for Birds of Prey – **Kids** *5666 W. Flying Hawk Lane off S. Cole Rd., 6mi south of Boise via I-84 Exit 50.* &. ▯ ☎ *208-362-8687. www.peregrinefund .org.* The Peregrine Fund was established in 1970 to save the once-endangered peregrine falcon from extinction. The Fund has now turned its captive-breeding efforts to reestablishing populations of other threatened birds, including the California condor, the South American harpy eagle and the aplamado falcon of the southwestern US. Video cameras and one-way mirrors enable guests to view incubation chambers and birds without disturbing them.

South of Boise, the world's highest concentration of raptors nest on bluffs overlooking the Snake River. The 755sq-mi **Snake River Birds of Prey National Conservation Area** is accessed via Swan Falls Road *(3mi west of Kuna and 23mi south of Boise via I-84 Exit 44; ☎ 208-384-3334).* Best times to visit are late spring, when the young have hatched, and early autumn, when birds congregate to migrate south.

★★ Hells Canyon National Recreation Area – *Description p 274* .

★★ Sun Valley Resort – *Rte. 75, 83mi north of Twin Falls & 151mi east of Boise.* △ ⑂ &. ▯ ☎ *208-725-2111. www.visitsunvalley.com.* The Wood River Valley was a sleepy backwoods until the 1870s, when the discovery of gold, silver and lead transformed it into a bustling mining district. Sheep ranching later drove the economy, the former tent town of **Ketchum** becoming the second-largest export center in the world. Later, W. Averell Harriman, then chief executive of the Union Pacific Railroad, purchased a 4,000-acre ranch and began building a European-style winter resort. When the **Sun Valley Lodge★★** *(1 Sun Valley Rd., Sun Valley; ☎ 208-622-4111)* opened in 1936, it attracted a Hollywood clientele and set the tone for what then was known as the world's finest ski area, complete with the first chair lift (patterned after a maritime banana hoist).

Sun Valley continues to expand and modernize around its core village. With 18 lifts on two mountains—including 9,150ft **Bald Mountain**, whose slopes drop 3,400ft directly into Ketchum—and cross-country runs on the 21mi **Wood River Trail System**, it remains a world-class destination. In summer, there are golf, tennis, horseback riding, bicycling and many other sports, as well as figure-skating exhibitions by some of the world's finest skaters.

Author Ernest Hemingway (1899-1961) spent his later years as a resident of Ketchum, where he is buried; he is remembered with a bust and epitaph at the **Ernest Hemingway Memorial** *(Trail Creek Rd., 1mi northeast of Sun Valley Lodge).*

★★ Sawtooth National Recreation Area – *Headquarters on Rte. 75, 8mi north of Sun Valley.* △ ⑂ &. ▯ ☎ *208-727-5013. www.northrim.net/sawtoothnf.* Embracing 1,180sq mi of rugged mountains—including 40 peaks of 10,000ft elevation, 1,000 lakes and the headwaters of four important rivers—this is one of the most spectacular yet least-known corners of the continental US. Route 75 climbs up the Wood River to 8,701ft **Galena Summit★★**, then descends the Salmon River drainage. To the east are the magnificent Boulder and White Cloud Mountains, swathed in a carpet of firs. To the west rise the awesome peaks of the Sawtooth Range, a dramatic granite-dominated fault scarp formed 50 million to 70 million years ago and carved by ice, wind and rain. Valleys and lakes were scoured from the rock.

The most developed of four large morainal lakes on the east slope of the Saw-tooths is **Redfish Lake★★**, named for the sockeye salmon that traditionally spawned in its waters. A visitor center, log-cabin lodge, marina and beach make this a pop-ular destination.

Tiny **Stanley★★** *(Rtes. 21 & 75, 61mi northwest of Ketchum & 134mi northeast of Boise)* is an American Switzerland. Among the 69 hardy souls (winter snowfall averages 8ft) who call this gorgeous basin home are 23 outfitters, who specialize in backpacking and horse packing, fishing and white-water rafting.

★**Craters of the Moon National Monument** – *US-20/26/93, 18mi southwest of Arco & 65mi southeast of Sun Valley.* ⛺ ♿ 🅿 ☎ *208-527-3257. www.nps .gov/crmo.* Nowhere is the volcanic history of the Snake River Plain more obvious. Established in 1924, the 83sq-mi preserve is intriguing and foreboding, a jumble of fissures, lava tubes, spatter and cinder cones, an outdoor museum so intimidat-ing, it has yet to be fully explored. Scientists believe this stark landscape was formed when basaltic lava oozed out of cracks in the earth's crust. So moonlike is the terrain that astronauts were trained here for lunar landings.

From a newly remodeled **visitor center**, 7mi of paved road thread through the vol-canic features. In late spring, the black cinder slopes are transformed into a car-pet of wildflowers. Daytime temperatures exceed 90°F in summer; when the park closes in winter, the area is a popular cross-country skiing destination.

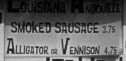

Hot Dog Stand, Venice, California

WORLD'S * LARGEST * HO

OD EMPORIUM... Pizza. H

ORDERS

POLISH KIELBAS

BUNSIZE $2   BIG 10" $4
INCLUDES OUR FAMOUS GRILLED ONIONS & PEPPERS
ADD 50 CENTS FOR AL

LOUISIANA ANDOUILLE

SMOKED SAUSAGE 3.75

ALLIGATOR or VENNISON 4.75

BIG 10" ITALIAN
SAUSAGE
$3.75

OAXACA
TACOS
FISH, CHICKEN, OR ASADA (BEEF)
$1.50 EACH

NACHOS
2.75 WITH CHEESE & JALAPENOS
CHICKEN OR BEEF ASADA 5.50

BUFFALO HOT
WINGS
3.99

SPICEY BEEF

POLISH 3.00

^ HOT SAUSAGES ^   ^^ HOT DOGS

HOMEMADE
ONION
RINGS
2.50

HOT DOG

KETCHUP

H SLICE CHEESE
PIZZA
$1

FRE
* LEMON
$1.

© David R. Frazier

Practical Information

Calendar of Events

Date	Event	Location

Spring

late Mar	Academy Awards	*Los Angeles CA*
	Cowboy Poetry & Music Festival	*Santa Clarita CA*
Mar or Apr	Easter Pageant	*Phoenix AZ*
Apr	Houston International Festival	*Houston TX*
	Azalea Festival	*Muskogee OK*
	Pole, Pedal, Paddle Triathlon	*Jackson Hole WY*
early Apr	Merrie Monarch Hula Festival	*Hilo HI*
mid-Apr	International Wildlife Film Festival	*Missoula MT*
	Toyota Grand Prix	*Long Beach CA*
	Orange Blossom Festival	*Riverside CA*
	Cherry Blossom Festival	*San Francisco CA*
mid-late Apr	Fiesta San Antonio	*San Antonio TX*
late Apr	Fiesta Broadway	*Los Angeles CA*
	Newport-Ensenada Yacht Race	*Newport Beach CA*
late Apr-early May	Buccaneer Days	*Corpus Christi TX*
	Apple Blossom Festival	*Wenatchee WA*
late Apr-mid-May	Ramona Pageant	*Hemet CA*
May	Molokai ka Hula Piko	*Molokai HI*
	Helldorado Days	*Las Vegas NV*
May 1	Lei Day	*Honolulu HI*
May 5	Cinco de Mayo	*cities near Mexican border*
early May	Mayfest	*Fort Worth TX*
mid-May	California Strawberry Festival	*Oxnard CA*
	Tejano Conjunto Festival en San Antonio	*San Antonio TX*
	Examiner Bay to Breakers Foot Race	*San Francisco CA*
	Calaveras County Fair & Jumping Frog Jubilee	*Angels Camp CA*
	Elk Antler Auction	*Jackson WY*
late May	Art Fest	*Dallas TX*
	Laguna Gloria Fiesta	*Austin TX*
	Carnaval	*San Francisco CA*
	Spring Festival of the Arts	*Santa Fe NM*
	Sacramento Jazz Jubilee	*Sacramento CA*
	Northwest Folklife Festival	*Seattle WA*
late May-early Jun	Seattle International Film Festival	*Seattle WA*
Jun	El Paso/Juarez International Mariachi Festival	*El Paso TX*
	King Kamehameha Day	*all islands HI*
	Portland Rose Festival	*Portland OR*
	Mormon Miracle Pageant	*Manti UT*
	The Great Cannery Row Sardine Festival	*Monterey CA*
early Jun	Red Earth Native American Cultural Festival	*Oklahoma City OK*
early-mid-Jun	Austin Jazz & Arts Festival	*Austin TX*
mid-Jun	Juneteenth African-American Festivals	*major cities*
	Telluride Bluegrass Festival	*Telluride CO*
	Smoky Hill River Festival	*Salina KS*
	Cannon Beach Sand Castle Contest	*Cannon Beach OR*
	La Jolla Festival of the Arts & Food Faire	*La Jolla CA*

Summer

Jun-Aug	Black Hills Passion Play	*Spearfish SD*
	Medora Musical	*Medora ND*
	Aspen Music Festival and School	*Aspen CO*
	Cody Nite Rodeo	*Cody WY*

Date	Event	Location
	The Britt Festivals	Jacksonville OR
Jun-early Sept	Summer Solstice Celebration	Fairbanks AK
late Jun	Little Big Horn Days	Hardin MT
	International Busker Fest	Denver CO
	Lewis & Clark Festival	Great Falls MT
	Lesbian/Gay/Bisexual/Transgender Pride Celebration	San Francisco CA
	Boise River Festival	Boise ID
late Jun-early Aug	Central City Opera	Central City CO
late Jun-late Aug	Santa Fe Opera	Santa Fe NM
late Jun-early Sept	Utah Shakespearean Festival	Cedar City UT
Jul	Cherry Creek Arts Festival	Denver CO
	Days of '47	Salt Lake City UT
	Taos Pueblo Powwow	Taos NM
	Green River Rendezvous	Pinedale WY
July 4	Independence Day Celebrations	every city and town

Native American Festival, New Mexico

	Independence Day Fireworks	Mt. Rushmore SD
early Jul	Pikes Peak International Hill Climb	Manitou Springs CO
	World Championship Timber Carnival	Albany OR
early-mid-Jul	North American Indian Days	Browning MT
mid-Jul	Cable Car Bell-Ringing Competition	San Francisco CA
	California Rodeo	Salinas CA
	International Climbers Festival	Lander WY
mid-late Jul	Cheyenne Frontier Days Rodeo	Cheyenne WY
late Jul	Golden Days & World Eskimo-Indian Olympics	Fairbanks AK
	Days of '76	Deadwood SD
	Last Chance Stampede	Helena MT
	US Open Surfing Championships	Huntington Beach CA
	Oregon Brewers Festival	Portland OR
	Gilroy Garlic Festival	Gilroy CA
	Spanish Market	Santa Fe NM
July 24	Pioneer Day	Utah
Jul Aug	Colorado Music Festival	Boulder CO
	Flagstaff Festival of the Arts	Flagstaff AZ
	Festival of Arts & Pageant of the Masters	Laguna Beach CA
	Festival of the American West	Logan UT
	Grand Teton Music Festival	Jackson WY

Date	Event	Location
mid-Jul-mid-Aug	Seafair Festival	Seattle WA
Aug	Hawaiian International Billfish Tournament	Kailua-Kona HI
	Kansas City Jazz Festival	Kansas City MO
	World's Oldest Continuous Rodeo	Payson AZ
	Texas Folklife Festival	San Antonio TX
	Fleet Week	San Diego CA
early Aug	Sturgis Rally and Races	Sturgis SD
	Festival of the Arts	Bigfork MT
	Old Spanish Days	Santa Barbara CA
	Park City Arts Festival	Park City UT
	Steinbeck Festival	Salinas CA
	Hot August Nights	Reno NV
	Festival of Nations	Red Lodge MT
early-mid-Aug	Inter-Tribal Indian Ceremonial	Gallup NM
mid-Aug	Indian Market	Santa Fe NM
mid-Aug-mid-Oct	State Fairs	every state
late Aug	World Body Surfing Championships	Oceanside CA
	Cherokee National Holiday	Tahlequah OK
Sept	Grand Canyon Music Festival	South Rim, Grand Canyon AZ
	Moab Music Festival	Moab UT
early Sept	Fiesta de las Flores	El Paso TX
	A Taste of Colorado	Denver CO
	All-American Futurity Race	Ruidoso NM
	Pioneer Days	Fort Worth TX
	Sausalito Art Festival	Sausalito CA
	La Fiesta de Santa Fe	Santa Fe NM
	Bumbershoot	Seattle WA
	Virginia City International Camel Races	Virginia City NV
mid-Sept	Mexican Independence Day	cities near Mexican border
	Navajo Nation Fair	Window Rock AZ
	Fiestas Patrias	Houston TX
	Pendleton Round-Up	Pendleton OR

Albuquerque International Balloon Festival, New Mexico

Date	Event	Location
	United Tribes International Pow Wow	Bismarck ND
	San Francisco Blues Festival	San Francisco CA
	Monterey Jazz Festival	Monterey CA
	Wooden Boat Festival	Port Townsend WA
	National Championship Air Races	Reno NV
	Jackson Hole Fall Arts Festival	Jackson WA

Fall

Date	Event	Location
late Sept	Gathering of Indian Nations Festival	Sedona AZ
	River City Roundup & Rodeo	Omaha NE
	Cabrillo Festival	San Diego CA
Sept-Oct	Aloha Festival	all islands HI
late Sept-early Oct	Taos Fall Arts Festival	Taos, NM
late Sept-mid-Oct	State Fair of Texas	Dallas TX
Oct	Festival of the Horse	Oklahoma City OK
early Oct	Albuquerque International Balloon Festival	Albuquerque NM
	Oklahoma International Bluegrass Festival	Guthrie OK
	Oktoberfest	Fredericksburg TX
mid-Oct	Alaska Day Festival	Sitka AK
	Canyonlands Fat Tire Festival	Moab UT
	Helldorado Days	Tombstone AZ
late Oct	Ironman Triathlon	Big Island HI
Oct 31	Halloween	most cities and towns
Nov	Kona Coffee Festival	Kailua-Kona HI
	Death Valley Fall Festival & '49er Encampment	Furnace Creek CA
early Nov	Will Rogers Days	Claremore OK
	Wurstfest	New Braunfels TX
late Nov	Hollywood Christmas Parade	Hollywood CA
	Doo Dah Parade	Pasadena CA
	River Parade & Lighting Ceremony	San Antonio TX
Nov-Dec	Triple Crown of Surfing	North Shore, Oahu HI
late Nov-mid-Dec	Feria de Santa Cecilia y Fiestas Navideñas	San Antonio TX
late Nov-early Jan	Red Rock Fantasy of Lights	Sedona AZ
early Dec	Bachelor Society Ball & Wilderness Women Contest	Talkeetna AK
	National Finals Rodeo	Las Vegas NV
	Weihnachtsfest	Carmel CA

Winter

Date	Event	Location
Dec	Christmas celebrations	every city and town
	La Mele o Maui	Maui HI
	Festival of Poinsettias	Lawrence KS
	Festival of Lights at the Grotto	Portland OR
	Fiesta Bowl Events	Phoenix AZ
	Yuletide in Taos	Taos NM
mid-Dec	Our Lady of Guadalupe Fiesta	Las Cruces NM
	Christmas Boat Parade	Newport Beach CA
Dec 16-24	Las Posadas	Los Angeles CA
Jan	Sundance Film Festival	Park City UT
	Seattle International Boat Show	Seattle WA
	National Western Stock Show and Rodeo	Denver CO
Jan 1	Tournament of Roses	Pasadena CA
mid-Jan	Winterfest	Aspen CO
late Jan-Feb	Chinese New Year Festival	Asian communities (espec. CA & HI)
Feb	Flagstaff Winterfest	Flagstaff AZ
	Mardi Gras! Galveston	Galveston TX
	San Antonio Stock Show and Rodeo	San Antonio TX
	Cowboy Ski Challenge	Jackson WY

Date	Event	Location
early Feb	Winter Carnival	*Steamboat Springs CO*
	Whitefish Winter Carnival	*Whitefish MT*
	Southwestern International Livestock Show	*El Paso TX*
	Festival of Whales	*Dana Point CA*
mid-Feb	Fur Rendezvous	*Anchorage AK*
	Race to the Sky Sled Dog Race	*Helena MT*
	Whale Week	*Maui HI*
	An Affair of the Heart	*Oklahoma City OK*
late Feb	National Date Festival	*Indio CA*
	La Fiesta de los Vaqueros	*Tucson AZ*
	Newport Seafood & Wine Festival	*Newport OR*
	Fat Tuesday, Seattle's Mardi Gras	*Seattle WA*
late Feb-end Oct	Oregon Shakespeare Festival	*Ashland OR*
early Mar	Iditarod Trail Sled Dog Race	*Anchorage to Nome AK*
	Snowfest	*Tahoe City CA*
mid-Mar	C.M. Russell Auction of Original Western Art	*Great Falls MT*
	Scottsdale Arts Festival	*Scottsdale AZ*
	World Snowmobile Expo	*West Yellowstone MT*
Mar 17	St. Patrick's Day	*many cities*
Mar 19	Return of the Swallows	*San Juan Capistrano CA*

Planning Your Trip

Consult the pages shown for detailed practical information about the following areas:
▶ Alaska p 62; Denver p 124; Hawaii p 178; Los Angeles p 218; San Francisco p 317.

Before You Go

In addition to the tourism offices, visitors from outside the US may obtain information from the nearest US embassy or consulate in their country of residence *(see table below)*. For a complete list of American consulates and embassies abroad, visit the US State Department Bureau of Consular Affairs listing on the Internet at http://travel.state.gov/links.html.

Country	Address of US Embassy	☏
Australia	Moonah Place Yaralumla ACT 2600	02 6214 5600
Belgium	27, boulevard du Régent 1000 Brussels	02 513 38 30
Canada	Consular Section 100 Wellington Street, Ottawa OntarioK1P 5T1	613-238-4470 800-529-4410 (US & Canada)
China	3 Xiu Shui Bei Jie Beijing 100600	10 6532 3431
France	2, avenue Gabriel 75008 Paris	01 43 12 22 22
	US Embassy tourism information line	01 48 60 57 15
Germany	4-5 Neustaetter Kirchstrasse 10117 Berlin	30 238 5174
Italy	Via Vittorio Veneto 119/A 00187 Rome	06 46 741

Country	Address of US Embassy	☎
Japan	10-5 Akasaka 1-Chome Minato-ku Tokyo 107-8420	03-3224-5000
Mexico	Paseo de la Reforma 305 Col. Cuauhtémoc 06500 México, D.F	01 5209 9100
Netherlands	Lange Voorhout 102 2514 EJ The Hague	70 310 9209
Spain	Serrano 75 28006 Madrid	91587 2200
Switzerland	Jubiläumsstrasse 93 3001 Bern	31 357 7011
United Kingdom	24 Grosvenor Square London, W1A 1AE	171 499 9000

Entry Requirements – Citizens of countries participating in the Visa Waiver Pilot Program (VWPP) are not required to obtain a visa to enter the US for visits of fewer than 90 days. They will, however, be required to furnish a current passport, round-trip ticket and the customs form distributed in the airplane. Canadian citizens are not required to present a passport or visa to enter the US, although identification and proof of citizenship may be requested (a passport or Canadian birth certificate and photo identification are usually acceptable). Naturalized Canadian citizens should carry their citizenship papers. Citizens of countries not participating in the VWPP must have a visitor's visa. For visa inquiries and applications, contact the nearest US embassy or consulate, or visit the US State Department Visa Services Internet site: http://travel.state.gov/visa_services.html.

Customs and Immigration – All articles brought into the US must be declared at time of entry. The following items are exempt from customs regulations: personal effects; one liter of alcoholic beverages (providing visitor is at least 21 years old); either 200 cigarettes, 50 cigars (additional 100 possible under gift exemption) or 2 kilograms of smoking tobacco; and gifts (to persons in the US) not exceeding $100 in value. Prohibited items include firearms and ammunition (if not intended for legitimate sporting purposes); plant materials, and meat or poultry products. For other prohibited items, exemptions and information, contact any of the following before departure; a US embassy or consulate, Customs Headquarters (US Customs Service, 1300 Pennsylvania Ave. NW, Washington DC 20229; ☎ 202-927-1000) or the US Customs Traveler Information page on the Internet: www.customs.gov/travel/ travel.htm. Note that most major cities have a local customs port; contact information is available from Customs Headquarters or from the Internet site.

Health Insurance – The United States does not have a national health program; doctors' visits and hospitalization costs may seem high to most visitors. Check with your insurance company to determine if your medical insurance covers doctors' visits, medication and hospitalization in the US. If not, it is strongly recommended to purchase a travel-insurance plan before departing. Prescription drugs should be properly identified and accompanied by a copy of the prescription.

Tourist Information

State tourism offices *(below)* provide information and brochures on points of interest, seasonal events and accommodations, as well as road and city maps. Local tourist offices *(telephone numbers and Web sites listed under each blue entry heading in the text)* provide additional information, free of charge, regarding accommodations, shopping, entertainment, festivals and recreation. Many countries have consular offices in major cities. Information centers are indicated on maps by the 🚹 symbol.

States	Tourism Offices	☎
Alaska (AK)	**Alaska Division of Tourism** P.O. Box 110801 Juneau AK 99811-0801	907-465-2010 www.commerce.state.ak.us/tourism
Arizona (AZ)	**Arizona Office of Tourism** 2702 N. 3rd St., Suite 4015 Phoenix AZ 85002	602-230-7733 www.arizonaguide.com

California (CA)	**California Division of Tourism** P.O. Box 1499 Sacramento CA 95812-1499	916-322-2881 www.gocalif.com
Colorado (CO)	**Colorado Travel and Tourism Authority** P.O. Box 3524 Englewood CO 80155-3524	800-265-6723 www.colorado.com
Hawaii (HI)	**Hawaii Visitors Bureau** 2201 Kalakaua Ave., Suite 401 Honolulu HI 96815	808-923-1811 www.gohawaii.com
Idaho (ID)	**Idaho Travel Council, Administrative Office** Idaho Department of Commerce 700 W. State St. Boise ID 83720-0093	208-334-2470 www.visitid.org
Kansas (KS)	**Kansas Travel and Tourism Development Division** 700 SW Harrison St., Suite 1300 Topeka KS 66603-3712	800-252-6727 www.kansascommerce.com
Montana (MT)	**Travel Montana** 1424 Ninth Ave. Helena MT 59620	406-444-2654 www.visitmt.gov
Nebraska (NE)	**Nebraska Tourism Office** Department of Economic Development P.O. Box 98907 Lincoln NE 68509-8907	402-471-3796 www.visitnebraska.org
Nevada (NV)	**Nevada Commission of Tourism** 401 N. Carson St. Carson City NV 89701	775-687-4322 www.travelnevada.com
New Mexico (NM)	**New Mexico Department of Tourism** 491 Old Santa Fe Trail Santa Fe NM 87503	505-827-7400 www.newmexico.org
North Dakota (ND)	**North Dakota Tourism** 604 E. Boulevard Ave. Bismarck ND 58505-0825	701-328-2525 www.ndtourism.com
Oklahoma (OK)	**Oklahoma Tourism and Recreation Department** Travel and Tourism Division 15 N. Robinson Blvd. Oklahoma City OK 73105	405-521-3988 www.travelok.com
Oregon (OR)	**Oregon Economic Development Department** Tourism Division P.O. Box 14070 Portland OR 97214	800-547-7842 www.traveloregon.com
South Dakota (SD)	**South Dakota Department of Tourism** 711 E. Wells Ave. Pierre SD 57501-3369	605-773-3301 www.travelsd.com
Texas (TX)	**Texas Department of Commerce** Tourism Division P.O. Box 12728 Austin TX 78711	512-483-3705 www.traveltex.com
Utah (UT)	**Utah Travel Council** Council Hall/Capitol Hill 300 N. State St. Salt Lake City UT 84114	801-538-1030 www.utah.com
Washington (WA)	**Washington State Tourism** Department of Community, Trade and Economic Development P.O. Box 42500 Olympia WA 98504-2500	360-586-2088 www.tourism.wa.gov
Wyoming (WY)	**Wyoming Division of Tourism** I-25 & College Drive Cheyenne WY 82002	307-777-7777 www.wyomingtourism.org

Tips for Special Visitors

Children – In this guide, sights of particular interest to children are indicated with a 🧒 symbol. Many of these attractions offer special children's programs. Most attractions offer discounted (if not free) admission to visitors under 12 years of age. In addition, many hotels and resorts boast special family discount packages, and some restaurants provide a special children's menu.

Travelers with Disabilities – Full wheelchair access to sights described in this guide is indicated in admission information by &. Federal law requires that existing businesses (including hotels and restaurants) increase accessibility and provide specially designed accommodations for the disabled. It also requires that wheelchair access, devices for the hearing impaired, and designated parking spaces be available at newly constructed hotels and restaurants. Many public buses are equipped with wheelchair lifts; many hotels have rooms designed for visitors with special needs. All national and most state **parks** have restrooms and other facilities for the disabled (such as wheelchair-accessible nature trails). The permanently disabled are eligible for the **Golden Access Passport** *(free to US citizens)*, which entitles the carrier to free admission to all national parks and a 50 percent discount on user fees (campsites, boat launches). The pass is available at any national-park entrance fee area with proper proof of disability. For details, contact the National Park Service, Office of Public Inquiries, P.O. Box 37127, Room 1013, Washington DC 20013-7127, ☏ 202-208-4747. Many attractions can also make special arrangements for disabled visitors. For information about travel for individuals or groups, contact the **Society for the Advancement of Travel for the Handicapped**, 347 5th Ave., Suite 610, New York NY 10016 ☏ 212-447-7284, www.sath.org.

Travel by Train – Train passengers who will need assistance should give 24hrs advance notice. Making reservations via phone is preferable to booking on-line since passenger's special needs can be noted on reservation by booking agent. The annual publication *Access Amtrak* providing detailed information on Amtrak's services for disabled travelers is available upon request *(☏ 800-872-7245 and 800-523-6590 TDD)* or may viewed on Amtrak's Web site: www.amtrak.com/trip/special.html.

Travel by Bus – Disabled travelers are encouraged to notify Greyhound 48hrs in advance. The annual publication *Greyhound Travel Policies* is available by request: ☏ 800-231-2222 or 800-345-3109 (TDD).

Rental Cars – Reservations for hand-controlled cars should be made well in advance.

Senior Citizens – Many hotels, attractions and restaurants offer discounts to visitors age 62 or older (proof of age may be required). Discounts and additional information are available to members of the American Association of Retired Persons (AARP), 601 E St. NW, Washington DC 20094, ☏ 202-434-2277, or the National Council of Senior Citizens, 8403 Colesville Rd., Silver Spring MD 20910, ☏ 301-578-8800.

When to Go

The diversity of **California**'s geographic regions promotes a dramatic variation in climatic conditions. Although coastal areas are subject to relatively little variation in seasonal temperatures, these tend to increase with distance from the coast, and drop quickly as elevation increases. Most rain falls between October and April. In the San Diego area, winter temperatures range from 60-70°F; summer temperatures average only 5-10°F more. The Los Angeles coastal area remains warm and pleasant year-round,

San Francisco Bay, California

while the inland areas are hot and hazy during the summer and fall. Average temperatures are 45-65°F in winter and 60-75°F in summer. San Francisco Bay Area weather can change suddenly in a single day, from warm and sunny to foggy and chilly. Thick fog is particularly characteristic of the summer months. Inland Bay Area cities are warmer, with pleasant, sometimes hot, summer temperatures. Average temperatures are 40-55°F in winter and 55-70°F in the summer.

West of the Cascade Range, the **Pacific Northwest** experiences very wet winters with strong winds and extensive cloud cover that promotes mild temperatures—40-50°F. Summers are usually sunny and rather comfortable with occasional heat waves reaching 90°F. The interior of the region is colder and drier in winter, hotter in summer.

Southwest winters produce mild days and cold nights with daytime temperatures typically in the 40s on the Colorado Plateau, 70s in the Sonoran Desert. Despite relatively mild conditions, heavy snows fall in the mountain areas. Mild winter days give way to long summer days of bright sunshine and hot temperatures that can exceed 100°F. In May, summers start out dry with little rain, but by mid-July the humidity increases and the area receives many thunderstorms as the summer progresses. Despite this rainfall, temperatures remain very hot.

Winters in the **Rocky Mountain states** usually include large amounts of snow, and temperatures fluctuate between days of extreme cold to more mild days depending on air currents. In summer, with temperatures around 90°F, days are warm while the nights are cool, with temperatures between 40-50°F. Thunderstorms and hail are common in the summer months.

In the **Central and Southern Plains**, winters fluctuate between spells of warm, pleasant weather and cold snaps that bring snow and ice. Summers can be similarly unpredictable, often with severe thunderstorms and strong winds. Summer temperatures are typically hot, ranging from 90-100°F.

Winters in the **Northern Great Plains** are cold and dry, as polar air masses deliver extensive snow cover and sub-zero temperatures. Winter's extreme conditions are sometimes softened by chinook winds that bring warmer temperatures. Summer heat may invite severe thunderstorms, hail and high winds. *Current weather conditions are on-line: www.weather.com or www.cnn.com/weather.*

Temperature Chart

City	January avg. high °F / °C	avg. low °F / °C	precip. in. / cm.	June avg. hi °F / °C	avg. low °F / °C	precip. in. / cm.
Albuquerque NM	47 / 8	22 / −6	0.4 / 1.1	90 / 32	58 / 14	0.6 / 1.5
Anchorage AK	21 / −6	8 / −13	0.8 / 2.0	62 / 17	47 / 8	1.1 / 2.9
Aspen CO	32 / 0	0 / −18	1.3 / 3.2	72 / 22	34 / 1	1.4 / 3.4
Billings MT	32 / 0	14 / −10	0.9 / 2.3	78 / 26	52 / 11	2.0 / 5.1
Boise ID	36 / 2	22 / −6	1.5 / 3.7	81 / 27	52 / 11	0.8 / 2.1
Dallas TX	54 / 12	33 / 1	1.8 / 4.6	92 / 33	70 / 21	3.0 / 7.6
Denver CO	43 / 6	16 / −9	0.5 / 1.3	81 / 27	52 / 11	1.8 / 4.5
El Paso TX	56 / 13	29 / −2	0.4 / 1.0	97 / 36	64 / 18	0.7 / 1.7
Grand Canyon AZ	42 / 5	18 / −8	1.4 / 3.7	78 / 27	45 / 7	0.5 / 1.3
Honolulu HI	80 / 27	66 / 19	3.6 / 9.0	87 / 31	72 / 22	0.5 / 1.3
Houston TX	61 / 16	40 / 4	3.3 / 8.4	90 / 32	71 / 22	5.0 / 12.6
Kansas City MO	35 / 2	17 / −8	1.1 / 2.8	83 / 28	63 / 17	4.7 / 12.0
Las Vegas NV	57 / 14	34 / 1	0.5 / 1.2	100 / 38	69 / 21	0.1 / 0.3
Los Angeles CA	66 / 19	48 / 9	2.4 / 6.1	72 / 22	60 / 16	0.0 / 0.1
Moab UT	42 / 6	18 / −8	0.6 / 1.4	93 / 34	50 / 14	0.4 / 1.1
Oklahoma City OK	47 / 8	25 / −4	1.1 / 2.9	87 / 31	66 / 19	4.3 / 10.9
Omaha NE	31 / −1	11 / −12	0.7 / 1.9	84 / 29	60 / 16	3.9 / 9.8
Phoenix AZ	66 / 19	41 / 5	0.7 / 1.7	104 / 40	73 / 23	0.1 / 0.3
Portland OR	45 / 7	34 / 1	5.4 / 13.6	74 / 23	53 / 12	1.5 / 3.8
Rapid City SD	34 / 1	11 / −12	0.4 / 1.0	78 / 26	52 / 11	3.1 / 7.8
Reno NV	45 / 7	21 / −6	1.1 / 2.7	83 / 28	47 / 8	0.5 / 1.2
Sacramento CA	53 / 12	38 / 3	3.7 / 9.5	88 / 31	55 / 13	0.1 / 0.3
Salt Lake City UT	36 / 2	19 / −7	1.1 / 2.8	83 / 28	55 / 13	0.9 / 2.4
San Antonio TX	61 / 16	38 / 3	1.7 / 4.3	92 / 33	73 / 23	3.8 / 9.7
San Diego CA	66 / 19	49 / 9	1.8 / 4.6	72 / 22	62 / 17	0.1 / 0.2
San Francisco CA	56 / 13	42 / 6	4.4 / 11.0	70 / 21	53 / 12	0.1 / 0.3

Temperature Chart

Santa Fe NM	47 / 8	14 / −10	1.1 / 2.8	82 / 28	47 / 9	4.4 / 11.1
Seattle WA	45 / 7	35 / 2	5.4 / 13.7	70 / 21	52 / 11	1.5 / 3.8
Tucson AZ	64 / 18	39 / 4	0.9 / 2.4	100 / 38	68 / 20	0.2 / 0.6
West Glacier MT	29 / −2	15 / −10	3.4 / 8.6	72 / 22	44 / 7	3.4 / 8.6

Getting There & Getting Around

By Air

Major US airlines serve most of the West's metropolitan areas.

Major airports

City	Location	Information ☎
Albuquerque NM Albuquerque International Sunport (ABQ)	3mi south of downtown	☎ 505-842-4366 www.cabq.gov/airport
Anchorage AK Anchorage International Airport (ANC)	6mi south of downtown	☎ 907-266-2525 www.dot.state.ak.us/external/aias/aia/aiawlcm.htm
Billings MT Billings Logan International Airport (BIL)	1.5mi north of downtown	☎ 406-657-8495 http://.cibillings.mt.us/government/air
Boise ID Boise Airport (BOI)	4mi south of downtown	☎ 208-383-3110 www.boise-airport.com
Dallas/Ft. Worth TX Dallas/Ft. Worth International Airport (DFW)	20mi northwest of Dallas; 25mi northeast of Ft. Worth	☎ 972-574-6000 www.dfwairport.com
Denver CO Denver International Airport (DEN)	23 mi northeast of downtown	☎ 303-342-2000 www.flydenver.com
El Paso TX El Paso International Airport (ELP)	5mi northeast of downtown	☎ 915-772-4271 www.citi-guide.com/elp
Honolulu HI Honolulu International Airport (HNL)	4mi west of downtown	☎ 808-836-6413 www.hawaii.gov/dot/hono.htm
Houston TX Houston Intercontinental Airport (IAH)	15mi north of downtown	☎ 281-233-3000 www.ci.houston.tx.us/departme/aviation/iah.htm
Kansas City MO Kansas City International Airport (MCI)	19mi north of downtown	☎ 816-243-3000 www.kcairports.com/kci
Las Vegas NV Las Vegas McCarran International Airport (LAS)	4mi southeast of central Strip	☎ 702 261 5211 www.mccarran.com
Los Angeles CA Los Angeles International Airport (LAX)	10mi southwest of downtown	☎ 310-646-5252 www.lawa.org
Oklahoma City OK Oklahoma City Will Rogers World Airport (OKC)	5mi west of downtown	☎ 405-680-3316 www.flyokc.com/w.r.w.a
Orange County CA John Wayne Airport (SNA)	13mi southeast of Anaheim	☎ 949-252-5200 www.ocair.com
Phoenix AZ Phoenix Skyharbor International Airport (PHX)	5mi east of downtown	☎ 602-273-3300 www.skyharbor.com

City	Location	Information ☎
Portland OR		
Portland International Airport (PDX)	*12mi east of downtown*	☎ 877-739-4636 www.portlandairportpdx.com
Reno NV		
Reno/Tahoe International Airport (RNO)	*4mi south of downtown*	☎ 775-328-6490 www.renoairport.com
Sacramento CA		
Sacramento International Airport (SMF)	*12mi north of downtown*	☎ 916-929-5411 www.sacairports.org
Salt Lake City UT		
Salt Lake City International Airport (SLC)	*5mi west of downtown*	☎ 801-575-2400 www.ci.slc.ut.us/services/ airport/index.html
San Antonio TX		
San Antonio International Airport (SAT)	*8mi north of downtown*	☎ 210-207-3450 www.ci.sat.tx.us/aviation/ index.html
San Diego CA		
San Diego International Airport (SAN)	*3mi northwest of downtown*	☎ 619-231-2100 www.portofsandiego.org/ sandiego_airport/index.html
San Francisco CA		
San Francisco International Airport (SFO)	*13.5mi south of downtown*	☎ 650-876-7809 www.sfoairport.com
Seattle WA		
Seattle-Tacoma International Airport (SEA)	*13mi south of downtown*	☎ 206-431-4444 www.portseattle.org/seatac

© J. McDermott/Tony Stone Images

By Train

The Amtrak rail network offers a relaxing alternative for travelers with time to spare. Advance reservations ensure reduced fares and availability of desired accommodations. On some trains, reservations are required; smoking is not allowed on any Amtrak trains. Passengers may choose from first-class, coach, or cars with panoramic windows.

The **Explore America Rail Pass** allows up to 45 days travel nationwide (limited to three stops). The **North America Rail Pass** links Amtrak train routes with Canada's VIARail system for 30 days with unlimited stops. The **USA RailPass** (not available to US or Canadian citizens) offers unlimited travel within designated regions at discounted rates; 15- and 30-day passes are available. For schedule, prices and route information: ☎ 800-872-7245 or www.amtrak.com *(outside North America, contact a travel agent)*.

In the West, service is provided along the following routes:

Train	Route	Along the Way
California Corridor	San Jose-Reno	*San Francisco, Sacramento*
California Zephyr	Chicago-San Francisco	*Denver, Salt Lake City, Sacramento*
Cascades	Vancouver-Eugene	*Seattle, Portland*
Coast Starlight	Seattle-Los Angeles	*Portland, San Francisco, Santa Barbara*
Empire Builder	Chicago-Seattle	*Minneapolis, Glacier Park*
Southwest Chief	Chicago-Los Angeles	*Kansas City, Santa Fe, Phoenix*

The Alaska Railroad links Seward, Anchorage, Denali National Park and Fairbanks (mid-May-mid-Sept daily; in winter, weekends only); for schedule and reservations: Alaska Railroad Corp., P.O. Box 107500, Anchorage AK 99510, ☎ 907-265-2494 or 800-544-0552.

Travelers may relive the romantic era of travel aboard one of **American Orient Express'** four trains in the West: Great Northwest (Seattle to Glacier National Park), Pacific Coast Explorer (Los Angeles to Seattle), *National Parks of the West* (Rockies and Southwest) or *Rockies & Yellowstone* (Denver to Portland). Each offers deluxe rail travel in large cabins with numerous sightseeing stops, and a dining car where meals prepared by expert chefs are served. For schedules and fares contact American Orient Express, 5100 Main St., Suite 300, Downers Grove IL 60515, ☎ 630-663-4550, www.americanorientexpress.com.

By Bus

Greyhound, the largest bus company in the US, offers access to most cities and communities. Overall, fares are lower than other forms of transportation. Some travelers may find long distance bus travel uncomfortable owing to a lack of sleeping accommodations. Advance reservations are suggested. Greyhound's Ameripass and **International Ameripass** allow unlimited travel of 7, 10, 15, 30, 45 or 60 days, allowing stops along the way. The Ameripass may be purchased at any Greyhound terminal; the International Ameripass is available through International travel agents. Both passes are available on line at Greyhound's Web site. Schedules, prices and route information: ☎ 800-231-2222 *(US only)*, www.greyhound.com; or Greyhound Lines, Inc., P.O. Box 660362, Dallas TX 75266. Information for disabled riders *(p 405)*.

By Car

Limited-access **interstate highways** crisscross the US. North-south highways have odd numbers (I-15, I-25); east-west interstates have even numbers (I 40, I-80). Numbers increase from west to east (I-5 along the West Coast and I-95 on the East Coast) and from south to north (I-8 runs east from San Diego CA; I-94 connects Billings MT with Milwaukee WI). Interstate **beltways** encircle cities and have three digits: the first is an even number and the last two name the interstate off which they branch (I 410 around San Antonio TX branches off I-10). There can be duplication across states (there are I-405 beltways around Seattle WA, Portland OR and Los Angeles CA) and exceptions to this general rule. Interstate **spurs** entering cities also have three digits: the first is an odd number and the last two represent the originating interstate.

A system of non-interstate highways and roads, predating the interstate system, includes US, state, county and Indian reservation routes. **US routes** and **state routes** range from major highways to winding two-lane roads. North-south roads have odd numbers (of one, two or three digits), east-west roads even numbers. **County routes** and **Indian reservation routes** typically are smaller local or connector roads. The US Forest Service and Bureau of Land Management (BLM) manage a system of backcountry roads (generally unpaved) with their own route numbering.

Rental Cars – National rental companies have offices at major airports and downtown locations. Aside from the agencies listed below, there also are local companies that offer reasonable rental rates. *See yellow pages for phone numbers.*

Renters must possess a major credit card (such as Visa/Carte Bleue, American Express or MasterCard/Eurocard), a valid driver's license (international license not required). Minimum age for rental is 21 in most states. A variety of service packages offer unlimited mileage and discounted prices, often in conjunction with major airlines or hotel chains. Since prices vary from one company to another, be sure to research different companies before you reserve. (To reserve a car from Europe, it is best to contact a local travel agent before departure.)

All rentals are subject to a local tax not included in quoted prices. Liability insurance is not automatically included in the terms of the lease. Be sure to check for proper insurance coverage, offered at an extra charge. Most large rental companies provide assistance in case of breakdown.

Cars may be rented per day, week or month, and mileage is usually unlimited. Only the person who signed the contract is authorized to drive the rental car, but for an additional fee, and upon presentation of the required papers, additional drivers may be approved. If a vehicle is returned at a different location from where it was rented, drop-off charges may be incurred. The gasoline tank of the car should be filled before it is returned; rental companies charge a much higher price per gallon than roadside gas stations.

Harbor Freeway, Los Angeles, California

Rental car **information and reservations** across the US may be accessed on the Internet at www.bnm.com, or by calling one of the companies listed below.

Alamo	☎ 800-327-9633	**Hertz**	☎ 800-654-3131
Avis	☎ 800-331-1212	**National**	☎ 800-227-7368
Budget	☎ 800-527-0700	**Thrifty**	☎ 800-331-4200
Dollar	☎ 800-421-6868	**Enterprise**	☎ 800-325-8007

Recreational Vehicle (RV) Rentals – One-way rentals range from a basic camper to full-size motor-homes that can accommodate up to seven people and offer a bath-room, shower and kitchen with microwave oven. Reservations should be made several months in advance. There may be a minimum number of rental days required. A drop fee is charged for one-way rentals. Cruise America RV (☎ *800-327-7799, www.cruiseamerica.com)* offers rentals with 24hr customer assistance. The **Recreational Vehicle Rental Association** (RVRA) publishes a directory *($10; $15 via international mail)* of RV rental locations in the US: 3930 University Dr., Fairfax VA 22030; ☎ 703-591-7130; www.rvra.org. **RV America** *(www.rvamerica.com)* offers an on-line database of RV rental companies as well as information on campgrounds and RV associations.

Road Regulations and Insurance – The speed limit on most interstate highways in the contiguous US ranges from 55mph (88km/h) to 70mph (112km/h), depending on the state. On state highways outside of populated areas the speed limit is 55mph (88km/h) unless otherwise posted. Within cities, speed limits are generally 35mph (56km/h), and average 25-30mph (40-48km/h) in residential areas. Headlights must be turned on when driving in fog and rain. Unless traveling on a divided road, the law requires that motorists in both directions bring their vehicle to a full stop when the warning signals on a school bus are activated. Parking spaces identified with ♿ are reserved for persons with disabilities only. Anyone parking in these spaces without proper identification will be ticketed and/or their vehicle will be towed.

The use of **seat belts** is mandatory for all persons in the car. Child safety seats are available at most rental-car agencies; indicate need when making reservations. In some states, motorcyclists and their passenger are required to wear helmets. Hitch-hiking along interstate highways, except at entrance ramps, is forbidden by law. Auto liability insurance is mandatory in all states.

In Case of Accident – If you are involved in an accident resulting in personal or property damage, you must notify local police and remain at the scene until dismissed. If blocking traffic, vehicles should be moved as soon as possible. Automobile associa-tions such as the **American Automobile Association (AAA)** ☎ 407-444-7000, **Mobil Auto Club**

☎ 800-621-5581 and **Shell Motorist Club** ☎ 800-852-0555 provide members with emergency road service. Members of reciprocal automobile clubs overseas may also benefit from AAA services:

Australia	Australian Automobile Association (AAA)	☎ 02 6247 7311
Belgium	Royal Automobile Club de Belgique (RACB)	☎ 02 287 09 11
	Touring Club de Belgique (TCB)	☎ 02 233 22 11
Canada	Canadian Automobile Association (CAA)	☎ 613 247 0117
France	Automobile-Club de France (ACF)	☎ 01 43 12 43 12
	Fédération Française des Automobile-Clubs (FFAC)	☎ 01 53 30 89 30
Germany	Allgemeiner Deutscher Automobil-Club E.V. (ADAC)	☎ 89 7676 0
	Automobilclub von Deutschland E.V. (AvD)	☎ 69 6606 610
Ireland	The Automobile Association Ireland Ltd. (AA Ireland)	☎ 01 617 9950
Italy	Automobile Club d'Italia (ACI)	☎ 06 49 98 1
	Federazione Italiana del Campeggio e del Caravanning (Federcampeggio)	☎ 55 88 23 91
	Touring Club Italiano (TCI)	☎ 02 85 26 1
Netherlands	Koninklijke Nederlandsche Automobiel Club (KNAC)	☎ 70 383 1612
	Koninklijke Nederlandse Toeristenbond ANWB (ANWB)	☎ 70 314 71 47
Spain	Real Automóvil Club de España (RACE)	☎ 91 594 74 00
Switzerland	Automobile Club de Suisse (ACS)	☎ 031 328 31 11
	Touring Club Suisse (TCS)	☎ 022 417 27 27
United Kingdom	The Automobile Association (AA)	☎ 1256 44 88 66
	The Camping & Caravanning Club (CCC)	☎ 203 694 995
	The Caravan Club (CC)	☎ 01 342 326 944
	The Royal Scottish Automobile Club (RSAC)	☎ 141 221 3850

Suggested Driving Tours in the USA West

Now that you've got your car, it's time to hit the road. We've outlined below several tours that take in highlights of the West, from Hollywood to Old Faithful, Mount St. Helens to The Alamo.

All sites indicated in bold type are listed in the index.

California Dreaming – *15 days; about 1,800mi. Any season, but Sierra parks are closed in winter.* Anchoring the southwest coast, California has a bit of everything, from surf-riddled beaches to alpine resorts, cosmopolitan cities to ghost towns.
Our tour begins in **San Francisco**, keeper of the Golden Gate, its cable cars scaling the hills from **Fisherman's Wharf** to **Chinatown**. Drive south to **Monterey**, its aquarium anchoring Cannery Row. Highway 1 weaves a cliffside path along the wild **Big Sur** coast to emerge at eclectic **Hearst Castle**. From the charming mission town of **Santa Barbara**, boats provide access to Channel Islands National Park.
Stay long enough in sprawling **Los Angeles** to spy movie stars in **Hollywood** or **Beverly Hills**; spend an afternoon at the **Getty Center** or another renowned art museum. Revisit your childhood at **Disneyland**, the world's most famous amusement park. Subtropical **San Diego** is a delight for animal lovers with its world-famous zoo, wild animal park and **Sea World**. Loop back to L.A. via Pacific Coast Highway (Rte. 1) through Laguna Beach and **Long Beach**, permanent home of the **Queen Mary**.
Northbound I-5 runs up the Central Valley, the richest farmland on earth, and lures outdoors lovers to the big trees of **Sequoia and Kings Canyon National Parks** and to the stark glacial valley and waterfalls of **Yosemite National Park**. Across the crest of the **Sierra Nevada**, year-round resorts surround deep-blue **Lake Tahoe**. A short drive from the casinos of **Reno**, Nevada, is historic **Virginia City**, built in the 1860s and 70s on the fabulously rich Comstock Lode. West is the **Gold Country**, many of whose towns—like quaint **Nevada City** and bustling Auburn—date from the 1850s gold-rush era. Miners traveled upriver from **Sacramento**, now the state capital.
In the **Wine Country** of Napa and Sonoma Counties, dozens of wineries welcome tasters. An easy drive down the Marin County coast, to rugged **Point Reyes National Seashore** and majestic **Muir Woods National Monument**, leads back to San Francisco.

Canyons and Casinos - *15 days; about 1,800mi. Best done in spring or fall.* Las Vegas is the gateway to the spectacular canyon country of the Southwest, but it is prudent to wait until this drive is over before investing in blackjack or roulette.
From **Las Vegas**, cross the great **Hoover Dam** and continue east via I-40 to the vast and colorful **Grand Canyon**. The largest chasm on earth is a mile deep, 10mi wide, 277mi long and nearly 2 billion years in the making. From Grand Canyon Village, touring roads extend east and west; dizzying trails descend to the canyon floor.
Delightful **Sedona**, in **Red Rock Country** south of **Oak Creek Canyon** via Rte. 89A, is a magnet for artists and New Age spiritual seekers. National monuments preserve ruins of

ancient civilizations. **Canyon de Chelly** and Navajo National Monuments are north and east on the broad Navajo Indian Reservation. Surrounded by Navajo lands, Hopi reservation residents pursue ancient cultural traditions.

The landscape of **Monument Valley** is well-known from myriad Western movies. US-191 continues to **Moab**, a center for mountain biking and rafting, and gateway to **Canyonlands** and **Arches National Parks**—the former a forbidding canyon wilderness, the latter preserving more than 2,000 sandstone arches. Southwest, drivers skirt the colorful backcountry of **Capitol Reef National Park** en route to **Bryce Canyon National Park**, a fairyland of rock spires and pinnacles. Two hours farther is **Zion National Park**, enclosing a steep canyon adorned with waterfalls and hanging gardens.

Returning to "Lost Wages," you now can gamble unspent cash in lavish casinos: On the world-famous **Las Vegas Strip**, you'll find the Eiffel Tower and Statue of Liberty, King Arthur's castle and King Tut's tomb.

The Heart of Texas – *8 days; about 1,100mi. Not suggested in summer.* Texas is the largest US state after Alaska. This tour, which starts and ends at the Dallas-Fort Worth airport, samples its cultural, historical and geographical diversity.

Begin in **Fort Worth**. The **Stockyards National Historic District** brings back to life the cowboy days of yore in western-wear stores, a rodeo arena and the world's largest honkytonk. The **Kimbell Art Museum** is outstanding. South via I-35 in **Austin**, the state capital, is the nationally famous Sixth Street Entertainment District. The **Lyndon Baines Johnson Presidential Library and Museum** on the University of Texas campus pays homage to a native son further remembered at historical parks in the nearby **Hill Country**. Settled by Germans, **Fredericksburg** retains its Teutonic heritage.

San Antonio, rich in Hispanic tradition, is the cradle of Texas freedom. **The Alamo** canonizes 189 patriots who died in its defense. Gondolas cruise past the 2.5mi **River Walk**, lined with shops and cafes. Southeast via I-37, on the Gulf Coast, **Corpus Christi** is the gateway to **Padre Island National Seashore**, a favorite of birdwatchers.

East of San Antonio via I-10 is **Houston**, fourth largest city in the US and home to **Space Center Houston**, where US space research and astronaut training takes place. Oil wealth helps to supports Houston's superb Museum District, highlighted by the Surrealist works of the **Menil Collection** and the energy exhibits of the **Houston Museum of Natural Science**. Seaside **Galveston** has a notable 19C historic district.

North via I-45 is **Dallas**. Shoppers love the Dallas Market Center, world's largest wholesale merchandise market. **The Sixth Floor Museum at Dealey Plaza** commemorates the life of President John F. Kennedy and analyzes his assassination here in 1963.

Peaks and Pueblos – *13 days; about 1,500mi. Best done in summer.* From the heights of the Rocky Mountains to the secrets of the ancient Anasazi heritage, this tour highlights two states: Colorado and New Mexico.

Start and finish in **Denver**, urban center of the Rockies. The **LoDo** district is a landmark of historic preservation; the **Denver Art Museum** has a renowned Native American Collection. Climb aross the Continental Divide on I-70. Colorful Victorian architecture in the thin air of **Breckenridge** and **Leadville** bears testimony to a silver-mining heritage. The ski resort of **Vail** is a playground for high society; chic **Aspen**, which nestles near the beautiful **Maroon Bells**, has a delightful 19C downtown.

Continue west to the stark geology of **Colorado National Monument** and **Black Canyon of the Gunnison National Park**, then follow spectacular US-550 through the San Juan Mountains to **Durango**, with its fine historic railway. At nearby **Mesa Verde National Park**, visitors walk through five major cliff dwellings dated AD 750-1300. New Mexico's **Chaco Culture National Historical Park** embraces ruins that formed a 9-12C trade and political hub. South, off I-40, clifftop **Sky City at Acoma Pueblo** has been continually inhabited since the 11C. The **Indian Pueblo Cultural Center** at Albuquerque represents 19 communities; the **National Atomic Museum** details the nuclear age.

Enchanting **Santa Fe** begs a lengthy stay. See the **Palace of the Governors**, in use since 1610, and the **Georgia O'Keeffe Museum**, displaying the works of the great artist. Marvel at the spiral staircase in the **Loretto Chapel** and take in a show at **The Santa Fe Opera**. Meander north to the artists' colony of **Taos**, packed with galleries, historic homes, the remarkable **Taos Pueblo** and the adobe **San Francisco de Asis Church**.

En route back to Denver via I-25, pause in **Colorado Springs**. Take a railway to the 14,110ft summit of **Pikes Peak**, learn about broncos at the ProRodeo Hall of Fame, and say a prayer beneath the spires of the Cadet Chapel at the **US Air Force Academy**.

Rocky Mountain High – *13 days; about 1,900mi. Best done in summer.* Several of America's most famous national parks and historic sites are a part of this high-elevation tour, which begins in Salt Lake City and concludes in Denver.

Salt Lake City fascinates visitors intrigued by the religion and culture of the Mormons, who founded the Utah city in 1847. Take I-80 east to the historic mining town of **Park City**, like Salt Lake preparing for the 2002 Winter Olympics, then head north. US-89 leads through **Jackson**, renowned for his cowboy ambience and its **National Museum**

Distance Chart

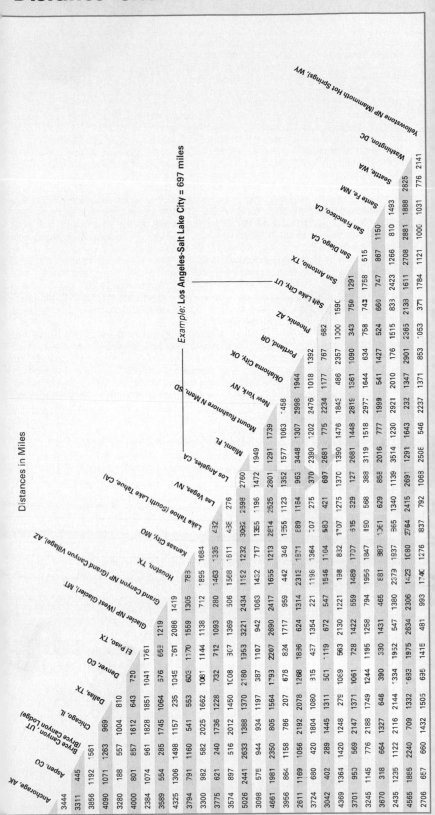

Distances in Miles

Example: Los Angeles–Salt Lake City = 697 miles

of Wildlife Art, and **Grand Teton National Park**, embracing a dramatic range of craggy mountains reflected in morainal lakes. It continues into **Yellowstone National Park**, whose unparalleled natural attractions—geysers, hot springs, canyons and rich wildlife—demand more than an overnight stay.

Turning east on US-14, pause in **Cody** to explore **Buffalo Bill Historical Center**, then proceed directly across the Big Horn Mountains to the fluted monolith of **Devils Tower National Monument** and into the **Black Hills**. After paying homage to the stone images of US presidents at **Mount Rushmore National Memorial**, detour to **Wind Cave National Park** and the once-rowdy mining town of **Deadwood**. Swing east through the geological curiosities of **Badlands National Park**, then south across western Nebraska to pick up the **Oregon Trail** near Scotts Bluff National Monument.

The historic trail follows US-26 past **Fort Laramie National Historic Site**. Turn south through **Cheyenne**, a quintessential rodeo town; detour via US-34 to pristine **Rocky Mountain National Park**. The tour ends in **Denver**, described in "Peaks and Pueblos."

Northwest Passages - *10 days; about 1,700mi. Best done in summer.* This tour starts and ends in Seattle and takes in the volcanic peaks of the Cascade Range, great rivers, redwood forests and an unforgettable Pacific coastline.

The futuristic **Space Needle** towers above **Seattle**, home of Microsoft and Boeing, grunge rock and Starbucks Coffee. The maritime city invites exploration of its **Pike Place Market**, its **Seattle Center** cultural complex, museums and gardens. Visitors view 747 jets under construction at the **Boeing Everett Site**. Alpine roads wind southeast through magnificent **Mount Rainier National Park** and fascinating **Mount St. Helens National Volcanic Monument**, which offers perspective on the peak's 1984 eruption.

In the shadow of **Mount Hood** is **Portland**, Oregon's "Rose City." The International Rose Test Garden is one of several gardens in **Washington Park**, which sprawls across hills near downtown. Outside Portland is the pinot-rich **Oregon Wine Country** and the **End of the Oregon Trail Interpretive Center**, documenting the journey of mid-19C pioneers. Panoramas extend east up I-84 through the **Columbia River Gorge**, host to myriad windsurfers and ribbon-like Multnomah Falls.

The hub of central Oregon is Bend, southeast of Portland on US-97. Drive the **Cascade Lakes Highway** en route to **Crater Lake National Park**, where a cobalt-blue lake, deepest in the US, fills a collapsed caldera. Continue southwest via Rte. 62 to taste the Shakespearean persona of Ashland, the 19C gold-rush flavor of **Jacksonville** and the labyrinths of **Oregon Caves National Monument**. Slide into northwest California on US-199 to see forests of giant redwood trees in **Redwoods National and State Parks**.

Then proceed straight up the coast, a gorgeous three-day drive on US-101 via **Oregon Dunes National Recreation Area** and the noted Oregon Coast Aquarium in Newport. **Olympic National Park** dominates Washington's Olympic Peninsula and includes the lush **Hoh Rain Forest** and unforgettable views from **Hurricane Ridge**. Visit the Victorian seaport of **Port Townsend** before boarding a ferry back to Seattle.

Basic Information

Time Zones – There are four standard time zones in the contiguous United States: Eastern, Central, Mountain and Pacific, and additional Alaska and Hawaii time zones. Daylight Savings Time is observed in all states—except Arizona, Hawaii and most of Indiana—from the first Sunday in April through the last Sunday in October; time is moved forward one hour, bringing an earlier dawn but also an earlier dusk. Pacific Standard Time (PST) is 8hrs behind Greenwich Mean Time (GMT), or Universal Time (UT); Pacific Daylight Time (PDT) is 7hrs behind GMT.

Major Holidays - Banks and government offices are closed on the following legal holidays:

New Year's Day	January 1
Martin Luther King Jr.'s Birthday*	3rd Monday in January
President's Day*	3rd Monday in February
Memorial Day*	last Monday in May
Independence Day	July 4
Labor Day*	1st Monday in September
Columbus Day*	2nd Monday in October
Veterans Day*	November 11
Thanksgiving Day	4th Thursday in November
Christmas Day	December 25

Many retail stores and restaurants stay open on these days.

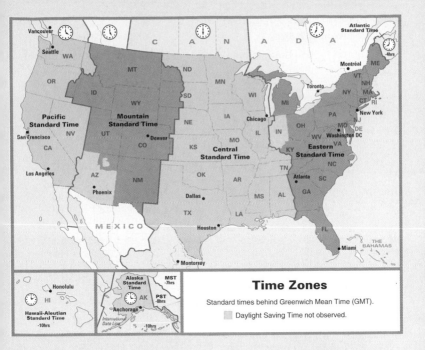

Time Zones

Standard times behind Greenwich Mean Time (GMT).

▨ Daylight Saving Time not observed.

Business Hours – Most businesses operate Mon-Fri 9am-5pm. Banking institutions are normally open Mon-Thu 9am-4:30pm, Fri until 5pm or 6pm. Some banks, especially in larger cities, may be open Saturday mornings. Most retail stores and specialty shops are open Mon-Sat 10am-6pm. Malls and shopping centers are usually open Mon-Sat 10am-9pm, Sun 10am-6pm.

Electricity – Voltage in the US is 120 volts AC, 60 Hz. Foreign-made appliances may need AC adapters (available at specialty travel and electronics stores) and North American flat-blade plugs.

Temperature and Measurement – In the US, temperatures are measured in degrees Fahrenheit and measurements are expressed according to the US Customary System of Weights and Measures.

Metric Conversion Chart

Degrees Fahrenheit	Degrees Celsius
95°	35°
86°	30°
77°	25°
68°	20°
59°	15°
50°	10°
41°	5°
32°	0°
23°	-5°
14°	-10°

1 inch (in.) = 2.54 centimeters
1 pound (lb.) = 0.454 kilogram

1 foot (ft.) = 30.48 centimeters
1 quart (qt.) = 0.946 liter

1 mile (mi.)= 1.609 kilometers
1 gallon (gal.) = 3.785 liters

Twin Girls at 4th of July Parade

	Women's Sizes				Men's Sizes		
	Europe	US	Great Britain		Europe	US	Great Britain
Shoes	35	4	2 1/2	Shoes	40	7 1/2	7
	36	5	3 1/2		41	8 1/2	8
	37	6	4 1/2		42	9 1/2	9
	38	7	5 1/2		43	10 1/2	10
	39	8	6 1/2		44	11 1/2	11
	40	9	7 1/2		45	12 1/2	12
	41	10	8 1/2		46	13 1/2	13
Dresses &	36	6	8	Suits	46	36	36
Suits	38	8	10		48	38	38
	40	10	12		50	40	40
	42	12	14		52	42	42
	44	14	16		54	44	44
	46	16	18		56	46	46
Blouses &	36	8	30	Shirts	37	14 1/2	14 1/2
Sweaters	38	10	32		38	15	15
	40	12	34		39	15 1/2	15 1/2
	42	14	36		40	15 1/2	15 1/2
	44	16	38		41	16	16
	46	18	40		42	16 1/2	16 1/2

Telephone – For **long-distance** calls in the US and Canada, dial 1 + area code (3 digits) + number (7 digits). To place **local calls**, dial the seven-digit number without 1 or the area code, unless the local calling area includes several area codes. To place an **international call**, dial 011 + country code + area code + number. To obtain help from an **operator**, dial 0 for local and 00 for long distance. For **information** on a number within your area code, dial 411. For long-distance information, dial 1 + area code + 555-1212. To place **collect calls**, dial 0 + area or country code + number. At the operator's prompt, give your name. For all **emergencies**, dial **911**.

Since most **hotels** add a surcharge for local and long-distance calls, it is often advantageous to use your calling card. Local calls from public telephones cost 35¢ unless otherwise posted (25¢ in New York City). **Public telephones** accept quarters, dimes and nickels. You may also use your calling card or credit card (recommended for long-distance calls to avoid the inconvenience of depositing large amounts of change). Instructions for using public telephones are listed on or near the phone.

> Unless otherwise indicated, telephone numbers that start with the area codes **800, 888** and **877** are toll-free within the US.

Correspondence – First-class postage rates within the US are: 33¢/letter (up to 1oz), 20¢/postcard. To Europe: 60¢/letter (up to .5oz), 50¢/postcard. Most post offices are open Mon-Fri 9am-5pm; some may open Sat 9am-noon. Companies such as Mail Boxes Etc., Mail Express USA and PAKMAIL *(consult the yellow pages in the phone book under Mailing Services)* also provide mail service for everything from postcards to large packages. These companies also sell boxes and other packaging material. For photocopying, fax service and computer access, Kinko's has locations throughout the US *(☎ 805-652-4022 or 800-254-6567, www.kinkos.com)* or consult the yellow pages in a local phone book under Copying Service for a listing of local companies.

Money – The American **dollar** ($1) is divided into 100 **cents**. A **penny** = 1 cent (1¢); a **nickel** = 5¢; a **dime** = 10¢; a **quarter** = 25¢. Most national banks and Thomas Cook *(locations throughout the US, ☎ 800-287-7362, www.thomascook.com)* **exchange foreign currency** at local offices and charge a fee for the service.

The simplest methods to obtain dollars are to use traveler's checks *(accepted in most banks, hotels, restaurants and businesses with presentation of a photo ID)* and to withdraw cash from **ATMs** (Automated Teller Machines) with a debit or credit card. Banks charge a fee *($1-$2)* for non-members who use their ATMs. For more information on the ATM network, call Cirrus *(☎ 800-424-7787)* or Plus System *(☎ 800-843-7587)*. In the event you **lose your credit card**: American Express, ☎ 800-528-4800; Diner's Club, ☎ 800-234-6377; MasterCard/ Eurocard, ☎ 800-307-7309; Visa/Carte Bleue, ☎ 800-336-8472.

It is also possible to send and receive cash via **Western Union** *(locations in more than 100 countries, ☎ 800-325-6000, www.westernunion.com)*.

Taxes and Tips – In the US, with the occasional exception of certain food products and gasoline, **sales tax** is not included in the quoted price and is added at the time of payment. Sales taxes vary by state and range from 3 to 8.5 percent (except for Alaska, Delaware, New Hampshire and Oregon, which charge no sales tax). Sales tax may often be higher in major cities due to local taxes. In some states, the **restaurant tax** appearing on your bill when you dine out may be higher than the state tax; also, expect additional **hotel taxes** and surcharges.

Tipping

In restaurants, it is customary to leave the server a gratuity, or tip, of 15-20 percent of the total bill (unless the menu specifies that gratuity is included). Taxi drivers are generally tipped 15 percent of the fare. In hotels, bellmen are tipped $1 per suitcase and housekeeping $1 per night. Hairdressers may be tipped at the client's discretion.

Liquor Laws – The minimum age for purchase and consumption of alcoholic beverages is 21; proof of age may be required. Local municipalities may limit and restrict sales, and laws differ among states. In many states, liquor stores sell beer, wine and liquor. Beer and wine may also be purchased in package-goods stores and grocery stores. Liquor is available at grocery stores in California. Beer may be purchased in gas station convenience stores in some states. However, in other states, wine and liquor are sold at state-operated shops and beer sold by licensed distributors. Certain states, such as Utah, do not permit alcohol sales on Sundays, even in restaurants (exceptions usually apply in metropolitan and tourist areas).

Accommodations

For a listing of lodging recommendations for areas described in this guide, consult the **Address Book** sections in each chapter.

Luxury **hotels** are generally found in major cities and resort communities, **motels** in clusters on the edges of towns and off the interstate highways. **Bed-and-breakfast inns** usually are found in residential areas of cities and towns, but also in more secluded natural areas. Many properties offer special packages and weekend rates that may not be extended during peak summer months *(late May – late Aug)* and holiday seasons, especially near ski resorts. Advance reservations are recommended during these times. Rates tend to be higher in cities and near coastal and resort areas.

Many resort properties include outdoor recreational facilities such as ski areas, golf courses, tennis courts, swimming pools and fitness centers, as well as gourmet dining and entertainment. Activities such as hiking, mountain biking and horseback riding may be arranged by contacting hotel staff.

Many cities and communities levy a hotel occupancy tax that is not reflected in hotel rates. Contact local tourist offices to request free brochures that give details about area accommodations. *(Telephone numbers and Web sites are listed under entry headings in each chapter.)*

Hotels & Motels - Rates for hotels and motels vary greatly according to season and location, tending to be higher during holiday and peak seasons. For deluxe hotels, plan to pay at least $175/night per room, double occupancy. Moderate hotels will charge $100-$175/night and budget motels range from $40-$100/night. In most hotels, children under 18 stay free when sharing a room with their parents. In-room efficiency kitchens are available at some hotels and motels. When reserving, ask about packages including meals, passes to local attractions and weekend specials. Typical amenities at hotels and motels include television, alarm clock, smoking/non-smoking rooms, restaurants and swimming pools. Always advise the reservations clerk of late arrival; unless confirmed with a credit card, rooms may not be held after 6pm. Contact state *(listing p 403)* or local *(numbers under each blue entry in this guide)* tourism agencies for free brochures on accommodations in an area.

Hotel & Motel Reservation services - Hotel reservation services are abundant, especially on the Internet. For a full listing, search the Internet using the keyword "reservation services" or ask your travel agent. Following is a brief selection.

Service	☏
Accommodations Express	609-391-2100 www.accommodationsexpress.com
Central Reservation Service	800-548-3311 www.reservation-services.com
Hotel Reservations Network	214-361-7311 www.hoteldiscount.com
Quikbook (certain major cities only)	800-789-9887 www.quikbook.com
StayUSA	813-895-4410 www.stayusa.com

Major US Hotel/Motel chains

Best Western	☏ 800-528-1234	Marriott	☏ 800-228-9290
Comfort Inn	☏ 800-228-5150	Motel 6	☏ 800-466-8356
Courtyard	☏ 800-321-2211	Nikko	☏ 800-645-5687
Days Inn	☏ 800-325-2525	Omni	☏ 800-843-6664
Econo Lodge	☏ 800-553-2666	Quality Inn	☏ 800-228-5151
Embassy Suites	☏ 800-362-2779	Radisson	☏ 800-333-3333
Fairfield Inn	☏ 800-228-2800	Ramada	☏ 800-272-6232
Four Seasons	☏ 800-332-3442	Red Roof	☏ 800-843-7663
Hampton Inn	☏ 800-426-7866	Residence Inn	☏ 800-331-3131
Hilton	☏ 800-445-8667	Ritz-Carlton	☏ 800-241-3333
Holiday Inn	☏ 800-465-4329	Sheraton	☏ 800-325-3535
Howard Johnson	☏ 800-446-4656	Super 8	☏ 800-525-2149
Hyatt	☏ 800-233-1234	Travelodge	☏ 800-578-7878
La Quinta	☏ 800-687-6667	Westin	☏ 800-228-3000

Bed & Breakfasts and Country Inns - Most B&Bs are privately owned historic residences. Bed-and-breakfast inns are typically cozy homes with fewer than 10 guest rooms; breakfast is usually the only meal provided. Country inns are larger establishments, often offering over 25 guest rooms; full-service dining is typically available. Both establishments include a breakfast ranging from continental fare to a gourmet repast; some offer afternoon tea and the use of sitting rooms with cozy fireplaces, or garden spots providing breathtaking panoramas of ocean shores or mountain vistas. Some lower-priced rooms may not have private baths. Especially during holiday and peak tourist seasons, reservations should be made well in advance. Minimum stay, cancellation and refund policies may be more stringent during these times. Most inns will accept major credit cards. Rates vary seasonally but range from $125 to $200 for a double room per night. Rates will be higher for rooms with such amenities as hot tubs, private entrances and scenic views.

Bed & Breakfast and Country Inn reservation services - Numerous organizations offer reservation services for B&Bs and country inns. Many services tend to be regional; following are some nationwide services. For a complete listing, search the Internet using keyword "bed and breakfast" or ask your travel agent. Also, the **Independent Innkeepers' Association** *(☏ 616-789-0393, www.innbook.com)* publishes an annual register listing B&Bs and country inns by state.

Bed and Breakfast Travel Associates, Inc.	716-696-6720 www.bbamerica.com
The National Network of Bed & Breakfast Reservation Services (TNN)	972-298-8586 www.go-lodging.com
Professional Association of Innkeepers International	805-569-1853 www.innplace.com
Wakeman & Costine's North American Bed & Breakfast Directory	828-387-3697 www.bbdirectory.com

Guest Ranches - In the late 19C, working farms and livestock ranches welcomed big-city friends eager to help with chores, or paying guests to help them through tough economic times. The romanticization of the American West to an eastern audience lent a mystique to the cowboy and the open range that persists to this day. The "dude ranch," as it became known, provided a unique window on the Western lifestyle. Today's dude ranches, now more frequently called "guest ranches," vary in style from rustic to posh. Catering to as few as 12 or as many as 125 guests, they may be working ranches that involve guests in cattle drives and branding; outfitting ranches that emphasize horseback riding; or resort ranches, where relaxation is the order of the day. Many guests return to the saddle year after year for spectacular scenery, riding and family-style meals.

© David Barnes/Tony Stone Images

Web sites have made these Western vacations readily accessible to a global market intrigued by the cowboy lifestyle. Organizations that provide information on guest ranches include The Dude Rancher's Association, P.O. Box 471, La Porte CO 80535 (☎ 970-223-0440, www.duderanch.org), and Guest Ranches of North America, P.O. Box 191625, Dallas TX 75219 (www.guestranches.com).

Spas – Modern spas offer a variety of programs – fitness, beauty and wellness; relaxation and stress relief, weight management, and adventure vacations. Guests are pampered with European mud baths, daily massages, state-of-the-art fitness and exercise programs, cooking classes and nutritional counseling. Spas offer luxurious facilities in beautiful settings that may include championship golf courses, equestrian centers and even formal gardens. Most offer packages for stays ranging from 2 to 10 nights, which include health and fitness programs, golf and tennis, and image enhancement. Most facilities have age restrictions. Most spas are informal, but check when making reservations.

Prices range from $800/week to $3,500/week depending on choice of program and season. (price per person, double occupancy). All meals, including special diets, use of facilities, tax, gratuities and airport transportation, are usually included. **Spa Finders**, 91 Fifth Ave., New York NY 10003, ☎ 212-924-6800 or your travel agent.

Condominiums – Furnished apartments or houses are more cost-effective than hotels for families with children. Amenities include separate living quarters, fully equipped kitchen with dining area, several bedrooms and bathrooms, and laundry facilities. Most condos provide televisions, basic linens and maid service. Depending on location, properties may include sports and recreational facilities, patios and beach access. Most require a minimum stay of three nights or one week, especially during peak season. When making reservations, ask about cancellation penalties and refund policies. Chambers of commerce and convention-and-visitors bureaus have listings of local property management agencies that can assist with the selection. A variety of private accommodations can be arranged through **Condo & Villa Authority**, 305 N. Pontiac Trail, Walled Lake MI 48390, ☎ 248-669-7500.

Hostels - A simple, no-frills alternative to hotels and inns, hostels are inexpensive dormitory-style accommodations with separate quarters for males and females. Many have private family/couples rooms, which may be reserved in advance. Amenities include fully equipped self-service kitchens, dining areas and common rooms. Hostelling International members receive discounts on room rates and other travel-related expenses (Alamo car rentals, and local attractions). Hostels often organize special programs and activities for guests. When booking, ask for available discounts at area attractions, rental car companies and restaurants. Rates average $14 to $45 per night. For information and a free directory, contact **Hostelling International American Youth Hostels** *(733 15th St., NW, Suite 840, Washington DC 20005, ☎ 202-783-6161, www.hiayh.org)*. For more general information on hostels: www.hostels.com.

From outside the US, contact the **Hostelling International** center in your country of residence.

Australia: Australian Youth Hostels Association, ☎ 2-9565-1699, www.yha.org.au.

Belgium: Les Auberges de Jeunesse, ☎ 02-219-56-76, www.planet.be/asbl/aubjeun.

Canada: Hostelling International-Canada, ☎ 613-237-7884, www.hostellingintl.ca.

France: Fédération Unie des Auberges de Jeunesse (FUAJ), ☎ 01-44-89-8727, www.fuaj.org.

Ireland (Northern): Hostelling International-Northern Ireland, ☎ 01232-315-435, www.hini.org.uk.

Italy: Associazione Italiana Alberghi per la Gioventù, ☎ 06-487-1152, www.hostels-aig.org.

Netherlands: Stichting Nederlandse Jeugdherberg Centrale, ☎ 20-5513155, www.njhc.org.

Spain: Red Española de Albergues Juveniles, ☎ 91-347-7700.

Switzerland: Schweizer Jugendherbergen, ☎ 01-360-1414, www.youthhostel.ch.

United Kingdom: YHA (England & Wales) Ltd., ☎ 0870-870-8808, www.yha.org.uk.

Camping & Recreational Vehicle (RV) Parks – *National and state park listings p 426.* Campsites are located in national parks, state parks, national forests, along beaches and in private campgrounds. The season for camping in the high country usually runs from Memorial Day to Labor Day; in lower elevations, campgrounds are open year-round. Most offer full utility hookups, lodges or cabins, backcountry sites and recreational facilities. Advance reservations are recommended, especially during summer and holidays. In most parks and forests, campgrounds are available on a first-come, first-served basis.

National park and state park campgrounds are relatively inexpensive, but fill quickly, especially during school holidays. Facilities range from simple tent sites to full RV hookups *(reserve 60 days in advance)* or rustic cabins

© Steve Bly

Campsite, Middle Fork of the Salmon River, Idaho

(reserve one year in advance). Fees vary according to season and available facilities (picnic tables, water/electric hookups, used-water disposal, recreational equipment, showers, restrooms): camping & RV sites $8-$21/day; cabins $20-$110/day. For all US national park reservations, contact the park you are visiting or the **US National Park Reservation Service** *(☎ 301-722-1257, http://reservations.nps.gov)*. For **state parks**, contact the state tourism office *(p 403)* for information.

Private campgrounds offering facilities from simple tent sites to full RV-hookups are plentiful. They are slightly more expensive *($10-$16/day for tent sites, $20-$25/day for RVs)* but may offer more sophisticated amenities: hot showers, laundry facilities, convenience stores, children's playgrounds, pools, air-conditioned cabins and outdoor recreational facilities. Most accept daily, weekly or monthly occupancy. In winter *(Nov-Apr)*, some campgrounds may be closed. Reservations are recommended, especially for longer stays and in popular resort areas. **Kampgrounds of America (KOA)** operates campsites for tents, cabins/cottages and RV-hookups throughout the United States. For a directory *(include $3 for shipping)*, contact KOA Kampgrounds, P.O. Box 30558, Billings MT 59114 *(☎ 406-248-7444, www.koakampgrounds.com)*. Directories of campgrounds throughout the US are easily found on the Internet. Following is a sample of some Internet **campground directories** covering the US:

Camping USA	www.camping-usa.com
CIS' RV-America Travel & Service Center	www.rv-america.com
Go Camping America Directory	www.gocampingamerica.com
(official site of National Association of RV Parks & Campgrounds)	
RVing Campground Directory	www.rving.com
USA Campgrounds & RV Parks	http://usacampgrounds.net

Recreation and Sports

Outdoor Recreation

Adventure Travel and Multi-Sport Excursions - The varying geography of the western US provides unlimited opportunities for outdoor adventure—from snorkeling off the California and Hawaii coasts to cross-country skiing in search of bison herds in Yellowstone National Park. Contact state tourism offices *(p 403)* for information on activities in specific geographic areas, or consider an organized tour. **Green-Travel.com** *(1611 Connecticut Ave. NW, Suite 4C, Washington DC 20009; www.green-travel.com)* promotes responsible nature tourism in conjunction with the nonprofit organization Conservation International and provides resources for finding adventure travel through its tour operator/trip database.

Following is a sampling of tour providers and programs available:

For exciting **all-inclusive vacations** involving activities such as bicycling, hiking and kayaking, contact **Backroads** *(801 Cedar St., Berkeley CA 94710-1800; ☎ 510-527-1555 or 800-462-2848, www.backroads.com)*. Programs include destinations in Alaska, Arizona, California, Colorado, Hawaii, Idaho, Montana, New Mexico, Utah, Washington and Wyoming.

For adventures on **horseback** throughout the USA West, including riding tours, cattle drives and visits to working ranches, contact **Hidden Trails** *(5936 Inverness St, Vancouver BC V5W 3P7, Canada; ☎ 604-323-1141, www.bcranches.com)*.

Multi-sport vacations are available from **The World Outside** *(2840 Wilderness Place, Suite F, Boulder CO 80301; ☎ 303-413-0938 or 800-488-8483, www.gorp.com/rlt)*. Destinations include Alaska, Arizona, California, Colorado, Hawaii, Montana, New Mexico, Utah, Washington and Wyoming.

AdventureQuest.com *(482 Congress St., Suite 101, Portland ME 04101; ☎ 207-871-1684 or 800-643-5630, www.adventurequest.com)* offers an on-line reservation service with bookings ranging from cultural tours and animal treks to more typical cruises and sporting adventures.

Covering the western US from Alaska to Arizona, **Backcountry, Ltd.** *(P.O. Box 4029, Bozeman MT 59772; ☎ 406-586-3556 or 800-575-1540, www.backcountrytours.com)* provides multi-sport vacations for active travelers.

Offering adventure trips throughout most of the USA West, **American Wilderness Experience** (*P.O. Box 1486, Boulder CO 80306;* ☎ *303-444-2622 or 800-444-0099, www.awetrips.com*) provides combination and single-activity vacation packages ranging from rafting and biking to covered wagon trips.

Cycling enthusiasts can see the US on tours offered by **America by Bicycle** (*P.O. Box 805, Atkinson NH 03811;* ☎ *603-382-1662 or 888-797-7057, www.abbike.com*). Tours range from 5-11 day mini-tours to 52-day coast-to-coast programs.

Wilderness Inquiry, Inc. (*808 14th Ave. NE, Minneapolis MN 55414,* ☎ *612-676-9400 or 800-728-0719, www.wildernessinquiry.org*) offers tours that include activities such as **kayaking** in Alaska's fjords, **rafting** in the Grand Canyon and **horsepacking** through the Rockies.

Llama Pack Trip, Beartooth Mountains, Montana

All but the most experienced **whitewater rafters and kayakers** book expert guides to lead them through rivers' perils. The following veteran outfitters know rivers not only in their home state but throughout the West: **All-Outdoors California Whitewater Rafting** (*1250 Pine St., Suite 103, Walnut Creek CA 94596;* ☎ *925-932-8993 or 800-247-2387, www.aorafting.com*); **Bill Dvorak Kayak & Rafting Expeditions** (*17921 US-285, Nathrop CO 81236;* ☎ *719-429-6851 or 800-824-3795, www.vtinet.com/dvorak*); **ECHO: The Wilderness Company** (*6529 Telegraph Ave., Oakland CA 94609;* ☎ *510-652-1600, www.echotrips.com*); **Nichols Expeditions** (*497 N. Main St., Moab UT 84532;* ☎ *801-259-3999 or 800-648-8488, www.NicholsExpeditions.com*); **OARS** (*P.O. Box 67, Angels Camp CA 95222;* ☎ *209-736-4678 or 800-346-6277, www.oars.com*); and **R.O.W.-River Odysseys West** (*P.O. Box 579, Coeur d'Alene ID 83816;* ☎ *208-765-0841 or 800-451-6034, www.rowinc.com*). In Hawaii: **Kayak Kaua'i** (*P.O. Box 508, Hanalei, Kauai HI 96714;* ☎ *808-826-9844 or 800-437-3507, http://planet-hawaii.com/outbound*).

Skiing the West - From the Rockies to the Cascades and Sierra Nevada, the peaks of the USA West offer any winter sport. Ski areas are abundant, ranging from small local hills (with perhaps a single tow) to major international resorts. Most western states—except those of the southern Great Plains—boast at least one ski area; associations count 161 in all, including 31 in California and 27 in Colorado. In **Hawaii**, intrepid skiers drive Jeeps to the summit of 13,796ft Mauna Kea, "The White Mountain," to play in winter snows. The **Ski Odyssey Online Resort Guide** (*www.skiodyssey.com*) has details on every North American resort and many overseas.

Major areas—with at least eight lifts and a 2,000ft vertical drop—include these:

Alaska: Anchorage area: Alyeska Resort (☎ *907-754-1111*).

California: Lake Tahoe: Heavenly (☎ *775-586-7000*), Kirkwood (☎ *209-258-6000*), Northstar-at-Tahoe (☎ *530-562-1010*), Sierra-at-Tahoe (☎ *530-659-7453*), Squaw Valley (☎ *530-583-6985*). Mammoth Lakes: June Mountain (☎ *760-648-7733*), Mammoth Mountain (☎ *760-934-0745*).

Colorado: Aspen/Snowmass *(☎ 970-925-1220)*. Crested Butte *(☎ 970-349-2323)*. San Juans: Purgatory *(☎ 970-247-9000)*, Telluride *(☎ 970-728-6900)*. Steamboat Springs: Steamboat *(☎ 970-879-6111)*. Summit County: Breckenridge *(☎ 970-453-5000)*, Copper Mountain *(☎ 970-968-2882)*, Keystone *(☎ 970-468-4111)*. Vail

Sightseeing & Tours

National and City Tours - Several national tour companies provide all-inclusive packages for motor-coach tours of the US *(see below)*. The scope of tours may vary among tour operators, but most offer packages of varying length, geographic coverage and cost. **TrekAmerica** *(P.O. Box 189, Rockaway NJ 07866; ☎ 973-983-1144 or 800-221-0596, www.trekamerica.com)* caters to travelers who prefer small groups, varied sightseeing/sporting activities and flexible itineraries. For those interested in more educational offerings, **Smithsonian Study Tours**, sponsored by the Smithsonian Institution, offers a variety of single- and multi day thematic tour programs covering topics such as architecture, history, the performing arts and cuisine. Educators specializing in related fields lead tours. For more information: ☎ 877-338-8687 or www.si.edu.

Information on **city tours** can be obtained from convention and visitors bureaus in most large US cities. **Gray Line Tours** provides half- and full-day sightseeing motor-coach tours for more than 70 cities: Gray Line Worldwide, 2460 W. 26th Ave., Suite C-300, Denver CO 80211 *(☎ 303-433-9800, www.grayline.com)*.

Grand Canyon Railroad

National Tour Companies

Brennan Tours, Joseph Vance Bldg., 1402 3rd Ave., Suite 717, Seattle WA 98101; ☎ 800-237-7249, www.brennantours.com.

Collette Tours, 162 Middle St., Pawtucket RI 02860; ☎ 800-248-8943, www.collettetours.com.

GoGo Worldwide Vacations, 69 Spring St., Ramsey NJ 07446; ☎ 800-229-4999, www.gogowwv.com.

Globus and Cosmos, 5301 S. Federal Circle, Littleton CO 80123; ☎ 888-218-8665, www.globusandcosmos.com.

Mayflower Tours, 1225 Warren Ave., Downers Grove IL 60515; ☎ 800-323-7604, www.mayflowertours.com.

Trafalgar Tours, 11 E. 26th St., Suite 1300, New York NY 10010; ☎ 800-854-0103, www.trafalgartours.com.

Tauck Tours, 276 Post Rd. W., Westport CT 06880; ☎ 800-788-7885, www.tauck.com.

area: Beaver Creek (☎ 970-476-5601), Vail (☎ 970-476-5601). Winter Park (☎ 970-726-5514).

Idaho: Panhandle: Schweitzer (☎ 208-263-9555). Sawtooths: Sun Valley (☎ 208-622-4111).

Montana: Glacier National Park area: Big Mountain (☎ 406-862-7669). Yellowstone National Park area: Big Sky (☎ 406-995-5000), Red Lodge (☎ 406-446-2610).

New Mexico: Sangre de Cristo Range: Taos Ski Valley (☎ 505-776-2291).

Oregon: Cascade Range: Mt. Bachelor (☎ 541-382-7888), Mt. Hood Meadows (☎ 503-337-2222).

Utah: Wasatch Range: Alta (☎ 801-359-1078), The Canyons (☎ 435-649-5400), Deer Valley (☎ 435-649-1000), Park City (☎ 435-649-8111), Snowbasin (☎ 801-399-1135), Snowbird (☎ 801-742-2222).

Washington: Cascade Range: Crystal Mountain (☎ 360-663-2526), The Summit at Snoqualmie (☎ 206-233-8182).

Wyoming: Jackson Hole (☎ 307-733-2292).

Guides and Outfitters - A list of accredited **mountaineering organizations** can be obtained from the nonprofit **American Mountain Guides Association** *(710 Tenth St., Suite 101, Golden CO 80401; ☎ 303-271-0984, www.amga.com)*. **America Outdoors** *(P.O. Box 10847, Knoxville TN 37939; ☎ 423-558-3595, www.americaoutdoors.org)* offers an outfitter database on its Web site and a free publication available by mail, listing US outfitters.

Nature and Safety

Wildlife - In most natural areas, tampering with plants or wildlife is prohibited by law. Although the disturbance caused by a single person may be small, the cumulative impact of a large number of visitors may be disastrous. Avoid direct contact with wildlife; any animal that does not shy from humans may be sick. Some wildlife, particularly bears, may approach cars or campsites out of curiosity or if they smell food. **Food storage guidelines:** hang food 12ft off the ground and 10ft away from a tree trunk, or store in a locking ice chest, in a car trunk or in lockers provided at some campgrounds. Improper storage of food is a violation of federal law and subject to a fine. If a bear approaches, try to frighten it by yelling and throwing rocks in its direction. Never approach a mother with cubs, as she will attack to protect her young.

Thunderstorms and Tornadoes - Prevalent across the Great Plains in summer, storm fronts can develop as quickly as they can dissipate. Some thunderstorms can be severe, featuring hail and dangerous lightning. Severe storms sometimes produce **tornadoes**, violently rotating air columns reaching from the storm clouds to the ground. Winds generated by tornadoes can reach 250-300mph.

Thunderstorm Safety Tips:

If outdoors, take cover and stay away from trees and metal objects.

If riding in a vehicle, remain inside until the storm has passed.

Avoid being in or near water.

If in a boat, head for the nearest shore.

Do not use electrical appliances, especially telephones.

Tornado Safety Tips:

If indoors, move to a predesignated shelter (usually a basement or stairwell); otherwise find an interior room without windows (such as a bathroom).

Stay away from windows.

Do not attempt to outrun the storm in a car. Get out of the automobile and lie flat in a ditch or low-lying area.

Beach and Water Safety - In the strong sun of coastal areas where white sand and water increases the sun's intensity, visitors run the risk of sunburn, even in winter. Apply sunscreen even on overcast days, as ultraviolet rays penetrate cloud cover. During summer months, when temperatures may be extreme, avoid strenuous midday exercise and drink plenty of liquids.

Along public beaches warning flags are posted every mile: blue flags signify calm waters; yellow flags indicate choppy waters; **red flags** indicate dangerous swimming conditions such as riptides, strong underlying currents that pull swimmers seaward. Take precautions even when venturing into calm waters: never swim, snorkel or scuba dive alone; and supervise children at all times. Most public beaches employ lifeguards seasonally; take care when swimming at an unguarded beach. Stinging creatures such as jellyfish, Portuguese men-of-war and sea urchins can inhabit shallow waters. Although most jellyfish stings produce little more than an itchy skin rash, some can cause painful swelling. Treating the affected area with papain-type meat tenderizer will give relief. Stingrays and Portuguese men-of-war can inflict a more serious sting; seek medical treatment immediately.

Oregon Dunes National Recreation Area, Oregon

Before beginning any watersports activity, check with local authorities for information on water and weather conditions. If you rent a canoe or charter a boat, familiarize yourself with the craft, obtain charts of the area and advise someone of your itinerary before setting out. **Life jackets** must be worn when boating. Many equipment-rental facilities also offer instruction. Be sure to choose a reputable outfitter.

Earthquake Precautions – Although severe earthquakes are infrequent, they are also unpredictable, making earthquake preparedness a fact of life in California and other Pacific-coast states. If you are **outside** when a quake occurs, stay clear of trees, buildings and power lines. If you are in a **vehicle**, pull to the side of the road and stop. Do not park on or under bridges; sit on the floor of the vehicle if possible. If you are in a **building**, stand inside a doorway or sit under a sturdy table; stay away from windows and outside walls. Be alert for aftershocks. If possible, tune to local radio or TV stations for advisories.

Desert Safety – When traveling through desert areas, particularly in summer, certain precautions are essential. Before driving or hiking in remote areas, notify someone of your destination and your planned return time.

For Your Vehicle – Always stay on marked roads; most unpaved roads are suitable only for four-wheel-drive vehicles. As service stations may be far apart, it is wise to keep your gas tank at least half full, and carry plenty of radiator water. If the vehicle is running hot, turn off the air conditioning. If it overheats, pull to the side of the road, turn on the heater and slowly pour water over the radiator core *(do not stop the engine)*. Refill the radiator after the engine has cooled. In the event of a breakdown, do not leave your vehicle to seek help; instead, stay with the vehicle and wait for passing traffic.

For You – Summer temperatures can reach above 120°F (48°C). It is imperative to carry plenty of water and drink it freely, at least once an hour. Do not lie or sit in the direct sunlight. Always wear loose-fitting clothes (preferably long-sleeved), a broad brimmed hat and sunglasses.

Heat exhaustion is caused by overexertion in high temperatures. Symptoms include cool, clammy skin and nausea. If experiencing either of these symptoms, rest in the shade and drink plenty of fluids. Symptoms of **heat stroke** include hot, dry skin, dizziness or headache; a victim may become delirious. To treat these symptoms, try to lower the body temperature with cold compresses (do not use analgesics) and seek medical assistance.

Abandoned mines are common in desert areas, and all are potentially dangerous. Never enter a tunnel without a flashlight. Watch for loose rock and do not touch support timbers. Be watchful for sudden storms that may produce flash floods.

Mountain Safety – Take particular care if you are traveling at high altitudes, whether driving across Trail Ridge Road at 12,183ft in Colorado's Rocky Mountain National Park or taking the cog railway to the 14,110ft summit of Pikes Peak. Your body does not immediately acclimate to the reduced oxygen level and lowered atmospheric pressure. One to four days may be necessary to fully adjust. Move slowly, get plenty of rest, avoid large meals, and drink lots of water. Senior citizens, pregnant women and travelers with a history of heart problems should consult their physicians before climbing too high.

Especially if you are hiking or skiing above 8,000ft, you may suffer **altitude sickness** caused by overexertion. Symptoms include headache, shortness of breath, appetite loss or nausea, tingling in fingers or toes (which may progress to swelling in feet and legs) and general weakness. If experiencing any of these symptoms, rest and eat high-energy foods such as raisins, trail mix or granola bars; take a couple of aspirin and slow your pace. If symptoms become more severe, descend to a lower altitude; if they do not disappear in 2-5 days, seek medical attention.

As the sun's rays are more direct in the thinner atmosphere of higher elevations, they cause sunburn more quickly, especially in winter when they reflect off snow. A good sunblock is essential.

It is important to keep yourself warm and your clothing dry any time of year. Hypothermia poses the greatest threat in winter, but even midsummer temperatures can drop below freezing at high altitude.

National and State Lands

The United States has an extensive network of federal and state lands, including national and state parks, that offer year-round recreational opportunities such as camping *(p 420)*, fishing, horseback riding, snowmobiling and boating. US federal land-management agencies support a comprehensive on-line database *(www.recreation.gov)* that supplies information on all recreation areas through a variety of search options and Internet links. The National Park Service provides a listing of all lands under its jurisdiction on its Web site *(www.nps.gov)*.

Both national and state parks offer **season passes** *(disabled travelers p 405)*. The **Golden Eagle Passport** *($50)* is good for one year and includes admission to all national parks, sites and areas. The pass may be purchased at any park entrance area or via mail: National Park Service, 1100 Ohio Dr. SW, Room 138, Washington DC 20242; Attention: Golden Eagle Passport. Most parks have information centers equipped with trail maps and informative literature on park facilities and activities. Contact the following agencies for further information:

National Forests
US Department of Agriculture
Forest Service, National Headquarters
PO Box 96090
Washington DC 20090-6090
☎ 202-205-1760 or www.fs.fed.us

National Parks
US Department of the Interior
National Park Service
Office of Public Inquiries
1849 C St. NW
Washington DC 20240
☎ 202-208-4747 or www.nps.gov

Tips for Visiting Public Lands

Spray clothes with insect repellent (particularly around cuffs and waistline) and check for ticks every 3-4hrs when participating in outdoor activities.

Do not feed wild animals.

Do not litter; pack out everything you pack in.

Boil (5min) or chemically treat water from streams and lakes.

Cutting wood for fires is prohibited; only dead or fallen wood should be used. Campfires are limited to fire pits.

All plants and animals within the parks are protected.

Taking natural objects (antlers/horns, historical items, plants, rocks) is prohibited.

State Park Divisions

Alaska Division of Parks & Outdoor Recreation
550 W. 7th Ave., Suite 1260
Anchorage AK 99501-3557
☎ 907-269-8400
www.dnr.state.ak.us/parks

Arizona State Parks
1300 W. Washington St., Suite 150
Phoenix AZ 85007
☎ 602-542-4174
www.pr.state.az.us

California Dept of Parks & Recreation
P.O. Box 942896
Sacramento CA 94296
☎ 916-653-6995
http://cal-parks.ca.gov

Colorado Parks & Outdoor Recreation Division
1313 Sherman St., Room 618
Denver CO 80203
☎ 303-866-3437
www.dnr.state.co.us/parks

Hawaii Div of State Parks
1151 Punchbowl St., Room 310
Honolulu HI 96813
☎ 808-587-0300
www.hawaii.gov/dlnr/dsp/dsp.html

Idaho State Parks & Recreation Department
5657 Warm Springs Ave.
Boise ID 83712
☎ 208-334-4199
www.idahoparks.org

Kansas Dept of Wildlife & Parks
512 SE 25th Ave.
Pratt KS 67124
☎ 316-672-5911
www.kdwp.state.ks.us

Montana Parks Division
P.O. Box 200701
Helena MT 59620
☎ 406-444-3750
www.fwp.state.mt.us/parks/parks.htm

Nebraska Game & Parks Commission
2200 N. 33rd St.
Lincoln NE 08503
☎ 402-471-5550
www.ngpc.state.ne.us/parks

Nevada State Parks
1300 S. Curry St.
Carson City NV 89703
☎ 775-687-4370
www.state.nv.us/stparks

New Mexico State Parks Division
P.O. Box 1147
Santa Fe NM 87504
☎ 505-827-7173
www.emnrd.state.nm.us/nmparks

North Dakota Parks & Recreation Department
1835 E. Bismarck Expressway
Bismarck ND 58504
☎ 701-328-5357
www.state.nd.us/ndparks

Oklahoma Parks Division
P.O. Box 52002
Oklahoma City OK 73152
☎ 405-521-3411
http://touroklahoma.com

Oregon State Parks & Recreation Department
1115 Commercial St. NE
Salem OR 97301
☎ 503-378-6305
www.prd.state.or.us/home.html

South Dakota Park & Recreation Division
523 E. Capitol Ave.
Pierre SD 57501
☎ 605-773-3391
www.state.sd.us/gfp/sdparks/index.htm

Texas Parks & Wildlife Department
4200 Smith School Rd.
Austin TX 78744
☎ 512-389-4800
www.tpwd.state.tx.us

Utah Parks & Recreation Division
P.O. Box 146001
Salt Lake City UT 84114
☎ 801-538-7220
www.nr.state.ut.us/parks/utahstpk.htm

**Washington State Parks
& Recreation Commission**
P.O. Box 42650
Olympia WA 98504
☎ 360-902-8500
www.parks.wa.gov

**Wyoming Division of State Parks
& Historic Sites**
1E. Herschler Bldg., 122 W. 25th St.
Cheyenne WY 82002
☎ 307-777-6323
http://commerce.state.wy.us/sphs

Hiking & Backpacking – The National Park Service, US Forest Service and Bureau of Land Management administer 17 national scenic and national historic trails in the US. For information, obtain the *National Trails System Map and Guide ($1.25)* from the Consumer Information Center, US General Services Administration *(Pueblo CO 81009;* ☎ *888 878 3256, www.pueblo.gsa.gov/travel.htm)* or contact agencies listed below.

🏃 National Trails System Branch of the National Park Service

1849 C St. NW, Washington DC 20240, ☎ 202-565-1177

🏃 Continental Divide National Scenic Trail

Continental Divide Trail Society, P.O. Box 30002, Bethesda MD 20814

US Forest Service, Northern Region, P.O. Box 7669, Missoula MT 59807; ☎ 406-329-3150 (Montana-Idaho); Rocky Mountain Region, 740 Sims St., Lakewood CO 80225; ☎ 303-275-5350 (Wyoming-Colorado-New Mexico)

Hikers in Haleakala National Park, Maui, Hawaii

© Robert Holmes

Pacific Crest National Scenic Trail

Pacific Crest Trail Conference, P.O. Box 2514, Lynnwood WA 98036-2514

Nature of the Northwest, 800 NE Oregon St., Room 177, Portland OR 97232, ☎ 503-872-2750

Iditarod National Historic Trail

Iditarod Trail Committee, P.O. Box 870800, Wasilla AK 99687, ☎ 907-376-5155

Juan Bautista de Anza National Historic Trail

National Park Service, Golden Gate National Recreation Area, Fort Mason, Bldg. 201, San Francisco CA 94123-1372, ☎ 415-556-0560

Lewis and Clark National Historic Trail

Lewis and Clark Trail Heritage Foundation, P.O. Box 3434, Great Falls MT 59403

National Park Service, Lewis and Clark National Historic Trail, 1709 Jackson St., Omaha, NE 68102, ☎ 402-221-3471

Mormon Pioneer National Historic Trail

National Park Service, Long Distance Trails Office, P.O. Box 45155, Salt Lake City UT 84145, ☎ 801-539-4095

Nez Percé (Nee-Me-Poo) National Historic Trail

Forest Service, Northern Region, Federal Bldg., P.O. Box 7669, Missoula MT 59807, ☎ 406-329-3590

Oregon National Historic Trail

Oregon Country Trails Assn., P.O. Box 1019, Independence MO 64051-0519, ☎ 816-252-2276

National Park Service, Pacific Northwest Region, Oregon National Historic Trail, 83 S. King St., Suite 212, Seattle WA 98104, ☎ 206-220-7450

Santa Fe National Historic Trail

Santa Fe Trail Assn., Santa Fe Trail Center, Rte. 3, Larned KS 67550; ☎ 316-285-2054

Trail of Tears National Historic Trail

National Park Service, Long Distance Trails Group Office, P.O. Box 728, Santa Fe NM 87504-0728, ☎ 505-988-6888

Hitting the Links

From multi-course complexes and resorts to municipal and daily-fee courses, US **golfing facilities** provide challenging play, beautiful natural scenery and gracious amenities for enthusiasts of all skill levels. Following is a list of some top rated public-access courses in the western US:

Course	Location	☏
Troon North	Scottsdale AZ	480-585-5300
Sedona	Sedona AZ	520-284-9355
Tahquitz Creek	Palm Springs CA	760-328-1005
Pebble Beach	Pebble Beach CA	831-625-8518
Meadows del Mar	San Diego CA	858-792-6200
Pasatiempo	Santa Cruz CA	831-459-9155
The Broadmoor	Colorado Springs CO	719-577-5790
The Prince	Kaua'i HI	808-826-5000
Mauna Kea Beach	Kohala Coast HI	808-882-7222
Coeur d'Alene	Coeur d'Alene ID	208-765-0218
Pumpkin Ridge	Cornelius OR	503-647-9977
Angel Park	Las Vegas NV	702-254-4653
Edgewood Tahoe	Stateline NV	775-588-3566
Piñon Hills	Farmington NM	505-326-6066
Del Lago	Conroe TX	409-582-7570
Horseshoe Bay	Burnet TX	830-598-2511
Las Colinas	Irving TX	972-717-0700
Entrada at Snow Canyon	St. George UT	435-674-7500
Teton Pines	Jackson WY	307-733-1733

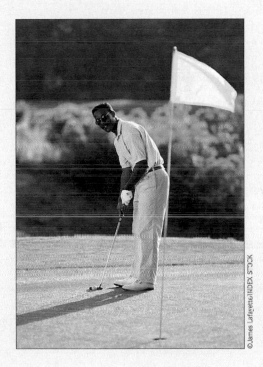

©James Lafayette/INDEX STOCK

Professional Team Sports

For ticket purchase, call the local **Ticketmaster** office.

BASEBALL   Apr-Oct

MLB (Major League Baseball) *www.majorleaguebaseball.com*

Team	Venue	☏
Anaheim Angels	Edison International Field	714-634-2000
Arizona Diamondbacks	Bank One Ballpark	602-514-8400

Team	Venue	☎
Colorado Rockies	Coors Field	303-762-5437
Houston Astros	Enron Field	713-627-8767
Kansas City Royals	Kauffman Stadium	816-921-8000
Los Angeles Dodgers	Dodger Stadium	323-224-1448
Oakland Athletics	Network Associates Coliseum	510-762-2255
San Diego Padres	Qualcomm Stadium	619-283-4494
San Francisco Giants	Pacific Bell Park	415-467-8000
Seattle Mariners	Safeco Field	206-346-4000
Texas Rangers	The Ballpark in Arlington	817-273-5100

BASKETBALL   Oct-Apr

NBA (National Basketball Association) www.nba.com

Team	Venue	☎
Dallas Mavericks	Reunion Arena	214-373-8000
Denver Nuggets	Pepsi Center	303-405-1212
Golden State Warriors	Arena in Oakland	510-986-2222
Houston Rockets	Compaq Center	713-627-3865
Los Angeles Clippers	Staples Center	213-742-7500
Los Angeles Lakers	Staples Center	213-480-3232
Phoenix Suns	America West Arena	602-379-7867
Portland Trail Blazers	The Rose Garden	503-231-8000
Sacramento Kings	ARCO Arena	916-928-6900
San Antonia Spurs	The Alamodome	210-554-7773
Seattle SuperSonics	KeyArena	206-281-5800
Utah Jazz	The Delta Center	801-355-3865

FOOTBALL   Sept-Jan

NFL (National Football League) www.nfl.com

Team	Venue	☎
Arizona Cardinals	Sun Devil Stadium	602-379-0102
Dallas Cowboys	Texas Stadium	214-953-1500
Denver Broncos	Mile High Stadium	303-433-7466
Kansas City Chiefs	Arrowhead Stadium	816-920-9300
Oakland Raiders	Network Associates Coliseum	800-225-2277
San Diego Chargers	Qualcomm Stadium	619-220-8497
San Francisco 49ers	3Com Park	415-656-4900
Seattle Seahawks	Husky Stadium	888-635-4295

HOCKEY   Oct-Apr

NHL (National Hockey League) www.nhl.com

Team	Venue	☎
Colorado Avalanche	Pepsi Center	303-893-6700
Dallas Stars	Reunion Arena	214-467-8277
Los Angeles Kings	Staples Center	310-673-1300
Mighty Ducks of Anaheim	Arrowhead Pond	714-704-2500
Phoenix Coyotes	America West Arena	602-379-7800
San Jose Sharks	San Jose Arena	408-287-9200

Index

Tacoma .... City, town, region or other point of interest

Bering, Vitus .... Person, historic event or term

Accommodations .... Practical information

Place and sight names are followed by state abbreviations: *AK* Alaska, *AZ* Arizona, *CA* California, *CO* Colorado, *HI* Hawaii, *ID* Idaho, *KS* Kansas, *MT* Montana, *NE* Nebraska, *NV* Nevada, *NM* New Mexico, *ND* North Dakota, *OK* Oklahoma, *OR* Oregon, *SD* South Dakota, *TX* Texas, *UT* Utah, *WA* Washington, *WY* Wyoming.

Abbreviations

NP	National Park	NPres	National Preserve
NRA	National Recreation Area	NWR	National Wildlife Reserve
NHS	National Historic Site	SP	State Park
NHP	National Historic Park	SR	State Reserve
NHR	National Historic Reserve	SHS	State Historic Site
NM	National Monument	SHP	State Historic Park
NMem	National Memorial	SHM	State Historic Monument

C

Notes